Intuition
How we think and act

Intuition
How we think and act

Tony Bastick

JOHN WILEY & SONS
Chichester · New York · Brisbane · Toronto · Singapore

British Library Cataloguing in Publication Data:

Bastick, Tony
  Intuition: How we think and act
  1. Intuition (Psychology)
  I. Title
  153.4'4   BF311   80-42060

  ISBN 0 471 27992 7

Typeset by Photo-Graphics, Yarcombe, Honiton, Devon.
Printed at The Pitman Press, Bath, Avon.

This book is dedicated to my family
who made it possible; and necessary.

Contents

List of Tables and Figures

Introduction

Creativity is the quintessence of man; and the spark of inspiration, the insight, the intuitive understanding on which our creativity depends is fundamental to both the fulfilment of the individual and the progress of humanity. This book includes an investigation into that fundamental intuitive process. But the investigation also leads to an encompassing description of how we think and act. This description includes a Theory of Intuitive Thought which develops from the investigation and explains the phenomenon of intuition. This description of how we think and act shows that intuition is a product of accepted psycho-physiological processes of thought and behaviour that occur under particular conditions of personality, environment, and experience. These conditions are not mystical; rather they are conditions with which we are all familiar. The encompassing description is a fundamental organization which synthesizes many and varied phenomena of thought and behaviour, including the phenomena of intuition and creativity.

It has been usual for other descriptions of integrated thought and behaviour each to have been open to many interpretations; mainly because their key words have slightly different meanings for readers from various backgrounds. These implicit, ambiguous interpretations have reduced the practical use of such descriptions. In order to increase the usefulness of this description of how we think and act, the terms used are closely defined; terms such as empathy, projection, and creativity, which in Chapter 9 are formally defined by probability statements. The investigation also reviews numerous experiments related to intuition showing how and why their methodology may be used by readers whose studies include the phenomenon of intuition; for example studies of creativity, of teaching, or of problem-solving.

We first consider how the words 'intuition' and 'insight' are used, in order to find a consensus meaning of these words. However, we find that the literature contains no precise definitions. For example some 'definitions' used by philosophers are metaphysical and some are even mystical; some even 'define' intuition as something that one cannot define. Generally 'definitions' from the literature are just descriptions in terms of associated properties which are themselves only loosely defined. From these descriptions we identify twenty properties commonly associated with intuition; properties such as empathy, creativity, etc. We then investigate how these twenty properties are associated with intuition. The phenomena of thought and behaviour that involve these properties are very varied and their interrelations are most complex. However, the fundamental organization presented in Chapter 9 synthesizes simply the findings of this investigation.

The range and variety of phenomena synthesized by this organization enable the organization to describe thought and behaviour in general and to include a Theory of Intuitive Thought which explains the phenomenon of intuition in particular.

1

Studies of Intuition

1.1 POWER AND PERVASION OF INTUITION

Insight or intuition is relevant to all fields of study and all walks of life. It is a universal experience, little understood but treasured and sought after by all. The intuitions of great men, the 'Eureka' experiences that have pushed forward the frontiers of knowledge, that have produced technologies moulding our civilization, are inspirations to the schoolboy, are guiding lights to the research worker. But there has been little investigation into intuition. There seems to have been a spiritual mystique surrounding this invaluable faculty. To delve too deeply would dispel, it was thought, not only the spiritual mystery but also the power giving the intuition.

However, pioneering investigations by early psychologists looked promising and the Gestalt Field Psychologists extensively used the concept of insight. Behavioural psychologies, being generally more easily demonstrated, rivalled Gestalt psychology in popularity. But they found insight has not been so easily demonstrable and the Behaviourists' inadequate description of it as 'one trial learning' caused much contention. Intuition became a highly emotive word in psychology and had been all but excluded from serious study. Unfashionable or not, intuition is too important to be ignored for we all have our intuitions. They may not be as important as those of the giants to whom we aspire, but in our own lives they are the sparks that short circuit mere reason, the flashes that illuminate our logical slogging, and leave a glowing satisfaction of true meaning.

The terms 'intuition' and 'insight' are now found increasingly in psychological writings and research experiments, but the terms are still 'semantic riddles'. However, if this common experience could be understood, if this elusive universal faculty could be developed, then each individual would have a powerful resource for understanding and creative invention. This investigation aims to provide such an understanding by defining intuition and producing a formal theory of intuitive thought processes. The theory has been verified by psychophysiological experiments and simulation (Bastick, T.,

1

1979). This theory can be applied in education and mathematics in realizing the individual's intuitive potential. A simulation of this theory may be used to program a computer analogy of man's intuition. Computers with the creative power of intuition to match their already superior analytic abilities would be tools with limitless potential.

Intuition is a powerful human faculty, perhaps the most universal natural ability we possess. Newton and the apple, Archimedes in the bath, Pythagoras gazing at his tiled wall and the many other legends of intuition illustrate the power of this ability.

> the history of mathematics and natural science is filled with illustrations of the spectacular display of imagination and intuition...imagination, fantasy, intuition, discovery by mental lightning flashes, constitute the supreme creative faculty or faculties of the scientist. The great scientist shares this god-like quality on equal terms with the poet, the dramatist, the painter, the sculptor, the philosopher. (Henderson, A., 1946)

Intuition has been called 'one of the most important cognitive faculties of man' (Lorenz, K.Z., 1951). The famous intuitions and millions of other intuitions are responsible for every creation, device, and man-made system of civilization to date. Some might say that it is our reason that has brought civilization this far, but reason is only the servant of our intuition. If '...We believe that in our reasonings we no longer appeal to intuition; the philosophers will tell us this is an illusion. Pure logic could never lead us to anything but tautologies; it could create nothing new; not from it alone can any science issue' (Poincaré, H., 1929, p. 208). The creative mathematician Henri Poincaré also says '...it is by logic that we prove. It is by intuition that we discover' (Arnheim, R., 1970, p. 274). In fact '...intuition is the foundation of the intellect' (Bahm, A. J., 1960, p. 1). Intuitive judgments of future events have added the mystical attributes of clairvoyancy to this awesome ability. To gain self-control of this power that touches us unbidden in its own whimsical place and time, and in an instant wreaks such changes in our lives; to retain its fleeting touch and direct it to demolish problems impervious to reason, problems of our own conscious choosing; this is the fascination of the alchemists. It is because of this fascination that I have written this book. 'If man is to use his capabilities to the full and with the confidence that fits his powers, he has no alternative but to recognise the importance and power of intuitive methods in all fields of inquiry — literature and mathematics, poetry and linguistics' (Bruner, J. and Clinchy, B., 1966, p. 82).

All of us have this ability. There is plenty of opportunity to study intuition for there is a lot of the 'raw material' about. Intuitions are very common. In various degrees they pervade everything we do. They vary from the scientist's awesome moments of creative inspiration to the day-to-day hunches and 'feelings' which guide our common actions.

The creative scientist's awesome moments of inspiration can change his whole life. They are the 'Eureka' experiences, the lights on our road to Damascus.

> Most of us who have attempted to advance science have had our all too brief and passing moments of inspiration; we have added a single brick to the mighty structure or finished some corner which the master in his impetuosity has overlooked. And though our tiny efforts rightly pass almost unnoticed by the rest of mankind, they have a value for ourselves beyond what we can tell; one instant we have stood with the great ones of the earth and shared their glory. (Williams, F.E., 1966, p. 119)

The lesser intuitions of our day-to-day lives are much more common. The Myers-Briggs Type Indicator is a test of the Jungian concept of thinking versus feeling for evaluating experience. Two postulated perceptual functions are sensation and intuition. It is found that as much as 25 per cent of the general population score as intuitive on this test (Myers, I.B., 1958). This day-to-day intuition includes phenomena like 'woman's intuition'. It is common folk lore that a 'woman's intuition' can judge a situation in which the evidence is insufficient or too complicated for a man to reason. 'Mental processes of this kind [intuitive] seem to be common wherever there are situations too complex for ready logical analysis' (Neisser, U., 1963).

We all make 'educated guesses' when the information is insufficient, too complicated or even when we are not aware of what priorities we should give to various information. Examples are judging people on acquaintance or when we must vote for politicians; then we are being asked to judge the pontifications of experts and a myriad of complex interrelated issues. We often need to make 'guesstimates', initial approximations to seed iterations or to make decisions too speedily for the process of data definition and logical analysis. These are some of the ways in which intuition pervades our lives.

The diverse forms of creativity which mark our humanity all start with the intuition that reason fashions into a creation. The process that produces the intuition is how we know: not only how we know the intuition but how to guide reason to fashion it into creativity. There is a vast literature on creativity but as Walkup points out the creativity literature is lacking in the study of *how* one knows (Walkup, L.E., 1965, p. 37). Edison said that creativity is 1 per cent inspiration and 99 per cent perspiration but not even 1 per cent of the creativity literature is concerned with intuition.

It is not least in research that this '...supposedly superior form of cognition called intuition' (Stocks, J. L., 1939, p. 2), is indispensable. From the initial curiosity, the insight into causes, intuitive choice of analogies, design of relevant original experiments, even to the choice and guidance of the techniques of analysis — intuition is all-pervasive.

The linguistic philosophers tell us that the language of reason is not transparent. Gödel has shown that a consistent system of reasoning cannot be sufficient to reason about reason. Intuition is needed to guide the blind steps of logic and give purpose to this direction.

Need for Research into Intuition

An overview of the development and current state of the literature on intuition reveals a professed, and to date largely unfulfilled, need for practical enquiry into the phenomenon of intuition. The literature repeatedly proclaims the need for investigations into intuition. There is, however, very little modern research into intuition. This is partially a result of the divisions between psychologists on the concept of insight and intuition; notably between the Gestalt and Behaviourist psychologists. The result of this controversy was to stymie research into intuition. Any reference to the concept avoided the term 'intuition' and was conducted under designations such as 'preconscious concept formation', 'preverbal concepts', 'instinctive knowledge', 'cognitive reorganization', etc. Even research under these synonyms did not use operational definitions of intuition embodying the properties commonly attributed to intuition. The need for research into intuition remains unfulfilled and becomes increasingly important with the development of other related fields of psychology.

Insight and intuition are central to creativity and learning, yet no suitable model or explanation exists for these concepts. Consequently writers on learning and creativity are completely at a loss in the many cases where their work directly relates to these concepts. Consequently, they frequently admit the need for research into insight and intuition. For example, Thurstone, studying creativity says 'Eventually a research program on creative and inventive talent should investigate what happens before the moment of insight' (Thurstone, L. L., 1962, p. 52). In his work on insight learning, Viesti also states this need for further research '...further research in this area is warranted' (Viesti, C. R. Jr., 1971, p. 182).

In spite of this need there is very little research in the literature on the process of intuition and insight. 'These processes have received remarkably little attention' (Davitz, J. R., and Ball, S., 1970, p. 70). Brady recognizes the importance of intuition in his particular field — psychotherapy — and also attests to the sparseness of research into this concept. 'The concept of insight, so basic in dynamic thinking, has proved elusive'; 'the role of insight in psychotherapy has been the focus of little research, and many issues remain unexplored and unsettled' (Brady, J. P., 1967, pp. 304 and 310). In reviewing the literature on intuition up to 1979 Ralph Frick concurs with his summary, 'In general, few writers go beyond an almost wistful contemplation of this mysterious trait and what potentially dramatic properties it may have. The few attempts to seek it out, to define and measure it, have up to this time met with only moderate success' (Frick, R. C., 1970, p. 2).

Gestalt versus Behaviourist 'Insight' Controversy and its Effect on the Literature

The concept of insight was used extensively by the Gestalt Field Psychologists. Their concept included many of the properties attributed to intuition (see

Table 1.3/1). They used the term to mean 'a sense of feeling of pattern, or relationships ... "sensed way through", "feel",' (Bigge, M. L. and Hunt, M. P., 1965). The S-R associationist psychologists gained popularity over the Gestalt psychologists mainly because their ideas were generally more easily amenable to experiment. One exception, however, was the problem of insight. The prolonged popularity of the Gestalt psychologists is partly due to the inability of the Behaviourists to match their explanation of this important psychological concept. 'It is probably fair to say that much of the vogue which Gestalt psychology, with its emphasis on insight, enjoyed in this country during the 1930s and 1940s arose from the manifest inadequacy of the notion that we learn only by doing' (Mowrer, O. H., 1960a, p. 18).

The Behaviourists inadequately tried to explain insight as 'one trial learning'. Mowrer for instance tried to explain insight completely in terms of learning principles (Mowrer, O. H., 1960b, Chapter 6). He refers to the controversy with those who contend that one can also learn by insight: 'There has been some controversy among psychologists about this progressive, step-by-step aspect of learning (Spence, B. 1940). Doubting that learning is essentially inductive, some writers (e.g. Krechevsky, 1938) have taken the position that this is instead a matter of "insight"' (Mowrer, O. H., 1960a, p. 439). [References only used by other authors are not in the Bibliography.] After considering the Gestalt criteria for insight learning Pechstein and Brown suggest that all these criteria for insight are equivalent to saying '...that all instances of alleged insight learning are merely examples of trial-and-error plus the transfer of past experience' (Pechstein, L. A. and Brown, F. D., 1939, p. 41).

The Gestalt psychologists agree that past experience is central to their concept of insight but refute the reductionism of the 'Gestalt' into gradual reinforcement through previous trials.

> What is intended by insight is a perception of the essential requirements of a problem so that past experience can be brought to bear in a manner appropriate to the present.... The fact that past experience affects insightful learning does not reduce insightful learning to trial and error. The real issue comes in describing *how* past experience is used appropriate to the demands of the problem. (Anderson, H.A., 1959, p. 165).

Piotrowski denies that intuition can even be explained in terms of other behaviours. 'The act of inter-relating concepts and empirical reference in meaningful propositions...is intuitive and cannot be explained as an inevitable result of other mental functions' (Piotrowski, Z. A., 1971, p. 10). The Gestalt psychologists contend that insight is not directly observable, it must be inferred, i.e. we cannot always accurately infer from a change in over-behaviour the full nature of the insight behind it (Eutsch, M. D., 1954, p. 191). They accuse the Behaviourists of being responsible for adverse developments in education. 'The emphasis of S-R associationists upon behaviour had led to educational practices designed to change overt behaviour and measures for it — and nothing else' (Bigge, M. L. and Hunt, M. P., 1965, p. 301).

Trying to avoid the controversy resulted in further confusion in the meaning of even basic accepted terms. For example, Mowrer tried to 'side-step' the controversy by admitting that insight learning was not learning!

> ...suggesting that although insight is real enough, it is not itself a form of learning, properly speaking. Therefore, the fact of insight does not go against the assumption that learning proper is progressive, inductive. Insight as we shall see, is a deductive procedure and thus complements the notion that learning is inductive. There is, it seems, no real contradiction here. (Mowrer, O. H., 1960a, p. 439)

The efforts of the S-R associationists to explain insight in behaviourist terms has caused only controversy. 'Attempts to define insight in terms of observable behaviour have produced controversy rather than clarification' (Jensen, K., 1960, p. 3).

An interesting possible explanation as to why such controversy could occur is proffered by the findings of Cohen in his recent book. He interviewed thirteen leading psychologists including Eysenck, Festinger, Broadbent, and Skinner, and noted the following personality characteristics associated with these psychologists. It could be these characteristics that were in part responsible for the controversy rather than any insurmountable difficulties intrinsic to the concept.

> These divisions are well known. What is less well known, and, perhaps, more disturbing, is the manner in which claims are presented. Cohen reveals an evangelistic egoism about individual claims and an apparent inability on the part of many of these psychologists to recognize the claims of others and cope with criticism. He notes a strange tendency on their part to strike an attitude of 'those who are not with me are against me' (quoted from a book review of Cohen, D., 1978)

The legacy of this controversy has been a dearth in the literature on intuition and a reluctance by psychologists to study the subject in spite of the continuing need and growing importance of doing so. The following results illustrate this lack of literature on intuition. An exhaustive computer-aided literature search was carried out on Wednesday 26 April 1978. The title and descriptions of all articles in the following five conglomerate files were searched for the word 'intuition'.

(1) ERIC from 1966, references 350 journals plus reports — 304,000 articles were searched.
(2) BIOSIS PREVIEWS from 1972, contains citations from Biological Abstracts and Bioresearch Index, references 8000 journals — 1,470,000 articles searched.

(3) ISMEC from 1973, the data base of the Information Services in Mechanical Engineering, referencing 250 journals — 50,000 articles searched.
(4) PSYCHOLOGICAL ABSTRACTS from 1967, produced by the American Psychological Association, references 900 journals — 276,000 articles searched.
(5) Comprehensive Dissertations Abstracts from 1861, covers United States and Canadian Doctorial Theses and other countries — 592,000 theses searched.

Result: of the 2,692,000 articles, reports and theses searched from these most likely sources only 91 had the word 'intuition' in the title or as a description. Of these 24 were studies of intuition. The others used the term in a casual sense. Similar results from computer searching of other files confirm this result.

It is plain, as Simonton says from his recent survey of the literature, '...there is relatively little work on intuition' (Simonton, D. K., 1975, p. 351). Similarly Westcott remarks, 'A look at the psychological literature indicates that it is unusual for anyone to be studying intuition' (Westcott, M. R., 1964, p. 47). Very few psychologists, as a result of the controversy, now use the term 'intuition'. 'The terminology "intuition" is often avoided in psychology as it is a term carrying excess emotional freight' (Allport, G. W., 1965, p. 545). Westcott, M. R. (1968) remarks, 'Relatively few writers have used the term "intuition" either in the title of their works or as a descriptive of the phenomenon studied' (p. 55). Also 'Empirical studies within the framework of general psychology which consider "intuition" — either as a problem or as a solution — are clearly few and far between' (p. 73). Similarly Baer, R. A. Jr. (1976) remarks '...there is very little emphasis upon intuition...' (p. 27). In serious psychological research involving the concept and properties of intuition, such synonyms as 'preconscious concept formation' are used. Apart from these rare serious studies the literature generally only contains vague references to the phenomenal power of intuition, '...aside from the Gestalt psychologists and the religious mystics, few have carefully isolated the phenomenon or come to grips with it as such. Most expositors have contented themselves with vague and hyperbolic reference to it' (Hutchinson, E.D., 1941, p. 32). Any practical research, rather than discussion of the term, is far rarer. 'It is a fact that it is exceedingly difficult to find commonly agreed upon examples of intuition in the literature' (Guiora, A. Z. et al., 1965, p. 110).

As psychology progresses in various fields related to intuition, the 'hole' caused by the lack of research into this key concept is becoming an increasing embarrassment. Its importance is increasingly recognized and the need for empirical research is crucial: '...little empirical information exists about this important psychological concept...' (Viesti, C. R. Jr., 1971, p. 182). Not least because of the controversy does insight in particular require investigation and its meaning clarified: '"insight" especially warranted close scrutiny because of its great variety of meaning and controversial history' (Jensen, K., 1960, p. 2). Further research is warranted to develop the potential of this basic individual ability for common use. 'Continued studies of intuition are warranted to attempt to reveal its potential for problem-solving, for conventional thinking, and for ordinary living' (Frick, R. C., 1970, p. 36). A development of the literature since Ornstein, R. E. (1972) is concerned with the different functions of the right and left cerebral hemispheres. The right is being considered broadly as intuitive and the left as analytic. This mainly neuro physiological work follows a classic philosophic and cultural dichotomy of consciousness related to the two halves of the body. Summers, Roni (1976) gives a good literature survey of how this relates to the study of intuition. Her work should be considered complementary to this aspect of the investigation and will not be duplicated here.

Need to Discover the How-What-When-and-Why of Intuition

There is a consensus that we need intuition in all fields of study: logic or reason is not enough. But the first aim is to find out exactly what is intuition. Henri Poincaré makes the same point: '...to make arithmetic, as to make geometry, or to make any science, something else than pure logic is necessary. To designate this something else we have no word other than intuition. But how many different ideas are hidden under this same word' (Poincaré, H., 1929, P. 208). It is necessary to find what properties are generally considered to be included under the term 'intuition'. Different schools of thought, from the Intuitionists to the Gestalt Psychologists, use the term in different ways: '...the concept of intuition seems to represent a broad variety of theories of knowledge, some of which characterize direct knowledge, some knowledge of unities, some telepathic or innate knowledge' (Allport, G. W., 1929, p. 15). He calls intuition '...this troublesome term...' (p. 15). After her literature survey on 'The measurement of intuitive thinking' Bouthilet, Lorraine (1948) still says the 'semantic riddle of intuition remains to be solved' (p. 49). Indeed the varieties of meaning are profuse and it is an aim of this investigation to categorize and analyse them. One of the most nebulous, verbose books on intuition — actually called *Intuition* — is by Buckminster Fuller. This book illustrates one extreme of its use. In fifty-nine pages of pseudo-scientific prose and word associations the author rambles on, culminating in naming a ship 'Intuition'. This pseudo-scientific jargon in the author's mind embodies 'intuition' as a vague universal term (Buckminster Fuller, R., 1972). At the other extreme are the many psychologists who succinctly 'define' intuition in terms of one of its non-unique properties using terminology that itself is ill-defined (see Section 1.3).

In order to settle the confusion this term has caused, a primary aim of this investigation is to define it in terms of its properties and to formalize any previously vague terms employed in its definition. 'Intuition has been a baffling and elusive subject for generations. The lack of clear-cut definition and the loose usage of the word has only added confusion to this nebulous matter' (Guiora, A. Z. *et al.,* 1965, p. 110).

This is not particularly easy because many descriptions from which definition must be derived consider intuition as mystical or as a negative tautology, e.g. as some power we cannot understand. Hence, according to such a tautology any understanding brought about by this investigation could not be an understanding of intuition. Perhaps it was as a result of the Gestalt versus Behaviourist 'insight' controversy (Section 1.1) that psychologists attributed elusive almost mystical aspects to intuition, e.g. as Hathaway says of 'intuition' that the source of the judgment cannot be specified (Hathaway, S. R., 1955). Similarly Piotrowski says 'The act of interrelating concepts and empirical reference in meaningful propositions...is intuitive and cannot be explained' (Piotrowski, Z. A., 1971, p. 10). Intuition has been linked with parapsychological phenomena, but little scientifically reproducible work at present exists. Watson, L. (1974) considers intuition in terms of ESP and telepathy but says '...so far, no tests of this kind have been done, and the connection between telepathy and intuition remains obscure. It is possible that there is no correlation between them at all' (pp. 276/277). Bigge and Hunt deny that the process of intuition is open to scientific scrutiny, 'no-one can describe objectively what happens during an act of intuition' (Bigge, M. L. and Hunt, M. P., 1965, p. 305). They actually categorize intuition as mystical: '...most behaviourists consider that insight connotes something intuitive and mystical' (p. 305). As Richard Board says, '...intuition was increasingly espoused as a method of thinking possessing almost mystical virtues which appealed to the irrational longings of romanticism' (Board, R., 1958, p. 234). These attitudes reinforce the mystical allusions of intuition and further dichotomize the philosophy of intuition into reason versus mystical intuition. Hutchinson reveals that philosophers have 'disputed endlessly about the relative value of these two modes of thought — the systematic or dialectical and the intuitive or mystical' (Hutchinson, E. D., 1941, p. 31). Western schools of thought have emphasized reason to the detriment of intuition because of this mystical connotation. In his tortuous book on the philosophy of intuition Archie Bahm notes 'Western philosophies, by and large, ignore or deny a need for intuition' (Bahm, A.J., 1960, p. 1).

This association is continued in the psychological literature. 'Lately, the term has been in use in psychiatry and other professions to indicate the unexplainable, unaccountable, instinctive, extrasensual, supernatural, or magical type of knowledge' (Szalita-Pemow, A. B., 1955, p. 7). Phillip Jackson, writing on psychology and educational practice, implied that there is some mystical power to intuition that would no longer be available if intuition were closely scrutinized. He observes a reluctance to analyse the intuitive process (Jackson, P. W., 1971, p. 10). Davitz and Ball say it is 'inaccessible to study' (Davitz, J. R. and Ball, S., 1970, p. 70). Perhaps the difficulties of precisely defining intuition from these descriptions are best illustrated by

Suzuki's view that intuition is so different and so much more than reason that reason could never comprehend it (Suzuki, D. T., 1957, p. 95).

In this book a precise definition of intuition will be presented in the form of a Theory of Intuitive Thought Processes. This theory may be used to describe how to develop instruments for recognizing those who have a high propensity for intuitive thinking. Ralph Frick at the conclusion of his study of intuition calls for such research. He also agrees that research is needed into the environment and conditions that facilitate intuition. 'Research is needed to develop instruments that will be more successful in identifying the intuitive thinker. Research is also needed to learn more about the conditions under which intuition operates' (Frick, R. C., 1970, p. 35). These are two main aims of this investigation.

The literature shows that a precise definition of intuition is needed. It is difficult to derive such a definition from some descriptions of intuition in the literature as they have mystical connotations and deny that such a definition is possible. Bouthilet, Lorraine (1948) concludes her review of the literature on intuition: 'the review of the meaning of intuition showed the futility of attempting to encompass the concept of intuitive thinking into one all-inclusive definition' (p. 50). This investigation, however, aims to produce such a definition in terms of the properties commonly attributed to intuition. Ill-defined terms used in the definition will be formalized. The process of intuition will be described by a theory that may be used to identify high-intuitive types and describe the personality characteristics and the type of environment that facilitates intuition. Thorsland, M. N. (1971) points to the need for such a theory: 'Since in this study it was possible only to *functionally* link the intuitive and analytic dimensions with various cognitive related variables, the establishment of any causal links in this regard would considerably clarify the mechanisms involved' (p. 18).

Applying Intuition in Education

Intuition is basic to the educational process. In both learning and teaching at all levels the intuitive process should be employed. As Bruner and Clinchy say: 'It is quite plain that learning and teaching must start from some intuitive level' (Bruner, J. and Clinchy, B., 1966, p. 71). They emphasize this is particularly true of anyone approaching a body of knowledge for the first time. This is essential for effective teaching. 'In summary, then, it seems that, if teaching is to be most effectual, the learning theory which should be employed is that which seeks consistently to develop insight' (Bayles, E. E., 1952, p. 71). However, at the moment although such a need is recognized little is known about how to train intuition: '...let it be said at the outset that nothing is known about the training of intuition and that very likely we are still too unclear about what is intended by the word to devise proper educational procedures' (Bruner, J. and Clinchy, B., 1966, p. 76).

The theory proposed in this book may be applied in general education by showing how to develop the natural ability of insight. Once the student has developed this ability, the teacher may then develop the student's reliance on and use of this intuitive ability. Not only is it intended that educational procedures will be developed to increase the student's natural intuitive ability, but the theory may suggest procedures to enable the student to use these abilities confidently for problem-solving, creativity, judgment, etc., etc. Although this is recognized as good educational practice, at present students are not encouraged to use their intuitive ability. For example, they are not taught how to use their intuitive abilities to integrate facts into personally meaningful understanding of the whole body of knowledge. Students are taught the 'analytic apparatus and none of the general intuitive feel that is needed to put the pieces into a coherent and understandable picture' (Bruner, J. and Clinchy, B., 1966, p. 75).

Rather than work with the child's intuition, some teachers' insistence on reason alone inhibits this natural intuition. 'Intuition is not allowed to operate freely in most school curricula: Because much emphasis has been placed on formalism, the child's intuitive approaches have been inhibited' (Bruner, J. S., 1963). It is hoped that the theory will be used by teachers to develop and work with a child's intuition. As Blythe Clinchy says 'We must deepen and discipline children's intuitive powers' (Clinchy, B., 1958, p. 37).

Teaching methods may be developed that are soundly based on the theory. 'A comprehensive learning theory must take into account both insight and creative activity' (Guilford, J. P., 1950). Which is what this investigation will do. These teaching methods should use intuitive techniques to increase the effectiveness of learning and the effectiveness of standard techniques by presentation, instruction, and use of environments all facilitating intuition. This would satisfy the following suggestion, that '...teachers should capitalize on what is known about intuition to increase the effectiveness of present educational procedures' (Frick, R. C., 1970, p. 36). For example, the techniques and advantages of the teachers' intuitive evaluation will be shown. The necessity of this technique is outlined in Conklin's paper on intuitive evaluation in education. 'This paper has attempted to show that a teacher's intuitive evaluation is fundamentally important.... Teachers should have more faith in their intuitive judgment...hopefully, a teacher's increased use of intuitive techniques of evaluation would stimulate students' (Conklin, K. R., 1970, p. 332).

The theory may be applied to subject independent teaching and learning by showing how intuitive ability may be developed and how it can be used in education. Also teaching methods may be described that use the teachers' intuitive abilities and capitalize on the students' developed intuitive capabilities. Teaching environments and techniques may be defined that work with and encourage the students' intuitive ability.

More than most subjects, mathematics seems difficult for children to learn. Children's intuitive understanding is not generally actively encouraged. Blythe Clinchy in her paper on 'The role of intuition in learning' says that teachers are not even aware of children's intuitive understanding (Clinchy, B., 1975). The structures of language that children intuitively acquire are far more complex than the early school mathematics they are taught. This intuitive ability should be used for the ease of understanding mathematics. New teaching methods using intuitive techniques applicable to mathematics education should be discussed. It is recognized that intuition is needed in the creation of mathematics and should be used in the teaching of the subject. 'Even if we could do without intuition in the creation of mathematics, it would be folly to try to do without it in the teaching of mathematics' (Adler, I., 1968, p. 80). Many children seem to fail in mathematics. By showing how to give intuitive support to the usual analytic work it is hoped that the enjoyment and deep understanding that accompanies intuition will save many of those who would otherwise fail in mathematics. 'It is absolutely essential to encourage the use of such intuitive support' (Fischbein, E., 1972).

By improving mathematics education in this way it is to be hoped that more and better mathematicians will be produced. Further, in training mathematicians in these new techniques of understanding and discovering mathematics, it is also hoped that new types of mathematics may be discovered. Bunge in his book *Intuition and Science* quotes Rey Pastor, who says of intuition in mathematics that it '...leads us to guess or to forbode a multitude of properties we would never discover otherwise' (Bunge, M., 1962, p. 110). Problem-solving success will be improved by the use of these techniques. As William Gordon says, understanding intuition will increase success in a problem-solving situation (Gordon, W. J. J., 1961, p. 6). With more mathematicians with new techniques the rate of research in mathematics should increase.

Particularly in science we have extended our analytic techniques and neglected our intuition. Some of our analytic tools are immensely powerful. For example, the linear step-by-step processing of digital computers is phenomenally fast by human comparison. The computer has been shown to be a powerful analytic tool, superior to us in accuracy as well as speed, with a vast memory of uniquely defined data. But it has no intuition. It cannot analyse the organization of its data to ask even the simplest meaningful question although it has the analytic capability to answer the most complex of questions. It has been called the fastest idiot we have.

In an age when man has developed machinery to run off the routine analytic tasks, it may well be that his best alternative is to develop inventive powers for dealing with the ill-formed and partly formed problems that remain. It is precisely in this domain that a vigorous and courageous intuitive gift, refined through practice, can serve man best. (Bruner, J. and Clinchy, B., 1966, p. 83)

Man's intuition at present guides computing power. The results of many common programing experiences '...suggest the desirability of using human intuition to cut down the number of alternatives that need to be examined systematically by a computer' (Schneider, J. B., 1971, p. 99). But if man's intuition can be defined in a way suitable for computer simulation then the intuitions output by such a program may be used as input to the analytic problem-solving capability of the machine. The Theory of Intuitive Thought Processes in an algorithmic form may be programed for computer simulation in order to output machine-generated intuitions.

This computer analogy of man's intuitive thought may be enhanced to surpass his natural ability in the same fashion as the speed for decision based on precise data has been enhanced in computing compared with the human brain. Such a device has unlimited potential.

1.2 SPECIALIST USE AND MEANINGS OF 'INTUITION'

The structures of other studies on intuition may be considered in terms of the variety of specialisms from which the investigators draw their information, the extent to which an explanatory theory is offered, experimental techniques used, and the applications of intuition considered. The literature shows that an investigation of intuition should embrace many fields of study. This is due to the basic psychological nature of intuition and its pervasiveness. In particular, the literature has suggested a wide range of specific research into intuition from diverse fields of study. However, studies of intuition both theoretical and operational in various fields, have tended to restrict the information base that they use to their own fields of study although the researchers infer their results to 'intuition' in a general context. Some studies have been misleading in that they have used properties of intuition specific to one field of study for an operational definition specific to another field of study, erroneously influencing subsequent research. We incorporate information used in studies of intuition from many fields as well as incorporating information not considered by other researchers on intuition.

We have discussed (Section 1.1) how intuition influences our day-to-day actions and judgments as well as all creativity. Because of this pervasion evidence for the study of intuition is to be found in day-to-day observations, the arts, history, science, etc., etc. — the whole spectrum of human endeavour. In particular as the intuitive process is such a basic psychological phenomenon many branches of psychology will be directly relevant to the study of intuition. This obvious observation is made by several writers. For example Alexander Guiora and his colleagues in their paper on intuition conclude: 'Even a cursory survey will reveal that a systematic study of intuition will have to be related to the main body of psychological knowledge. Thinking and emotions pertain to it, consequently the entire range of psychological research will have a bearing on intuition' (Guiora, A. Z. *et al.,* 1965, p. 117).

Researchers working in specialist fields soon realize that intuition is relevant to many other branches of study, and call for specific research into these fields to complement their own work. These specific research suggestions, as noted here, are a guide to how intuition may be studied. For example, Guiora *et al.*, concerned with psychiatry, found the lack of research into the use of intuition in psychiatry and related fields inhibited their research. They specifically suggest that finding remote associates and operantly conditioning remote associations '...could be conducive to an experimental study of the idiosyncratic association aspect of intuition' (Guiora, A. Z. *et al.*, 1965, p. 118). They suggest that research into intuition should centre around the following variety of topics: '...need systems correlating with areas of intuition-competency; ...the role of process and content in the allo-logical principle; ...the question of preferred modes of communication, that is, auditory, visual, tactile in intuition; the tracking down of idiosyncratic associations in the intuitive under sodium pentothal; ...sensory deprivation and intuition...' (p. 120). Later we will consider these research suggestions. In a review of the research on insight in the field of psychotherapy Roback found writers linked insight with problem-solving processes, creativity, empathy, and awareness of relationships (Roback, H. B., 1974, p. 62). In this book we will consider these links with insight.

From the debris of the Gestalt versus Behaviourist 'insight' controversy (Section 1.1) comes the need to study how past experience is involved with insight. The effect on intuition of organization of past experience has not been satisfactorily explained by other studies of intuition, yet it is central to any application of intuition. Those who try to apply intuition in their own specialist studies soon recognize this need. For example Allport applies the 'Intuitive Method' to the study of personality but suggests that further research is necessary into the organizing role of past experience on intuition (Allport, G. W., 1929, p. 27). He also says, 'Any intuitionism which denies the obvious role of inference based on previous experience is unpsychological (p. 26). In this book we investigate the effect on intuition of the organization of past experience, property 5 Section 2.4.

Anxiety and behaviour shifts affect the intuitive process and have bedevilled those researchers whose experiments include subjects instructed in some problem that is to be solved intuitively. Cowen is one who found that psychological stress inhibited intuitive solutions 'It now remains to inquire somewhat more deeply into the possible underlying psychodynamic factors capable of throwing additional light on this finding' (Cowen, E. L., 1952, p. 516). The Theory of Intuitive Thought proposed in this investigation follows this suggestion by describing how anxiety affects intuitive behaviour.

The intuitive process is a whole body process (Section 3.1) and so research into intuition should consider the physiology of the organism during the intuitive process. '...intuitive events can be studied in the laboratory...I believe that we need, for example, autonomic studies and behavioural shift studies of great artists and poets, mathematicians and scientists; we need studies of unconscious concept formation among chemists in the field of chemistry, among architects in the field of design etc.... Some day we may have them'

(Westcott, M. R., 1964, p. 41). This investigation into intuition answers this need by reporting physiologically monitored behavioural shifts during intuitive problem solving and unconscious concept formation.

The role and interaction of memory and feelings in intuition is relevant to the many experiments where subjects must intuitively estimate or recall emotionally involving information. Experimenters like Milton Blake realize the limitations placed on their findings by the lack of research into these aspects of intuition. Blake suggests research...to try to uncover a possible relationship between temporal coding and the feeling of knowing' (Blake, M., 1973, p. 318). The theory presented in this book proposes such a relationship.

Those who use intuition in the fields of Counselling, Human Simulation (business games, role-play, etc.), and Psychotherapy are concerned with the lack of research on the role of empathy in intuition. Hathaway considering 'clinical intuition' proposes that if more relevant data were available intuition would be found to be equivalent in many aspects to empathy and projection. 'It is possible, however, that some features of all empathy, projection, and the like, would turn out to be intuitional if the pertinent data were available' (Hathaway, S. R., 1955, p. 224). In Bastick, T. (1979) experiments and instruments are designed to measure empathy and projection. These concepts are formalized and included in the Theory of Intuitive Thought proposed here. David Rapaport similarly considered the importance and need for research into intuition and empathy in the field of *Organization and Pathology of Thought*. He says 'Though empathy and intuition certainly are the archetypes of our knowledge about our fellow human beings, their nature is still a closed book to us' (Rapaport, D., 1951). Cooper, reviewing the literature on empathy — one of the properties of intuition, property 12 in Table 1.3/1 — notes the need for a definition, reliable experimental methods, and a formalized concept: '...a great deal of the results in the research is confounded by hazy conceptualization and methodology...its conceptualization is quite ambiguous.... The primary characteristics of the research, however, are its inconclusive and ambiguous results and its nonclinical nature' (Cooper, L., 1970, p. 169).

Research into the accuracy of empathy as a component of intuition is reported in many diverse studies that employ it, from the field of verbal learning where Blake suggests research into '...how feeling-of-knowing accuracy could be further improved' (Blake, M., 1973, p. 318) to the field of psychiatry where Guiora *et al.* suggest research into 'the question of accuracy; the problem and meaning of empathy involved in intuition' (Guiora, A. Z. *et al.*, 1965, p. 120). We answer these requests for research into the accuracy and importance of the role of empathy in intuition and will show later that empathic ability is basic to the intuitive process.

Other studies of intuition fall into five categories:

(1) religious and philosophical studies;
(2) literature surveys on the meaning of the term;

(3) consideration of its nature and use in psychotherapy — including role-play;
(4) intuitive problem-solving experiments;
(5) its role in education and creativity.

Surveys of its meaning often precede studies in categories (3), (4), and (5) but the surveys are mainly limited to the field of the application considered although the results are erroneously applied to 'intuition' in general. Studies rarely cross-reference relevant research findings from other categories. However, cross-references out of context have been made and are misleading to subsequent researchers.

Studies Involving Religious Views of Intuition

'Religious experience is characteristically intuitive, going beyond reason, conveying certainty, understanding and joy' (Clark, F. V., 1973, p. 158). The religious studies consider the mystical aspects of intuition namely in Yoga and Zen Buddhism and other Eastern religions. They discuss properties of intuition such as the opposition of intuition (Prajna in Zen) with reason (Vignana in Zen) and the 'wholeness' of intuition. Buddhism offers the notion of the intuitive mind or 'Manas' (Govinda, L. A., 1974, pp. 74 ff). It is a seventh class of consciousness following the five senses and intelligence. The practical applications are through states of meditation. There is a direct association between these meditation states and the regressive ego states and the primary processes of Western psychology. The techniques of achieving these meditation states are akin to the biofeedback methods for increasing theta waves. The teaching methods of Eastern religions train intuition through techniques that would not be out of place in a modern progressive primary school. However, these and many other cross-references between religious considerations of intuition and studies in other categories have not been made in the literature because of the tendencies to isolate the study of intuition to the specialism of the investigator.

Philosophic Studies of Intuition

The later philosophic studies are humanistic extensions of the religious considerations of intuition. They consider the 'oneness' of self and nature which in psychological or psychoanalytic studies would be considered in terms of empathy, projection, identification, sympathy, etc. However, the teaching and techniques of intuition do not benefit by cross-reference to the more behavioural approach, scientific equipment, and techniques of Western psychology and psychoanalysis.

The early philosophical studies of intuition in the literature are European, mainly from German philosophers. They are concerned with epistemology and the construction of knowledge through ultimate reference to the senses.

Summers, Roni (1976) gives an excellent concise history of the philosophy of intuition (pp. 15-24). Her source is Copleston's series on the history of philosophy (1962-65). She outlines the contribution of Aristotle (384-322 BC) to the recent European philosophy of Descartes (1596-1650), Locke (1632-1704), Hume (1711-76), Kant (1724-1804), and those who consider intuition as the path to ultimate reality, namely Bergson (1859-1941), Spinoza (1632-77) and Croce (1866-1952). In mathematics intuitionists forbade themselves the use of the principle of the excluded middle and existence proofs. They have, however, managed laboriously literally to construct a great deal of mathematics without these tools. The concrete nature of their philosophy parallels the concrete symbolism of Eastern philosophy and is an aspect of intuition considered later in this book.

Literature Reviews on the Meaning of Intuition

Wild's classic survey on the meaning of intuition was finished before it could be affected by the Gestalt versus Behaviourist 'insight' controversy (Section 1.1). Wild's book on intuition was published in 1938. He considers the views of philosophers and psychologists on intuition. The psychologists he included would today be mainly classed as Gestalt Psychologists. In all he only considered thirty people's view of intuition and found that two-thirds of philosophers subscribed to an abnormal non-sensory view of intuition. Wild is quoted in most bibliographies of studies on intuition. There has not been a systematic survey since Wild's that started with writers and categorized their views of intuition. There have been reviews that consider first selected aspects of intuition and sometimes relate these aspects to the literature. These studies tend only to select aspects of intuition closely related to the specialism of the researcher. This kind of survey is most common and most restricted where it precedes an experiment on intuition. The restricted properties selected in the literature surveys preceding the experiments are so drastically reduced for the operational definition of intuition on which the subsequent experiments are designed, that claims that the results do apply to 'intuition' in general cannot be substantiated.

Studies of Intuition in Psychotherapy and Related Fields

The understanding of the psychodynamics of the intuitive process is best represented in the literature that categorizes studies dealing with intuition in psychotherapy and the related field of psychiatry and to a lesser extent counselling. Perhaps it is the introspective nature of the subject that encourages the research psychotherapist to examine his own intuitive processes. The terms 'insight' and 'intuition' have caused some confusion in these fields. In reviewing the psychotherapy literature on insight Roback concludes: 'The investigations do not shed much light! The body of knowledge comprising the insight psychotherapies is a "semantic jungle" through which the reviewer could not emerge with perspicacity. Many authors discuss the concept of "insight" in poetic language and appear to assume that everyone agrees about its empirical definition' (Roback, H. B., 1974, p. 83). There are papers devoted to clarifying the meaning of the terms. Loosely a psychotherapist uses his intuition to give the patient insight into his mental illness. The patient's knowledge of his illness, of its effect on others, and of its origins represent three different specialist meanings of insight. The effect of some degree of insight is to affect the desired behavioural change in the patient. The psychotherapist's intuition is developed through a 'controlled' empathy in which he evokes feelings subjectively similar to the patient's as 'emotional information' upon which his supposedly unaffected professional judgment may act. The definitions, however, do not have the rigour for operational use and, as in other specialisms, researchers have avoided studying insight. 'Undoubtedly, many investigators have avoided studying "insight" and related variables because of the enormous difficulties in operationalizing for scientific usage the major constructs to eloquently described in the theoretical literature of the insight psychotherapies' (Roback, H. B., 1974, p. 83).

These views of intuition emphasize the accuracy of the subjective empathy. This is increasingly so in modern counselling literature. They also necessitate that intuition and reason should be concurrent yet independent in process but not in information. However, these concepts are not well-defined, as for example in the study of information theory. Some aspects of the original concepts of insight and empathy have been extended by these specialisms to become specific subject-related terms having little to do with the use of the same terms in their original form or as used by other categories of studies on intuition. For example, intuition based on empathy in psychotherapy is between people and imbued with interpersonal relations, but in the scientific creativity literature intuition is based on empathy with inanimate objects or systems and involves different personality characteristics and cognitive styles (Gordon, W. J. J., 1961).

Applications of intuition in the literature are in religious and philosophical, education and creativity studies. Studies on intuition consisting of reviews of the literature on its meaning, and studies that employ experiments based on operational definitions of the term do not generally concern themselves with applications of intuition.

The religious and Eastern philosophic studies apply their 'wholeness' views of intuition to living in accord with nature and becoming part of this 'wholeness' — one with nature. They employ concrete symbols and teach by analogy, encouraging oneness of thought and feeling with the environment. Similar techniques are used to encourage intuitive problem-solving in synectics (Gordon, W. J. J., 1961). The Western philosophies use their definition of the intuitive method to construct and verify knowledge.

Intuition and insight are used as tools in psychotherapy. Insight is used to change a patient's behaviour and the psychotherapist's intuition is used as a means for encouraging a patient's insight and directing the change of behaviour to recovery.

These techniques of controlled empathy are useful in scientific problem-solving. The terms 'empathy', 'insight', and 'intuition' have specialized meanings in psychotherapy with emphasis on accurate interpersonal empathy. Without this emphasis the same intuitive methods may be profitably applied in teaching and creativity, as they are in this study.

It has been shown elsewhere in this book that intuitive methods should be used in education but are not used and that little is known about such methods. 'In these areas [studies of the intuitive process] research opportunities abound, because so much of the empirical data on which sound educational policy should be founded is missing' (Baldwin, A., 1966, p. 85). There are no other studies involving investigative experiments on intuition that also apply intuition to education. The studies that do apply intuition in education use idiosyncratic observations on intuition and do not make a thorough investigation of the topic.

Robert Rose, studying memory processes, says '...intuitions are phenomena worthy of study in their own right, and perhaps more importantly they may lead to the discovery of important cognitive mechanisms' (Rose, R. G., 1975, p. 149). These 'mechanisms' are important because they explain many general findings in the specialist fields they cross-reference.

'Intuition' Definitions Specific to one Specialism are Misleadingly Applied to Another

Westcott has taken a definition of intuition used in clinical psychology and applied it as an operational definition in analytic problem-solving. He takes a definition of Hathaway's, who uses intuition in the specialist sense outlined in the preceding paragraph, that is inferences made relative to a target person in which the source of the inference cannot be identified with satisfactory completeness (Hathaway, S. R., 1955, p. 233).

Hathaway asked an audience to tick the same three words from a list as ticked by a 'target subject' being observed by them. The information on which intuitive judgment would be based in such a situation would be subliminal personal reactions of the target person. However, Westcott uses this definition in a completely different analytical problem-solving situation, where a subject has to uncover terms of a series in order to guess in as few terms as possible, the completion of a partially given term, e.g. find x in x: 25 given successively the following consecutive terms 2 : 4, 3 : 9, 4 : 16. See Section 8.1 for examples of Westcott's measure of intuitive thinking. It may be a consequence of the need for a quantitative measure of intuition, which Westcott provides by counting the terms uncovered, that subsequent researchers have continued to use this very limited property of intuition out of its context and misleadingly infer their results to 'intuition' in general. (For example Kaplan, H. A., 1973.)

Practical Studies on Intuition and Insight

There are a group of experiments on 'insight' which involve the Behaviourist concept of incremental learning. These consist of trials where the subject must 'guess the rule' usually for some sorting procedure. The subject is told on each trial if he was successful or not, according to the unknown rule. A sudden rise in the learning curve, shown by a marked increase in successful trials, indicates the acquisition of 'insight'. The subject obviously finds the rule before he can say what it is, but this fact is used by the experimenters to label insight as 'preverbal concept formation' or 'preconscious concept acquisition'.

There is also a series of logic experiments using the term insight. They have little to do with the concept of insight as generally used except they use the term insight as a synonym for understanding of a logical relationship, e.g. Goodwin, R. Q., and Wason, P. C., 1972; Johnson-Laird, P. N. and Wason, P. C., 1970a, b.

Another series of insight experiments into problem-solving involves the subject being given a practical problem to solve using apparatus in a 'novel' way. The subject is observed while using the apparatus. These experiments give almost no consideration to any properties of intuition. The experiments are far from 'clinical', uncontrolled with many variables unconsidered, e.g. the subject's experimental history, experience with similar apparatus, social taboos on using the apparatus, etc., that effect an insight solution.

Studies concerned solely with problem-solving applications of intuition and not using experiments as a means, for understanding intuition, are mainly in education and creativity. Properties of intuition relevant to problem-solving are introduced through the researchers' observations rather than through psychological theory or understanding of intuition. Little if any understanding of the psychodynamics of the process is considered. No experiments are done to substantiate the validity of the observations. However, procedures based on these observations are recommended.

Understanding the psychology of intuition together with its application to creativity is found in the sections of the works of creative scientists and artists, e.g. Poincaré, Einstein, etc., whose observations are derived from introspection and their intuitive processes sometimes described. These are not in themselves primarily investigations into intuition, although books/papers of these collected works may be considered so. These introspections of creative people have had a major influence in this investigation by giving priority to the inclusion of information processing in the Theory of Intuitive Thought Processes.

In education, observations of intuition are concerned almost exclusively with young children. Bruner, J. S., Clinchy, B., and recently Griffiths and Howson are the main contributors in that order, both in quality of their contribution and in chronology. The works of the educational psychologists, e.g. Piaget, Skemp, Deans, etc., are very wide and although, like most other psychology their work is very relevant to intuition in young children's education, they mention it only superficially, e.g. *Intuitive and Reflective Intelligence* (Skemp, R. R., 1971, pp. 54 ff).

In applications of intuition to creativity, the literature consists of numerous minor references of idiosyncratic observations. Studies on problem-solving that are not primarily studies of intuition do shed light on the intuitive process in problem-solving, e.g. Duncker, K. (1945), as do the peripheral applications of observations on intuition in 'think tank' studies. Notably Gordon has used these observations to create environments and give training that is relevant to the use of intuition in creative problem-solving. His work is relevant to teaching, mathematical creativity, and education in general but is not cross-referenced by studies of intuition in these fields.

Because of the Gestalt versus Behaviourist insight controversy (Section 1.1) it has been assumed by psychologists that intuition was not amenable to study in the laboratory. However, surveying the literature on intuition up to 1948 Lorraine Bouthilet proposes that it is possible to devise experiments to study intuition: '...it is proposed that a situation can be so devised and so presented that a form of behaviour from which intuitive thinking may be inferred, can be demonstrated' (Bouthilet, L., 1948, p. 49). Since then there have been experiments devised to observe intuitive thinking both in the West and in the USSR. These are the 'insight' learning experiments in which subjects try to guess a rule for some sorting procedure. Also included are the experiments involving 'novel' use of apparatus to solve a practical problem and also the logic problems just criticized as having a too restricted view of intuition.

Although the importance of insight is fully recognized there have been few attempts to measure it. Grossman noted how unfortunate it is that despite the vast importance and controversial nature of 'insight' in psychodynamic thinking, there have been so few attempts at direct, objective measurement of this concept (Grossman, D., 1951). The problems of finding a measure of insight or intuition are problems of definition, 'technique and methodology' (Bouthilet, L., 1948, p. 49).

Roback wrote a paper on 'Insight: a bridging of the theoretical and research literatures'. He is restricted to the measurement of insight in psychotherapy — his own specialism. However, he summarizes his review of the empirical measures of insight used in psychotherapy as follows: 'In spite of diverse efforts at developing a useful insight measure, each measure reviewed appears to present major problems of definition, relevance and methodology' (Roback, H. B., 1974, p. 65). This problem of definition is solved in the present investigation by the proposed Theory of Intuitive Thought Processes.

Confidence in the subject's intuitive solution to a problem is one of the properties of the intuitive process. The only studies that purport to measure this confidence are those of Westcott's. He measures this confidence by the lack of evidence a subject has when he arrives at his answer. These experiments are criticized elsewhere on many counts in the relevant sections of this book (Sections 1.2, 1.3, 4.3 and elsewhere).

The majority of this investigation is concerned with the role of the body in the intuitive process. Body reference is a major integral part of the intuitive process. The studies of intuition in psychology and introspective studies of intuition in creativity realize this indispensable role of the body in intuitive processes. Many of the writers studying intuition in these categories call for research into this phenomenon: '...by elucidating the way our bodily processes participate in our perceptions we will throw light on the bodily roots of all thought, including man's highest creative powers' (Polanyi, M., 1966, p. 15). (See also Section 3.1 on emotional interaction in the intuitive process.)

Techniques of monitoring physiological change during the intuitive process should be used in experiments on intuition. This is shown to be necessary, not only from the importance given to bodily responses in those categories of studies above, but in other categories that show the preconscious nature of the process and the inhibiting effects of the process of other methods of study, e.g. from applications in education and creativity, it is found that introspection halts the process, in psychology cross-modal interference of the senses negates the value of cognitive insight measures, etc.

'Intuition' factors have arisen in some studies that were not initially concerned with intuition. An experimenter may construct a questionnaire-type instrument and on factor analysis find a factor with high loadings from items, that to his mind, are related to intuition. He then calls this an intuitive factor. This is rather loose usage of the term. The test items loading on the 'intuitive factor' would be used in this study as an indicator of the meaning the experimenter ascribes to 'intuition' but would not be used as a test to identify the 'intuitive type'.

Studies of intuition are isolated in their own specialisms and do not profit from relevant findings in other fields. Being aware of the difficulties and restrictions of other studies due to their highly subject-selective information base, this investigation uses an extensive information base crossing these specialisms.

An example of the restrictions of a subject-specific information base is the lack of use of an excellent paper on insight by Hutchinson, E. D. (1941). This concerns observations of insight in creative problem-solving and is extremely relevant to studies on applications and on experiments using intuition. However, it was published in a psychiatric journal. Not fitting the specialist use of the term 'insight' as used in psychiatry, it has been practically ignored by psychotherapists. Also workers in other categories isolated in their own specialisms have ignored this important contribution.

This study incorporates the information base of all previous major studies on intuition and the majority of minor articles on intuition. Not only does it combine the information from the isolated specialisms of previous studies on intuition, but it also draws on much previously unconsidered information from diverse sources that is directly relevant to the properties of intuition. This information base has been generated through personal observation, personal communications, manual literature searching and extensive international computer-aided literature searching of literally millions of articles, papers, books, theses, etc.

The computer-aided literature searching technique utilized in this investigation not only provides an extensive information base, but allows a degree of confidence in the exhaustive nature of the survey not usually expressed in studies of the scientific type.

The information most relevant to the intuitive process and explicitly used in this investigation has been collated on to magnetic tapes for computer processing. Computer sorting and searching of this investigation's extensive bibliography files affords efficient and comprehensive integration of information, consistency, and cross-referencing. The large manipulative information base allows much of the information to be cross-referenced in novel ways indicating new relationships by this organization. Some idiosyncratic examples illustrating the wide range of topics considered are method acting, chess-playing, computer programs, Zen Buddhism, curriculum design, effects of drugs on the sympathetic nervous system, etc.

It has been shown that there is a need for a Theory of Intuitive Thought Processes (Section 1.1). This need is felt primarily by researchers who use intuition practically, either in experiments or in applications to education, creativity, or psychotherapy. Religious and philosophical studies are not concerned with behavioural explanations of the intuitive process.

Ralph Frick concludes his review and experiments on 'Intuition as inference' by calling for research into the nature of intuition, emphasizing its importance in education and creativity:

> Finally, additional research ought to be conducted to attempt to determine whether intuition is a single, somewhat complete cognitive function or whether it is a step in the whole creative process. The answer to this question has implications for those who emphasize independence, creativity, and problem solving as major components of the education endeavor. (Frick, R. C., 1970, p. 36)

A comprehensive theory of the intuitive process is needed to explain the intuitive products that researchers have been unable to explain in other ways. 'The word "intuition" has been used for some time now to fill in a gap whenever it is apparently not possible to explain in other ways how a certain body of knowledge has been obtained' (Szalita-Pemow, A. B., 1955, p. 7).

Studies on intuition in the literature contain observations on aspects of the intuitive process derived almost exclusively from the specialism of the researcher. For example, psychoanalysts consider behaviour change following insight. Educationalists consider the quality of understanding given by insight. Behaviourists consider the relations of insight to past experience. Those applying insight to creativity are concerned with the novel associations made. Although studies in each specialism contain observations similar to these on insight, they offer no encompassing theory of the intuitive process. By combining the different aspects of the properties of intuition from all the categories under which intuition is studied, this investigation has been able to propose a comprehensive theory of the intuitive thought process.

1.3 PROPERTIES ATTRIBUTED TO 'INTUITION' AND 'INSIGHT'

Using a convenience sample of views, definitions, and descriptions of 'intuition' and of 'insight' we now list the properties commonly attributed to these terms so that we may in Section 1.4 compare their meanings in terms of these properties and later in Chapters 2 to 8 use what is common among these properties as the basis of further investigation of these terms with a view to synthesizing this information in the theory presented in Chapter 9.

To define intuition one should describe a unique set of its properties, showing also that such a set is unique. 'Definitions' in the literature are by this criterion only descriptions and some of the descriptions are most ambivalent. However, using an unbiased selection of the most readily available literature — public or university libraries rather than say computer search for specialist information — for a survey of definitions and descriptions of intuition it is possible to find a set of properties satisfying a consensus meaning of intuition and from which an operational definition and theory may be developed. These properties will be enumerated in this section and later compared and contrasted in Section 1.4. A list of numbered properties from this survey is given in Table 1.3/1.

Theoretical Considerations of Intuition

This section enumerates the listed properties of intuition apparent from 'definitions' and descriptions of the term 'intuition' when used not as an operational definition but in general usage and in theoretical considerations.

The impression noted above may be why Drever, J. (1974) does not regard intuition as a scientific term. 'Intuition. Immediate perception or judgment usually with some emotional colouring without any conscious mental steps in preparation; a popular rather than scientific term.'
Properties 1, 2, 3.

The nearest scientific term is 'insight' in some of its uses. Webster's Third *New International Dictionary* defines intuition as 'Revelation by insight or innate knowledge, a form of knowing that is akin to instinct or a divining empathy and gives direct insight. Quick and ready insight. The act or process of coming to direct knowledge or certainty without reasoning or inferring'. Webster defines insight as 'seeing intuitively'.
Properties 12, 13, 1, 10, 4.

The *Oxford Dictionary* also defines 'Intuitive apprehension or faculty; insight. Of knowledge or mental perception that consists in immediate apprehension without the intervening of any reasoning process'. It gives many historical uses of the term.

Table 1.3/1   Numbered Properties of Intuition and Insight

No.	Properties
1	Quick, immediate, sudden appearance
2	Emotional involvement
3	Preconscious process
4	Contrast with abstract reasoning, logic, or analytic thought
5	Influenced by experience
6	Understanding by feeling — emotive not tactile
7	Associations with creativity
8	Associations with egocentricity
9	Intuition need not be correct
10	Subjective certainty of correctness
11	Recentring
12	Empathy, kinaesthetic or other
13	Innate, instinctive knowledge or ability
14	Preverbal concept
15	Global knowledge
16	Incomplete knowledge
17	Hypnogogic reverie
18	Sense of relations
19	Dependence on environment
20	Transfer and transposition

Properties 1, 4.

Some of the earliest scientific thoughts on intuition are cited by Hamlyn, D. W. (1961). They are those of Ockham, Descartes, Locke, and Kant (p. 52). William of Ockham's view is that knowledge is based on intuition: '...intuition gives us knowledge whether a thing exists or not'. He opposes intuition with 'abstractive cognition...thinking of something...apart from the conditions of its existence', i.e. abstract thinking. He distinguishes perfect intuition 'constituted by an immediate experience' and imperfect intuition which also utilizes past experience (p. 64).

Properties 4, 5.

Hamlyn says Descartes considers extension by intuition 'inspectiomentis' as one of the 'simple natures' by which we have direct knowledge of a mental substance.

Property 3.

Where 'direct' is interpreted to mean that we have the knowledge without awareness of it coming to us, i.e. a preconscious process (p. 95), Locke claims three degrees of knowledge the first of which is intuitive by which we know of our existence (pp. 132 ff). Kant defines intuition as any awareness of an object through experience of it. 'Intuition is the awareness of the object mediated by sensation.'

Properties 2, 5.

Jung (Dry, A. M., 1961) defines intuition as 'perception by way of the unconscious irrational aimed at pure perception'.
Properties 3, 4.

Messer, E. A. (1967) says 'Intuition is also an irrational function: it is a perception of realities which are not known to consciousness, a perception therefore which comes by way of the unconscious. To Jung, it is also an active creative process, which comes into play when judgments are made without conscious decision' (p. 40).
Properties 3, 4, 7.

Piaget, J. and Inhelder, B. (1956) in explaining children's errors in judgment of the views of other observers, equate intuition and egocentricity '...intuitively — which is to say, egocentrically —'.
Property 8.

Sarbin, T. R. *et al.* (1960) believe all types of intuition are inferential processes that are similar to ordinary perception. They think stimuli are classified according to Piaget-type schemata — which they call modules. They say that this assigning of the characteristics of a whole class to a particular cue is a preconscious level process.
Property 3.

Bigge, M. L. and Hunt, M. P. (1965) define intuitive judgments and describe intuitive thought as: 'intuitive judgments are hypotheses based on personal convictions, supporting evidence is hidden and vague. Intuitive thought does not make use of publicly verifiable data, runs no tests on its hypotheses and totally ignores the fact that its assumptions may be false or debatable. The subject believes his assumptions to be true' (p. 105).
Properties 2, 9, 10.

Guilford, J. P. (1966, pp. 88/89) defines intuition as a form of recentring:

(1) returning information in a radically different form to the input of information — showing a high degree of novelty; or
(2) not so much the degree of alteration but the surprisingly remote connections between the original and the reproduced information.

Property 11.

Eyring, H. (1959) relates an anecdote illustrating the use of empathy in intuition. 'It is interesting to consider what qualifications make for scientific intuition. The familiar story of the racehorse that was lost is instructive. The lost horse was sought for all day by the entire town, unsuccessfully. On the second day the village fool went out and in an hour returned with the horse. In response to inquiry as to his procedure, he explained that the first day he sat and thought what he would do were he a horse. On the second day he went to the point where he himself would have gone. The horse was there' (p. 6).
Property 12.

Taft, R. (1960) also recognizes the empathic component in intuition. 'Probably these [intuitive] judgments carry their sense of immediacy and

conviction because of empathic components, i.e. kinaesthetic and affective responses in the judge.'
Properties 10, 12.

Intuition shares certain properties with the creative process. Tauber, E. S. and Green, M. R. (1959) consider them essentially identical, and group them together with dreams and subliminal perception as 'prelogical' experience, opposed to the 'logical' processes of reason. Piotrowski, Z. A. (1971) also notes the non-logical properties of intuition. On intuition he says: 'In every empirical reference of a concept, there is an intuitive, non-rational, qualitive element — non-rational meaning, everything that cannot be duplicated by a mechanical device'.
Property 4.

This contrast with the logical process is also noted by Garard, R. W. (1962). 'The brute power of logic is useless somehow, you get the clue and that's that. The moment it comes there is no question about the right solution. It carries with it a strong feeling of certainty. Occasionally you are wrong, but most of the time you are correct.'
Properties 2, 9, 10.

De Groot, A. D. (1965) refers to chess intuition as unlike other knowledge in that it cannot be verbalized but is activated by situations. He says most skills depend largely on 'intuitive experience' i.e. on a system of methods that one cannot explicitly describe (p. 147). He notes that when knowledge is incomplete intuition can give the confidence for a decision. 'In chess nearly every argumentation is incomplete and decisions are based on necessarily incomplete evidence. There is a strong need for "intuitive completion" to enable the subject to build up the subjective certainty he requires for actual decisions' (p. 150).
Properties 5, 10, 14.

Bartlett, F. C. (1968) also thinks that in an intuitive kind of thinking, the steps are not articulated or stated but they could be. See also Cartwright, M. L. (1955, pp. 9-12) who agrees with this.
Property 14.

Bruner, J. S. (1960) says of intuitive thinking: 'Intuitive thinking characteristically does not advance in careful, well-planned steps. Indeed, it tends to involve manoeuvres based seemingly on an implicit perception of the total problem. The thinker arrives at an answer, which may be right or wrong, with little if any awareness of the process by which he reached it' (pp. 57/58).
Properties 3, 4, 15.

It is widely recognized that intuition uses global knowledge, e.g. 'Such inspirations, it is well recognized, rarely come unless an individual has immersed himself in a subject. He must have a rich background of knowledge and experience in it...without this flash the creative process might never have been able to get started' (Sinnott, E. W., 1959, pp. 24/25).
Properties 5, 7, 15.

Gagne, R. M. (1965) wrote in agreement with the previous reference that

intuitive thought requires a wide knowledge of the subject matter in which the problem is set: '...the great discoverers almost always had a great grasp of the field in which they were working'.
Property 15.

Another author who contrasts reason and intuition is Arnheim, R. (1970) who says that there are two kinds of perceptive thinking, intuitive and intellectual cognition. By intuitive cognition he means relations between various components in a perceptual field mostly at a preconscious level. 'A good deal of thinking and problem-solving goes on in, and by means of intuitive cognition' (p. 233).
Properties 3, 4.

Vernon, P. E. (1972) also points to the preconscious properties of intuition. 'Those intuitive judgments of people are essentially the same as any others but they depend on less fully instantiated cues, i.e. unconscious, and processed by less explicit concepts and principles' (p. 51).
Property 3.

Based on the Jungian concept of thinking versus feeling for evaluating experience the Myers-Briggs-type indicator using two postulated perceptions of sensation and intuition scores 25 per cent of the general population as intuitive (Myers, I. B., 1962).
Property 6.

Neisser, U. (1963b) notes that when logical processing cannot be used intuitive processing is used by default. 'Mental processes of this kind [intuitive] seem to be common wherever there are situations too complex for ready logical analysis' (p. 308).
Property 4.

In psychoanalytic writings the word intuition is used in the sense of insight into a patient's feelings — diagnosis on little quantitive evidence (Berne, E., 1957, p. 614).
Property 16.

In another paper, Berne (1955) defined a particular use of the word 'intuition'. 'A primal image is the image of an infantile object relationship, that is, of the use of the function of an erogenous zone for social expression. A primal judgment is the understanding (correct or incorrect) of the potentialities of the object relationship represented by the image. In the normal adult, under ordinary conditions, neither the primal image nor the primal judgment comes into awareness. Instead, a more or less distant derivative, which is called here an intuition, may become conscious' (p. 1).
Properties 3, 9.

On page 10 of *Productive Thinking,* Wertheimer, M. (1959) contrasts intuition and logic. He criticizes logical thought as being in 'danger of being empty and senseless, though exact' relative to intuitive thought.
Property 4.

A common dictionary definition of intuition is: 'Conscious awareness without logical reasons'.
Property 4.

Fischbein, E. (1972) defines intuition as 'His [pupil's] own means of direct comprehension'. He distinguishes between two types of intuition in mathematics:

(1) intuitions of adhesion — a feeling of evidence such that the need for a mathematical proof is not felt;
(2) intuitions of anticipation — a global vision of the solution to a problem that precedes the vigorous and explicit construction of the solution.

He says 'Intuitions base themselves on mental habits'.
Properties 4, 5, 6, 10, 13, 15.
Fischbein further defines:

(1) primary intuitions which are constructed during the subject's onto-genesis before and outside any systematic intuition; and
(2) secondary intuitions which are academically learnt, e.g. intuitions based on Newton's Laws. He says these are new intuitions and not altered old ones. He uses 'intuition' to mean 'model' in this context.

Fischbein quotes Bergson's view that 'intelligence and intuition are opposing and irreducible modalities of knowledge'. Bergson's definition of intuition is that intuition is a direct knowledge of vital phenomena and is an extension of the instinct. However, these words are ill-defined in this context. Fischbein (1972) says in his paper '...long familiarisation with a certain field of knowledge transforms it into an immediate form of synthetic global knowledge having the characteristics of intuition'.
Properties 4, 5, 15, 16.

Theoretical Considerations of Insight

Varieties of meaning are attached to the word 'insight' by different authors in different fields (Hartmann, G. W., 1931, p. 249). This section enumerates the listed properties of insight as used in theoretical psychological, psychoanalytic, and general theoretical literature rather than as used in operational situations. Where the attributed properties contradict properties elsewhere positively attributed to insight, this is indicated by a negative sign in the properties list.

Hartmann in his 1931 survey of insight, notes three categories of meaning of the term insight.

(1) A form of intuitive knowledge of a complex situation — the Geistes-wissenschaft school implies a meaning ordinarily attached to empathy.
(2) A person's ability to appraise his individual resources in agreement with others. 'Insight in this case has fundamentally an egocentric reference' (p. 243).
(3) A type of learning giving novel solutions to puzzle situations — con-figurational learning.

Hartmann gives a review of other writers' pertinent criteria for insight but not definitions of insight. He asks: 'Is the moment of insight emotionally toned?' (p. 252). Originally he notes that the criterion of insight was the occurrence of complete solutions with reference to the total organization of the field.

Properties 2, 8, 11, 12, 15.

Watson, G. (1964) gives four conditions under which insight occurs. 'The experience of learning by sudden insight into a previously confused or puzzling situation arises when

(a) there has been a sufficient background and preparation,
(b) attention is given to the relationships operative in the whole situation,
(c) the perceptual structure "frees" the key elements to be shifted into new patterns,
(d) the task is meaningful and within the range of ability of the subject.

The term "cognitive reorganization" is sometimes applied to this experience. Suddenly the scene changes into one that seems familiar and can be coped with.' This process is also called recentring.

Properties 1, 5, 11, 15.

Neisser, U. (1963a) says that in insightful thinking the situation is viewed as a whole, simultaneously rather than one isolated part at a time. Also '"insight" seems to involve building a novel hierarchy of existing processes. There is ample evidence already that the "components" of insightful behaviour must be established in advance. The present suggestion is that their potential existence is not enough, they must be simultaneously operative if a novel recombination is to emerge' (p. 307). Birch, H. G. (1945) also sees insight as a global reorganization of existing experience.

Properties 5, 11.

On the relation of insight to experience Bigge, M. L. and Hunt, M. P. (1965) say: 'Insights are dependent not only on the nature of the environment, or confronting situation, but also on the influence of one's experience and one's purposes at a time' (p. 497). The authors shift to different meanings of 'insight' throughout the book. Here they are using 'insight' in the same context as the Gestalt Field Psychologists.

Properties 5, 19.

One of the founders of the Gestalt School of Psychology, Köhler, W. (1947) gives several personal examples of insight and observes that: 'The layman believes that he often feels directly why he wants to do certain things in a first situation...' (p. 188). From several examples of 'insight' from his own experience, he notes how one better understands by feeling and how direct experience is more formative than 'scientific induction' (p. 190). 'My experience told me more than any scientific induction could.' (Referring to appreciation of an opera singer.) He uses 'insight' in a different sense from some authors to mean instinctive understanding of experience; understanding through emotional appreciation.

Properties 6, 12.

The Gestalt Field Psychologists' view of insight is put forward by Bigge, M. L. and Hunt, M. P. (1965) as a sense of feeling of pattern, or relationships, 'sensed way through' 'feel'. Insights they say are not necessarily true. They give a concise definition of insight (p. 341) as 'feeling for, basic sense of relationships'.

Properties 6, 18.

This is similar to the insight definition by Bigge, M. L. (1968). 'Basic sense of, or feeling for, relationships. Gestalt Field Psychologists' definition: Insight development is a change in cognitive structure of a life space' (pp. 177/178). Much of this work repeats his earlier joint book (Bigge, M. L. and Hunt, M. P., 1965).

Properties 6, 9, 18.

Contrasting with the idea that insights might be wrong is the following definition from Woodworth, R. S. (1940): 'Some penetration into the true nature of things'.

Property 9.

Insight was defined originally as the sudden awareness of the relationships among various elements in a situation, though 'the "sudden" idea is no longer felt necessary' (English, H. B. and English, Ava C., 1958). (Also see Ausubel, D. P., 1968.)

Property 1.

Most writers in the past have held to the idea of the suddeness of insight — the ha! ha! experience or the 'Eureka' experience. 'The breakthrough type of insight comes by sudden arrival, because it is not susceptible to logical attack and can gain consideration only in a relaxed mental state or in disassociated thought' (Haefele, J. W., 1962, p. 86).

Properties 1, 4, 17.

There are many observations of creativity associated with hypnogogic reverie, also there are anecdotes of many insights occurring during this state, e.g. Kekule's conception of the benzene ring (Green, E. *et al.,* 1970).

Property 17.

In learning theory the idea of insight has caused many problems. The controversy of Gestalt with the Behaviourist view of insight learning is discussed in Section 1·1. However, Bigge, M. L. and Hunt, M. P. (1965) offer a learning-theory-type description saying that transfer in learning is generalizing insights gained in one situation to use in other situations. They give the following two examples of insightful learning:

(1) simplification of $\sqrt{(dog)^2}$;
(2) the readjustment of a Tennessee Sharpshooter using a modern rifle.

Both these examples illustrate well-learnt rules applied to superficially similar

situations. They say results may be satisfying but wrong. The authors' definition of insightful learning here seems to have degenerated to mean the finding of patterns and applying this relationship to other situations.
Property 20.

Reese, H. W. (1968) says, however: 'Transposition does not necessarily indicate the presence of reasoning or insight. Insight is not only perception of relations, but also awareness of relations, particularly cause-effect relations' (p. 239).
Properties 18, 20.

Studying the creativity of adults, Sliker, Gretchen P. (1972) says: 'It is agreed that the flash of insight referred to by many writers occurs when the mind is in a relaxed state.... This relaxed mental state immediately suggests Piaget's concept of flexibility between the mental processes of accommodation and assimilation in the young mind, a condition essential for the manifestation of egocentricity' (p. 16).
Properties 8, 17.

Wheeler, R. H. (1931) uses the term insight in a very wide sense to cover most learning situations (p. 126). He gives the term insight to any appropriate responses already organized with respect to a goal at the level of conscious behaviour. He says: 'Tensions are established and resolved in the form of configurational responses which the term, insight, serves well to describe' (pp. 259/260).
Properties 2, 18.

'Intuition' used in Experiments

Relatively few experiments have been done specifically mentioning 'intuition'. Although there are experimental studies of intuition under other titles only those researchers using the term 'intuition' will be surveyed in this section, and since consideration of the methodology of these rare experiments is particularly relevant to an understanding and any scientific investigation of intuition, they will be commented on and considered in more detail.

Kahneman, D. and Tversky, A. (1973) used the term 'intuitive judgments' to mean guessing estimators from statistical data. E's showed that S's used representativeness for statistical prediction and that S's confidence depends on how representative his selection of the input data is, i.e. the more consistent the input data, then the more confident the prediction because the prediction is then more representative. Extremities of data values, it was found, falsely influenced intuitive judgments. This result may be explained if people assume a normal population. This idea of S's assessment of probability is used in several experiments in intuition.
Property 10.

Westcott, M. R. (1961) required subjects to uncover tabs, each showing a consecutive number from a series. They had to guess the next number. He also measured confidence of his subject's prediction on a five-point scale by interviewing. From the number of tabs uncovered before the subject made his prediction, Westcott was able to distinguish between high and low information demanders. This was relevant as Westcott considers that an intuitive type is willing to make inferences based on little information (p. 268). Solutions may have been, and almost certainly were reached through the use of the subject's IQ and previous knowledge; e.g. if the subject was very familiar with the series of squares, he was more likely to complete this. 16 : ? given 4 : 2, 9 : 3, 25 : 5, similarly ACEGI : ? are typical IQ-type questions; (see section 8.1 for other examples). Confidence is a measure of previous experience in this type of problem, and so it may have been better to use problems with no answers to avoid the use of known techniques. Westcott also used the FL and IE scales from the Vassar College Attitude Inventory (Sanford, R.N. *et al.,* 1957), and the Taylor Scale (Taylor, Janet, 1953). The following is not reported in the above paper but in Westcott, M. R. (1964, p. 43).

The above tests failed to discriminate very successfully between the groups, as did verbal and mathematical aptitude tests from the College Entrance Board, etc. However, an item analysis of the personality scales showed that high information demanders, regardless of success, tended to show caution, conservatism, compliance, and relative unawareness of inner states, though successful problem-solvers were more variable. Low information demanders tended to be moody, introspective, unconventional, tensely involved in what they were doing. Unsuccessful subjects were defensive and unrealistic. Personality characteristics of low information demanders may be indicative of an 'intuitive type'. A criticism of this experiment is that accuracy is the measure of success.

Properties 10, 18, 20.

Gray, C. W. (1968) writing on 'Man as an intuitive statistician' devised an experiment in which subjects had to predict from seeing pairs of cards with a number on each, which number went with a presented card. There was a linear relationship between the pairs and numbers. Gray found that there was a correlation between the predicted and presented numbers but that matching rather than optimization was used for prediction.

Properties 18, 20.

One of Thurstone's students, Bouthilet, Lorraine (1948), devised an experiment in which the hidden criterion was to associate words containing the same letters. Subjects were trained and tested. She found that success rose above chance before the point at which the subject stated the criterion. There were one to two steps on the success curves that she considered represented intuition. This type of learning curve is considered typical of intuitive learning.

Properties 14, 18, 20.

Earle, T. C. (1972) also devised a numerical prediction experiment and introduced degrees of randomness in some of the matched pairs. Subjects had to predict a value C (between 1 and 20) dependent on given values A and B (both between 1 and 10). An intuitive approach was elicited by an instruction to use the 'intuitive approach characterized by speed and lack of analytical thought'. *A* and *B* were presented using heights of bar graphs. The group working under the intuitive approach were told not to use the numerical values in finding the relationships between *A, B,* and *C.* 'The analytical approach is characterized by slow careful reasoning.' A pencil and paper were given to subjects on the analytic trials — ninety in all. Self-reports were classed as 'intuitive' if by default no analytic method was used. Results showed that intuitive methods were inaccurate compared with analytic methods but that analytic methods were equally inaccurate when used on inconsistent tasks. Earle defines an intuitive task as one with few cognitive aids (p. 41). A criticism of Earle's definition of intuition (by default of being analytic) is that it is negative and involves only one property of intuition. Also he should have avoided possibly inducing an intuitive approach in non-intuitive types by blocking on personality types in his experimental design.

Properties 14, 18, 20.

Rossman, B. B. and Horn, J. J. (1972) used one hundred and eighty-eight arts and engineering students to whom they gave tests on ninety variables. In a factor analysis they found that the fifth factor was one of 'rule-orientated' versus 'intuitive': '...for creative people are often said to be intuitive and not rule bound' (p. 280). This factor represented a major distinction between engineering and arts students. It had positive loading with general reasoning and a negative loading with the sixteen personality factor test's factor one, *viz.* sensitivity.

Properties 4, 7.

Westcott, M. R. and Ranzoni, J. H. (1963), in an experiment to find correlates of intuitive thinking, used data from a previous experiment of Westcott's (1961) with interviewers (see above). They describe 'intuition' as '...reaching a conclusion on the basis of little information which is normally reached on the basis of significantly more information' (p. 595). They found (p. 610) that successful intuitive thinkers are 'deeply involved emotionally in what they are doing'. Otherwise they found the same personality correlates for intuitive thinking as have been found elsewhere for creativity, e.g. tolerance of ambiguity, etc.

Properties 2, 7.

Thorsland, M. N. and Novak, J. D. (1972), using twenty-five subjects, compared two problem-solving approaches to problems in physics:

(1) analytic approach — step-by-step analysis; and
(2) intuitive approach — implicit 'feel' for the subject with little or no conscious awareness of the steps used in arriving at an answer.

This definition of the intuitive approach can be criticized as was Earle's above as a definition by default of not being analytic, and indeed the authors found when compared with interview information on the type of approach used this method of defining an intuitive approach was not so reliable as the method of defining an analytic approach (analytic $p < 0.01$, intuitive $p < 0.05$) 'indicating

that the intuitive ratings assigned varied somewhat more than the analytic ratings from problem to problem' (p. 4). Results showed that the intuitive and analytic type is at an advantage in both learning time spent and resultant learning efficiency. Authors also quote Ausubel, D. P. (1968): '...intuitive dimension being a manifestation of the existence and utilization of over-all superordinate concepts' (p. 9).
Properties 3, 4, 6, 15.

'Insight' used in Experiments

The listed properties of intuition and insight are now enumerated as they are attributed to operational definitions of insight. Insight experiments generally use practical problems to test insight or they expect the subject to guess unknown criteria, usually for sorting. Some experiments are logic tasks in which the experimenters operationally define insight in terms of knowing how to falsify a statement. There are also animal experiments where the term insight is operationally defined in behaviourial terms.

Experiments Using Practical Insight Problems

Many experiments on 'insight' use practical problems, where the subject is given some apparatus to be used in the problem. Solution is usually by recentring where the subject uses the apparatus in an unconventional way.

The following problem (Maier, N. R. F., 1931) has been used in several investigations on insight. Two strings are hung from the ceiling from opposite sides of the room. Each string is too short to carry over to the other. The problem is to tie the ends. One solution is to tie a weight on to one string and make it into a pendulum.
Property 11.

In an attempt to predict success on an insight problem Burke, R. J. and Maier, N. R. F. (1965) chose the above pendulum problem as their 'insight problem' and measured many suggested predictors of insightful ability, but say that different abilities from the ones they measured are needed for the solution of insightful problems. They did not measure empathy or the other properties listed in Table 1.3/1.

A similar example of a practical test often used is the hat rack problem. The subject, in an empty room, is presented with two sticks, a G-clamp, and a hat. He is instructed to make a stable structure on which to hang the hat. There are many solutions which Duncker, K. (1945) examines in detail, one of which is to clamp the two sticks so as to make one strut long enough to wedge between the ceiling and floor of the room. The hat is hung on the clamp.

Dominowski, R.L. and Jenrick, Regina (1972) in studying the effect of hints and interpolated activity on the solution of an insight problem used the hat rack problem. They discovered that the effect of hints was not to put *S* on the right track but to stop *S* from following wrong leads. The Gestalt transformation test was used as a measure of problem-solving ability. Some interaction was found between hints and interpolated activity for high-ability subjects.

Property 11.

The hat rack problem was also used by Maier, N. R. F. and Burke, R. J. (1967) who were interested in the preconscious incubation period before the realization of the insight, specifically the influence of timing of hints on their effectiveness in problem-solving. Three hundred and eighty-three subjects were tested. It was found that the value of each hint depends upon the incorrect activity it eliminates. Timing of hints did not affect problem-solving activity. Hence if no activity, or no wrong activity, is in process then the hint is no use.

Property 11.

Another practical problem was used by Murray, G. H. and Denny, P. J. (1969) in a study of the interaction of ability level and interpolated activity (opportunity for incubation) in human problem-solving. The experimenters placed balls in a cylinder on a tray which had to be placed in another cylinder which was immovable. Both were out of reach. Tools for the insightful solution were string, a wire coat hanger and lots of newspapers. A solution was to make a hook from the coat hanger, tie it to the string, then holding one end of the string to throw the hook to catch the tray which could then be pulled to within the subject's reach. The subject then rolls the newspapers so as to make a telescopic tube down which the balls may be rolled into the immovable cylinder. These 'insight' problems at the human ability level are analogous to Köhler's chimpanzee insight problems.

Property 11.

There are practical problems similar to this given by Wertheimer, M. (1959), e.g. the bridge problem — where S must span two blocks with lintels that are too short. However, Wertheimer calls this type of problem an 'intuitively' solved problem not an insight problem. A criticism of this type of insight experiment is that no account has been taken of the subject's practical experience which most probably influences his ability to solve such practical problems.

Insight Experiments Requiring Subjects to Discover Rules

A different group of insight experiments are of the 'guess the rule' genre. The S makes a choice and is reinforced if the choice is correct according to some criteria unknown to him. Success curves are plotted. Success rises above chance before S can verbalize the criteria. Jumps on the learning curves are interpreted as the indication of occurrence of 'insight'.

This type of experiment was used by Snapper, A. (1956). Working under Eric Heinemann, Snapper required S to sort four hundred different cards into boxes with reference to a sample card pasted on the front of the correct box. There was also a rejection box. Subjects were told if they were right or wrong. Twenty-five successive correct sortings was the stringent criterion for success.

The curves of increasing success for the fifty-two subjects were similar to simple learning curves. Six subjects had slow increasing success to criterion. Thirteen of the subjects gave an insight curve with a sharp jump in success occurring after some trials. The other thirty-three subjects failed to reach criterion. Subjects who reached criterion in small increments average fewer trials than the insight subjects but the insight subjects were able to state the criteria involved whereas those who reached criterion slowly could not as a rule offer a reason for their success. The non-verbalizers treated the test as 'fun' in a relaxed casual way as opposed to the hypothesis-testing procedure of the verbalizers. This experiment may be criticized as being a direct result of operant conditioning of a sensory-motor discrimination response. It is unusual that in this experiment some subjects were never explicitly aware of the criterion.

Properties 18, 20.

Pickford, R. (1938) showed subjects various polygons which they had to put into preselected but undefined categories — e.g. a category of having a right angle — without being told that this was the defining characteristic of the group. Subjects were told if they were correct or not on each trial. Subjects were asked to state the criterion for choice as soon as it was known to them. Pickford also found that success rate rose above chance before the subjects could verbalize their criteria.

Properties 14, 18.

Drever, J. I. (1934) used the same criterion as Pickford (1938) above. The subject was presented with polygons and had to guess the rule that the 'correct' ones had a right angle. Insight was judged to have occurred when they guessed the rule. Eight subjects did not guess the rule. Drever offers as explanation of successful subjects, not that trial and error or chance could explain his results, but that 'it [the learning curve] suggests a preliminary adaptation without which no further progress is possible'. He uses the word 'orientation'.

Properties 18, 20.

Prentice, W. C. H. (1949) showed subjects a circle and a square, side by side, on a glass fibre panel. The figures on each showing differed in a number of ways not identified for the subjects. On each showing the subjects were required to 'choose' one picture thought to be 'correct' according to the unknown criteria. To test the Continuity Theory (that presolution or pre-insight trials are of no significance) false reinforcement was given but no effect of negative transfer was noticed.

Properties 18, 20.

Hartmann, G. W. (1933), in a comparison of insight versus trial and error in the solution of problems, designed ten tests so that 100 per cent failure preceded the insight which was followed by 100 per cent success. All tests required subjects to 'find the principle underlying each series'. The principles were:

(1) *E* points to a dot at each end of a line of dots hidden in a random pattern of dots;

(2) *E* selects the innermost concave indentation of the left member of a pair of figures and the outermost convex projection of the right member;

(3) *E* underlines words which have a particular relation to the rest of the sentence;

(4) *E* shows three triangles and points to the smallest, middle, and largest angles of each respectively;

(5) inverted analogies, etc.;

(6) syllogisms.

From his results Hartmann notes: 'Even "false" insights occur, i.e. they arise suddenly and carry emotional conviction as intense as the "real" ones...' However, he did not use this fact for recognizing insight occurring during his experiments.

Properties 2, 9, 18.

In an experimental enquiry into the existence and nature of 'insight' Bulbrook, Mary E. (1932) used a series of experiments most of which contained an implied taboo, e.g. the solution required breaking *E*'s beads in order to rearrange them. This is an example of an inhibiting factor which is an acceptance of inferred restrictions in many 'insight' experiments. The 'trick' is to ignore these restrictions so that a recentring may take place and lead to a solution. Other experiments required a solution derived from putting objects that were outside the experimental apparatus into a new relationship with the objects in the experiment, whereas I believe in such experiments the solution should be contained in the solver and/or the experiments. An example is that ink was left 'handy' for colouring some beads black so as to meet the requirement of a specific black/white ordering. Emotional involvement was observed by Bulbrook: 'There is always an accompaniment of pleased pride in solution.... In failure there is frustration...' (p. 415).

Other experiments were of the 'guess the rule' type. The rule being the order of tapping a line of boxes to indicate which box in the line should be opened. *E* designed a closure experiment where exploded and ill-proportioned letters, e.g.

representing R, were to be recognized. Kinaesthetic physiognomy was noted from some subjects (p. 421). A recentring experiment where *S* has to make four triangles with six matches was also used; the solution being a tetrahedron. One experiment required the rearrangement of letters to form a word. To reach the solution one letter had to be rotated.

Properties 2, 11, 18.

Insight Experiments using Logic Relations

A series of experiments by Wason, P. C. and various colleagues using logical reasoning tasks, purport to be concerned with 'insight'. Johnson-Laird, P. N. and Wason, P. C. (1970a) presented subjects with cards bearing the characters

A, D, 4, or 7. Subjects had to choose which cards to turn so as to prove or disprove the statement — 'if a card has a vowel on one side, then it has an even number on the other side'. Authors call 'insight' the realization that cards must be chosen so as to falsify the condition. They also devised a similar experiment using coloured triangles.
Property 11.

Johnson-Laird, P. N. and Wason, P. C. (1970b) did two similar experiments on 'insight into a logical relation'. By choosing black or white triangles subjects had to prove true or false the proposition 'all the triangles are black' or 'if they are triangles then they are black'. The other experiment used types of diagrams hidden inside envelopes which subjects had to choose in order to prove a similar proposition true or false. Authors showed (p. 49) that insight depends upon the complexity of the material and that insight is gained more easily by using concrete materials.
Properties 5, 11.

Similar abstract reasoning tests using coloured cards bearing triangles or squares were used by Goodwin, R. Q. and Wason, P. C. (1972) in a study of 'degrees of insight'.
Property 11.

When Wason, P. C. and Shapiro, D. (1971) presented the same logical reasoning tasks in concrete terms, they found 'it became markedly easier to solve, compared with presentation in terms of abstract, unconnected material'. This is a general finding that reasoning is easier with concrete analogies.
Property 5.

In his strongly flavoured Gestalt book on the psychology of practical and mathematical problem-solving, Duncker, K. (1945) discusses in detail the pendulum problem and other similar problems. He makes the observation that some 'insight' problems are reached only by a dodge, i.e. the solution is obtainable only by a rare recentring of the given facts. On pages 64 and 65 Duncker discusses two types of insight in problem-solving:

(1) insight as a realization that things belong in a common category;
(2) why they are thus connected.

Property 11.

Dymond, R. F. (1948) used the term 'insight' as in psychotherapy: '...intellectual and emotional realization by the subject of the circumstances and relationships out of which his symptoms arose'. *E* talks of *S*'s 'expectation response patterns which he brings to a new ambiguous situation', but these are developed by *S*'s observation of how others react to him. Subjects were twenty students of high IQ. They were given TAT cards for which *E* used the standard instructions as in the manual. The ten pictures were shown at each of two weekly interviews. On the results *E* was able to split subjects into high and low empathy groups, and compared with his interview results *E* found 'these

conditions suggest that empathy may be one of the underlying mechanisims on which insight is based'. A criticism is that a very small number of subjects was used and the paper gives an impression of *ad hoc* theories to interpret her inconsistent results found from little statistical analysis.
Properties 2, 12.

Experiments on 'Animal Insight'

There is a literature on 'animal insight' which is usually discussed in terms of Behaviourist learning theories. From their experiments Kumberger, D. and Kardash, K. (1948) arrive at the conclusion that insight is a short-cut to conditioned learning by using secondary reinforcement. The authors gave secondary reinforcement of a 'signal' to a group of rats on pressing a bar to obtain food. This group learnt faster than the second group who only pressed the bar and so only received primary reinforcement.
Property 5.

Harlow, H. F. (1949) worked with monkeys solving a protracted series of discrimination problems and came to the conclusion that they seem to 'learn to learn'. He interpreted the data — before the formation of a discrimination set, a single training trial produces negligible gain, after the formation of a discrimination learning set, a single training trial constitutes problem solution — as showing 'clearly' that animals can gradually learn insight. By insight he means combining something in the situation with something that is temporarily or spatially remote, and as the experimental history of the monkey is well known he can indicate what it is the monkey brings to and combines with the significant features of the immediate situation.
Property 18.

Helson, H. (1927) studying 'insight' in rats considered the occurrence of relational responses to be a criterion of insight.
Property 18.

Numerical Comparison of the Terms 'Intuition' and 'Insight' in Theoretical and Operational Use, by their Attributed Properties

The twenty listed properties are not exhaustive or independent — see the introduction to properties attributed to intuition and insight, Section 1.3. As categories they are ill-defined, their occurrence not strictly counted, and the original cursory survey was from a 'convenience' sample rather than from a controlled sample of the literature. It follows that a robust statistical analysis based on these properties as here enumerated is not possible. Further, in several papers experimenters discuss properties of intuition and insight that are not used or implied in their experiments. As these properties are included with their operational use of the words intuition and insight, a robust statistical comparison of the categories 'theoretical usage' and 'operational usage' is also here not possible. However, a cursory numerical description will illustrate the more marked similarities and dissimilarities between these two usages of the words as found in the literature.

The following refers to Table 1.3/2, the tabulation of properties of intuition and insight in theoretical and operational usage.

The properties mentioned in the previous section (Table 1.3/1) are tabulated under the four categories:

Category 1 (C1)   Intuition in Theoretical Usage.
Category 2 (C2)   Insight in Theoretical Usage.
Category 3 (C3)   Intuition in Operational Usage.
Category 4 (C4)   Insight in Operational Usage.

'Intuition' an Older and More Generally Used Term than 'Insight'

Assuming the 'definitions' and descriptions presented here are a representative selection from the general literature, the row of totals for C1 and C2, *viz.* sixty-four references to intuition versus twenty-seven references to insight, reflects the fact that the theoretical usage of the term intuition is much older and more widespread than theoretical usage of the term insight. Many anecdotes concerning intuition appear in work of general public interest — other than psychological works. Also writers use the word commonly in a general imprecise descriptive manner, e.g. in novels. The term insight came into general usage much later and in a more definite psychological sense with the publication of Gestalt Psychology. The imprecision associated with its use as a recent psychological term is reflected in this category (C2) being the only one of the four categories to show completely opposing views from the literature, *viz.* properties 9 and 20.

The columns showing the totals are derived in the following way:

Total usage of Insight   (T1) = C2 + C4
Total usage of Intuition   (T2) = C1 + C3
Total Theoretical usage   (T3) = C1 + C2
Total Operational usage   (T4) = C3 + C4
Overall total   (T5) = C1 + C2
                                    + C3 + C4
                                    = T1 + T2
                                    = T3 + T4

The attendant percentages in the totals columns T1 to T4 show each property as a percentage of the total references to the properties in that column — for the purpose of comparison of a property between column categories, e.g. property 5 column T1 occurred a total of six times in connection with insight so 10·7 per cent of the usage of the term 'insight' is accounted for by property

42

5 (10·7% = 6 ÷ 56 × 100%). But although property 5 also occurred six times in the usage of the word 'intuition' column T2, it accounts for only 7·1 per cent of the total usage of this term (7·1% = 6 ÷ 84 × 100%).

The longer and more general use of the term intuition is shown by comparison of the totals of columns T2 and T1, *viz.* eighty-four references to properties of intuition versus only fifty-six references to properties of insight. This contrasts with the operational use of the word intuition. The total for C3, *viz.* twenty is the lowest for all four columns C1 to C4, illustrating a lack of experimental literature on intuition due mainly to the Gestalt-Behaviourists controversy — Section 1.1.

That insight is a more 'scientific term' is shown by the fact that there are approximately as many references to its theoretical usage as to its operational usage, *viz.* totals of C2 and C4 with twenty-seven and four versus twenty-nine respectively. Whereas the total theoretical usage (T3) is nearly twice as great as the total operational usage (T4), *viz.* ninety-one versus forty-nine. This is again due to the more general use of 'intuition'.

Similarities and Differences in the Meaning and Usage of 'Insight' and 'Intuition' in Terms of Their Properties

Difference columns D1 and D2 are calculated as follows:

Difference between total usage of insight and total usage of intuition (D1) = mod (T1% − T2%);
Difference between total psychological usage and total operational usage of both terms (D2) = mod (T3% − T4%).

The purpose of these columns is to highlight the properties most responsible for the similarities or dissimilarities between the meanings and usage of the words.

An indication of the similarities between categories C1-C4 and the total and operational usage of the words intuition and insight may be given by comparing the order of the priority that the literature gives to the properties in each category. The priority being inversely proportional to the number of references to the property. This can be quantified by the correlation coefficient. For example if the twenty properties have the same order of importance in two particular categories — indicated by the order of the number of references to the properties in these categories — than these two particular categories may be considered similar in terms of these properties. Spearman's rank order correlation coefficient, which is used as the absolute difference between the number of references, that decides the priority of the property within a category, is not demonstrably stable enough for the use of Pearson's product moment correlation coefficient, and cells are too small for chi-squared-based statistics.

Table 1.3/2 Tabulation of references to properties of intuition and insight in theoretical and in operational use

No.	C1	C2	C3	C4	T1	%	T2	%	T3	%	T4	%	T5	D1%	D2%
1	3	1	0	0	1	1·8	3	3·6	4	4·4	0	0·0	4	1·8	4·4
2	4	2	1	3	5	8·9	5	6·0	6	6·6	4	8·2	10	2·9	1·6
3	9	0	1	0	0	0·0	10	12·0	9	9·9	1	2·0	10	12·0	7·9
4	13	1	2	0	1	1·8	15	17·9	14	15·4	2	4·1	16	16·1	11·3
5	6	3	0	3	6	10·7	6	7·1	9	9·9	3	6·1	12	3·6	3·8
6	2	3	1	0	3	5·4	3	3·6	5	5·5	1	2·0	6	1·8	3·5
7	2	0	2	0	0	0·0	4	4·8	2	2·2	2	4·1	4	4·8	1·9
8	1	2	0	0	2	3·6	1	1·2	3	3·3	0	0·0	3	2·4	3·3
9	3	−2·0	0	1	1	1·8	3	3·6	3	3·3	1	2·0	4	1·6	1·3
10	6	0	2	0	0	0·0	8	9·5	6	6·6	2	4·1	8	9·5	2·5
11	1	3	0	9	12	21·4	1	1·2	4	4·4	9	18·4	13	20·2	14·0
12	3	2	0	1	3	5·4	3	3·6	5	5·5	1	2·0	6	1·8	3·5
13	2	0	0	0	0	0·0	2	2·4	2	2·2	0	0·0	2	2·4	2·2
14	2	0	2	1	1	1·8	4	4·8	2	2·2	3	6·1	5	3·0	3·9
15	5	2	1	0	2	3·6	6	7·1	7	7·7	1	2·0	8	3·5	5·7
16	2	0	0	0	0	0·0	2	2·4	2	2·2	0	0·0	2	2·4	2·2
17	0	3	0	0	3	5·4	0	0·0	3	3·3	0	0·0	3	5·4	3·3
18	0	4	4	8	12	21·4	4	4·8	4	4·4	12	24·5	16	16·6	20·1
19	0	1	0	0	1	1·8	0	0·0	1	1·1	0	0·0	1	1·8	1·1
20	0	−2·0	4	3	3	5·4	4	4·8	0	0·0	7	14·3	7	0·6	14·3
	64	−4·27	20	29	56		84		91		49		140		

Key:

C1 Intuition in theoretical use
C2 Insight in theoretical use
C3 Intuition in operational use
C4 Insight in operational use

T1 Total insight use
T2 Total intuition use
T3 Total theoretical use
T4 Total operational use
T5 Overall total

D1 Difference in insight and intuition use
D2 Difference in theoretical and operational use

The following notation is used:

$R(S)$ (a, b) is the rank correlation coefficient between columns a and b where $a, b \in$ C1 to C4, T1 to T5, D1, D2 in Table 1.3/3. The significance levels are from Guilford, J. P. and Fruchter, B. (1973, p. 528 appendix B, table K).

Although there is some agreement between the total usage of words intuition and insight in terms of the priority of these properties — $R(S)$ (T1, T2) = 0·538, this is the smallest but still significant ($p < 0·01$) agreement between the categories of interest. Compare this with the agreement between the theoretical usage of the terms $R(S)$ (C1, C2) = 0·741.

The operational properties of intuition and insight are in high agreement $R(S)$ (C3, C4) = 0·903 as would be expected for operational definitions have to be well-defined and admit only properties that may be explored in the experiment, thus excluding properties more difficult to define and measure, e.g. properties 1, 8, 13, 16, 17, and 19. The operational usages of insight and intuition are both in high agreement with the theoretical use of the term insight. This shows that in experimental considerations the terms are most equivalent — $R(S)$ (C2, C3) = 0·945, and $R(S)$ (C2, C4) = 0·929. Whereas the total agreement between theoretical and operational usage of the terms combined is relatively low — $R(S)$ (T3, T4) = 0·611 but still significantly ($p < 0·01$).

Table 1.3/4 is derived from Table 1.3/2 by ordering properties on D1 per cent. As can be seen from this Table (1.3/4), property 11, recentring, is most responsible for the difference between the general usage of the words insight and intuition.

Recentring is prominent in experiments on insight because it is one of the easier properties to recognize in an experimental situation. This is closely connected with property 18, sense of relations, which is also easily testable. The third property in order of dissimilarity property 4, the contrast with abstract reasoning, logic or analytic thought, is more associated with intuition, having fifteen references, than it is with insight which has only one reference. The same is true of the next in order of difference, property 3, preconscious process, with a difference of twelve. The terms are most similar in respect of property 20 — difference of only 0·6 per cent — but this similarity is due entirely to the similarity of their operational meanings.

Table 1.3/5 is derived from Table 1.3/2 by ordering properties on D2 per cent. It highlights the properties that make the combined operational use of the words different from their combined theoretical usage.

From Table 1.3/5 it is seen that property 18 is most responsible for the difference in operation and theoretical usage of the terms insight and intuition. It is noticed from Table 1.3/2 that property 18, sense of relations, with a difference of 20·1 per cent is used relatively more in operational usage than the theoretical literature would merit. Property 20 secondly separates the

Table 1.3/3 Matrix of Spearman's R(S) rank correlation of insight and intuition in theoretical and in operational use — showing similarity by properties of insight or intuition ranked on number of references to properties in these categories

	C1	C2	C3	C4	T1	T2	T3	T4	T5	D1	D2
C1	1·000	0·741	0·750	0·629	0·565	0·961	0·947	0·616	0·550	0·449	0·373
C2		1·000	0·945	0·929	0·868	0·640	0·690	0·854	0·276	0·267	0·383
C3			1·000	0·903	0·773	0·690	0·631	0·868	0·217	0·214	0·392
C4				1·000	0·947	0·565	0·586	0·961	0·357	0·402	0·539
T1					1·000	0·538	0·629	0·945	0·552	0·535	0·671
T2						1·000	0·945	0·629	0·701	0·545	0·529
T3							1·000	0·611	0·756	0·593	0·516
T4								1·000	0·533	0·523	0·720
T5									1·000	0·776	0·777
D1										1·000	0·728
D2											1·000

$N = 20$ df $= 18$

R(S) $= 0·377$ at $p = 0·05$

R(S) $= 0·534$ at $p = 0·01$

Table 1.3/4 Dissimilarity in general meaning of the terms intuition and insight, in theoretical and operational use: as shown by their properties ranked according to their relative contribution to this dissimilarity

Most dissimilar

Order	1	2	3	4	5	6	7
Property no.	11	18	4	3	10	17	7
D1% ordered	20·2	16·6	16·1	12·0	9·5	5·4	4·8

Order	8	9	10	11	12	13	14
Property no.	5	15	14	2	8	13	16
D1% ordered	3·6	3·5	3·0	2·9	2·4	2·4	2·4

Order	15	16	17	18	19	20	
Property no.	1	6	12	19	9	20	
D1% ordered	1·8	1·8	1·8	1·8	1·6	0·6	

Most similar

operational and theoretical usage of the terms because — from Table 1.3/2 — it does not occur positively in theoretical usage, but as noted above it occurs approximately equally in the operational use of both terms. Thirdly, property 11, recentring, is used more in experiments — 18·4 per cent of operational references — than the theoretical literature would indicate — 4·4 per cent of theoretical references. The property in most agreement and which also has a fair amount of references is property 2, with ten references and a difference of only 1·6 per cent. However, this is a contamination as although experimenters mention this property in their practical work, they use it less in operation than the inflated figure of 8·2 per cent of operational references would indicate. The disagreement of properties 9 and 19 — 1·3 per cent in Table 1.3/5 — is insignificant due to lack of references — 3 to 1 and 1 to 0 respectively from Table 1.3/2.

Summary of the Comparisons of 'Insight' and 'Intuition'

From a 'convenience' sample of generally available literature giving definitions and descriptions of insight and intuition, twenty properties were enumerated under the categories of insight or intuition in theoretical or operational use. Comparisons of these categories by the number of references to each of the twenty properties within each category give the following results.

The meanings of insight and intuition are most similar where used in experiments — R(S) (C3, C4) = 0·903 from Table 1.3/3 where R(S) = 0·534 at $p = 0·01$. They are quite similar in theoretical usage R(S) (C1, C2) = 0·741.

Table 1.3/5 Dissimilarity in the use of the terms intuition and insight (in theoretical compared with operational use): as shown by their properties ranked according to their relative contribution to this dissimilarity

Most dissimilar

Order	1	2	3	4	5	6	7
Property no.	18	20	11	4	3	15	1
D2% ordered	20·1	14·3	14·0	11·3	7·9	5·7	4·4

Order	8	9	10	11	12	13	14
Property no.	14	5	6	12	8	17	10
D2% ordered	3·9	3·8	3·5	3·5	3·3	3·3	2·5

Order	15	16	17	18	19	20	
Property no.	13	16	7	2	9	19	
D2% ordered	2·2	2·2	1·9	1·6	1·3	1·1	

Most similar

Insight in theoretical use coincides with intuition in experimental use R(S) (C2, C3) = 0·945. But the *overall* agreement between the terms is significant ($p < 0.01$) but relatively low R(S) (T1, T2) = 0·538.

The difference between the general meaning of the terms insight and intuition is mainly due to the difference in their theoretical and operational use. This is indicated by the rank correlation of the properties contributing to this difference in intuition and insight with the properties contributing to the difference in theoretical and operational use R(S) (D1, D2) = 0·728. This difference arises because the properties most difficult to define, measure or control that are attributed to intuition or insight in theory are ignored in operational definitions, to the advantage of the properties more amenable to experiment which, because of the more recent use of the term insight in the psychological literature, tend to be more common to the theoretical use of the term insight. Guiora, A. Z. *et al.* (1965) also note: 'General psychology concentrates on certain aspects of the phenomenon which are amenable to experimental investigation like the problems of minimal cues and remoteness of associations' (p. 118).

As this is a methodological shortcoming of the experimental literature rather than a conceptual difference, the terms intuition and insight will be considered synonymously in this investigation. Indeed other writers also consider these terms to be equivalent (Hartmann, G. W., 1931; Lorenz, K. Z., 1951; Webster's Dictionary and Oxford Dictionary) and others recognize their similarity, using the terms interchangeably in theoretical considerations (Conklin, K. R., 1970, p. 331).

Having identified this difference, special consideration is given by Bastick,

T. (1979) to the definitions, measurements or control of the relevant properties, e.g. experimental techniques are developed to formalize and measure properties 2, 9, and 10, (pp. 644 and 678). His design of the insight experiment controls for subjects' experimental history, property 5. Each property is next considered in detail and the literature on intuition is considered in depth (Chapters 2 to 8) to develop a theory of intuitive thought synthesizing the literature on these properties of intuition and to indicate experimental procedures for testing this theory.

The literature concerning intuition and insight is considered with the literature on each of the twenty properties of intuition. A simple theory of intuitive thought is developed that synthesizes this literature. The theory gives explanations of previously unexplained characteristics of intuition and some alternative explanations of the properties: explanations relating to the extant body of psychophysiological knowledge, with supporting evidence from the literature of each new or alternative explanation.

It is seen in this chapter how the developing theory of intuitive thought links these twenty diverse properties, and through its simple structure enables the findings associated with some properties to illuminate the previously unrelated observations associated with other properties. As the theory develops in terms of these diverse properties, it is seen that intuitive thought is so fundamental that it encompasses much more than what is generally accepted as intuition and that it may be considered a basic encompassing psychophysiological theory of thought and behaviour.

The twenty properties listed were chosen as those best descriptive of 'intuition' and 'insight' as used in the general literature and far from being independent they are related in complex ways.

Preconscious processes are a subset of all mental processes some of which are preverbal concepts $3 \cap 14 \neq \phi$.

Abstract reasoning and logic or analytic thought is no part of hypnogogic reverie. Property 4 states that intuition does not exhibit abstract and logic or analytic thought.

Hypnogogic reverie is part of those thoughts that are not abstract reasoning or logic and analytic thought $17 \subset 4$.

No reasoning or analytic thought is a preconscious process $4 \cap 3 \neq \phi$.

A concept is defined as: 'That type or level of cognitive process which is characterized by the thinking of qualities, aspects, and relations of objects, at which therefore, comparison, generalization, abstraction, and reasoning become possible...' (Drever, J., 1974, p. 47).

So hypnogogic reverie and any form of concept are disjoint $17 \cap 14 \neq \phi$.

Innate, instinctive knowledge or ability seems to be a contradiction as instinct is congenital and knowledge is not. However, we may consider instinctive knowledge as 'animal impulse', i.e. having complex instinctive responses for specific situations rather than a cognitive knowledge of the correct behaviour to be adopted in that situation. Knowledge is usually defined as 'cognition, familiarity gained by actual experience' (Hayward, A. L. and Sparkes, J. J., 1970). Considering this meaning, instinct must be disjoint to reasoning and logic and concepts. $13 \cap 4 \neq \phi$ $13 \cap 14 \neq \phi$, i.e. is contained in property 4 $13 \subset 4$.

If hypnogogic reverie is instinctive then $17 \cap 13 \neq \phi$ but this is a complex issue not completely understood.

Properties 3, 4, 14, and 17 are affected by experience but property 13 is not affected by experience $5 \cap A \neq \phi$, $\forall A \subset \{3, 4, 14, 17, \sim 13\}$. The relations between these six properties may be illustrated as shown in Figure 1.3/6. The universal set is the psychophysiological responses of the individual.

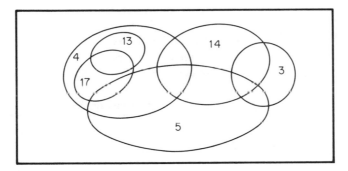

Fig. 1.3/6 Illustration of part of the complex interdependence between just six properties of intuition

The interrelations become more complex as more properties are considered, and difficulties arise from the contrasting views of these properties as found in the literature.

Table 1.3/7 gives the twenty properties of intuition listed according to the total number of references to them in Section 1.3, ordered by column T5 of Table 1.3/2. The twenty properties are now discussed in this order of priority to develop a simple theory incorporating all these properties and their complex interrelations and to indicate experimental procedures for testing the theory. The theory will offer a definition which, being the first definition consistent with all these properties generally attributed to intuition, may be considered as the first consensus definition of intuition.

Table 1.3/7 Numbered properties of intuition and insight ordered by total number of references to them in column T5 of Table 1.3/2

Section order	Number of references	Property number	Name of property
2.1	16	4	Contrast with abstract reasoning, logic, or analytic thought
2.2	16	18	Sense of relations
2.3	13	11	Recentring
2.4	12	5	Influenced by experience
3	10	2	Emotional involvement
4.1	10	3	Preconscious process
4.2	8	10	Subjective certainty of correctness
5	8	15	Global knowledge
6.1	7	20	Transfer and transposition
6.2	6	6	Understanding by feeling
6.3	6	12	Empathy, kinaesthetic or other
7.1	5	14	Preverbal concept
7.2	4	1	Quick, immediate, sudden appearance
7.3	4	7	Associations with creativity
8.1	4	9	Intuition need not be correct
8.2	3	8	Associations with egocentricity
8.2	3	17	Hypnogogic reverie
8.3	2	13	Innate, instinctive knowledge or ability
8.3	2	16	Incomplete knowledge
8.4	1	19	Dependence on environment

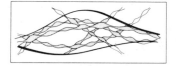

2

Experienced Sense of Relationships

2.1 INTUITION CONTRASTS WITH LOGIC

This contrast is one of the most noticed properties of intuition: property 4 with sixteen references to it in Section 1.3, Table 1.3/2.

'The issue of logical versus the intuitive approach is a major one and warrants a book-sized discussion' (Kline, M., 1976, p. 451). The intuitive thought process is contrasted with analytical thought on several properties of intuition. Intuition has emotional involvement: property 2, Chapter 3. Analytic thought is 'cold' and emotion-free. Intuitive thought is dependent on the past experiences and the present situation of the intuiter, property 19, Section 8.3, whereas analytic thought is considered independent of personal experience, property 5, Section 2.4, and independent of the immediate environment. The intuitive process is preconscious but analytic thought is entirely a conscious discipline. Pure analytic thought, being devoid of feeling, cannot share the subjective feeling of certainty that accompanies even wrong intuitions, property 10, Section 4.2. Analytic thought is a linear step-by-step often slow process whereas intuitive thought is sudden, property 1, Section 7.2, and depends on parallel processing of a global field of knowledge, property 15, Chapter 5, whereas analytic thought only compares two elements at a time.

Intuition depends on physiological functions, e.g. understanding by feeling and instinct, property 6 and property 13, also hypnogogic reveries, property 17, and most importantly empathy, property 12, Section 6.3. Most of these contrasts are detailed in the relevant sections rather than in this section. However, pure analytic thought, pure reason, or pure intellect in contrast to intuition is considered to be entirely independent of our physiology, e.g. machine intelligence. It is considered in this investigation, however, that what is generally called analytic thought is, like all thought, interwoven with our intuitive processes and cannot exist independently; see Section 7.3 on intuitively guided analysis. Many analyses, as processes, can of course exist independently of human thought.

Baer, R.A. Jr. (1976) tells us that the contrast between intuitive and rational thought was present even in the middle ages. 'The Middle Ages distinguished between ratio (the power of discursive, logical thought) and intellectus (the power of direct intuition)... open to the gift of inner understanding' (p. 27). Poincaré, H. (1969) is a mathematician who contrasts intuition with logical thought and comments on the insufficiency of logic alone. 'This shows us that logic is not enough; that the science of demonstration is not all science and that intuition must retain its role as complement, I was about to say as counterpoise or as antidote of logic' (p. 209). Berne, E. (1949) in *The Nature of Intuition* writes that logical thinking interferes with the intuitive process. Hutchinson, E.D. (1941) in *The Nature of Insight* contrasts intuitive thought with analytic thought on its property of suddenness. He compares 'the more systematic constructive processes on the one hand, and the insightful or intuitive... on the other. The logical progressive, steadily integrating process of thought merges by imperceptible degrees into the intuitive, the suddenly integrating, the a-logical' (p. 31). Koestler, A. (1959) reports that scientists like Copernicus, Kepler, and Galileo resist the 'obvious' and use the 'illogical' for their creations.

Unlike the analytic process of reasoning, intuition is not logical but categorizes on common associated feelings rather than common logical properties; see Section 8.1 on allo-logical errors of the intuitive process. Allport, G.W. (1929) quotes writers who also '...make a sharp distinction between intuitive and intellectual knowledge' (p. 17). Clark, F.V. (1973) says: 'However, intuition remains primarily a cognitive function outside of the province of reason...' (p. 159). Giordana, G. (1976) recommends the study of organizational structures as: 'They create an awarness that there are intuitive and logical organizational structures and that these structures have different functions' (p. 7). Skinner, B.F. (1969) posits a twofold view of cognition. He sees a rule following analytic strategy contrasted with an intuitive contingent mode. Board, R. (1958) writing on intuition contrasts it with methodical thinking '...an antirationalistic alternative to methodical thinking... intuitive rather than systematic approach as intuition is used to replace methodological thinking...' (p. 223). Bartlett, F.C. (1958) also contrasts intuitive processes with the step-by-step analytic process.

Analytic versus Intuitive Thought Construed as Discrete Consecutive Binary Relations versus Continuous Simultaneous Multirelations

The analytic process may be considered as a step-by-step process comparing just two elements at a time. This contrasts with the intuitive process which uses feedback feelings for the whole field of knowledge simultaneously. This intuitive parallel process results in, among other things, a marked difference in the speed of processing; see Section 5.4 on non-linear parallel processing of global multicategorized information giving the speed and error distributions

Fig. 2.1/1 Comparing three sizes intuitively and analytically

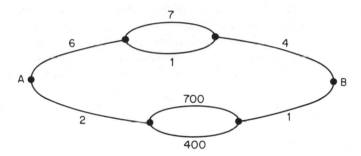

Fig. 2.1/2 Analytic solutions of the shortest route given by
pairwise comparisons

characteristic of intuitive processes, and Section 7.2 on the speed of the
intuitive process.

Consecutive discrete binary relations are characteristic of analytic thoughts
and logical reasoning, involving two elements at a time in a linear manner.
Where many elements are used in an analytical analysis they are either grouped
into sets for binary operations or are considered pairwise; in contrast is the
three-body problem from dynamics. Similarly 'the components of intuitive
thought processes act within a continuous field' (Arnheim, R., 1970, p. 234).
In illustration Arnheim compares the intellectual and intuitive comparison of
three sizes. Intuitive thought takes the whole field when comparing the three
sizes. Intellectual (analytic) thought compares two at a time. When a non-
linear data structure is analytically analysed, liner branches are reasoned
separately not simultaneously, or the properties of branches are grouped for
pairwise analysis. This grouping for pairwise analytic analysis is illustrated in
the process of solution in finding the quickest route between nodes A and B in
the network of Fig. 2.1/2. Also complex analytic groupings can be dissembled,
e.g. tensor operations reduce to binary operations on elements. The example
above illustrates the point made in the literature that analytic thought uses a
restrictive field, *viz.* two elements at a time.

Intuitive thought in contrast seems to use the whole field of knowledge;
reference property 15, global knowledge, in Chapter 5. Associated ideas and
feelings affect one another in a non-linear simultaneous feedback process,
detailed in Section 6.2 on feedback systems of the body and their interaction

54

with cognitive events. This process is often preconscious — property 3. Concepts formed preconsciously are called, by Vygotsky, L.S. (1962), 'spontaneous concepts as opposed to analytically derived scientific concepts'. An analogous example for contrast with the structure of the above examples on analytic thought is the global feedback effect on the distribution and quantity of charges on the plates of a charging condenser. The building charge on one plate induces charge on the other which in turn reduces the charge on the plate connected to source. The smoothed exponential build up is described by the usual differential equations. Also the changing charges on the plates affect the distribution of the many neighbouring charges simultaneously.

Another analogy of the global feedback effect within the field of knowledge during intuitive thought, is the simultaneous relocating of elements in a stable system on the introduction of a new element. For example, imagine isolated north magnetic poles floating in a north ring magnet. They will float to a stable position. Now introduce another north pole. Each magnet's subsequent movement affects every other magnet in a global probablistic feedback process which eventually stabilizes.

Fig. 2.1/3 Analogous example of global feedback in the intuitive process contrasting with the analytic process

The interrelations become more complex as more properties are considered, and difficulties arise from the contrasting views of these properties as found in the literature. The contrast between the linear detailed analytic information processing and the intuitive parallel global information processing is reflected in the individual's cognitive style. The intuitive type prefers complexity and multidimensional categorizing in contrast to the analytic type who prefers simplicity and symmetry and who is more intolerant of ambiguous categorization. Hence by considering from the literature cognitive styles in terms of analytic versus intuitive processes and other properties of intuition, it might be possible to use extant indicators of these cognitive styles to predict the intuitive versus analytic type; see Section 5.2 on cognitive style and intuitive perception.

Thorsland, M.N. (1971, p. 286) gives the following criteria for distinguishing, using an interview, a student's analytic approach to problem-solving from an intuitive approach to problem-solving;

Analytic approach —
    Student proceeds a step at a time. Steps are reasonably explicit. Student often uses mathematics, equations or logic and an explicit plan of attack.

Intuitive approach —
   Student tends to use manoeuvre based seemingly on an implicit perception of the problem. Student may not be able to provide an adequate account of how he got an answer. Student seems to grasp the meaning or significance of a problem without necessarily relying on analytic means.

Thorsland applied this interview method of categorizing subject's responses to four problems with each of twenty-five students and found no significant correlation between the analytic and intuitive ratings for each problem but a significant correlation with ratings of $p < 0.01$ for analytic ratings and $p < 0.0505$ for intuitive ratings, showing that the interview method was reliable.

   Intuitive thought alone, even if correct, does not give detailed accuracy as seen from the probability assessment experiments in Section 7.3. (See also the Section 2.2 on Hadamard, J., 1945 and the imprecision of physiognomic perception.) It rather recalls ideas associated with the emotive feeling. The logical connections between these ideas are then analytically demonstrated. In false intuitions no logical connections can be demonstrated. The fact that an intuitive individual is more tolerant of analytically ambiguous ideas has been found in studies of creativity. It may be that in the intuitive mode there are close subjective unambiguous links with the emotive feelings. These are the intuitive individual's nonconsensus criterion for associating ideas. This would explain the tolerance of ambiguity in creative types.

   Thorsland, M.N. (1971) refers to non-analytic (global) versus analytic cognitive style, which he also refers to as field-independent versus field-dependent cognitive style (p. 18). Kagan, J. *et al.* (1964) define the analytic style as grouping familiar objects together on the basis of objective elements of the total stimulus rather than by subjective elements. Grouping by subjective elements is a characteristic of intuitive thought. Frederick, W.C. (1967) also found a contrast between non-analytic (global) style and analytic cognitive style which he said increased with age. Bereiter, C. and Hidi, Suzanne (1977) also found from their experiments that: 'Younger subjects were seen as reasoning in an intuitive, factual manner, while older ones were seen as reasoning from a logical system,' supporting Frederick's finding of the tendency away from the choice of the intuitive mode to using the analytic mode to increase with age.

   Whether during problem-solving one uses an analytic approach based on a restrictive field or whether one uses an intuitive approach based on a wide field, is related to the personality of the problem-solver (Bloom, B.S., 1956). This is one of many determinates of cognitive style which may be analysed on an analytic versus intuitive dimension. Pettigrew, T.F. (1958) defines cognitive style as 'broad versus narrow categorizing'. Similarly Kelly, G.A. (1955) defines cognitive style as 'simplified versus multidimensional construing'. Ausubel, D.P. (1968) gives a list of various classifications of cognitive style.

One definition is 'field independence, i.e. analytic versus global field dependent'. Whether one is intuitive or analytic is related to one's cognitive style.

It is apparently difficult to modify cognitive style (Witkin, H.A. *et al.*, 1954). This points to the stability of a possible 'intuitive type' and has implications against universally teaching only an intuitive approach to problem-solving.

Poincaré, H. (1969) also considers that it is not the type of their mathematics that makes mathematicians either analytic or intuitive but that their approach is an inherent characteristic: 'It is the very nature of their mind which makes them logicians or intuitionalists, and they cannot lay it aside when they approach a new subject' (p. 205). He gives examples contrasting the analytic and intuitive approaches of various mathematicians. It has been found that when presented with a mass of data, one personality style is to select a part of a complex situation that can be handled, and attend to this. Subjects with other personality styles break down, become immobilized, collapse into tears, or discharge tension in undirected motor activity (Davitz, J.R. and Ball, S., 1970, p. 327). The failures may have been intuitive types who relied on an intuitive approach personally too limited to handle such a large field of knowledge.

Intuitive/Analytic Continuum

In the second phase of creativity, intuitive thought seems to alternate with analytic thought; Section 7.3. Perhaps it is this intuitive guidance of analytic thought that has led some writers, notably Brunswik, E. (1966), to consider intuitive thought and analytic thought as two ends of one continuum. Other writers disagree with this and consider intuition and reason as two different modes of thought. This is the view taken in this investigation, for logical reasoning even 'slightly' adulterated by allo-logical associations or given slight emphasis through feelings, is no longer pure logical reasoning. Reasoning is seen here as the abstraction from intuitive thought of coincidental logical relations without their attendant feeling associations. Devoid of these feeling associations one may wonder how a logical edifice was constructed. The face-value assumption that logical structure can be created without associated feelings has done a disservice to the place of intuition in Western education, particularly in recent mathematical education.

Brunswik, E. (1966) considered intuitive and analytic thought processes as a continuum. His ideas are summarized in the following four points.

(1) There is a continuum of cognitive functions ranging from intuitive to analytical thinking. Most thinking is quasirational, consisting of some mix of intuition and analysis.

(2) Thinking towards the intuitive end of the continuum is relatively unaided, perception-like thinking. Operating in the intuitive mode, a person does not consciously impose transformations on information.

(3) Thinking toward the analytical end of the continuum is relatively aided thinking. Operating in the analytic mode, a person consciously imposes transformations on information.

(4) As consequences of the three preceding points: (a) thinking in the intuitive mode is fast, uses a variety of information, has a low degree of awareness, and is seldom precisely correct or drastically wrong; (b) thinking in the analytical mode is slow, uses a limited range of information, has a high degree of awareness, and when wrong produces large errors.

Baumgardner, S.R. (1973) also considers an analytic/intuitive continuum on which he rated student's career decisions (p. 9). Point 4(a) above on the distribution of intuitive errors is in disagreement with the results of an experiment on problem-solving by Whitfield, J.W. (1951). 'An attempt at solving the "insight" problem is almost certain to be either completely right or completely wrong. When wrong so little information is gained that the problem remains approximately of the same difficulty.'

The idea of insight producing a 100 per cent correct response was used in an experimental design by Hartmann, G.W. (1933) as a criterion for recognizing insight solutions as opposed to trial and error solutions on ten 'puzzle tasks'.

Earle, T.C. (1972) based his study of intuitive/analytical thinking on Brunswik's treatment of analytical and intuitive thought as a continuum. Earle induced an intuitive approach by instruction and later tried to confirm by interview that an intuitive approach had been used. An approach was called intuitive if it was not analytic. His result of a low significance of this confirmation may be due to trying to induce intuitive styles in analytic types whose cognitive styles were little influenced by the instructions. Although this is a methodological shortcoming, not having a positive method of recognizing an intuitive approach and blocking subjects by cognitive style, it may be conceptually fortuitous in that people do use intuitive methods only when analytical or previously tried methods are not available, through technical inability, inconsistent or incomplete knowledge, property 16. A lens model system was used by Earle (pp. 14/15) to illustrate intuitive and analytical situations. It is based on subject/task interaction but does not allow for the main properties of intuition and therefore is inadequate for this study.

Ausubel, D.P. (1968) proposed a model that allowed for analytic thinking and intuitive thinking as two distinct modes of thought, not two ends of a continuum, that may, however, be mixed to give the resultant appearance of a continuum. He uses the model of Fig. 2.1/4 to account for the fact that linear processing occurs in analytic cognitive processes but not in intuitive cognitive processes.

Referring to Fig. 2.1/4 high-intuitive individuals move freely from one superordinate concept to another with frequent referral primarily to, and less frequently from, subordinate exemplars.

Compared with this is his model for the highly analytic individual (Fig.

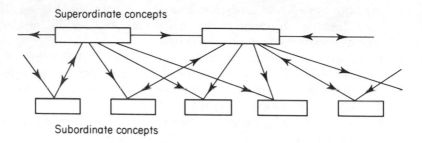

Fig. 2.1/4 Ausubel's model of intuitive thinking as primarily referral
between superordinate concepts

2.1/5). High-analytic individuals move primarily within subordinate concepts
and to superordinate concepts, with referral back to subordinate concepts,
thus expanding the subordinate concepts. Very little, if any, exchange is
between superordinate concepts.

It is presumed that the arrows indicate the order in which superordinate or
subordinate concepts occupy the individual's consciousness. However, the
process of intuition is preconscious, only the product is conscious. No such
distinction is made in this model. However, the model would better explain the
facts if amended so that the superordinate concepts are interpreted as 'emotive
feelings' with the subordinate concepts associated with these. In the intuitive
mode these emotive feelings are aroused perhaps by some physiognomic
perception, and the intuitive individual can drift more freely between these
feelings than the analytic individual, recalling the associated ideas as the
feelings change. These ideas will have subjective associations with the emotive
feeling so will be very varied according to the individual's unique experience.
Unusual and original preconscious transformations characteristic of intuition
would occur in this way. Such an amended model is the basis of the theory of
intuitive thought proposed in Chapter 9.

Comparing analytical and intuitive problem-solving approaches Thorsland,
M.N. and Novak, J.D. (1972) found that the intuitive and analytical type is at
an advantage in both learning time spent and resulting learning efficiency (p.
10). They explained their results with the help of Ausubel's structure:
'...intuitive dimension being a manifestation of the existence and utilization
of over-all superordinate concepts'. In an earlier work Thorsland, M.N. (1971)
found results that flatly contradicted Brunswik's notion of an
analytic/intuitive continuum: 'The intuitive and analytic dimensions are
separate and distinct and not two ends of a continuum' (p. 181).

Intuition is Dependent on 'Feelings', Reason is Not

One main contrast between intuition and reason is that pure reason is
considered to be independent of feelings and impressions, machine-like and
not 'clouded' by our emotions whereas intuition is dependent on our feelings

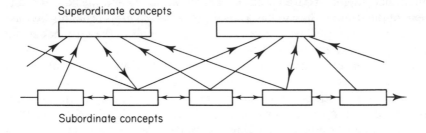

Fig. 2.1/5 Ausubel's model of analytic thinking as primarily referral
between subordinate concepts

at all stages from the initial perception where feeling impressions of the information are created: through the intuitive processing where feelings may change, to the final intuition which has its accompanying feeling of certainty. Feelings are involved with each property of intuition and this is discussed in more detail where each property is separately considered.

In experiments requiring subjects to make intuitive probability assessments, it has been found that judgments have been made from 'impressions' of the information given. This is a source of error in intuitive judgments which is discussed in Section 8.1 on distortions during intuitive perception. Kahneman, D. and Tversky, A. (1973) showed that subjects use representativeness for statistical prediction. A subject's confidence depends upon how representative is his selection of the input data. The more consistent the input then the more confident the prediction as the prediction is then more representative. Extremities of data values falsely influence intuitive judgments. Probably because the subjects would have assumed a normal distribution for their input data.

Peterson, C.R. and Beach, L.R. (1957) noticed that subjective and objective probability is usually not a linear relation and is somewhat dependent on the decision situation involvement of the subject. One's subjective evaluation of the probability 'one-sixth' might be greater when playing Russian Roulette than when playing Ludo! They asked a number of college students to estimate intuitively certain statistical parameters; the resulting estimates were frequently conservative and the students failed to gain all the information from the samples, which shows intuitive thoughts are not as precisely detailed as analytic thoughts.

The physiological mechanism of adaptation also modified subjective judgment (Lollo, V. di and Cassedy, J. H., 1965; Costello, C. G., 1961). The cognitive effect of an anchor stimulus also has a modifying effect in subjective judgments of the intuitive type, because it falsifies the impressions from which the judgments are made. For a full discussion and experiments on anchors see Johnson, D.M. (1972).

Anchoring effects explain the results of Parducci, A. and Sandusky, A. (1965) from their experiments on intuitive probability assessments. They found that judgments are based on range (midpoint) and median, not on the mean of the stimuli. Spread has a secondary effect. This is probably because of the decay of the significance given to repeated stimuli so the extremes are given more significance than their frequency deserves.

No feeling of certainty of correctness accompanies an analytic solution. The answer is not its own confirmation as is the case with an intuitive answer. There is the uncertainty that one has made a technical error in the analytic process or has operated on inappropriate data. Confidence is given by consistency checks either internal to the process, or external to the result. For example, if the result is in agreement with other findings. But in contrast an intuitive solution alone carries a subjective certainty of its correctness. A theory of intuition must explain this difference between analytic and intuitive thought. It is explained by the Theory of Intuitive Thought in Section 4.2 on subjective certainty of correctness.

Expectancy theory, for considering physiological effects on detecting repeated signals, can also be used to allow for the physiological effects of subjective probability assessments. In an intuitive judgment the subject expects to be correct, property 10. To ensure that any measure of expectancy of being correct is based on the subject's intuitive judgment only, and that there is no interaction with probability assessments from the subject's experimental history, an experiment should use a problem unique to the subject. If not, expectancy of being correct on similar problems in his experience will have an effect, e.g. 'I usually get this type of problem wrong so I expect I am wrong again this time'.

There are ways of processing information other than by abstract reasoning or analytic thought, e.g. comparing feelings. Intuition is one of these processes which includes the use of kinaesthesis; see Section 6.3 on kinaesthetic empathy. Kinaesthetic experiences are commonly used in evaluating information. There is a literature on kinaesthetic experience used in comparison judgments and in the processing of spatial forms.

Kinaesthesis may be physiologically differentiated from touch. Usually kinaesthetic stimuli mean those which cause displacement or compression of joint capsules. Touch receptors respond to tactile stimuli and are fast-adapting, befitting a receptor that is subject to continuous stimulation. Kinaesthetic receptors are slowly adapting. Touch fibres are of different diameters. Usually the larger the diameter the more sensitive is its receptor. Kinaesthetic receptors are located in muscles, the spindles or tendon organs of Golgi (Campbell, H.J. and Eayrs, J.T., 1965). The kinaesthetic receptors in the eye muscles are closely related to visual imagery; see Section 3.2 on body reference and kinaesthetic judgments. A definition of touch is '...tactile stimuli are those which cause displacement of hairs or deformation of skin without injury' (Rose, J. and Mountcastle, Y.B., 1959).

Bishop, A.J. (1973) found an interesting relationship between structural apparatus and spatial ability. He gave NFER spatial test 1 to four hundred and sixteen pupils from a Nuffield and a non-Nuffield school. There was a significant difference in their performance ($p < 0.05$) though there was no significant difference in IQ. Also a like/dislike five-point scale for arithmetic, algebra, and geometry, showed the children who had used structural apparatus preferred geometry. There were no preferences among the others. The use of structural apparatus, e.g. Dienes, Cuisenaire, Stern and Colour factor, can build up kinaesthetic experiences used in intuitive processing of spatial forms which supports their pedagogic use.

Fig. 2.1/6 Objects intuitively assessed by active touch and kinaesthesis

Gibson, J.J. (1962) calls active touch 'tactile scanning'. His subjects had to identify by touch shapes of the type shown in Fig. 2.1/6. The mean diameter was one inch and E compared active and passive touch. He found: 'Active touch, however, is an excellent channel of spatial information in that the arrangement of surfaces is readily picked up. The solid geometry of things is best got by feeling them'. He then gives observations to support this assertion (p. 484). Such observations indicate the use of kinaesthetic information input for experiments on intuition.

Summary of the Contrasts Between Intuitive Thought and Abstract Reason

The contrast between intuitive thought and abstract reasoning is apparent in most properties of intuition and is further discussed where these properties are individually considered. There is evidence to show that an intuitive or analytic approach to problem-solving is a stable cognitive style.

Analytic thought is based on detailed defined relations between two elements at a time. Intuitive thought is based on an emotional state associated with all the elements in the field of knowledge (overall impression).

The difference between intuitive and analytic thought suggests the following model. In intuitive thought, elements are related by their associated feelings being concordant with the overall emotional state. Each element contributes to this emotional state. As the emotional state drifts and changes, new elements associated with the new states are juxtaposed with old elements. Because the concordant feelings associated with the elements have been associated by the individual's unique experience, original juxtapositions of elements can result. These elements are related by a common subjective feeling, not by logic. This agrees with intuitive types being emotionally more variable and more tolerant of logical ambiguity.

The intuition is a relation between elements due to their associated feelings being concordant. The intuition may be wrong in that no logical connection may exist between the elements. This may be because the feelings associated with the elements, one's impression of things, may be inaccurate. Even if correct, the intuition only presents the elements in a subjective relationship, not a detailed analytic relationship. Intuitive thought categorizes elements by common subjective associated feelings, e.g. metaphors such as 'Juliet is the sun' whereas analytic thought categorizes elements by common consensus properties, e.g. Juliet is female.

It has been shown that kinaesthetic experiences can be used in intuitive judgments on spatial forms. This distinction from analytic judgments may be used in experiments on intuition. Conscious use of kinaesthetic information in problem-solving is novel to most subjects and in agreement with the above may be used in an experiment as input for intuitive judgments. It is preferable to use large movements designated as kinaesthetic rather than small finger movements, i.e. tactile scanning movements such as these would probably be processed in an analytic way. (See Hoff, Phyllis, A., 1971.)

2.2   INTUITIVE SENSE OF RELATIONS

This is property 18 and with sixteen references is of equal importance with the previous property.

'Insight involves the organization of perception and the apprehension of relations' (George, F.H., 1962, p. 36). Helson, H. (1927) considered the occurrence of relational responses to be a criterion of insight. Stang, D.J. (1974) equates intuition with insight in agreement with the conclusion of Section 1.4 when he describes intuition as '...intuitions really being insight into causal relationship' (p. 652). Pechstein, L. A. and Brown, F. D. (1939) give as a criterion of insight the response to the meaningful relationships in a situation. 'The advocates of insight consider the response to relations between the elements in a situation as a criterion of insight' (p. 40).

Also Köhler, W. (1925) defines insight as '...grasp of a material inner relationship of two things to each other' (p. 229).

Physiognomic Perception Gives the Intuitive Sense of Relations

Sense of relation, one thing to another and their relation to the whole, during intuitive thought, seems to come from a physiognomy of the whole situation. Introspective reports of inspired moments of artists, scientists, and mathematicians in the literature, clearly show this is the case. The theoretical literature on physiognomic perception shows also that this proposal is consistent with the other properties and characteristics of intuitive thought, e.g. physiognomic perception like intuition is a primary process which involves the whole field of knowledge (property 15, global knowledge). Both physiognomic perception and intuition involve a preconscious (property 3) emotional involvement (property 2) which is brought about by empathic projection usually involving kinaesthetic empathy (property 6).

A sense of relations is more than cognitive knowledge of relations in this context. It is an awareness arising from an emotional state of the individual: a state that subjectively corresponds to a physiognomic perception of the objects in the relationship. Werner and other Gestalt psychologists consider physiognomic perception as the seeing of emotional qualities in peoples' expressions, works of art, or physical objects (Werner, H., 1948). Vernon, Lee (1912) says that physiognomic perception is: 'The attribution of our own moods of dynamic experience, motor ideas, to shapes. We attribute to lines not only balance, direction, velocity, but also thrust, strain, feeling, intention and character.' See also experiments on physiognomic perception of lines by Krauss, R. (1930) reported in the next subsection.

Examples of physiognomy from the literature follow: '...sound of machines may present itself with a strong expression of personality' (Feilberg, L. and Skrifter, S., 1949, pp. 284ff).

Lehmann, A. (1913) describes threatening clouds, friendly landscapes, majestic mountains. He analysed to what extent these moods depend upon associations and previous experience. He found '...that the feeling for the exalted in nature on the whole, depends upon reproduced kinaesthetic sensations'. See also Section 6.3 on kinaesthetic empathy giving rise to intuitive understanding.

The following illustrative example of physiognomic perception comes from the Father Brown story 'The Wrong Shape' (Chesterton, G.K., 1950). It is about an oriental knife. 'It's the wrong shape in the abstract. Don't you ever feel that about Eastern art? The colours are intoxicatingly lovely; but the shapes are mean and bad — deliberately mean and bad. I have seen wicked things in a Turkey carpet' (p. 92).

Mathematical, Artistic, and Scientific Relationships Intuitively Sensed Through Physiognomic Perception

There are numerous examples in art, literature, and science of physiognomic perception. These examples incidently show that physiognomic perception has much in common with the properties and characteristics of intuition. In mathematics Chase, W.G. (1973), studying the function of visual imagery in elementary mathematics, recorded that with reference to the flash card shown in Fig. 2.2/1: 'One subject said that he had to remove the bars in order to move the symbols and two others said that they felt constrained to move the symbols as if they were tiles in a frame. For example, subject 10 said, "I don't

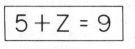

Fig. 2.2/1 Physiognomy of flash card giving intuitive sense of mathematical relations

64

swing things around because the bar doesn't let me. I shift the symbols horizontally'' '.

Physiognomic perceptions of situations are personal and subjective. They vary between and within individuals with mood and time so that one individual may not emotionally appreciate the physiognomic perceptions of another, or even his own remembered perceptions. See Section 6.2 on personalized feeling models.

Item from the test match problems

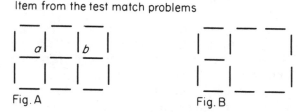

Fig. A   Fig. B

<u>Problem</u> : Take away four matches from Fig. A leaving
three squares and nothing more. Answer is Fig. B

Fig. 2.2/2 Item whose solution is suggested by its physiognomy

A personal example of the use of physiognomy in a mental problem of the type used in IQ tests (given on p. 55, Ripple, R. E., 1964) is illustrated in Fig. 2.2/2. Identifying with Fig. A, the heart or centre is at *a* or *b*, so the figure is most sensitive here and can be changed most by removing matches from here. Hence a large change could be effected here at the heart; the most dense place. If the problem required a small change then it should occur at the periphery. Fig. B looks as though it has its heart missing. This, like all physiognomic perceptions is a 'one off' personal physiognomic perception that may not be appreciated by others or by the same subject at another time.

Iron   Silver   Gold

Fig. 2.2/3 Geometric properties of lines different from
their physiognomic properties

Werner, H. (1948, pp. 70/71) reports an experiment on physiognomic perception by Krauss, R. (1930). Fifty subjects matched eight lines to represent gaiety, melancholy or sadness, rage, darkness, dawn, gold, iron, or glass in which two hundred and forty-two subject choices agreed to an extent of 73·6 per cent of unanimity in the physiognomic meaning of the lines, for example see Fig. 2.2/3. He notes that the geometric properties of lines are different from their physiognomic properties. It is interesting that although physiognomic perception is subjective such a detailed agreement between individuals can be found. It would be interesting to group subjects by culture, experience, etc., to find if some common cause is responsible for this agreement. There are cultural stereotypes, e.g. film mood music, advertising, etc.

Werner notes 'the self-descriptions of artists often reveal that it is normal for them to perceive things physiognomically' (p. 71). It is part of the creative process. The following passage from Werner shows how basic is physiognomic perception and how during physiognomic perception the feelings and perceptions are inextricable, particularly in childhood. This is part of the child's way of seeing things. A part that creative adults seem to have retained:

> One speaks only too readily of the anthropomorphism of the child. But physiognomic perception is something more general, more deeply rooted, than anthropomorphism. The latter is itself a definite interpretation of the world. It must be borne in mind that anthropomorphism, in the strict sense, can be spoken of only when there is a consciousness of a polarity between the personal and the impersonal. During the physiognomic period of childhood however, it is the very absence of polarity and the high degree of fusion between person and thing, subject and object, which are characteristic. The average adult generally has a physiognomic experience only in his perception of other human beings, their faces and bodies. The child, on the other hand, frequently sees physiognomic qualities in all objects, animate or inanimate. And this experience is by no means identical with the idea of anthropomorphizing objects, with the personification of the inanimate with the reading of human qualities into lifeless things. Physiognomic experience is genetically precedent to anthropomorphism. ...the child grasping the world as he does through his motor-affective activity, will understand the world in terms of physiognomics. (p. 72)

This tendency away from physiognomic perception with age, particularly in non-creative adults, is consistent with the findings of Frederick, W.C. (1967) and Bereiter, C. and Hidi, Suzanne (1977) — reported in Section 2.1 — of a trend away from the choice of the intuitive mode towards the analytic mode of thought with increasing age. In creative adults this return to physiognomic perception type of thought is termed 'regression' but is considered in this investigation to be a developed rather than a residual mode of thought in creative types. This is discussed in Section 8.2. It is further seen from these extracts of Werner's work that physiognomic perception involves a temporary identification as occurs during the intuitive process, see Section 6.3 on temporary identification during the intuitive process.

In children's drawn copies of sharp or pointed objects '...the angularity and pointedness are exerienced psychophysically by the whole body...

children very often experience such objects physiognomically as conditioned by their affective and bodily response'. See in agreement the discussion of intuition as a whole body process in Chapter 3 on emotional involvement, property 2.

An example is given of the four-year-old girl, who upon seeing some cards on which angular figures were drawn, cried out, 'Ugh! what a lot of prickles and thorns!' And she hesitated to pick up the cards lest the thorns stick into her fingers.

Many examples can be given of physiognomic perception, but as they are personal and subjective, dependent upon personal experience, their content is not universally appreciated. An exception in art and literature is when an artist can use his material to induce a physiognomic perception which many can appreciate because it involves a common experience. Failure in communication between art critics and the public may in part be due to the critic not realizing the subjectiveness of his physiognomic perceptions.

In his book on the psychology of invention in the mathematical field, Hadamard, J. (1945) gives many examples of how famous mathematicians have an intuitive sense of mathematical relations, '. . . they are felt rather than formulated' (p. 31).

He gives the following account of physiognomic perceptions giving a sense of relations that may then be formulated as a mathematical proof. In this account Hadamard makes these points:

(1) Physiognomic perception is necessary for him in understanding mathematical research.
(2) Physiognomic perception has the effect of simultaneously processing the field of knowledge (global knowledge, property 15).
(3) Physiognomic perception holds associated ideas but not the analytic links between these ideas (contrast between analytic and intuitive thought, property 4; compare the Theory of Intuitive Thought which shows ideas are associated by common feelings).
(4) Physiognomic perception is dynamic in that it changes while the object is constant, and is related to the mood of the moment. (The Theory of Intuitive Thought uses drifting emotional sets and changing physiological states to account for this.)

'. . . let us take an elementary and well-known proof in arithmetic, the theorem to be proved being: 'The sequence of prime numbers is unlimited'. I shall repeat the successive steps of the classic proof of that theorem, writing opposite each of them the corresponding mental picture in my mind. We have for instance, to prove that there is a prime greater than 11.

Steps in the proof	My mental pictures
I consider all primes from 2 to 11, say, 2,3,5,7,11	I see a confused mass
I form their product $2 \times 3 \times 5 \times 7 \times 11 = N$	N being a rather large number, I imagine a point rather remote from the confused mass
I increase that product by 1, say N plus 1	I see a second point a little beyond the first
That number, if not a prime, must admit of a prime divisor, which is the required number	I see a place somewhere between the confused mass and the first point

(pp. 76/77)

He admits to the imprecision and inaccuracies of such images which is an agreement with the above distinction between analytic and intuitive thought and consistent with property 9 that intuition need not be correct, see Section 8.1.

But at the same time, one can easily realize how such a mechanism or an analogous one may be necessary to me for the understanding of the above proof. I need it in order to have a simultaneous view of all elements of the argument, to hold them together, to make a whole of them — in short, to achieve that synthesis which we spoke of in the beginning of this section and give the problem its physiognomy. It does not inform me on any link of the argument (i.e. on any property of divisibility or primes); but it reminds me how these links are to be brought together... indeed, every mathematical research compels me to build such a schema. (p. 77)

This is the global knowledge property of intuition, Chapter 5.

In the following observation Hadamard notes how an individual may not appreciate his own recalled physiognomic perceptions: The Theory of Intuitive Thought accounts for this through utilizing drifting emotional sets (changing moods) to an emotional set that no longer has relevant feeling responses common to the set in which the perception occurred.

I do not take time to write the equations completely, only caring to see, so to speak, how they look. These equations, or some terms of them are often disposed in a peculiar and funny order like actors in a scenario, by means of which they 'speak' to me, as long as I continue to consider them. But if, after having been interrupted in my calculations, I resume them on the following day, what I have written in that way is as if 'dead' for me (p. 82).

Empathy and Projection Giving Physiognomy Necessary for Intuitive Sense of Relations

It has been seen from the introspective, theoretical, and experimental reports above that physiognomic perception has so many properties in common with the intuitive process that it may be considered part of it. We now further support this proposal by reporting evidence showing that empathic projection essential to the intuitive process (see Section 6.3 on empathic projection, a temporary identification through empathy and projection being essential to the intuitive process) is also the process allowing physiognomic perception.

Klein, G.S. (1970, pp. 154/155) points to the relationship between physiognomic perception and kinaesthetic empathy — property 12. 'Perhaps a gift for physiognomic organization is implied in behaviour usually described as "empathic". Perceptual components are ignored in speculations about "empathy", most of which have emphasized motor "identification". But the colouring of percepts by subtle affects may be a precondition of "empathic" experience.'

In a patient who was incapable of physiognomic perception, Klein noticed an incapacity for empathy. 'If the physiognomic attitude in some form is one requirement of emotional communication and empathy, then we should not be surprised by the emotional poverty that this patient showed under clinical scrutiny'.

Physiognomic perception and empathy give the sense of relations, feeling for relations, characteristic of intuition. Physiognomic perception is a superficial, less involved form of empathic projection (defined in Section 6.3) in that the perception, commonly kinaesthetic, induces or recalls a light emotional state. This is intuitive perception as explained in Section 3.1.

One's feelings and associated thoughts are so 'fused' with the perception of the object that they are attributed to the object, i.e. projected on to it. The difference between physiognomic perception and empathic projection is one of degree, in that the emotional state involved with physiognomic perception is not sufficiently physiologically extreme to have associated organized physiological responses, e.g. motor activity.

Physiognomic perception is also closely related to the processes of cross-modal transposition, transfer and other transposition; detailed later in Section 6.1 on cross-modal transposition facilitating transfer and intuitive thought.

Summary of Intuitive Sense of Relations

The basic ability of physiognomic perception enables one to associate emotions with perceived, imagined and remembered elements. This involves empathy and projection in that the emotion and perception occur together and are so interrelated that one feels it is possible to imagine how the element of the perception feels.

These associated feelings are how the subject intuitively experiences the elements of his perception. These feelings are interdependent with mood and dependent upon environment and are commonly dependent upon reproduced kinaesthetic sensations.

If the feelings associated with elements in a relationship are concordant one has an intuitive sense of the relationship. This is necessary for intuitive understanding. See Section 6.2 on intuitive understanding through feeling.

The following example illustrates how the concordance of feeling evoked in physiognomic perception can give an intuitive sense of relations. Analytically 'IRON CLOUD' is a cloud made of iron. The physiognomic perception of 'IRON' as a metal, heavy and cold, together with the physiognomic perception of 'CLOUD' as light floating puffs of white vapour in a blue summer sky, make 'IRON CLOUD' an intuitively unacceptable relation. However, if the physiognomic perception of 'IRON' changes to iron-colour grey, cold, and heavy and the physiognomic perception of cloud changes to thunder clouds of a threatening grey and heavy with winter rain, then 'IRON CLOUDS' has concordant feelings, · both being associated with a common emotional experience, and so conveys an intuitive sense of the relation.

2.3   RESTRUCTURING RELATIONSHIPS

This is the eleventh property of intuition with thirteen references to it in Section 1.4.

Recentring is a new permutation of relations between ideas. Often it is caused by the introduction of the new idea and the new permutation of relations is brought about by including relations between and with new and old ideas. This is illustrated in the above analogy to intuitive thought of floating magnets (Fig. 2.1/3). The existing relations between them are changed to accommodate the newly introduced magnet. The relationships in which the magnets now stand relative to one another are not necessarily completely different from their original relationships. Some relations between elements may be topologically invariant. For example, a particular group of three magnets may still be together in the new arrangement. So it is with recentring that some subsets within the original relationships may remain the same but the overall relationships have changed. The central cause of the change being the inclusion of relationships with the new element.

The Theory of Intuitive Thought explains that the rearrangement of relationships between responses conditioned to emotional sets takes place whenever emotional sets are combined. One of the three methods of combining emotional sets, outlined in Section 5.4, is specifically called 'recentring' in this investigation. Recentring is an unlikely combination of two similar emotional sets. It is called recentring because this method of combining emotional sets has associated with it the extreme phenomena usually associated with the term recentring as used in the literature. The structure by which the Theory of Intuitive Thought explains recentring is detailed in Section 5.4. The accompanying feelings of elation typical of the 'Eureka' experience, the extreme form of recentring, are discussed in Section 3.2. The suddenness with which intuition appears resulting from recentring is outlined in Section 7.2 and its emergence after a preconscious incubation period is discussed in section 4.1. This present section discusses how new relations are produced by recentring.

Recentring is the Unlikely Combination of Similar Emotional Sets

In problem-solving the elements of the problem are known and an end condition is required. This condition is called the 'means-end relationship' (Ausubel, D.P., 1968: Hutchinson, E.D., 1941, etc.). The problem is solved when a relationship is found between the elements of the problem and the end condition. An intuitive solution involves satisfying subjective feelings which is the relationship between elements. In contrast an analytic solution involves demonstrable logical connections as the relationship between elements. In a correct intuitive solution both relationships exist. In an incorrect intuitive solution the elements are related by satisfying subjective feelings of association within the emotional set of the solution, but the logical connections between the elements are incomplete, not demonstrable, or are non-existent.

The emotional set of a person is dynamic, is gradually changing, sometimes slowly, sometimes quickly. It does not change discontinuously into another discrete state, but transforms continuously. Each slight transformation to a new emotional set results from a combination of the concordant responses in common between two extant emotional sets, that is the emotional set which the subject has just occupied and the next emotional set he would have moved into. This is diagrammed in Fig. 5.4/6 and further discussed in that section. The subject transverses his network of emotional sets whose transition probabilities give the most probable paths. As he transverses his network he 'refreshes' that part of the network in the same sense of refreshing a cathode ray tube display but changes it by this rehearsal. Some concordant responses' concomitant stimuli are carried along with the changing occupation of each emotional set. The carried response tendencies and present response tendencies combined with the concordant response tendencies of the next extant emotional set in the network give continuity and reinforce the transition probability to the next emotional set. This combination leaves the emotional set slightly changed. During time, usually referred to as the incubation period, some feelings that code the initial problem are gradually dropped from the changing present emotional sets.

There are three methods of combination depending on the similarity of the two emotional sets that enter into combination. When recentring occurs by the introduction of a new element to produce an intuitive solution, the problem 'feelings' have been completely dropped from the present emotional set, i.e. there is a low transition probability from the emotional set of the problem to the present emotional set. That new element causes recentring because of its subjective feelings of association with the same or a similar emotional set to which the problem elements were associated. In the recentring type of combination the transition probability from the original 'problem' emotional set to the present emotional set is very low as this is not a likely pathway in the extant network of emotional sets. But when an emotional set occurs which is similar to the original 'problem' emotional set, i.e. has the same 'feel', then a new link is made. The pathway is opened up and the present 'solution' emotional set is combined with the 'problem' emotional set to produce recentring insight with its recognition of the present emotional set as the solution. This is often triggered by some slight kinaesthetic experience giving that final similarity of feeling causing recentring. See Section 7.2 which reports slight kinaesthetic experiences, particularly in permissive ego states, causing recentring. Similarly slight kinaesthetic experiences with environmental factors sparking the 'Eureka' experience are discussed in Section 8.3.

When ideas associated with emotional states of low transition probability are found to be compatible their combination by recentring is subjectively most noticeable. 'I now see things in a completely different light!' If the new responses causing the recentring are associated with the same emotional set as the problem elements because of an uncommon experience, a rare recentring occurs, in that others are unlikely to have experienced this association. If this is a correct insight, i.e. an analytical connection between the elements can be demonstrated, it is inventive. This process satisfies Guilford J.P.'s, (1966) definition of intuition:

(1) Returning information in a radically different form to the input of information — showing a high degree of novelty.
   or
(2) Not so much the degree of alteration but the surprisingly remote connections between the original and the reproduced information.

(pp. 88/89)

If no analytical connection can be demonstrated this rare idiosyncratic recentring is fictional fantasy and considered eccentric and the unusual subjective connections cannot be generally appreciated.

It may be that what distinguishes scientific intuition from artistic intuition is not that scientific intuition is restricted by the need for demonstrability, but that the scientist also uses, not only logic, but feelings about logic with which his solution and problem feelings must be concordant — see Section 7.3 on the difference in scientific and artistic creativity.

In many of the insight problems detailed in Section 1.3 on experiments using practical insight problems, the insight is reached as Duncker, K. (1945) says 'by a dodge, i.e. the solution is only obtainable by a rare *recentring* of the facts' (p. 23). He gives as an example, the problem of making four triangles with six matches. The solution is a tetrehedron. The idea of moving from two to three dimensions is what causes the recentring, i.e. the four triangles in a new relation to each other. It seems probable that this idea is often recalled because it is associated with an emotional set initiated by the trial and error kinaesthetic experiences of holding the matches in space above the surface on which the others are placed. The more practical insight problems, e.g. the hat rack and pendulum problems (Maier, N.R.F., 1931; Dominowski, R.L. and Jenrick, Regina, 1972) are obviously more dependent on the practical experiences of the subject. The more practical experiences the subject has, then the more associated ideas the experience of the problem will make available for recentring. In such practical experiments extreme intuitive recentring is prevented from occurring as the incubation time allowed and the change in environment and physiological set is too restrictive for all feelings associated with the problem to be dropped from the subject's chain of refreshed emotional sets.

The following example illustrates the restructuring of the 'sense' of relations in recentring. There is a tenuous relationship between the problem elements 1-9 and the solution idea 10 as illustrated in Fig. 2.3/1, A, B, and C. The strength of the relationships between the elements is illustrated by the arcs. Various transformations may produce different relationships. The linear connection 1, 2, 6, 7, 8, 10 may give rise to a circular pattern, as illustrated in Fig. 2.3/1B. If associations represented by the dotted links were then apparent, this would be a more satisfying arrangement than that shown in Fig. 2.3/1A. The physiognomic perception of the relation between 1, 2, and 3 in Fig. 2.3/1A is similar to that of Pascal's triangle, which may lead to the restructuring in Fig. 2.3/1C which would probably result from a recentring.

The relationships resulting from the recentring Fig. 2.3/1C 'feel' better as they incorporate the number sequence and a regular pattern which is less tension-producing than the asymmetries of Fig. 2.3/1B. Also fewer new associations, represented by dotted lines, are needed to make this a more satisfying recentring, corresponding to the selection betweeen two equally explanatory hypotheses on the criterion of simplicity.

Recentring during intuitive problem-solving involves a restructuring of relationships defining the problem to give a structure maximizing redundant feeling associations. This is identified in Section 5.5 with maximizing redundant information between the problem elements.

Functional Fixation Inhibits Intuitive Recentring

When an object is shown in its common use this inhibits novel ideas for other uses. The subject loses flexibility because he has a course of action that is plausible. In experiments by Duncker, K. (1945), repeated by Adamson, R.E. (1952), this process is called 'functional fixation'. This is related to field dependence; see Section 2.1 on the contrast between intuitive and analytic

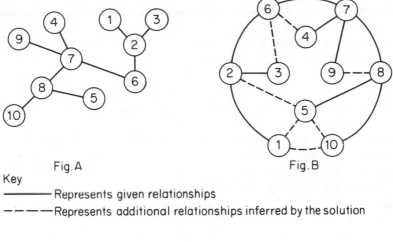

Fig. A

Fig. B

Key

————— Represents given relationships

— — — — Represents additional relationships inferred by the solution

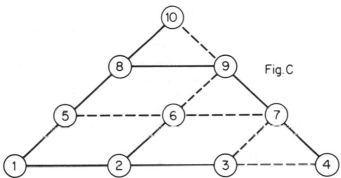

Fig. C

Fig. 2.3/1 Restructuring of relations in recentring

thought in relation to field dependence. Functional fixation acts in opposition to recentring.

Functional fixation as it is used in problem-solving is explained here as the possession of a solution that reduces any tension that might otherwise give intrinsic motivation to find another solution. The feelings, i.e. emotional set, associated with the function of the problem element are so satisfying (habitual) that they restrict the transition from the emotional set to an oscillation about the low-tension state. Few new ideas can be brought into relation with the problem elements and no recentring can take place. Subjects who are emotionally more variable have more chance of escaping this emotional set, for example, creative personality types.

A descriptive analogy of an oscillating, stable emotional state due to functional fixation is that of the centre of probability of the motion of an electron 'fixed' in its energy and motion by its nucleus. Its fixation to the nucleus is too great to be overcome by its varying associations with other nuclei. Unless a quantum jump can be made the association will continue between the electron's probable motion and the nucleus. So analogously the same subjective association will exist between the probable oscillating changes in emotional state and the nucleus of the emotional set because of the function of the problem element that fixes the association.

As functional fixedness inhibits intuition, it would be expected that abilities and personality correlates opposing functional fixation would correspond to the abilities and personality correlates of the intuitive type. The following reported literature supports this expectation.

Particularly in the field of mathematics, Duncker, K. (1945, p. 111) notes: 'Functional fixedness inhibits mathematics, as an element often necessarily changes its function in a mathematical process'. He gives examples of field dependence inhibiting mathematical thought.

This is consistent with our earlier discussion in Section 2.1 on field-independent cognitive style corresponding to intuitive thinking. This is also in agreement with inferences from correlations found between spatial ability and mathematical ability, where low field dependence is related to high spatial ability, especially those spatial abilities loading on k factor (Macfarlane Smith, I., 1964). The literature on this indicates the use of a kinaesthetic spatial problem in experiments on intuitive mathematical judgments. See also Section 3.1 on 'intuitive type', spatial k factor, and cognitive style.

Flexibility is measured by divergent thinking tests. Factor analysis shows that fluency and flexibility load on the same factor (Child, D. and Smithers, A., 1971). These are reported in Section 7.3 on correlates of intuition and creativity.

Richards, P.N. and Bolton, N. (1971) showed that the three factors of fluency, flexibility, and originality do not appear to be independent as Guilford's model implies. (Guilford, J.P., 1956, and Guilford, J.P., 1967). Richards and Bolton made up problem tests to include uses of objects test, circles test, uses and consequences. Their work also showed that 'progressive' environments facilitate divergent thinking. It is reported in Sections 8.1, 8.2, 8.3 and elsewhere that such environments also facilitate intuition, further supporting the association between divergent thinking and intuition.

Not only is divergent thinking and its personality correlates associated with recentring and intuitive thought, but also the test environment and test instructions for divergent thinking tests affect their results in a similar way as test instructions and environment affect the choice of the intuitive mode rather than the analytic mode for problem-solving. In fact experimenters manipulate test instructions and test environments to elicit an analytic or intuitive mode in the experiments involving intuition. This is seen from the descriptions of experiments involving intuition reported in Section 1.3 and also from Section 5.1 on the use of instructions to evoke the intuitive mode for problem-solving.

For divergent thinking tests, instructions are given that change the goal from finding a solution to the problem, to finding a maximum number of solutions to the problem. If the subject is satisfied with a particular solution, the instructions, rather than the original problem, become his motivation for continuing.

The mean correlation between divergent thinking tests is about 0·74 (Nuttall, D.L., 1971). This lack of reliability between tests is due to their dependence upon the form of the instructions (Nuttall, D.L., 1973, pp. 112-129), as the above discussion would indicate. Nicholls, J.G. (1972), also found the reliability of the tests to be dependent on the conditions of the tests. This is not only the instructions but also the environment in which the tests are held. Instructions and environment greatly affect intuitive thinking, see Section 5.1.

Vernon, P.E. (1971), who studied the effects of administration and scoring on divergent thinking tests, found more similarity than other workers have found in the scoring procedures which also account in part for this low reliability.

Generally, as found by Wallach, M.A. and Kogan, N. (1965), different results are obtained when the tests are administered under test-like versus game-like conditions. The studies by Gopal Rao G.S. *et al.* (1970) and Richards, P.N. and Bolton, N. (1971) are consistent in showing that students in progressive environments score higher on divergent thinking tests than their peers in traditional schools. Haddon, F.A. and Lytton, H. (1968) gave four tests to match subjects in formal versus informal school environments. They found that there was no significant difference on the four tests; a significant difference in the 'complete circles' test in favour of formal schools; and a significant difference in favour of the informal schools on the 'imaginative stories' test. However, these negative findings may be due to the inappropriateness of the labels informal and formal. Similar results were found for types of teachers, i.e. permissive versus dictatorial.

Because of the connections between permissive environment and flexibility, the 'atmosphere' for an experiment on intuition should be free from personal anxiety, not a test-like situation.

Divergent thinking tests are used in tests of creativity (Guilford, J.P., 1959) and have been found also to correlate with empathy scores (Hudson, L., 1968). Both empathy and associations with creativity are properties of intuition, properties 7 and 12 respectively.

Humour Involves Recentring

Humour often involves recentring. Often the narrative of a joke builds a relation between the elements that the 'punch line' reverses. For example two Irishmen driving along the motorway to London, saw the sign 'Clean Toilets Ahead' and cleaned thirty-five before reaching London. The double function of 'Clean' as adjective and verb, allows a change in the relationship between the men and the toilets: the toilets serving the purpose of the men is reversed to the men serving the 'purpose' of the toilets. Many jokes involve recentring.

Humour has much in common with intuition, in particular recentring and the accompanying feelings of certainty which encourage intuitive acceptance. These are used through humour to promote acceptance in advertising, see Section 5.5 on intuitive acceptance.

Kris, E. (1950) explains that

> ...ego regression (primitivisation of ego functions) occurs not only when the ego is weak — in sleep, in falling asleep, in fantasy, in intoxication, and in the psychoses — but also during many types of creative processes. This suggested to me years ago that the ego may use the primary process and not be overwhelmed by it. The idea was rooted in Freud's explanation of wit according to which a preconscious thought is 'entrusted for a moment to unconscious elaboration' and it seemed to account for a variety of creative or other inventive processes.

Epstein, S. and Smith, R. (1956) used the difference in self-rating and group rating of hostility to categorize thirty-two subjects into two categories, (a) 'lacking in insight' and (b) 'relatively insightful' (p. 392). These categories were compared with subjects' ratings of cartoons for 'funniness'. The insight categories correlated with 'sense of humour' which was indicated by the subjects' expressions whilst they sorted the cartoons. The experimenters conclude: 'The most striking correlate of insight is the sense of humour' (p. 222). They quote similar studies with highly significant correlations.

This recentring in humour is difficult to use as a measure of the person's ability to recentre because, as with the practical insight experiments, it requires a specific recentring dependent on common experience. It does not follow that those capable of common recentring have the ability to produce the rare idiosyncratic recentrings indicative of highly creative subjects. Also the subjective appreciation of the emotional response to humourous recentring introduces many variables experimentally difficult to control.

Summary of Recentring

Recentring is a change in the structure of the subjective relationships between elements associated with an emotional set. This is often caused by incorporating an element whose subjective associations are with a different emotional set.

The restructuring may relate elements whose analytic connections are remote and novel, a common product of insight. Through familiar experience functional fixation places an element in such a satisfying relationship with other elements associated with an emotional set that the natural drift and change of emotional sets is inhibited. Other elements associated with new sets are unlikely to be available to cause recentring. Emotionally variable types, e.g. creative individuals, have more chance of changing their emotional set and overcoming this functional fixation.

Functional fixation is related to field dependence which is indicative of analytic cognitive style and so opposes intuitive cognitive style. Low field dependence indicative of intuitive cognitive style seems commonly related to high spatial abilities loading on k factor. A permissive environment is conducive to intuitive recentring. The last two points should be incorporated into the experimental methodology used in experiments on intuition.

2.4   INTUITION IS INFLUENCED BY EXPERIENCE

This is the fifth property of intuition with twelve references to it in Section 1.4. Berne, E. (1949) defines intuition as: 'Knowledge based on experiences and acquired through sensory contact...'

The dependence of insight on experience has caused much controversy between Behaviourists and Gestalt psychologists. The Behaviourists have called insight 'one trial learning', but recognize 'the fact that past experience affects insightful learning... the real issue comes in describing *how* past experience is used appropriate to the demands of the problem' (Hilgard, E.R., 1959, p. 165). This investigation attempts to settle the issue through the Theory of Intuitive Thought.

The Theory of Intuitive Thought explains that past experiences condition response to contiguous emotional states, producing emotional sets. These emotional sets are the attitudes with which we approach present situations. The perception of present stimuli is moderated by our present emotional set: see Section 3.1 on emotional states influencing perceptions. An insight may be triggered through some present experience causing a recentring of the present emotional set to which the solution responses are associated, on to some past emotional set to which the problem elements are conditioned. Thus past experience conditions the problem to an emotional set and present experience can make the solution contiguous with the problem by recentring the present solution emotional set with the problem emotional set.

De Groot, A.D. (1965, p. 147) says that intuition is 'activated by situations'. Also in agreement with this Davis, G.A. and Scott, J.A. (1971, p. 175) say 'insight is triggered by a specific experience, whether that experience is in the form of an actual event, a dream, or a vision'.

Affective Coding of Cognitions

At any time in any situation what is then being experienced is one's emotional state. ' "Experiences" are not in general crystallized in statements but in attributes of objects. For example general functional characters are "heavy", "impenetrable", "mobile", "sensitive", "hindering" ' (Duncker, K., 1945, p. 73).

These functional characteristics of objects are emotionally experienced as part of their perception. One most common body response which is part of perception is kinaesthetic sensations. Allport, F.H. (1955, pp. 75-79) reports that Titchener assigned considerable importance to kinaesthetic sensations,

In Titchener's view there is one special type of sensation that is paramount as a contextual meaning-providing process, namely, kinaesthesis. As the organism faces the situation it adopts an attitude toward it, and the kinaesthetic sensations resulting from this attitude (assuming it to be a muscular tension or reaction) give the context and meaning of the object to which the organism is reacting.

This psychophysiological attitude, including its motor, affective, and cognitive components, etc. in this investigation is called the emotional set; see Section 3.2 on the development of emotional sets.

An example of how kinaesthetic sensations may produce a physiognomic perception experience in a subject is the watching of Moire patterns expanding and contracting; the subject sets up rhythmic breathing and expands and contracts himself as the patterns do and thus associates these feelings with the patterns. The patterns seem to breathe. Objects can gain kinaesthetic associations by observers tracing the shape or outline of an object with their tongue or toe whilst following the outline with the eyes. This associates a movement pattern with the object.

Emotional Sets Conditioned by Past Experience are Intuitively Used to Evaluate Present Experience

'. . . a person could best intuit about one or more particular areas, touching on corresponding sensitive areas in his past experiences (Guiora, A.Z. *et al.*, 1965, p. 119).

Past experience can also interfere with the perceptions of a situation through anxiety, adaptation, anchoring, or emotional blocking, etc. — 'none so blind as those who do not want to see' — so the physiognomic perception will not be representative of the situation (see the discussion on emotional involvement in intuition).

The process of intuition relates these present experiences to past experiences. 'What is intended by insight is a perception of the essential requirements of a problem so that past experience can be brought to bear in a manner appropriate to the present' (Hilgard, E.R., 1959, p. 164). 'Insights are dependent not only on the nature of the environment, or confronting situation, but also on the influence of one's experience and one's purposes at the time' (Bigge, M.L. and Hunt, M.P., 1965, p. 497). A theory of intuition must explain how present and past experiences are associated. As Becker, J.D. (1970) points out, 'an intermediate level cognitive theory must explain how past experience is used to define present goals'. Similarly Birch, H.G. (1945) writing on 'The relation of previous experience to insightful problem solving' says '. . . there remains very little basis for doubting the validity of the term insight as descriptive of a distinct category of behaviour. . . However, there still remains lacking any conclusive evidence concerning the genetic development of insightful problem solutions and the part played by the previous experiences . . .' (p. 370). The Theory of Intuitive Thought explains this association through past experience conditioning emotional sets that are used to evaluate present experience — and are changed in the process of this evaluation.

Lehmann, A. (1913) concluded that reproduced kinaesthetic sensations of previous associations and experiences are 'on the whole' responsible for our present moods.

Allport, G. W. (1937) also points to the important part played by kin-aesthetic sensations in relating past and present experience: 'Kinaesthetic cues were originally associated with subjective experience, and... when the cues recur in an imitative response they reinstate the same original experiences'.

Harlow, H.F. (1949), in his experiments on monkeys, used this combining of something in present experience with something in past experience as his operational criterion of insight. Comparison of past and present experience is exploited in intuitive analogies detailed later.

An emotional state may have many experiences associated with it, e.g. the emotional state of 'fear' will have experiences associated with it that were fearful to the subject. The emotional state of fear induced by a fearful experience like being followed along a dark lonely street, may recall similar associations of an experience being alone in a haunted house or locked in a cupboard, etc.

That similar experiences are related has been used by the associationists' learning theory. In particular the S - S contiguity theory as used by Woodworth, R.S. (1947) in a wider emotional sense than Prentice, W.C.H. (1949) used it in his insight experiment. Conditioning, i.e. the associating of specific responses with the emotional state corresponding to an experience, is conceived by Woodworth as a development of perceptions, expectations, anticipations, meanings, emotions — these terms all being more or less equivalent to him in this use. An emotional state together with these associated conditioned responses is called an emotional set in this book.

The importance of experience of kinaesthetic sensations in intuitive understanding has been shown by modern discovery-learning techniques, eg. an emphasis on 'learning by doing', especially kinaesthetic experiences with structural apparatus associating ideas with experiences that can later be recalled and used intuitively. 'During the early years, it seems necessary and appropriate to emphasize training through sensory-motor modalities for subsequent intellectual and personality development' (Yamamoto, K., 1972, p. 68).

Montessori has written extensively on intellectual training through sensory-motor modalities at ages from three to six (Montessori, M., 1965a, b, 1969).

Emotional Experience Used for Intuitive Recall

Once an emotional set has the elements of experience associated with it, these elements will be brought into consideration with the elements of any new experience that induces this emotional set. The subjective associations (feelings) between the elements and the emotional set help to hold the elements in mind for global processing. These feelings act as 'memory hooks'. The role of emotional cues in recall seems generally to have been neglected in laboratory experiments on memory. There are many reports of how one exciting or emotional experience can long be remembered. In these cases the feelings of association are acting as memory hooks. 'Situations that prove embarrassing or in which one is the center of attention likewise appear to be better remembered than less "ego-involved" experiences' (Bugelski, B., 1956).

This phenomenon can help to explain the results of a memory experiment by Camp, B.W. and Zimet, Sara, G. (1973) in which they presented a list of verbs each rated as either high or low in aggressive effects, to twenty-eight kindergarten children. They also administered the Knox Cube Test: Arthur revision. Results showed significantly more high-aggressive verbs were remembered than low-aggressive verbs. There was no correlation between IQ and recall. Frequency of usage was a significant influence on recall. I suggest the more aggressive verbs were easier to remember because of their higher emotional involvement.

Relationships which have been experienced can be used for problem-solving when induced by the physiognomic perception of problem elements. This explains why during problem-solving subjects prefer to consider relations between concrete objects rather than to coniser the same relations abstractly. Miller, R. (1973) used two groups, forty-five first-graders and forty-five undergraduates. He forced them to choose between abstract and concrete presentations of a problem. Irrespective of their age, he found results mostly supporting the preference for concrete presentation over abstract presentation.

Emotional states rich in associated experiences are induced more easily by concrete objects than by abstract thought. This was found by Johnson-Laird, P.N. and Wason, P.C. (1970b) who showed that insight depends upon the complexity of the material (p. 49). They showed insight is gained more easily by using concrete materials. See also Section 6.2 on intuition facilitated by concrete exemplars.

The effect of subjective feelings of association between elements of experience and the relevant emotional state acting as 'memory hooks' was noted earlier by Hadamard, J. (1945). It is a way of coding a large field of knowledge for use in intuitive problem-solving. The code being a common concordant feeling about all elements. Miller, G.A. (1956) considers that meaningful and understood relationships are coded in a manner that keeps them ready for use. Miscellaneous uncoded facts, stored in memory as isolated fragments, overtax our systems, so that we cannot use these facts well in problem-solving. The above coding process by emotional sets avoids this effect. This method of coding is illustrated by a party game of remembering many objects. The objects can be related to one another, e.g. in a story or picture. Recalling the experience of this relation will recall the objects.

Experience Can Reinforce the Appropriateness of Empathic Responses

The emotional set for evaluating a present experience is evoked through empathy. The present empathic feelings evoke emotional sets with similar associated feelings. The accuracy of the intuitive evaluation will of course depend on the appropriateness of the feelings empathically aroused. If the feelings are inappropriate, then an emotional set with inappropriate responses will be used to evaluate the present experience intuitively, resulting in incorrect intuitions. See Section 8.1 on distortions during intuitive perception.

The appropriateness of the feelings evoked may be learnt from reinforcement of correct intuitive evaluation. However, as the intuitive process is preconscious (property 3) the more removed from the initial feelings is the reinforcement then the less effect it will have in influencing the appropriateness of these initial feelings: see Section 8.2 on empathic projection as developed egocentricity.

If feelings associated with evaluation — not the evaluation itself — can be incorporated concordantly with the feelings empathically aroused, then there will be more chance of a demonstrably correct intuition. The inclusion of these feelings of evaluation may, as noted in Section 2.3, distinguish scientific from artistic intuitions.

Empathy is a major constituent of intuitive thought (property 12) and is dependent on past experience: '...we employ our own past experience in empathy...' (Allport, G.W., 1965, p. 536). Empathy is a process we use in understanding present experiences. Taft, R. (1960) says we use ourselves as a frame of reference in object perception and use empathy, i.e. kinaesthetic and affective responses, in intuitive judgments. Empathy relates past and present experiences.

Experiences of two situations producing similar emotional states enable one to consider these situations as intuitively analogous. Two situations may be considered intuitively analogous if similar emotional states (feelings) are associated with each. It is highly probable that some of the analytic relations between elements in one situation will be isomorphic with some of the analytic relations between elements in the other situation: because experience is not of isolated elements but of elements grouped by some relationship. The power of the analogy depends upon the extent and relevance of this isomorphism.

Synectics consciously emphasizes the similar feelings between intuitive analogies in order to exploit any analytic isomorphism. For example:

All the synectics groups (within as well as outside the parent group) had shown a recurrent tendency to identify, as the altimeter inventor did when he asked himself: 'What would I feel like if I were a spring?' 'How would a spring feel if it were human?' We deliberately fed this tendency back into group sessions, and since its use led to successful solutions we concluded that this was one mechanism for initiating and sustaining inventive effort. This particular mechanism was injected by persuading participants to imagine how they would feel if they were the inanimate elements of the problem under consideration. For instance, in a session devoted to the invention of an unbreakable yet translucent plastic glass the group was encouraged to describe their subjective response at 'being' an actual piece of glass. How did they feel? Which way were they pulled? Did they want to stay close to their brother particles? (Gordon, W. J. J., 1961, p. 28).

These subjective responses are clearly dependent upon experience — usually kinaesthetic experience — which allows identification; see Section 6.3 on temporary identification during the intuitive process. Identification with a fantasy experience is less likely to produce 'correct' insight as the elements of the fantasy experience are not governed by logically consistent rules as are natural occurrences. This point may also be relevant to the differences between creative scientists and artists in relation to their training and experiences, e.g. drama and fantasy role-playing (artists empathize with their fantasy experiences versus scientists empathize with their remembered actual reality experiences). Intuitions of artists do not have to be 'true', only to relate to common experience or common fantasy experience. The opposite is true for the intuitions of scientists.

The emotional matching in intuitive analogies is similar to the concept of resonance (Duncker, K., 1945, p. 46), where a recognition is made because the recognized object has similar properties to the internalized model of the thing being sought. An emotional resonance is also possible, e.g. a husband and wife playing 'password' would tend to give specific common experience clues rather than analytic clues.

This discussion on how experience affects intuitive thought and how experience is used in intuitive thought, indicates that tests that score specific recentrings as correct are too restrictive as an individual's experiences may not be attuned to that particular recentring. The discussion also indicates that tests that score only common associations as correct, e.g. some creativity tests, are sampling at best only common experience. In order to leave the individual free to make his own associations between ideas and his experiences, a projective test or slightly structured fantasy instrument is more suitable, e.g. TAT or Rorschach. Suitable tests are discussed in Section 6.3 on measuring empathy with projective and fantasy tests.

Summary of How Intuition is Influenced by Experience

Functional characteristics of objects are experienced emotionally as part of their perception. These feelings are associated with the objects. Thus past experience provides, through empathy, the associated feelings used in the process of insight.

Insight is triggered by specific objects through empathic experience of them. In particular reproduced kinaesthetic sensations reinstate the original experience to give meaning and context to a situation. So insight relates past and present experience.

Experience conditions specific responses to an emotional state to give an emotional set, which is the complete psychophysiological attitude adopted when a subject faces a familiar situation.

The emotional set common to many elements, that is the overall impression to which they all contribute, acts as a means of retaining the whole field of knowledge for the intuitive thought processes. If one or more elements is excluded or new elements included, the emotional state drifts and changes. The overall impression is different. With this change in emotional state comes the intuitive realization that one is considering a different set of elements.

Two situations may be considered analogous if they are both associated with similar emotional sets. The insight is the subjective feeling of relation incorporating the two situations. The intuition may be analytically exploited because of the high probability that the relationships defining each situation are isomorphic when conditioned by naturally occurring experiences of the environment, rather than by fantasy experiences.

Projective and fantasy tests and measures of subjective correctness are more suitable instruments for investigating intuition than are measures of absolute correctness.

3

Dependence on Emotional Involvement

3.1 EMOTIONAL/COGNITIVE INTERACTION IN THE INTUITIVE PROCESS

This is property 2, with ten references to it in Section 1.3. It is a particularly important property in that emotional involvement is central to all aspects of intuition and the relevant literature reviewed in this chapter affords major contributions to the Theory of Intuitive Thought.

Emotions are involved with thoughts. The psychology and physiology of the body are so interrelated that by only considering one or the other one neglects the synergism, antagonism, and feedback between the two systems that modifies much of behaviour. Intuition is a mind-body process in that cognitive processes are modified by emotional states through activity of the voluntary neuromuscular system, hormonal activity, digestions, intro-organic tensions, autonomic nervous system, internal stimulation of glands, etc.

Insight has been thought of in terms of emotional involvement by many writers. Dymond, R.F. (1948) considers insight as '...emotional realization...' The role of emotional involvement in intuitive processes is recognized by Westcott, M.R. (1964) who admits: 'I am a long-time devotee of autonomic responses so I consider them as having a central role in intuitive leaps. I believe very strongly in the importance of the gut reaction' (p. 52).

Baumgardner, S.R. (1976) writes: 'Intuitive thinking was defined by global feelings and judgments not proceeding from objectively specifiable premises... Emotional involvement and global feelings are thus taken as definitive for this mode of thought' (p. 41). This definition of intuition also refers to property 15, global knowledge and property 6, understanding by feeling. Brady, J.P. (1967) says that: 'To be meaningful, the qualifying term emotional must denote insight accompanied by the perception and expression of appropriate affective charge' (p. 305).

Guilford, J.P. (1966) considers emotion and intuition together, '...the emotionally sensitive individual, the intuitive thinker' (pp. 88/89). Jung uses the degree of emotional involvement to distinguish between two forms of intuition, 'concrete' and 'abstract', '...according to the degree of participation on the part of sensation' (Dry, A.M., 1961, p. 568).

Emotional involvement is most obvious in intuitive processes that result in invention and discovery 'That an affective element is an essential part in every discovery or invention is only too evident, and has been insisted upon by several thinkers' (Hadamard, J., 1945, p. 31).

Gordon, W.J.J. (1961) asserts as one hypothesis of synectics that: 'In the creative process the emotional component is more important than the intellectual' (p. 6). Elsewhere Gordon states that emotional involvement is a condition for insight, even emotional involvement with abstractions. 'Synectics uses one's own highly personal emotions and characteristics to gain insight into purely technological or abstract problems' (p. 36). Emotional involvement is an integral part of intuitive processes.

Referring to the 'moments of insight', Gerard, R.W. (1966) points out that: 'One always gets that element of closure and satisfaction...' (p. 116). This is one of the three subjective feelings that result from emotional involvement in intuitive processes. The three subjective feelings are of:

(i) Correctness of intuition (see property 10, subjective certainty of correctness).
(ii) Confidence in the result (see Section 4.3 on confidence in intuitive products).
(iii) 'The warm feeling of "being right" long before rationality occurs — as with Blake's intuition' (Courtney, R., 1968, p. 230).

These feelings are some of the results due to reduction in tension when the discordance of the emotional state initiating the intuitive process is resolved. 'The solution (intuitive) carries with it a great deal of pleasure, a great feeling of relief from tension (Garard, R.W., 1962, p. 118).

Two further results of this reduction in emotional tension accompanying insight are:

(i) To give intrinsic motivation — 'that tendency to activity which arises when the resolution of tension is to be found in mastering the learning task itself' (Bigge, M.L., 1968, p. 290). This is relevant to teaching intuitive methods.
(ii) Most important to intuitive processes is the building of emotional sets by associating percepts and response tendencies with emotional states using the reinforcement afforded by this reduction in emotional tension — detailed later in Section 3.2. '...the self-administered satisfaction, the drop in emotional tension experienced at the moment is none the less real or effective in reinforcing the responses which have preceded it' (Mowrer, O.H., 1946, p. 218).

Intuitive processes are 'whole body' psychophysiological processes in that they result from the interaction, by feedback modification, of cognitive and emotional processes. Strongman, K.T. (1973) reviews and summarizes the work of Lazurus, R.S. on what he calls 'direct action' which supports the interaction of emotion and cognition, '...direct action; this is essential to emotion since its success or failure or any feedback from it changes the cognition and hence the emotion' (p. 84). Robinson, G. (1973) also says '...the muscular as well as the nervous apparatus participates in the thinking process' (p. 79); '...the central nervous system is so constructed as to make interactions of cognitive, affective, and motor components inevitable' (Murphy, G., 1965, p. 451). Melzack, R. and Casey, K.L. (1970) illustrate the complicated interplay of sensory input, level of arousal, and central mediating processes in emotion, with the example of tickling a child and noting its response whilst varying pressure, expression, or relation of the person doing the tickling (p. 62). Separating the study of these processes has severely hampered the study of 'whole body' processes like intuition, and there is a need for a unifying theory, see Section 1.1 reviewing literature proclaiming the need for research into intuition. Samples, R. (1976) remarks that: 'In fact the use of the terms cognitive and affective may well be a millstone to progress' (p. 9). Murphy, G. (1965) remarks '...the "mental" versus "physical" way of looking at matters, has merely confused us' (p. 453). Cognition and emotion must accompany one another. This is stated by Kilpatrick, D.G.(1972): 'It is reasonable to assume that perceptual activity or autonomic emotional arousal cannot occur without some degree of accompanying cognitive activity' (p. 225).

The interactive feedback between emotion and cognition is used in our most effective high-level thinking. Insight and intuition are referred to as 'higher mental events' relative to stimulus response learning. The emotional involvement during 'higher emotional events' has been physiologically monitored by McGuigan, F.J. (1973) whose experimental results support this argument for feedback between emotion and cognition. See also Section 6.2 on feedback systems of the body and their interaction with cognitive events. He says of his results: 'In conclusion, I think the data do indicate that humans in their most effective thinking, use widespread feedback loops, including responses. Earlier I mentioned McCulloch's (1951) good paper entitled, "Why the Mind is in the Head!". With apologies to him, perhaps mine should have been entitled "Why only Part of the Mind is in the Head" ' (p. 376).

There are ample examples of this use of emotion in high-level effective thinking from all fields of creative research — from art, literature, science, and mathematics. Hadamard, J. (1945) states that in the field of creative mathematical research although

It may be surprising to see emotional sensibility invoked à propos of mathematical demonstrations which it would seem can interest only the intellect, this interaction of emotion and cognition is responsible for the intuitive choices of mathematical elements in insightful combinations. This is a true feeling that all real mathematicians know, and surely it belongs to emotional sensibility (p. 31).

In Section 2.2, discussing mathematical, artistic, and scientific relationships intuitively sensed through physiognomic perception, it was noted that in mathematics this emotional involvement is often through kinaesthesis. Wheeler, R.H. (1931) also recognizes the importance of the physiological process of kinaesthesis not only in mathematics, but in all intelligent behaviour. 'Intelligent behaviour involves kinaesthesis throughout ...kinaesthesis is an essential condition of conscious behaviour.' Wheeler also considers emotion and cognition to be inseparable, '...the instant a person exhibits feelings and emotion in a learning situation, the learning process has already commenced... it is arbitrary to separate the emotion from the learning' (p. 251). 'Thinking occurs also in terms of conscious or motor attitudes: acceptance, rejection, doubt, belief, anticipation, expectancy, certainty, uncertainty, assurance and many others' (p. 433).

The 'whole body' is influenced by the environment (see property 19, dependence of intuition on the environment). As George, F.H. (1962) says, '...it seems clear that psychological data is directly dependent on physiological states as well as on the environment' (p. 142). In comparing his own work, using electrophysiological investigations, with that of Watson, J.B. (1930); McGuigan, F.J. (1973) agrees that there is a participation of 'whole body' interactions with thought: 'these complex, interacting covert processes is what Watson meant by the phrase that we think with our whole bodies. And I believe that we do, when one considers the massive amount of evidence that implicates the eyes, arms, GSR, heart, etc., in thought processes' (p. 373). As indicated by the above-mentioned work of McGuigan it is considered suitable, because of this emotional interaction with cognition, to use the measurement of physiological responses during intuitive processes as an experimental methodology. Block, J. and Petersen, P. (1955) have also used autonomic measures in a study involving intuitive thought as did Springbett, B. (1957) in his approach to the measurement of creative thinking.

The literature substantiates this interaction between emotional states and cognitive processes. In substantiation are the following reports on:

  (i) perceptions inducing and influencing emotional states;
  (ii) emotional states influencing perceptions;
  (iii) interactions between emotional states and perceptions;
  (iv) psychophysiological experiments that measure the results of these
     interactions.

Perceptions Inducing and Influencing Emotional States

Griesinger, D.W. (1974) points out: 'Despite the frequent use of the terms [emotional state] there is little consensus among behavioural scientists on an operational definition' (p. 44). The term 'emotional state' is used here to include the same meaning as Schachter, S. and Singer, J.E. (1962) used, namely: 'It is suggested that emotional states may be considered a function of a state of physiological arousal and of a cognition appropriate to this state of arousal' (p. 398).

Melzack, R. and Casey, K.L. (1970) state that: 'Cognitive processes such as thoughts and past experience however, may not only influence emotion; they may evoke it' (p. 63). This is the case presented in this present book.

As early as 1947 the Gestalt psychologist Köhler had made observations on how perceptions can spark off emotional states (Köhler, W., 1947, p. 197). One of these observations was of how the handwriting of a friend on an envelope may produce a happy emotional response. He uses many personal observations to illustrate his points. Gordon, W.J.J. (1961), discussing Einstein's self-report of his mental activities, notes how mathematical thoughts produce corresponding emotional states: 'Here a great man of science working in the most abstract area of thought admits "muscular" identifications even with *a priori* constructs of mathematics' (p. 23). Even the S-R Associationists in 1960 considered cognition and emotion as a stimulus pairing. 'And it is even probable that in "purely cognitive" learning there is a "response" of some sort within the central nervous system' (Mowrer, O.H., 1960a, p. 281).

An early worker, Jacobson, E. (1932), was one of the first to measure the response of parts of the body to imagination. Using relatively primitive equipment he showed, for example, that a man who imagines himself running will make small movements of the legs even while he is relaxing in a chair, or similarly if he imagines himself hammering, the relevant arm will move a small distance. The arm averaged $0 \cdot 07$ to $0 \cdot 32$mm of movement. I have found that relaxed subjects' physiological responses as recorded on a polygraph, shift from basal level when they imagine vigorous exercise.

Jaensch demonstrated that the eidetic image (vivid recall) of a straight horizontal line will expand considerably in length if a pull is exerted on the horizontally outstretched arms of the subject. And vice versa, the sensation of the scanning motions performed by the eye, and of the other subliminal muscle impulses and stresses, all interfere with perception, particularly tactile values and the feel of texture. (Jaensch, E.R., 1930). This again indicates the use of tactile and texture information input for experiments involving intuition.

A more modern and now widely similar field of study is in lingual electromyography where the covert responses to linguistically directed thought are measured; see Blumenthal, M. (1959), also Bassin, F.V. and Bein, E.S. (1961) and many others.

The effect of emotional states on perception has been noted by Köhler, W. (1947, p. 192), who showed how the observer's emotional state affects the Gestalt of a simple figure, e.g. patterns of dots may appear to have varying priorities of groupings (Fig. 3.1/1).

Figure A in Fig. 3.1/1 may be perceived in any of the groupings illustrated, e.g. the line groupings in figures B and C or the main group of C with an

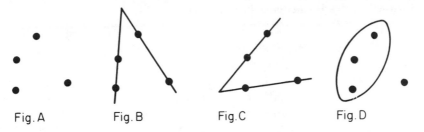

Fig. A   Fig. B   Fig. C   Fig. D

Fig. 3.1/1 Emotional sets influencing perceived groupings

'outsider' as in figure D. There are more complex and famous drawings which may be seen in different ways, sometimes called figure ground optical illusions, e.g. Boring's young/old woman figure and the Rubin's Vase illusion which alternates between perception of two facing profiles or a vase. Records of eye movements show that a subject perceives that part of a visual stimulus field with which he is most emotionally involved.

Brosgole, L. and Neylon, Ann (1973) arranged for seven subjects to move their hands in total darkness. This gave rise to a sense of visual motion (kinaesthetic visual imagery) followed by the impression of being able to see the hand. This experience was also reported by one of my subjects during the pretest of an insight experiment where subjects were required to feel a model without being able to see it.

One of the earlier attempts to explain this was a theory proposed by Werner, H. and Wapner, S. (1949). They proposed a sensory tonic theory of perception in which the body is fairly explicitly assigned important reference point functions, e.g. as used in the judgment of the true vertical of a strip light in a darkened room. It was demonstrated to appear to tilt in the direction opposite to that side of the subject's body subjected to electrical stimulation, producing increased muscular tonus on that side.

Since then other experiments have been done that illustrate this emotional influence over perception. McFarland, J.H. (1962) exposed three groups of sixteen subjects to a 20° tilted luminous line in a darkened room. During exposure subjects ' "felt" their bodies tilted or wanted to tilt their bodies in the direction of the tilted line'. McFarland says 'these findings suggest that the tendency towards movement occurring during exposure to the tilted visual object plays a role in the observed perceptual changes'.

The use of projective tests, e.g. TAT, Rorschach and SPEAK illustrates how subjects' emotional states vary their perceptions of the same visual stimulus and force personal priorities on the organization of the visual field. This again indicates the use of such tests in the study of intuition. When using TAT cards Bellak, L. (1944) found 'hungry subjects project ideas pertaining to food and have been found to perceive objects actually pertaining to food as presented so as to be perceived only with difficulty when not hungry (p. 365). Bellak gives several other examples of emotion affecting cognition and perception.

Emotional States Influencing Perceptions

Simon, H.A. (1967) comments that a general theory of thinking and problem-solving must incorporate the influence of emotions and cognitions. The Theory of Intuitive Thought attempts to do this.

The accuracy of perception as well as the way in which we organize our perceptions, is greatly influenced by our emotional states. Accuracy is improved when one is more interested in what one is doing. 'There are now data in Rorschach protocols, for example, that indicate that people can observe more accurately precisely when they are emotionally involved; that is to say, reason works better when emotions are present, the person sees more acutely, sharply, accurately when his emotions are engaged' (Anderson, H.A., 1959, p. 65). Beck, S.J. (1967) writes '. . . we do not know until we experience with the emotions. All the current evidence in the study of personality, both integrated and disordered, leads to this conclusion' (p. 106).

The emotional state of the body influences the perception which provides the data for cognitive processing, including intuitive thought. 'I think it can be demonstrated that we cannot really see the object unless we have some emotional involvement with it' (Anderson, H.A., 1959, p. 65).

This effect of the emotional state of the body modifying perception is particularly noticeable in 'person perception', where the perception must be processed so that the processing is also modified by the emotional state. Shrauger, S. and Altrocchi, J. (1964) give many examples of how perception of others is altered by the process of assuming that others are the same as the perceiver, e.g. authoritarians see others as more authoritarian, etc. There is a natural tendency to see others in our own likeness. Self-concept can change perception of objects and systems, as well as perceptions of people, similarly to how it rationalizes motives.

We perceive what we expect to perceive, and the organization of this perception is a determinate of cognitive style. Subject's protocols on projective tests may be used to assess cognitive style. Shrauger and Altrocchi emphasize that 'motivational interpersonal variables may be important in drawing inferences from cues'.

Intuitive judgments of other people may be wrong — property 9 — but it has been found that accuracy in the judgment of other people is positively correlated with intellectual skills (Taft, R., 1955). These contrast with intuitive skills — property 4.

In a comprehensive review of the perception of people Bruner, J.S. and Tagiuri, R. (1954) also concluded that accuracy is positively correlated with intellectual and social skills and adjustments. This illustrates that accuracy of perception of people is not so much a measure of intuitive ability as of intellectual skill. As noted in the previous discussion on how experience affects and is used in intuition, accuracy tests in general are not suitable for measuring intuitive ability. Projective tests are preferable. See the criticism of accurate rating given in Section 6.3.

Ego Threat Inhibits Intuition

Although mild emotion has an integrating effect on perception, extreme emotions — e.g. due to ego threat — can produce the disorganization of emotional blocking, giving inaccurate perception. In an experiment on the effect of 'Psychological stress and intuitive problem solving' Daniels, U.P. (1973) used Westcott's (1968) Problem Scale to measure intuitive thinking and he increased stress by increasing the rate of presentation of cues. Seventy-nine male students solved ten problems in paced or unpaced conditions. Results included highly significant main effects for stress on intuitive problem-solving. He concludes that increased stress inhibits intuitive problem-solving.

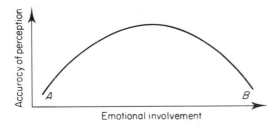

Fig. 3.1/2 Yerkes-Dobson Law applied to accuracy of perception varying with emotional involvement

If one is too highly motivated accuracy of perception decreases, according to an inverted 'U' function. In Fig. 3.1/2 point A represents apathy, point B represents emotional blocking. 'Emotional blocking can interfere with reflection by producing a deficiency in perception' (Bigge, M. L. and Hunt, M. P., 1965, p. 497). This emotional blocking may be the result of emotional and personality disturbance which adversely affects accuracy of perception, e.g. as shown in IQ scores.

Emotional involvement also adversely interferes with accuracy of perception when the subject is under threat, e.g. ego threat, threat to the integrity of the personality. In these circumstances the subject's perception and experience of his environment is distorted, by rejecting parts of this experience: '...experience which if assimilated, would involve a change in the organization of self, tends to be resisted through denial or distortion of symbolization' (Rogers, C.R., 1951, p. 390). An example of this inaccurate perception of experience is rationalization, a defence mechanism against accusation (Drever, J., 1974, p. 239). Rogers showed that under threat it is more difficult to modify the current organization of 'self'. This is a non-permissive ego situation where priority of categorizing thoughts shifts from the criterion of emotional association to the criterion of analytic association. Under ego threat intuitive processes are inhibited. In particular the cognizance of ego-threatening environments inhibits the intuitive process.

The environment, being the external source of stimuli, can give rise to different types of anxiety states. Some anxiety states encourage intuitive processes and some anxiety states inhibit intuitive processes. Inhibiting to intuitive processes are environments giving rise to non-permissive ego states, e.g. anxieties caused by threat to self-preservation, primary anxiety conditions (lack of food, electric shock) or secondary threat by expectation and/or anticipation of primary anxiety conditions. Manso, A.V. *et al.* (1977) identify one of the factors inhibiting to intuition as 'debilitating anxiety' (p. 190). Environments that encourage intuitive processes give rise to permissive ego states, e.g. anxiety caused by subjects' association of the stimulus with incongruous emotional states, giving rise to intrinsic motivation, 'fun' and 'game-like' environments. In test or concept-learning situations the environment appropriate to rote or intuitive materials should be selected respectively. 'Experiments show that for the most accurate perception non-threatening emotional atmospheres are better. That is non-threatening to the beliefs of the subject' (Rogers, C. R., 1951, p. 390). See also Section 8.3 on non-repressive environments facilitating intuitive thought.

The association between ego-permissive environments and the predominance of intuitive associations over analytic associations can be seen from the results of an exploratory factor, a study of peak experiences and ego permissiveness by Taft, R. (1969). He considers 'ego permissiveness' is the analytic control allowing expression of unanalysed thoughts, intuitions, unconventional and novel associations. These are the expressions of free floating emotions (allowed because of relaxed ego control). He quotes (p. 30) a paper by As (1962) which finds role absorption and tolerance of unusual states are related to ego permissiveness. Taft gave a many-itemed test of agree/disagree items to measure ego permissiveness. The close relation between intuitive processes and ego-permissive states as described in the present study is illustrated by item 14 of Taft's test (Taft, R., 1969, p. 51) which measures ego permissiveness. 'I would rather rely on my own intuition than try to think things out by logic.' Thirty-two per cent of respondents agreed to this item.

The concomitants of insight and intuition all have the same favourable environments, e.g. concomitants such as creativity, empathy, field independence, and related personality factors. Bruner, J. (1962, p. 102) says of intuition that: 'It is found on a kind of combination playfulness that is possible only when the consequences of error are not overpowering or sinful'. Favourable conditions are the opposite of this for rote learning, analytic tasks, field dependence, authoritarianism personality responses, etc., and other personality characteristics not associated with insight or intuition. This classification by 'favourable environment' is an indication of psychophysiological phenomena that may be associated with the intuitive process.

Psychophysiological Experiments Involving the Perception/Emotion Interaction

The psychophysiological experiments that monitor the interaction of emotional states with cognitive activities fall into three categories depending upon the type of variable producing the physiological responses. These variables may be:

(i) cognitive, or
(ii) emotional, or
(iii) personality variables.

The theory of intuitive processes presented in this study uses ideas of secondary reinforcement of emotional states interacting with these three types of cognitive variables. This theory is in agreement with Mowrer's work which is also an example of a much needed 'whole body' unifying theory. 'One of the most attractive features of Mowrer's work (two-factor theory and secondary reinforcement, e.g. hope, etc.), is the gradual interlinking of emotional and personality factors with cognitive ones' (George, F.H., 1962).

Psychophysiological Experiments Involving Cognitive Functions in Various Degrees of Complexity, Activational Peaking, and Kinaesthesis

The psychophysiological experiments which involve cognition as the cause of the monitored physiological responses use various cognitive functions in varying degrees of complexity, giving instructional requirements for the subject to:

(a)   imagine movement;
(b)   read;
(c)   learn a rote task;
(d)   learn, involving concept identification; and
(e)   think generally, involving visual attending, etc.

These experiments give indications of variables and analyses that may be used in psychophysiological investigations of intuition, which unfortunately, apart from Bastick, T. (1979), do not seem to exist.

The Wursberg group, (Kulpe, Marbe, Ach, Watt) showed that kinaesthetic sensations from the body played an important role in judgments relating to various psychophysical tasks. These sensations result from proprioceptive feedback from the musculature (Festinger, L. and Kirkpatrick Canon, L., 1965, p. 373) and from 'Feelings of innervation' (James, W., 1950, p. 493) during actual movement that occur whilst the subject is thinking as mentioned above. These small movements are easily demonstrated during physiological monitoring. They were measured by Jacobson, E. (1932) who found 'movement of eyeballs at the moment of visual imagination' (p. 690) and measured the 'interaction of muscular regions and mental activity' (p. 694).

The musculature responds to the cognitive act of reading. There are many experiments that measure covert activity whilst reading. An example is McGuigan, F.J.'s (1973) study of covert oral behaviour during the silent

94

performance of language tasks. One of the earliest was by Jacobson, E. and Kraft, F.L. (1942) who measured contraction potentials in the right *quadriceps femoris* whilst subjects were relaxing and reading. They used platinum iridium wires 11mm deep in the thighs of one hundred subjects for measuring tonus in the muscle. They only recorded voltage at a particular frequency.

Psychophysiological experiments concerning rote learning use the cognitive associations of alphameric or numeric characters. An experiment with an arithmetic bias was designed by Kahneman, D. *et al.* (1969). A modification of this experiment was used by Bastick T. (1979).

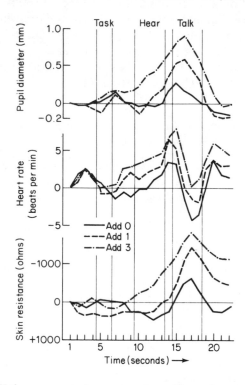

Fig. 3.1/3 Pupillary, heart-rate, and skin resistance changes while adding up to four digits (from Kahneman, D. *et al.*, 1969)

Kahneman *et al.* measured pupillary, heart-rate, and skin-resistance changes during a mental task. Ten subjects were required to add the digits 0, 1, or 3 to the digit 4. The numbers to be added were serially presented and the answer was read out after a two-second pause. The results were taken on polygraph and analogue tape which was later digitalized and computer-processed. They found that the degree of response was ordered by the difficulty of the task and that there was a much greater response during hearing and talking than that due to task difficulty, see Fig. 3.1/3. Each subject took five trials. Respiration was recorded but not measured. It was used as an indication of artefacts.

Physiological responses to the emotional involvement at different levels of difficulty of a task may be due to the satisfaction and lack of anxiety that accompanies more frequent success on the simpler tasks. Some physiological correlates of verbal learning task difficulty were measured by Andreassi, J.L. (1966). He recorded muscle action potentials (MAPS), palmar skin conductance (PSC), heart rate, and GSR over thirty-second intervals whilst eight subjects had to learn lists at three levels of difficulty. He defined GSR as resistance change greater than 1000 ohms within a two-second period, and found these changes by eye. Results were that GSR and PSC increased whilst learning. He found more activity on easier tasks. The author suggested the possibility that the men's increased physiological activity might indicate greater involvement in the learning task when their performance was more successful. With only eight subjects this was rather a small experiment.

These size restrictions, due to the inordinate work involved in manual coding of traces, should now be outmoded by the availability of microcomputer physiological monitoring equipment. The verbal rote-learning tasks usually involve associating pairs of nonsense syllables. The cognitive act of learning the association between pairs of nonsense syllables is influenced by emotional involvement and the resulting physiological responses have been measured by several workers. Paired association not controlled for emotional content should not be used in experiments on intuition, but a modification of the design, methodology, and analysis of the following experiments may be used in the development of psychophysiological experiments to study intuition.

Furth, H.G. and Terry, R.A. (1961) have measured autonomic responses during serial learning. They measured GSR and pulse pressure. The GSR measure used was the difference in conductance level (CL) from the beginning to the end of the trials taking two measures for each subject, one at the initial exposure trial and the other at the extreme value. Z scores were used in analysis. Forty subjects, with controlled immediate experimental history, e.g. no meal within an hour of the experiment and thirty minutes rest before the experiment, used sets of twelve nonsense syllables with four-second anticipation between exposures. Results were that the conductance level rose during learning and pulse pressure fell. There was no significant correlation between pulse pressure and conductance level. Being a rote task there was not a great deal of emotional involvement. A log-conductance transformation was used. Z scores and controlled immediate experimental history should be used in psychophysiological experiments comparing the intuitive ability of subjects. Much experimental research has been done connecting the orientating response and EEG (see Germana, J., 1968, pp. 107/108). Brain rhythms will be considered later in Section 6.2. Kintsch, W. (1965) investigated the GSR component of orientating response during paired associate learning before and after learning had taken place. He used thirty-two subjects; twelve nonsense syllables as stimuli; numbers one and two as responses; four-second anticipation interval; two-second interitem interval; thirty-second intertrial interval and ten trials. GSR was measured in mm from base line to maximum deflection, which occurred during presentation of each item. Results were that GSR increased on non-learning trials (due to frustration?) with a maximum on the trial of the last error. Basal resistance slightly decreased during the experiment for most subjects. Behavioural response latencies became shorter after learning. Half the subjects had high GSR on errors. This was the opposite case for the other half of subjects.

In a second experiment using thirty-six subjects, ten items and two-digit numbers paired with nonsense words, Kintsch found that GSR decreased when subjects were correct. 'The fact that the orientating reaction is stronger in the intermediate state than at the very beginning of learning agrees well with the interpretation of the first stage of the learning process as stimulus encoding.' As long as an item is completely new, a moderate orientating reflex is evoked. This reflex reaches maximum strength after the subject already knows something about the item but recall is either still incomplete or unreliable. In terms of Sokolov E.N.'s (1960), neuronal model one could say that a neural representation has been built up but does not yet coincide perfectly with all the parameters of the stimulation. After an item enters the learning state habituation sets in.

Andreassi, J.L. and Whalen, P.M. (1967) measured some physiological correlates of learning and overlearning. They recorded measures of heart rate, palmar skin conductance, and phasic GSR, whilst fifteen subjects were learning nonsense syllables. All measures were taken for ten seconds and averaged over ten trials giving one hundred seconds total measurement time per subject. There were two-minute rests between thirty two-second trials. GSR was defined as a change in basal skin resistance greater than 1000 ohms in two seconds. PSC was found by eye over each of the ten-second intervals. The experimenters used the transformation inverse of PSC × 1,000,000 micromhos. Electrodes were fitted at the base of the index and little fingers 5 cm apart. Heart-rate electrodes were placed on each arm and grounded by an ear-lobe clip. Results showed that all measures went down on overlearning and up again on new learning. Experiment two showed a further drop with 'double overlearning' the same list. Analysis used t-tests not Anovar.

Brown, C.H. (1937) found that greater GSRs are associated with learning (a list of nonsense syllables) than with correct anticipations *per se*. He found $0 \cdot 8$ group correlation with the order of learning the items.

Germana, J. (1968) found the consistency in his review of relevant experiments that activational responses to conditioned stimuli increase during early phases of learning, peak at the point of response acquisition, then decrease with continued practice. He called this activational peaking (AP). Germana, J. (1966) defined activational peaking as follows: 'AP may therefore be defined as consisting of the following sequence of events: as a stimulus takes on the properties of CS, i.e. during the initial stages of conditioning, ARs to the stimulus increase over the level of responsiveness characteristic of the preconditioning stage. Further elaboration of the conditioned response results in AR decrement to the CS' (pp. 2/3). He interprets activational peaking effect as a change in 'emotional state', or subject apprehension. This is a redescription of AP equalling change in emotional state, showing that a measure of AP is a measure of emotional involvement. Hence, in experiments on intuition activational peaking may be taken as an indication of emotional involvement.

In an investigation of activational peaking during concept identification Spencer, W.B. and Olmedo, E.L. (1969), using only six subjects, found that learners exhibited a lower absolute resistance level and a higher GSR magnitude throughout the experimental session than did non-learners.

The most complicated cognitive activity investigated during psychophysiological experiments is that of concept formation and identification. If during these experiments the experimental conditions and methodology are inducive to intuitive processes as outlined in this study, then it is possible that the physiological responses measured in these experiments result from intuition or insight.

There are two types of concept formation experiment in the literature where physiological responses are recorded.

(1) The subject is presented with a succession of stimuli each of which contains a pattern. The subject has to guess the criteria defining the pattern and is reinforced by information of his success or failure on each trial. This is the same design as the insight experiments reviewed in Section 1.3 on insight experiments requiring subjects to discover rules.

(2) The subject works through a problem task and his behaviour in different sections of the task is monitored and compared.

Typical of the first type is an experiment by Germana, J. and Pavlik, W.B. (1964) who required seventy-five subjects to discover the criteria that the middle number of seven presented digits was correct. Subjects were reinforced on five groups of 4, 8, 12, 16, or 32 acquisition trials followed by 10 extinction trials. GSR was defined as greater than 0·5mm deflection. Results were that the magnitude of GSR in log conductance scores increased to the point of learning then decreased to the base line and the magnitude of GSR on the first extinction trial increased with the number of reinforcements. A criticism of the above and many such experiments is that one cannot say whether the peaking of GSR is due to stimulus or behavioural response as the subjects were responding simultaneously as the stimulus was presented.

In an experiment monitoring electrodermal and electromyographic parameters during concept identification, Pishkin, V. and Shurley, J.T. (1968) showed that spontaneous GSR is related to successful information intake. They required thirty subjects to categorize geometric patterns of various difficulties in two sets, one solvable and the other unsolvable. They measured muscle action potential (MAP) and specific GSR magnitude in conductance units and spontaneous GSRs were defined as a change greater or equal to 0·001 of basal resistance. The concepts used were some properties of geometrical shapes presented in pairs, e.g. colour, number of sides, etc. Subjects pressed a key to choose which one of each pair had the criteria defined by the concept they had to guess the rule. Two sets were used. One set was unsolvable as false feedback was given to the subjects. The sets used three levels of criterion complexity.

Results show the harder the task the fewer were the spontaneous GSRs, giving a correlation of -0.56 ($p < 0.01$) between the number of errors and spontaneous GSR. Also changes in conductance of resulting MAPs indicated internal disturbance associated with an inability to process information. Spontaneous GSRs indicated successful information intake. Specific GSR was not effected. This could be due to the poor units used, i.e. a constant current was used followed by a transformation to conductance units using change in conductance equals change in resistance divided by R^2 where R is basal resistance at the onset of response. Spontaneous GSR was defined as greater than 0.001 of basal resistance. In conclusion authors state that: 'Spontaneous GSR's are positively and monotonically related to successful information intake while muscle tension probably represents internal disturbance associated with inability to process information as a combined function of unsolvable set and amount of irrelevant information'.

A criticism of the methodology of the above experiment is that it would have been much improved if it had resembled more that of Lykken, D.T. and Venables, P.H. (1971), e.g. the use of constant voltage, not conductance, etc.

A more ambitious experiment was an investigation of the relationship between three measures of GSR and activational peaking in two concept-identification tasks by Spencer, B. (1972). He tested two concepts. They were (1) numerical: (2) spatial: the three measures of GSR were tonic SCL measured prior to experiment, phasic SCR in two parts:

(a)   S — SCR, the GSR accompanying stimulus presentation; and
(b)   R — SCR, the GSR accompanying the behavioural response;

thus avoiding the methodology criticized above (Germana, J. and Pavlik, W.B., 1964).

The spatial concept was whether or not two illuminated bulbs in a 3×3 matrix were in the same row or column. E delayed the stimulus and response in order to isolate the GSRs accompanying each but this does not prevent covert response so that only GSR due to physical overt response such as moving, is isolated, not GSR due to mental activity during delay. E had S press a lever when 100 per cent certain that S had learnt the correct concept. 100 per cent correct response is a Behaviourist's criterion for insight, as noted in Section 1.3.

E picked up GSR through zinc electrodes on the volor surfaces of the first and third fingers of the non-preferred hand. E used zinc sulphate electrolytic jelly for good skin contact and to minimize measurement errors associated with the battery effect. E left S in a soundproof room and monitoring equipment was in another room. Equipment was a board on which there was a 3×3 pattern of lights numbered 1 to 9. Two lighted numbers were shown, the correct numerical concept was if their sum or difference was even: compare with its space concept of whether two lights are in the same row or column. The lights were on for ten seconds and S was expected to respond within five seconds of switching off the lights. A blue lamp came on when the concept was recognized which acted as the reinforcement. E used a polygraph with an event marker on the GSR record at the beginning and the end of the experiment. AP was found to be related to S-SCR, reflecting successful information intake. The results were that activational peaking (AP) was found only on S-SCR. Also the SCL measure reflected cognitive activity and the SCR measure reflected psychological stress accompanying the unsuccessful utilization of information. The activation level of non-learners in the spatial task was higher than that of learners, see Fig. 3.1/4.

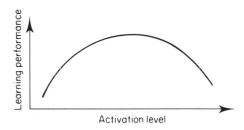

Fig. 3.1/4 Graph of activation level against learning performance on a spatial learning task

Increments in activation, arousal, excitation, etc., are commonly taken to be reflected by increments in skin conductance, heart rate, etc. Activational level (AL) is the tonic state of the whole organism. Activational response (AR) is phasic change of the whole or part of the structure of the organism. Spencer's paper is on AR to external or internal stimulation. His conclusions support the general thesis of this present study, that of the interaction of emotion and purely cognitive activity.

> The data for both conditions supports the interpretation that the psycho-physiological arousal accompanying cognitive activity increases during learning and shortly after learning, while the emotional arousal accompanying the intake of information shows an increase during learning, but declines rapidly after learning. The sharp decrease in the number of spontaneous SCRs after the 100% response is probably indicative of a release of emotional arousal due to the fact that the concept has been learned. (Spencer, B., 1972, p. 52).

These results indicate the suitability of electrodermal measures for monitoring emotional involvement during intuitive processes.

> '...the results of this experiment support the hypothesis that the tonic electrodermal activity reflects the psychophysiological arousal associated with cognitive activity.' (Spencer, B., 1972, p. 47).

An experiment involving the type of cognitive activity involved in a problem-solving task was designed by Blatt, S. (1961). He conducted an experiment using a Psi Apparatus (or Logical Analysis Device) in which subjects pressed buttons to get information about its internal circuitry through flashing lights. Using this information subjects had to find the correct sequence to switch on the centre light. Each problem takes about an hour. Blatt explored variations in cardiac activity only, that were asssociated with problem-solving behaviour. He found that efficient problem-solvers, that is the ones who asked the fewest questions, which corresponds to Westcott's definition of intuitive types as low information demanders (Westcott, M.R., 1961, 1964, 1966, 1968), showed a marked cardiac change at three points:

(1)   when all the information had been gained;
(2)   when their behaviour shifted from analysis to synthesis in button pressing;
(3)   as they approached the final solution.

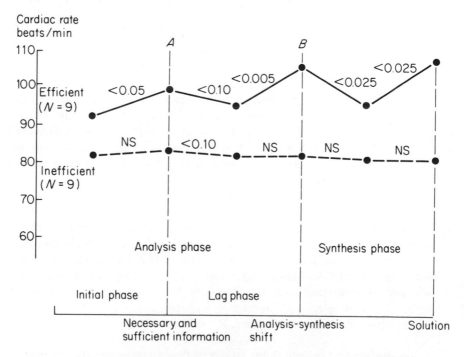

Cardiac rate of efficient and inefficient groups during the three phases and three points of the experimental problem

Fig. 3.1/5 Activational peaking of low information demanders but not high information demanders, on a problem-solving task (from Blatt, S., 1961)

They had two distinct highs, see Fig. 3.1/5, that coincided with two distinct parts of the problem-solving process:

(1) where the necessary and sufficient information had been gathered; and

(2) where the method changed from analysis to synthesis.

This was a logical problem and did not contain concrete elements with which the subject could easily empathize through any modality. Indeed the 'concept' could be identified by an analytic search process, although subjects need not have used this rote process. Hence, the APs at A and B in Fig. 3.1/5 could represent the emotional involvement during intuitive processes. In response to a questionnaire about their feelings during the experimental problem task, efficient subjects frequently commented in retrospect:

'satisfaction of working out the problem'
'elation as solution was reached' and
'the problem was lots of fun, I enjoyed it'.

Inefficient subjects referred to:

'annoyance' and
'frustration'.

This agrees with the theory presented in the present study on the attitudes inducive to intuitive processes and reported attitudes of intuiters versus analysers on intuitive tasks. This indicates the advantage of using interviews or questionnaires as collaborative qualitative evidence of an intuitive versus analytic approach in experiments on intuitive problem-solving.

With reference to the points of AP representing involvement in intuitive processes, in an earlier paper on a similar experiment Blatt, S. (1960) stated: 'Cardiac arousal at these crucial points in the thought process which are not reported by subjects has been discussed as the intuitive, sensitive, effect-laden functioning frequently conceptualized as preconscious'.

Activational peaking was also a result of an experiment by Trabasso T. and Bower G.H. (1964) who found that the magnitude of GSR increased up to the criterion of 100 per cent correct concept identification; the behavioural insight criterion then dropped; also that GSR were related to the number of errors (frustration again?). Colgan, D.M. (1970) in a study of the effects of instructions upon the skin resistance response also found that cognitive perception of the subject determines the direction and magnitude of electrodermal response. Generally HR and palmar conductance are affected by various cognitive activities as shown in Fig. 3.1/6. It is interesting to note the opposite directions of the HR and GSR responses in the intuitive related tasks of visual attention and empathic listening. Such a result might be expected from physiological experiments on intuition.

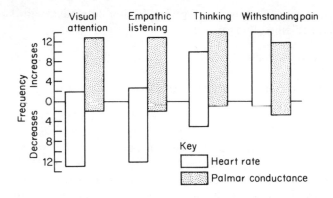

Fig. 3.1/6 Directional fractionation response according to the nature of subjects' tasks, for fifteen subjects (from Sternbach, R. A., 1966, p. 88)

Psychophysiological Experiments which Monitor the Physiological Effects of Emotions

There are a few experiments in the literature that monitor physiological effects of different emotions. The effect of threat on GSR levels was investigated by Bridger, W.H. and Mandel, I.J.A. (1964) who compared the GSR fear responses produced by threat and electric shock. They measured GSR for two groups of subjects. Both groups wore electrodes for receiving electric shocks and were told that shock would occur after a particular stimulus. One group was given the shock, the other group only threatened. GSRs of both groups were greater than the psuedo-conditioned control groups.

This is confirmed by many experiments; that the threat produces as good if not a better GSR expectancy reading than the actual stimulus. This idea may be used in experiments on intuition to measure the emotional involvement caused by a threat of electric shock. An advantage of using a threat rather than the actual shock is not only that it produces the same type of GSR effect, but that in the experimental situation it is easier to return to a permissive atmosphere of the subject's trust in the experimenter than it would be if a shock had actually been given. This friendly experimental environment is a requisite for the study of intuitive processes, see Section 8.3. A further methodological advantage relies upon another finding of Bridger, W.H. and Mandel, I.J.A. (1964). Both groups were told there would be no more shocks and the 'threatened group' extinguished rapidly whereas the shocked group did not. This means that subjects return to basal levels sooner after threat than after shock, thus allowing the next section of an experiment to begin sooner.

However, threat may cause fear and/or anxiety. It has previously been said that threat to the ego would be inhibitive to intuitive processes but that some forms of anxiety could give intrinsic motivation which encourages intuitive processes. It has been found that HR and different components of the GSR response are indicative of these two emotions. Ax, A. (1953) found different physiological responses due to fear and anxiety. The number of increases in GSR conductance was greater for anger than for fear. There was a similar decrease in heart rate, greater for anger than fear. The amount of skin conductance increases was greater for fear than anger. Confirmation of the experiment was found by Schachter, J. (1957).

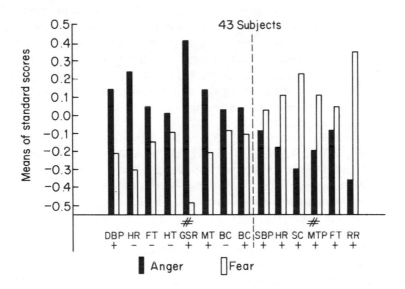

Fig. 3.1/7 Graph of differing effects of fear and anger on means of fourteen physiological responses (from Sternbach, R. A., 1966, p. 85)

Fig. 3.1/7 (Sternbach, R.A., 1966, p. 85) illustrates the differing effects of anger and fear on the means of the standard scores of fourteen physiological responses. In the figure plus signs (+) indicate increases in the variable, minus signs (−) indicate decreases. Greater average responses for anger appear in diastolic blood pressure rises (DBP +), heart rate decreases (HR-), the number of galvanic skin responses (GSR) and muscle tension increase (MT +); greater average responses for fear appear in skin conductance increases (SC +), the number of muscle tension peaks (MTP), and increases in respiration rate (RR +).

From the above results it is seen that the three responses most affected are phasic GSR, respiration rate, and heart rate, which indicates the suitability of these measures for recording subjects' physiology during experiments on intuition. These various physiological responses characteristic of different emotional states are controlled by the central nervous system (CNS) through its peripheral system the autonomic nervous system (ANS), by the feedback interaction between the para-sympathetic nervous system (PNS) and the sympathetic nervous system (SNS) responses, influencing the action of the body chemically with adrenaline and noradrenaline. For example, when an increase in heart rate is observed it may be due to either increased activity of the SNS cardiac accelerators (adrenaline) or an increase in the activity of the PNS decelerators (noradrenaline).

Wenger, M.A. and Cullen, T.D. (1958) measured nine variable responses to fourteen stimuli and compared them to the base-line responses during sleep. The results suggest different mixed adrenaline and noradrenaline patterns to different stimuli. Although the quantity of emotion has been measured, the fine graduations of emotion produced by finely graduated proportions of adrenaline and noradrenaline mixture produce fine graduations of emotional response which have not yet, to my present knowledge, been measured.

It is the montage of the emotional responses to innumerable stimuli that forms the emotional state of the organism. For example, a subject relaxing in a chair responds to innumerable physical stimuli, e.g. changing pressures on his body from the chair, patterns of light, sound and temperature, and his own thoughts, etc., which all define his unique emotional state at any moment. The gradual changes in each component emotional response alter the emotional state to another unique, but so similar emotional state that this change can be described as a continuous drift of emotion. The changes are stable in that a slight change in one direction by the PNS is compensated by a change in the other direction by the SNS producing a distribution of emotional states whose central tendency is the homeostasis of the organism.

A descriptive analogy of the above processes might be the motion of a wobbling vibrating jelly on the end of a stick. The shape at any time depicting the emotional state of the organism, the cause of the wobbling and vibration representating external and internal stimuli. The restriction and wobbling motion given by the stick being analogous to the dependences of the emotional state on the environment and the stimulation of the emotional state by the environment. Homeostasis being represented by the shape defined by the mean motion of every part of the surface of the jelly relative to the end of this stick. These fine graduations of response have not been measured, as subtle emotions do not produce statistically significant changes in coarse physiological recordings of the ANS. An attempt, however, was made to assess these differential autonomic patterns in emotions by Sternbach, R.A. (1962). He measured responses of children to viewing the film *Bambi,* and found no difference between their reactions to sad and funny parts on ANS measures. He compared scenes which made the children happiest, saddest, etc., and compared concomitant physiological measures with their prestimulus levels. The difference between the scores for the scenes showed an insignificant ANS response but eye-blink response decreased significantly with sadness and skin resistance increased significantly, showing that skin resistance is a sensitive measure, another reason for its use in physiological experiments on intuition.

Personality Correlates of Physiological Responses and the Intuitive Type

Some cognitive variables that define personality, e.g. cognitive style, authoritarianism, fantasy ability, etc., have an interaction with emotion and are also independently associated with intuitive processes, see Sections 5.2 and 7.3. The personality variables that facilitate the intuitive process define an intuitive type. The emotional interaction with these cognitive variables has been monitored through various physiological responses. The physiological responses of the personality variables concomitant with the intuitive process should all be of the same type and in the same direction. The following illustrate these two points:

(1) cognitive personality characteristics and emotion interact and the interaction has been monitored through physiological responses;

(2) the physiological measures associated by the Theory of Intuitive Thought with the personality concomitants of the intuitive process are of the same type and in the same direction. This is physiological support for the theory.

It is shown in Section 7.3 that the personality variables associated with the intuitive process are intercorrelated. The consistency of these findings is one of the ways in which the literature adds supporting evidence to the theory of intuitive processes presented in this study.

A subject's $\overline{A}$ score is a useful index that may be correlated with personality variables. $\overline{A}$ is the total of a subject's basal physiological responses standardized across subjects: see Wenger, M.A. (1941) for a method of measuring individual differences in autonomic balance($\overline{A}$).

Eysenck, H.J. (1953) found that neuroticism is correlated with deviation from $\overline{A}$ in either direction, i.e. individuals' differences in their $\overline{A}$ from the mean $\overline{A}$ (in either the SNS or PNS direction) reflected their neuroticism. Eysenck thinks extroverts are SNS-dominant, i.e. high on GSR. Note that sweat glands receive only SNS fibres (similarly so do hair follicles which cause goose bumps).

Another study relating subjects' $\overline{A}$ scores with their emotional characteristics, natural activity, and fantasy ability was done by Wenger, M.A. (1947) who found that children on the tails of the $\overline{A}$ distribution had significantly different personality traits. Strong PNS dominance is related to emotional inhibition and less emotional excitability, low frequency of activity, and less fantasy. This implies that intuitive types, who have opposing characteristics, will have strong SNS dominance.

Natural activity or alertness was also found to have physiological correlates by Cattell, R.B. (1946) who found a factor characterized by high GSR. This factor is psychologically associated with alertness, activity, and excitement. Low GSR correlates with sleepiness and passivity. Similarly Sanford, R.N. *et al.* (1943) found a positive correlation of similar measures with conscientious work, and negative correlation with timidity. Wishner, J. (1955) also showed that GSR correlated with alertness. The Rorschach test was also used by Wishner, J. (1953) in a study of neurosis and tension; using the relationship of physiological and Rorschach measures, his results confirm the above conclusions.

In a study of personality correlates of electrodermal resistance to type of response, Seymour, R.B. (1950) showed that subjects with high GSR are significantly more interested in achievement and are more forceful in their behaviour than children with low reactivity. Subjects' Need for Achievement (nACH) score may also be derived using McClelland, D. C. *et al.*'s (1949) and (1953) methods of scoring the French Insight Test (French, Elizabeth, 1958); thus relating insight and nACH to GSR response.

Barrier scores (detailed in Section 3.3) are a measure of subjects' cognizance of their own bodies for which many personality correlates have been found. Herring, F.H. (1956) found that high barrier scorers have a minimum HR during surgery and incidently have a high basal metabolic rate which may be associated with the finding of alertness from the above experiments.

A study that directly relates personality variables with kinaesthetic emotional involvement in cognitive judgments involves the fact that in a dark room a stationary light seems to move. Byrne, D. (1966, p. 266) reports that Millon (1957) showed that subjects soon settled on a personal norm of the distance the light appears to move. He took the number of trials to form the norm as a measure of intolerance of ambiguity. Subjects high in authoritarianism formed norms significantly faster than those low in authoritarianism. Body reference gives the information that the light is moving. High authoritarian types rely little on the internal body sensations giving this information, so formed norms faster. Personality concomitants of intuitive processes, given by the theory of intuitive processes, are completely in agreement with this result.

The foregoing all show that intuitive processes are 'whole body' processes resulting from the psychophysiologial interaction of emotion and cognition. Sternbach, R.A. (1966) at the beginning of his book defines 'psychophysiology' as: 'Mental or emotional or behavioural activities are made to occur while physiological events are being observed. Correlations between the activities and the observed physiological events are noted and some intervening internal event is postulated.'

From this study psychophysiological experiments on intuition may be designed which involve mental, emotional, and behavioural activities whilst the physiological events indicated above are being observed. The experiments may be designed so that the internal event can only be postulated to be intuition.

Early psychologists considered the whole personality. Over the last few decades the S-R associationists and others have fragmented the personality by making successful studies of its specialized substructures. The trend now is back to 'whole body' personality theories to which this study subscribes. Experimental psychology and physiology is now again considering the integrated person; 'the wheel's turned full circle' (George, F.H., 1962, p. 290).

3.2   DEVELOPMENT AND USE OF EMOTIONAL SETS

At any one time the organism is in some emotional state. At the next moment the organism has drifted through continuous change to another unique emotional state. The normal rate of change from one emotional state to another varies between individuals and is affected by stimuli from the environment. Intuitive types tend to be more emotionally variable (moody) than the 'cool' analytic types and they are more emotionally sensitive to the environment.

It has previously been discussed in this study how perception affects emotion, how emotion affects perception and how it is in fact not possible to separate emotion and perception because of the modifying effect they have upon one another.

The succession of transient emotional states immediately before and after the present emotional state have many responses in common and form an emotional set of these concordant responses. It is shown in this section that specific perceptions tend to induce emotional sets specifically paired with these perceptions and that the reverse is also true, that emotional sets tend to induce secondary perceptions (memories) specifically paired with these emotional sets. It is also shown that, through processes of conditioning, response tendencies are associated with some emotional states, thus forming emotional sets. Hence a perception can induce an emotional set. The organism then has a tendency to behave in a way preconditioned by its experience.

Conditioning Of Percepts To Emotional States

Perceptions have associated emotions. Physiognomic perception is a common part of the intuitive process in which perceptions arouse specific emotional sets. There are many examples of this, some given in this study, e.g. Section 2.2 on mathematical, artistic, and scientific relationships intuitively sensed through physiognomic perception. However, a new perception will evoke a different emotional state, thus changing the emotional set associated with the first perception. There is little literature on this change and drift of emotional states: '. . . we know a good deal about the way signs, symbols, and situations may serve to arouse emotional states of various kinds, we know comparatively little about the way in which they may also serve to terminate such states' (Mowrer, O.H., 1946, p. 218).

This specific emotional arousal that accompanies a perception was monitored by Spencer, B. (1972) using a GSR measurement: '. . . the S-SCR measure reflects the emotional arousal accompanying the perceptual and cognitive activities set into motion by the presentation of the stimulus' (p. 49).

These associated emotional states, linked through contiguity conditioning with the original perception, are a method of memory coding the perceptions so that when the specific emotional state reoccurs, it induces a copy (memory) of this perception. This is supported by findings cited by Bandura, A. (1969, p.

133) indicating that in the course of observation, transitory perceptual phenomena produce relatively enduring retrievable images of modelled sequences of behaviour.

Findings cited by Bandura show that a verbal coding helps the subject to remember complex perceptions, both of external stimuli and of secondary image stimuli, e.g. memories, fantasies, dreams, etc.: '...these [images] are transferred to long-term memory with the help of verbal coding'.

However, this verbal coding itself uses emotional interactions which are felt throughout the whole body and so are associated by the conditioning of repeated experience to be remembered when the emotional set again occurs; an example is rhythmic chanting, e.g. of multiplication tables. See the later discussion on how the association of emotional sets is used for intuitive recall. This 'whole body' emotional interaction involved in verbal coding has been found by McGuigan, F.J. (1973, p. 373) and others. 'We have some good evidence that covert oral behaviour is intimately linked with covert non-oral responses and these patterns develop, as Novikova (1961) put it, into a "single functional system with the motor speech analyser". This is, we can well expect that a linguistic stimulus becomes conditioned to widespread responses through the body, including autonomic, as well as skeletal responses.''

The specific association between perceptions of external stimuli — visual and verbal — with related emotional states and also the association between specific emotional states and perceptions of imagery and memory was clearly demonstrated by the following two studies. Peters, G.A. and Merrifield, P.R. (1958) in their experiment titled 'Graphic representation of emotional feelings' had one hundred and eighty-eight male subjects draw lines to represent twenty-four emotive adjectives, e.g. strong, sad, faint, hard, etc. The lines were categorized according to their form, e.g. straight, curved, wavy, or angular and by their direction, e.g. horizontal, upward or downward and also categorized by their intensity of line, e.g. light, medium, or heavy stroke. It was found that direction was related to social desirability, e.g. dead related to down, strong related to up. Form was related to overt activity, i.e. irregular or wavy lines for angry and lively and straight lines for quiet, idle. Intensity was related to strength of emotional feeling, i.e. furious and cruel being hard heavy lines (note the natural physiognomies of the description) and light lines for delicate and quiet. Words were scored by comparison with mean scores for all words. These results are explained here by the words inducing emotional states which have perceptions of visual meanings associated with them.

Common experiences tend to produce common pairings of perception and emotional states, as exploited by advertisers. The perception of a word has specific associated emotional connotations. Again through common experiences these specific pairings are similar throughout a particular culture. Osgood, C.E. (1952) uses his semantic differential to compare the emotional meaning of words. The word is rated on an n-point scale on N independent emotional dimensions, e.g. for the word 'socialism' with n-7 and N-3 the schematic Fig. 3.2/1 would represent such a rating.

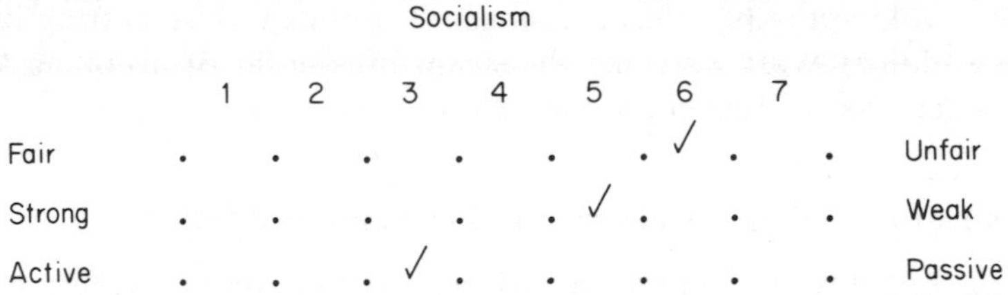

Socialism

	1	2	3	4	5	6	7	
Fair	.	.	.	.	.	✓	.	.	Unfair
Strong	.	.	.	.	. ✓	.	.	.	Weak
Active	.	.	. ✓	.	.	.	.	.	Passive

Fig. 3.2/1 Semantic differential rating of 'Socialism' on seven-point scale of three 'Independent' emotional dimensions (from Osgood, C. E., 1952)

An example is of how the word 'socialism' was rated by a group of American Mid-western voters in 1952 (Osgood, C.E., 1952). The emotional connotations of the word are represented by the point in the N dimension space to which this scheme maps it, e.g. 'socialism' on these scales is mapped to the point socialism (6, 5, 3). Osgood uses the point defined by the mean of many subjects' responses to the same word, and the Euclidean distance between mean points as the semantic differential between the emotional connotations of words. By taking the mean of subjects he is considering common experience.

This test, as a consequence of the theory discussed here could also be used as a psychiatric instrument to measure the emotional disturbance of a patient by quantifying the divergence of his free emotional word associations from those of the normal population, e.g. sum the differences between his emotional associations to common key words and those of the normal populations to find the dimensions on which the patient is most at variance with normality. As a further consequence of the Theory of Intuitive Thought Processes, this system could also be used to define subcultures and personality types by clustering the subjects on the criterion of total similar variance of ratings, on all dimensions, of the emotional connotation of words. The words chosen should of course be relevant to the culture or personality.

These common emotional state/perception pairings result from similar experiences in a common environment. The pairings of emotional states with perception are, however, results of personal experiences and contribute to the uniqueness of an individual's personality. Some creative workers exploit this pairing by placing themselves in a specific environment, to induce emotional sets in which they have previously experienced insights, e.g. working in a particular room or with a particular coloured ink — see Section 8.4 on eccentricities of intuitives explained as the need to create internal and external environments facilitating the intuitive process.

There are numerous anecodatal examples of a specific perception of a stimulus from the environment inducing an emotional set to which the individual's experience has previously associated a different perception. The novel coincidence of the perception of the environment and the perception induced by evoking the previous emotional set results in a recentring type of insight, e.g. James Watt watching the steam lift the lid of a boiling kettle, which he associated with engines powered by steam.

Conditioning of Response Tendencies to Give Emotional Sets

Our experiences of responding to an environment condition these responses to the emotional state associated with our perception of this environment. These associations of response tendencies with the similar consecutive emotional states form emotional sets. A subject's emotional sets are described by Dymond, R.F. (1948) as the '. . . expectation-response patterns which he brings to a new and ambiguous situation'. 'Now let us consider the role of insight. The acquisition (and extinction) of conditioned emotional responses in human subjects is facilitated by awareness of stimulus contingencies, i.e. being able to discriminate the conditions under which adversive stimulation occurs and has occurred in the past' (Lacey, J.I. and Smith, R.I., 1954). The work of Fuhrer, M.J. and Baer, P.E. (1965) supports this. Further, it is shown in Section 4.1 that this awareness may be preconscious.

However, not all responses have to be conditioned to an emotional state. Some responses are instinctive. When one is in particular physical environments, for example involving danger, one acts instinctively. The emotional states corresponding to these environments have these instinctive response tendencies associated with them. The body makes small motor responses and mental attitude shifts which do not have to be learnt. One only has to imagine a state of physical danger to evoke an emotional set with these instinctive responses. These responses immediately provide a course of action. The conscious products of these instinctive responses are intuitions and insights, usually of a course of action or decision. This type of intuition or insight fits the description of 'instinctive knowledge' or 'innate knowledge', property 13.

The emotional state that is finally associated with an external stimulus has been modified from the initial emotional state induced by the perception of the external stimulus through the feedback interaction between emotion and perception. The response tendencies are conditioned to the most modified recent emotional state associated with the perception. Being in this emotional state tends to induce the modified perception of the original stimulus; see the discussion of intuitive recall using associated emotional sets which follows in this section. Fig. 3.2/2 shows the schematic make up of an emotional set. Conditioning gives the structure, association gives the process.

Fig. 3.2/2 illustrates, not only the fact that percepts induce emotional set and vice versa, but also that emotional sets have associated response tendencies, and that a generation of these responses can induce the associated emotional set. Kinaesthetic memory of systems and objects can be used to recall emotional sets. When the responses are percepts Fig. 3.2/2 folds about A/B.

The emotional set includes what Schachtel, E.G. (1950) calls 'a neuromuscular set':

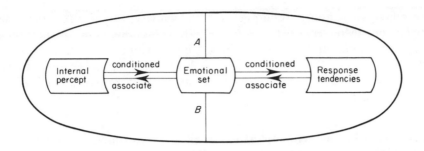

Fig. 3.2/2 Conditioned structure and association process of an emotional
set

If a person has the tendency to react with a certain, typical attitude or striving to the world around him or to his own drives, then this attitude will also find expression in a neuromuscular set which could be described as the physical side of the attitude, a readiness to perform such motor activity as will be suitable to realize the goal of the attitude or striving. This 'goal' of a person's general attitude or orientation (E. Fromm's term) is either not all in awareness or, at least, not in focal and full awareness. It is not a goal in the same sense as is the purpose which a person consciously wants to reach by a specific, consciously planned and executed series of acts. The neuromuscular set which is the physical aspect of a habitual, lingering readiness to react in a certain way to the world and to oneself is at the basis of both the inadvertent expressive movements and physiognomic expressions of people and their kinaesthetic responses. (p. 77)

Professor Mira's technique (Mira, E., 1940) for detecting cognitive trends of personality is based on an assumption similar to the above, that every mental attitude implies in the human subject a corresponding muscular attitude, in which the movements leading to the realization of the purpose contained in the mental attitude are to be facilitated and those opposite to it are to be rendered difficult.

There are extant psychological concepts of the process by which these proposed emotional sets are created. Associating response tendencies with emotional states to give emotional sets has been called 'emotive learning'. The internal percepts of imagery, memory, etc., which are induced by emotional sets and the covert physiological responses associated with them further reinforce this association. This reinforcement results in 'secondary learning'. These ideas are in agreement with those of Woodworth, R.S. (1947) as presented in his paper 'Reinforcement of perception' in which he considers learning as the development of certain perceptions, expectations, anticipations, meanings, and emotions.

The above formulations of secondary learning are in agreement with the 'law of effect': '...current formulations of the law of effect include the possibility of learning resulting from secondary, or purely emotional, satisfaction' (Mowrer, O.H., 1946, p. 217). This is one point of the present study that interprets Gestalt ideas in behaviouristic terms. Other Behaviourists, e.g. Rice and Thorndike, also consider reinforcement in terms of 'wants', 'interests', and 'attitudes' as well as in terms of external stimulus/response connections.

Reduction in Tension Accompanying Insight Gives Learning, Confidence, Intrinsic Motivation and Organization of Perception

The conditioning of response tendencies in usually thought of as a conditioning arising from resolution of tension (Bigge, M.L., 1968, p. 290). Stimuli produce internal tensions whose resolution results in learning and are described by Wheeler, R.H. (1931) as follows:

> First, there are stimulus-patterns which arouse intra-organic tensions together with tensions of the voluntary neuromuscular system. Second, there is an organic structure composed of an autonomic nervous system, a digestive tract and a chain of glands which furnish the organism with internal stimulation. When these conditions function in a learning situation, emotive learning occurs. (p. 255)

Novel perceptions of problems, e.g. inconsistencies seen for the first time, induce an emotional state which does not have a novel solution as represented by concordant associated response tendencies, as they are novel, conditioning could not yet have occurred. If the state involves tensions, such as might be caused by the perception of a novel problem situation, then the person needs to form a novel response to reduce this tension. An insight solution, necessarily novel, reduces this tension and gives the feeling of relief and satisfaction associated with insight solutions. 'Tensions are established and resolved in the form of configurational response which the term, insight, serves well to describe' (Wheeler, R.H., 1931). Conflicting response tendencies can cause the initial emotional tensions whose resolution directs the intuitive process. The theories of Hebb, D.O. (1949) and Brown, J.J. and Farber, I.E. (1951) introduce theoretical constructs relating to the conflict between response tendencies. Hebb introduced constructs in terms of hypothetical neural processes that direct the normal behaviour of the organism but that, when antagonistic, result in emotional behaviour. Brown and Farber introduced their construct referring to conflict, that is 'frustration state', in terms of antagonistic response tendencies that are in turn defined by specific antecedent conditions.

The pleasant feelings resulting from this reduction of tension accompanying an insight solution have three main effects:

(1) learning by conditioning the response to the emotional set;

(2) felt confidence as confirmation of insight;
(3) intrinsic motivation

The first effect is to condition the successful response to the novel emotional set, producing a changed emotional set that allows transference to analogous situations, i.e. situations again involving this emotional set. The set is retained for future use. 'Behaviour patterns invoked to resolve conflict are often retained as a favoured means of adaptation after the conflict subsides' (Hartmann, H., 1939). This effect can be observed in children — and sadly, also in students, who, having had this reinforcement of a successful response, continue to give this response in inappropriate situations that evoke similar emotional sets. Miller, N.E. and Dollard, J. (1941) agree that this conditioning mechanism operates 'in cases involving insight... If this response is rewarded, it will be learned as the response to that situation. If the insight is not rewarded it will be abandoned' (p. 27). It is proposed here that the reduction in tension accompanying an insight is reward enough to condition the insightful response to the emotional set. If the insightful response later meets with non-reward when produced in an inappropriate situation its response tendency within that emotional set will diminish.

A second effect of the reduction in tension accompanying an insight is to give the confidence needed on which the person may support an intuitive action as in a situation in which a decision to act is a result of the intuitive process; see Section 4.3 on confidence in intuitive products.

A third effect applies to those who frequently experience this satisfaction associated with insight. It has the effect of intrinsic motivation to work along the same lines as those which in the past have produced insights. This applies particularly to academics, see Section 4.3 on anxiety and its reduction as learned intrinsic motivation.

This present interpretation implies that if for any reason a person resists the internal tensions associated with novel perceptions, then he will inaccurately perceive the novel situations so that his perception will induce an emotional set which has response tendencies which may rapidly reduce his tensions. This misperception acts as a defence mechanism in the Freudian sense. Causes of this resistance might be environmental, non-permissive ego environments, e.g. competitive speed tests, or a result of an individual's cognitive organization. Intuitive types are more tolerant of physical discomfort that this tension might involve and are also more tolerant of cognitive ambiguity than are non-intuitive types. These deductions agree with the literature reviewed in Section 7.3 on personality correlates of intuition and creativity that are explained by the Theory of Intuitive Thought.

Once these emotional sets have been established, their use is the basis of the intuitive process and other behaviour. The sets are used to associate the correct behaviour with a specific stimulus: '...stimulus is presented and reflexive initiation of an extensive preparation for behaviour results' (Germana, J., 1968).

Inaccurate perception or unusual conditioning may produce the bizarre behaviour responses found in some psychiatric patients. A tolerance for associating one of many partially similar sets with the emotional set evoked by a particular stimulus can produce the novel intuitive behaviours found in creative types.

The established emotional sets are also used for organizing an ambiguous visual field as in TAT and Rorschach tests. Bellak notes the connection between this use and tension reduction. 'In an ambiguous picture, personality variables will determine mainly what becomes figure and what becomes ground. This cognitive function is greatly influenced by a tendency toward tension-reduction' (Bellak, L., 1944, p. 365).

The established emotional set may have response tendencies that are cognitive and/or physiological: '...the response may consist of an idea, a mood, a liking, a craving as well as a motor act' (Mowrer, O.H., 1946, p. 214). An example of a widespread body response of this type is the common experience of feeling better after being reassured by someone with whose reassurance the appropriate emotional set is associated.

Emotional Sets Used for Intuitive Recognition

A stimulus is recognized when it evokes an emotional set. The responses of this set give the context of the recognition. When a percept is part of this response the stimulus is literally re-cognized, i.e. its perception is put into mind. How the detailed structure of the Theory of Intuitive Thought gives intuitive recognition is shown in Section 5.5.

A wrong recognition occurs when the wrong emotional set is associated with a stimulus. It may be through inaccurate perception that a set corresponding to the accurate perception of another stimulus is selected. It may be that the set has become ill-defined through lack of refreshing, i.e. lack of experience conditioning its response tendencies, as when something has been put out of mind for a long time.

Forgetting is not recognizing a stimulus whose perception has been associated with an emotional set in the past. This is because the response tendencies to the evoked emotional set are weakly conditioned, maybe through lack of experience as in an undertrained situation where lack of practice or changing emotional environment during practice makes response conditioning weak. Another cause of forgetting might be that the changes in the emotional set through secondary learning, e.g. frequent inaccurate recall, are so great that the emotional set evoked by the external stimulus is no longer concordant with the changed set. An example is how upon returning to some house or place years later, one is struck by how it does not resemble one's memories: time has rewritten it, by successively refreshing without reference to the original stimuli.

Recognition is through the mediating structure of the emotional set with its response tendencies of which commonly kinaesthetic responses are prominent:

see Section 2.4 on kinaesthetic experiences commonly predominating in conditioning emotional sets and predominant in evoking these emotional sets to evaluate present experiences intuitively. Referring to the kinaesthetic response Wheeler, R.H. (1931) observes: 'It is merely perceived as "feeling". It is found in recognizing, in making comparative judgments and in choosing' (p. 433). The organization of perceptions through the mediating structure of emotional sets is a prerequisite for insight. 'The achievement of more comprehensive insight requires, we think, the building of a mediating representational structure that transcends such immediate imagery, that renders a sequence of acts and images unitary and simultaneous' (Bruner, J.S. and Keney, H.J., 1965).

This form of recognition, by associations of stimuli with emotional sets, describes what Lorenz, K.Z. (1951) means by Gestalt insight, which he equates with intuition.

I hold that Gestalt perception of this type (of extricating the essential constant factor by abstracting from the inessential variable sensory data) is identical with that mysterious function which is generally called 'Intuition' and which indubitably is one of the most important cognitive faculties of man. When the scientist, confronted with. a multitude of irregular and apparently irreconcilable facts, suddenly 'sees' the general regularity ruling them all, when the explanation of the hitherto inexplicable all 'at once' jumps out at him with the suddenness of a revelation, the experience of this happening is fundamentally similar to that other when the hidden Gestalt in a puzzle-picture surprisingly starts out from the confusing background of irrelevant detail. The German expression in die Augen springen* is very descriptive of this process. (*To spring to the eyes.)

In a study of the pre-insight period in learning Drever, J.I. (1934) designed an experiment to show the effect of experience on insight, which illustrates the formation of an emotional set and its use for intuitive recognition. Subjects had to choose geometrical shapes according to an unknown criteria. At intervals subjects were asked to draw figures and state the principle upon which they were working. Drever concludes that what happens before insight is essentially an orientation towards the problem. 'Some sort of organization seems to take place but this organization was not primarily a conscious idea or concept. It is difficult to characterize it further, but although certain of its effects resembled those of a concept, it functioned rather less efficiently' (p. 202).

This organization is described most suitably by the formation of an emotional set, even to its relative efficiency of accuracy compared with an analytic concept. Drever gave information of the subject's success which reinforced the correct choice response to the emotional set evoked by the perception of the shapes at this time. Without the gradual building of an emotional set incorporating solution responses, success after the initial chance success would not have been possible. Drever concurs with this in offering the following explanation of successful subjects' results in that trial and error or chance could not explain these results but that "it [the learning curve] suggests a preliminary adaptation without which no further progress is possible'.

Emotional sets are clearly used in the intuitive recognition of music themes. In some people, music produces strong motor responses, not just tapping the feet but emotional tensions and resolution of tensions that the music is composed to produce. Popular music is rarely recognized analytically by comparing syntax, etc. It is commonly recognized intuitively, by the resemblance of past with present feelings it produces. Hence in the intuitive recognition of music, these response tendencies have an obvious role. These patterns of physiological response are termed 'feeling sets' or 'neuromuscular sets' which help in orientating the organism to a situation through recognition by emotional involvement with perception of its environment.

Emotional Sets Used for Intuitive Acceptance

This intuitive recognition allows us intuitively to accept a novel stimulus without analytically questioning it. How the detailed structure of the Theory of Intuitive Thought explains intuitive acceptance is shown in Section 5.5. This is how, for example, brand names and commercial goods are presented in advertisements, so as to be intuitively accepted without trial by reason. The item is presented in a situation that evokes an emotional set with culturally common response pairings. Some advertisements of this kind are not suitable for other cultures for, of the numerous stimuli presented, only one has to be positively associated with an incompatible set for the item to be intuitively rejected. An example illustrating intuitive rejection because of an incongruous detail might be a British advertisment trying to induce an emotional set associated with childhood country nostalgia in which the mother stimulus has an incongruent American accent. To be intuitively accepted the mother's voice should be dubbed with a British accent.

The process of intuitive acceptance is used generally in assimilating knowledge, for we cannot possibly justify analytically every detail of what we accept and believe to be true. The point is illustrated particularly in the field of mathematics by Cartwright, Mary L. (1955) in the following passage which shows that we accept the perception of stimuli that may be associated with established emotinal sets without analytic justification, even in the analytic setting of mathematics.

> We may get a general idea of the sort of thing an expert in another field of mathematics is doing and of the possible repercussions, but he could say that 2 + 2 = 5 in disguised terms and we would be none the wiser...
> [because]... The process of reading and understanding mathematical

work is slow and difficult even for the expert, and we do not nowadays expect to understand important new work without a very considerable expenditure of time and energy. For this reason non-mathematicians seem to us to be unduly worried if they cannot understand. After all if I only get a vague impression of similarity to something I once understood, why should they be worried if they do not understand after practically no work at all. (p. 11)

Emotional Sets Used for Intuitive Judgments and Decisions

Intuitive judgments are made by comparing the emotional sets associated with the perceptions of the groups of stimuli about which the judgments are to be made. The ability to do this depends on one's development of empathic projection, an ability to evoke the emotional set associated with a group of stimuli. Judgments of similarity or suitability are made by the relative ease with which one may go from being in one emotional set to being in another, a subjective evaluation of the transition probability of going to emotional set B given being in emotional set A. An example is an intuitive test of the consistency of the statement 'a sunrise in a coal mine'. The emotional set corresponding to 'sunrise' is so different from that corresponding to 'in a coal mine' that the probability of a direct transition between the emotional sets is very low, this discordance marking their coincidence as intuitively unacceptable. However, it is possible to transfer via other emotional sets with higher transition probabilities. The intermediate emotional sets offer the associations that make the original connection tenable. For example, for this connection to be tenable, one or both of the situations must be unreal, imaginary. Starting at the 'sunrise' emotional set personal experience might associate dreaming and then dreaming of being in a coal mine and waking at sunrise. Starting at the 'in a coal mine' emotional set, personal experience of danger may associate ideas concerning concussion from falling coal which causes the dream of the 'sunrise'. This type of transition is noted in responses to questionnaires of the type: 'Find a connection between phrase A and phrase B'. The stimulus defining the starting emotional set is the anchor stimulus, and the starting emotional set is the anchor emotional set. The judgment is more satisfactory if fewer transitions from the anchor set are involved. How the detailed structure of the Theory of Intuitive Thought shows intuitive judgment of similarity is given in Section 5.5.

So the intuitive judgment of consistency is based on the relative ease of transition from one emotional state to the other. This implies that intuitive types having a greater ease of transition between emotional states will probably find more subjective consistency between two situations than would analytic types. This agrees with many findings of intolerance of ambiguity in non-creative types.

The judgment based on relative ease of changing from one emotional set to another is different from that based on the resolution of the tension of an emotional state by associating a set that would resolve the tension, which is the process behind intuitive judgment of the type 'how would you like it to happen to you?' By empathic projection the emotional set corresponding to 'it happening to you' is evoked with its associated tensions. Transition to one's original state resolves the tension. The degree of resolution of tension is the basis of the judgment. Further consideration of the ease of transition may give rise to the supplementary judgment 'but it couldn't happen to me'.

This method of resolving tension by evoking new emotional sets rather than by finding suitable response tendencies to resolve the present discordant emotional state by combining emotional sets reinforces withdrawal in psychiatric patients who escape the tensions of reality by evoking fantasy emotional sets for which they have tension-reducing responses. The Theory of Intuitive Thought Processes suggests that a remedial treatment would be to encourage the combining of emotional sets by role play which are gradual approximations to the patient's actual role, emotional sets to which suitable responses may be conditioned during treatment.

Intuitive judgment through the above use of emotional sets is facilitated by concrete experience, see Section 6.2. Preference for concrete experience can be used as one determinate of cognitive style, of intuitive cognitive style versus analytic cognitive style; see Section 2.1 on 'analytic type' versus 'intuitive type' being indicated by cognitive style. This determinate of the difference in style has been observed by many workers, one of whom is Hanfmann, E. (1941). He required subjects to group blocks by unknown criteria of size and height. Verbal reports of subjects whose approach was to group the blocks first, then deduce the rule, were 'seemed natural', 'just look right'. This approach is termed one in which the subjects 'intuitively grouped the blocks and then formulated the principle' (p. 315). The other style was to hypothesize without contact with the blocks.

As intuitive judgments are based on emotional sets, processes affecting these sets will affect the judgments. The formation of inappropriate sets by misperception may give rise to unusable insights: '...usability of insights depends on how well they take into account the physical environment' (Bigge, M.L. and Hunt, M.P., 1965). See also Section 8.1 on distortions during intuitive perception.

In the type of intuitive judgment utilizing the relative difficulty of changing from an anchor emotional set to another emotional set, the anchor emotional set is often evoked predominantly by kinaesthetic stimuli, see Section 2.4. This anchor emotional set of the body is then the body reference. Body references are used as internal anchors in intuitive judgments. The anchor stimulus is judged with less variability than other stimuli. Johnson, D.M. (1972, p. 403) mentions that variability and errors in judgment decrease as the anchor is approached. An example of how body reference may be used as an internal anchor is in the estimation of angles or distances, etc. For example in Fig. 3.2/3 a subject could identify with the horizontal line which would then be the anchor. So small angles will be judged with less variability of error.

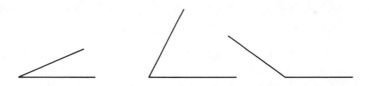

Fig. 3.2/3 Errors in intuitive estimation decrease approaching the
emotional set of the anchor stimulus

The same phenomenon explains the results of an experiment by De Soto, C.
et al (1965). The authors compared the number of different presentations of
transitive relations correctly ordered in ten seconds and found the relation
'better than' had 61 per cent success compared to 'worse than' at 43 per cent
success. They also found that end anchoring had an effect, i.e. starting at an
end and moving towards the middle had 62 per cent success, while starting at
the middle and moving out had only 38 per cent success. Identification with
the terms defining the relationship and with the anchor point would account
for these results. For example, results of 'type A is better than B and C is worse
than B', solved at 62 per cent success compared with 'type B is better than C
and B is worse than A', solved at 38 per cent success.

The use of body reference has been monitored by Spencer, B., (1972) using a
GSR measure. 'The R-SCR measure, however, reflects the emotional arousal
accompanying the behavioural response and the importance of the feedback
concerning the correctness of the response' (p. 49). This 'feedback concerning
the correctness of the response' which is derived from successive reduction in
tension, evoked through initial emotional involvement of the intuitive process,
guides the intuitive process through the selection of suitable anxiety-reducing
emotional sets. This guidance by reduction in tension is discussed in detail as
accompanying increased redundancy of information in Section 5.4 on
intuition as a global process directed by increasing redundancy.

The following experiments show the results of judgment using body
reference with kinaesthetic information input. Results and inferences from
these experiments should be instrumental in designing the information input
for experiments on intuition, which as shown by the preceding discussion
should preferably be kinaesthetic information. A three-dimensional nonsense
model would be very suitable.

Hoff, Phyllis A. (1971) required fifty male subjects to make judgments of:

(1) thickness by finger span;
(2) extent by arm movement;
(3) heaviness by lifting weights;
(4) force by hand grip;
(5) speed by arm movement.

She plotted actual measure (A say) against subjective judgment of the measure (M say) and fitted a linear log graph to the results, giving a relation of the type $A = a\,M^b$. The range of b is an indication of whether

(1) subjective judgment progressively underestimates as the actual measure increases: b less than 1;
(2) subjective judgment is independent of size of the actual measure: $b = 1$;
(3) subjective judgment progressively overestimates actual measures of increasing size: b greater than 1.

To test (1) subjects were given a pad of paper $63 \cdot 7$mm thick and had to halve it by feel. This was the most accurate of the five types of judgment. Results of (2) show that the psychological extent of movement grows more rapidly than physical distance: $a = 0 \cdot 134$, $b = 1 \cdot 21$. Test (3) shows that subjective weight grows more rapidly than physical weight: $a = 0 \cdot 00131$, $b\ 1 \cdot 43$. This was also true for force by hand grip (4), $a = 0 \cdot 0249$, $b = 1 \cdot 56$. Similar results were found for speed (5), $a = 0 \cdot 283$, $b = 1 \cdot 54$.

Results 1 and 2 considered with other results previously mentioned on kinaesthetic feedback from joint movements (Section 2.1) indicate that a model used in an intuition experiment should be designed to be larger than could be measured by finger span. However, parts of it should be within finger-span range to be subjectively most accurately judged — these parts to be separated by a structure large enough to require arm movements to relate them. Subjective finger-span evaluation of different parts of the model and the relation of these parts to each other should be found by arm movement only so that the overall task may be accurate. Further, as the accuracy of the judgment of the different measures varies with the absolute size of the measures, only judgment of the relative proportions should be required.

The next consideration is whether passive movement or active movement should be used, i.e. whether the subject should be guided or left to explore an insight experiment model by himself. From the physiological theory it seems that self-generated movements would give more body reference, as a record of the signals given to the musculature instructing it where to move, would be available. In impassive movement only proprioceptive feedback would be available.

Two experiments are now reported that are relevant to this point of design and theory of an insight experiment model. Jones, B. (1973), using fifteen subjects, considered passive movement (E moves S's arms) and active movement (S felt the distance to be matched). Results were found that showed the two methods are asymmetric. Active touch is more accurate, showing 'the motor cortex may monitor the state of cutaneous receptors'. This result is in agreement with the above theory.

The second experiment is also by Jones, B. (1972) in which he considered outflow information in movement duplication. Three subjects were compared blindfolded in three groups:

(1) constrained active movement: *S* moved a thimble to a stop on a rod;

(2) unconstrained active movement: *S* moved it as far as he liked;

(3) passive movement: *E* moved *S*'s finger in the thimble.

Results were that when duplicating movement group (2) was most accurate. No correlation between distance and accuracy of reproduction was noticed, unlike the results of Posner, M.I. (1967) and Hoff, Phyllis A. (1971 above). This was attributed to the fact that in this experiment arm movement was at the side of the body and not in front.

Results of the above type have been explained in terms of body reference using the idea of remembered efferent impulses. Holst, E. Von. (1954) used this idea to explain how the organism differentiates between self-generated movements of a part of the body and an identical movement generated by external forces. He proposed the idea of an 'efferent copy' of outgoing signals which are compared by matching with incoming afferent signals. If they matched perfectly then the motion was entirely self-generated. Results reported above indicate that kinaesthetic information input for intuitive experiments should be gathered by free active touch with the arm movement to the side of the subject.

Piaget says that this use of body reference state is a passing phase and less importance is given to body sensations as the child develops. However, Pufall, P.B. (1973), using a Piaget-type 'what does it look like from there' experiment has shown that: 'Self-reference, then rather than decreasing, in its functional importance seems to be more encompassing' (p. 174) — see Section 8.1 on a developmental model of egocentricity. The ability to develop emotional sets and use them in the way described above is necessary for intuitive judgments.

Emotional sets may also be used to give intuitions of decisions or courses of action. In particular the instinctive response tendencies may accelerate the change in emotional sets by producing small motor responses and hormonal changes that are associated with other emotional sets. The percepts associated with these new emotional sets may be conscious decisions or courses of action. For example, if a situation has a physiognomy of imminent personal danger the emotional set evoked has the instinctive responses of flight. These responses are actually made minutely through the body — as measured by Jacobson, E. (1932). The instructions for these responses and the responses themselves evoke, using proprioceptive feedback and information from efferent impulses, a very similar emotional set which also has the perceptual response of flight. This percept is the conscious intuitive decision 'to flee'.

Analysis of a personal observation of the solution to a concrete problem illustrates this process.

The problem was to fit a bookcase into a cupboard. First, I judged by eye that it might just fit by comparing sizes, and tried the simplest method of fitting it. This proved unsuccessful so I try different rotations in the mind. All these are analytic conscious thought processes involving size comparisons. Each solution seems unsatisfying and meets emotional resistance but each process is carried consciously to its conclusion. The last solution tried is the successful one and has a different thought process asociated with it. The successful rotation is consciously chosen then so immediately is it obviously the correct solution that I am already physically fitting the bookcase in the time that I had previously spent in analytic consideration of the other unsuccessful rotations.

This successful solution met no emotional resistance as the others did. It needed no analytical confirmation (by comparison of distances or otherwise). The way I think of it 'slipping' through the restricting space makes me realize in hindsight that the intuitive process which derived the successful solution was produced by my associating myself physically with the bookcase. I was the bookcase and I was trying to get through the space.

Was I using the same 'instinctive' thought processes to solve this problem as I would use if I was physically trapped, but guided by the restraints of the situation, e.g. the invariant size and shape of the bookcase, priority of solutions needing least lifting, possible damage, etc.? This is possibly so, as before the original analytic considerations of the rotations, I am aware that I wanted to change the shape of the bookcase in ways in which I can change my own shape, e.g. pull in an awkward corner as I pull in my arms, squash it in just as I breathe in, etc., to physically get out of the same type of situation as I would be in if I were the bookcase. After these almost instant easy thoughts came similar analytic thoughts, e.g. will it help to take off the legs or doors etc...

Conclusions from this and similar observations are that the process is organized as follows:

(1) Initial identification with the problem.
(2) Using well-learnt or instinctive behaviours to arrive at a solution, e.g. behaviours associated with self-preservation.
(3) These initially erratic behaviour possibilities are guided more and more towards an acceptable solution by a growing awareness of the restraints of the situation. Correctly forming solutions (i.e. solutions that reduce an anxiety) is encouraged by the feedback of feelings deeply, reflexively associated with the behaviours involved, until a successful solution is felt to be right.

Conclusions (1) and (2) illustrate the way emotional sets are used to give intuitive decisions. Conclusion (3) is relevant to the guidance towards the solution due to conscious restrictions of the problem.

The emotional set with instinctive responses need not be evoked preconsciously but it may be evoked consciously through empathy, as is done in synectics, and the resulting intuitive responses are then directed towards a problem solution. One of the key psychological states in synectics theory is 'involvement' (Gordon, W.J.J., 1961, p. 18). To encourage emotional involvement, group leaders would say 'I find myself right inside this problem. My ears and eyes and arms are elements of it' (p. 21). The following is an example from a recording of an inventor trying to simplify an aircraft altimeter. It illustrates this emotional involvement:

'. . . but what is the spring? What does it mean to say of a spring that it is a spring? How would I feel if I were a spring? I find myself very mixed up with this spring. I can't get away from my own springiness. . . even if I wanted to. But I don't want to. I am folding in and then expanding, folding in and then expanding. . . or I'm being pulled out and then I'm pushed back in. Tight! This I don't like. I don't like this tight feeling. . . I don't like this feeling of being pulled way out either. Someone's got me by the hands and the legs. Stretching me over a rack, torturing me. . .'

The process of evoking these responses through empathy and associating them with the objects is called empathic projection. It is used consciously and preconsciously particularly in concrete situations, e.g. hat rack and pendulum problems — see Section 6.3 on intuitive understanding using empathic projection.

Insight as 'Single Trial Learning'

Emotional sets are also used in secondary learning. The response is associated with the percept through use of an appropriate emotional set. Being in this set reinforces the association, i.e. refreshing an emotional set is secondary learning. Hebb, D.O. (1968), considering imagery, proposed that such mental processes may replicate the more central aspects of perceptual experiences so that they are both distinguishable from perceptual experience and yet of the same type. Combining emotional sets corresponding to these 'perceptual experiences' gives reduction in tension through their conditioned responses. This is the secondary reinforcement used in secondary learning. This idea can be seen from a comment by Bruner, J.S. (1964, Chapter 19) who says that learning as a response produced by reduction in primary drive state is greatly extended by the idea of secondary reinforcement: '. . . any state associated even remotely with the reduction of a primary drive could also have the effect of producing learning' (p. 242).

This use of secondary learning helps to explain insight in Behaviourists' terminology. Behaviourists have had difficulty in explaining insight as 'single trial learning', in that it is not affected by previous trials, as insight curves show. However, this is only true for experiments which do not condition the response tendencies to the emotional set associated with the problem, e.g. hat rack and pendulum problems (Section 1.3). It is not true for experiments in which information of success on each trial does condition these responses, e.g.

'guess-the-rule'-type experiments (again see Section 1.3). On these experiments insight is 'learnt' as the learning curves show. Behaviourists have used secondary learning from imagery, etc., to explain insight as a short cut to learning without trials involving environmental experience (see Miller, N.E. and Dollard, J., 1941).

From their behaviour experiments Kumberger, D. and Kardash, K. (1948) arrive at the same conclusion, that insight is a short cut to conditioned learning by using secondary reinforcement.

Another use of emotional sets is to give motivation. The reduction in tension afforded by the responses acts as a secondary reward. This can motivate the organism to seek situations offering stimuli that will induce an emotional set whose response tendencies offer this secondary reward. The situation sought may even offer uncomfortable primary stimuli whose comparison with the secondary rewards make the rewards even more desirable. Examples are, seeking dangerous experiences with the reward of exhilaration, continued trial for future success and being helpful for the sake of feeling good.

Intuitive Recall and Problem-Solving

We have discussed the intuitive uses of emotional sets, as memory hooks to give novel associations and analogies, and in recentring. This aspect of their involvement with emotion is now further detailed. Emotional sets are used as memory hooks (Section 2.4). They can be used to code a lot of information by associating this information with some emotional set so that being in that emotional set recalls this information. The recall of this information is part of the response to being in this emotional set. See the end of Section 2.2 where it is reported how Hadamard, J. (1945) finds emotional involvement necessary '...in order to have a simultaneous view of all elements of the argument, to hold them together, to make a whole of them — in short to achieve that synthesis...' (p. 77).

Shepard, R.N. and Chipman, Susan (1970) showed that spatial information has a second-order isomorphic internal representation. Coding by emotional sets is such a representation. Considering the representation of a square and a triangle. First-order isomorphic representation would be something square in the brain as the internal representation of the square. Second-order isomorphic representations of the triangle and square would have a similar relation to that between the reality of the two shapes. In their experiment Shepard and Chipman used shapes of the States of the United States of America and considered the similarity of these shapes.

The slow rate of physiological change relative to change of thought enables many thoughts associated with one emotional set to be brought into intuitive processing. The emotional set 'holds' the global field of knowledge. If an intuitive type is asked to explain some concept he is observed to make subconscious overt copies of the motor responses associated with the emotional set used to 'hold' the concept that he is explaining. Observe the movement of the hands, face, and body of people explaining. Most of these motions are obviously kinaesthetic associations of visual models. For example observe the motions of people describing a helix (spiral staircase) or a one-man band.

Walkup, L.E. (1965) suggests that the visual intensity of creative persons may be indicated by asking them to describe their thought processes in the following two problems.

(1) A cube is painted and cut into twenty-seven smaller cubes. How many of the smaller cubes are painted on 0, 1, 2, and 3 faces?

(2) What is visualized mentally when verbal directions are given for driving a car from one place to another?

Verbal street directions are frequently expressed with the kinaesthetic responses that accompany the internal representation of the experiences which lead to the directed place. These kinaesthetic responses enable the director to give very complicated directions that the enquirer, not having the same kinaesthetic experientially conditioned responses, is unable to follow. The directions, however, may easily be followed by someone with an equivalent emotional set, i.e. someone who knows the district.

It has been explained in Section 2.1 how personal experiential associations between thought and emotional sets may produce novel associations. This has been called affective association, '...affective association where ideas are linked on the basis of common feeling' (Drever, J., 1974, p. 11).

We have also explained how the strong experiential association of functional fixedness inhibits changes of emotional set and so reduces the probability of novel associations. This is related to field dependence, a determinate of cognitive style, and is a concomitant of the other characteristics of the non-intuitive type. Adamson, R.E. and Taylor, D.W. (1954) and Adamson, R.E. (1952) found that functional fixedness reduces with time. This is in agreement with insights occurring after long incubation periods. After some time the inhibiting effect of functional fixation on the drift of emotional sets is reduced, thus increasing the probability of the occurrence of insights by novel associations and recentring.

The transition between emotional sets may be restricted during a problem-solving situation by giving hints. However, new emotional sets are not created by these hints so that the hints do not open new channels of thought, they only eliminate wrong ones already contemplated. This description explains the results of an experiment by Maier, N.R.F. and Burke, R.J. (1967) on the influence of the timing of hints on their effectiveness in solving an insight problem, actually the hat rack problem. 'The analysis of activity following the hint supported an earlier study demonstrating that the effect of the hint was to eliminate activity incongruous with it. Thus the value of each hint depended upon the incorrect activity it eliminated' (p. 2).

The transition probabilities between emotional sets may be explored for a particular subject by asking for a story that starts with a sentence containing phrase A and by association ends with a sentence containing phrase B. Interview will clarify which of the associations are experiential rather than analytic. The nature of the experience defines an emotional set for each association. With enough responses and judicious choice of the start and finish emotional sets evoked by phrases A and B, a map of the emotional sets and their transition probabilities can be built up and tested by predicting experiential associations.

A recentring results in a change in the transition probabilities between emotional sets, see Section 4.1. This recentring should be evident from a comparison of the maps of emotional sets and their transition probabilities before and after recentring.

Summary of the Use of Emotional Sets in the Intuitive Process

Once emotional sets have been established they are used in the intuitive process in many ways. The literature affords examples of these uses and many experimental results can be better explained in the light of the Theory of Intuitive Thought Processes. Several explanations and descriptions of psychophysiological processes can be translated from the terminologies of various psychological schools into the terms of this Theory of Intuitive Thought Processes.

Intuitive products of the use of emotional sets in the intuitive process include:

intuitive —   recognition,
            acceptance,
            judgments,
            memories,
            associations,
            analogies,
            recentring,
            learning.

In this study 'intuition' is closely defined. However, in general the reply to 'how did you come to that conclusion?' is 'Intuition!' when the conclusion is a specific example of any of the above products of the intuitive process.

These products of the intuitive process result, in part, from whichever source of stimuli evokes the emotional state. The emotional state of the organism may be evoked by:

(a) perception of, or empathic projection with, external stimuli;
(b) perception of, or empathic projection with, internal stimuli;
(c) natural drift due to competing control of (a) and (b) or due to retaining an appropriate state of the organism — homeostasis.

How empathic projection with stimuli induces emotional states is detailed in Section 6.3 on empathic projection as a temporary identification through empathy and projection which is essential to the intuitive process.

This section reviews evidence supporting the following proposals. When two discordant emotional sets vie for control of the organism response tendencies interfere with each other. These conflicting tendencies cause tension. This is the source of tension initiating the intuitive process.

The speed with which physiological states can change is slow relative to the speed of mental association and general thought. This allows many thoughts to be associated with a particular feeling. The thoughts representing a field of knowledge are 'held together' by being in a particular emotional set. In the case of an insight solution the problem has a distinct physiognomy which is slow to change. This point is supported by the observation that one cannot go rapidly with deep insight from one problem to another, as one may in analytic associations, for to do so would require too rapid an emotional change for the natural latency of compound physiological responses. It is this fact that allows 'global knowledge' to be available in intuitive processing whereas reason progresses linearly from one thought to the next.

3.3   PERSONALITY CONCOMITANTS OF EMOTIONAL INVOLVEMENT IN INTUITIVE PROCESSES

The personality concomitants of emotional involvement in intuitive processes are a subset of the characteristics that define the cognitive style of the intuitive type. The ones discussed here are body image and barrier scores, spatial abilities that load on the spatial k factor, and common personality traits.

Body Reference, Body Image, and Barrier Score Concomitants of the Intuitive Type

Because of the role of body reference in intuitive processes, it is reasonable to expect intuitive types to be more sensitive to body reactions and to body boundaries as firm and definite rather than indefinite and vague. It is reported in Section 6.3 that this awareness of body boundary is used in the intuitive process by the imagined extension of body boundary to include the object of the intuition. The barrier score is a measure of the degree to which a person experiences body boundaries as firm and definite. The score is derived from Rorschach protocols. The protocols are scored on the number of inferences to penetration of boundaries, e.g. '...with a hole or cut in it...' and scored on firmness of boundaries, e.g. 'knight in armour'. High penetration indicates low barrier scores which shows that the body boundaries are experienced as vague and indefinite, and vice versa for high barrier scores. The Theory of Intuitive Thought Processes indicates that intuitive types should have a high barrier score. In the following studies experimenters have used Rorschach records to obtain barrier scores of subjects, which they have then correlated with other tests on the same subjects. Barrier scores should correlate positively with tests on which intuitive types score highly. Barrier score is not determined by actual body characteristics, e.g. Sheldon's somato-types.

Fisher, S.A. and Cleveland, S.E. (1968) found that barrier scores do not correlate with verbal IQ (three tests, p. 78), but they do correlate with the façade aspect of drawing a house (p. 104). This elaboration also correlates with creativity which includes some use of intuitive processes. They also found (p. 100) that high barrier scores correlate with the number of sentence completions with body vulnerability indicating high-barrier-scoring subjects.

Atkinson, J.W. (1951) observed that barrier score is correlated with achievement score and that achievement score is positively correlated with a tendency to recall more ego-involving uncompleted tasks than completed tasks. The recall of ego-involving experiences is expected from an intuitive type and is used in the Selected Phrase Empathic Key (SPEAK) test to measure intuitive thinking. An unexpected result was found by Holtzman, W.H. and Bitterman, M.E. (1956). They found that there is no barrier and Rorschach scores related to scores from rod and frame spatial orientation experiments.

The work of Roe, Ann (1953) relates the subject matter of different occupations and interests to barrier score. Her results show that mathematicians have the lowest barrier score and psychologists the highest barrier score. This agrees with her table of barrier versus interests. High barrier scores correlate with interest in people, low barrier scores correlate with interest in exact quantative sciences, i.e. high barrier scores are linked with interest in personal communicative interaction with others. The low barrier scores she found for physicists prompted her to raise the question as to whether or not the theoretical physicist's superior ability to manipulate size concepts so abstractly, not necessarily intuitively, is a function of the fact that he can freely separate them from his body image, which she conjectures is relatively poorly developed. She observed a very high incidence of severe childhood illnesses among the theoretical physicists and wondered if this might lead to an impairment of body image. She suggests that it would be easier to discard an unsatisfactory body image because of its relative uselessness and thus be free to manipulate size concepts loosely and without reference to body standards. Artists have very high barrier scores and they are undoubtedly intuitively creative. For such results to be consistent, they can only be interpreted to mean that artists rely more on intuition than do scientists. This may be because a larger proportion of art is intuitive and a large part of science is analytic, which allows scientists to be assessed by their analytic rather than by their intuitive ability. A connection between measured physical sensitivity of the body, rather than sensitivity inferred from psychological variables, as above, was found by Haber, W.B. (1956). He related the body image concept to tactile sensitivity variables, viz. light touch and two-point discrimination. The degree of sensitivity indicated a direct relationship between the way an individual pictures an area of his body and the degree of tactile sensitivity he shows in that area. This indicates that tactile stimuli are important in building up body images. See also Section 6.2, describing how sensitivity to feeling facilitates intuition.

Actual physiological correlates of barrier scores have been measured by the following three researchers. Herring, F.H. (1956) showed that high barrier scorers have a low heart rate — and a high metabolism which would agree with the high natural activity and alertness of intuitive types implied from results of studies previously mentioned in Section 3.1.

High barrier scorers are more GSR-sensitive than low barrier scorers. Also low barrier scorers are more heart-rate sensitive than high barrier scorers. This was confirmed in an experiment by Fisher, S.A. (1959) and independently by Armstrong, H. (1964), who also found that high barrier subjects had a high GSR and low barrier subjects had a high heart rate. Bastick, T. (1979) found this same low heart-rate sensitivity and high GSR-sensitivity in high-intuitive types as compared with low-intuitive types, giving physiological evidence associating high barrier scores with intuitive ability. For further correlates of body image see Fisher, S.A. (1958, 1963, 1964, 1968).

Spatial *k* Factor and Cognitive Style Concomitants of the Intuitive Type

Throughout this study reference has been made to the use of kinaesthesis, particularly in the common ability modality of imagery. It is common for intuitive types to have a high spatial ability. The connection between intuition, high spatial ability, and reduction of tensions by insight is seen in the work of MacFarlane Smith, I. (1964) who gives the following concomitants of high spatial ability. These agree with Lorenz K.Z.'s (1951) definition of intuition. 'The person with relatively high spatial ability has a marked tendency to seek for and recognize regularities and patterns in his experience. He tends to experience tensions when he becomes aware of a lack of completeness in any of these patterns and he continues to search until he achieves the most satisfactory completion or "closure" ' (p. 230).

The use of emotional sets with imagery responses is common in creative mathematics, see Section 2.2. MacFarlane Smith, I. (1964) reports that 'Einstein used imagery which was mainly visual but might be muscular (kinaesthetic)' (p. 317). Hadamard, J. (1945) also quotes Einstein's introspections on his use of kinaesthetic imagery: 'The physical entities which seem to serve as elements in thought are certain signs and more or less clear images which can be "voluntarily" reproduced and combined... this combinatory play seems to be the essential feature in productive thought... The above mentioned elements are, in my case, of visual and some of muscular type' (pp. 142/143). It is noted in Section 6.2 that tuning into bodily responses, particularly kinaesthetic imagery, gives extra information that might otherwise be blocked from awareness (Clark, F.V., 1973, p. 161). According to Hadamard, J. (1945), the mathematicians Riemann, Klein, Bertrand, and Hilbert had pronounced spatial intuition. Although intuition in mathematics is commonly spatial it need not be geometric. 'Hermite was remarkable in that he had a positive hatred of geometry and yet had a highly intuitive mind' (MacFarlane Smith, I., 1964, p. 317).

The movement of the extraocular muscles gives the kinaesthetic sensations for body reference used in intuitive spatial judgments: 'Wundt — emphasized kinaesthetic sensations from eyes and body, in explaining the experience of spatial continuity' (Fisher, S.Λ. and Cleveland, S.E., 1968, p. 40). As previously mentioned, actual body responses that accompany imagery have been measured. The eye also responds to imagery. 'Kinaesthesis is involved in visual imagery. When a near object and then a far one are visualized there occur changes of accommodation and convergence as in actual vision' (Wheeler, R.H., 1931, p. 433).

The results of the following two experiments taken together explain how kinaesthetic information is made available by these preconscious eye movements that accompany imagery. Brindley, G.S. and Merton, P.A. (1960), trying to find if there was any proprioceptive feedback from the extraocular muscles, did the following. They anaesthetized the surface of the eyes and the inner surface of the eyelids of subjects and covered the corneas with opaque caps so that the subjects received no visual information, then mechanically moved both eyes simultaneously. The subjects did not know that their eyes were moving, i.e. this demonstrated absence of position sense in the eye based solely on proprioception from the extraocular muscles. Merton, P.A. (1964) concluded that: 'A subject is only conscious of his intention to move his eye and does not know whether the movement has in fact taken place or not' (p. 318).

Secondly, Festinger, L. and Kirkpatrick Canon, L. (1965) devised an experiment which compared locating a light source target after tracking and after saccadic eye movements. In their logic they used the above conclusions of Merton, P.A. (1964) and the results of Rashbass, C. (1961), who showed that only saccadic movements were caused by location of the visual target on the retina. The authors inferred from Rashbass's work that an efferent record of position would be available from the saccadic movements but not after tracking. On comparing accuracy of twenty-eight subjects on twenty-eight trials their data supported this hypothesis. The authors concluded that: '...information based on some kind of record of efferent impulses (i.e. outflow information) is available to the organism' (p. 382).

A criticism of their methodology is that adaptation to the exposure of the light whilst tracking would cause inaccuracies in locating the terminus position of the light. The inaccuracies would be in the direction from which the light approached the terminus point. The authors' results support this criticism as the mean error for each subject was in this direction, even though the directions of tracking, left versus right, were randomized.

The following psychological tests give results compatible with the above physiological and theoretical results. Kinaesthetic imagery, a common component of intuitive thought, has been isolated by several workers as a subdivision of the spatial factor (Macfarlane Smith, I., 1964, pp. 84ff). It has been given various labels, commonly Visualization Factor V or Kinaesthetic Factor k. It is categorized by 'the ability to think about those spatial relations in which the body orientation of the observer is an essential part of the problem: '...the ability to imagine the movement or internal displacement among the parts of a configuration'. '...to involve a person's ability to remain unconfused by the varying orientations in which a spatial pattern may be presented'; '...the ability to comprehend imaginary movement in three-dimensional space, or the ability to manipulate objects in imagination'. Spatial kinaesthesis is a common ability mode for the intuitive type who generally should score highly on tests using these abilities. Visualization items requiring these abilities often appear in reasoning tests, e.g. Mazes or Kohs' Block Design Test is highly k-loaded but considered by some, e.g. Rapaport, D. (1950), to require the analytic processes involved in conceptual thinking. In contrast the Flags test and SRA spatial relations do not have items that are k-loading.

A test of k-loading spatial abilities, which uses mental paper-folding, was given in an experiment by Shepard, R.N. and Feng, Christine (1972) who used nets of cubes with arrows on some of the squares. S had to say if the arrows would be adjacent when the net was folded into a cube. The results were that the mean reaction time increased with the number of mental folds needed. Interviews with the ten subjects used could have established if they had used body reference. The increased length of time required for the greater number of mental folds would be in agreement with such an interpretation.

A similar experiment on mental rotations was performed by Shepard, R.N. and Metzler, Jacqueline (1971). Es used a computer to produce graphic output of 3D shapes of twelve cubes joined in various ways, from rotational views in 20° increments. Ss were presented with these views in pairs and had to decide if the views were of the same arrangement in each of the pairs. Sixteen thousand pairs were possible and it was found that recognition time is linearly proportional to the angle of rotation needed to align the views in each pair and ranged from one second to five seconds and 0° to 180° of rotation. Again interview transcripts are not available but as this test is highly k-loading the interpretation of body reference fits these results.

Simple rotations are done analytically but complex rotations use body reference. This is similar to the finding that intuitive processes are used in default of not being able to use an analytic technique through insufficient data or through complexity. Results of this kind were found by Zimmerman, W.S. (1954) who gave a Visualization of Manoeuvres test at three levels of complexity to aviation students who also took a large battery of classification tests. The students had to recognize the position of an aeroplane after one, two, or three successive manoeuvres corresponding to the three levels of difficulty. Zimmerman found that the third level of difficulty measured the visualization factor Vz or k. None of the tests loaded significantly on the reasoning factor.

This result is concordant with visualization processes being intuitive and not analytical. Further it shows that reasoning tests employing items of this type are allowing intuition to contribute to a reasoning measure. 'Intuitive reasoning' is a contradiction in terms. Spatial items requiring analytical analysis, e.g. progressive matrices, tend to measure the general factor g. MacFarlane Smith, I. (1964, p. 97) says that it is only when the subject is compelled to rely on the perception of a configuration as a whole that the test involves k. This again connects kinaesthetic imagery with the Gestalt definition of insight. 'Such tests [loading on a k or v factor] involve an ability to perceive and retain in mind a figure as an organized whole' (MacFarlane Smith, I. 1964, p. 98).

The literature shows that the use of body reference, dependence on sensations from within the body, and ability on k-loading spatial tests are concomitants of an intuitive cognitive style, characterized as field-independent, low functional fixedness, and with emotional involvement.

Gupta, G.C. (1973) relates body reference for spatial judgments with cognitive style. He showed how body reference is used to judge the apparent vertical. Subjects were seated on a tilted chair and instructed E on how to turn a rod so that it was vertical. The results of this experiment were interpreted in terms of (a) 'the notion of a spatial reference system of external space differentiating out of a global functioning defined by reference to the body', and (b) cognitive styles. Both (a) and (b) are related to intuition.

Two studies by Witkin, H.A. *et al.* (1954 and 1962) relate the following concomitants of intuitive style: spatial ability, dependence on body sensations, success on insight problems, and low persuadability. Witkin *et al.* found that field-dependent persons were less successful than field-independent persons in 'hidden figures' tests of the Gottschaldt type, block design, and picture completion (all k-loading), and in imposing structure on Rorschach ink blots. They tended to be guided by the surrounding visual field 'rather than by sensations from within the body'. They were poor on Duncker's 'insight problems' (alternative uses). They tended to favour occupations popular within their groups which involved contact with people. They seemed particularly attentive to faces and therefore were better at recognizing people only briefly met previously. They tended to change their views in the direction of attitudes of an authority. The result on favoured occupations agrees with Roe, Anne's, (1953) results using barrier scores. The other results are consistent with non-intuitive types.

These findings are in agreement with the following results of Gardner, R.W. *et al.* (1959) whose work shows that the use of body sensations and emotional reactions as a source of information is related to lack of functional fixedness and ability to change emotional sets, and less dependence upon the environment. In a series of tests (colour-word test, incidental recall test, size estimation test 11, free association test) the authors found constrained-cognitive control subjects 'tended to avoid using feelings or emotional reactions as a source of information. A constrained-control subject also seemed resistant to change, preferring to maintain sets long after they were appropriate', i.e. were prone to functional fixedness (p. 53). Also flexible control subjects in a free association test veered towards remote associations and were less committed to the stimulus word, e.g. the stimulus word 'dry' for thirsty subjects had less effect on the flexible control group.

On an insight task Snapper, A. (1956) reports finding different emotional attitudes to be indicative of intuitive versus the analytical approach. He found that successful non-verbalizers treated the insight test as 'fun' in a relaxed casual way as opposed to the hypothesis-testing procedure of the verbalizers. Blatt, S. (1960), in agreement with the above finding, also observed that efficient problem-solvers consider the task more in terms of 'fun' than do the inefficient problem-solvers. This behaviour seems common to creative situations. The above work relates the following personality traits commonly found in intuitive types. The high-intuitive type has field-independent cognitive style, is good at hidden figure tests and spatial k or V-loading items. He relies on body sensations as a source of information more than the low-intuitive type. Also in contrast to the law-intuitive type he tends to be a non-verbalizer, can more easily structure Rorschach items, is less prone to functional fixation, is less influenced by authority, veers more towards remote associations, and prefers a permissive 'fun' type environment. See also for comparison the personality traits associated with creativity which are reported in Section 7.3.

Summary of Emotional Involvement in the Intuitive Process

The property of emotional involvement has, through its related literature, contributed more than most properties of intuition to the Theory of Intuitive Thought Processes. In particular, evidence has been presented to support the following points. The intuitive process is dependent upon the interaction of emotional states and cognitive processes. It is evident from the feeling of satisfaction and reductions in tensions that accompany an insight that emotional involvement plays a part in intuitive processes.

Cognitive activity and emotional arousal do occur together. The interactive feedback between them is used in our most effective thinking, e.g. in intuitive mathematics. A 'whole body' unifying theory is needed to describe intuitive processes. Because we 'think with our whole bodies' intuitive processes can be monitored by physiological measures. The literature testifies to this interactive feedback between emotional states and cognitive activities, *viz.* perception inducing and influencing emotional states, emotional sets influencing perceptions, interactions of emotional states with perceptions, and psychophysiological experiments that monitor the extent of these interactions.

These findings on the causes and types of interaction allow a comprehensive explanatory and consistent theory of emotional involvement in intuitive processes to be developed. Various aspects of the emotional states associated with cognitive activity have been measured. The accuracy and organization of perception is influenced by changing emotional sets. It is proposed that these emotional sets act as a body reference for cognitive activity.

Self-concept and motivation also influence perception. Absolute accurate perception correlates with analytic skills and not with intuitive skills. Projective tests, e.g. TAT and Rorschach, are more suitable for measuring emotional interaction with perception than are tests of accuracy. Emotion interferes with perception in many ways, e.g. blocking, ego-threat, anxiety, etc. Non-permissive ego states inhibit experiential associations and so give priority to thought based on analytic associations. Threat environments cause anxiety and non-permissive ego states, but anxiety due to associating a stimulus with two incongruous states gives intrinsic motivation used in the intuitive process. Environments for experiments in intuitive processes should be permissive and game-like. The concomitants of intuitive processes have common favourable environments. This may be used as a consistency test on concomitants of intuition.

Results of psychophysiological experiments are available in which emotional interactions have been monitored associating physiological responses to cognitive, emotional, and personality variables. The use of cognitive variables, at various levels of complexity, has shown that kinaesthetic sensations from the body are used in judgments. The small body movements accompanying cognition give proprioceptive feedback from the musculature, and give information based on a record of efferent impulses that are associated with emotional states and are used for body reference in intuitive judgments: particularly in orientation as discussed later. There are widespread body responses associated with cognitive activity. These responses interact with cognitions through feedback systems, including those systems used to retain homeostasis. This dynamic state of cognitions, body responses, and internal stimuli at any one moment defines the emotional state of the body at that moment.

Physiological evidence has been reported here, supporting the proposed explanation of emotional involvement in intuitive thought and giving indications of procedures for experiments on intuition. Learning involves these emotional states and autonomic responses have been monitored and associated with learning. Activational peaking may be used in suitable experimental circumstances as an indication of emotional involvement during intuitive processes. Low absolute skin resistance is related to cognitive activity. High phasic GSR is related to successful information intake. Enjoyable attitudes are associated with intuitive problem-solving. Threat of electric shock produces as good a GSR expectancy as the actual shock and return to basal levels is quicker. This makes GSR to threat of punishment if the solution is wrong suitable for measures of confidence in intuitive solutions. Different mixtures of adrenaline and noradrenaline are associated with different physiological responses, distinguishing emotional states. The montage of widespread emotional responses to innumerable stimuli forms the emotional state of the organism. Successive emotional states preserving common responses are an emotional set. Changes in stimuli change the emotional set, through continuous transformation, into another unique emotional set.

Some cognitive variables that define personality interact with emotion and are associated with the intuitive process. Those that facilitate it define an intuitive type. Physiological responses associated with personality variables concomitant with the intuitive processes are of the same type and in the same direction. This is an independent physiological consistency check on the personality variables describing the intuitive type. Some personality variables that correlate with physiological responses of the same type and direction are alertness, neurotic extrovertness, high fantasy, high barrier score, low authoritariansim, sensitivity, and reliance on body sensations. The rate of change of the moment-to-moment drift from one emotional set to another is affected by stimuli and personality, intuitive types being more emotionally variable.

A specific perception tends to evoke an emotional set associated with it. This stimulus response pairing is conditioned when the perception occurred when the organism was in that emotional set. A return to this emotional set will evoke the associated secondary perception, i.e. memory of the original perception.

Emotional states, with or without associated perceptions, may have tensions associated with them. A course of action may reduce these tensions. The tendency to respond in such a way as to reduce these tensions, becomes conditioned to the emotional set incorporating the emotional state by the relief or reduction in these tensions. Successive emotional states that share these response tendencies are an emotional set. Some instinctive response tendencies are innately associated with some emotional sets without the need of conditioning. Use of these sets in intuitive processes explains the common definition of intuition as 'instinctive knowledge'. The tensions of a particular state may be resolved by drifting to an emotional set with similar tensions and using the response tendencies of that set to reduce the tensions. So some perceptions are associated, through a mediating emotional set, with response tendencies.

The manipulation of emotional sets is of use as follows. Emotional sets encode complex perceptions and act as memory 'hooks'. Verbal coding is part of this process. Environments are chosen for creative work that experience has previously associated with emotional sets in which insights have occurred. The resolution of tensions acts as secondary reinforcement to secondary perceptions associated with the emotional sets. This is secondary learning through 'mental' rehearsal. Reduction in tension gives subjective confidence in an intuitive decision. The reduction in tension associated with insight also acts as an intrinsic motivation for creative workers. Intuitive types are more tolerant of the physical discomfort that this self-induced tension involves. Associating the wrong emotional set with a stimulus, through inaccurate perception or unusual conditioning, may produce bizarre behaviour responses. Emotional sets are used for organizing an ambiguous perceptual field as in TAT, Rorschach tests and figure ground perception.

The intuitive process involves many ways of operating with emotional states to bring about the products of the intuitive process: intuitive-recognition, acceptance, judgments, memories, associations, analogies, recentring and learning, etc. These operations depend on the sources of stimuli evoking the emotional state, internal or external, and two physiological properties. One is that efferent information is available about the change in sets. The other is that because of the latencies of physiological responses, thoughts may change faster than emotional sets. The three sources evoking the state may be:

(1) perception of, or empathic projection with, external stimuli;
(2) perception of, or empathic projection with, internal stimuli;
(3) natural drift due to competing control of (1) and (2) or due to maintaining an appropriate state of the organism (homeostasis).

Combinations of these sources and the physiological properties outlined produce, through their effect on emotional sets, different products of the intuitive process as illustrated below.

The relatively slow change of emotional set allows the many associated thoughts defining the field of knowledge to be considered in the intuitive process. Encoding of information by associating it with an emotional set and the slow change in the emotional set gives context to concepts. Movements that are responses in the emotional set are observed to be duplicated when someone is using this emotional set as a memory hook to explain associated thoughts and the context of a concept.

The use of emotional sets with instinctive response tendencies gives rise to 'insight' as one-trial learning. The insight is usually a decision or course of action. Insights based on emotional sets with conditioned response tendencies are affected by learning. This type of insight is found in the 'guess-the-rule'-type of experiment. Insight is a short cut to learning through secondary reinforcement by the reduction in tension through the responses conditioned to the recalled and combined emotional sets.

External stimuli are intuitively recognized when they evoke an emotional set rather than a discordant emotional state. The lack of tension afforded by the responses is the feeling of recognition. This intuitive recognition allows us to accept a novel stimulus, for which we have no emotional set, by presenting it with stimuli for which we do have emotional sets. The concordant response tendencies of these emotional sets are then associated with the novel stimulus. This is used in advertising, and in accepting knowledge that we cannot analytically justify.

If the novel stimulus tends to evoke a slightly discordant emotional state similar to some extant emotional set, natural intolerance of tension may cause the similar emotional set to be associated with the stimulus rather than the discordant emotional state. This is because the novel emotional state has no conditioned response tendencies to resolve the tension but the conditioned response tendencies of the similar emotional set will resolve this tension, so we see what we expect to see. This classifies the stimulus by its Gestalt, e.g. ⌒

is perceived as ◯ or enables us to classify the stimulus without our having
an analytic definition of the class, e.g. recognizing one of the many types of
tree as a tree without a definition of a tree.

Intuitive judgments comparing two sets of stimuli are made on the
subjective feeling of the relative difficulty of going from the emotional set
associated with one group of stimuli to the emotional set associated with the
other group of stimuli. Judgments of this kind are about the truth of statements of the following sort: (1) 'if *a* then *b*' and (2) '*a* is equivalent to *b*'.
If the groups of stimuli evoke the same emotional set then they are intuitively
judged as equivalent, i.e. (2) is true. If there is a natural flow from one
emotional set to the other then (1) is true. If an intermediate set is required
for the transition then the responses to this emotional set give a condition
for (1) to be true, e.g. 'will you wear your raincoat when you go out walking
today?' Here one may go from the emotional set associated with 'wearing
a raincoat' to the emotional set associated with 'out walking today' via the
emotional set associated with 'being in the rain'. Hence this becomes the
condition to make the statement true. The greater the relative change from
one emotional set to another then the greater is the intuitive judgment of the
subjective difference between the groups of stimuli. The greater the number of
intermediate transition emotional sets, i.e. the lower transition probability
from the emotional set associated with *a* to the emotional set associated with *b*,
then the more unsatisfying is the judgment of the truth of (1).

The anchor state is an emotional state in which the transition starts. The
anchor state is used as body reference in judgments of difference. Intuitive
types, being emotionally more variable, find transition between emotional sets
easier and so find a greater consistency between groups of stimuli than analytic
types would find, i.e. intuitive types could give more subjective reasons for the
similarity or the two groups of stimuli. Resolving tensions by changing from
the evoked emotional state to an emotional set with convenient responses
rather than finding suitable responses to the evoked emotional state, reinforces
withdrawal.

Kinaesthetic information input is a common preference modality for
intuitive processing because the motor responses associated with the emotional
sets are, in part, copies of the input information and thus avoid the effort and
possible errors involved in transposition to another modality. This shows the
suitability of kinaesthetic input information for experiments on intuition. The
type of information should be structured so that parts may be evaluated by
finger span and associated into a whole relationship one to another by
unconstrained active arm movement at the side of the body.

Combining of emotional sets is used in intuitive problem-solving. Novel
associations may arise by the juxtaposition of thoughts associated through
personal experience with emotional sets combined into one emotional set. The

138

reduction of functional fixedness with time allows for the occurrence of insights after long incubation periods. The reduction in fixation lessens the restriction on emotional drift thus increasing the probability of novel association of responses conditioned to combined emotional sets. Hints in problem-solving change emotional drift by rejecting transition to incongruous emotional scts. They do not otherwise positively encourage drift to emotional sets associated with a solution.

A subject's emotional sets and transition probabilities may be mapped by the use of experiential association tests. Recentring, a restructuring of the emotional sets and transition probabilities, may be examined by comparing maps of free associations before and after recentring.

High barrier scores are associated with many concomitants of the intuitive process, e.g. measures of creativity, reliance on information from the body, sensitivity to the environment, memory related to ego involvement, alertness, high GSR, and low heart-rate sensitivity. Barrier scores show that scientists are significantly less intuitive than artists.

The common use of kinaesthetic visual imagery in intuitive processes would generally give intuitive types a high spatial score on k-loading test items. Emotional sets accompanying visual images include motor and hormonal activity. Information from proprioceptive feedback and the efferent impulses that cause this activity is the basis of kinaesthetic body reference in intuitive processes. The record of this information as the emotional sets change gives orientation information, particularly the spatial orientation used in kinaesthetic visual imagery.

Because k-loading test items are solved intuitively and intuition is in contrast to analytic reasoning, these k-loading test items should not be included in tests purporting only to measure analytical reasoning. High spatial orientation also has been found to have many correlates that are concomitants of the intuitive process, e.g. field-independent cognitive style, dependence on body sensations, low authoritarianism, low functional fixedness, ease of change of emotional sets, and a 'fun' approach to problem-solving, etc.

The Theory of Intuitive Thought Processes developed in this study describes and explains emotive involvement in behaviour as observed by different schools of psychology. Its terminology and concepts offer a common translation of the different ways in which the schools describe these phenomena. This part of the theory concerning emotional involvement offers testable predictions and applications to a wide variety of fields of study.

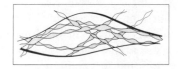

4

Preconscious, Anxiety-reducing Process

4.1 INTUITION IS A PRECONSCIOUS PROCESS

This is the joint fifth property in order of priority with ten references to it from the definitions of insight and intuition previously cited from the literature in Section 1.3.

In this section on the preconscious aspects of intuition 'preconscious' and other equivalent terms used in descriptions and definitions of insight and intuition are reported. To illustrate the preconscious aspects of these equivalent terms, examples will be given of these terms in definitions, descriptions, and experiments on insight and intuition. Also physiological experiments will be cited where during insightful behaviour subjects exhibit activational peaking (AP) of which they are unaware and which they cannot consciously control.

It will be noted that 'preconscious process', referring to intuition in the literature, may be dichotomized into:

(1) preconscious information intake;
(2) preconscious intuitive processing of this information.

Examples will be given indicating how information may be gained preconsciously using subliminal stimulation, hypnotic recall, and incidental learning. This will be contrasted with the intuitive problem situation where some information intake is conscious and used with the preconsciously gained information to arrive at insight. The intuitive process will be considered with references indicating the preconscious aspects of each part of the process, *viz.* of changing emotional states and preconscious contiguity conditioning to give emotional sets (incidental learning), preconscious aspects of empathic projection, instinctive responses, the role of the preconscious during the incubation period preceding the recentring type of insight, preconscious

139

setting of subgoals in intuitive processes, and inferences about the preconscious processes that may be made from introspection of the conscious products of the intuitive process.

Preconscious Criterion of Intuition

'Preconscious' is used to refer to material, which, though at the moment it may be unconscious, is available, and ready to become conscious (Drever, J., 1974, p. 219). This use of the term 'preconscious' is appropriate to intuition, as the intuitive products like insights, intuitions, Eureka experiences, etc., seem to be the conscious products of information often gathered and processed subconsciously, i.e. 'occurring outside of personal awareness' (Drever, J., 1974, p. 285).

Some other terms used for 'intuition' indicate its preconscious aspects, e.g. Westcott, M.R. (1964) calls intuition 'unconscious concept formation'. It is also called 'preverbal concept formation'. Other names for intuition in the field of interpersonal judgments where information about people is gained and processed preconsciously are 'social perception' and 'judgment of character' (Valentine, C., 1929). Valentine explicitly states that intuition is unconscious. 'I shall use intuition as implying judgments of which the grounds are unconscious...' (p. 215). Similarly Simonton, D.K. (1975) says when contrasting intuitive processes with analytic processes that intuition is unconscious (property 4, contrast with logic or analytic thought). 'Intuition is unconscious and behavioural whereas analysis is conscious and logico-symbolic' (p. 351).

Writers also infer that intuition is preconscious by stating that the subject does not know the source of his intuitions and cannot specify how he completed the intuitive process: '...[intuition] in which the inferences have their source in cues or cognitive processes that the percipient is unable to identify or specify with satisfactory completeness' (Hathaway, S.R., 1955, p. 233). Clinchy, Blythe (1975) defines intuitive understanding in terms of this property of preconsciousness: 'I think we mean [by intuition] that we know something without knowing how we came to know it and without being able to prove it' (p. 48). Myers, I.B. (1962) defines the '...process of intuition, which is understood as indirect perception by way of the unconscious, with the emphasis on ideas or associations which the unconscious tacks on to the outside things perceived' (pp. 1/2).

In experiments involving intuition or insight the preconscious aspect of intuition has been used as the criterion for the involvement of intuition or insight. Pickford's experiment on insight (Pickford, R., 1938) where subjects had to 'guess the rule' that some polygons had right-angles in order to categorize them correctly, showed that with reinforcement subjects could obtain a success rate above chance although they were unable to verbalize the rule they were successfully using.

Simonton, D.K. (1975) included Pickford's experiment as a 'simple' task combined with a more 'complex' categorization task, namely that of categorizing views as A, B, not A or not B on the unknown criterion that one set was an interior view and the other was an exterior view. The pictures were presented as pages in a book with the correct category marked on the back of each page. After guessing a picture's category the subject turned the page to see if he was correct. Simonton used forty subjects defined as high or low creatives by the Barron-Welsh Art Scale. He instructed half of each group of high and low creatives to intuit the answers and the other half of each group to categorize by analysis and hypothesis testing. This is consistent with property 4, contrast with logic or analytic thought. His instruction to be intuitive was: 'Intuit each prediction... relying solely on a subconscious grasp of the task' (p. 352). This indicates that Simonton considers intuition as 'subconscious'.

In many laboratory situations in which intuition is 'demonstrated', it seems that the criterion for intuition is that the subject reaches his conclusion, solution, formulation, etc., without being aware of how he reached it. Viesti, C.R. Jr. (1971) writing on 'Insight learning' summarizes the literature: 'In agreement with the prevailing view of these investigators, it is held that Ss can acquire a working concept of these relationships without awareness of what they are' (p. 181). For further examples see the experiments quoted in Section 1.3 on properties attributed to the term intuition in operational use.

Several physiological experiments are cited in Section 3.1 that show activational peaking associated with insightful behaviour. These experiments also show two preconscious aspects of the intuitive process; that the subject lacks conscious awareness of the activational peaking accompanying insight, and the subject's lack of conscious control of the physiological process on which intuition depends.

Another experiment which demonstrated this AP associated with insightful behaviour was an experiment similar to Simonton's insight experiment above conducted by White, S.H. and Plum, G. (1964) who also monitored the eye movements of subjects during the experiment. They asked sixteen children (3½ to 5-years-old), in a series of discrimination tasks to choose between two pictures. They photographed eye movements at three-second intervals while children were working on the selections. The children's eyes moved most rapidly just before they solved the problem. GSR AP was also demonstrated by Finesmith, S. (1959) who identified the trial on which each correct response first occurred in a paired-associates learning task. He found GSRs to stimulus items increased up to the point of learning then decreased with practice.

These recorded physiological responses are difficult to control consciously. Stern, R.M. (1973) showed in particular that GSR was difficult to control voluntarily. In an experiment to find the conscious ability of subjects to change their physiological reactions Barber, T.X. and Hahn, K.W. Jr. (1962) measured muscular potential, respiration irregularities, heart rate and skin resistance on four groups of subjects: (i) hypnotized subjects, (ii) subjects instructed to fake hypnosis, (iii) an uninstructed group of subjects, and (iv) a control group. They found that heart rate and skin resistance were the only variables which showed no significant difference between the groups, i.e. could not be consciously or subconsciously controlled. All other measures, e.g. breathing and muscular control, were under 'voluntary' control. This indicates that heart rate and GSR are suitable variables to choose for monitoring psychophysiological experiments on intuition.

In interviews with subjects after the experiments involving AP, reports show that the subjects were not aware of their AP. 'Efficient problem-solvers showed a marked cardiac change. Inefficient problem-solvers did not show these marked anatomic changes. Subjects were unaware of these changes' (Blatt, S., 1960). 'The subjects were unable to report these changes' (Blatt, S., 1961).

These experiments indicate that both the cognitive and physiological aspects of the intuitive process can be preconscious. The experiments designed for psychophysiological studies of intuition should, therefore, involve the recording of selective physiological responses (HR and GSR à la Barber and Hahn, 1962, above) to monitor the preconscious intuitive process.

Preconscious Intake and Storage of Information for the Intuitive Process

Although it has been shown that the intuitive process is a 'whole body process' and that the intake of information should not be considered independently from the processing of that information, see emotional and cognitive interactions in intuitive processes discussed in Section 3.2; the literature relevant to the preconscious processes of intuition may be divided into these two aspects. The preconscious intake and storing of information used in intuition is considered first.

Board, R. (1958) uses this preconscious aspect in his 'definition' of intuition. 'Intuition is a concept composed of a theoretical relation-structure some of whose empirical observations and symbols are unconscious or otherwise unavailable for conscious delineation' (p. 237). Clark, F.V. (1973) attributes the following to Jung and Fordham: 'More simply, intuition is defined as a perception of realities which are not known to consciousness' (p. 159). In an analysis of the intuitive processes of recognition, Hebb, D.O. (1946) also observes that preconscious information is used in intuition. 'The fact is evident that one frequently reaches a right conclusion without being able to state the evidence which really determines it' (p. 89).

Jung used this concept of preconscious perception of information in his idea of intuition as 'perception by way of the unconscious' (Dry, A.M., 1961). Jung's definition of intuition is as follows: 'Intuition is also an irrational function: it is a perception of realities which are not known to consciousness, a perception therefore, which comes by way of the unconsicous' (Messer, E.A., 1967, p. 40).

It is well established that an individual may take in information preconsciously, retain and process it preconsciously. Westcott, M.R. (1968) in his book *Toward a Contemporary Psychology of Intuition* gives a short review of some of the literature on learning without awareness, subliminal stimulation, and reinforcement of preconscious behaviours (pp. 82ff).

Controlled experiments on subliminal perception have been related to intuition and intuitive types by several researchers. Because of the properties that intuition has in common with dreams and subliminal perception Tauber, E.S. and Green, M.R. (1959) group them together as 'prelogical' experience which they say is opposed to the 'logical', and therefore conscious, process of reasoning agreeing with property 4, contrast with logic or analytic thought. This point of view comes close to the positions of Freud and Kubie.

Eagle, M. (1962) studied the personality correlates of persons sensitive to subliminal stimulation. His results are concordant with the personality correlates of the intuitive type as pictured from the literature reviewed in Sections 3.3 and 7.3.

Eagle describes the subject who is sensitive to subliminal stimulation as follows: '...he is receptive to "inner cues" in the sense of being intuitive, introspective, and insightful...' (p. 3). This is consistent with the sensitivity of feeling typical of the intuitive type, see Section 6.2 showing that sensitivity to feeling facilitates intuition. Eagle also found that the subliminal effect is most likely to be facilitated under conditions which also facilitate intuitive responses, namely non-repressive environments facilitating intuitive thought: see Section 8.3.

Primary-Process Thinking

In Section 7.3 intuitive thought is considered to be primary-process thinking. It is reported here that during relaxed states, occasioning hypnogogic reverie (property 17) typical of primary-process thinking, particularly in the first intuitive stage of creativity and during light hypnosis, information recall and associations are not consciously directed.

Fox, Muriel (1960) worked on regression as an aid to subliminal sensitivity. She found that highly sensitive subjects were more capable of regression and the subliminal effects were 'more likely to develop when subjects minimize the demand of reality', as in primary thinking. There are many anecdotes of insights occurring during these semi-conscious states (spindling sleep), e.g. Kekule's conception of the benzene ring.

Creative insights are not consciously directed: '...it is still clear that creativity goes on with varying degrees of intensity on levels not directly under the control of conscious willing' (Rollo, May, 1959, p. 62).

Theta rhythms (4-7HZ) occur whilst in this state (Foulkes, D., 1966) and it has been suggested that theta conditioning, by biofeedback and muscle relaxation, etc., might facilitate insightful problem-solving (Stoyva, J., 1973, p. 410); see also Section 6.2, on intuition being facilitated through the use of biofeedback.

That this preconsciously gained information is also held preconsciously has been demonstrated in experiments where subjects have improved recall whilst under hypnosis. In one experiment (Kubie, L.S., 1958) subjects were shown a room and later asked to recall items. The conscious recall was twenty to thirty items but under hypnosis a further two hundred items were remembered.

In the problem situation where a problem is given and an insight solution is expected, (e.g. the practical recentring insight experiments like the bridge problem, the hat rack problem, the pendulum problem, etc., mentioned in Section 1.3 on experiments using practical insight problems,) information is consciously gained about the problem elements, but the recentring is caused by incorporating other information gained preconsciously in the problem situation and included with information brought subconsciously to the problem situation by the subject. It is because of the lack of control of these preconscious aspects of the subject's experimental history that I consider these practical insight experiments to be poorly designed.

Preconscious Processing of Information Resulting in Intuition

The intuitive process is preconscious. Writing in 1938 Wild, K.W. considered the views of thirty writers on intuition, both scientific and philosophical. He concluded that common to most definitions is the idea of reaching a conclusion, a synthesis, a formulation, or a solution to a problem without being aware of the processes which this conclusion or synthesis is reached. Hebb, D.O. (1946) also refers to this preconscious process when writing of intuition. 'Intuitive is used to refer to judgments which follow premises or steps of which the judge is unaware.' Bruner, J.S. (1960) has written more than most about intuitive thinking and he also indicates that intuition is a preconscious process. 'The thinker arrives at an answer, which may be right or wrong, with little if any awareness of the process by which he reached it': also supporting property 9, intuition need not be correct. Jung, C.G. (1969) includes in his definition of intuition: '...without being able to explain or discover in what way this content [the intuition] has been arrived at' (p. 263). Bahm, A.J. (1960) writes of the intuiter that: 'Intuition occurs without his being aware of it' (p. 4).

Writing on intuition Board, R. (1958) remarks on '...its intimate connection with unconscious processes...' (p. 234), and notes the following three preconscious aspects of the intuitive process:

(i) the person is unaware of the concept's connection with a previous train of thought;
(ii) he is unaware of how he came to entertain the concept;
(iii) he is unaware of any systematic effort to formulate the concept (Board, R., 1958, p. 234).

The literature refers to intuition as instinctive knowledge which is property 13, innate instinctive knowledge or ability. This may be because the intuitive process, like an instinctive response, is preconscious. It may also be because instinctive as well as conditioned responses are available as part of emotional sets, that intuition is thought of as instinctive knowledge: see Section 3.2 on intuitive decision and action derived from instinctive responses to evoked emotional sets.

It appears from the literature that the intuitive process is dependent on a structure which may be summarized in a theory of intuitive thought process as the conditioning of responses (sensations, cognitions, and behaviours) to changing emotional states to give emotional sets. The subject is aware of the conditioned sensations which are the responses to emotional sets and which result in the behavioural products of the intuitive process, i.e. sensations, cognitions, and behaviours. The intuitive process itself is the association of the emotional sets in order to obtain their conditioned sensations. The associations of emotional sets are partially dependent on the changing physiological states of the organism guided by the selections of subgoals, which are emotional sets with sensations most similar to the final sensation sought. The consecutive emotional sets in the associations are evoked by empathy, projection, and responses in common with the previous emotional set. The literature indicates that each part of this intuitive process can be preconscious except for some of the gross sensations of which the subject must become consciously aware, and which are the intuition: see Section 7.2 on intuition suddenly erupting into consciousness.

The physiological and cognitive responses are part of the subject's emotional set and since it has been shown that the subject is sometimes unaware of these responses during the intuitive process it follows that the subject is sometimes unaware of his emotional sets during an intuitive process.

Incidental learning experiments and transfer learning experiments have shown that the subject is unaware of much of the conditioning of his responses to emotional sets.

Crutchfield, R.S. (1960) tested two groups of one hundred and seventy-nine experimental subjects and one hundred and ninety-nine control subjects on three spatial reorganization puzzles. Immediately beforehand the experimental subjects worked on three tasks containing spatial cues relevant to the puzzle solution whereas the controls worked on similar tasks not containing such cues. The results showed that the experimental group did significantly better than the control group in the percentage of solutions they reached. '...and this occurred without awareness of the relevant cues' (p. 429).

Crutchfield calls this the 'intuitive use of cues'. There are numerous experiments in the literature that illustrate this preconscious conditioning and transfer.

The preconscious combinations of emotional sets mediate the subject's responses. Being unaware of this part of the intuitive process the subject is not consciously aware of how he arrived at his intuitions through the sensations, cognitive and affective responses, etc., conditioned to these mediating emotional sets. 'The inability to verbalize an intuitive process may be due to lack of awareness of the mediating process' (Baldwin, A., 1966, p. 87). The particular combinations of similar emotional sets can be clearly inferred from a subject's free associations under conditions facilitating the intuitive process. The work of Pollio, H.R. (1974) illustrates this. He used a protocol from a psychoanalysis session (by Knight, J., 1950). The subject breaks from talking about his father to talking about a policeman then returns to talking about his father. 'The mediating elements (authority + anxiety) are common to both, and the seemingly chaotic leap in the stream of association is given coherence by the relationship of Topics A and B to the same mediating element' (p. 152).

This is an example of preconsciously categorizing elements (policeman and father) by a common emotional set (anxiety + authority). If a cue is associated with an emotional set then the characteristics of the other stimuli in that set will also be associated with the cue, giving a physiognomic perception. Sarbin, T.R. et al. (1960) say that this assigning of the characteristics of the whole class to a particular cue is a preconscious process. In a review of the relevant literature Pollio also says that all the present explanations of how these associative connections are made '...involve the assumption of an unconscious — unverbalizable — process and its associated mental manoeuvering that keeps events and ideas out of awareness' (p. 152).

A stimulus may evoke an emotional set through preconscious empathic projection so that the responses, cognitions, and sensations conditioned to the emotional set are also associated with the stimulus, giving a physiognomic perception. 'This, his personal kinaesthetic or other feeling, aroused by what he sees, is projected on to the person or object seen and merges completely, without the subject's being aware of it, with the percept of the person or object empathically perceived' (Schachtel, E.G., 1950, p. 73).

The sensations may be available to the conscious but the process is preconscious: '...while the content of the projection may or may not be conscious to the person as being part of himself, the process of projection usually takes place outside of awareness' (Schachtel, E.G., 1950, p. 74).

As detailed in Section 3.2 on the development of emotional sets, these responses conditioned to the emotional set may be cognitions, associated sensations, motor actions, etc., and adults may become aware of this association. 'Thus the awareness of a tendency to act can be treated merely as an "associated sign" of emotion, though it may be more ...Adults become used to associated signs of imagery and bodily sensations' (Cantril, H. and Hunt, W.A., 1932). It is suggested in Section 8.1 that this awareness is preconsciously developed and preconsciously used as directed egocentricity in 'correct adult' intuition. It is the relatively large reduction in tension brought about by combining suitable emotional sets during the intuitive process that brings about the conscious awareness of the conglomerate emotional set responsible for the reduced tension which terminates the preconscious intuitive process and whose responses are the intuition. It is because of the awareness of these sensations that they may act as preconscious goals in the intuitive process, e.g., feelings of confidence in attaining an intuitive solution, reduction in tension associated with closure. This awareness of sensation may also be used to select, preconsciously, as subgoals emotional sets with sensations similar to the goal sensation. This awareness of sensation is a prerequisite for directing the combinations of emotional sets towards attaining the goal. If combinations in a certain direction do not give the required sensations then the direction will be changed to select a more suitable emotional set to enter into combination. Because this is a preconscious process part way between lower motor behaviour and higher reasoning it is classed as Intermediate Level Cognition (ILC). It is driven by the seeking of pleasant sensations and avoidance of anxiety sensations. This compares with Festinger's Dissonance Theory. Becker, J.D. (1970) gives the following examples of situations in which ILC applies and preconscious gathering and processing of information is clearly evident: '. . . when we look around the room for a book we have set down somewhere, or when we steer a car, or when we turn on a faucet in order to get water, or when we understand what a friend is saying to us, or when we understand the friend's mood without his saying anything' (p. 4).

These examples illustrate many of the previous points made about the preconscious aspects of the intuitive process and show that it is so basic to our existence that desirable specific intuitive products like the Eureka experience and transfer of learning, etc., cannot be considered in isolation. 'Most skills depend largely on "intuitive experience", i.e. on a system of methods that one cannot explicitly describe' (De Groot, A.D., 1965, p. 147). This leads us in Chapter 9 to consider the theory of intuitive thought as but a particular mode of processing an organization for describing general thought and behaviour.

The Role of Preconscious Incubation in Insight

The incubation period is the name given to the time in which the intuition develops, the time between realizing the problem and arriving at an intuitive solution. The word 'incubation' implies that the intuitive processing is going on 'out of awareness' and as a result of this 'hidden' processing the intuition comes to light fully formed like the incubation process of an egg where the chick develops unseen and comes to light fully formed. Section 5.4 shows how the length of the incubation period varies with the three processes of combining emotional sets. This section only considers the longest incubation period which results in combining emotional sets through recentring.

The Eureka experience type of insight is often preceded by a lengthy incubation period. The usual scenario is that the subject has involved himself in the problem but being unable to find a solution he has consciously 'shelved' or 'forgotten' the problem. Hours, days, weeks or even years later he suddenly becomes aware of the problem and its solution. This incubation period has given writers the idea that the subconscious mind has been somehow 'reasoning' or working on the information in the same way as the conscious mind would reason, and when the answer is reached it pops into consciousness. Hence they wrongly infer that intuition is the same type of process as analytic reasoning but at a preconscious level.

Bartlett, F.C. considers that in the intuitive kind of thinking, although the

148

steps are not articulated or stated, they could be (Bartlett, F. C., 1968). Cartwright, M.L. (1955), in discussing the mathematical mind, is also of this opinion. Bunge, M. (1962) also presents this as his view: 'Intuition is very fast reasoning, so fast that the process is not appreciated as reasoning' (pp. 89/90). These ideas of intuition as fast reasoning and reasoning 'preconsciously' during an incubation period, are contradictory for if intuition was 'very fast reasoning' then a lengthy incubation period would not be necessary.

Cobb, S. (1952) also mistakenly defines intuition in this way. 'Intuition can be defined as reasoning from premises and by processes that are forgotten. It is an extreme example of what goes on in most reasoning' (p. 250). How can he compare reasoning with a forgotten process? If it is forgotten one cannot compare with it.

Intuitions that follow long incubation periods usually involve drastic recentring. This occurs when responses that have previously been conditioned

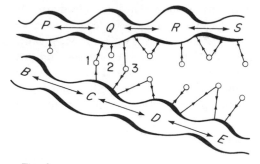

Fig. A
Emotional sets before recentring

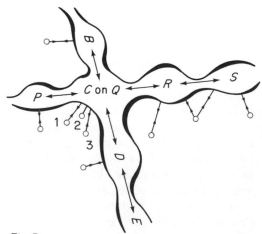

Fig.B
Emotional sets after recentring

Fig. 4.1/1 Structure of drastic recentring 'Eureka' experience

to two similar emotional sets in different chains of associations are so similar that these similar emotional sets are combined as one emotional set. A chain of emotional sets is a probable path of emotional sets that a person may occupy because of their high transition probability, i.e. because of their many shared response tendencies. In the combination of emotional sets the responses of each emotional set are available to the other emotional set and the linking of the two chains of 'adjacent' emotional sets provides new paths for future emotional drift (where 'adjacent' is defined by high transition probability between the emotional sets). In Fig. 4.1/1 P, Q, R, S and B, C, D, E illustrate two chains of emotional sets. Responses 3 and 1 are common to emotional sets C and Q causing recentring of emotional sets C on Q so that the response 2 initially only associated with Q is now available to C and Q. The new chains of probable emotional drift are now [P, C on Q, D, E] or [P, C on Q, B] or [B, C on Q, R, S] etc. The additional responses that were not in common before recentring are in common after recentring, viz. 2 . The availability of these new responses gives the new insights (sensations, etc.), resulting from the recentring.

The anecodotal literature indicates that these Eureka experiences are 'fired' by concrete experiences — see Section 8.3 on how experiences can trigger Eureka experiences. De Groot agrees that intuitions are activated by situations (De Groot, A.D., 1965, p. 147). The responses in the new situation are so similar to the responses in the previous problem situation that the recentring occurs. An example might be that many of the motor actions and associated behaviours in the new situations are similar to those produced by empathic projection in the previous problem situation, and the additional responses relieve any tensions of the emotional state originally evoked by the problem. If the initial emotional state did not have the unresolved tensions evoked through personal involvement with an unsolved problem then the transient experience of recentring would not be reinforced as in déjà vu, i.e. déjà vu is recentring without release of tension associated with the intuitive process. Similarly daydreaming is the combination of emotional sets by drifting without the resolution of the tension initiating the intuitive process.

From this interpretation it is seen that the incubation period resulting in recentring only allows time for the subject to be involved in a different chain of emotional sets from those associated with the problem. The information is not necessarily being preconsciously restructured during the incubation period. Maier, N.R.F. and Burke, R.J. (1967) used an insight problem, the hat rack problem, to find the influence of timing of hints on their effectiveness in problem-solving. They tested three hundred and eighty-three subjects and found that the timing of the hint did not affect the problem-solving as it would if information relevant to the problem were being preconsciously structured during the incubation period. They found that the value of a hint depends on the incorrect activity it eliminates. So if there is no activity or no wrong activity the hint is of no use.

Using the present interpretation of the intuitive process as combining emotional sets in a direction to reduce the initiating tension of the emotional state evoked by the problem, the hint would halt the combination in the present direction but not initiate new combinations of emotional sets, as would be the case if the hint were more emotionally involving. However, during the incubation period new responses may be conditioned to the emotional sets of the problem or of the solution if the subject happens to be in one of these emotional sets. For having more responses conditioned to the emotional sets would very slightly increase the probability of having responses in common between the two emotional sets, thus increasing the likelihood of recentring. It is more probable that recentring will occur if the individual occupies as many different emotional sets as possible, each rich in conditioned responses, during the incubation period, i.e. providing a variety of enriched familiar emotionally involving environments is more likely to lead to an intuitive solution than merely providing hints.

4.2 INTUITION USES SUBJECTIVE CERTAINTY

This is property number 10. It is the seventh in order of priority with eight references to it in Section 1.3.

Intuitions are often incorrect (property 9, Section 8.1) but independently of their objective validity a person who experiences an intuition has an accompanying subjective feeling that his intuition is correct. 'Subjective certainty is a hallmark of intuition' (Westcott, M.R., 1968, p. 185). This confidence accompanies all the products of the intuitive process.

This section evidences this subjective certainty and the feelings of exhilaration that often accompany it. It is shown that the following properties of the intuitive process necessarily impose subjectiveness on this certainty: intuition is not the product of analytical logical development (property 4, Section 2.1), the process is preconscious (property 3, Section 4.1), is preverbal so cannot be publicly justified and confidence is dependent upon 'body reference' feelings that are not easily communicated (property 6, Section 6.2). These properties are detailed in the sections indicated.

This section also relates feelings of confidence to physiological effects during problem-solving, viz. activational peaking (AP), induction and reduction of anxiety. This literature provides some further indications for developing suitable physiological experiments which may be used in investigations of intuition.

Evidence is given that tensions, anxiety, and frustration are induced initially in the intuitive process and the resolution of these tensions and a lack of anxiety and frustration accompanies the intuitive product. It is proposed that the subjective certainty of correctness is a result of this resolution of tension, lack of anxiety, etc. It is shown how the idea of emotional sets arising from the discussion of property 2 (emotional involvement, Section 2.2) may account for this induced anxiety and its resolution in respect of intuitive products. The effects of this induction and resolution of anxiety on such a model are discussed in terms of increased conditioning of responses and changes in transition probabilities between emotional sets. Finally, personality concomitants predicted by these effects, e.g. willingness to take intuitive leaps, authoritarianism, emotional blocking and aspects of cognitive style, are compared with those found by other writers on intuition.

Confidence Accompanying Intuitions

Irrespective of the objective correctness of the intuition it brings with it a feeling of confidence accompanied by a felt release of tension: '...moment of insight [involves]... the surge of self-confidence.. release of tension...' (Hutchinson, E.D., 1941, p. 38). In her enquiry into the existence and nature of insight Mary Bulbrook observed this emotional accompaniment of an intuitive solution and the frustration that persists if a solution is not found. 'There is always an accompaniment of pleased pride in solution... In failure there is frustration' (Bulbrook, Mary E., 1932, p. 415). These feelings of satisfaction that accompany the intuitive product are indicators that the process is complete. 'Exhilaration marks such moments of insight, a glow or elation goes with them, a feeling of adequacy, finality, accomplishment' (Hutchinson, E.D., 1941, p. 31). Archie Bahm, considering 'Types of intuition' also links this feeling with confidence: '...feelings of satisfaction found in believing that what appears to be so is so' (Bahm, A.J., 1960, p. 8).

There is evidence to show that as a general psychological principle intentions are accompanied by anxieties that when resolved indicate the completion of the intention. If the intention is to solve a problem the intuitive solution with its accompanying lack of anxiety, feelings of satisfaction, etc., indicates that the solution is acceptable: '...an intention is aroused when one is set to discriminate, to remember, to image, etc. Also tied up with the intention are standards of adaptive adequacy which tell a person that the intention has been met and which serve as termini to his behaviour' (Gardner, R.W. *et al.,* 1959, p. 11). In the intuitive process these feelings of relief of tension act as terminators and give the subjective confidence in the solution. 'Inspirations are described as accompanied by the feeling of tension and anxiety... There is a certain amount of relief in arriving at initial ideas (more so in inspirations)'; '...inspirations are associated with a greater sense of relief ...Such inspirations are said to "solve" aesthetic problems and are experienced with relief and pleasure' (Rothenberg, A., 1970, pp. 176, 181).

Basing confidence in the intuitive products because of these accompanying subjective feelings is a frequent technique used by creative mathematicians. 'This seems to be what mathematicians mean when they say that things are "intuitively obvious" — that they are convinced but lack the formal language of a proof' (Griffiths, H.B. and Howson, A.G., 1974, p. 218). Although intuitions are not guaranteed to be correct it has been shown that the confidence accompanying these 'feelings of knowing' is not misplaced as they tend to accompany correct intuitive solutions. In two meticulously designed experiments Milton Blake explored the relation between 'feeling of knowing' and later recognition of trigrams. He showed a trigram to a subject for one second then filled an eighteen-second retention interval by the subject pronouncing the colour (not the word) on a random succession of Stroop items. The subject was then asked to recall the three letters of the trigram. If unsuccessful he was asked whether 'he felt he knew the target well enough to recognize it among a set of seven lures' (Blake, M., 1973, p. 313). Regardless of how correctly the trigram was initially recalled, those subjects who had 'the feeling of knowing' were significantly more accurate in their later recognition. In the second experiment the lures were designed to contain the letters initially correctly remembered so that the probability of a chance hit was constant at 0·125 irrespective of whether none, one, or two letters were correctly remembered from the initial trigram. Subjects were aware of this but it did not make them less likely to report their 'feeling of knowing', showing that this 'feeling of knowing' was not totally based on partial recall. Even without the benefit of partial recall Blake found that this 'feeling of knowing' was still a good predictor of successful intuitive recognition.

However, Hathaway's work shows that only in certain circumstances is confidence a predictor of accuracy. He asked an audience to tick the same three words from a list as ticked by a 'target' subject being observed by them. He found (Hathaway, S.R., 1955, p. 233), that confidence in results and sympathy with the target were related, but both were independent of accuracy. This result also confirms that sympathy is part of the intuitive process.

Intuitive products are associated with reduction in tensions, anxiety, and frustrations. The intuitive process is initiated by evoking emotional states with unresolved mild tensions, anxiety, and frustrations. Emotional sets are combined until a conglomerate emotional set occurs whose conditioned responses allow the resolution of this mild anxiety state to terminate the intuitive process. The responses of this terminating emotional set form the intuitive product. The resolution of tension, satisfaction, and lack of anxiety and frustration is the confidence in the intuitive product. Under certain conditions (further detailed in correctness of intuition, property 9, Section 8.1) the subjective confidence tends to predict correct intuitions.

Subjectivity of the Certainty That Accompanies Intuition

To verify objectively the correctness of an intuitive product the process and the evidence processed would need to be public, or else some verification independent of the process would be needed. The intuiter is unaware of the process, indeed audio-tape recordings show that forced introspection during intuitive problem-solving halts the intuitive process. The intuiter uses evidence from his personal experience and also interprets evidence in the light of his personal experiences of which he is often unaware and unable to communicate (detailed in intuition influenced by experience, property 5, Section 2.4). 'No-one can describe objectively what happens during an act of intuition. Intuitive thought does not make use of publicly verifiable data...' (Bigge, M.L. and Hunt, M.P., 1965, p. 305). Hebb makes this point in 'An analysis of the intuitive processes of recognition' (Hebb, D.O., 1946, p. 89). 'Intuition is used to refer to judgments which follow premises or steps of inference of which the judge is unaware and especially those which he cannot put into words.' Thus the correctness of intuitions is always independently verified.

The experiential evidence people use in their intuitive process has connotations in more than one modality. An intuitively appraised situation is often said to 'feel right' or 'smell right' before it is intuitively accepted. The experiential evidence from all modalities must be represented by concordant response tendencies within one emotional set to allow the acceptance of an intuition. The intuiter could not relax while entertaining discordant associations from different modalities, for the release of tension and anxiety that marks the termination of the intuitive process and gives certainty of correctness, could not occur. When the level of concordance is acceptable the process is sometimes described as 'it all comes together' or 'it gels' and the intuitive process is terminated.

This is hardly a precise verbal description of the evidence and process that allows objective analysis.

The level of concordance is objectively judged by the anxiety state of the body when in the emotional state whose responses' concordance is being judged. 'The subjective features of emotion derive from the appraised condition of the organism, including alternatives to action and the coping impulses actually generated, feedback from bodily reaction and the perceived consequences of the act' (Lazarus, R.S. et al., 1970, p. 218).

The intuiter cannot detail the evidence as it is a multiplicity of non-discrete feelings, with their associated cognitions, from more than one modality. As Blythe Clinchy says of intuition; 'I think we mean that we know something without knowing how we came to know it and without being able to prove it... Intuitive judgments are hard to put into words and they are hard to justify'. 'To explain the basis of the intuitive judgment is difficult' (Clinchy, Blythe, 1975, pp. 48, 50). In the intuitive mode evidence is perceived subliminally and included in the preconscious intuitive process. 'There is experimental evidence that fine discriminations may be made by humans without awareness or correct verbal labelling' (Brady, J.P., 1967, p. 308); see also evidence presented in Section 4.1 on preconscious process, property 3). Confidence in such a process using subliminal evidence could only be subjective. 'Intuitive judgments are hypotheses based on personal convictions, supporting evidence is hidden and vague' (Bigge, M.L. and Hunt, M.P., 1965, p. 305).

The release of tension and anxiety that terminates the intuitive process is 'labelled' by the conscious cognitions associated with that terminating emotional set. This process is in agreement with the work of Schachter, S., 1964; Cantril, H. and Hunt. W.A., 1932; Schachter, S. and Singer, J.E., 1962; Dunlap, K., 1932; Landis, C., 1924 and others' experiments on cognitive labelling of emotional states. In this way, at the termination of the process the 'insight' becomes conscious: '...insight and inspiration are psychodynamically similar or equivalent, i.e. both involve overcoming repression and rendering unconscious and preconscious material into consciousness' (Rothenberg, A., 1970, p. 176).

The creative worker still uses his intuitive processes to guide his choice of analytic techniques and the directions of their use in his public verification of his intuition. The public language and its use, mathematical or whatever, is chosen to maximize the concordance of its associated 'feelings' with those of the original intuition. For example, '...Weierstrass in his development of analysis, was showing the ability to model a subjective feeling [about graphs] in an objective language — here in the language of mathematics' (Griffiths, H.B. and Howson, A.G., 1974, p. 216). The lack of anxiety and tension associated with a particular choice of technique and its direction of use gives the subjective confidence that the chosen analytic method is successfully independently verifying the original intuition, giving one the feeling of 'being on the right track'.

In the more mundane situation of a problem-solving exercise where the solution is given and has to be proved to be the solution, this given solution replaces the original intuition. The 'feeling' associations to the given answer are used intuitively to select the technique of analysis and its direction of use. The method then becomes an 'ends/means' logic path; leading towards the given answer and guided by it. The feelings evoked by a given answer will tend not to be so varied and strongly conditioned to emotional sets as the experiential associations are to an intuitive answer. Hence the chosen methods of solution will tend not to bring about as much subjective confidence. Their form would tend to be less objectively novel.

The correctness of an intuitive product is judged by the intuiter according to the release in tension, anxiety, and frustration afforded by the product. This judgment based on body reference is necessarily subjective. Further, the evidence from which the intuitive product is derived is complex in its source, quantity, and combination. It is experiential and spans more than one modality and thus is not verbalized. As some evidence is subliminal and all experiential evidence has subconscious associations, it is not possible to verbalize all the evidence used in deriving an intuitive product. These conditions made the evidence subjective. The intuitive process of idiosyncratic combinations of emotional sets, involving this evidence and physiological drift, is similarly subjective. The cognitive and behavioural responses conditioned to the present emotional set, terminating the intuitive process by resolving the initially evoked anxiety, are the conscious intuitive products of this preconscious intuitive process. Body reference, the type of evidence, and the preconscious process result in the subjectivity of the correctness of these intuitive products.

The induction of anxiety initiating the intuitive process, and the reduction of anxiety at the termination of the process that gives the subjective certainty of correctness in the intuitive product, are physiological effects that can be monitored. Similarly the changing emotional state of the organism during problem-solving involves fluctuating anxiety that can be identified with shifts in the problem-solving behaviour and also physiologically monitored. The subjective certainty of the correctness of an intuitive product may be measured by the relative lack of anxiety maintained by the subject under repetition of the conditions that originally evoked the anxiety state that the intuitive product resolved. For example, if the subject is confident in his solution to a problem then the problem will no longer evoke the anxiety that the solution was developed to resolve. This lack of anxiety reflects his confidence in the solution. To date I am not aware of any research, other than Bastick T. (1979), that monitors physiological change during insight, although the literature surveyed in Section 3.1 (on emotional involvement, property 9) and the literature surveyed here, clearly indicate the importance of the emotional component of insight and the need to consider it: 'Consideration needs to be given also to the quality of the emotional reactions which follow certain insights. Initially, the effect may be one of anxiety or guilt. However, these reactions are often followed by one of great emotional relief' (Brady, J.P., 1967, p. 309).

Some intuitive products, e.g. drastic recentring (the Eureka experience) have such a marked accompanying release of tension that overt physiological responses of excited movement or exclamation occur. As Rothenberg maintains in describing inspiration, '...an impulse to action... and an associated transient emotional relief often associated with an actual physical sigh or explication of "AHA" (Rothenberg, A., 1970, pp. 173/174). It has been noted that in some cases the change in physiological state, from the induced frustration to the resolution of tension, is most extreme. 'The accompanying emotional transformation is at times almost miraculous. Joy, zest, gratification, elation, enthusiasm and, in the extreme, even rapture, replace the disruptive and disintegrative reactions of the period of frustration' (Hutchinson, E. D., 1941, p. 37).

This terminating emotional set involves tendencies to action related to the insight, often an urge to tell someone or anyone about it. The marked resolution of anxiety and the action tendencies of this terminating emotional set of the intuitive product, involve gross physiological changes that may be monitored as indicators, in suitable circumstances of insight having occurred. 'The point is that each emotion involves its own particular kind of appraisal, its own particular kinds of action tendencies, and hence its own particular constellation of physiological changes which are part of the mobilization to action, whether or not these action tendencies are actually expressed or inhibited' (Lazarus, R.S. et al., 1970, p. 218). The 'suitable circumstances' will be detailed in Section 8.3, on dependence on environment, property 19, and should be included in the design of experiments on intuition.

The individual physiological variables should not be considered independently as indicators of subjects' certainty of the correctness of their intuitive products as subjects have different patterns of physiological response to reduction in anxiety. Martin concludes his review of approximately fifty papers with the following summary to this effect: 'These studies do point to the possible subtleties in autonomic patterns associated with various kinds of stimulation or arousal states, and caution against any too ready acceptance of some particular pattern as being the anxiety or the anger pattern'. 'Research thus far gives little ground for optimism that these variables will correlate very highly, if at all' (Martin, B., 1961, pp. 239, 243).

We might expect that the physiological change accompanying insight might maximally affect the GSR of one subject but maximally affect say the heart rate or respiration of another, indicating that an analysis should not compare or group subjects during an insight response on only one physiological variable but consider responses across physiological variables. Martin has been able to distinguish between induced anxiety and other arousal states, e.g. anger. He cites studies that show heart-rate increases more in anxiety than in anger, cardiac-output increases more in anxiety than in anger, and the number of discrete GSRs in experiments was significantly higher in anger than anxiety. Similarly respiration rate was greater in anxiety than in anger. Whenever we consider the neurophysiological basis of the intuitive process the hypothalamus and the sympathetic nervous system seem to be implicated. Martin also gives as the neurophysiological basis of anxiety functions of '...the posterior hypothalamus and its effects upon the sympathetic nervous system, the adrenal medulla, and the pituitary-adrenocortical system' (Martin, B., 1961, p. 234). The hormones that activate and inhibit the sympathetic system complicate a subject's relative physiological responses. 'The fact that these two hormones [epinephrine and norepinephrine from the adrenal medulla] produce quite different reactions points up what has long been known: namely, that it is a great oversimplification to speak of sympathetic arousal as if it were a unitary function' (Martin, B., 1961, p. 238).

The dependence of intuitive processes on the sympathetic nervous system, and the effect of these hormones on this system, invite the possibility of actively increasing the propensity for intuitive products by the use of drugs.

From the above, we would expect that change in heart rate indicating the occurrence of insight would be in a direction different from the change in GSR and respiration rate indicating an insight, which agrees with the results of Bastick T. (1979). The initial effect of the reduction of tension accompanying insight on conditioning response tendencies to emotional states is further discussed in Section 3.2 under property 2, emotional involvement. The effect of continued reduction in tension on emotional sets is to reinforce this conditioning and is further discussed in Section 5.4.

The physiological monitoring of the emotional changes, e.g. reduction of anxiety, etc., accompanying the subjective certainty of the correctness of an insight may be used as an indicator that an insight has occurred. Neurophysiological considerations indicate that the direction of change of GSR during reduction of anxiety would be opposite to the direction of HR.

Further, in an analysis subjects should not be compared by their responses on only one physiological variable.

Fluctuating Anxiety States During the Intuitive Process

During the intuitive process towards a solution a 'wrong turn' may be taken when an emotional set enters a combination that does not further reduce tension but perhaps even adds to the anxiety, thus indicating that this direction of combining emotional sets is not leading to a suitable terminating set of the solution. 'The rise and fall of emotion, and the shifts in its quality, reflect this continuing cognitive activity of appraisal and reappraisal' (Lazarus, R.S. *et al.*, 1970, p. 220). The fluctuating anxiety during the intuitive process is felt as conviction and directs the intuitive associations to the terminating emotional set.

During the intuitive process, as emotional sets are combined, the continuing resolution of tension through realizing conditioned responses to these sets gives subjective confidence that indicates the chain of combinations is leading to the formation of an emotional set that will bring acceptable reduction in tension and terminate the process. The cognitive and other associations of this terminating set are the intuitive product labelled as responsible for the subjective feeling of confidence that is the final resolution of tension.

Hutchinson remarks on this evidence of conviction of a maturing solution being available during the intuitive process, '...this conviction of ideas attached to larger systems of unconscious thought, this evidence that some solution is maturing, that some integration is taking place, heralds itself by a certain emotional excitation, or satisfaction, often felt prior to the complete conscious realization of the full insight itself' (Hutchinson, E.D., 1941, p. 36). The feelings of certainty that guide the intuitive process are also discussed in Section 7.3, where creativity is considered as intuition verified by intuitively guided analysis.

Gordon, W.J.J. (1961) reports these pleasurable feelings guiding the intuitive process from interviews after creativity sessions.

However, it is our conclusion that this pleasure-sense of direction is purposeful and is a psychological state subject to cultivation as a skill in pursuit of the successful climax of the inventive process. We observed that certain people repeatedly selected ways of thinking about a problem which led to elegant solutions. These people confessed to a pleasurable feeling, a feeling of 'being on the track', long before their intuition was proved correct. They said that they regarded this pleasurable feeling as a signal telling them they were headed in the right direction. (p 29)

These fluctuating changes in anxiety during the intuitive process can be physiologically monitored. When, during the intuitive process, the conditioned response tendencies associated with a present emotional set are inhibited, because they are discordant and conflict with other conditioned response tendencies associated to a different but equally suitable emotional set, the resulting anxiety would increase the GSR. Waller noticed this increase in GSR with suppression of emotion: '...the more perfectly an examinee can control the visible signs of the emotion, the more violently is the galvanometer deflected through the palm of the hand by reason of this suppressed emotion' (Waller, A.D., 1919). Abel considered GSR during problem-solving and similarly suggested that when, during phases of problem-solving, impulses are inhibited GSR increases. His studies suggest a connection between galvanic skin response and 'certain reportable attitudes which mark sudden, decided, and momentary checks in the course of the comprehension and solution of simple problems of an elaborative sort' (Abel, I.M., 1930). These continued proportional reductions in anxiety, felt as continued confidence and conviction, guide the combination of emotional sets. The subject knows he is 'on the right track' but does not know what the goal is: commonly expressed as 'I'll know it when I see it'.

Rather than an absolute change in anxiety the subject could better appraise a proportional change in anxiety (compare the law of initial values, Sternbach, R.A., 1966, p. 46). Thus the subject would be less aware of initial absolute decreases than latter absolute decreases of the same size. Initially these smaller proportionate changes in anxiety, brought about by combining emotional sets, would be preconscious. As Rothenberg says, during the creative process '...inspirations that occur at the beginning or along the way are... preconscious emotional conflicts' (Rothenberg, A., 1970, p. 176). However, nearer the 'moment of insight' much of the initially induced absolute anxiety has been reduced, so even a small absolute release in tension would be appraised as a large proportionate change in anxiety and even border on awareness. Hutchinson recognized this as part of the 'complicated experience of insight' that is 'a tenuous and fleeting intimation that insight is about to appear... [and]... is usually not far in advance of actual illumination' (Hutchinson, E.D., 1941, p. 36).

In a controlled problem-solving environment, changing to a different emotional set, partially induced by subjective associations to the controlled introduction of a new element, may be identified with monitored physiological changes in anxiety. This is one category of physiological experiments considered by Joseph Germana (Germana, J., 1968) which may be used in psychophysiological studies of intuition; namely, physiological measures are correlated with identifying activational peaking (AP) with a particular activity. Activational peaking in the intuitive process results in changes due to the response tendencies conditioned to the succession of combining emotional sets being inhibited or facilitated according to the proportions of conflicting response tendencies conditioned to the conglomerate sets. Germana gives interpretations of AP in agreement with this and also finds that AP is a consistent correlate of CR formation. In his master's thesis Germana found that GSRs were consistently larger for responses to stimuli than to the stimuli presentations and that only GSRs occurring to conditioned stimuli demonstrated activational peaking (Germana, J., 1964). Further considerations of AP during problem-solving and its relation to the study of intuition are discussed under emotional involvement, property 2, Section 3.1, discussing psychophysiological experiments on the perception/emotion interaction.

The subjective confidence associated with fluctuating anxiety during the intuitive process directs the combining of emotional sets whose response tendencies progressively proportionately reduce this anxiety. This proportionate reduction in anxiety is appraised by the subject and felt as subjective confidence that the direction of intuitive associations is correct. Appraisal of large proportionate decreases in anxiety becomes conscious and results in that emotional set which reduces tension to a maximally accepted anxiety level terminating the process. The subject's need to 'cognitively label' his felt confidence is satisfied by the conviction that the conscious cognitive responses to this terminating emotional set are correct. These cognitive and behavioural responses are the conscious intuitive products. The fluctuations in anxiety during the intuitive process can be monitored and associated with the changing of emotional sets by identifying them with other observable and reported behaviour changes, that is with response tendencies also conditioned to these same emotional sets.

Inhibition of Anxiety Under Threat as a Physiological Predictor of Confidence in an Intuitive Product

Threat conditions related to the intuitive product that initially would have caused anxiety, cannot cause anxiety when the subject can freely evoke an emotional set with conditioned response tendencies that will resolve this particular anxiety. Thus presence of anxiety after threat may be used to test whether the solution to a problem was found intuitively or otherwise.

Anxiety caused by threat related to the original problem would indicate the absence of response tendencies capable of resolving this anxiety. If no other source of confirmation were available to the subject it may be inferred from this anxiety that no intuitive solution has been found, i.e. insight has not occurred. Similarly a self-report of the subject's lack of confidence, in the face of no external verification, would indicate no intuitive solution, again insight has not occurred. 'Observable responses from which one might infer the strength of the anxiety reaction are of two basic types: physiological-behavioural responses and self-report responses' (Martin, B., 1961, p. 235). Thus investigations of intuition may use both these methods to assess absence of anxiety as an indicator that insight has occurred.

The subject's assessment of his anxiety during the intuitive process is preconscious. The fluctuations in anxiety are assessed by the feelings of accompanying emotional relief. As Rothenberg observes; in the creation of a poem: 'Although it is not immediately obvious, the true inspirations that occur during the creation of a poem are actually accompanied by a certain amount of anxiety. The sense of relief is so dramatic that anxiety is not apparent to the poet himself or to a possible observer (Rothenberg, A., 1970, p. 175). For this reason self-report of anxiety is not experimentally feasible. Physiological recording of anxiety is needed. However, self-report of the emotional relief in terms of self-assessed confidence is experimentally feasible.

The strength of this confidence following an insight solution will inhibit the anxiety that a threat related to the problem could induce. As Brady remarks about the emotional relief following insight: 'This strong positive emotional response is inhibitory to the anxiety aroused by the material being "worked through" ' (Brady, J.P., 1967, p. 309).

The assessment of absence of anxiety under problem-related threat and self-report of confidence in the subject's solution should advisedly be included in the design of physiological insight experiments and used as a consistency check that insight has occurred.

4.3   CONFIDENCE IN INTUITION

Confidence in intuitive products is derived from the reduction in anxiety brought about by combining emotional sets to give a concordant emotional set.

An emotional state may be discordant because at least one concurrent stimulus response is tending to evoke another emotional set whose responses conflict with those of the present emotional set. For example, if in a present situation a sitting posture has always been an appropriate response but on this occasion some different elements indicate a sitting posture is not suitable, then the inhibition of the sitting response by the conflicting tendencies to not sit causes anxiety, felt as lack of confidence in this situation. It is this tendency of some stimulus/response elements to evoke conflicting response tendencies that is the discord preventing the present emotional set from being the terminating set associated with the intuitive product.

The intuitive process of combining intermediate emotional sets which have elements with less conflicting response tendencies eventually reduces this anxiety and gives confidence. The emotional set terminating the intuitive process has an acceptable level of anxiety due to its elements having reduced the tendencies to evoke conflicting responses.

The tendency of some dissimilar elements to have conflicting responses may be reduced by the following methods of combination which change the relative conditioning of these tendencies within the emotional set.

(1) Instrumental learning: the dissimilar elements are conditioned to the present emotional set. This is not considered as an intuitive process as emotional sets are not combined in order to change the relative tendencies of the elements to evoke conflicting responses.

(2) Drifting by continuing combination to a different concordant emotional set: the responses evoked by the dissimilar elements do not conflict with the responses of this final conglomerate emotional set.

(3) Recentring: the responses to the emotional set with the dissimilar elements are so similar to those of another emotional set, and the physiological state so similar, that the two sets are 'centred' on one another, integrated, and considered as one set. The conditioning of the common responses is dramatically increased compared to that of the dissimilar elements.

(4) Generalization: (Embedding) the hierarchy of the emotional set is changed by including similar concordant emotional sets. The relative tendency of the different elements to evoke conflicting responses within the enlarged emotional set is thus reduced.

The intuitive products and many other observations of the results of mental behaviour may be explained by these four methods of changing the relative tendencies of some elements to evoke conflicting responses within the present emotional set.

Arieti agrees that the obstruction of these responses gives rise to tension. He defines tension as '. . . tension — a feeling of discomfort caused by different situations, like . . . obstructed physiological or instinctual response' (Arieti, S., 1970, p. 136). He says the reduction in tension requires presymbolic and, in some cases, symbolic cognitive activity (p. 137). Both these types of cognitive activity are associated with the intuitive process.

Subjective Confidence Accompanying the Intuitive Phase of Creativity

The reduction in anxiety accompanying the intuitive phase of creativity gives self-confidence and satisfaction to the creator.

The combining of emotional sets carries along both the affective elements of frustration and the cognitive elements of systems of ideas in the changing present emotional set. 'Its process [intuitive process] is psychologically obscure; but what we know of it leads us to think of insights — intuitions — not as single ideas arriving along in consciousness, but rather as we have seen, tied to whole systems of ideas, "complexes" that is, generated by the frustrations of the problem situations' (Hutchinson, E.D., 1941, p. 36). In the intuitive phase of the creative process emotional sets are combined whose responses are most likely to reduce these frustrations and tensions: '. . . in cases of genuine creative work one is usually dealing with the psychology of temporary frustration, he may expect that periods of illumination will be fostered best by those activities which relieve such conditions of tension' (Hutchinson, E.D., 1941, p. 32).

Recentring, the combining of similar emotional sets from different chains, i.e. with low transition probability, gives the greatest rate of anxiety reduction of the four methods. It is the *Eureka Experience,* the release of anxiety, enjoyment, tension, and energy on combining emotional sets. Hutchinson also describes this 'energy released by the new integration at the moment of insight' (p. 39). This feeling of enjoyment accompanying creativity was used by Torrance to measure creative thinking.

He used a ten-point, self-rating scale of feelings of stimulation and enjoyment (Torrance, E.P., 1973). In his PhD thesis Rossman found, from an extensive survey of the creativity literature, seven attributes representative of creativity among which he included this 'Lack of anxiety' (Rossman, B.B., 1970). This lack of anxiety gives the creator confidence in his creative judgment. As this confidence is based on body reference it is initially little affected by the opinions of others. The creative type tends to stick with his original opinions. Some creative social scientists have been known to devote their life's work to supporting, with emotional fervour, their original insights that in the face of new analytic evidence are no longer tenable. Barron noticed this independence of group judgment and associated emotional reaction in the creative type. In experiments on the relation between creativity and independence of group judgment he found 25 per cent of his subjects clung to their own opinions. These he called 'independents' and the others he called 'yielders'. The 'independents' showed more of the attributes of creativity than the 'yielders', including a high degree of emotional reactivity (Barron, F., 1963a, Chapter 14).

The intuitive phase of creativity may include many intuitive products, e.g. recognition, acceptance, judgments, memories, associations, analogies, recentring, learning, etc. Only the subjective certainty during the intuitive phase of creativity is discussed in this section. Other intuitive products associated with creativity (property 7), are discussed in Section 7.3.

Under emotional involvement, property 2 in Section 3.2, two methods of intuitive judgment and their dependence upon body reference are discussed. Two sets of elements, whose similarity is to be judged, tend to evoke conflicting responses. The first method of intuitive judgment is the assessment of the anxiety due to these conflicting responses, as the judgment of their dissimilarity. Surrealist images can evoke this anxiety as elements within the images induce conflicting responses, e.g. Dali's 'Soft Watches' or 'Flat Iron with Protruding Nails', etc. In the second method the confidence and satisfaction obtained in resolving this anxiety have used as indicators of the degree of synthesis achieved.

Arnold uses the words 'liking or disliking' rather than anxiety 'reduction' or 'confidence' as a measure of intuitive judgments, but this dependence on body reference is still asserted. 'When we see or hear something or experience it in another modality, we intuitively appraise it as good or bad (guided by affective memory) and this appraisal is experienced as liking or dislike' (Arnold, M.B., 1970, p. 179). Stocks also agrees to the affective appraisal in intuitive judgment. 'Judgments possessing some such [intuitive] character may be found in very close relation to sensation' (Stocks, J.L., 1939, p. 11). However, Guiora et al. specifically refer to the affective appraisal in intuitive judgments as one of anxiety reduction. 'The areas of intuitive judgment-making will be selected in accordance with the principle of utility, which is nothing but anxiety reduction' (Guiora, A.S. *et al.,* 1965, p. 119).

It is through his empathic ability that the subject is able to allow the elements, whose similarity is to be judged, to evoke a subjectively appropriate emotional state with its discordant cognitive and affective response tendencies whose resolution is felt as confidence (see property 12, empathy, Section 6.3). 'Probably these [intuitive] judgments carry their sense of immediacy and conviction because of empathic components, i.e. kinaesthetic and affective responses in the judge' (Taft, R., 1960).

The confidence felt as reduction in anxiety is brought about by changing the relative tendency of elements to evoke conflicting responses. Reducing this relative tendency can be achieved by:

(1) further conditoning: instrumental learning;
(2) including more concordant response tendencies into the emotional set: generalization; (embedding)
(3) drifting by combining with increasingly different emotional sets to another emotional set whose responses were discordant with the emotional set initially evoked;
(4) dramatically increasing the conditioning of the non-discordant responses by recentring.

These methods are presented in order of their ability to reduce conflicting response tendencies, recentring being the most efficient in rate of decrease of anxiety with time. Combinations of these methods may be used in the intuitive phase of creativity. Intuitive judgment of the similarity of two groups of elements is assessed by the anxiety induced by their conflicting response tendencies or by the degree of confidence when this anxiety is resolved. In either case the anxiety or confidence is dependent on the empathic abilty of the subject to allow the groups of elements, whose similarity is being judged, to evoke a subjectively appropriate emotional state whose conflicting response tendencies are appraised as this anxiety, or whose resolution is appraised as this confidence.

Effects of Confidence and Anxiety Reduction on the Intuitive Process

One of the effects of the reduction of tension in the intuitive process is to increase the conditioning of some responses to emotional sets. The alterations in relative response tendencies also result in changes in the relative probability of different emotional sets being combined, i.e. changes in their transition probability. Another effect is that the intuitive type learns to evoke goal-related anxiety whose reduction is the intrinsic motivation for reaching the goal. Successful experience with the intuitive process gives continued confidence in its use.

Confidence Reinforcing Choice of the Intuitive Mode for Problem-Solving

The confidence associated with successful use of the intuitive process reinforces the selection of the intuitive process as a future problem-solving mode. Bruner and Clinchy noted that this confidence in the subjects' ability to solve problems was a feature of being an intuitive thinker (Bruner, J. and Clinchy, B., 1966, p. 73). Just as confidence acts as the reward reinforcing the selection of the intuitive process, unresolved anxiety associated with its unsuccessful use would inhibit its choice as a future problem-solving mode. The anticipation of satisfaction, etc., as a reward, will be reduced by maintained anxiety experienced in the unsuccessful use of the intuitive process: '...anticipatory reward extinguishes as a function of experience with non-reward' (Ryan, T.J. and Watson, P., 1968). Similarly drive '...is related to the magnitude of the anticipatory reward' (Strongman, K.T., 1973, p. 103).

A case history of success reinforces choice of the intuitive mode, which in any case becomes mandatory as evidence becomes too complex or insufficient for the analytic mode (see property 4, contrast with abstract reasoning, logical or analytial thought, Section 2.1). As Bruner and Clinchy say '...intuition ...is based upon a confidence in one's ability to operate with insufficient data' (Bruner, J. and Clinchy, B., 1966, p. 71).

This fact has been used by Malcolm Westcott to design an experiment to measure 'intuitive leaps'. He uses the fact that confidence in their choice of the intuitive mode for problem-solving would tend to make intuitive types take intuitive leaps to solutions on the basis of data that would be insufficient for use in the analytic mode. Westcott is one of the foremost modern writers on intuition but I consider his work to be unrepresentative of the consensus meaning of the word 'intuition'. Indeed his view of intuition is so limited as to be misleading except when applied to his own work. Westcott's work on intuition in problem-solving is based on a definition of Hathaway's of intuition as used in psychoanalysis. The situations for which these writers use the same term are hardly commensurate. Further, he considers that if the result of the intuitive leap is not accurate then the intuitive process has not been used. This ignores property 9, that intuitions need not be correct. More importantly his experiments designed on the confidence of subjects to take intuitive leaps are tested on items similar to: complete the following pair 16: given '4:2, 9:3, 25:5' or complete 'ACEGI '. The subject uncovers successive clues of this type until he considers he has enough information to make an 'intuitive leap'. Westcott measures the intuitive leap by the number of clues uncovered for correct solutions (Westcott, M.R., 1961). A criticism is that these items do not require the use of intuition (having no affective component, etc., also see criticisms elsewhere, e.g. Fig. 8.1/1), and the subject's willingness to give the answer depends on his successful experience with similar IQ-type items. The items should be emotionally involving, novel with affective components and answers should force cross-modal transfer of information. Then they would more probably require intuitive processing.

Conditioning Effect of Confidence on Emotional Sets

The effect of reduction in tension on emotional sets is here interpreted in the terms of Hullian Theory as drive and avoidance learning. The reduction in tension conditions contiguity responses to the emotional set and reinforces the responses that successfully reduced the anxiety.

The term 'set' is used here as it corresponds to the state elicited by a conditioned stimulus which Mowrer designated by the term 'set' (Mowrer, O.H., 1950). Miller thought of emotion in general under the following three headings which show the properties of emotion relevant to the concept of conditioning in the emotional set and hence its name 'emotional set':

(1) an unconditioned reflex, mainly an ANS reaction which can be brought under stimulus control;
(2) a discriminative stimulus; and
(3) a drive: new responses can be learnt by the reduction of tension. (Miller, N.E., 1951)

In this investigation the stimuli eliciting the anxiety are considered distinct from the responses that are associated with the reduction in tension in the intuitive process and which are conditioned (learnt) or further conditioned to the emotional set. 'It is sometimes convenient to consider as conceptually distinct stimuli (external or internal) which elicit the anxiety response and those responses which have been learned because they reduce or avoid the anxiety response' (Martin, B., 1961, p. 235). Mowrer, O.H. (1950) postulated a learning process to account for the learning of responses that are instrumental in reducing these anxieties.

If the responses are not available to reduce the anxiety, then frustration will result. Brown and Farber use the term 'frustration' in a technical sense — its properties being mainly to increase drive and arouse internal 'emotional stimuli' (Brown, J.J. and Farber, I.E., 1951). Maier says the state of frustration is characterized by autonomic feedback, feelings will dominate consciousness: '...as a result, perceptions and thoughts will have subjective rather than objective reference. The frustrated person, therefore, must be unusually aware of a mass of feelings or sensations of internal origin. When these sensations are excessive, they would occupy his attention and consequently make him less aware of the external world as well as insensitive to the feelings of other persons' (Maier, N.R.F., 1956, p. 384). These behaviours are facilitative to the intuitive process in overcoming frustration. These processes affect the subject by increasing the variability of his physiological state, thus increasing the probability of combining another emotional set which has suitable tension-reducing responses.

If the subject continues to associate the same emotional states from a small group of similar emotional states, then functional fixedness occurs, indicated by repetitive behaviour and elaboration, rather than original and flexible behaviour as in the intuitive phase of creativity. Continuance of this frustration can cause 'abnormal fixation' (Maier, N.R.F., 1956, pp. 371 ff). This is not a 'habit' that may be easily reconditioned but a 'behaviour' that may not be changed after an amount of trials far in excess of those needed to change a similar habitual behaviour. Maintained anxiety, like punishment, '...may serve either as a negative incentive or as a frustrating agent, depending on its intensity' (p. 373). Maier summarizes that '...punishment and experience of failure are associated with situations producing high rates of fixation' (p. 375). It has been shown in this investigation that these properties mitigate against the intuitive process. The partial reinforcement afforded by some fortunate combinations of emotional sets, which partly reduce the tension but then end in frustration, could be more inhibiting than an unsolvable problem for which the intuitive process was not initiated as being an inappropriate process. An unsolved problem on which no intuition attempt is made, is less inhibiting than partial intuitive success followed by failure of the intuitive process. Wilcoxon, H.C. (1952) has shown that such partial reinforcement causes fixation more than insoluble problems. Further, if the initial anxiety is too great then the regressive generalizing behaviour state necessary for the intuitive process will differentiate into distinctive arousal states such as anger, hunger, sex or other 'motivational states' (Martin, B., 1961, pp. 234/235). It is shown elsewhere (Section 3.1 on how perception of ego-threatening environments inhibits the intuitive process), how these high motivation states inhibit the intuitive process. Fromm-Reichmann studied intuitive processes in psychoanalysis and came to the same conclusions that mild anxiety stimulates the intuitive process whereas severe anxiety inhibits it. 'Severe anxiety in the analyst and his defenses against it, constitute a serious source of interference [in the intuitive process], mild anxiety a potential source of stimulation of the successful operation of the analyst's intuitive processes' (Fromm-Reichmann, F., 1955).

Anxiety and its Reduction as Learned Intrinsic Motivation

In this section it is proposed that, because of the satisfaction derived from the intuitive process, the subject in an 'end/means' situation learns to evoke anxiety whose resolution, by use of the intuitive process, acts as intrinsic motivation in a problem situation. This evoked, goal-directed anxiety is commonly called 'curiosity'.

It is recognized that the intuitive process is motivated by an internal need. 'In the writer's understanding, intuitive behaviour is prompted by an internal need' (Guiora, A.S. *et al.*, 1965, p. 119). They also suggest that research should centre around 'need-systems correlating with areas of intuition (p. 120). The 'highly learnable' nature of anxiety is consistent with this proposal. 'Anxiety also possesses the property of being highly learnable: that is, the hypothetical response becomes readily conditioned to stimuli that do not innately elicit the response' (Martin, B., 1961, p. 235). Martin also says that '...clinicians frequently infer anxiety on the basis of these "defenses" against anxiety as much as from direct expression of the anxiety itself' (p. 235). Projection, basic to the intuitive process (Section 3.2 and elsewhere) is considered by classical psychoanalysts to have a defensive function (Freud, S., 1916). If, as proposed, the subject learns to use the intuitive process as a 'defense' against this self-induced anxiety so as to be rewarded by the satisfaction of the intuitive product, then this gives a basis for training intuition.

Schachtel terms the motor associations conditioned to the emotional set as a 'neuromuscular set'. He also relates it to unconscious goal-setting and to two other aspects of intuition, *viz.* physiognomic perception and kinaesthesis.

If a person has the tendency to react with a certain, typical attitude or striving to the world around him or to his own drives, then this attitude will also find expression in a neuromuscular set which could be described as the physical side of the attitude, a readiness to perform such motor activity as will be suitable to realize the goal of the attitude or striving. This 'goal' of a person's general attitude or orientation is either not at all in awareness or, at least, not in focal and full awareness. It is not a goal in the same sense as is the purpose which a person consciously wants to reach by a specific, consciously planned and executed series of acts. The neuromuscular set which is the physical aspect of a habitual, lingering readiness to react in a certain way to the world and to oneself is at the basis of both the inadvertent, expressive movements and physiognomic expressions of people and their kinaesthetic responses. (Schachtel, E.G., 1950, p.77)

Confidence in the use of the intuitive process is learnt by its repeated successful use. Unsuccessful intuitive experience inhibits its use. The confidence conditions contiguity responses and tension-reducing responses to the emotional sets. The name 'emotinal set' is chosen because of the conditioning and other properties of emotion that are consistent with the concept of emotional sets. If no emotional set can be associated which has suitable anxiety-reducing responses then the resulting frustration would cause fixations and repetitive or elaborating behaviour. If anxiety is too high it would differentiate the general behavioural state into highly motivational states inhibitive to the intuitive process. It is proposed that high-intuitive types have learnt to evoke anxiety (curiosity) associated with some goal in order that the reduction in this anxiety can act as intrinsic motivation for achieving the set goal. This proposal has implications for training in intuition.

Personality Concomitants of Confidence in the Intuitive Process

The evidence of correlation between the attributes of intuition presented in this section is inferential support rather than deductive support for their common association with intuition. This is because there is no evidence that they are unique to intuition. Fig. 4.3/1 illustrates this logic. The relationships between

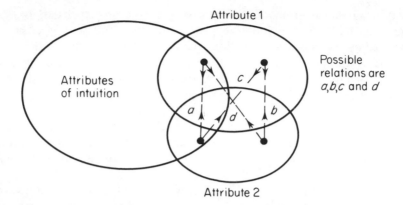

Fig. 4.3/1 Four possible types of relationships between two non-unique attributes of intuition

attributes of intuition presented in this section are assumed to be of type *a* in Fig. 4.3/1. This evidence of consistency supports the common association of the attributes with intuition.

Researchers have considered personality correlates of the concomitants of confidence in the intuitive process that we have previously discussed. They are the personality correlates of the intuitive type. This is indirect evidence further associating confidence with the intuitive process.

The confidence in the intuitive process is derived by reduction in the anxiety initially evoked. From what has been presented here one would expect high-intuitive types, like creative geniuses, to be capable of self-excitation of this anxiety. Cattell and Butcher, in agreement with this, found in their personality studies of the bibliographies of creative geniuses, e.g. Priestly, Darwin, Kepler, etc., that: 'High anxiety and excitability appear common' (Cattell, R.B. and Butcher, H.J., 1968).

High-intuitive types, because of their confidence in the intuitive process, are prepared to take risks by giving answers based on information insufficient for an analytic solution. In contrast, low-intuitive types lacking this confidence would be more cautious. Westcott, by defining low-intuitive types as high information demanders, got the following tautological results using the F1 and IE scales from the Vassar College Attitude Inventory and the Taylor scale (Westcott, M.R., 1961): that high information demanders, regardless of success, tended to show caution. A further connection between anxiety and risk-taking was found by Kogan and Wallach who showed that test anxiety correlates with risk-taking (Kogan, N. and Wallach, M., 1964).

Frustration in the intuitive process is due to the unavailability of emotional sets with suitable tension-reducing responses. Frustration is more likely to arise in scientific than in artistic creativity because of the restriction that the creative scientific product has to be consistent with the existing body of scientific knowledge. This limits the possible responses that could release tension. There is little restriction of this type on artistic creativity unless it is self-imposed. From this it is predicted that creative scientists tend to be more prone to frustration than creative artists. Confirming this prediction, the personality correlates of being anti-social and preferrings things to people were found to be characteristic of those prone to frustration (Maier, N.R.F., 1956, p. 384), which are the same personality correlates that distinguish the creative scientist from the creative artist (Roe, Anne, 1953; see also Section 3.1 on personality concomitants of emotional involvement in the intuitive process and elsewhere).

The emotional excitability of the intuitive type and the effect of threat on GSR have been separately noted as related to confidence in the intuitive process: see Sections 4.2 and 4.3.

The results of Learmonth, *et al.* bring these effects together in agreement. They monitored the GSR of twenty subjects on three types of stress: (1) whilst completing emotionally involving sentences, e.g. 'I hate my mother when. . .'; (2) during stressful interview about past feelings of great intensity, anxiety, fear, etc.; and (3) when a blank gun was fired and a mild electric shock was given. Afterwards the twenty subjects completed the Minnesota Multiphasic Personality Inventory (MMPI) and a Rorschach test scored for *M* and *C*, etc. All the scores were ranked for a Spearman's correlation analysis. From this analysis the authors conclude: 'The increase of fluctuation of palmar potential in response to stress is negatively correlated with a group of personality variables that have in common the element of expressivity' (Learmonth, C.J. *et al.,* 1959, p. 153).

The emotional energy and personal feelings which result in confidence have been previously mentioned, as has the influence on the intuitive process of hormones in the sympathetic nervous system (Section 4.2). Fox and his colleagues found an association between excretion of these hormones and the emotional behaviours of the intuitive type. They found significant differences between individuals in levels of their adrenocortical activity measured daily over a five-week period. They noted also the following personality differences associated with high and low autonomic activity: 'The more a person reacts emotionally, the higher his level of the 17-hydroxycorticosteriods. . . At one extreme, there are individuals with vivid personal feelings who experience a sense of emotional urgency and, at the other extreme, those who are relatively guarded and withdrawn' (Fox, H.M. *et al.,* 1961, p. 38).

It was shown (in Section 4.2) that one reason for the subjectivity of the certainty of correctness is that the evidence used in intuitive processing is often subliminal. Elsewhere in this chapter it has been shown that the intuitive type is confident in his behaviour, that his reliance on body reference requires affective openness, requires appraisal of these feelings, and that he also has physiological defences against anxiety. Eagle found that the personality correlates of subjects sensitive to subliminal stimulation are in agreement with those of the intuitive type among which are that the subject '. . . appears to be confident in his behaviour; he is more concerned with his own aggressive impulses than with being aggressed against from without; he shows cognitive and affective openness rather than constriction; he tends to use non-cognitive defenses — that is, defenses in which action rather than thought is prominent; . . .' (Eagle, M., 1962, p. 3).

The co-relation between such diverse attributes of confidence in the intuitive process supports the inference of their nature and role in the intuitive process.

Summary of Subjective Certainty of Correctness

The confidence that attends the intuitive product and guides the process is the result of proportionate reduction in the mild anxiety that initiates the process. This anxiety is reduced by various methods of combining emotional sets with their tension-reducing responses. The various methods and combinations of methods of combining emotional sets explain the degree of anxiety reduction accompanying the different emotional products from the Eureka experience to hypnogogic reverie.

The final proportionate reduction in anxiety is so marked by this confidence that the person's affective and cognitive responses present at that time are consciously labelled as the intuitive product. This confidence is based on feelings and incommunicable evidence and so is necessarily subjective though frequently an accurate predictor of correct insights or intuitions.

The changing anxiety can be monitored during the intuitive process by changes in GSR, heart rate, and respiration. These measures will also indicate the subject's lack of anxiety due to his confidence in his intuition, particularly in the face of a stress related to the original anxiety-evoking problem. The confidence measured physiologically and by self-report may be used in investigations to confirm the occurrence of insight.

Confidence acting as a reward for successful use of the intuitive process reinforces its choice as a problem-solving mode. It also indicates that intuitive types may learn to create goal-related anxiety, termed 'curiosity', whose satisfaction is the intrinsic motivation for reaching the goal. Maintained anxiety associated with unsuccessful use of the intuitive process has the opposite effect of discouraging its use as a problem-solving mode, as do external agents that reduce this confidence. If the initial anxiety is too high, or due to ego threat, the generalized behaving state facilitating intuition will differentiate into high motivational states that inhibit the intuitive process.

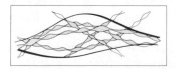

5

Global Knowledge
Property of Intuition

This chapter shows how the literature relating to the global knowledge property of intuition suggests further development of a simple model of intuitive thought processes consistent in its explanation of this property and the other properties of intuition. Further, the direction, duration, and feelings accompanying the intuitive process and the emergence of intuitions are explained through this model by identifying the key factor of increasingly redundant information.

By collating theories and experimental results from the literature relevant to the psychophysiological effects of increasingly redundant information during behavioural states corresponding to identified aspects of the intuitive process, *viz.* global perception of internal and external stimuli, internal organization of information and final intuition, it is possible to show how the simple model of intuitive thought processes gives a consistent interpretation to these varied works, explains intuitions and the intuitive process in the accepted concepts of previous research, gives novel interpretations of behaviours related to intuition and suggests connections between findings previously considered unrelated.

5.1 GLOBAL NATURE OF INTUITION

There are many references in the literature to the global nature of intuition; on wholeness of perception, completeness of ideas, involvement of associated feelings, and well-rounded experiences. Ann Lewis considers what she calls the tradition of studying intuition in a 'global or holistic' sense as articulated by Carl Jung and his predecessors. She says that intuition 'is a perception of the whole rather than the parts' (Lewis, Ann T.C., 1976). Suzanne Langer expounds Locke's view of intuition as a holistic perception (Locke, J., 1690): '...the perception of form, pattern, unity of form, wholesness, Gestalt' (Langer, Suzanne K., 1969). Clark, F.V. (1973) says Assagioli, R. (1965): 'Has

171

also considered intuition primarily as a cognitive function which apprehends reality directly as a whole' (p. 159). Jung, C.G. (1969) defines intuition as: 'A non-judgmental irrational mental activity through which an individual can perceive an internal or external event or object in its entirety...' (p. 263). Jung describes the intuitor as 'Forming global concepts, integrating experiences' (Bledsoe, J.L., 1976, p. 18). Stocks, J.L. (1939) refers to '...intuition in its characteristic function of making possible the keeping of the whole in mind' (p. 9). Pechstein, L.A. and Brown, F.D. (1939) give as a criterion of insight: 'Responses to the situation as a whole. The insight theory holds that the learner sees and responds from the beginning to the situation as a whole' (p. 40). Cooper, writing on empathy, a property of intuition, expounds the Gestalt notion of empathy as explicated by Köhler, W. (1947) which shows this global nature of intuition. 'What is involved is a direct and intuitive experiencing of the other person; the experience is most frequently not verbalized within the empathizer. The intuition seems to be a global undifferentiated, but internal perceptual experience' (Cooper, L., 1970, p. 171).

Intuition Integrates Perception, Emotional Involvement, and Experience

'An "intuition" may fairly be said to be based upon a felt awareness of, or for, a situation as a whole,' (Reid, L.A., 1976). The personal involvement is global in that it is experienced throughout the whole body: '...intuitively which is to feel through one's whole being with a total conviction' (Burden, Virginia, 1975, pp. 29/30). Clark, F.V. (1973) also states: 'The intuitive is likely to perceive and comprehend the whole at the expense of sensory detail'. The directness of perception will be shown here to be due to the interaction of the perception of internal, and the perception of external, stimuli in empathic projection.

In his book *Types of Intuition* Bahm notes the global nature of perception of information for the intuitive process and how its wholeness is used by the process to make intuitive judgments. 'Intuition involves apprehending something both directly and all-at-once... so, when one grasps directly and all-at-once both a whole and its parts, including apparent parts and missing parts, these missing parts are thereby intuited as missing' (Bahm, A.J., 1960, p. 5).

The process of intuition is not a linear step-by-step process, but a global non-linear process using information from global perception. 'Intuitive thinking characteristically does not advance in careful, well-planned steps. Indeed, it tends to involve manoeuvres based seemingly on an implicit perception of the total problem' (Bruner, J.S., 1960). The intuitive process integrates the information that one already has, the new associations between this information constituting new insights: '...shreds of information that earlier had had no meaning became prominent in light of new conclusions' (Clark, J., 1973, p. 215). Indeed, processes which depend on this integration for their meaning lose this meaning when attention is paid to their details rather than their global nature. 'Repeat a word several times, attending carefully to the motion of your tongue and lips, add to the sound you make, and soon the word will sound hollow and eventually lose its meaning. Motion studies tend to paralyse skill. The meticulous dismembering of a text, which can kill its appreciation...' (Polanyi, M., 1966, pp. 18/19).

In the intuitive process ideas come in a complete form speeded by the non-linear processing. Hutchinson quotes five creative workers whose first-hand descriptions of their insights illustrate these two aspects of the global nature of intuition; '...whole and at once... ideas come to me as a whole' etc. (Hutchinson, E.D., 1941, p. 38). The completeness of the final idea is an aspect of the global nature of intuition that is necessary for intuitive invention. It is necessary for the inventor to enable him to invent and to enable others to understand the 'inventing'. This is particularly true in mathematical invention where the global nature of the intuition gives guidance and purpose to the analytic methods of verification. Poincaré points out that the step-by-step dissectionist demonstrations of the logician or analyst do not give this necessary understanding and unity to their proofs. There are many methods of analysis available but:

> Who shall tell us which to choose? We need a faculty which makes us see the end from afar, and intuition is this faculty... This view of the aggregate is necessary for the inventor; it is equally necessary for whoever wishes really to comprehend the inventor. Can logic give it to us? No; the name mathematicians give it would suffice to prove this. In mathematics logic is called analysis and analysis means division, dissection (Poincaré, H., 1969, p. 210).

The verbal mode is linear and a less suitable mode for intuition which is non-linear and global. Baldwin suggests that the inability to verbalize the intuitive process may be due to 'vague and global ideas that are not codifiable' (Baldwin, A., 1966, p. 87). It is the global nature, particularly the affective components of intuition, that make it difficult or impossible to explain in the linear verbal mode; property 14, preverbal concept. The engrossing feelings associated with the overall pattern are taken by Bayles as a criteria of insight. 'Perhaps insight should be defined as a sense of, or feeling for, pattern' (Bayles, E.E., 1952, p. 67). He gives examples among which is that of a study of a violin passage with insight, where he says it is necessary to '...imagine the feel of the passage as a whole... the feel for pattern' (pp. 67/68).

From fifty-six written accounts of subjects' experiences of intuition Roni Summers frequently found this theme: 'A very strong intensity to the experience which was felt overall or totally throughout one's body' (Summers, Roni, 1976). This global feeling was used to define operationally the intuitive mode of thought in experiments by Baumgardner whose judges categorized subjects' reasons for career choices as intuitive versus analytic: 'Intuitive thinking was defined by global feelings and judgments... Emotional involvement and global feelings are thus taken as definitive for this mode of thought' (Baumgardner, S.R., 1973, p. 16).

These global feelings are related to past and comprehensive experience in the subject field. 'Such inspirations, it is well recognized, rarely come unless an individual has immersed himself in a subject. He must have a rich background of knowledge and experience in it' (Sinnott, E.W., 1959, p. 24). Tom Comella also says: 'Preoccupation, conscious or unconscious is a prerequisite for insight' (Comella, T., 1971, p. 176). This often obsessive and dedicated immersion in the subject over some time conditions many feelings to ideas which become associated and integrated during the intuitive process into a global inclusion resulting in the intuition: 'Hunches, global grasps, and other forms of intuition occur as a result of the careful analysis of problems, as a reward for patient and often obsessive preoccupation with them' (Bunge, M., 1962, p. 117).

The global knowledge property of intuition is evident from perception in the intuitive mode which takes the whole external stimulus field combined with diverse, pervasive internal stimuli, affective and cognitive bonds conditioned from comprehensive experience, which are integrated by the speedy non-linear process into a complete idea. The global knowledge property of intuition results from this whole perception, whole body emotional involvement (property 2), comprehensive experience (property 5), integrating process and completeness of the final idea. 'The intuitive process differs from other thinking in that it erupts into consciousness in a ready to use form' (Szalita-Pemow, A.B., 1955, p. 317).

Global Information

Multimodal Physiognomy

The intuitive process does not use a succession of separate parts of the total information as an analytic process would. It processes simultaneously an apperceptive mass of information as defined by its physiognomy. (See the detailed discussion of physiognomy in Section 2.2). This physiognomy is later formalized in this book as an emotional set evoked by external stimuli.

Assagioli uses the global nature of intuition to define it. 'It [intuition] is a synthetic function in the sense that it apprehends the totality of a given situation or psychological reality. It does not work from the part to the whole — as the analytical mind does — but apprehends a totality directly in its living existence' (Assagioli, R., 1971). The interactive modification of perception of external stimuli by internal stimuli during the perceptual part of the intuitive process gives the physiognomy of the information used in the integrating part of the intuitive process. The affective and cognitive associations which are the internal stimuli interact with the perceptions of external stimuli, giving subjective relative importance to different external stimuli in defining the physiognomy. Information-impoverished external stimuli have a physiognomy in intuitive perception but in such a case the majority of the information in the physiognomy will be constituted from internal stimuli. Information from the perception of additional external stimuli will change this balance according to the subjective importance of this information, i.e. the strength, number, and redundancy of its associations. The external stimuli that duplicate associations (redundancy) contribute most to the physiognomy — see the interpretation of Dinero's research in this section under 'Redundancy of intuitive global information'.

The physiognomy changes to incorporate additional external information. So the total global information may be included in the physiognomy. Thus the physiognomy avoids the degradation of rapidly presented analytical information.

Information contributing to the physiognomy comes from perception through all senses. Joan Bissel *et al.* list these sensory modalities, based on the five senses for perceiving the world (Bissell, Joan *et al.*, 1971, p. 131). In the intuitive mode modalities are preferred that are capable of carrying much simultaneous information, e.g. visual or kinaesthetic versus verbal. An example of the verbal mode is remembering through words or spoken thought, (Bartlett, F.C., 1932) or '...thinking in terms of words, as though you are talking to yourself. You don't actually say the words but you hear them in your mind as though they were being said' (Roe, Anne, 1952, p. 145).

George Krebs studied the utilization of verbal versus non-verbal communication and hypothesized that an intuitive mode of perception is related to greater responsiveness to non-verbal communication. He was unable to support this hypothesis (Krebs, G.M., 1975). Similarly, Davitz tried to identify subjects sensitive to non-verbal cues in terms of a battery of thirty-three personality measures (MMPI, Allport-Vernon-Lindsey Study of Values) but failed to find such a relationship. Such a personality profile would have corresponded to that of the intuitive type (Davitz, J.R., 1964). Mehrabian and Ferris, studying the relative importance of verbal content versus facial expression in communication of anxiety, proposed a model for summarizing communicational significance of such multichannelled communication. Their model takes into account both the separate components of a communication and gives independent weights to the components. On the basis of the data it was determined that the weight assigned to the content component of the equation was the smallest for limited information. For example, whereas the designated coefficient for the verbal component was 0·07, the coefficient of the facial component was 0·55 (Mehrabian, A. and Ferris, S. R., 1967). This result shows that the physiognomic component is more prominent where there is little information.

Experimenters who endeavour to show that intuitive types are more sensitive to non-verbal cues generally get non-significant or even paradoxical results possibly because the instruments they use are not developed in accordance with a consistent theory of intuitive thought processes, as is presented in this book. The most common fault is to use accuracy measures of intuition and other unsuitable tests. The disappointing results of Krebs, G.M., 1975, Bodnar, W.A., 1975, Lewis, Ann T.C., 1976, Aldenbrand, Martha L., 1974, and many others can be explained in this way. Krebs used the Myers-Briggs Type Indicator (MBTI) as did Bodnar; Ann Lewis also used the MBTI and she also used Westcott's Intuitive Problem Solving Scale (WIPSS) but in explaining her disappointing results she realized that Westcott's scale does not indicate Jungian-type intuition.

A similar criticism of the MBTI explains the lack of confirmation of the hypotheses proposed by the above users including Martha Aldenbrand, who also uses this criticism of Westcott's scale to explain her disappointing results. She gave a similar criticism of the MBTI to explain the lack of conformation of her hypotheses. She recognized this mistake as a common error in this field of research and admits that she also considered the obtained products of these tests whilst giving little attention to the underlying processes. Krebs, who failed to confirm his hypothesis '. . . that an intuitive perceptual preference is related to greater responsiveness to non-verbal communication cues,' (p. 44) using intuitive types being defined by the MBTI, similarly concludes '. . . the hypothesis involving perceptual preference was less clearly grounded on prior research and was, therefore, more speculative. . . it is most parsimonious to assume that the dimension tapped by the sensory-intuition scale (MBTI) is unrelated to the differential utilization of non-verbal communication cues'. He notes his selected questions from MBTI on pages 64 to 67. (His publishing university, Missouri, offer the helpful facility of duplicating his video recordings if researchers send blank tapes.)

The 'direct' experiencing and 'self-knowledge' descriptions of intuitive perception are here attributed to the multichannel perceptions contributing the information to the intuitive process. Bissell et al. (1971) discuss the cross-modal transposition of this information (pp. 133, 145). Suzuki, D.T. (1957, p. 85) uses the global self-knowledge characteristic to define intuition and to contrast it with reason. He says intuition 'is the self-knowledge of the whole' in contrast to reason '. . . which busies itself with parts'; intuition 'never loses its unitive totality' (p. 95).

The idea that information perceived physiognomically may be coded in terms of multimodal connotations for intuitive processing combines ideas from the works of Shiffrin, R.M., 1970, Norman, D.A. and Rumelhart, D.E., 1970, and Bower, G.H., 1967. These researchers have produced models of human memory. Shiffrin considers organization effects of perception of stimuli into internal 'images', which corresponds to emotional sets in this book. Norman and Rumelhart say that memory may be coded by feelings: 'The memory of an item often is related to its psychological encoding rather than to its actual physical form' (pp. 19/20). Bower's multicomponent model of memory suggests the multimodal coding of the perception of stimuli.

Redundancy of Intuitive Global Information

Redundancy may be considered as repeated information. Miller, G.A. (1964) defines redundancy as shared information (pp. 179ff). For example, as explained more fully in Section 9.1, there is no redundancy in a nonsense trigram as the three letters chosen at random are independent, the information in each letter being $\log_2 26 = 4 \cdot 7$ BITS. However, the spelling structure of English limits the choice of following letters in permissable words, e.g. 'Q' is always followed by 'U', so the letters in English are not independent but the average information of a letter in written English is approximately $1 \cdot 4$ BITS. This is only about a quarter of the information that the alphabet allows. The other three-quarters is shared redundant information which may be used as a check. Hence it is possible to recognize probable spelling mistakes in words that one does not know. This example is analogous to how redundancy may be used in intuitive recognition. As one's judgment about the misspelling may be wrong so may one's intuitions based on redundancy be wrong. (See property 9, correctness of intuition, Section 8.1) Further, the context of written English reduces the choice of subsequent letters, e.g. one hundred letters in context reduces the choice of the next letter on average to one in three, further increasing redundancy (Miller, G. A., 1964, p. 118). Intuitive information is also context-bound which gives it high redundancy. In the intuitive mode perception organizes stimuli by context and information is coded by its context; it is also processed by its context in such a way as to increase its redundancy. The increase in redundancy is the one function common to each part of the intuitive process.

The work of Dinero, T.E. (1970) shows that physiognomy, as used in the perception stage of the intuitive process, is highly redundant. The cross-modal transfer of duplicate information in multimodal perception would add to the redundancy of a physiognomy. Dinero was working on a model for word meaning. He produced a 'physiognomic model' where 'meaning' is defined as the process that transfers locations of words in denotive space to locations in connotive space. He refers to an 'organismic state' of internal response patterns associated with words. This is similar to that which I call an emotional set (see Section 3.2). He indicates the difference between connotative and denotive as being the affective component which contributes to the connotative meaning, whereas the sensory-motor component contributes to the denotive meaning. 'If the organismic state were deprived of its affective components, the remaining response patterns would entirely consist of sensory-motor constituents. Were these alone then used for encoding, the overt response would be entirely denotive' (p. 59). Dinero completes his research by suggesting how a subject evaluates a word on Osgood's Semantic Differential Scale (see Fig. 3.2/1). 'Osgood's mediating process is the generation of internal physiognomic substates from the concept network' (p. 65). Dinero suggests a weighting process which may be interpreted as emphasizing the redundancy of the physiognomy at the expense of the non-redundancy information, describing the change in the physiognomy to incorporate new information: '...points of agreement are mutually supportive and points of dissonance are cancelled out, there still remains some on-going affective state that is translated to overt scaling behaviour' (p. 67).

The physiognomy of constant external stimulus elements may be different on each occasion they are perceived, because of the intervening change in the internal state that interacts with the perception of external stimuli to produce the physiognomy. Perception of the same situation will vary with one's mood, with 'which side of the bed you get out'. So the encoding of even the same stimuli is variable. This variability of the encoding further increases the redundancy of the coded information. The same stimulus may be conditioned to different affective/cognitive contexts (emotional sets). This increase in redundancy due to variability of encoding explains how different experiences with the same stimuli facilitate insight, i.e. seeing the same thing from different points of view facilitates insightful understanding. Viesti, C. R. Jr. (1971), who regards insight as the processing of information rather than its perception (p. 181), concludes his paper on insight learning in agreement with this explanation that to facilitate an early appearance of insight one should increase the subject's experience with similar kinds of tasks (p. 182). Thus the effect of experience is to increase redundancy due to variability of encoding. This supports my criticism of practical insight experiments where the experience of the subjects with similar apparatus is not taken into account by the experimenter.

The intuitive process is directed towards increasing redundancy. Four methods of manipulating emotional sets which increase redundancy are discussed in Section 5.4, the most dramatic being recentring or the Eureka experience, where two contexts are considered identical so their shared information is redundant. The concordance of the elements of an emotional set can be measured by their redundancy. The increase in redundancy during the intuitive process is proportional to the reduction in the induced anxiety. A marked increase in redundancy accompanies the marked decrease in anxiety that makes one aware of the present emotional set whose cognitions are taken as the public, conscious intuition, the thoughts we try to communicate.

Common to all the psychophysiological processes during intuition is the increase in redundancy of the contextual information. Global knowledge is characterized by its redundancy. Physiognomic perception is characterized by its redundancy. Variability of encoding these perceptions increases redundancy. The manipulation of emotional sets (the contextual information) is directed by the tendency to increase redundancy. The final conscious intuition is marked by a present emotional set with acceptable redundancy. Hence 'intuition' may be defined as psychophysiological processes that increase the redundancy of contextual information. These processes are discussed in Section 5.4.

*Controlled Global Information used in Experiments to Encourage
Intuitive Thinking*

In experiments on intuition where the subjects are required to process
information in the intuitive mode, the global characteristics of intuitive
information are used as instructions to elicit intuitive thinking: complex
information or instructions are given, information is given too quickly for
analytic processing, information is given in non-verbal modes (kinaesthetic,
tactile, commonly visual), or insufficient information is given (sometimes
utilizing subliminal or peripheral cues).

Most commonly, non-linear information is given in visual form. Peters,
Joan T. *et al.* (1974) explored the effect of visual versus written information on
the tendency to use 'intuitive versus analytic thinking'. They asked fifteen
subjects to find the resultant of two forces under three methods of
presentation: (i) intuitive condition where two forces are given as points on a
plain sheet and *S* guesses the vertex of the parallelogram giving the resultant;
(ii) the forces are given as co-ordinates only; and (iii) the same presentation as
the intuitive condition but including a grid overlay. The authors say that the
results indicate that 'if an individual is reatricted to perceptual cues (condition i)
an intuitive mode is likely to result' (p. 130). Benjafield, J. (1969) offered both
visual and written information under two conditions, *viz.* a difficult or simple
instruction. Under difficult instruction the subjects relied significantly more
on visual information. Benjafield asked forty-eight subjects to compare the
total lengths of *PAEF* and *PCEF* in Fig. 5.1/1 where *P* is the unmarked centre
of *AC*. This amounts to comparing *AE* with *CE*. He was interested in knowing
how the strength of the illusion and the ease of deduction might influence the
subject's method of comparison, i.e. logical deduction (analytic) depending on
written cues or a perceptual comparison (empirical) depending on visual cues.
He used a strong and weak illusion making the angle *ADF* 50° and 85°. He
used two types of logic data, (i) angle *CAE* = angle *ACE* versus (ii) angle *CAE*
= angle *CEF*; the second requiring more analytic steps for deduction. He used
a 2 × 2 contingency table with six males and six females per cell. Subjects were
encouraged to 'think aloud' so that their type of method, analytic or

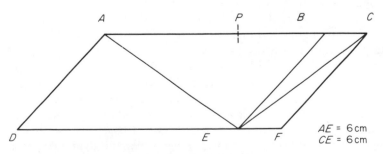

Fig. 5.1/1 Sander parallelogram

perceptual, could be decided from the protocols. Benjafield concludes that when simple instructions are given subjects tend to use them but are influenced by the strong perceptual effects, which sometimes make their logic go wrong (p. 286).

The tendency to use the intuitive mode in complex situations was also noted by Neisser, U. (1963b); 'Mental processes of this kind [intuitive] seem to be common wherever there are situations too complex for ready logical analysis' (p. 308).

Instructions encouraging a low-anxiety environment allow more peripheral cues to be used, internal as well as external, which supports the redundancy of the present information being processed. Instructions allowing tolerance of wrong answers also support inferential answers based on redundancy, like the judgment of misspelling example under 'Redundancy' in this section. Harold Kaplan used these types of instructions to create 'active' versus 'relaxed' attitudes whilst exploring the effect of anxiety on the choice of the intuitive mode in problem-solving. Kaplan arranged two groups of subjects chosen as high and low scorers on the Myers-Brigg Type Indicator (fifty-minute test in three parts). These he referred to as subjects who prefer intuitive strategies and subjects who prefer logical strategies in problem-solving (pp. 22/23). Subjects were assigned to one of three types of experimental condition: (i) active, (ii) relaxed and (iii) controlled. Instruction tapes were used to give the level of arousal defined as active by asking for rapid answers or were used to define relaxed condition (ii) and to work logically or intuitively, e.g. 'relax and attend to inner cues, ideas and associations' (p. 23). The 'relaxed' instructions included 'don't be afraid to go on a hunch. Just flow with your hunches and inner feelings' (p. 45). Therefore implying guessing wrong answers would be tolerated. In condition (i) one would expect subjects to take more cues to ensure accuracy and avoid censure. This may explain the result that the anxious group took more cues on the Westcott Intuitive Problem Solving Scale. Kaplan used a 2×3 analysis variance and a t-test on subjects' responses to the Manifest Anxiety Scale which showed that the instructions were effective in causing anxiety (Kaplan, H.A., 1973).

When little information from an external source is available for necessary processing, particularly when the information is incomplete for an analysis, then the subject' internal redundancy-rich subjective associations contribute more to the physiognomy than does the information from the external source. During the intuitive process more internal associations are included to be further integrated by combining emotional sets further increasing redundancy. This further facilitates processing in the intuitive mode. The adding of one's own redundancy-rich associations to the meagre available information during the perception and processing of the information explains Hathaway's definition of clinical intuition on which Westcott bases his Intuitive Problem Solving Scale. 'Intuition is involved either when the available information seems inadequate to produce the inferences drawn by the recipient or when the integrative powers of the recipient seem to exceed ordinary rational analysis' (Hathaway, S.R., 1955, p. 233).

Bruner points out that both in science and in life there are instances when we must act with incomplete knowledge. He says that the plausibility of our guesses may well depend on how intuitive we are (Bruner, J.S., 1963). As the experimental results of Mehrabian, A. and Ferris, S.R. (1967) have shown, with limited information physiognomic cues take preference over verbal content. In these cases of little external information the physiognomy contains much internal information. Consequently insight experiments designed for the investigation of intuition should not use only a verbal input of information.

Wagennar, W.A. and Sabato, S.D. (1975) required subjects to extrapolate the terms of an exponential series. The information available to the subjects was sufficient for an analytic solution. However, to encourage subjects to 'intuitively extrapolate' the experimenters gave little time for the estimates (one minute only) and discouraged use of analysis. 'In the instruction, it was stressed that the subject should give his best intuitive estimate; application of strict arithmetic rules was not encouraged' (p. 416). Subjects always underestimated even after a training lecture. Farmer, C. (1961) also used the device of limiting time to evoke intuitive processing. Twenty-two subjects had to select correct conclusions to forty-eight syllogisms from a presented list. Farmer defines a fifteen-second timed test as 'intuitive' and an untimed test as a 'power' test. In subsequent interviews all subjects agreed that fifteen seconds was insufficient for an analytic approach. Subjects reported finding the intuitive task frustrating and anxiety-provoking. This is consistent with assuming that intuition is used as a defence against self-induced, task-associated anxiety.

The intuitive mode of thought, even when information is available for an analytic solution, is the mode of thought that is most naturally chosen, unless an analysis is specified either directly or by conditions inhibiting intuition. 'Faced with any novel, complex problem we all tend to fall back on intuitive modes of thought' (Clinchy, Blythe, 1975, p. 49). Of the analytic and intuitive modes of thought the intuitive mode is the default mode.

Information is derived from perception of the external stimuli interacting with the perception of internal stimuli to give the physiognomy which is the cognitive and affective, predominately non-verbal information being processed at any time by the intuitive process. This information is redundancy-rich and the intuitive process, by integrating subjectively associated information, increases this redundancy. The natural limit of our memory capacity and analytic processing capacity causes degradation to realistic quantities of non-redundant analytic information. Holding information in the form of its physiognomy with much redundancy enables more information, global information, to be available for the intuitive process. This quantity of information is not available for processing in the analytic mode.

An example which illustrates how holding information in the form of its physiognomy enables more information to be available for intuitive thought is given by Everitt, B. (1978, pp. 87 ff). He shows how multivariate data may be scanned to 'provide useful and informative insights into the structure of such

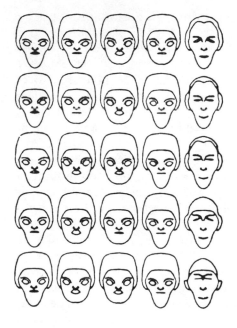

Fig. 5.1/2 Physiognomy of multivariate data (from Everitt, B., 1978, p. 94)

data' (p. 94). For example, points in nine-dimensional space may be intuitively scanned for patterns by representing each point as a face composed of nine features; a feature for each dimension. The mouth say, may be used to represent one of the dimensions. The two extreme positions of smiling and drooping may represent the two extremes of the data so that the chosen shape of the mouth is decided by interpolation. Fig. 5.1/2 illustrates nine measurements of each of twenty-five ships. Everitt quotes a computer program that draws such traces from multivariate data. He says '...people are used to studying and reacting to faces and, hopefully, they are able to filter out insignificant visual phenomena and focus on the potentially important. Certain major characteristics of the faces are instantly observed, and finer details become apparent after studying the faces for some time. The awareness of these does not drive out of mind the original major impressions' (p. 89). Such a representation of multivariate trend data may be used to spot intuitively a sudden change which would be noticed as an abrupt change in the physiognomy of the series of faces representing the trend data.

Experimental conditions incorporating these characteristics of global knowledge, inhibitive to analytic thought but facilitative to intuitive thought, are used by researchers to encourage the intuitive mode of thought in their subjects. This is done either by giving complex redundancy-rich information, by giving so little information that the subject must add his own redundancy-rich associations to the sparse information given, or by allowing too little time for a linear analytic process. In any case the most natural mode a subject chooses is the intuitive mode of thought unless an analytic solution is particularly called for.

5.2 GLOBAL PERCEPTION

Peripheral Cue Utilization Increases Contextual Information

Global perception of the environment is faciliated in relaxed states. Such states allow a receptivity to peripheral cues, increasing the information and its redundancy, further facilitating intuition. 'A certain alertness and receptivity with relatively little interference from perceptive ego function seems to be important in establishing intuitive capacity' (Guiora, A.Z. *et al.*, 1965, p. 115). The perception, i.e. sensing and organization, of these cues is preconscious. (Reference preconscious process, property 3.) The multimodal perception involves all the senses. 'Intuition like sensation is perceived unconsciously' (Guiora, A.Z. *et al.*, 1965, p. 113). In an extensive search of the creativity literature Rossman, B.B. (1970) also found that 'Perceptual receptivity' was a major attribute of creativity; intuition being the inspirational stage of creativity.

Crutchfield, R.S. (1960) found that in his sample of subjects males were unaware of their 'intuitive' use of spatial reorganization cues in a puzzle-solving task. It is relatively simple to design experiments studying the use of minimal cues and minimal attending, hence this aspect of intuition is better represented in the literature than other aspects of intuition. 'General psychology concentrates on certain aspects of the [intuitive] phenomenon which are amenable to experimental investigation like the problems of minimal cues...' (Guiora, A.Z. *et al.*, 1965, p. 118). However, despite this emphasis in the literature, Aldenbrand, Martha L. (1974), studying the effects of intuition and feeling on empathy ignored her subject's perception of peripheral cues. She attributes her disappointing results to ignoring the subjects' 'minimally attending to new cues'. The range of cue utilization appears to be reduced by ageing (Birren, J.E., 1952; Griew, S., 1958; Kirchmer, W.K., 1958; Welford, A.T., 1951). This could mean that people become less intuitive as they become older, unless other parts of the intuitive process are emphasized during ageing in compensation, e.g. a compensating increase in experience, etc.

The literature on search models of human memory indicates that contextual information of the environment is coded in memory and unassociated information on individual objects in the environment is not. Writing on intuition Guiora, A.Z. *et al.* (1965) say '...what is intuited is not an object, but a situation...' (p. 113). It is the peripheral cue sensations, subliminally perceived, that give the information corresponding to the external situation, and a relaxed state helps this perception. In agreement with this, Muriel Fox found that subjects sensitive to subliminal stimulation gave significantly more regressive verbal responses using subjects' protocols scored on a seven-point scale of regression, than did subjects of low subliminal sensitivity (Fox, Muriel, 1960). Kris, E. (1952) views intuition as a voluntary departure from established standards of perception. He thinks intuition may be understood as a regression from secondary to primary processes, and this regression is a

'regression in the service of the ego'. There may be stimuli in the environment on which the subject imposes conflicting contexts. Klein, G.S. (1970)
explains that in primary process thinking '...contradictory ideas are tolerated
side by side...' (p. 282). This is relevant to creative people's tolerance of
ambiguity.

Wider awareness of the environment through all modalities characterizes the
perceptual part of the intuitive process. Increased awareness and bodily
sensations were central themes in fifty-six subjects' written accounts of their
intuitive experiences phenomenologically analysed by Summers, Roni (1976).
In spite of cultural/educational emphasis on the verbal mode: Still all
individuals seem to maintain a sizeable stake in all three modalities', viz.
kinaesthetic, visual, and verbal (Bissell, Joan et al., 1971, p. 145). The
following two papers on stimulus word recall also indicate that multimodal
attributes are used as contextual information in encoding even disassociated
types of external stimuli. Brown, R. and McNeill, D. (1966) found that
although words may not be remembered some of their attributes might be, e.g.
initial letter, sound pattern, etc. When the attributes were identified but not
the word itself, the subjects often reported the word to be on the 'tip-of-the-
tongue'. Similarly Yavuz, H.S. and Bousfield, W.A. (1959) found that to
some extent the connotative meanings of unrecallable words can be
remembered even though the words themselves cannot. This suggests attribute coding of the connotations.

Dittman attempted to apply the concept of information processing to a
person's perception of the emotional messages, grimaces, stance, etc., sent by
another. This application of information theory is helpful in understanding
the conditions changing the relative information load on different channels
(modalities) both in input (perception) and during output (communication). In
particular, contextual coding may reduce noise (non-relevant information)
during global perception: '...coding helps the operator to resist the
interfering effects of extraneous input...' (Dittman, A.T., 1972, p. 54).

Contextual coding will prevent a 'fledgling thought' or relevant 'snippet of
information' from proactive interference by further external information
input in the intermediate stage of intuitive processing. Papers on the
interference to memory of intermediate tasks are common, and it is
informative to consider their results in the light of the attributes of the initial
stimuli (even nonsense trigrams) that may be used for contextual coding. This
is seldom considered by the researchers. As intuition is a primary process the
environment that facilitates the primary process will encourage intuition,
particularly the global physiognomic perception part of the process. There is
evidence to show that hallucinogen LSD-25 increases susceptibility to total
physiognomic cues. Klein, G.S. (1970, p. 410) describes an experiment where
subjects drugged with LSD-25 were compared with placebo subjects on their
descriptions of the personalities of a 'south American native' whose face was
depicted by a line drawing and whose name was either 'Takete' or 'Uloomu'.

The standard physiognomic connotations of the names had a greater tendency to anchor the personality descriptions in the LSD subjects than they did for the placebo subjects. There is a possible connection here between the effects on thought processes of drugs producing ego-permissive states and drugs blocking SNS or lesions that prevent SNS feedback.

Traditionally the mechanisms eliciting the secondary or primary processes are classed as inhibitory or disinhibitory respectively: '...effective-secondary process thinking [analytic] is essentially inhibitive' (Klein, G.S., 1970, p. 285). High motivation is inhibitory and favours the analytic mode over the intuitive mode of perception. Viesti's experiment on insight learning showed that increased drive, by increasing payment, did not increase the insightful problem-solving results, it actually inhibited insightful problem-solving. 'Those subjects who were not offered money performed significantly better than those who were paid... The result would seem to indicate that, regardless of their size, monetary utilities do not appreciably increase performance on insight learning tasks, rather, their presence may interfere with such performance' (Viesti, C.R. Jr., 1971, p. 182).

Easterbrook, J.A. (1959) reviews experiments that illustrate the inhibitory effect of high motivation on cue utilization (e.g. Bahrick, H.P. *et al.,* 1952). 'The interesting finding was that proficiency at the peripheral tasks was inferior under high motivation, despite the fact that they too were more rewarded' (p. 184). As intuitive judgments are dependent on the physiognomy of the total perceptual field and use peripheral cues, when the use of these cues is suppressed as in high-drive environments the intuitive process is correspondingly suppressed. This is one reason why the environment and the instructions so affect the choice of analytic or intuitive modes of thought. This suppression effect is directly proportional to the peripheral versus central content of the tasks. 'The benefits attributable to motivation were obtained on the central task at the cost of proficiency on the broader (central + peripheral) task.' '...Perception of threat raises drive level, reduces the range of cue utilization...' (pp. 184/185, 187).

Easterbrook reviews several papers that show the reduction of the perceptual field due to anxiety (pp. 188/189). Anxiety would inhibit the perception of cues for the intuitive process. Perceptual tasks which require a large number of cues have been constructed in the laboratory. By reducing the definition of the cues available in easy tasks, e.g. reducing exposure, or reducing illumination, etc., the intuitive mode would tend to operate, and some experimenters have used this 'stimuli degradation' to induce the intuitive mode, but under anxiety the intuitive mode would be inhibited and the joint result would be an impairment of discrimination. (See Yerkes, R.M. and Dodson, J.D.'s classic experiments.) Easterbrook's conclusions on his review are: 'In all of these cases the use of cues was impaired by increase of drive' (p. 189). On analytic tasks, however, reduction in irrelevant cue utilization improves performance.

Organizational Characteristics of Global Perception Define Cognitive Styles and Personality Traits Commensurate with the Intuitive Type

An assumption fundamental to personality theory of the purpose of behaviour, is to discover the most general regulatory principles that determine a person's responses and account for individual differences between people. One of these regulatory principles is cognitive control, from the field of psychoanalytic ego psychology, that is features of organization more general than any specific structural components underlying perception, recall, and judgment (Gardner, R.W. *et al.,* 1959, p. 6). Intuitive processes are a cognitive control. Intuitive organizing tendencies are an example of 'adaptive control' and intuitions, their behavioural consequences, are 'adaptive solutions' (Gardner, R.W. *et al.,* 1959. p. 1). The structure of cognitive controls coexisting within a personality is termed 'cognitive style'.

An individual's method of coping with particular structural frameworks and his intuitive organization of perception has been used to define his cognitive style. Bodnar, W.A. (1975) investigated the relationship of cognitive controls to Jungian 'intuitive' versus 'sensation' types. He considered the hypothesis that intuitive types would show significantly higher levels of scanning, sharpening, field independence and flexible control, than would sensation types. These perceptual oranizations are not all, however, commensurate with global, holistic intuitive perception. Sharpeners are attentive to details and attend to differences in stimuli whereas levellers make global judgments and are inattentive to details (Israel, N.R., 1969). Intuitive types would therefore be levellers in this context whereas in category sorting they might be considered sharpeners.

Unfortunately Bodnar used the Myers-Briggs Type Inventory to indicate the intuitive type and this inappropriate instrument may have been responsible for his contradictory and non-significant results, his most significant result being at 0·1 level. Gaughran, E. (1963) defines cognitive style as a person's readiness to respond to physiognomic qualities of inanimate stimuli (p. 1). It has been shown here that intuitive perception is the physiognomy of the whole stimulus field.

Personality correlates of the cognitive styles commensurate with global perception are also personality correlates of intuitive types. Kvascev and Popov (1972) found that creative subjects were able to base imaginative ideas on non-structured material. They also found creative subjects had a tolerance of vagueness and ambiguity consistent with the physiognomy of global perception. Klein, G.S. (1970, p. 282), found that contradictory ideas are tolerated side by side in primary-process thinking. Intuitive thought is primary-process thinking. Aldenbrand, Martha L (1974) found that the opposite personality trait of dogmatism unduly influenced the categorizing of 'intuitive' versus 'sensory' types on the Myers-Briggs Type Inventory. Dogmatism/authoritarianism/conservatism is frequently considered as opposing the intuitive process. The same positive relations between field independence, complexity, affective receptivity, and creativity all negatively related to dogmatism, were found by Gerber, L.A. (1972). Gerber used the Affect-Cognition Scale to rate forty subjects' responses to the six TAT cards. He also administered other personality tests and from the ranked correlations found: 'The positive correlations between the Affect-Cognition scores and cognitive complexity, field independence, and originality and the negative correlation with dogmatism suggest that the Affect-Cognition Scale taps an inner, creative process involving affect and cognition as well as some degree of "openmindedness" '.

The wholeness of intuition lies in the interaction of internal and external perception and the continuing integration of the information with internal affective cognitive contexts. But for the sake of discussion we have considered separately in this, and the immediately following section, perception of external stimuli, perception of internal stimuli, and the interaction of the two.

Perception is one organizing part of the intuitive process. It is considered here as the selective sensing of stimuli both internal and external. The selectivity results from the ongoing interaction of the perception of external and continually changing internal stimuli. The varying sensitivity of the senses from person to person and within a person at various times, e.g. periodic, time of day and month as well as variations with age, will determine preference and ability modes. These variations affect the intuitive process in so much as it depends on global perception, i.e. peripheral cue utilization and subliminal perception of external cues through non-linear modalities. This is matched by global perception of internal stimuli, i.e. appraisal of body feeling and memory. The interaction between the two changes the emotional state. The intuitive person is said to be sensitive to these perceptions in that the feedback of the interaction between perceptions and changing emotional states may be affective. These processes vary between individuals, producing intuitive and non-intuitive types. They vary with age so that the young have a different emphasis in their intuitive processes to the old. Environment and biorhythms affect the process so that an individual will be more intuitive in some surroundings at some times than at others. There are many anecdotes of creative people who prefer to work at odd times in peculiar environments conducive to their intuition.

External anxiety-provoking pressures should be minimal for a subject to utilize a wide field of perception, including subliminal perception using all modalities. The wider the cue utilization then the more redundancy will be contained in the information. Similarly, information duplicated across modalities is highly redundant. With many modalities acting as channels receiving information, more information may be received more quickly.

Intuition is referred to in the literature as a 'primary process' or a 'regressive ego state'. There is a minimum of drive and ego autonomy in such a relaxed state. Physiological changes peculiar to these states include an increase in theta waves. Psychologically one may experience hypnogogic reverie. It is quite possible that biofeedback theta-wave training, making this state more attainable, would, when other properties of intuition are also considered (e.g. increased awareness and sensibility), make intuition more controllable. The environments that affect the maintenance of primary-process thinking will facilitate the intuitive process. Environments offering external threat-producing anxiety will inhibit the intuitive process by reducing external cue utilization and inhibiting other integrative parts of the process. Similarly, high external motivation does not facilitate insight and has been shown to inhibit it.

How a person perceives his environment, as well as the organization he imposes on the information from this perception, has been used to define his cognitive style. Particularly relevant to this section are 'focusing' and 'levelling versus sharpening' cognitive styles that relate to the range of cue utilization. Other cognitive styles relating to other parts of the intuitive process, e.g. 'field dependence' relating to the priority given to internal versus external stimuli, are to be discussed in another section. Test batteries have given personality factors concomitant with the global style of external perception. These factors also describe the intuitive type as low on dogmatism, high on tolerance and the mixing of contradictory ideas, etc.

The changes in sensitivity and relative priority of preference and ability modes with age affect the perception of external stimuli for intuitive information. These alterations are reflected in modifications in cognitive style, personality profiles, and in models of child development.

Intuition as a Function of the Right Cerebral Hemisphere

Global perception and many other properties of intuition have been considered to be the province of the right cerebral hemisphere. Sudjanen, W.W. (1976) contrasts the left cerebral hemisphere as linear, time-orientated, rational, analytic, and verbal, with the right cerebral hemisphere as non-linear, lateral-thinking, intuitive, artistic, and creative (p. 23): '...it helps us to see the forest rather than the trees' (p. 23) — see property 4, contrast with abstract reasoning, logic or analytic thought, Section 2.1, for similar contrasts. The idea of regarding these different specializations of the two hemispheres of the brain seems to originate in the work of Ornstein, R.E. (1972). Similarly Samples, R. (1976) says the intuitive holistic functions reside in the right cerebral hemisphere.

> Recent findings have verified a long-known notion that humans have two modes of knowing in their minds. Some of the data are powerfully aligned with the notion that these two modes of knowing, relational-linear and metaphoric-intuitive, are located in opposite cerebral hemispheres ... The metaphoric-intuitive, more holistic mind functions, are conversely linked to the right cerebral hemisphere. (p. 8)

He uses recent neurophysiological findings to conclude: 'The left side was tied to the logical-linear convergent functions that were best exemplified by the rational side of reading, writing and arithmetic. The right side on the other hand tended to be more holistic, more intuitive and metaphoric' (p. 8).

The following experiments of Franco, Laura and Sperry, R.W. (1977) similarly show that many of the properties of intuition are associated with the right cerebral hemisphere, e.g. holistic properties, speed, confidence. Franco and Sperry investigated 'hemispheric lateralization for intuitive processing of geometrical relations' (p. 107). They required five commissurotomy patients and five normal patients to select one from three shapes, by touch only, that was most similar to a displayed set of five shapes.

There were eight sets comprising four in two dimensions and four in three dimensions, each of the four representing either Euclidean, affine, projective, or topological characteristics. They found: 'The speed and also the degree of apparent confidence with which the subjects worked with the left hand reinforces further the evidence for superiority of the left hand-right hemisphere system' (p. 109). The difference in success of left versus right hand on the different geometric tasks reflected the 'ease of verbalization' of the mathematical constraints defining the sets, i.e. the more fundamental, the more loosely structured and the fewer the limitations, then the more successful, was the left hand.

> The close correlation of left hemisphere performance with the number of defining geometrical constraints may suggest that what has been referred to as 'ease of verbalization' of a task may correspond to varying degrees of mathematical limitations which can be ordered in terms of class logic ...loosely structured shapes are entirely suited for right hemisphere processing which is not diverted by the search for details and therefore more readily captures holistic properties of sets independently of structural constraints. (pp. 112/113)

Bruner, J. and Clinchy, B. (1966) also noted that an informal structural basis, that cannot be verbalized by the subject, is a feature of intuitive thinking (p. 73).

The experiments and literature surveyed by James Dwyer, (1975) also support the conclusion that intuitive functions of holistic perception, parallel processing, and recognition of complex visual and audio patterns pertain to the right cerebral hemisphere. Dwyer investigated the non-verbal/verbal, i.e. connotative/denotive communication dichotomy with reference to the part played by the left versus the right cerebral hemispheres. He reports many interesting experiments on commissuratory patients. He paid fifty males and fifty females two dollars each to take part in an experiment which fed different information into the left and right ears and noted which the subject reported. He found an asymmetry sensitivity to various contents which he interprets as being consistent with his literature survey, i.e. '...the right hemisphere specializes — to some unknown extent — in making inferences about the context of speech' (p. 103). He summarizes from his literature survey that the right hemisphere specializes in the following functions which are all relevant to intuition:

   (1) parallel processing as opposed to serial processing;
   (2) processing of more than seven elements in a short span of time;
   (3) recognizing musical patterns and chords;
   (4) making pitch discriminations;
   (5) recognizing complex visual forms (such as faces);
   (6) discerning the form of a whole from its parts.

(pp. 114/115)

Similarly Robert Samples (1976) says that we should replace the cognitive/affective dichotomy '...with the more accurate one of "rational/intuitive" — a distinction based on research into the two hemispheres of the brain' (p. 25). He says the left-hand side of the brain is logical, rational, digital whereas the right-hand side is intuitive, metaphorical, analogical. Sherman, V. (1977) names right hemisphere skills such as poetry, music, dance, and other art forms (p. 1). Blakeslee, T.R. (1980) has written a specialist 'popular' book on the subject of the right hemisphere of the brain. Summers, Roni (1976) lists examples of duality of consciousness relevant to intuition which include the left/right hemisphere dichotomy (pp. 75, 76, 87). Humour, a primary process, is a form of intuitive recentring (Section 2.3, recentring, property 11) and so is linked with the right cerebral hemisphere. 'Humour has its roots in the kind of functions performed by the right cerebral hemisphere, it depends on metaphor and intuition' (p. 27). Brown, R. (1975) also recognizes a holistic and metaphorical level of the human mind that he calls the '...intuitive centers from which arise our emotions, our attitudes, and many of our opinions' (p. 28). He also links this with the processing of visual material. (See Section 5.2 on the superiority of imagery for cognitive representation and global transformation of intuitive information).

Schwartz, G.E. et al. (1975) found that spatial and emotional responses which have been associated with intuition were also associated with the right cerebral hemisphere, whereas verbal non-emotional responses which have been associated with non-intuitive types, they found were associated with the left hemisphere of the brain. Using lateral eye movement (LEM) to the left to indicate subjects' use of right brain hemisphere and LEM to the right to indicate subjects' use of left hemisphere, the authors presented 24 right-handed subjects with four classes of stimuli:

   (1) verbal non-emotional, 'what is the primary difference between meanings of the word "recognize" and "remember"?'
   (2) verbal emotional, 'For you, is anger or hate a stronger emotion?'
   (3) spatial non-emotional, 'Imagine a rectangle. Draw a line from the upper left-hand corner to the lower right-hand corner. What two figures do you now see?'
   (4) spatial emotional, 'When you visualize your father's face, what emotion first strikes you?'

Results showed a highly significant preference for spatial and emotional responses to be associated with the right hemisphere while verbal and non-emotional responses were associated with the left hemisphere.

We find that questions requiring both spatial and emotional processing result in accentuated right hemispheric activation, whereas questions demanding both verbal and non-emotional processes result in the greatest left hemispheric activation. The remaining two types of questions (verbal-emotional and spatial non-emotional) fall predictably in between (p. 287).

Parkinson, A.M. (1970) found that the right cerebral hemisphere tended to be used for the identification of intended emotional tone in content-free speech. This understanding of emotional tone in contrast to content is well illustrated by the following quote from *Othello,* Act IV: 'I understand a fury in your words/But not the words'. In studies using EEG alpha asymmetry, Doktor, R. and Bloom, D.M. (1977) reported: 'Language and analytic tasks were expected to engage primarily the left hemisphere; spatial and intuitive tasks were expected to engage primarily the right hemisphere, consistent with earlier findings with normal Ss'. Blake, R.W. (1976) says that the intuitive stage of creative writing 'involves unconsious, personal, irrational, intuitive writing which may be called "writing for the left hand" since it involves the type of mental activity controlled by the right hemisphere of the brain'. He says: 'The stage of revising the first draft involves conscious, impersonal, rational, and intellectual writing', which involves the right hemisphere.

These results indicate that an insight experiment using kinaesthetic/tactile stimuli should input this information through the left arm/hand of right-handed subjects.

Superiority of Imagery for Cognitive Representation and Global Transformation of Intuitive Information

From the analysis of fifty-six written accounts of intuitive experiences Summers, Roni (1976) found that intuition was experienced through many mediums: including images, dreams, day-dreams, as well as feelings, bodily sensations, and thoughts. Visual representation is a common cognitive accompaniment to the affective connotations of the representation. Szalita-Pemow, A.B. (1955) says that intuition depends 'on the capacity to use visual images' (p. 17). 'As for natural endowment [for intuitive thought], that depends predominantly, I think, on the degree of the capacity for using visual images as a type of shorthand intermingled with organized thinking' (p. 10). Farmer, C. (1961) in 'An experimental approach to the measurement of intuition' found that the highest scorers on his intuitive task tended to represent problems visually. Peters, J.T. *et al.* (1974) investigating 'Intuitive versus analytic thinking' used visual representations of a problem as their intuitive condition for problem-solving. Mednick, S.A. (1962) uses the 'visualizer-verbalizer dimension' as defining a cognitive style. He says: 'The visualizer is one who tends to call up relatively complete memorial sensory representations of the relevant concrete aspects of problems' (p. 224).

It is the advantage of the simultaneous representation of visual information over serial verbal representation that gives the visual-ability mode superiority in intuitive processing. It seems that Poincaré, H. (1969) distinguished between intuitive and analytic mathematicians by their ability modes; intuitive being spatial and analytic being verbal. He said that analysts reject 'the aid of the imagination' (p. 211). He noted the rarity of analytic invention in mathematics (p. 211). This is consistent with the spatial mode being a common ability mode for intuitive invention. Bruner, J. and Clinchy, B. (1966) in 'Towards a disciplined intuition' noted that 'visualization — imagery... non-verbalizability...' (p. 73) were features of intuition. They say intuition is 'more visual or "ikonic", more oriented to the whole problem than to particular parts, less verbalized...' (p. 71). Writing in *Organization of Memory,* Collins, A.M. and Quillian, M.R. (1972b) observe:

> Perhaps interaction between separately stored concepts and their properties can be evaluated more readily if the concepts are generated together in imagery... Several subjects reported that they rejected 'A limousine has a rudder' as false by imagining the rudder on the back of a limousine. It is an imagined interaction that produces a mismatch with memory. (p. 340)

The imagery and affective components of fantasy in primary-process thinking are free from the physical restrictions reality places on the objects they represent. Global transformations can result in original cognitive and affective associations contributing to a final intuition. This internal representation allows simultaneous processing of the whole physiognomy.

> Imagery that allows comparison of events actually separated in time, the dreamlike fantasy of telescoping time and other dimensions, is a useful intuitive tool. It enables the subject to integrate temporary discrete experiences and allows the recognition of features of experience that are invariant under temporal change. It enables the subject to comprehend reversability, commutivity, associativity. (p. 90)

In intuition '...perceptions take the form of fantasies, images, hallucinations' (Guiora, A.Z. *et al.,* 1965, p. 113). Baldwin, A. (1966) analysed three aspects of intuition, one of which was '...ikonic cognitive representations of environmental phenomena' (p. 85). Fantasy representation of the environment has been fostered by Gordon to encourage intuition in practical situations. 'Fantasy analogy' is one of four methods used in synectics for producing creative solutions to given problems (Gordon, W.J.J., 1961, p.

23). Zavalishina, D.N. (1973) identified an analytic and intuitive function of visualization during problem-solving. The intuitive function was used '...to fix knowledge' rather than '...as a means of analysing logical conditions'. Visualization is used in the intuitive process for integration and the patterning of information. Zavalishina found that both functions of visualization were required for an integral configuration in visual patterning corresponding to an optimum way of solving problems (p. 27).

Appraisal of Affective and Cognitive States

Emotions are the internal contexts of information used in the intuitive process; see Section 3.1 on emotional/cognitive interactions in the intuitive process. These comprise physiological and cognitive stimuli allowing appraisal of mood and sensation, the affective components of the intuitive process. Physiological stimuli may be hormonal, kinaesthetic or other stimuli, sometimes changing, slowing relative to rapidly changing cognitive associations. The slowly changing physiological state acts as a 'memory hook' enabling concordant connotations of rapidly associated cognitions to be retained, increasing the information available for intuitive processing. Gathering of affectively concordant associations reinforces the physiognomy of the intuitive information. The physiological state with the cognitive associations is a concrete 'feeling model' of the information. No matter how abstract the information may publicly be considered, a person represents it as a personalized concrete feeling model for intuitive processing.

The physiological representation of the affect components of the physiognomy has a parallel not a serial structure in that different aspects of the information are felt simultaneously. Similarly the cognitive associations are predominantly visual as this too allows parallel internal representation of information. Together the two, visual imagery and feeling model, constitute fantasy for processing intuitive information. It is probable that intuitive types with the serial verbal-ability mode have proncounced body-feeling models of their information to compensate for their lack of parallel image representation. This is supported by Bastick, T. (1979) from transcripts of subject interviews during insight experiments.

'Information obtained through one modality comes to be related to and modified by ongoing activity in the others' (Bissell, Joan et al., 1971, p. 133). The internal cross-modal transference of information not only increases redundancy but supports the unity of the appraised body state.

The physiognomy of intuitive information is represented internally by physiological connotations. Underwood, B.J. (1969) considers that memory does not contain the same engramic representation of input information but a set of attributes of the content of the input. In his short history of the term 'intuition' Stocks, J.L. (1939) says that: 'Intuition now includes sensation' (p. 4). The sensations are the attributes that code the information into memory.

This encoding is subject to some variability, to the advantage of the intuitive process, see Section 5.3 on variability of encoding.

This representation of a physiognomy by the whole body is in agreement with the views of two writers quoted by Allport, G.W. (1929). They alleged that '...intuitive knowledge retains its grasp upon the self as a whole' (p. 17). The structuring of information in this way, i.e. categorizing by emotional sets, facilitates the global search strategies of information-processing models of human memory (Shiffrin, R.M., 1970; Norman, D.A. and Rumelhart, D.E., 1970). It should be possible to show that the speed of search is commensurate with experience of intuitive recall, and the variability of error is in agreement with results of experiments on the distribution of intuitive versus analytic errors (Peter, Joan T. *et al.,* 1974; Brunswik, E., 1956; Earle, T.C., 1972).

5.3   ORGANIZATION OF GLOBAL INFORMATION

Intuitive perception of the external stimulus field categorizes the stimuli by subjective contexts influenced by perception of internal stimuli. Cognitions conditioned to the appraised physiological set that are associated with perception of external stimuli reinforce the subjective categorization. The priority that a subject gives to the internal or external stimuli in defining the categorization of the external stimulus field may be considered as a cognitive style which some researchers refer to by the term 'field independence versus field dependence'. An extreme field-independent subject would 'see what he expects to see' rather than what is there. He would 'rationalize' the reality to fit his preconceptions.

The internal and external information is integrated into a physiognomy of the situation. Cross-modal transfer of information increases the redundancy of the physiognomy, further reinforcing the criteria for categorization. In intuitive perception internal and external information merge into a global whole through continuous feedback as the reinforced criteria for subjective categorization are further applied to the external stimulus field to the extent that affective components of the categorization are attributed to the external source. This is a temporary projection imbuing the external source with the emotional set of the observer. Integration of internal and external stimuli is complete when the observer temporarily identifies with the external source as an extension of himself, see Section 6.3, on temporary identification during the intuitive process. Results of the intuitive processing of this integrated information will subjectively apply to the external source as much as they do to the subject.

Information is organized, i.e. selected and categorized, for intuitive processing on criteria which give maximum redundancy. Affective and contiguous cognitive contexts in an emotional state tend to be associated by contiguity conditioning into an emotional set as shown in Section 3.2 on the development of emotional sets. As the concordance (redundancy) of the perception of external stimuli with these emotional sets reinforces the criteria for categorizing the external stimulus field, then the subjective criteria used in classification experiments can indicate the map of a subject's emotional sets. That is, his probabilistic tendencies to combine particular affective and cognitive contexts (emotional sets) with other affective and cognitive contexts can be indicated by the subjective criteria he uses in categorizing complex stimuli. These criteria give the subjective importance to selected stimuli which defines the physiognomy of the global situation.

There are experimental methods which have been used for other purposes which may, however, be used to map the idiosyncratic associations within and between a subject's emotional sets. Such work is important in the study of problem-solving as it shows the intuitive associations responsible for a creative solution. A powerful technique for the advancement of knowledge would be to superimpose the idiosyncratic associations of specialists in a particular field; specialists who have similar personalities. Experimental methods that are now being used and that may be applied to this mapping are, for example, experiments on levelling/sharpening cognitive style where a subject sorts cards bearing concepts into categories. The number and criteria of the classifications are noted. Reaction times between free associations and the criteria for associating can be used. Osgood's semantic differential can be used to quantify these criteria. The change in criteria and reaction time of free associations under drugs that inhibit or facilitate body appraisal through the sympathetic nervous system is suggested from neurophysiology and from the qualitative emotional content of interviews with patients with varying degrees of spinal cord lesions (Hohmann, G.W., 1962, 1966). One might speculate on the use of a vector of physiological measures to indicate a subject's probable associations of affective and cognitive contexts.

The above experimental techniques may be used for mapping idiosyncratic probable associations of affective and cognitive contexts, by which a subject organizes his global knowledge for intuitive processing. However, criticisms of the above experimental techniques can be considered in terms of variability of encoding stimuli, both across subjects and within the subject across time and stimuli. Although we are aware of a great variety and graduation of personal emotion, the literature is prolific with examples of failure to find corresponding physiological indicators of any but the most extreme of a few emotional states. The view expressed here is in agreement with other physiological experiments that show, however, that a different pattern of physiological responses exists between subjects experiencing similar emotions, e.g. for a particular emotion one subject may respond maximally on GSR and minimally on HR whereas for another subject and the same experienced emotion, the reverse might be the case. Such results explain why analysis on single physiological measures across subjects shows no specific differentiated physiological pattern to variety and graduation of emotion. However, a vector of physiological measures may be a meaningful indicator of graduation and variety of emotion within the subject.

The encoding of cognitive events by components of their affective associations has been criticized (Hebb, D.O., 1946, p. 99. and others) because the same stimulus may give rise to different affective components at different times so there can be no one-to-one correspondence suitable for unique recall. In fact the work of Schachter, S. and his collaborators (e.g. Singer, J.E.) on the cognitive labelling of emotion has shown by some fascinating experiments that the same physiological responses may be labelled as different emotions because of different cognitive associations at various times. It is this very variability of encoding cognitive events that facilitates intuitive processing. That unconnected cognitive events may be conditioned at different times to similar affective states explains how novel associations of these cognitive events may occur when the subject is again in that affective state. The encoding, to a limited extent, of the same stimulus with different physiological states, cross-modal transposition conditioning information to different components of an affective state, and the encoding of different stimuli to similar physiological states all increase the redundancy of the information. It is this redundancy (cross-categorization and duplicated categorization) that decides the probable chaining of emotional sets and consequent association of ideas, e.g. as in hypnogogic reverie, that occur in the intuitive processing of the global information.

The facilitating effect on the intuitive process of variability in encoding information has pedagogic implications for the transfer of learning, in that to aid transfer similar stimuli should be associated, through a variety of experiences, with many emotional sets.

External Stimuli Organized for Intuitive Processing through Encoding by Internal Events

It is recognized in the literature that external information is combined with internal information for intuitive processing. Some authors who independently expound this primarily Jungian view of intuition are Ann Lewis and Alexander Guiora and his colleagues. Guiora, A.Z. *et al.* (1965) in their paper entitled 'Intuition' say that intuition is perceiving a situation '...together with what is in the unconscious mind' (p. 113). Ann Lewis interprets Carl Jung's 'global or holistic sense' of the word intuition as: 'Intuition represents a mode of perception which involves the sensing of possibilities in both external and internal events' (Lewis, Ann T.L., 1976).

Michael Polanyi says that physiologists accept that appraisal of the internal state gives meaning to the perception of external stimuli.

Physiologists long ago established that the way we see an object is determined by our awareness of certain efforts inside our body, efforts which we cannot feel in themselves. We are aware of these things going on inside our body in terms of the position, size, shape, and motion of an object, to which we are attending. In other words we are attending from these internal processes to the qualities of things outside. These qualities are what those internal processes mean to us. The transposition of bodily

experiences into the perception of things outside may now appear, therefore, as an instance of the transposition of meaning away from us, which we have found to be present to some extent in all tacit knowing...
(Polanyi, M., 1966, p. 14)

By 'tacit knowing' he means intuition. Klein cites several sources that agree '...that percepts are often subtly suffused with emotional or expressive qualities' (Klein, G.S., 1970, p. 151).

It is proposed here that the internal events are used to encode the external events for intuitive processing, including recall and other responses. Because the contiguity conditioning responsible for the encoding is symmetrical, this proposal is also suggested from an inversion of Schachter's (1964, 1971 and Schachter, S. and Singer, T.E., 1962) ideas that externally instigated cognitive events are used to label emotion, i.e. inversion to: emotion can label (encode) externally instigated cognitive events. This proposal is supported by Voss, J.F. (1972), writing in *Organization of Memory*. He writes that external stimuli may be encoded in terms of contexts and internal stimuli. 'Furthermore, two other factors are probably involved which shall be termed external and internal context. The former refer to contextual events which may be encoded with, or as part of, the particular stimulus event; the latter refer to other encodings which occur with or are a part of the encoding of the particular event' (p. 174). This concept of similar encoding for stimulus and response is in accordance with general models of associative learning: '...in the context of associative learning, one of the hypotheses generated is that the encoding of a stimulus item should not be independent of the response encoding' (p. 188).

General writers, as opposed to research psychologists, recognize that internal events organize the perception of external events for the process of intuition, but writing in fields other than behavioural psychology they do not concern themselves with models of how this might occur. Polanyi, M. (1966), a general writer, not only notes the effect of internal events on perception, he also emphasizes the use of these internal events for integrating and understanding the global information.

Because our body is involved in the perception of objects, it participates thereby in our knowing of all other things outside. Moreover, we keep expanding our body into the world, by assimilating to it sets of particulars which we integrate into reasonable entities. Thus do we form, intellectually and practically, an interpreted universe populated by entities, the particulars of which we have interiorized for the sake of comprehending their meaning in the shape of coherent entities. (p. 29)

His idea of 'expanding our body into the world' is further discussed under empathy and projection in Section 6.3, empathy, property 12. This idea of 'expanding our body into the world' is also consistent with the Eastern philosophic ideas of intuition as a oneness or unity with the environment which gives global knowledge as mentioned in Section 1.2 under philosophic studies of intuition.

Priority of Internal Versus External Contexts for Categorizing Corresponds to Field-independence Versus Field-dependence Cognitive Style

Researchers have identified a cognitive style of 'field dependence versus field independence'. These styles may be explained by the priority a subject attaches to external or internal contexts in categorizing the external stimulus field. Subjects giving priority to external contexts being field-dependent, and subjects with field-independent cognitive style being thought of as giving priority to internal contexts for categorizing external stimuli.

In Section 5.2 intuitive processes were considered as a cognitive control resulting in other cognitive styles associated with organizing global perception. The work of Witkin, H.A. *et al.* (1954) describes the cognitive style of 'field dependence versus field independence' and this description is very similar to that of constricted versus flexible cognitive control. The constricted versus flexible-cognitive control dimension is relevant to functional fixedness in intuitive problem-solving (Birch, H.G., 1945; Maier, N.R.F., 1956; Duncker, K., 1945).

About half of Martin Thorsland's PhD thesis is concerned with intuitive and analytic problem-solving approaches. He considers the literature on non-content-specific cognitive styles of subjects with intuitive problem-solving approaches. He equates field dependence versus field independence with global style versus analytic style. 'One of these general cognitive styles is referred to as analytic versus non analytic (global), also referred to as field-independent versus field-dependent' (Thorsland, M.N., 1971, p. 18). 'The analytic dimension as studied is characterized by a preference to group familiar objects together on a basis of objective elements of the total stimulus' (p. 18). Some tests to identify the analytic dimension are Siegel's Styles of Categorizing Stimuli Test, the Cognitive Style Test (Kagan, J. *et al.,* 1963), the Hidden Figures Test (Kagan, J. *et al.,* 1964) and various embodied figures tests.

Gilbert, G.S. and Rappaport, L. (1975) used an embodied figure in their demonstration experiment on 'Categories of thought and variations in meaning'. The embodied figure was a face composed of nine dots embedded in a matrix of two hundred dots. They compared the effects of different sets of conditions under which three groups of ten students estimated the number of dots. The first 'pure-analytic' condition and the third 'aesthetic' condition are relevant to this section. In the first pure-analytic condition subjects were instructed to estimate the total number of dots. In the third aesthetic condition subjects were told to look at the card as a whole and 'get a feeling for it'. Analyses of subjects' reproductions of 'any identifiable pattern' indicated that analytically oriented subjects missed the embedded figure entirely. Results also showed that the aesthetically oriented subjects found the embedded figure significantly more often. As the subjects were not grouped on cognitive style, this result indicates the importance of instruction in influencing field-independent towards field-dependent cognitive style, which is generally assumed to be relatively invariant except with age, e.g. occurrence of the analytic dimension increasing with age (Kagen, J. *et al.*, 1963), information-processing ability becomes increasingly related to the analytic dimension with increasing age (Frederick, W.C., 1967).

Subjects more sensitive to their affective states tend to be more attuned to external emotional contexts. Zimring, F. *et al.* (1970) found that the Affect Cognition Scale differentiated between subjects' ability to hear target emotional and neutral sentences when played simultaneously with E reading a biography over binaural headphones. The affect cognition scale is derived from the six TAT cards (1, 2, 3BM, 5, 6BM, 8BM) in the following way.

Category 1 (Affect Content) is given to a vague statement or impression of emotion which is not attributed to any character or developed in any context or with any rationale. 'This picture is sad', is a statement that would fall within Category I. Category II (Attributed Affect) is given when a simple statement of emotion is written and attributed to an individual in the TAT story (e.g. 'He is angry'). Category III (Defined Affect) is used as an individual increasingly specifies how the story character feels (e.g. 'He felt waves of anger and embarrassment rising within himself'). Category IV (Developed Affect) is used as an individual connects the feeling with the context and/or with ensuing behaviour (e.g. 'He felt ashamed of himself for wanting to touch her and so backed away').

Gerber, L.A. (1972) found a positive correlation between this Affect Cognition Scale and field independence which further supports our thesis that intuitive types being field-independent and using their sensitivity to internal events can appraise external contexts.

Witkin, H.A. *et al.* (1954 and 1962) used TAT and Rorschach cards with psychiatric patients. They found different responses for field-dependent and field-independent patients; there are similar references in Section 5.2. Differences were also noted in the symptoms of field-dependent and field-independent patients that again relate extreme 'rationalization', due to giving priority of classification to internal states, to schizophrenics, *viz.* field-independent patients were more prone to delusions bordering on schizophrenia and unrealistic attempts at maintenance of identity. The effect of experiment instructions on varying field-dependent to field-independent cognitive style and inducing an internal emotional set for appropriate organization of external stimuli is relevant to the use of experimenters' instructions to encourage the intuitive mode, discussed in Section 5.1. It is also relevant to the presentation of classroom material for intuitive versus analytic processing and applications to problem-solving.

Mood, Kinaesthesis, and Affective Sensitivity Integrate External Stimuli into a Physiognomy of the Whole

Global information is organized into a physiognomy for intuitive processing. The physiognomy includes emotional contexts that structure the information. It is not surprising therefore, that mood and kinaesthesis that are dimensions of emotional contexts, and affective sensitivity that assesses the emotional context along these dimensions, are instrumental in integrating external stimuli into a physiognomy of the total information.

Allport, in his study of personality by the 'intuitive method' remarked on the function of mood in structuring stimuli by contexts. 'Any satisfactory theory as to "how we know people" must recognize that inference and context are always in the service of the inherent tendency of mood to structure its content into wholes, and therefore, in a sense, to perceive intuitively' (Allport, G.W., 1929, p. 27). Allport equates intuition with Eduard Spranger's term 'Verstechen' as meaning the integrating function of emotional context. 'Verstechen according to the definition of Eduard Spranger, is the mental process of "grasping events as fraught with meaning in relation to a totality" ' (p. 14). Allport says that a possible English equivalent to Verstechen is intuition.

The work of Werner, H. and Kaplan, B. (1967) shows the unity achieved by emotional contexts integrating stimuli into the physiognomy of the whole. It also shows the interrelatedness of physiognomic categories which is relevant to criteria defined by category-sorting experiments. It was earlier mentioned that it is the interrelatedness of categories, i.e. their redundancy of contextual coding, that defines their probable intuitive association with other categories by the probability of combining emotional sets of the categories. Werner and Kaplan discuss in some detail 'the physiognomic apprehension of language forms'. They consider categories based on physiognomies and compare them to grammatical categories. From experiments they found (p. 232) that physiognomized categories were less differentiated from each other compared with the degree of categorical distinctiveness of words at the non-physiognomic level. The authors found that nouns and adjectives as well as verbs tend to be physiognomically imbued with dynamic properties. The physiognomic versus linguistic appreciation of a sentence compares with analytic versus intuitive appreciation:

> '. . . linguistically seen, a sentence consists of discrete vocables related to each other through morphological indices and abstract order arrangements, but the unity of a sentence is achieved physiognomically through a successively changing accentuation within a global event, that is, with syncretic rather than discrete categorical forms constituting the sentiential integration.' (p. 233)

Werner and Kaplan give the following examples from the protocols of normal adults that illustrate how body referents, e.g. mood and kinaesthesis, are categorizing contexts. 'Dusk, for me is something unsympathetic to the high degree. Yellow is agility and bounciness. Longing is reaching in all directions. Red is something prickling and stirring. Wood is something splintery, rugged' (p. 342).

The organizing effect on the external stimulus field of body referents is most noticeable in psychoanalytic clinical projective studies. In fact kinaesthesia is scored in the Rorschach test on the basis of movement in perceived whole human figures: '. . .emphasis on whole figures is built into the scoring criteria for *M,* a tendency to perceive the whole. . .' (Urist, J., 1976, p. 577). Several writers (e.g. Arnheim, R., 1949; Werner, H., 1954; Schachtel, E.G., 1959) have indicated that the tendency to perceive physiognomically is closely related to the perception of movement in static stimuli. Gaughran, E. (1963) studied physiognomic perception as a cognitive style related to qualities of body experience. He talked about the 'psychophysical undifferentiatedness' of physiognomic perception 'or the tendency to treat physical and psychological realms of experience as phenomenally similar . . .Expressive Lines and Colour Mood involve a merging of aspects of visual stimuli with feeling and emotion' (p. 9). The Rorschach *M* human movement response is used to measure empathy (King, G.F., 1958; Frankle, A.H., 1953): see Section 6.3 on measuring empathy with projective and fantasy tests.

Cooper, L. (1970) expounds the Gestalt notion of empathy as intuition explicated by Köhler, W. (1947): 'What is involved is a direct and intuitive experiencing of the other person; the experience is most frequently not verbalized within the empathizer' (p. 171). Rorschach *M* is used by Bastick, T. (1979) as an indicator of empathy and intuition.

Gaughran, E. (1963) defines cognitive style as a person's readiness to respond to physiognomic qualities of inanimate stimuli (p. 1). He outlines the Gestalt view of physiognomic perception in accordance with the view presented here, that affective, sensitive persons use body referents as internal contexts, particularly mood and kinaesthesis, for categorizing external stimuli and integrating the categories into a physiognomy of the total information.

> The subject reacts directly (i.e. with immediacy and not necessarily with awareness) to a similarity between properties of objects and characteristics of inner experience (e.g. between a heavy, jagged line, or a harsh, dissonant sound and his own body movements in the expression of anger); and this co-ordination of inner and outer experience gives rise to the impression that animation intention or meaning reside in the field itself. (p. 1)

Gaughran, quotes Werner, H. (1940) on analytic versus intuitive thought. He says Werner refers to analytic thinking as '. . .the literal mode where objects are comprehended in terms of their spatial, temporal and objective properties' (p. 3). Gaughran refers to intuitive thinking by the term physiognomic mode where 'differentiation between self and object is not so firmly maintained and the organismic state of the perceiver plays a more active role in the organization and understanding of the present' (p. 2). Gaughran further quotes Werner, (1954), he '. . .contrasts the physiognomic mode with literal perceiving. . . Differentiations between objectively or conventionally different spheres of experience (animate-inanimate, visual-auditory, etc.), are not firmly maintained' (p. 3). This is consistent with cross-modal transposition of information processing as described in Section 6.1. He gives the Gestalt theory requirements of physiognomic perception as:

> If physiognomic perception arises from the co-ordination of external percepts with the relatively subtle experiences of bodily changes occurring during the expression of emotion (expressive movements), a person would not only have to be sensitive to bodily experiences, but would need well-differentiated, stable, and clearcut knowledge of subtle body changes and cues. (p. 7)

Physiognomy integrates details into a whole. 'Gestalt psychology has demonstrated that we may know a physiognomy by integrating our awareness of its particulars without being able to identify these particulars' (Polanyi, M., 1966, p. 6).

Affective sensitivity, mentioned by Gaughran, E. (1963) above and used for integrating external stimuli through emotional contexts into a physiognomy of the total information, was also found to be an attribute of creative problem-solving by Rossman, B.B. and Horn, J.J. (1972). From an extensive search of the creativity literature, Rossman, B.B. (1970) found affective or aesthetic sensitivity, attitudinal openness and sensitivity to problems to be attributes representative of creativity. These are also proposed as personality correlates of the intuitive type. Similarly illustrating the organization of perception by bodily responses for creativity, Michael Polanyi says perceptions form '. . .the bridge between the higher creative powers of man and the bodily processes which are prominent in the operations of perception' (p. 7).

Categorizing Global Information by Emotional Sets

We categorize our environment using the conditioned emotional contexts of emotional sets. These contexts and probable combinations of emotional sets may be mapped using standard associative procedures and other techniques. The variability of encoding stimuli by emotional contexts facilitates intuitive associations.

In first confrontations with our environment we most naturally categorize it intuitively. This flexible categorization may later suggest analytic criteria for categorizing. When the criteria are complex integrated common emotional contexts they may be difficult to translate into consensus analytic terms. 'All descriptive sciences study physiognomies that cannot be fully described in words or even by pictures' (Polanyi, M., 1966, p. 5). But in science when this is achieved advancement is made. Such common intuitive criteria for taxonomy are implicitly included in science or even sometimes explicitly included as in the Ranganathan intuitive method of library classification which is assumed necessary because of the complex cross-referencing of subjects (Chappell, Marcia, H., 1976).

The process is always relative and the extremes of our public and personal knowledge are of this kind. Idiosyncratic physiognomic categorization of even our analytic knowledge gives it meaning for us. In simple illustration, the number fact '1 + 1 = 2' has an emotional context that varies between individuals and within an individual. The momentary emotional context of the fact is its transient meaning. Its total meaning (its concept) to the individual would be the net of probable associated emotional contexts or emotional sets. One cat plus one mouse means more than two animals. It carries the idiosyncratic emotional contexts of the reader, e.g. it may be part of the food chain; it might be a 'Tom and Jerry' cartoon. In a group of mathematics teachers one common response I received was the feeling of easiness epitomized by the common simile 'as easy as one and one is two'. Similarly the meaning of the probability of one-sixth varies when playing ludo or when playing Russian roulette. The gradient of a hill has different meanings when one is driving up or running up. 'Pure quantity is most drastically illustrated by groupings of things that have nothing in common but quantity. Other groupings produce results that have properties different from quantity, e.g. one mother plus one child equals more than two people — it adds a relationship and all it connotes' (Arnheim, R., 1970, p. 210).

In Fig. 5.3/1 regions *A, B,* and *C* might represent three persons' emotional associations with the number fact '1 + 1 = 2'. The intersection of all such

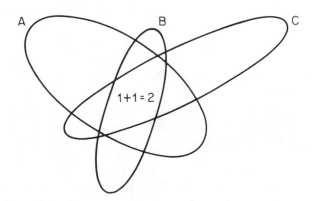

Fig. 5.3/1 'Mathematical fact' as the intersection of people's connotations with the fact: and an 'abstract concept' as the intersection of a person's contextual exemplars

regions is the bare mathematical fact. The analogy might be extended to more people so that the intersection shrinks to meaningless definition. In one subject where the regions represent different emotional contexts of the same fact, the union might represent the subject's concept and the intersection represent what is called the 'abstract concept'; the abstractness from the contextual exemplars being relative.

It is generally accepted that people organize information from stimuli by categorizing into groups for processing. Sarbin, T.R. *et al.* (1960) believe all types of intuition are inferential processes that are similar to ordinary perception. They think that stimuli are classified according to Piaget-type schemata, which they call modules. Mandler, G. and Pearlstone, Z. (1966) put forward a unitization hypothesis that subjects arrange lists of words into stable categories for recall. Miller's idea of encoding stimuli is similar to this unitization hypothesis, but due to some limits on our capacity to process information, he considers that words from a single category are recoded into a single 'chunk' and that the subject recalls the chunk and not the individual words (Miller, G.A., 1956). He mentions that the literature is very vague as to how the chunks are encoded and decoded. This book proposes the mediation of emotional contexts for this process and extends Miller's ideas to the embeddability of these emotional contexts in a hierarchical model of emotional sets as presented in Chapter 9.

Norman, D.A. (1970), studying models of human memory, suggests a six-part information-processing model. The first part is that presented information would appear to be transformed by the sensory system into its physiological representations (p. 2). Although it is generally accepted that various contexts code stimuli into memory, and I here propose that its physiological representation is the affective components of emotional contexts, many models seek to explain recall or recognition of paired nonsense or non-contextual words and so miss the point of memory organization, i.e. that it is the context that codes the items for memory. Information may be taken into long-term memory through suitable contexts during relaxed ego states, e.g. during sleep, when minimum ego control allows combinations of maximally redundant emotional sets with their dreamlike illogical inconsistencies to weave the new context among those we already have.

The emotional contexts of information are complex and unique to the individual, a product of his experience and physiology. However, categorization to some extent is culturally determined, e.g. the use of mass nouns whose perceptual criteria are texture, or the categorization of females by sexual taboos (see Triandis, H.C., 1964, 22 ff). However, there are pan-human tendencies of association due, one would presume, to common experience. Rosenzweig, M.R. (1957, 1961), used the Kent-Rosanoff list of primary words in French, German, English, and Italian and found that the greater the frequency of the primary response in one language, the more likely it is to be equivalent in meaning to the corresponding primary response in another language. It is the contiguity of common experience and usual physiological states that binds ideas into culturally accepted emotional contexts producing expected associations resulting from cross-subject experiments.

In an experiment on 'Information integration in numerical judgments and decision processes' Irwin Levin used an unusual approach in experiments on intuitive estimation. By using common emotional contexts his results showed that subjects weighted the importance of information accordingly. Other experiments on intuitive estimation may be criticized for not considering the weighting given by the subjective importance of the information to be estimated (Kahneman, D. and Tversky, A., 1973; Parducci, A. and Sandusky, A., 1965 Peterson, C.R. and Beach, L.R., 1957; Wolfe, Mary L., 1975). However, Levin used as data the percentage increase in food prices of various foods from different stores and subjects had to estimate the mean prices and which was the better store in which to shop. They also had to compare food prices. The information was given subjective importance by the subjects who could weight its value according to this subjective importance. 'This approach allowed the inclusion of affective rating responses and the manipulation of variables such as category importance... Category importance was shown to affect the weight of psychological importance of the information within a given category' (Levin, I.P., 1975, p. 39).

This use of subjective values is formally used in business decisions to assess utilities for valuing facilities and for comparative decisions, e.g. the utility of an extra £1000 is more to a man who has nothing than it is to a man who is already a millionaire. Similarly it is frequently preferable to decide on policies that minimize possible maximum losses rather than follow policies that maximize possible profits, because the disutility of loss subjectively exceeds the utility of a similar profit.

The unusual emotional contexts of the eccentric that are interesting for the study of original creative problem-solving, e.g. witness the unique experience, odd mannerisms, moodiness, etc., of the eccentric that are the dimensions of his unique emotional contexts.

In a weighty volume, *Human Problem Solving,* running to 920 pages, Newell, A. and Simon, H.A. (1972) do not even consider categorization of problem stimuli by emotional contexts but only by logical analysis. However, they report several interesting chess-playing programmes, one of which uses as a criterion for selection of moves priority for protection of pieces from the folk lore of chess-playing, not from any logical or analytic consideration of the game. This leads to the suggestion consonant with the above interpretation of the literature, that chess-playing programmes could use recognition of physiognomic patterns as criteria of move selection. Simon, H.A. and Barenfield, M. (1969) produced an 'Information processing analysis of perceptual processes in problem solving' through a chess-playing programme. The authors used a computer program PERCEIVER, that describes the position of chess pieces using seven formats of overlapping patterns with which I think a player may identify. They call these formats 'memory chunks'.

The programme simulates the eye movements of an actual player. For the importance of this they cite evidence that the initial structuring activity in problem-solving is 'perceptual' rather than 'cognitive'. In recalling chess positions they give evidence that 'meaningfulness' is an important factor, e.g. in replacing pieces correctly: '...with random boards, the performances of grand masters and masters sink to the level of weak players, while the weak players perform as well (or as poorly) with random boards as with boards from game positions' (p. 480). 'Hence, the short-term memory, limited to holding a specified maximum number of chunks, can retain many more relations if they occur in familiar configurations than if they must be held independently in memory' (p. 481); '...less skilled players have to describe the boards in a larger number of simpler chunks — hence cannot hold all the information required to reproduce the board in short-term memory.' The authors do not interpret their method in terms of physiognomies or emotional content. However, it is in agreement with the above cited work of Miller, G.A. (1956) on the combination of memory chunks and with my extension of the idea to a hierarchy of embeddable emotional contexts. Simon and Barnfield's programming method may be interpreted in terms of physiognomies rather than 'overlapping patterns with which a player may identify'. The more overlapping then the greater would be the redundancy of the physiognomies and hence the more flexible would be the programme selections. Chess programmes using heuristic search and means-end with subgoal analysis have recently plateaued in performance and could perhaps benefit from this programming approach. This idea of programming probable associations between information categorized by redundant physiognomies is used by Bastick, T. (1979) to verify the Theory of Intuitive Thought Process through computer simulation.

Formalized Emotional Sets

The emotional contexts comprising emotional sets are used by a subject as criteria for categorizing his environment. Hence categorization experiments with individual subjects on controlled stimuli will exhibit these criteria. Overlapping criteria partially define the probability of combining emotional sets. Physiological change also contributes to this probability of combining emotional sets. The two Figs. 5.3/2 and 5.3/3 illustrate the organization of global knowledge by emotional sets for intuitive processing.

In Fig. 5.3/2 the dotted region A represents the emotional set of the subject at any one instant. It comprises the changing physiological state $B,$ the conditioned and instinctive cognitive and affective responses a to f and the occasional unconditioned contiguous stimuli x to z. This emotional set is the emotional context of any of the stimuli/responses a to z; stimuli and responses being similarly coded in agreement with the requirements of general models of associative learning.

Responses a to f may be iteratively synthesized using standard and other

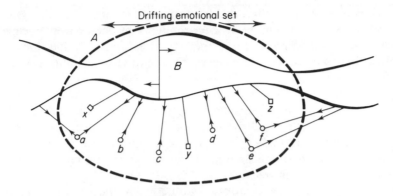

Fig. 5.3/2 Diagram of an emotional set

techniques of experiments described in this section. Responses *a, e,* and *f* illustrate responses that are conditioned to other emotional sets as well. These are the overlapping responses that encourage association of stimuli/responses by combination with other emotional sets. Newton, J.R. (1963) defines intuition as a '...process based on multiple systems of intersubstitutible cues having probabilistic relations with the environment' (p.1). The probability of a subject being in emotional set A and then next combining with emotional set I say, is here called the transition probability of emotional set A to emotional set I denoted as T_{AI}. The multiencoding of these responses is redundancy. The need to increase redundancy drives all aspects of the intuitive process.

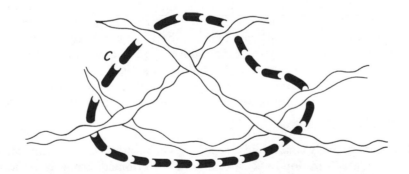

Fig. 5.3/3 Network of emotional sets with high transition probabilities

Fig. 5.3/3 illustrates part of the network of emotional sets whose links are their probability of combination, their transition probability. It is an extraction from the dense net, illustrating those few emotional sets with the highest transition probabilities. Dotted region C illustrates 'a concept' as a part of this network including emotional sets that categorize some specific 'abstract fact': '...meaning of a concept... is a reflection of probability relationships among and within the referents of the concepts' (Solley, C.M. and Messick, S.J., 1957, p. 161). The 'referents of the concept' being the affective and cognitive context of the emotional sets; 'It has long been recognized that some concepts are closely related to sensory-motor primitives, while others are put together from many primitive elements. Thus, concepts "red" and "moveeys" [sic] are, even in humans, known to correlate with functional elements in the sensory-motor system, whereas the concepts "cat" and "crochet" are complexly structured combinations of primitive sensations and actions' (Becker, J.D., 1970, p. 25). The transition probabilities between emotional sets, and/or those defining a subject's specific concept, may be mapped using the following techniques.

The subject's specific associations within this proposed organization of global information for intuitive processing may be ascertained from the theory of clustering within a concept. 'Since clustering is a consequence of organizational processes, an adequate theory of clustering should shed some light on the nature of organization as this function operates on a comparatively high level' (Bousfield, W.A. *et al.,* 1964, p. 206). Bousfield *et al.* used free associational norms for the prediction of clustering. Unfortunately they used an *ad hoc* empirical rule that did not work too well and was unsupported by theory.

The responses in an emotional set are not all equally conditioned. Some are more instrumental in defining the emotional set and this will be reflected in their ease of recall. The work of Collins and Quillian contributes to this proposed organization.

In fact, human concepts are probably more like hooks or nodes in a network from which many different properties hang. The properties hanging from a node are not likely to be all equally accessible; some properties are more important than others, and so may be reached more easily or quickly. In such a representation, going from one concept to another does not involve scanning a list but rather activating a path via some property from one to the other. (Collins, A.M. and Quillian, M.R., 1972b, p. 314).

The more strongly conditioned responses will naturally be more immediately used for categorization and so may be ascertained from classification experiments. Miller, G.A. (1967) asked subjects to sort packs of cards, each bearing a word, into as many sets as they wished. Miller repeated this with many subjects and did a cluster analysis on the frequencies of each pair. Thus having the individual's organization he found a group organization. The same technique could be repeated on the individual subject to describe more closely his idiosyncratic associations.

The organization of a subject's cognitive structure by experiments involving writing attributes on cards and grouping them is reported by Duval, S. and

Wickland, R.A. (1972, p. 174). Cognitive structure is defined in terms of

(1) differentiation: the number of attributes used in describing the object;
(2) complexity: the number of categories of attributes;
(3) unity: organization susceptible to change.

In their experiments E compared subjects who were required to receive information only, and those who were later required to transmit it. In agreement with our theory they found that the way subjects structured information was related to their attitude of subjective or objective self-awareness. Duval and Wickland's book does not give a physiological basis of self-awareness and mainly considers conscious self-awareness or evaluation.

The time taken for a subject to include a stimulus in one or another category is called Choice Reaction Time (Bertelson, P. and Tisseyre, F., 1966). This time may be used to ascertain the relative probability with which a subject associated the controlled stimulus with his chosen category. Reaction time has been used to structure concepts on tree models of memory (Bower, G.H., 1972). Distributions of reaction times have been extensively studied using exponential and Gaussian distributions (Hohle, R.H., 1965) in contradiction to McGill, W.J. (1963), also gamma distributions (Laming, D.R.J., 1968; Christie, L.S. and Luce, R.D., 1956; Restle, F., 1961). Some of these writers have inferred components of reaction times from these distributions.

Free associations may be used to map content and combinations of emotional sets. The speed and clustering as well as the time between clusters of free associations may be used to explore '...the idiosyncratic association aspect of intuition' (Guiora, A.Z. et al., 1965, p. 118). The use of drugs like Sodium Pentothal could aid associations. Comparison of the mapping before and after the recentring type of intuition might highlight the reorganization of emotional sets giving this Eureka-type experience.

Dinero, T.E. (1970) concerns himself with the affective components contributing to the connotation of a term. 'Osgood had defined connotation as almost synonymous with affect, an internal state corresponding to the linguist's emotive factors' (pp. 11/12). Dinero postulates that the affective-sensory-motor patterns associated with words, that he calls the 'organismic state' (which is similar to that which I call the emotional set) is composed of internalized response patterns: '...this state is physiognomic, some of the responses will reflect sensory and some affective substates. If these substates are activated, then in a given context they may serve to direct behaviour' (p. 61). Building on Osgood's model, he lets the internal responses r_m be gross responses 'reflecting a cognitive map or conceptual network. ...the individual r_m would then be nodes in such an internalized network' (p. 63). He equates the r_m with the concept network which he says the word evokes through a search process. He does not say how the search process 'act of reference' works. Nor does he elaborate the introduced ideas of nodes and networks. Neurophysiological evidence is reported in Section 6.2 to show that the central nervous system can mimic the action of physiological stimuli and may work as an 'act of reference' (e.g. Cohen, M.J., 1964, pp. 284 ff). Osgood's semantic differential is hence another tool for investigating a subject's organization of global information by emotional contexts.

The physiological components of an individual's emotional contexts may be more directly coded using the associated vector of physiological measures. It is a novel suggestion that the above quantitative indicators of emotional contexts, i.e. physiological vectors and associative probabilities, may be analysed using say factor analysis to account for their variability and so publicly reproduce idiosyncratic organizations of information. The super-imposition of the idiosyncratic organizations of similar creative workers in some specialism may be processed through these quantitative indicators to simulate an enhanced intuitive process.

Variable Encoding Increases Facilitating Redundancy

In analytic models of encoding information, search processes require unique sort keys for exact recall. The many algorithms for searching such organizations do not fit the speed and error distribution for intuitive recall (Brunswik, E., 1956; Newton, J.R., 1963; Peters, Joan T. *et al.*, 1974). For intuitive searching a probabilistic model is required where there is some multiclassification and variability of encoding information. This variability of encoding information clearly exists; '...there is a great variability in the mode of registering perceptions, in the exactness, intensity, richness and originality of combinations' (Szalita-Pemow, A.B., 1955, pp. 10/11). Within the same individual a similar stimulus may be encoded differently at various times, '...the position is adopted that repeated presentations of A-B are not encoded in an identical manner because of fluctuations both with respect to the external environment and with respect of the internal state of the organism' (Voss, J.F., 1972, p. 186); '...the functioning of the memory system is inextricably intertwined with the functioning of the total organism' (Anderson, J.R. and Bower, G.H., 1973, p. 44). The physiognomy of a symbol may vary depending on the mood of the observer. If one is in an unhappy mood a symbol is likely to have an unhappy physiognomy, whereas when in a happy mood the same symbol may have a happy physiognomy. As the emotional state is always changing along continuous multivariate dimensions no two states are identical, but due to individuals' restricted affective sensitivity, some similar emotional states may be indistinguishable. So not only may the same symbol be encoded by indistinguishable emotional states, but it may also be encoded by radically different emotional states.

This idea that similar stimuli may be encoded by different emotions is symmetrical with the findings that different emotions may be labelled by similar stimuli. This reflects the symmetry of contiguity conditioning, the process by which the encoding takes place. In support of this Dunlap, K. (1932) says that emotions are nothing more than an estimation of the situations in which they arise, either by an observer or by the subject himself. Also Landis, C. (1924) says that in every case it seems that the name given to an emotion is one which is assigned to some particular configuration or type of situation.

The fascinating experiments where subjects' physiology is changed, e.g. by adrenalin injections, and they are then placed in various environments, have shown that subjects need to label their new affective state and readily use environmental contexts (Cantril, H. and Hunt, W.A., 1932). The work of Valins, S. (1966), points to the apparent need for subjects to account for their body changes in some meaningful way. Valins showed two groups of subjects ten slides of female nudes. During viewing five of the ten slides, one group heard recordings of increased heart rate, the other group heard recordings of decreased heart rate. Both groups were led to believe that they were hearing their own heart beats. When asked to rate the attractiveness of the nudes the five slides shown during the increased heart rate recordings were significantly preferred. One month later these preferences were still significant. No consistent preferences were shown by the control groups. Similarly Weiskrantz, L. (1968) argues that the situational context must be considered when studying emotional states. Schachter, S. (1971) found that in states of physiological arousal subjects who had nothing to which to attribute their emotional state, would label the state according to cognitive variables. Subjects were injected with a drug or with a saline solution and informed, misinformed, or uninformed about the effects of the drug. They were then exposed to an actor who acted happy or angry. Pulse observation and self-reports were used to find the above results. Self-informed and informed subjects did not label emotional states according to socially induced moods of happiness or anger. Schachter, S. (1964) quotes researchers and experimental results that suggest

...that cognitive factors may be major determinants of emotional states... a general pattern of sympathetic discharge is characteristic of emotional states. Given such a state arousal, it is suggested that one labels, interprets and identifies this stirred-up state in terms of the characteristics of the precipitating situation and one's apperceptive mass. This suggests, that an emotional state may be considered a function of a state of physiological arousal. The cognition, in a sense, exerts a steering function. Cognitions arising from the immediate situation as interpreted by past experience provide the framework within which one understands and labels his feelings. (pp. 50/51)

There has been much effort in trying to classify emotions and identify physiological states corresponding to emotions. Allport, G.W. and Odbert,

H.S. (1936) produced a list of 2500 terms, most of which refer to feeling states or emotion. Darwin, C. (1872) lists thirty feeling states that are organized into eight general categories based on their intensity of emotion or concomitant facial expressions. Titchener, E.B. (1900) considered only two emotional states, *viz.* pleasant or unpleasant. This is consistent with a review of recent studies using varied techniques from introspection to factor analysis, that have also found this pleasantness/unpleasantness as a dimension (Dittman, A.T., 1972). Motor activity is a major component of the emotional state but Hebb sums up: 'All that has been shown is that there is no characteristic pattern of coexistent motor activity for a particular emotional state' (Hebb, D.O., 1946, p. 99). Schachter, S. and Singer, J.E. (1962) theorize two necessary factors for any emotional state are (1) a physiological component of autonomic arousal and (2) a cognitive component to label and explain arousal. The nature of the cognitive component is a function of the perception of environmental clues and past learning. Perhaps it is because this cognitive component to emotion gives so many combinations with the physiological state that it has not been possible to classify using objective indicators — e.g. concomitant plasma 17 hydroxycorticosteroid levels — any but extreme emotions, and it has not been possible to uniquely identify physiological states with the subjective nature of emotions. However, it is the view here that given a multiplicity of dimensions such as individual physiological vectors, probabilistic mapping of emotional sets' associations and contents as suggested in the section on 'formalized' emotional set, then it will be possible to distinguish between less extreme emotional states. Lazarus is in agreement with this view, his opinions being summarized by Strongman as: 'He [Lazarus, R.S.] believes, however, that ultimately emotional states will be distinguished from one another by the identification of specific physiological, cognitive and behavioural patterns, and eliciting events. On the other hand, he realizes that at present this is not possible' (Strongman, K.T., 1973, p. 84).

These many possible combinations of physiological states and cognitive contexts that comprise an emotional set, further increase the variability of encoding, as a specific stimulus may appear in different cognitive contexts. This may be deliberately encouraged to facilitate transfer. The ideas of Klein illustrate how the permutations of affective responses increase variability of cognitive associations:

> ... by a train of thought, I mean a temporarily extended series of events linked to stimulation by exteroceptors and visceroceptors, to motor activity by affective and effector processes, and to one another by facilitative and inhibitive signals in a patterned sequence. I assume, too, that these structural elements of a train of thought are connected flexibly and not in a fixed anatomical network; the same elements in different permutations may participate in many trains of thought. (Klein, G.S., 1970, p. 364)

Similarly: 'The stimulus for the formation of the new combinations (of thoughts and sensory perceptions) comes from the emotional sphere' (Szalita-Pemow, A.B., 1955, p. 8).

The need to label the emotional state encourages conditioning of the contiguent external stimuli to that state. This conditioning creates an emotional set. When internal or external stimuli again evoke this, or a similar emotional set, these labels will be instrumental in categorizing the present stimuli, i.e. defining the physiognomy. Wilkins presents the '. . . argument that the presence of autonomic arousal motivates an organism to search its environment for information which will account for the subjectively felt arousal. . . If no adequate explanation is found through veridical perception, the individual may distort reality in order to provide such an adequate account' (Wilkins III, W.W., 1970, p. 1). Perhaps this distortion gives the integration of the Gestalt, and its extreme is socially unacceptable in the schizophrenic. 'Emotional tuning' is a name given by Gellhorn, E. (1957) to this bias introduced in sensory reception and in motor expression by the establishment of an emotional state, involving the inhibition of some patterns of responses and the facilitation of others which provide the recurrent functional uniformity which characterizes each subjective emotion.

Newell and Simon say that Bartlett, F.C. (1958) made motor skills the key to understanding thinking (Newell, A. and Simon, H.A., 1972, p. 8), but they echo a general criticism of this in that motor skills in considerable part seem to be non-symbolic and that makes them a poor model for a system where symbols are central. However, motor skills are only some dimensions of the emotional context. Together with the effective dimensions they more accurately, though not uniquely, describe a symbol. It is the non-uniqueness of encoding, not the inaccuracy of encoding, that contributes to the redundancy. Lee, W. (1971) in his book *Decision Theory and Human Behaviour* suggests that the variability of subjective sensitivity and classification may be described by distributional theory and decision theory respectively, (p. 207). This leads to an information-processing basis for the Theory of Intuitive Thought Processes.

There is neurophysiological literature that describes processes which would enable the encoding, recall, and intuitive processing of information organized by emotional sets, as proposed here. Cohen, M.J. (1962) discusses research that shows how the central nervous system uses the continuous discharge of the sense organs, particularly from movement. These processes can encode the external stimuli. He also shows how the central nervous system can mimic the action of the original stimulus. This can effect a recall by reproducing the emotional context 'independently' of the present environment; but affected by imagery. Cohen cites (p. 274) experiments which monitor the discharge of sensory neurons due to joint movement (p. 277), and static position of the joints. The signal varies with the direction of joint movement (p. 279). He suggests that '. . .the presence of special phasic channels may be needed where delicate, precisely controlled responses must be evoked with a latency short enough to be relevant to the changing stimulus. This would apply to proprioceptive and spatial-equilibrium systems, in which separate phasic and tonic channels are known to occur' (p. 279); '...most sense organs send a continuous background discharge into the central nervous system ...The generalized tonic effect of receptors on motor function, demonstrated by behavioural experiments, can be ascribed to this continuous background barrage impinging on the central nervous system' (p. 285). The afferent systems have two kinds of activity. Both have been measured (pp. 284 ff). They are

(1) providing specific information about the environment, and
(2) setting excitability levels within the central nervous system.

Two information channels are used. The characteristics of this background discharge in vertebrates are under the control of the central nervous system. 'In other sensory systems, most notably certain proprioceptors in the vertebrates and invertebrates, the excitability of the receptor can be altered directly by the central discharge, which may be independent of the adequate environmental stimulus' (p. 286). 'Thus electrical stimulation of the efferent nerve can mimic the sensory response evoked by moving the joint. Presumably the central nervous system is also capable, therefore, of mimicking the action of the usual physiological stimulus for the sensory system... the sensory symbol of the external world can be evoked by the central nervous system independent of what is happening in the environment' (p. 287). Cohen further explains, by considering the structure of receptors, how reality and reproduced internal stimuli are differentiated (p. 288) and quotes work that shows that in vertebrates sense organs can duplicate information for reference. (p. 288).

Delgado, J.M.R. (1970) uses a model of constellations of functionally related neurol groups that determine an emotional state capable of duplicating emotional contextual information. 'At the central level, motor skills and other patterns of activity are stored in the nervous system as ideokinetic formulas which are similar during neural and during emotional displays' (p. 190).

Stimuli are variably encoded by different emotional sets, either due to appearing in a novel stimulus field, through being distorted through perception, or through being presented to the subject who is in a novel emotional set. This variable encoding increases the permutation of probable combinations of emotional sets. The possible increased permutations of combinations also increase the speed of recall (see Section 5.4). An analytic process minimizes redundancy but an intuitive process maximizes redundancy. Coding of stimuli through emotional contexts has been criticized under the assumption of being an analytic process but is acceptable as an intuitive process.

5.4   GLOBAL NATURE OF THE INTUITIVE PROCESS

The intuitive process is a non-linear parallel process effecting increasing redundancy by associating and integrating large conglomerations of information encoded into emotional sets through emotional contexts which pervade the whole body. This section outlines two aspects of non-linearity that contribute to the speed of intuitive association, *viz.* multimodal associations and hierarchical combinations of emotional sets. It shows how this non-linear process, in conjunction with the parallel processes of the tendency of concurrent stimuli to evoke emotional sets and the simultaneous tendencies to combine emotional sets, results in transformations of the global information corresponding to the notion of 'fantasy'.

In this section we also discuss how emotional sets are made more global, encompassing the information, by the three proposed methods of combining them and how this process is restricted by anxiety.

Non-linear Parallel Processing of Global Multicategorized Information Gives the Speed and Error Distributions Characteristic of Intuitive Processes

The two analogies and the references given in Section 2.1 contrasting intuition with abstract reasoning, logic or analytic thought, (property 4), illustrate that the intuitive process is viewed in the literature mainly as a continuous rather than a discrete process. Arnheim, R. (1970, p. 234) also refers to the intuitive thought processes as interacting within a continuous field. he alludes to intuition as the development of a network of relationships more appropriate to the nature of things than the operations of reason that 'are step-wise connections between fixed entities' (pp. 234/5). The 'sudden' attainment of insight has often seemed to contradict the continuous nature of the intuitive process. However, this apparent discreteness has been explained here in terms of the speed of the process, the insensitivity of the subject to continuous small changes in emotion causing a discrete approximation by a series of mean emotional states, and the noticeable large reduction in anxiety resulting in the cognitive associations of the present emotional set being taken as the sudden conscious insight responsible for this reduction in anxiety.

Section 2.1 also contrasts the linear nature of analytic thought with the non-linear nature of the intuitive process. The intuitive process is non-linear because of its global simultaneous interactive feedback nature, the many simultaneous changes throughout the body influencing cognitive associations and perceptions which continue to change the state of the body; '. . .the insights available in this mode cannot always be translated into sequential terms' (Ornstein, R.E., 1972, p. 138). This again contrasts with the analytic mode. Clark, J. (1973) in a non-mathematical paper contrasts this multimodal simultaneous process with the linear analytic process; 'In contrast to the linear movement of reason, intuition appears multi-dimensional' (p. 217).

The speed of non-linear parallel processing of information, reordering, associating and recall, will generally be much greater when the information is organized intuitively into overlapping multidimensional categories than will be the speed of linear non-parallel processing of information organized for analytic processing on a single dimension or sort key, into non-overlapping categories. The speed of processing generally increases with:

(1) the number of dimensions along which the processing may proceed;
(2) the size of the information base readily available, e.g. compare efficiencies of computers sorting algorithms having varying proportions of core to backing store-held information; and
(3) the multicategorization, i.e. redundancy, of the information.

Analytic processing however, correctly applied, gives an absolute accuracy and objective certainty which the probabilistic processing of the intuitive organization, also when correctly applied, just cannot match. 'The intuitive process depends on the rapidity of connections and availability of channels of communications' (Szalita-Pemow, A.B., 1955, p. 317). These differences in organization of analytic and intuitive information partially account for the characteristic differences in processing speed and error distribution of the two modes. A simple computer simulation of information organized by these two methods should reproduce the speed and error differences between the analytic and intuitive modes. I believe such a simulation has not yet been done; there are, however, many experiments on speed and accuracy of recall of information under conditions approximating those above whose results support the expected increased speed and error typical of intuitive recall suggested by increasing the organizational factors (1) to (3) above.

Emotion is multidimensional (Section 5.3). A series of experiments reported by Pollio, H.R. (1974, pp. 369 ff); illustrate how emotion is used to categorize thoughts. Subjects are asked to give continuous free recall to a particular stimulus word. The interword gaps are analysed so that the words can be split into fast and slow sequences. Using the semantic differential the words in the fast sequence are shown to be emotionally more similar than those in the slow sequence, illustrating that they are likely to be from one emotional category which was used for rapid recall. The same effect is noticed in learning sets of words (Weingartner, H., 1963). Words in one emotional subcluster require fewer trials to learn than sets of words from several emotional subclusters. A trick of mnemonists is to structure the relations between objects into emotionally meaningful wholes.

Choice Reaction Time reduces with the semantic distance. This mitigates against Net Theories of Memory — where words or concepts are nodes in some tree and their relations are the links between the nodes (Smith, E.E. *et al.*, 1974), although Collins, A.M. and Quillian, M.R. (1972b) say: 'It is important to keep in mind that semantic distance between concepts is not simply proportional to the number of nodes along the path between the concepts' (p. 314). These difficulties are avoided in this book by proposing the organization by emotional sets which combines the Net Models with the Set Theoretic

Models (Smith, E.E. *et al.,* 1974) so that concepts are reproduced by sets of elements, images, exemplars or attributes (see Meyer, D.E., 1970). In this investigation for example, concepts are represented by part of a network of emotional sets each of which is defined by non-unique attributes (see Section 5.3). As emotional sets are enlarged to incorporate other multicategorized attributes, the possible associations and hence the speed of association increases factorially.

It is misleading to use combinatorics to calculate the speed of choice of a response as a function of the number of responses available. For organic systems do not need this delay for a succession of binary choices, in the way that computer simulations of them do, because drive acts like a simultaneous pressure-head on all probable responses, giving instantaneous choice of response outlets.

Atkinson, R.C. and Shiffrin, R.M. (1968) mention two effects of encoding information by emotional sets that are relevant to the speed of intuitive recall and to the non-habituation of idiosyncratic memory responses. Being in a particular emotional set reduces the information available only to that categorized by that particular emotional set: 'The encoding might greatly decrease the effective area of memory which must be searched' (p. 118). Also '. . .the encoding might protect a fledgling association from interference by succeeding items. Thus if one encodes a particular pair through an image of, say, a specific room in one's home, it is unlikely that future inputs will have any relation to that image; hence they will not interfere with it' (p. 118). This multimodal, i.e. multidimensional, categorization distinguishes similar cognitions by their different affective attributes but will cluster unusual cognitions by their similar affective attributes, giving novel associations while protecting the possibly slight conditioning of novel experiences. The errors of intuitive recall, where for instance subjectively similar information is wrongly recalled, may be due in part to the similarity being on dimensions or modalities that do not coincide with those used to define the information objectively. This is supported by the results of an experiment by Conrad, R. (1964), who found that in short-term memory experiments when subjects were presented with visual stimuli acoustic confusions occurred, suggesting that visual items to be remembered are recoded by attributes associated with their sound or articulation and these substitution codes contribute to the incorrect recall. See also Section 8.1, intuitions need not be correct, property 9.

Embedding Emotional Sets Increases Selected Information

Emotional sets are embeddable. Fig. 5.4/1 illustrates how a person drifting between similar emotional sets A and B may retain the defining attributes of a previous set A and combine them with another set B to form a 'larger' emotional set C. The probable common responses to emotional set A and B, *viz. a* and *b,* will be reinforced at the expense of the probable responses not in common between the sets, *viz. c* to *f.* The common responses are instrumental

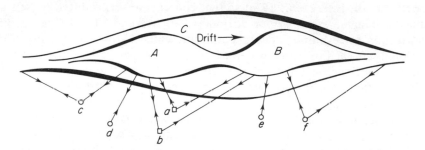

Fig. 5.4/1 Embeddable emotional sets

in defining the physiognomy of the new emotional set *C*. This reinforcement gives these defining features a higher priority as possible responses. This idea is in line with a paper on 'Structure and process in semantic memory' by Smith, E.E. *et al.* (1974). They call the notion of giving priority to defining features a '...characteristic feature assumption' (p. 216). They consider some threshold value for a probable response. Defining attributes above this they call 'defining features' and ones below this threshold value they call 'characteristics'. They would probably consider the greater response tendencies in Fig. 5.4/1 as 'defining features' and the lesser response tendencies in the same figure as 'characteristics'. The authors present two types of evidence for this theory, firstly linguistic analysis using hedges like 'technically speaking', and secondly, experimental findings of the typicality of an instance, i.e. a category pair on a semantic differential (p. 219). These results are typical of superordinate and subordinate categories and are not explained by the tree net structure of memory. The authors however present a theory which accounts for much of the data on categorization in memory. It is proposed here that it is the attributes in common between similar emotional sets, i.e. multicategorized stimuli, that encourage this embedding. Hence deliberately conditioning the same stimuli to different emotional sets will facilitate this part of the intuitive process. This has obvious application to teaching practice.

The notion of organizing lists of words into stable categories for recall is called the 'unitization hypothesis'. It is here supposed that stimuli are categorized into modifiable categories, i.e. into emotional sets, for recall. However, because of the similarity of these suppositions, results from experiments on the unitization hypothesis support this proposed organization for intuitive processing. Mandler, G. and Pearlstone, Z. (1966) concluded from the following experiment that such a hypothesis was a sufficient condition for a high level of recall. They required two groups of subjects to sort fifty-two cards, each bearing a word, into sets of similar meanings. The cards were then randomized and the exercise repeated until subjects duplicated their ordering on two consecutive trials. One group was previously asked to remember the cards for later recall, the other group was not. However, both groups did equally well in subsequent recall. Miller, G.A. (1956) put forward the unitization hypothesis and suggested a limit on our memories of 7 ± 2 'chunks' or categories. To account for large memories he introduced the idea of 'superchunks' which combine smaller chunks. Miller considers coding of cues where groups of cues may come to form larger perceptual units, attached to larger response units, so that the number of cues required for proficient performance might fall. Thus a subject may have a small number of larger 'chunks' to account for a larger memory. Mandler, G. (1967) discusses this embedding in relation to his own work (p. 332). Miller's G.A. (1956) concept of embeddable chunks into superchunks parallels my proposed organization of embeddable emotional sets allowing more global information to be available for intuitive processing.

Experimental results on the speed and accuracy of recall in relation to the number of categories have been contradictory, e.g. Underwood, B.J. (1964) in free recall experiments found better recall in words organized into a small number of conceptual categories, whereas Mandler, G. (1972) in his sorting and recall experiments has shown that, without overload on the number of categories, '...recall is in fact a linear function of the number of categories used during sorting' (p. 140). These contradictions may in part be due to experimenters not accounting for the encoding attributes implicit in the material and in its interaction with the subjects; see the note on this in Section 3.2. Some experimenters use nonsense trigrams. In contrast others use emotionally involving material but few experimenters record subject interviews on the mnemonics used. In illustration is the work of Simon, H.A. (1972). He produced a computer simulation, called EPAM, of his information-processing interpretation of visual imagery. Simon defines meaning by how many 'chunks' are involved in the meaning. EPAM uses the number of chunks involved in a stimulus to calculate learning speed. However, it fails to predict learning speed for emotionally involving stimuli, e.g. 'a whale smoking a cigar' (p. 189) presented visually. This is a novel discordance emotionally easy to resolve and is therefore fast to learn, but according to EPAM it is in three chunks and so is relatively slow to learn. Simon makes some good points on redundant representation of images, e.g. storing all attributes of an image at each node with its associations, so that the complete image may be recalled at any node (pp. 190 ff). His nodes correspond loosely to the concept of emotional sets as used in this book but the presently proposed organization modifies his by storing some attributes redundantly at various nodes, i.e. multicategorizing stimuli by emotional sets.

Solley, C.M. and Snyder, F.W. (1958) did a series of experiments on information processing and problem-solving to find a relationship between the number of bits of visual information and the time required to organize it. The task was for subjects to discriminate between the size and form of randomly distributed jigsaw pieces. The authors found a relation between the time taken to solve the jigsaw puzzle and the number of pieces. Their 'discrimination time' also involved time for movement. Experiment One involved eight subjects. From a thirty-five-piece grey jigsaw puzzle, two, four, eight, sixteen, and thirty-two pieces were chosen so that each joined with at least one other piece. One piece was handed to S who had to select one other piece to join it. The time taken was recorded. Results were that time t was a linear function of the number of pieces n. Namely $t = 0 \cdot 025n + 0 \cdot 080$. The authors then hypothesized that to complete a k-piece puzzle would just be the k sums of such linear functions with $n \geqslant k \geqslant 1$. This takes no account of memory but treats each selection as an independent task. The cumulative time was recorded for the two, four, eight, sixteen, and thirty-two piece puzzles. Results surprisingly agreed with prediction, although the residues for the least squares fit were not given. From these two results a prediction was made for the amount of time T to solve a puzzle of size n, namely

$$\text{Log}_2 T = 1 \cdot 6664 \qquad \text{Log}_2 n - 4 \cdot 2960$$

where $\text{Log}_2 n$ is the number of BITs of information in n pieces. Four subjects each did twenty-five puzzles of two, four, eight, sixteen, and thirty-two pieces, i.e. of one, two, three, four, and five BITs, and the authors did a five-hundred piece approximately nine-bit puzzle. Results were as expected, i.e. a linear log function. Log solution time is a linear function of the number of bits of information. No tests of significance were made. The authors say it is a linear log function rather than a log log function as other experiments have shown, because of spatial 'noise', i.e. interference of the patterns of randomly presented pieces with visual discrimination. 'Although the present studies do show a link between information theory and a type of problem-solving, there are also a large number of other problem-solving situations where information theory cannot be so clearly applied, e.g. the pendulum problem of Duncker' (p. 387) and other insight problems.

Stimuli have Simultaneous Competing Tendencies to Evoke and Combine Different Emotional Sets

Two other simultaneous tendencies operate on emotional sets to make the intuitive process a parallel rather than a linear process. In a stimulus field many stimuli are simultaneously competing in the subject's perception to evoke different emotional sets.

Fig. 5.4/2 illustrates emotional sets A and B with their conditioned responses a to d. Stimuli $x, y,$ and z are concurrently in the stimulus field and are simultaneously tending to evoke different emotional sets A or B according to the subject's previous experience. Concurrent stimuli cause dissonance when they tend to evoke very physiologically different emotional sets which will have discordant response tendencies. When in a particular emotional set there is also a simultaneous tendency to drift consecutively to a set with a high transition probability.

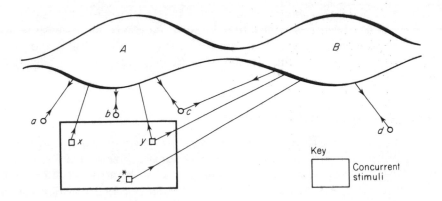

Fig. 5.4/2 Tendency of concurrent stimuli to evoke different emotional sets
simultaneously

Fig. 5.4/3 illustrates how when being in emotional set *A* there is a simultaneous tendency to drift next to emotional sets *B* and *C,* conditioned attributes *a, b,* and *c* contributing to the tendency to drift to emotional set *B* while conditioned attributes *d* and *e* are simultaneously contributing to the tendency to drift to emotional set *C.* Although only two possibilities are illustrated here the model proposes many such high-probability transition states; the direction of the physiological change also contributing.

The embedding of emotional sets and associating of visual responses to emotional sets on multimodal and multidimension criteria may be responsible for the surrealist transformation in space and time of the visual fantasy accompanying hypnogogic reverie and dreams. Such transformation being necessary for their affective components to be concordant with the changed emotional set, e.g. how much easier it is, in a relaxed state, to visualize growing into a giant while breathing in than while breathing out. Fantasy and movement are closely related. Davitz, J.R. and Ball, S. (1970) found:

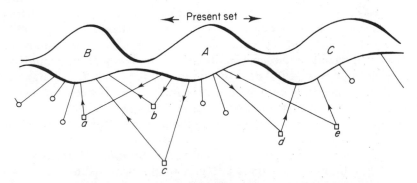

Fig. 5.4/3 Conditioned elements causing simultaneous tendencies to bring
alternative emotional sets into consecutive combinations

'Hyperactive children's ability to wait is closely related to growth of fantasy' (p. 327). It has been mentioned that intuitive types are more sensitive to subliminal stimulation (Section 5.2). Crutchfield, R.S. (1960) found that subjects sensitive to subliminal stimulation were more guided by fantasy than by reality cues.

Intuitive Process Increases Redundancy

This section shows the three methods of operating on emotional sets proposed as part of the intuitive process, *viz.* generalizing by increasing hierarchy, drifting to other sets, and combining similar sets by recentring each of these combinations is directed so as to increase redundancy of information which makes the intuitive process more global.

Through their personal experience people develop idiosyncratic relations among symbolic units. Anderson, J.R. (1972, p. 319) defines information as the connections among these symbolic units, e.g. ordered pairs like 'cat-dog' 'table-chair'. He says that it is these relationships that are stored in memory. In free recall paradigm, where individually presented words are allowed to be recalled in any order, subjects' conceptual organization of the associations between words makes them easier to recall. When E minimizes these relationships '...subjects apparently still impose their own idiosyncratic organization upon the word list' (p. 316). The interdependent cognitive and affective components (Harvey, O.J., 1965, p. 242) of these relationships are used to organize these relationships into emotional sets for intuitive processing. 'Intuitive thought processes are methods by which an individual when facing a situation of personal relevance will differentiate and integrate it, to structure or make meaning out of it. That individuals do this is one of the best documented and most pervasive assumptions in psychology' (Harvey, O.J., 1965, p. 243).

Redundancy occurs when relationships between elements conditioned to an emotional set are enhanced by the relationships between other elements conditioned to the same emotional set, i.e. they share constituents. For example, as illustrated in Fig. 5.4/4A 'soup' and 'plate' through experience may be related by being conditioned to a particular emotional set. Similarly 'soup' and 'spoon' may be conditioned through common cognitive and affective components to the same emotional set. As many of the cognitive and affective components will be in common between the two pairs, these indirectly associate plate with spoon. Any further experiences not involving part of these common cognitive and affective components relating 'plate' with 'spoon' will be reinforcing the direct conditioning of 'plate' with 'soup' or of 'soup' with 'spoon'.

Any novel direct experience that enhances an inferred relationship is redundant conditioning. Region A in Fig. 5.4/4B represents the cognitive and affective components that condition the symbol 'soup' to some emotional set. Similarly regions B and C represent the cognitive and affective components

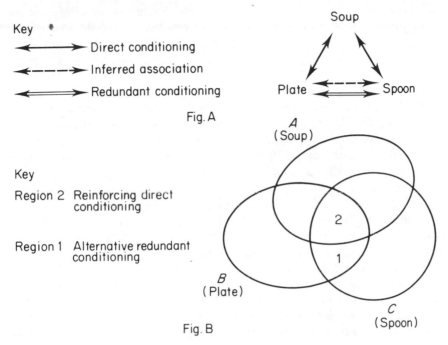

Key ●

⟵⟶ Direct conditioning

⟵----→ Inferred association

⟸⟹ Redundant conditioning

Fig. A

Key

Region 2 Reinforcing direct conditioning

Region 1 Alternative redundant conditioning

Fig. B

Fig. 5.4/4 Illustrating redundancy as alternative conditioning

that condition the symbols 'plate' and 'spoon' to that same emotional set. Common components $A \cap B$ relate 'soup' with 'plate'. Similarly $A \cap C$ relates 'soup' with 'spoon' and $A \cap B \cap C$, region 2 above which is part of the two previous experiences, i.e. $A \cap B \cap C \subset (A \cap B) \cup (A \cap C)$ also indirectly relates 'plate' with 'spoon'. Any new experience which also relates 'plate' and 'spoon', e.g. $A' \cap (B \cap C)$, region 1 in Fig. 5.4/4, will be redundant conditioning.

In neurophysiological terms such new alternative conditioning offers further responses for release of the self-induced anxiety state previously reduced only by responses represented by region 2 in Fig. 5.4/4B. Note that experiences which fall into this region, $A \cap B \cap C$, only reinforce existing responses and will have different psychological consequences from those experiences which fall into region 1 above, e.g. functional fixation due to the direct conditioning.

The enhancing of the inferred relationships between elements by these alternative anxiety-reducing responses further coalesces the information contained in the emotional set around this relationship, i.e. the physiognomy is altered in favour of the 'plate' 'spoon' relationship, and the emotional sets are altered in the direction of increased redundancy. The experiences to create such alternative redundant conditioning must occur whilst the subject is in the 'plate soup spoon' emotional set or else this experience will cause compartmentalization by a direct conditioning of 'soup' with 'spoon' in another emotional set. This is relevant to 'setting the scene' for teaching.

The additional alternative responses for reduction in anxiety within a subset of the original group of elements are experienced as simplicity, elegance, beauty, or harmony during the intuitive process, i.e. conceiving interconfirmed relationships within a smaller number of categories. Bruner, J.S. (1962) reports that in the opinion of the mathematician Poincaré the heuristic that guides one to fruitful combinations and distinguishes the good theorist from the mere formalist is 'emotional sensibility', 'physical intuition', or 'intuitive familiarity', i.e. 'the feeling of mathematical beauty, of the harmony of numbers and forms, of geometric elegance. It is this that guides one in making combinations in mathematics' (pp. 20/21). This is a common experience where the suitability of intuitive products is judged by such subjective criteria, e.g. 'I don't know what I want but I recognize it when I see it' (see Section 5.5 on intuitive recognition).

One method of altering emotional sets, not included in the three methods of intuitive processing above, is to alter by further conditioning the relative importance of responses in evoking and categorizing emotional sets.

Fig. 5.4/2 showed that concurrent stimuli tend to evoke different emotional sets simultaneously, possibly resulting in dissonance. Similarly redundancy allows a single stimulus to tend to evoke one of two similar but distinct emotional sets, perhaps from different chains of emotional sets. Further conditioning of a particular bond will strengthen the tendency of the stimulus concerned to evoke a particular emotional set at the expense of the tendency of the stimulus to evoke some other emotional set. This is illustrated in Fig. 5.4/5, where c represents a stimulus simultaneously tending to evoke emotional sets A or B. P_{cA} and P_{cB} represent its tendency to evoke emotional sets A and B respectively. Further conditioning of the association of c with emotional set B (say) will increase the probability P_{cB} relative to P_{cA} so that when the subject encounters stimulus c again, emotional set B with its associations (context B) will tend to be evoked rather than emotional set A and its associations (context A). Similarly if the probability P_{aA}, which is the

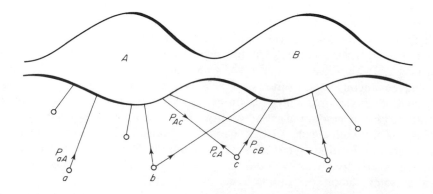

Fig. 5.4/5 Altering the relative importance of elements to evoke and categorize emotional sets by reinforcing conditioning

tendency of stimulus a to evoke emotional set A, is reinforced relative to P_{cA} so that $P_{aA} > P_{cA}$ then as stimulus a more readily evokes emotional set A and its associations than does stimulus c, stimulus a is more instrumental in categorizing context A than is stimulus c.

Among the many experimental results that show further conditioning of selected elements to contexts makes these elements more likely to be used in categorizing the contexts, is the following by Solley, C.M. and Messick, S.J. (1957). They showed forty subjects the concept of 'tribes', using as exemplars combinations of tall-short, happy-sad, fat-skinny, and black-white. Subjects' verbal descriptions of tribe members reflected the most frequently occurring combination of traits. 'We assume that the probability of a response in a given category increases if it is positively reinforced and decreases if it is negatively reinforced' (Malone, T.W., 1975, p. 263).

This further conditioning of existing responses is of the type falling into region 2 in Fig. 5.4/4B and will tend to produce functional fixation by reducing the drift of emotional sets by increasing the tendency of a present stimulus to hold the present emotional set and its associated stimuli/responses. This functional fixation is further expanded in Section 9.2.

In Fig. 5.4/5 the arrow from emotional set A to stimulus/response c illustrates P_{Ac} which is the tendency, when in emotional A, of giving response c. P_{Ac} is a monotonically increasing function of P_{cA} due to the physiological similarity of coding and representing stimuli and responses, their contiguity etc. When P_{cA} is comparable in size with P_{cB} then stimulus response c relieves the tension of emotional set A, including elements b, c, and d. Response c also reduces the tension of emotional set B, including the same elements b, c, and d. Hence in relation to these elements b, c, and d, P_{cB} and P_{cA} are mutually redundant. The effect of reinforcing conditioning which results in say $P_{cA} >> P_{cB}$ is to reduce this redundancy by tending to associate c only with emotional set A, especially in ego-threatening anxiety states where the threshold sensitivity to such low probabilities will have been raised. By reducing redundancy, reinforcing conditioning will facilitate analytic rather than intuitive thought.

Intuitive Learning versus Rote Learning Resulting from Redundancy-Increasing Alternative Conditioning versus Reinforcing Direct Conditioning

By combining the diagram of similar emotional sets (Fig. 5.4/5) with the diagram of the cognitive and affective components in common between elements conditioned to similar emotional sets (Fig. 5.4/4) it is possible to illustrate the increasing redundancy that directs the three operations on emotional sets terminating in the conscious intuition, Fig. 5.4/6. This diagram also illustrates how reinforcing direct conditioning enhances rote learning whereas alternative conditioning enhances intuitive learning.

Regions A, B, and C in Figs 5.4/4 and 5.4/6 correspond to conditioned attributes b, c, and d in Fig. 5.4/5. Similarly emotional sets P and Q in Fig. 5.4/3 correspond to emotional sets A and B in Fig. 5.4/5.

In Fig. 5.4/6 region B represents, as it does in Fig. 5.4/4B, some cognitive

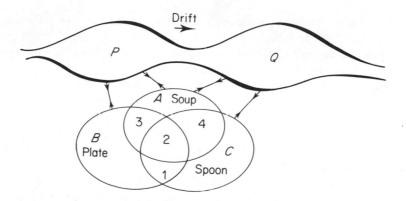

Fig. 5.4/6 Cognitive and affective attributes in common between similar emotional sets

and affective attributes of the symbol 'plate'. Similarly regions A and C represent some cognitive and affective components of the symbols 'soup' and 'spoon' respectively. Note that 'plate' is conditioned to extant emotional set P not Q, and 'spoon' is conditioned to the extant emotional set Q not P, whereas 'soup' is conditioned to both extant emotional sets. The attributes conditioned to extant emotional sets will of course be changed as the organism combines the emotional sets. This represents the basic learning process. As we continuously drift through emotional sets the conditioning of our affective and cognitive responses is modified and so through this basic learning process we are different from one moment to the next. This chapter outlines the variables affecting this drift and conditioning.

Some of the attributes of the symbols 'plate', 'spoon', and 'soup' may also be conditioned to other emotional sets not shown in Fig. 5.4/6. The attributes in regions 2 and 3 are in emotional set P. 'Soup' and 'plate' are related because they have these attributes in common in the emotional set. Similarly the attributes in regions 2 and 4 are in emotional set Q. However, as the organism drifts from emotional set P to the similar emotional set Q by combining P with Q many attributes from emotional set P are carried over to Q; like mown grass under the rake, most is dragged along but some falls behind. How many attributes continue into the next emotional set depends on the similarity of the emotional sets, remembering that this model approximates a continuous change by mean emotional sets whose difference depends on the sensitivity of the subject to this change.

The drift from present emotional set P to the next emotional set Q associates attributes in region 3 with those in the extant emotional set Q. The internal or external stimuli that are responsible for the drift also contribute attributes in region 1 to the new emotional set Q formed by the combination resulting in redundant conditioning of, in this example, 'plate' with 'spoon'. The new emotional set Q now contains attributes in the regions 1 to 4. Q now becomes the present emotional set and the drift continues.

In 'pure' rote learning region 1 is null but responses in region 2 have been reinforced. In the intuitive process the amount of redundant conditioning carried along increases until it is sufficient to terminate the process in an intuitive product. The flow diagram in Fig. 5.4/7 illustrates this where:

The shaded area represents the emotional state first evoked by the 'problem' stimulus.

The shaded area represents the next extant emotional set into which the organism will drift. Some attributes in region A, being in common with the last emotional set, contribute to the transition to this set.

The shaded area and dot (o) represent the combining of the emotional sets by drift, embedding, or recentring and become the new present emotional set.

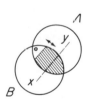

The shaded area and dot represent this present emotional set. The dot region represents the proportion of the emotional set which is redundant alternative conditioning. This redundancy may increase or decrease depending on whether or not the responses previously conditioned to the last extant emotional set to be combined were 'solution' responses or not — i.e. whether or not the previous conditioned responses reduced the self-induced anxiety accompanying the original problem stimuli. The dashed line xy (x_ _ _ _y) represents the fixed threshold value above which the proportional increase in redundancy is sufficient to terminate in a conscious intuition.

'It may be that what then emerges is an attitude towards the massive effects of a series of past reactions. Remembering is a constructive justification of this attitude' (Bartlett, F.C., 1932, p. 208). In Schachter's terms, the terminating intuition is a cognitive labelling of the emotional set concurrent with the proportional increase in redundancy above the threshold value; see Section 4.2 on fluctuating anxiety states. Experiments by Schachter, S. and Singer, J.E. (1962) have shown: 'Given a state of physiological arousal for which an individual has no immediate explanation, he will label this state and describe his feelings in terms of the cognitions available to him' (p. 398).

Although we will now deal separately with the three methods of combining emotional sets, during any one example of the intuitive process all three methods may be in operation.

228

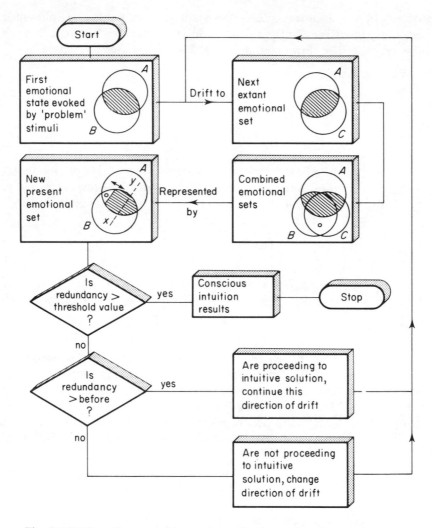

Fig. 5.4/7 Flow diagram of increasing redundancy directing combinations of emotional sets to the terminating conscious intuition

Increasing Redundancy by Hierarchical Embedding of Emotional Sets

Hierarchical embedding of emotional sets produces the least rate of increase in redundancy of the three methods of combining emotional sets. This is because the most similar emotional sets, which already have the majority of their responses in common, are combined and hence, as few other responses are available to be related by the combination, only a small amount of alternative redundant conditioning occurs.

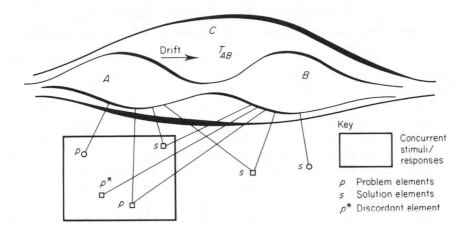

Fig. 5.4/8 Increased redundancy by hierarchical embedding of similar emotional sets with a high transition probability

Problem elements are of two types. There are stimuli that tend to evoke similar emotional sets of previously low transition probability and there are concurrent stimuli that tend to evoke different emotional sets. The former encourage combination of emotional sets. The latter are the cause of dissonance whose resolution reinforces the direction of drift. Without the elements causing dissonance the process would result in other thought and behaviour rather than resulting in intuitive thought and behaviour.

Fig. 5.4/8 illustrates the conditions under which embedding is likely to occur. A represents the present emotional set and B represents a very similar emotional set so that the transition probability T_{AB} is very high.

Emotional set A has many of the problem elements conditioned to it and some of the solution elements. Similarly emotional set B has many of the solution elements conditioned to it and some of the problem elements. Both emotional sets have many problem and solution elements in common and this similarity, which is reinforced by the drift, prevents the subject from being able to differentiate between them. A and B are embedded in one emotional set, C. The few elements that were not in common are now associated, producing a small amount of redundancy. Psychologically the subject has generalized by including all the elements in the same emotional context, under the same category label, e.g. realizing that an ostrich is also a bird. As detailed in Section 5.4 this generalization allows more selected information (responses) to be immediately available for the intuitive process. Hierarchical embedding requires little or no incubation period as the drift to an emotional set of high transition probability is the shortest emotional change. The new emotional set C may later be further combined into a higher echelon of the hierarchy, a more inclusive category, or by either of the following two processes; drifting or recentring.

230

Increasing Redundancy by Drifting Through Emotional Sets of High Transition Probability

The process of drifting from the emotional set evoked by the 'problem' elements, through increasingly different extant emotional sets of high transition probability to form the new emotional set to which the 'solution' elements are conditioned, produces a higher redundancy than the process of embedding emotional sets. This is because the embedded emotional sets, being very similar, have few elements not in common which may be associated by embedding. However, by drifting through increasingly dissimilar emotional sets the terminating emotional set will be so different from the initial emotional set that the increasing association of the many disjoint elements will result in a high redundancy.

In Fig. 5.4/9 emotional set *A* is evoked by the 'problem' elements with its accompanying non-ego-threatening anxiety. Solution responses that reduce this anxiety are conditioned along the chain of emotional sets with high transition probability, *viz. A* to *G*. The link elements in common along the chain aid the transition. The new elements may be included in the 'solution' while they reduce the initial anxiety by being concordant with the present emotional set and any of the originally discordant elements. By increasing redundancy they give direction to the drift of emotional sets. This answers the problem of giving direction to the search for an intuitive solution without the subject knowing what the solution is. Without the original discordance that makes this the intuitive process the natural direction of physiological change would be more prominent in directing the combinations of emotional sets. However, increasing redundancy felt as progressive reduction in tension confirms the direction of combination gives, with the aid of the link elements, direction to the intuiter who feels that he is 'instinctively' on the right path to an unknown destination. (See Section 4.2 on fluctuating anxiety states.)

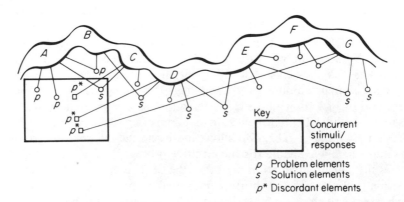

Fig. 5.4/9 Drifting through a chain of emotional sets with high transition probabilities

In a contribution entitled 'A preliminary study of insight' Greeno, J.G. (1972) reports on an experiment showing that linking contexts brings together component ideas in a way characteristic of insight. Subjects were taught the use of the Binomial Theorem to calculate the probability of suitable sequences. It was found that the wording of a test question had to be similar to previous examples before subjects could apply the Binomial Theorem in a given circumstance. Seven out of eight subjects answered a syntactically complex question containing the linking context phrase but none could answer the same question phrased simply without the context-linking phrase. Greeno says '...we apparently have an especially clear case of insightful behaviour to work with, and we may have evidence that, in general, insightful behaviour requires some sort of linking or bridging between the component ideas that are brought together in the process of solving a problem' (pp. 374/5).

Successfully terminating such a drift by a reduction of tension alternatively conditions elements in common between more dissimilar emotional sets. In Fig. 5.4/9 this would be represented by more and longer bonds between the elements and emotional sets. Such conditioning of elements in common to dissimilar emotional sets enhances the intuitive process increasing the redundancy in the organization of the high-intuitive type, whereas traversing the chain from an emotional set with no initial non-ego-threatening anxiety to resolve, as in non-intuitive thought and behaviour, will only reinforce direct conditioning of the existing link elements, making such a chain of thoughts and feelings more likely to recur. This conditioning is discussed in Section 3.2 on conditioning response tendencies to emotional states.

Experiments on the recall of word sets and word pairs illustrate how this linking makes the chain easier to retraverse for recall. For example Deese, J. (1959) found that frequently sets of associated words are easier to recall than sets of words that are not interassociated. Similarly in free recall of twenty-four pairs of words, a stimulus word and its highest frequency associate, not presented adjacently, Jenkins, J.J. and Russell, W.A. (1952) found a high probability that the words would be recalled together in pairs.

Intuition resulting solely from this drifting process requires a longer incubation period than intuition resulting from the embedding process. This is because of the time required for the organism to drift through the emotional sets. As no new external stimuli are necessary for this preconscious process, the intuition may result during a continuous interval in which the subject is involved with the problem.

Increasing Redundancy by Recentring Emotional Sets with Low Transition Probability

Recentring of emotional sets results in the greatest rate of increase in redundancy and accompanying anxiety reduction. It is felt as the Eureka experience. Section 4.1 describes recentring to illustrate the role of incubation in insight. Fig. 4.1/1 illustrates chains of emotional sets before and after recentring. Recentring gives the most redundancy because the two emotional sets that are combined by being recentred on one another come from two separate chains of emotional sets so that the transition probability between the two emotional sets is very low and they have many elements not in common. When the two emotional sets are combined, drastically changing the transition probabilities by forming a node between the two chains, it is the association of these many elements not previously held in common that results in this increased redundancy and felt release in tension.

The recentring experience often occurs after a long incubation period when the problem has been consciously 'shelved', i.e. the subject is no longer in the chain of emotional sets with high transition probability that includes the emotional set to which the problem elements are conditioned. Referring to Fig. 4.1/3 in illustration of this, emotional set C with the problem elements 1 and 3 may have been 'shelved' so that now sometime later the subject is drifting in chain $PQRS$. When in emotional set Q, which is physiologically similar to C but which contains solution elements, an external stimulus evokes emotional set C. The combining of the two emotional sets C on Q allows the solution elements to be instantly associated with the problem elements. The association of the many elements not previously in common gives 'new insights'. These new insights and the new 'paths of thought' opened by this node linking the chains of emotional sets explain the new relationships mentioned in the literature and reviewed in Section 2.3 under property 11, recentring. Without the discordant elements to be resolved, such recentring would be transient as in the experience of *déjà vu*.

Ego Threat Inhibits Intuition by Partitioning Global Knowledge

The literature is replete with reports of high motivation, anxiety, or threat inhibiting insight and creativity, disorganizing complex responses, reducing peripheral cue utilization, increasing rigidity of cognitive organization and functional fixedness, etc. There is also much physiological evidence that threat to the integrity of the ego produces autonomic changes accompanying such behaviour inhibitive to the intuitive process, giving less sensitivity to body changes, differentiation of general behaving states into specific arousal states, and/or increased internal noise, e.g. heart amplitude and rate, etc. This section uses the documented evidence of loss of sensitivity to internal body changes accompanying ego threat to explain the restrictive effect of ego threat on the intuitive process by proposing that the lack of sensitivity to internal peripheral cues, physiological components of a response that are far from the physiological mean of the present emotional set, makes that response and similar responses unattainable. It has been discussed that these redundant responses with peripheral physiological components contribute to the transition between emotional sets and their combination. As the transition between emotional sets and their combination is the basis of the intuitive process, the unavailability of these responses will severely inhibit the process.

Increased drive does not necessarily increase insight. Viesti, C.R. Jr. (1971, p. 182) showed that increasing drive by offering higher payment for insight solutions did not increase insightful problem-solving. The intuitive process involves learning, memory, objectively novel responses and many incorrect competing responses, some only slightly conditioned by peripheral physiological components to their emotional sets. Martin reviews approximately fifty papers on the effect of anxiety on memory and learning and concludes that it is precisely such tasks with these characteristics that are most affected by anxiety. 'A loose empirical generalization that emerges from studies in this area is that the kinds of tasks most likely to be affected by stress are learning and memory tasks involving novel or relatively poorly learned responses where incorrect competing responses are both numerous and relatively strong; or perceptual tasks in which conditions are imposed that make appropriate discriminations difficult' (Martin, B., 1961, p. 246). Cowen, E.L. (1952) indeed, found that increased stress inhibits insightful problem-solving. In his paper on 'The influence of varying degrees of psychological stress on problem solving rigidity' he reports: 'Statistical analysis reveals that under increasingly stressful psychological conditions there is a greater tendency to adhere to an induced behaviour which has become inappropriate' (p. 516), i.e. functional fixedness.

Under threat the cognitive organization by emotional sets becomes more rigid, the combination of emotional sets being inhibited. 'The structure and organization of self appears to become more rigid under threat' (Rogers, C.R., 1951, p. 390). Figs 5.4/10 and 5.4/11 illustrate the effect of ego threat on the repertoire of responses available to the subject.

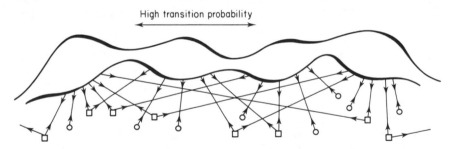

Fig. 5.4/10 High redundant responses available under low ego threat

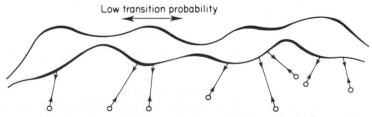

Fig. 5.4/11 Low redundant responses available under high ego threat

Increasingly high ego threat makes increasingly unattainable the responses in common between emotional sets. Without any such responses, the transition probability between emotional sets will depend only on the physiological drift of the organism. Under ego threat the generalized behavioural state differentiates into specific arousal states (Martin, B., 1961, pp. 234/5, also see Section 3.1) which are less variable and more discrete. When the subject is in a particular emotional set under ego threat, the transition probability is low. There is less probability of changing his present emotional set as the physiological state is less variable and the redundant responses are unavailable.

As Fig. 5.4/11 illustrates, under ego threat only the dominant responses, with physiological components near the mean of their emotional sets, are available. This is in concert with the 'behavioural law' of classical Behavioural Psychology that asserts the probability of occurrence of a dominant response is raised by increased drive (Hull, C.L., 1943). In the literature on problem-solving this restriction of responses to those only in the present low redundant emotional set is called functional fixation. Animal experiments have shown that fixations increase to 'abnormal fixation' under high anxiety (Maier, N.R.F., 1956).

Griesinger proposes a quantum mechanical description of behaviour which connects through the Schrödinger equation the propensity to action with perceived rewards. His model has properties in common with mine, namely that under high anxiety (high perceived rewards) emotional sets become increasingly discrete, making less probable the change from one emotional set to another. Griesinger uses the energy states described by the eigenvalues as being analogous to emotional states. This view coincides with the concept presented in this book of mean emotional states being subjectively discrete. Properties of the equations are as follows:

> There exists a set of states which are more aversive than λ_0. These states may form a discrete set or a continuum, depending on the form of the return potential. The values of λ depend on the return potential. If the return potential tends to constrain behaviour to a particular behavioural region, then at least some of the states will be discrete. The stronger the forces of contraint, the greater is the magnitude of the separation between discrete states. In a steady state... an individual will tend to be found in one particular emotional state; which state he will be found in depends on the history of interaction with the environment. Transitions between states occur only when there is some change in the force field. The greater the magnitude and the rate of change of the field, the greater is the probability that transitions to higher states of excitation will occur. (Griesinger, D.W. 1974, pp. 44/45)

Here 'return potential' is analogous to the perceived reward for action. Interpreting this model in terms of the effect of the environment on intuitive processes, it indicates that the stronger the response tendencies the greater is the tendency to a discrete emotional state.

The literature on anxiety is concerned with the differential effects of high versus low anxiety: 'The literature on emotional stress and performance is replete with examples of the motivating characteristics of low levels of arousal and the degradation of performance with excessively high levels of arousal' (Griesinger, D.W., 1974, p. 44). Solomon, R.L. and Wynne, L.C. (1954) have also considered the differential effects of mild and severe threat as applicable to conditioning of autonomic responses, such as fear reactions and instrumental trial and error learning. They have used this dual nature of learning as a point of departure for explaining the rapid acquisition and unusual persistent of avoidance responses. They believe that different sets of learning concepts must be used when pain-fear stimulation is intense enough to cause trauma, and when dealing with mild avoidance-producing stimuli. Also there is a threshold that has to be exceeded to obtain the change and they indicate that a state of anxiety, with the resultant autonomic responses and feedback, is produced with such stimuli. However, in Section 3.1 there was reported another dimension to anxiety other than high versus low, *viz.* ego-threatening versus non-ego-threatening, e.g. fear, hunger versus curiosity, self-competition. Even mild secondary ego threat can cause autonomic changes comparable with high primary ego threat because of the mediation of cognitive variables in secondary threat, e.g. anticipation of an electric shock or even the verbal threat of an electric shock produces as great a GSR response as the shock itself (Folkins, C.H., 1970). Grings, W.W. (1973) demonstrated a clear dominance of cognitive variables in three response categories: (1) orienting response, (2) anticipatory response and (3) the UCS-omission response. He summarizes: '...the results of the data just presented suggest a strong capability for verbally instituted expectations to determine autonomic behaviour in the direction of the verbalized expectancy' (p. 248). This technique is used by Bastick, T. (1979) in the threat sequence of an experiment to confirm a physiological measure of intuition.

Even a mild ego threat can be disorganizing as is shown by Coombs, A.W. and Taylor, C. (1952). In their work on the 'Effect of the perception of mild degrees of threat on performance' they asked subjects to encode neutral and threatening statements, e.g. offensive remarks about their mothers. They found that errors and time taken on encoding threatening statements were significantly greater than for the neutral statements. They take this as evidence that perception of threat to the self is expected to reduce the perceptive field to the area of the perceived threat. The authors emphasize the threat was only a mild one. The existence of the two dimensions of threat illustrates how misleading it is to extrapolate from rat insight experiments to human insight behaviour as has been done in the literature. The rat 'insight' responses are elicited under high-drive, ego-threat environments in which human insight could not operate.

5.5   GLOBAL NATURE OF INTUITIVE PRODUCTS

The literature attests that intuitions come in a 'whole' form. As intuitive products are the final state of the global intuitive process, this section uses the global nature of this process to explain the 'wholeness' of the final products. It is shown how the intuitive process by selecting redundant information increases the global nature of the process, resulting in the intuitive products of:

(1) intuitive recognition;
(2) intuitive acceptance — with recognition, and
without recognition;
(3) intuitive judgments — of similarity, and
of suitability.

The subjective impression of an intuition is that it is whole, complete or almost so. Sigmund Freud, writing on the intuitions of Goethe and Helmholtz, said: 'What is essential and new in their creations came to them without premeditation and as an almost ready-made whole' (Jones, E., 1953, p. 327). This impression is due to the sudden awareness of the mass of redundant cognitive and affective information constituting intuition, i.e. three points are responsible for the subjective 'wholeness' of the final intuition:

 (i) the mass of information available;
(ii) the suddenness with which it is available; and
(iii) the large proportion of redundancy giving a unity and interlinking to the information.

These points are individually detailed elsewhere in this book. Section 5.1 considered the global nature of the information stored by emotional contexts on multimodal attributes. The suddenness of awareness is further discussed in Section 7.2 under property 1, quick, immediate, sudden appearance. The third point is considered in the previous section, 5.4. Here the three points are considered jointly. The suddenness with which so much parallel structured information is available has a tendency to overload the subject's linear channels of communication. This is particularly noticeable in the energetic gesticulations accompanying an attempted verbal communication of the intuition. Poincaré, H. (1969) observes this with intuitive mathematicians. 'While speaking, M. Bertrand is always in motion; now he seems in combat with some outside enemy, now he outlines with a gesture of the hand the figures he studies. Plainly he sees and he is eager to paint, this is why he calls gesture to his aid' (p. 206). Dittman, A.T. (1972) considers these external emotional signals as containing information and uses information theory to measure the redundancy of such signals. These movements tend to bunch within non-fluent clauses to give $21 \cdot 9$ per cent redundancy compared with $5 \cdot 3$ per cent redundancy during fluent clauses. 'The concentration of movements around the non-fluencies, themselves, yields even higher figures of redundancy, up to $50 \cdot 2$ per cent for movement pairs where the first movement occurs just before the non-fluency' (p. 181). Dittman also reviews Broadbent's filter theory (Broadbent, D.E., 1958) which is relevant to interference through overloading human information channels.

The redundancy of the information available for an intuitive process at any one time may be increased by adding associated external or internal information to external perception, or combining emotional sets, or redundancy may be increased by reordering present available information by combining emotional sets: '...it is possible to show that the actual redundancy of a particularly ordered set can be appreciably less than the actual redundancy of that set differently ordered' (John, E.R., 1957, p. 19). The Eureka experience has been explained by increasing redundancy through drastically reordering the transition probabilities of emotional sets by combination through recentring (Section 5.4). Increasing redundancy through the other methods of combining emotional sets, hierarchical embedding, and drifting has also been discussed in Section 5.4. It is now shown how the intuitive products (1) to (3) above may be achieved by adding associated information through external perception or by these three methods of combining emotional sets.

The intuitive products (1) to (3) above all involve the concordant matching of a stimulus or stimuli with the present emotional set. If the stimulus is discordant with the present emotional set, then it will not be intuitively recognized, intuitively accepted, or intuitively judged to be similar to the other elements of that emotional set or to be of equivalent suitability. Two elements conditioned to the same emotional set are concordant because through their shared attributes (multimodal physiological components) both contribute to the physiological set, i.e. the same physiological variable does not contribute to their constituents in opposing directions simultaneously. In Fig. 5.4/5 these shared attributes are illustrated by the region in common between the regions representing the attributes of the elements conditioned to an emotional set. In this section these attributes in common between elements are represented by a dashed line linking the redundant elements that are associated by having these attributes in common, see Fig. 5.5/1. The explanation of the intuitive products will be in terms of increasing these links representing joint associations. 'We talk as if we store, remember, and retrieve individual attributes. Actually, we operate only on their links and associations' (Norman, D.A. and Rumelhart, D.E., 1970, p. 27).

These links will include redundant alternative conditioning (Section 5.4). By increasing the common attributes, i.e. associations represented by links, between a set of stimuli and the elements conditioned to an emotional set, redundancy will increase and the stimuli will become more concordant within that emotional set. This may be achieved by adding jointly associated elements to either the internal emotional set or to the stimuli as illustrated in Fig. 5.5/2. If i internal elements are associated with j stimuli the redundancy represented

238

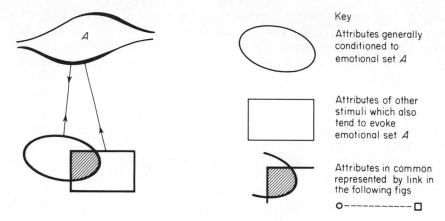

Key

Attributes generally
conditioned to
emotional set *A*

Attributes of other
stimuli which also
tend to evoke
emotional set *A*

Attributes in common
represented by link in
the following figs

Fig. 5.5/1 Experienced cognitive and affective attributes in common between
stimuli represented by links

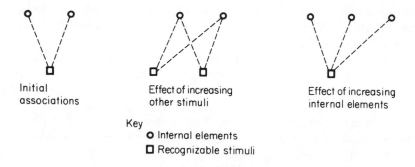

Initial
associations

Effect of increasing
other stimuli

Effect of increasing
internal elements

Key
○ Internal elements
□ Recognizable stimuli

Fig. 5.5/2 Increased redundancy by adding jointly associated
information

Internal
elements

Common
associated
elements

Element
novel to
internal
elements

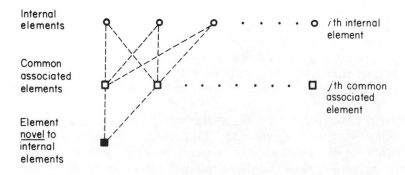

○ *i*th internal
element

□ *j*th common
associated
element

Fig. 5.5/3 Associating a novel stimulus with an emotional set by adding
associated elements

by the number of links of equal common association will be $R = ij$. Greater redundancy ensues by increasing the smaller set, i.e. if $i > j$ then $(i+1)\, j > i\, (j+1)$. But if $i > j$ then $(i+1)\, j > i\, (j+1)$. This has implications for learning and problem-solving in indicating whether the subject's experiential knowledge should be increased or more information about the problem should be given to encourage an intuition rather than over-learning.

In certain circumstances a novel stimulus that has no experiential association with the present internal context may be associated with the present emotional set by increasing its indirect associations with that emotional set, as illustrated in Fig. 5.5/3.

A truly novel stimulus, with no previous experiential association with any emotional set, will of course not be discordant with any emotional set and by being contiguous with a particular emotional set will be conditioned as a possible future response in that emotional set. In the following 'novel' means novel to the present emotional set.

The amount of redundancy is represented by the number of links which are considered to be of equal associative strength for simplicity. With i elements in the emotional set associated with j stimuli each associated with the novel stimulus gives redundancy $R = j + ij$ links from the novel stimulus to the emotional set. Redundancy may be increased by adding to the internally associated elements i through combinations of emotional sets or by adding to the associated stimuli j by increasing the stimulus field, e.g. giving more external information. The most efficient method depends on the relation of j to i. Redundancy is best augmented by increasing i if $i + 1 > j$ or adding to j if $i + 1 > j$, i.e. within one element, add to the smaller set * as in the case of no novel stimulus (see previous paragraph).

[Note. From $R = j + ij$, $\dfrac{\partial R}{\partial i} = j$ and $\dfrac{\partial R}{\partial j} = 1 + i$ $\dfrac{\partial R}{\partial i} > \dfrac{\partial R}{\partial j} \Rightarrow j > i + 1$ where $\dfrac{\partial R}{\partial i}$ and $\dfrac{\partial R}{\partial j}$ are the rates of change of redundancy with respect to the number of i and j respectively.]

Increased Redundancy Leading to Immediate and Delayed Intuitive Recognition

Recognition of a stimulus is taken to mean 'to know it again as experienced before'. As the stimulus has been experienced before, it is conditioned to at least one emotional set. The stimulus will be intuitively recognized when the subject is in one of these emotional sets; for then it will be concordant with the other elements of that emotional set, i.e. in one of its usual contexts. 'In recognition, we are given the attributes, and we try to recover the contextual information' (Norman, D.A. and Rumelhart, D.E., 1970, p. 27).

Two types of recognition are considered, firstly immediate recognition, and secondly recognition delayed through the incubation period. A stimulus will be immediately recognized if the subject's present emotional set is concordant

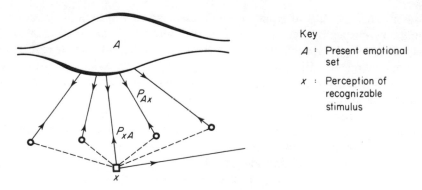

Key

A : Present emotional set

x : Perception of recognizable stimulus

Fig. 5.5/4 Immediate intuitive recognition

with the present perception of the stimulus, e.g. food associations are more easily recognized when the subject is hungry. Many cognitive and affective attributes of the perception of a stimulus (x say in Fig. 5.5/4 are in common with those of the present emotional set A. These redundant alternative associations sufficiently support the originally conditioned association of x which evokes A (*viz.* P_{xA}) for x to be recognized, i.e. to be a stimulus/response with physiological constituents concordant with the same response as before, *viz.* P_{Ax}.

If, however, the cognitive and affective attributes of the perception of x have little in common with the present emotional set A and more in common with other emotional sets (e.g. B and C in Fig. 5.5/5) then x will be discordant with the elements already conditioned to A.

In such a case P_{xA} will be small or zero, tending rather to evoke other emotional sets through its comon attributes which are peripheral to emotional set A. Here the emotional sets have to be combined in the ways previously

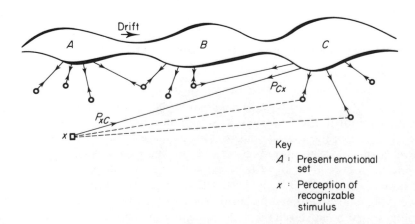

Key

A : Present emotional set

x : Perception of recognizable stimulus

Fig. 5.5/5 Intuitive recognition after an incubation period

described (Section 5.4) until the increasing redundancy of such a combination results in a situation as represented in Fig. 5.5/4 where the attributes of the elements of the present emotional set have sufficient in common with the attributes of the stimulus x to result in its recognition. Intuitive recognition of x in context C is signified by re-experiencing response P_{Cx}. Note the common cross-links in Fig. 5.5/5 indicate how the extant emotional set C will change in the process of combination to become the present emotional set C, the emotional context in which stimulus x may be recognized. Such combinations require time which corresponds to the 'incubation period' referred to in the literature.

It is possible for a novel stimulus, e.g. a stimulus not previously experienced in a specific context, to be mistakenly intuitively recognized as belonging to that context under circumstances of great redundancy. Where the novel stimulus is highly associated with a group of recognized stimuli, it might intuitively be recognized as one of this group because of its many associations with the group. Fig. 5.5/6 illustrates this.

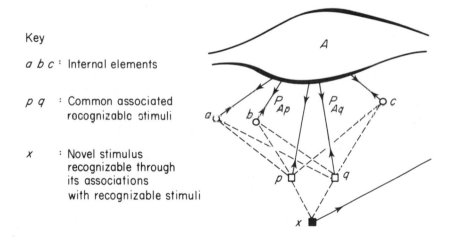

Fig. 5.5/6 Incorrect intuitive recognition resulting from high redundancy in common associations

This is the same structure as in Fig. 5.5/3 where the number of redundant links are shown to be best augumented by adding to the smaller group (within one). Such incorrect recognition is not marked by repeating a specific response as in correct recognition, but is marked by more defused feelings contributed to by responses of the associated recognized stimuli, P_{Ap} and P_{Aq} in Fig. 5.5/6. This and other factors contributing to wrong intuitions are discussed in detail in Section 8.1 under property 9, correctness of intuition.

Recognition of a stimulus, novel or not, further conditions that stimulus to the emotional set and probably introduces new associations, making later recognition more likely.

242

Increased Redundancy Leading to the Intuitive Judgment of Similarity of Recognized and Novel Stimuli

If two recognizable stimuli are concordant with the present emotional set they will be immediately judged as similar. Fig. 5.5/7 illustrates such a case, where x and y perceived concurrently while in emotional set A have many attributes in common with the elements already conditioned to emotional set A. They are both recognized as belonging to the same emotional context, i.e. the common attributes support the previous conditioning enabling both x and y to evoke the same emotional set A through P_{xA} and P_{yA}, resulting in the re-experiencing of such responses further conditioning their similarity, which then becomes an element of the new extant emotional set to be remembered in any future consideration of the similarity of x and y, i.e. the experience of recognition of the joint similarity has been abstracted as an element to be remembered as a fact that they are similar, in preference to reliving the original situation.

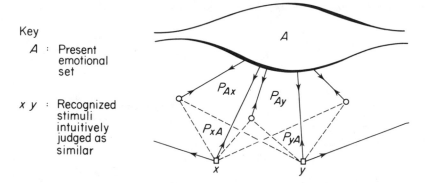

Fig. 5.5/7 Recognized stimuli intuitively judged as similar

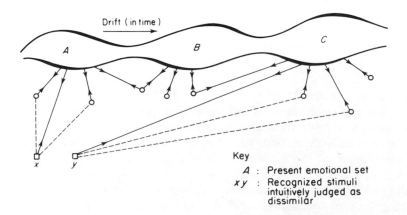

Fig. 5.5/8 Recognized stimuli intuitively judged as dissimilar

If x and y are recognized in two different emotional contexts, i.e. they are concordant with two different emotional sets (A and C say in Fig. 5.5/8) then they are judged dissimilar to the degree of the dissimilarity of the responses P_{xA} and P_{yC}.

The more remote the emotional sets A and C, i.e. the smaller the transition probability T_{AC} then the more dissimilar are x and y judged to be. If there is no point of similarity, which is an ideal limiting case, x and y will never appear concordant in the same emotional set, but at different times may be recognized in the context of their own emotional sets.

The recognition of both elements at different times, when the emotoinal set to which each is associated becomes the present emotional set, may give confidence and satisfaction that the difference is 'understood'. That is, by incorporating x and y separately into their respective emotional sets which maximize the redundancy of their common association with these separate sets, the different contexts of x and y are understood. The combination of emotional sets to achieve such understanding again requires an incubation period. However, a less satisfying impression of the difference in x and y is available from the discordant tension of the present emotional set in which only one is recognized but both are perceived. The subject's sensitivity to this unresolved tension is a basis of his immediate intuitive judgment, but not understanding, of this dissimilarity. This tension conditions an element of dissimilarity to A which may be remembered later when A is evoked rather than reliving the intuitive judgment of dissimilarity.

The similarity of novel stimuli has to be judged on the similarity of their associated recognizable stimuli. In Fig. 5.5/9 concurrently perceived novel stimuli x and y are intuitively judged to be similar because the stimuli to which they are associated, p and q, are, through their shared attributes with the inter-

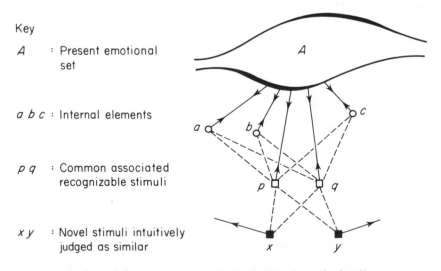

Key

A : Present emotional set

$a\,b\,c$: Internal elements

$p\,q$: Common associated recognizable stimuli

$x\,y$: Novel stimuli intuitively judged as similar

Fig. 5.5/9 Intuitive judgment of the similarity of novel stimuli

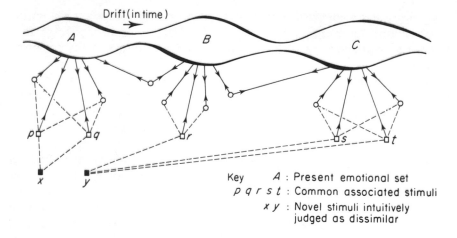

Fig. 5.5/10 Intuitive judgment of the dissimilarity of novel stimuli

nal elements a, b, and c, concordant within the same emotional set A. In future evocations of emotional set A, x and y will not be novel stimuli. Through the previous judgment of their similarity and experienced shared attributes they and the fact of their similarity are conditioned to emotional set A.

As illustrated in Fig. 5.5/10, if the two novel stimuli x and y are mainly associated with stimuli recognizable in different emotional sets then the difference between the dissimilar responses of the two emotional sets acts as the basis for the intuitive judgment of the dissimilarity of the two novel stimuli. As with two dissimilar recognizable stimuli, two dissimilar novel stimuli will have their recognizable associated stimuli in disaccord. The tension accompanying this discordance gives immediate awareness of their dissimilarity but not the satisfaction of understanding this difference. Such understanding may be afforded by the resolution in tension when the common associated stimuli p to t above, are recognized in the maximally redundant contexts of specific emotional sets, e.g. a conglomeration of A and C above. The tension due to the dissimilarity of x and y in emotional set A conditions this dissimilarity as an element in A for future remembrance, i.e. if in future the subject is in emotional set A, this will tend to evoke the memory that x and y are dissimilar through the response of second-order slight anxiety accompanying their cognition. That is, remembering anxiety bedomes less anxiety-evoking because each act of remembering involves combinations of emotional sets that successively defuse the anxiety so that progressively more general feelings of uneasiness become symbolic of the initial anxiety which was originally more intensely defined on fewer physiological dimensions of greater amplitude.

Increased Redundancy Leading to Intuitive Acceptance

Intuitive acceptance of a group of stimuli is achieved when each stimulus of the group is recognized in the same context. Fig. 5.5/11 illustrates such a

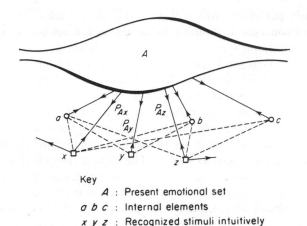

Key

A : Present emotional set

a b c : Internal elements

x y z : Recognized stimuli intuitively
accepted as a group

Fig. 5.5/11 Intuitive acceptance of a group of
recognized stimuli

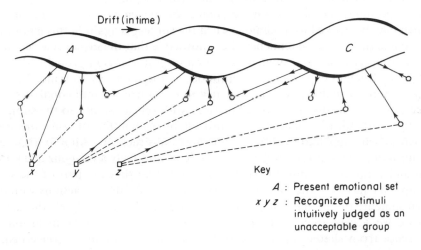

Key

A : Present emotional set

x y z : Recognized stimuli
intuitively judged as an
unacceptable group

Fig. 5.5/12 Intuitive unacceptance of a group of recognized stimuli

situation, where x, y, and z are the stimuli of the group which is immediately accepted through each of them being recognized as concordant with emotional set A, because of their attributes in common with the other elements of the emotional set, *viz.* a, b, and c.

The group of stimuli x, y, and z are mutually similar within the context of the emotional set A; consistent with the general inference that elements of any accepted group will be similar in the context in which they are accepted, *viz.* common properties defining the group. If the group of external stimuli are dissimilar, i.e. can only be recognized in different contexts, then they will be intuitively unacceptable as a group. Fig. 5.5/12 illustrates this.

Concurrently perceived stimuli *x, y,* and *z* above, are mutually dissimilar with respect to contexts *A, B,* and *C* because they are not concordant with any one of these emotional sets. As the three stimuli are perceived concurrently whilst the subject is in present emotional set *A* then instant awareness of this dissimilarity will be felt by their discordance and will be conditioned as a possible future response to emotional set *A*. However, by the three methods of combining emotional sets, an incubation period may result in a combined present emotional set highly redundant in containing the common attributes of *x, y,* and *z*. Such an emotional set would be a context in which *x, y,* and *z* would be intuitively accepted as similar. The large accompanying proportional reduction in anxiety would make these subject aware of these common attributes making available conscious information on the common attributes that make the stimuli acceptable as one group, i.e. the intuition follows the incubation period. Delayed intuitive recognition of a group is more satisfying than recognition of any single member of a group because the sum of the anxiety-reducing responses P_{Ax} to P_{Az} is greater than any single one of these responses.

The anxiety reduction marking the intuitive acceptance of the group within the emotional set conditions this acceptance as an element of the emotional set which may be evoked as a memory when the subject is again in this emotional set. While this response tendency, i.e. knowledge that the group is acceptable, remains larger than each single recognition response, it is improbable that the subject will again experience the intuition, as the tendency to remember this fact is more probable than the tendency to recognize the individual elements successively. This disparity would increase with rehearsal and so the subject's cognitive organization matures; the process of recognition of constituent experiences being replaced by the remembering of abstractions. An important use of our intuitive faculties is to be able to accept intuitively a recognizable group containing novel stimuli if 'it seems reasonable that they are part of the same group'. We have not the time during the majority of our interactions with our environment, or the natural inclination, to check analytically all the details before we accept their inclusion. We intuitively accept their inclusion on inference from shared attributes. Where one novel stimulus is concerned, if these common associations with the stimulus predominate over its tendency to evoke a different emotional set, then the stimulus will be incorrectly recognized as part of the group (see Fig. 5.5/6) and so the group will be intuitively accepted as one of mutually similar stimuli. Where the recognizable group of stimuli contains many novel stimuli the common associations have to be stronger than the many possible tendencies to evoke other emotional sets. Fig. 5.5/9 illustrates this, where the novel stimuli *x* and *y* have both been wrongly recognized as being similar to the group *p, q,* and *r* through their many common associations with *p, q,* and *r*. Attributes in common between novel stimuli concordant with the emotional set will obviously aid their acceptance.

'Gut advertising', to achieve intuitive acceptance of novel products, uses devices to achieve the structure illustrated in Fig. 5.5/9 from the structure of unacceptable novel stimuli illustrated in Fig. 5.5/10, *viz.* they increase the redundancy $R = j + ij$ by showing their novel product in a recognizable stimulus field, by increasing j, and then make the stimulus field more acceptable by encouraging the combination of emotional sets in the direction of increased redundancy, by increasing i. All available modalities are used to ensure many physiological components of the common attributes are employed. For example presenting the product in a recognizable situation such as circumstances identifiable with those of the target customer, and then evoking related highly redundant global emotional sets, e.g. centred on Mother, nostalgia, patriotism.

Increased Redundancy Leading to Intuitive Judgment of Suitability

The intuitive judgment of suitability has most import for creativity and problem-solving, as these endeavours are based on the intuitive judgment of a group of 'solution' elements being suitable for a group of problem 'requirement' elements. The requirement elements are usually novel aspects of a recognized stimulus field. The solution elements define a context in which the requirements are similar. An optimum intuitive solution will have maximum redundancy, i.e. the most attributes in common between the fewest elements. The range in degree of satisfaction accompanying the intuition, which is a subjective measure of the importance of the intuition, is large for it depends on the dissimilarity of the requirements and the transition probability to the solution context, both having a large range of opposite to equivalent and of 0 to 1 respectively.

The most mundane intuitive judgment of suitability is where the simultaneously perceived novel requirements are concordant with the current emotional set because of their shared attributes with the stimuli evoking the emotional set. Fig. 5.5/9 illustrates this. The recognized stimuli p,q,r and the other elements of the emotional set a,b, and c, are intuitively suitable for the novel requirement stimuli x and y, as x and y are judged as similar within the context of emotional set A. Few new associations have been created to obtain this structure, consequently little satisfaction and reduction of anxiety accompanies the small increase in redundancy.

Resolving a structure illustrated by Fig. 5.5/10 to that illustrated by Fig. 5.5/9 results in more satisfaction, because here the requirement stimuli x and y are initially dissimilar. As previously explained, drifting to emotional set C resolves the tension of this dissimilarity by recognizing the similarity of x and y in the context of the present emotional set C, a conglomeration formed by combining selected responses from A, B, and C, which will probably contain most of the recognizable stimuli p to t and some of their associated elements carried along in the drift to C. These elements are recognizable stimuli of the present emotional set C and are constituents of the solution suitable to the requirements x and y. The views of Sarnoff Mednick as expressed in his

'Associative basis of the creative process' are in agreement with this model: 'When the set of consequents of a new combination achieves a close fit with the set of problem requirements, this combination is selected. When there is a complete overlap of sets, "search behaviour" is terminated' (Mednick, S.A., 1962, p. 225). The length of the incubation period required to obtain this suitable solution by drift would be inversely proportional to the transition probability between the emotional set concurrent with the requirements and the emotional set containing the solution, *viz.* T_{AC}. If T_{AC} were large, hierarchical embedding of A and C into one larger context may occur. Although this is a solution and redundancy has been increased by associating the solution and requirements, the number of elements has also been increased so that there is more dissimilarity between peripheral elements in this larger context, thus reducing the overall gain in redundancy. Subjectively, a solution by intuitive judgment of suitability in a larger context is correspondingly less satisfying.

As the requirements become more dissimilar, possibly with increasing number, the transition probability to an emotional set containing the solution will be reduced. This is because being dissimilar the requirements are tending to evoke emotional sets of greater dissimilarity, i.e. 'pulling' in different directions and not contributing to the same transition probability. In such a situation, no solution might result from the drift process as the incubation time is so long that the discordance of the requirements is gradually 'dropped' and not carried along with the drift as other anxieties are evoked and take precedence. The emotional state of discordant requirements remains extant.

Resolution of such an extant emotional state of discordant requirements results in the most awesome intuition, *viz.* the Eureka experience. Here the direction of the process is different in that the initial emotional set is not the one containing the requirements but the one containing the solution. The two emotional sets have not previously been combined as they have a near zero transition probability, see Section 5.4 on recentring. However, the two emotional sets are very similar in physiological state and in duplicated response tendencies. It is the common associations of some new stimulus while in the present emotional set of the solution that causes the combination of the requirements and solution in the same context of the combined emotional sets giving the recentring.

Biographical accounts of Eureka experiences relate many examples where the stimulus catalysing the recentring has been an external event, seemingly analytically unconnected with the problem requirements, e.g. a body posture or movement, which has sufficient physiological components equivalent to the attributes of the requirements to cause the recentring of the present emotional set and the extant emotional state of discordant requirements. This recentring is not preceded by a gradual decrease of anxiety as in the combination of emotional sets by drifting. The sudden release of anxiety accompanying the recentring makes the Eureka experience the most awesome and powerful learning experience of the intuitive products.

Summary of the Global Knowledge Property of Intuition

Global knowledge is the fifteenth property of intuition considered in Chapter 1. In this book redundancy is identified as the characteristic of global knowledge facilitating the intuitive mode of thought, directing the intuitive process and determining the intuitive product. Redundancy is used here to mean combinations of concordant conglomerations of stimuli, contributing to response tendencies, being constituents of more than one stimulus/response and of more than one emotional set, so that components of response tendencies are duplicated in other response tendencies and in other emotional sets. These combinations of concordant conglomerations of stimuli comprised of less integrated affective, cognitive, motor, hormonal, visceral stimuli responses, etc. are the coded information for the intuitive process. Hence redundancy refers to the duplication of this information. Simply, the stimuli/responses that make up thoughts and feelings are components of response tendencies. Concordant response tendencies are similar on their physiological dimensions and are organized into emotional sets. The intuitive process, in contrast with secondary thinking, is proposed here to involve the combination of emotional sets containing many concordant responses. These emotional sets therefore tend to be highly redundant. The combination of large masses of redundant information is consistent with evidence of the global knowledge property of intuition presented in this chapter and contrasts with the characteristics of analytic or logical thought discussed in Chapter 2.

Reference to the literature supports the following statements. The intuitive process involves global perception of all the relevant information which comprises the whole information field for the intuitive process comprising both external and internal stimuli. Ideas come in a completed form. Intuition involves general feelings. The intuiter has much experience in the field of the intuition. This contrasts with the analytic mode of thought in which information is used part by part. Analytic ideas are constructed by adding parts. They are independent of affective components in the thinker. Analysis proceeds from a self-consistency independent of the concrete experiences of the analyst.

The global nature of the information used in the intuitive process markedly contrasts with the use of information in the analytic process. The total information being used at any time in the intuitive process is defined by its physiognomy, that is its associated feelings and ideas. Information may be contributed simultaneously through all modalities, speeding the process. Particularly non-verbal modalities are used, commonly spatial.

In subjects with a verbal preference mode, kinaesthetic representation of the information is commonly made. The verbal mode is restrictive in intuitive thought because of its linear nature. In the analytic mode one's limit in memory capacity implies a degradation of information as features of stimuli are extracted near one's maximum capacity. The noise in such degraded information inhibits the analytic process which gives equal importance to each precise detailed piece of information, i.e. in an analysis the details must be precise because one small contradicting detail negates an argument. However, in the intuitive process the total information being used at any time is defined by its physiognomy and so additional information can be incorporated into this physiognomy by changing the physiognomy according to the subjective associations of the thinker. Hence there is no limit to the amount of information that may be included in the physiognomy, but the relative subjective importance of the information will vary in the physiognomy of the whole. Physiognomy allows global knowledge to be available for the intuitive process.

Redundancy is shared or duplicated information. The information used in the intuitive process is redundancy-rich. The two extreme cases of information content where the intuitive process is used are:

(1) Complex information: a vast amount of interrelated information is redundancy-rich owing to the overlapping nature of the information. It is natural to choose the intuitive mode to process such complex information.

(2) Very little information: when the new information or time available for processing is too little for an analytic solution or if a subject is not predisposed to use analysis he naturally associates his own redundancy-rich information and intuitively processes the total information.

These aspects of global knowledge, *viz.* physiognomy, use of non-verbal modalities, redundancy, and degradation of overloaded analytic information, are used as experimental conditions to encourage subjects to use the intuitive mode during some experiments in the literature that involve intuitive thought. This is done by giving subjects complex information or very little information or allowing a time too short for any analytic solution. The intuitive mode is the default mode of thought, naturally used in all situations that do not specify an analytic solution.

Information may be organized into emotional sets for intuitive processing during perception. Both internal and external stimuli provide information for the intuitive process. The information from these sources interacts during the intuitive process by varying the encoding of constant stimuli, increasing the possible combinations of the available information and affecting the chaining of associations. These three effects of the interaction increase the global nature of the knowledge used in the intuitive process. In particular the interaction increases the redundancy of the information. The global nature of the perception of external stimuli, of internal stimuli and the addition to the global knowledge of their interaction, have been considered in this chapter.

The physiognomy of all the elements is absorbed during perception of external stimuli in order to extract features as information for the intuitive process. This involves much peripheral perception and subliminal perception in many modalities. Cross-modal transfer of equivalent information adds to the total redundancy. The literature shows that the personality characteristics of those sensitive to subliminal information are similar to the personality characteristics of the intuitive type. Subliminal sensitivity reduces with age as does flexibility in intuitive problem-solving. Both intuition and subliminal perception are considered as primary processes, the same constructs of the environment, e.g. causing anxiety, high motivation, etc., are inhibitory to both. It is proposed that the reduction in peripheral cue utilization in anxiety and high motivation states, found during experiments on subliminal perception and elsewhere, has the effect of making global knowledge unobtainable for intuitive processing, i.e. reduces redundancy of the information extracted from external stimuli. Focusing need not necessarily reduce the total information which may be accumulated by successively focusing on various aspects of the stimulus field. Such information, however, would tend to be more compartmentalized, i.e. sparsely redundant. External cue utilization has been used to define cognitive styles, e.g. focusing, levelling, tolerance of contradicting stimuli, etc. The literature illustrates that the cognitive styles and their concomitant personality characteristics that are associated with global perception also describe the intuitive type.

Appraisal of the whole body state is a result of perception of internal stimuli and is information for the intuitive process. Physiological conditions, e.g. kinaesthetic, hormonal, etc., as well as cognitive associations are some of the internal stimuli contributing to this information. The difference in rates of change of the relatively slowly changing physiological states and relatively fast changing cognitive associations conditioned to the physiological states aids the collection of cognitive information into the physiognomy primarily associated with a particular physiological state.

Such an information structure explains how global knowledge is available at the speed of recall consistent with intuitive processing. It is a psychophysiological interpretation and extension of the memory structures proposed in recent information-processing models of human memory.

The need for global non-linear internal representation of information in intuitive processing naturally favours imagery and visual fantasy against verbal representation. It is proposed that intuitive types with verbal rather than spatial ability modes use kinaesthetic and other bodily representations of the information. This has been confirmed by experiment.

The perception of internal and external stimuli cannot meaningfully be separated as the continued presence of internal stimuli interacts with the perception of external stimuli and it is this altered perception of the external stimuli that provides information on which the organism acts, not the external stimuli themselves. Further, the perception of external stimuli affects the internal state so that there is a feedback between the two. The priority a subject attributes to the internal or external stimuli may be described in terms of field-dependent cognitive style. The influence of perception of external stimuli on the internal state is here considered in terms of empathy, whereas the influence of the perception of internal stimuli on the perception of the external stimuli is considered in terms of projection. Between the two, the dynamic feedback process of empathic projection results in the changing physiognomy of the environment. The outcome of the perception of stimuli as information for the intuitive process is to structure the information in categories associated with emotional sets. The literature shows many methods have been used for mapping a subject's network of subjective categories. Such methods are used in experiments on memory structure, some in experiments on cognitive style, etc. For example, subjects sort cards bearing the concepts contained in the categories to be mapped, or experimenters time true or false responses to inclusion statements, or experimenters group subjects' free associations by the rate of their association, or elicit associations under drugs, etc.

All such methods assume a static network of associated categories. However, the posited direction of increasing redundancy in intuitive processing implies that category definitions change, overlap, recombine, embed, etc. Encoding variability, increase in possible combinations, and cross-modal transfer of information are just three of the factors facilitating this category fluidity, contributing to novel intuitions and even to different intuitions resulting from the same external stimuli.

The interactive perception of the stimuli and the variable categorization of the information contribute to the characteristics of redundancy in the global knowledge property of intuition. The processing of the information is also global in that it is non-linear and multimodal. It is here suggested that there are anxiety-producing simultaneous tendencies to evoke and combine emotional sets. These methods of combination resolve the anxiety and include non-linear hierarchical combinations embedding emotional sets. The resolution of problem-evoking anxiety confirms that the direction of combining emotional sets is leading to an intuitive solution. Combining emotional sets without the initial anxiety results in other than intuitive thought and behaviour. This explanation of the global nature of intuition provides for the numerous multichannel combinations of associations of categories facilitating the efficiency of recall of the global knowledge in the intuitive process. The association of information during the non-linear transformation of categories affected by the search frequently gives rise to visual fantasy like telescoping time, absurd juxtapositions, dream-like associations, etc.

The association of emotional sets proceeds in such a way as to tend to increase their redundancy. The methods of associating emotional sets, *viz.* generalizing by hierarchical embedding, recentring, and drifting to other sets, are restricted by high anxiety, high external motivation, and in a similar fashion as these restrict peripheral cue utilization. It has been shown here how intuitive recognition comes with increased redundancy, how redundancy increases the probability of intuitive acceptance, both with and without recognition of what is to be accepted. It has been shown how intuitive judgments of similarity and suitability are made on the redundancy of the emotional sets to which the relevant information is linked.

The literature attests to the completeness of the final intuition which emerges into consciousness in a complete form accompanied by feelings of confidence and lack of anxiety. In this book such intuitive products are not considered as separate from the intuitive process but simply the state of the system at the end of the intuitive process when the redundancy of the present emotional set, both physiological and cognitive redundancy, is sufficient to make such a marked proportional change in anxiety and release in tension that the subject is consciously aware of the change. The present cognitions are then the cognitive aspect of the intuition, part of which the intuiter may attempt to communicate. The present cognitions are subjectively attributed with being responsible for the marked attendant affective and reported state of confidence.

The intuiter may assume these cognitions alone to be his intuition. However, the global multimodal multidimensional content of the final intuition is apparent when the subject tries to communicate his intuition. Observe the speed of verbal communication as he endeavours to translate non-linear information into a linear form: 'A picture is worth a thousand words'; the gesticulations corresponding to phrases of low information content and the final dissatisfaction with the completed communication as being an inadequate translation of the original intuition. Visual artists may come closer to the original intuition because of the non-linear nature of their communication. However, even in such cases the visual representation of a global intuition is markedly different from the analytic building of a design piecemeal, part by consistent part into a self-consistent whole, as practised by some visual artists, e.g. Paul Klee.

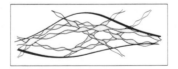

Intuitive Feelings, Empathy, and Projection

6.1 INTUITION FACILITATES TRANSFER AND TRANSPOSITION

Transfer and transposition is the twentieth property of intuition with seven references to it in Section 1.3, which makes it ninth in priority. Transfer of learning is used by some behavioural psychologists as a criterion for insight. However, the degree of transfer is relative and because in 'real-life' situations, as opposed to 'laboratory-test' situations, previous learning must be assumed and recognized in its complex transformations, which is a logical and operational difficulty, this criterion is controversial.

Transfer corresponds in the Model of Intuitive Thought to the combining of emotional sets. This is facilitated by conditioning similar responses (retrieval cues) to dissimilar emotional sets. This conditioning is on a multitude of physiological variables, non-exclusive conglomerations of which form the sensory modes. Because of individual modal preferences and different idiosyncratic dimensioning within modes, a transfer (combination of emotional set) is dependent on highly individualistic cues. This indicates that experiments dependent on such idiosyncratic conditioning, including experiments on creativity, word association, and experiments using psychophysiological recordings, should not be analysed in terms of cues and their dimensioning across subjects unless they can in some way first be standardized within the subject.

Transfer of Learning as Behaviourists' Criterion of Insight

Behavioural psychologists give transfer of learning as a criterion of insight. 'Insightful. This is finding a means-end relationship underlying the solution. It involves transposition of previous learning to analogous situations... Transferability is perhaps the most important criterion of insight' (Ausubel, D.P., 1968). Similarly Bigge, M.L. and Hunt, M.P. (1965) say: 'Transfer is generalizing insights gained in one situation to use in other situations' (p. 357). Kaufman, M.L. (1972) considers 'affective insight' as a transferable behavioural mode (p. 41). Cronbach, L.J. and Meehl, P.E. (1955) did a critical analysis of projective tests of insight and criticized them as not being valid for inference on transfer to other situations.

However, there is some controversy on whether transfer of learning is a necessary condition for confirmation that insight has occurred. This is particularly so for insights in 'real-life' complex non-experimentally controlled situations. 'What is necessary for intuitive behaviour is that one clearly senses current circumstances. At all costs one must withstand the temptation to view present reality as exactly like previous events in life' (Clark, J., 1973, p. 216).

Transfer of learning seems to satisfy Behaviourists that the subject has 'insight' into the relationships that make his behaviour appropriate. Examples satisfying this condition are where a subject learns behaviours appropriate to one situation and correctly chooses these behaviours as appropriate to some other situation, appropriateness being judged by correctly performing a task characterizing the situation. An assumption is made that there is a choice of behaviours. For example, if a subject learns to solve correctly a type of algebraic equation and then chooses the same method to solve correctly a different form of the same equation, the Behaviourist asserts that the subject has 'insight'. This seems to mean that the method is learnt in terms of the relations between the things to which it applies. It is, however, possible that the method is learnt in terms of relations between things unrelated to the properties about which the insight is assumed and these relations being coincidentally present in the test situations allow the method to give correct solutions. Many such examples exist in the teaching of mathematics where a rule is found to give correct answers to problems in different forms and it is believed by the teacher that the rule must be in terms of the properties of the problems about which insight is assumed, but eventually an unrecognized exception to the rule disproves this assumption. For example, a child might use a spatial relation rule to answer correctly a page of the following type of problems, e.g. the answer is the one different from the other row, but the teacher might assume these correct answers show 'insight' into subtraction as the inverse of addition through believing the correct answers result from use of number rules.

$$7 + 4 = \qquad 9 + 3 = \qquad 6 + 8 =$$
$$11 - 4 = \qquad 12 - 3 = \qquad 14 - 8 =$$

In experimental situations these rules are often formed from idiosyncratic experiences not incorporated into the experimental design. (Reference the criticism of practical insight experiments elsewhere in this book.) General insights occurring outside these relatively parochial experimental situations involve so much idiosyncratic experience that the type II error of assuming insight becomes more probable. Further, any previous learning is so transformed that its recognition is highly speculative. Hence the inadequacy and controversy of this criterion for insight in 'real-life' situations.

Cross-modal Transposition Facilitates Transfer of Intuitive Thought

> ...intuitive perception may be translated into any sensory modality. Intuition may become accessible to consciousness through visual imagery, auditory imagery and kinaesthetic response as well as vague undifferentiated feelings. (Clark, F.V., 1973, p. 160)

It is consistent with the model being developed in these chapters that transfer is the combining of emotional sets in the three ways detailed in Section 5.4. It was shown how such combinations are encouraged by conditioning a variety of retrieval cues to different emotional sets. Hence this procedure will facilitate insight and transfer of learning. This is supported by Gordon, F.R. and Flavell, J.H. (1977) in their paper on 'The development of intuitions about cognitive cueing'. The authors suggest ways in which associations may be used to encode and recall concepts.

> An example at the encoding end would be deliberately trying to provide the to-be-remembered information with a variety of future retrieval cues by processing it deeply — purposely assimilating it to a variety of knowledge schemes, intentionally relating it to other bodies of information, etc. An example at the retrieval end would be deliberately trying to think of related but nontarget information in hopes that doing so might cue retrieval of the target information. (p. 1028)

It is proposed here that these retrieval cues are responses conditioned to emotional sets on a multitude of physiological dimensions, each being any physiological change that can be detected (most subconsciously) by the individual, the common sensory modalities being overlapping conglomerations of these dimensions analogous to, say, oblique factors. The variety of retrieval cues for the same information was referred to in Section 5.4 as redundancy. This redundancy is increased by cross-modal transposition of the information. In his book Reese, H.W. (1968) considers theories of cross-modal transposition. He defines it as '...a kind of transfer that appears to result from response to relations among stimuli or to patterns of stimulus quantities, e.g. recognition of melody in another key or of shape or form when presented in a different colour or another spatial orientation' (p. 9).

Following are examples of experiments illustrating cross-modal transposition. Scheerer, M. and Lyons, J. (1957) asked subjects to match the names Waleula and Quidikaka with the line drawings in Fig. 6.1/1A. They found the total auditory style of Waleula corresponds to the total visual style of the drawing so labelled. Similarly with Quidikaka, there is a physiognomic correspondence.

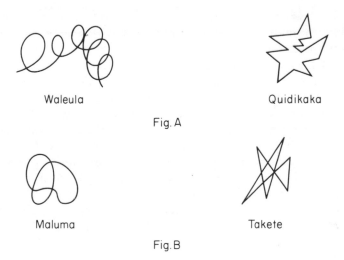

Waleula   Quidikaka

Fig. A

Maluma   Takete

Fig. B

Fig. 6.1/1 Visual/auditory cross-modal transposition

Honkavaara, S. (1961) used the names Maluma and Takete with the drawings in Figs. 6.1/1B which he presented to adults and children. He found that 90 per cent named the figures correctly but of five to six-year-olds only 9 per cent named them correctly, and of nine to fourteen-year-olds only half to two-thirds were correct. I have repeated Honkavaara's experiment with two hundred FE students using the same shapes on a form which also asked for the reasons for the subject's choice. Results were 100 per cent matched as shown in Fig. 6.1/1B and the responses supported the above reported conclusions of Scheerer, M. and Lyons, J. (1957). Wolff and Precker also did experiments in cross-modal transposition in which young children were asked to draw how music sounded. The children tended to interpret the expressive qualities of music by intensity of graphic movements and characteristic forms. The experimenters found that the children could also interpret social situations by scribblings or drawings (Wolff, W. and Precker, J.A., 1951, p. 490).

The distinction between modalities becomes blurred in conditions facilitating intuition (Gaughran, E., 1963). Multimodal retrieval is then experienced as a physiognomy; see Section 2.2 on physiognomic perception.

The theoretical background of Osgood's Semantic Differential supports the proposed multimodal coding of retrieval cues. Further: 'It is possible to infer the modality of stored information from the nature of the confusion in recall of similar stimuli in that modality' (Simon, H.A., 1972, p. 194). In illustration, card-players find talking, more than listening, interferes with counting cards whilst dealing. If, however, the count is by one-to-one correspondence with a spatial number pattern, e.g. covering imaginary domino dots, rather than a one-to-one correspondence with number names then talking and counting do not interfere. Try it! Cross-modal transposition of information is also supported by evidence of interference between modalities. As Dittman, A.T. (1972, pp. 156/163) says in his information-processing interpretation of the modalities as information channels; if one channel is overloaded with information, it influences the other channels.

It seems that a common cross-modal transposition is between the visual and kinaesthetic modes. Laabs, G.J. (1971) has shown that location in space when arising from kinaesthetic cues behaves like a visual code. It is this fact together with results of experiments on cross-modal kinaesthetic/visual judgment (e.g. Teghtsoonian, Martha and Teghtsoonian, R., 1965; Posner M.I., 1967) that further suggest cross-modal transposition of kinaesthetic and visual information should be incorporated into problems designed to elicit an intuitive solution in experiments on intuition.

Training in cross-modal transposition is a feature of pedagogy that encourages transfer and hence intuitive thought. Common examples are found in Montessori's techniques, e.g. the prelude to writing by feeling large sandpaper letters: '...a seeking for symbolic equivalents of experience in the widest possible number of sensory and imaginal modalities... exercises in imaginative play... these and still other emphasis in the learning would, I believe, strengthen the disposition to intuitive perception as well as intuitive thinking' (Ripple, R.E., 1964, p. 321). To train intuition Bruner, J. and Clinchy, B. (1966) suggest cross-modal transformation exercises: 'Training in transformations such as are needed in the Flags test. Multidimensional ordering using all modalities to encourage subtle sensory discriminations. Subjective transformation in graphic display, e.g. drawing the teacher as huge compared with little sister who is represented as a dot' (p. 78). Elder, Connie Z. (1973) discusses sandplay for the development of visual concepts and tactile development of nursery children. Cross-modal transposition is explicitly encouraged in nursery schools. It takes on less importance through middle school education and is unfortunately implicitly discouraged in the later teaching of 'abstract' mathematics. As cross-modal transposition encourages transfer and intuitive thought its inhibition in the teaching of higher mathematics may in part explain the generally recognized lack of creativity in mathematics students and suggests that the few who are intuitive have developed idiosyncratic cross-modal 'feeling models'. This is a testable supposition.

Transfer of Idiosyncratic Dimensions

There is evidence to show that transfer, interpreted by the Model of Intuitive Thought Processes as combination of emotional sets, is on highly idiosyncratic dimensions, similar responses (retrieval cues) being conditioned to different emotional sets in various intensities on a multitude of physiological dimensions. There is some variety among individuals in the priority given to different dimensions within modalities as well as among modalities. 'It is possible that individuals learn to deploy available energy in characteristic patterns. Thus some people may come to invest their deployable energy in one sense modality or another' (Solley, C.M. and Murphy, G., 1960, p. 188).

The concept of Sensory Type, of Ability and Preference Modes, supports this view as do the following experiments which compare input and output in various modalities. In an experiment with one hundred and nineteen bilingual students Rose, R.G. (1975) found a significant difference in confidence between input and output, i.e. listening and reading versus speaking and writing: but no significant difference in subjects' confidence between oral and graphic modes, i.e. speaking and listening versus reading and writing. This experiment was not sufficiently sensitive to indicate any difference in Preference or Ability Modes. Krebs, G.M. (1975) gave incongruent information in verbal and non-verbal modes. He identified the preference mode as being indicated by which information the subject chose to utilize. On instructional approaches Younie, W.J. (1967) says: 'The multisensory approach also takes note of the fact that all persons tend to have a sense learning preference... and it allows each child to use consistently that sense through which he learns best' (p. 28). Fernald, Grace M. (1943) tested twenty teachers and found that ten had visual preference in image recall, nine had auditory preference and one had kinaesthetic imagery preference in recall. Even physiological recording intensity varies with modal preference. Lanzetta, J.T. and Kleck, R.E. (1970) found that the degree of physiological arousal is related to a subject's differential responsiveness to non-verbal cues. Garvill, J. and Milander, B. (1968) using two sets of three-dimensional nonsense objects showed asymmetric cross-transfer effects '...higher transfer from tactual to visual presentation than from visual to tactual...'. Again relevant to kinaesthesis as a common preference mode, Mialaret, G. (1966) quotes A. Michotte on discussing the relative effects of modal transformations in cartoons: 'In particular, kinetic impressions remain unchanged despite radical changes of colour, form, dimensions which the moving bodies themselves are made to undergo' (p. 131).

The idiosyncratic dimensioning of cues even within common preference modes explains the following experimental result. Maier, N.R.F. and Casselman, G.G. (1970) gave six insight problems to three hundred and eleven male and two hundred and thirty-three female subjects in both the standard and easy version. The easy version was designed to give a hint which in each problem the authors thought might remove any blocks to insight

Results suggested that a single hint cannot provide significant improvement since a problem appears to be difficult for different people for a variety of reasons. Chance factors also play a part in successful problem-solving. Results also confirmed earlier findings showing that hints or suggestions which seem helpful when the solution is known may serve as distractions to an individual attempting to discover the solution. (p. 103)

It is a common observation that the same stimuli produce different physiological effects in different subjects, e.g. in stage fright one subject might sweat on his palms whereas another may experience a dry mouth. The physiological recordings in investigations of intuition should similarly show that subjects respond maximally on different physiological variables to the same stimulus. This observation is important for the analysis of experiments involving idiosyncratic conditioning. Many such experiments compare a variable across subjects so that this individual effect is unintentionally lost. Thus transfer on idiosyncratic physiological dimensions indicates that analysis on variables should be within subjects and/or standardized within each subject before comparison across subjects.

6.2   INTUITIVE UNDERSTANDING THROUGH FEELING

Understanding by feeling is the sixth property of intuition with six references to it in Section 1.3.

Fisher, S.A. and Cleveland, S.E. (1968) write '...there has been such limited success in finding psychological models that are meaningfully related to physiological models' (p. 307). At the moment there seems to be no psychophysiological/behavioural theory of emotion. There are, however, many other theories of emotion: 'They are physiological, cognitive or behavioural, or sometimes any two of these, but never all three. There appears to be no theory which successfully provides a description of experiential feelings, physiological change and emotional behaviour' (Strongman, K.T., 1973, p. 193). The Theory of Intuitive Thought Processes is an attempt to do this.

This section reviews work to show that we do understand intuitively through our feelings. It presents evidence to support the following simple explanation of how we intuitively understand through feeling, evidence which, being consistent with other evidence presented in this book on which the Theory of Intuitive Thought is based, allows this explanation to be incorporated into the theory.

It has been shown in previous sections that information used in the intuitive process is partially encoded and retrieved through its affective associations. It is proposed that the body uses highly sensitive feedback systems to assess these feelings on a multitude of physiological dimensions and thus access and process this information.

Feelings of Relation, Feelings of Confidence, and Feelings Resulting in Intuitive Products

'Those of us who rely more readily on the inner tools are more richly endowed with intuitive abilities' (Szalita-Pemow, A.B., 1955, p. 12). Feelings are used in the intuitive process to give a subjective measure of how correct the intuition is: 'It [intuition] carries with it a strong feeling of certainty' (Garard, R.W.,

1962). This use of feeling in the intuitive process is detailed in Section 4.2 on the subjective certainty of correctness of intuitions. However, intuition also involves a sense of relations, property 18, Section 2.2. This sense of relations, when it becomes conscious (property 3, Section 4.1 on preconscious intuitive process) commonly manifests itself as a diffuse feeling influencing our thoughts '. . . we have a capacity of conceiving objects: and to those capacities all that is intellectual in our nature is reducible' (Brown, T., 1860, p. 337).

Later authors have come to consider 'feelings' and 'intuition' contiguously (Davitz, J.R., 1964, p. 2). For example, Reid, L.A. (1976) asserts: 'I want to say that the intuitions and feelings we have in these matters are cognitive experiences, and that they make knowledge claims' (p. 12). Similarly Manso, A.V. *et al.* (1977), deploring the inhibition of intuition in teaching, write: 'It must be emphasized, for any who might misconstrue the intention of this article, that it is primarily a return to feeling and intuition which we advocate' (p. 194).

Bayles, E.E. (1952) defines insight in terms of this feeling sense of relations: 'It [development of insight] is the feeling for pattern which is caught during a performance — the insight gained — that counts' (p. 71). Other authors associate specific products of the intuitive process with the use of feeling. Feelings are induced by perception and modify perception particularly in ego states facilitating intuitive thought (see Section 3.1). 'The first fruit of perception, the first affective experience, seems to be a feeling. . .' (Arnold, Magda B., 1961, p. 36). Stocks, J.L. (1939) writing on the relation of 'reason and intuition' notes that the feelings associated with propositions in mathematics enable them to be intuitively accepted as relevant to the whole argument: 'Each proposition, as it is asserted, has its felt source and confirmation in an intuition of the relevant whole' (p. 9). Intuitive acceptance, of which this is an example, has been explained in Section 5.5 in terms of concordant feelings conditioned to changing emotional sets. The feelings are continuously modified by combining emotional sets to increase concordance resulting in the intuitive acceptance. This dynamic view is supported by Suzuki, D.T.'s (1957) interpretation of 'Intuition in Buddhist philosophy', called Prajna. 'Prajna is therefore dynamic and not static; it is not mere activity-feeling but activity itself' (p. 100). This again emphasizes the kinaesthetic mode of feeling. Szalita-Pemow, A.B. (1955) writing on the 'intuitive process' specifically relates feeling with intuitive understanding: '. . . intuitive understanding. . . is felt most of the time, certainly at first, as a forethought' (p. 9).

How feelings are used for intuitive judgment is shown in Section 5.5. That feelings are used in intuitive judgment is supported not only by references given in that section but also by Jung's concept of intuition as a perceptual function where feelings are used for evaluating experience (Myers, I.B., 1958). The Myers-Briggs Type Indicator, a test reportedly based on this concept, shows 25 per cent of the general population score as intuitive (Myers, I.B., 1962). See also Section 6.3 on intuitive understanding through feelings evoked by empathy with objects. Rosenbloom, P.C. (1972), discussing the nature of mathematics, considers that it consists largely of a '...feeling of what ought to be true ...At an elementary level one would want a child to feel that 1/67823·5 is a small number even if he cannot calculate it to seven decimal places, or that the error in calculating the area of a rectangle is small if the errors in measuring the sides are small, even if he cannot estimate the error rigorously' (p. 88).

The result of assessment of feelings associated with some 'object' is perceived as the physiognomy of the 'object'. The relevance of physiognomy to the intuitive process is discussed elsewhere in this book in Sections 2.2, 5.1, and 5.3.

Intuitive recall relies upon the feelings associated with the memory to be recalled, feelings used as retrieval cues (Section 3.2). The writing of Blake, M. (1973) on the 'feeling-of-knowing phenomenon' supports this part of the Theory of Intuitive Thought Processes. 'The weight of the feeling-of-knowing phenomenon seems to be carried by a knowledge of specific attributes of the inaccessible target memory' (p. 317); '...with regard to common experience, an individual trying to remember a forgotten name or event often receives a feeling that the sought-after information is known, laying in readiness, as it were, for the appropriate accessing to occur' (p. 311).

In this book we have seen some of the problems of defining and measuring intuition. As intuition is a necessary commencement to creativity (detailed in Section 7.3 where intuition is considered as the first phase of creativity) such problems must necessarily be transferred to definitions and measurements of creativity. It may be that the feelings associated with intuition will become the criteria of creativity and the predictors of creative types. Westcott, M.R. (1964) in a recorded conversation at the Fifth Utah Creativity Research Conference speculates: *'Westcott,* "The criterion evaluation of creativity may turn out to be essentially a gut reaction." *Participant* "Now we are completing the cycle by getting the gut reaction into the predictor's side." ' Following this suggestion these two uses of feeling during the intuitive process, *viz.* to feel relations and feel confidence in the intuitive solution, are included as criteria of insight in the experimental design of Bastick's, T. (1979) psychophysiological investigation of intuition, *viz.* intuition is indicated by the differences in physiological recordings during an insight and rote task and confirmed by psychophysiological recordings of confidence in the indicated intuition.

Both Witkin, H.A. *et al.* (1954) and Jacobson, R.W. (1944) have shown that age and sex are sources of variation in such experiments and therefore age was recorded in Bastick's (1979) investigation.

Feelings Give Intuitive Understanding

'Long before one has realized that the colour of the scene has changed, one may feel that the character of the scene has undergone change' (Asch, S.E.,

1946b, p. 85). We now explain that we understand by feeling by considering the body as extremely self-sensitive to the multitude of physiological dimensions that constitute our feelings. Evidence will now be reviewed showing that the ease and non-specificity with which these feelings are conditioned allows them to non-uniquely categorize cognitive events. This psychology allows for the construction of emotional sets whose redundancy-increasing combinations are the intuitive thought process. Later in this section we discuss some of the feedback systems by which the body is sensitive to these feelings.

Self-sensitivity to Feelings on a Multitude of Physiological Dimensions

I am considering here self-sensitivity to feelings that are more differentiated than those involved in stroking of the hand, a touch of a finger, the sound of a word, *viz.* the many visceral, skeletal experiences that are internally sensed subconsciously and used to maintain homeostasis. As Schachter, S. (1964) says: 'Since we are aware of a great variety of feeling and emotion states it must follow from a purely visceral formulation that the variety of emotions will be accompanied by an equal variety of differentiable bodily states' (p. 70).

However, searches for psychophysiological concomitance of feeling have concentrated on the extreme gross conglomerations of such finely differentiated feelings, namely emotions. Such investigations do not consider the interaction of more subtle feelings with chains of thought. So physiological differences to match even the multitude of feeling of which we are conscious have not yet been found.

In reviewing the literature on physiological determinants of emotional states, Schachter, S. and Singer, J.E. (1962) found that no fine physiological differentiation of human emotions has yet been discovered. 'Whether or not there are physiological distinctions among the various emotional states must be considered an open question. Recent work might be taken to indicate that such differences are at best rather subtle and that the variety of emotion, mood and feeling states are by no means matched by an equal variety of visceral arousal' (pp. 379/380). Also 'Some writers on the topic of emotion insist that there is no characteristic conscious event that can be called an emotion, nor any simple conscious index of an emotion, and explicitly or by inference deny that emotions have intrinsic conscious content that can identify them' (Hebb, D.O., 1946, p. 101).

By taking coarse measures of emotion, such as the related activity of the adrenal cortex found by concomitant plasma 17-hydroxycorticosteroid level measures, researchers have found that emotional states are undifferentiated, supporting evidence being cited by Wilkins, W.W. III (1970, p. 3). More recent work on the cognitive labelling of emotional states allows for greater differentiation of emotional states through their association with cognitive events, discussed later in this section. Wilkins overviews the literature on cognitive labelling of emotions (pp. 11 ff), and concludes of subjects '...the more subtle discrimination of which emotion they are experiencing is under the control of external cues' (p. 18). The results of his own experiment did not support this. Wilkins' experiment was to feed subjects false GSR and heart rate indicating false emotional arousal and ask them to rate a garbled recording for its emotional content. Results were a lack of expected association which was blamed on coincidental environmental distractions.

Wilkins also highlights the difficulties of inferring internal emotional states from external measures as possibly being responsible for the lack of success in physiologically identifying highly subjective emotional states, e.g. internal sensations and private events, by these public events used for operationally defining an emotion (p. 1). Hebb, D.O. (1946) refers to these internal events as '...certain neurophysiological states, inferred from behaviour about which little is known except that by definition they redispose toward certain specific kinds of action' (p. 89). But he allows that the subject must be aware of concomitant feelings: 'There must be other associated signs which the subject comes to notice in himself' (p. 103). Kantor, J.R. (1966, p. 393) testifies to the uniqueness and range of affective intensities.

Cognitive Events Conditioned to Feelings

The above paragraph and the 'whole body' references in Section 3.1 support the concept of the interaction of feelngs with cognitive events: '...it is our basic assumption that emotional states are a function of the integration of such cognitive factors with a state of physiological arousal' (Schachter, S. and Singer, J.E., 1962, p. 381). Also '...each emotional reaction, regardless of its content, is a function of a particular kind of cognition or appraisal' (Lazarus, R.S. *et al.* 1970, p. 218). Similarly Strongman, K.T. (1973) comments: 'Under some circumstances a stimulus, perhaps a mild one, might have some of its emotional effects more cognitively than in any other way. And, as the organism is dynamic rather than static, changed cognitions might affect subsequent emotional responses. Equally, physiological or behavioural changes could affect one another, or cognition' (p. 191). Neisser, U. (1963a) also supports this intimate association of the feelings and cognitive events: '...human thinking begins in an intimate association with emotions and feelings which is never entirely lost' (p. 195).

Further support for the conditioning of ideas with feelings on physiological dimensions into emotional sets, as presented by the Theory of Intuitive Thought Processes, is offered by Tomkins, S.S. (1965) who used the concept of feelings resonating with ideas which he calls 'Ideoaffective Resonance' (p. 74). Similar views may be found in Cannon W.B.'s (1932) theory of 'homeostasis and wisdom of the body' (p. 38).

The terms 'emotion', 'mood' and 'feeling' have been used here almost synonymously. Strongman, K.T. (1973) reviewing the works of Nowlis, shows that Nowlis also considers mood and emotion to be synonymous. 'Nowlis believes the "entire" individual to be involved in mood. He also suggests that the determinants of mood are often obscure or inaccessible although its main function is to monitor or control behaviour. Hence, in its breadth, the concept of mood is more or less equal to that of emotion' (p. 78).

Kantor, J.R. (1966) does, however, distinguish between feelings and emotion as affective and effective respectively. Effective behaviour brings about a change in the stimulus whereas affective behaviour brings about a change in the organism, e.g. glandular, smooth muscle action, secretion, increase or decrease in salivation, tear flow, adrenalin secretion, heart rate, blood pressure, respiration, etc. Kantor lists some salient characteristics of affective events which include completeness and smoothness of affective behaviour segments, i.e. feelings are complete responses: '...the specific affective reaction system constitutes the consummatory factor in a complex response. This consummatory phase is preceded by the attentional and the perceptive reaction systems' (p. 393). This distinguishes feelings from emotions. Bartlett, E.S. (1971) in an 'Investigation of the subjective experience of emotion' found results implying that felt experience is partially independent of the emotional process. However, affective and effective behaviour occur together.

Thus affective reaction systems that ordinarily are consummatory acts may in the complex perceiving, thinking, and reasoning behavioural fields serve as precurrent factors integrated with cognitive or other types of behavioural fields. In this case the behaviour segment will not be called an affective one. It is this sort of complication of complex behaviour segments that forms the basis for the intermixture of judgment and reasoning with affective components. (Kantor, J.R., 1966, p. 393)

That is, feelings and emotions occur together and involve cognition, hence I will continue to use the term 'emotional set', as opposed to feeling set.

Brady, J.V. (1970a) follows Kantor in this distinction between feeling and emotion.

Emotional behaviour seems most usefully considered as part of a broad class of effective interactions, the primary consequences of which appear to change the organism's relationship to its external environment. Feelings or affective behaviour, on the other hand, can be distinguished as a generic class of interactions, the principal effects of which are localizable within the reacting organism rather than in the exteroceptive environment. (p. 70)

However, as stated, because emotions and feelings are simultaneous I will continue to use the term 'emotional set' as analogous to the use of 'mental set' rather than the term 'feeling set' which would imply an affective restriction on the conditioned responses to the set.

There is evidence to show that these feelings are easily conditioned: 'An outstanding characteristic of affective behaviour is that the responses are very easily conditioned' (Kantor, J.R., 1966, p. 394). Apart from the responses previously mentioned, motor response tendencies conditioned to emotional sets, being noticeably effective, are particularly considered as a part of emotional behaviour. But these have been associated with autonomic visceral proprioceptive and endocrine activity in studies quoted by Brady, J.V. (1970a,b). That these response tendencies are conditioned has been shown by these introceptive events acquiring discriminatory control over behaviour (see Katkin, E.S. and Murray, E.N., 1968).

The ease with which feelings are conditioned, and their interpretation in this study as non-exclusive conglomerations on physiological dimensions, allows non-unique conditioning to different emotional sets, which is the source of redundancy used in the Theory of Intuitive Thought Processes. A review of relevant work by Brady, J.V. (1970b) supports this interpretation.

In keeping with their internal orientation, the feelings can be intimately associated with autonomic-visceral, proprioceptive, and endocrine activity. A host of recent conditioning studies [five references given] have documented the ease with which such interoceptive events can acquire discriminative control over behaviour and the flexibility which characterizes the loose integration of feeling responses with exteroceptive environmental stimuli. (p. 70)

Kantor's work also supports this aspect of the Theory of Intuitive Thought Processes.

The loose and flexible organization of affective fields with consequent ease of conditioning may be attributed to the fact that affective responses are less closely integrated with their stimulus objects inasmuch as the consequences of the reactions are localizable in the reacting organism. Responses in which visceral actions are prominent as compared with saliently skeletal patterns of action are less rigorously bound to the objects and situations to which they are connected at any particular time. (p. 394)

In agreement with our previous discussion Kantor also attests to cultural and personal experiences in conditioning these responses: 'Feeling interbehaviours are both idiosyncratic and cultural' (p. 394).

Rommetveit, R. (1968) notes the specificity of conditioning feelings to cognitive events with the example of 'words'. He argues that when a child learns a word he also comes to associate a particular 'organismic state' or a complex affective-sensory-motor pattern with that word; this state 'may persist as a covert physiognomic component of the adult's word meaning' (p. 157). In marking a semantic differential scale position, Rommetveit says that a subject's behaviour may be '...interpreted as a purely expressive act by which the respondent communicates fragments of a pattern of feelings and response tendencies' (p. 150). He points out that 'transparent' words carry a consensus effect both positive and negative. Perhaps these are conditioned by common or cultural experiences, which would agree with Kantor p. 394 cited above. The juxtaposition of words with positive and negative affect associations Rommetveit says is clearly untenable out of context, e.g. 'bad success' or 'iron cloud'. The model of Intuitive Thought Processes explains the intuitive unacceptability of such juxtapositions by the discordance of their associated feelings, see Section 5.5.

Indications of how the Body is Self-sensitive to Feeling

There are systems in the body that endeavour to maintain homeostasis against the unstabilizing effects of external stimuli. It is proposed here that not only does the peripheral sensing of these external stimuli influence the emotional state but that the feedback due to this sensing through these systems also contributes to the emotional state. Together the sensing of external stimuli, the sensing of internal stimuli, and change in internal stimuli constitute the feelings or the affective components of the responses conditioned to the emotional set. As a response is considered partly defined by the physiological dimensions of its affective components, any change in these will define a different response.

There are many feedback systems for assessing feelings, as listed in this section. The Theory of Intuitive Thought proposes that information for the intuitive process is accessed by feeling-retrieval cues hence a desensitization of the feedback systems which assess these feelings will inhibit intuitive thought. In this section evidence is cited to support this. The reverse also seems to be true.

The feedback systems of the body are analogous to engineering feedback systems described by differential equations. They are analogous to psychological feedback systems, e.g. where it is possible to increase motivation by giving subjects knowledge of their results (Mackworth, N.H., 1950). They include the biofeedback systems where a subject may control, both consciously or subconsciously, responses such as blinking, heart rate, alpha and theta rhythms (Foulkes, D., 1966). For example Hefferline, R.F. et al. (1959, 1963) operantly conditioned subjects' spontaneous muscular twitches to the cessation of an unpleasant noise. The twitches were unfelt by the subject but amplified for this experiment. When presented with the unpleasant noise after conditioning, subjects would unknowingly increase the frequency of the twitches to cut out the noise. Also Lazarus, R.S. and McCleary, R.A. (1949) presented subjects with nonsensical words and after certain syllables gave an electric shock. Subjects later anticipated the shock at the sight of the 'shock syllables' yet on questioning subjects could not identify the shock syllables. Similarly Eriksen, C.W. and Keuthe, J.L. (1956) shocked subjects when they uttered any associations to certain 'shock words'. The subjects learnt to avoid these associations without knowing it.

Commonly the associations between self-sensed changes and cognitive events are subconscious. I have asked relaxed subjects connected to polygraphs to imagine they are running. They later report that they were unaware of their physiological responses immediately departing from basal level. Similarly Jacobson, E. (1932) recorded slight movements in the limbs of subjects imagining they were hammering or running.

> A shift of attention from the right leg to the left arm will produce a minute movement of the eyes; thinking, an interior conversation, causes a dancing pattern of tension in the speech muscles. Jacobson (1967) used needle electrodes to show that imagery and verbal thought were always accompanied by slight tensional patterns in the eye and speech muscles respectively. (Grim, P.F., 1975, p. 127)

There is much evidence showing that imagery and motor patterns are commonly closely interdependent, see Section 3.3. Similarly feelings and motor patterns are closely associated: '...emotions are facilitated through appropriate posture and facial expression' (Gellhorn, E., 1964, p. 467). Gellhorn quotes experiments involving hypnosis to support his interpretation of the relationship between posture, mood, and emotional responsiveness. 'In numerous tests it has been impossible to induce a certain feeling which is unrelated to the directly suggested motor attitude. If, for instance, the posture accompanying "triumph" is suggested and "locked" in hypnosis, a depressive mood cannot be brought about unless the postural setting is changed' (p. 463).

The feedback systems of the body are interdependent and therefore kinaesthetic sensations sensed through proprioceptive feedback will influence the hormonal system. Gellhorn gives references that

> ...have clearly shown that the anterior hypothalamus primarily influences parasympathetic activity whereas the posterior hypothalamus regulates sympathetic processes... Bearing in mind that proprioceptive impulses are effective stimulants of the posterior hypothalamus, it is concluded that the excitation of the sympathetic division of the hypothalamus in emotion leads to movements reinforced by a positive feedback mechanism, ...The low intensity of proprioceptive impulses prevailing in a state of sadness would seem to contribute to the shift in hypothalamic balance to the para-sympathetic side and to its maintenance, and a corresponding statement would apply to the role of increased proprioceptive discharges and the state of sympathetic hypothalamic dominance in some forms of the happy state. Although a specific stimulus, mostly in the form of symbols, words seen or heard, appears to be the direct cause of mood or emotion, the setting of the hypothalamic balance through the total quantity of proprioceptive

impulses impinging on the hypothalamus per unit of time is of considerable importance. (pp. 458, 461, 463)

Gellhorn suggests that emotional states affect the skeletel muscles and vice versa (p. 463).

It seems not improbable, therefore, that in sensory-hypothalamic interaction the neocortex accounts also for the qualitative changes in sensations and perceptions during emotional excitation. The fact that this facilitative action of hypothalamic-cortical discharges is not confined to the sensory projection areas and to the motor cortex, but extends to the association areas as well suggesting that it might play a role in recalling past events. It should also be remembered that memory processes as well as perceptions are facilitated in the emotional state. (p. 466)

Fehr, F.S. and Stern, J.A. (1970) also maintain that primary feelings and immediate reflexes might now be seen a hypothalamic discharges which inhibit the cortex and excite the ANS. Emotion has been considered above in terms of effector responses and therefore dependent on the ANS whereas feelings have been considered in terms of affective responses and therefore dependent on the CNS. However, these are far from independent. The ANS is not solely an effector system but contains 'vast systems of visceral afferent fibers receiving messages from innervated receptors within the body cavity and sending them forward to the CNS.' (Lacey, J.I. and Lacey, B.C. 1970, p. 206). So palmar GSR, which is an ANS response, is recommended for investigations to monitor feeling in studies of intuition.

Many writers implicate the hypothalamus in the hormonal feedback system monitoring feelings and influencing cognitive events. Fehr, F.S. and Stern, J.A. (1970) say that the hypothalamus is important to emotion as physiological mechanisms that are in effect during emotion can be brought about by hormonal change — see also Gellhorn's theory of emotion in Gellhorn, E. and Loufbourrow, G.N. (1963). Similarly Strongman, K.T. (1973), reviewing the literature on psychology of emotion, summarizes

...we can be certain that the brain stem, the thalamus and hypothalamus, the limbic system and, to an extent, the neocortex are implicated in emotion. We can also say the endocrine changes are important and that the periphery has a part to play and that there are underlying neurochemical changes. However, we cannot say how these possible mechanisms interact. (p. 65)

Pribram, K.H. (1970) makes a suggestion towards a possible explanation of the above. He suggests that brain structures are suitable for monitoring chemical changes in the blood:

Because of the multisynaptic nature of the neuronal aggregates involved, they are in themselves especially sensitive to chemical substances circulating in the surrounding blood stream and thus are ideally constituted to serve as receptor sites. This special combination of control and sensitivity could be expected to make of these brain structures superb instruments for continuously monitoring their own state, a requirement basic to any conception of mood. (p. 51)

Because intuitive information is accessed through feeling-retrieval cues, desensitizing the feedback systems for assessing feelings should inhibit intuitive thought. The hypothalamic hormonal feedback system may be desensitized with drugs and the physical contributors to the feedback may be lesioned. It has been found that such desensitization does not inhibit the effective emotional behaviour, only the affective feelings.

The result of desensitization on emotional behaviour has been observed in animals. Bonvallet, M. and Allen, M.B. (1963) argue that there is a hypothesized area centred on the nucleus of the *tractus solitarious* which is involved with autonomic function and has many cardiovascular afferents. Impulses from this region should suppress any emotional activity, e.g. cortical, motor or autonomic activity. Experiments with animals have shown this, e.g. stimulation stops sham rage shown by decorticated cats, see Baccelli, G. *et al.* (1965). Solomon, R.L. and Wynne, L.C. (1950) similarly showed that sympathectomized dogs required many more trials (six hundred and fifty) to extinguish a conditioned avoidance response than did unoperated animals, thus also implicating the SNS in learning. Hammond, L.J. (1970) suggests that it is possible that lesioned animals perseverate due to an enhanced emotionality.

In humans desensitization has produced simulated emotional behaviour with lack of feelings. Hohmann, G.W. (1962, 1966) interviewed paraplegics and quadriplegics about their experienced feelings and emotions. He found that although emotional behaviour was maintained where physically possible, the reported accompanying feelings were reduced according to the degree of disfunction of the subject's ANS. Gellhorn, E. (1964) says: 'Moreover, a reduction or inhibition of proprioceptive impulses through blocking of the neuromuscular junction reduces sympathetic and increases parasympathetic discharges' (p. 468).

Increasing sympathetic activity using injections of adrenalin seems to enhance feeling whereas chlorpromagine, which is a tranquilizer, has the opposite effect. Schachter, S. (1971) injected either adrenaline, a placebo or a tranquillizer into subjects who watched a slapstick film. Subjects were observed and questioned and the results showed adrenaline-injected subjects enjoyed the film most, placebo-injected subjects enjoyed the film less, and tranquillized subjects enjoyed the film the least. This evidence seems to indicate that non-intuitive types would tend to have a less active sympathetic system. It would have been interesting to consider the number and quality of the intuitions of Schachter's tranquillized subjects and Hohmann's paraplegics compared to normal subjects.

There is evidence to show that animals deprived of visceral innervation are slow to learn. Schachter, S. (1964) quotes experimental results that show '...when deprived of visceral innervation, animals are quite slow in acquiring emotionally linked avoidance responses' (p. 73). The evidence is that humans also depend upon their feedback systems for cognitive acquisitions.

Abstract Thought as Intuitive Processing of Personalized Feeling Models of Originally Concrete Analogies

There is evidence to show we think better in concrete examples or analogies because one can empathize, become emotionally involved with the situations, and use the evoked feelings for intuitive thought. The ease with which one can empathize with a concrete situation makes that concrete situation or analogy more suitable for intuitive thought. The more modalities involved, then the more accessible is the intuitive information which has been encoded by the physiological dimensions comprising these modalities.

'Abstraction' seems to have two meanings, particularly in mathematics. Increasingly abstract mathematics means increasingly generalized mathematics, i.e. more inclusive of other mathematical concepts. However, I believe that to think abstractly as opposed to concretely means to think in feeling models more removed from the immediate perception of the specific external stimuli. The Theory of Intuitive Thought Processes shows this 'more removed' to be idiosyncratic transformations of the feelings originally associated with the perception. These transformations occur through the successive combinations of emotional sets to which the information is conditioned by these feelings. Each rehearsal further transforms the feelings producing a more personalized 'feeling model'. More abstract thought through the use of more personalized 'feeling models' is greatly transformed, by combination of emotional sets, from the original feelings associated with the original perception. Thus it is possible to think abstractly about concrete situations or to have concrete representations of abstract, i.e. generalized, ideas.

Along with the resolution of the anxiety initially evoked by concurrent discordant stimuli intuitive thought transforms the concordant feelings we have and which we initially associate with a concrete situation: '...at least one of the meanings of this troublesome term [intuition] signifies perceptions which are in the highest degree individual, concrete, and harmonious within themselves' (Allport, G.W., 1929, p. 15). 'Perhaps the first thing that can be said about intuition when applied to mathematics is that it involves the embodiment or concretization of an idea, not yet stated, in the form of some sort of operation of example' (Bruner, J.S., 1962, p. 103). In the essential intuitive commencement to creativity we manipulate the slightly different feelings associated with an analogy. 'The essential fundamental element of creative imagination is the capacity to think by analogy' (Ribot, T., 1906). The similarity of the feelings associated with aspects of the two groups of stimuli defines these two groups as analogous on these aspects.

There is evidence that shows we think more effectively when we include the intuitive process by involving our feelings through empathizing directly with the problem situation or through a concrete analogy, see Section 3.1. This principle is used in teaching particularly young children: 'When dealing with very young children it is difficult to unravel the "intellectual acquisition-affective resonance" complex. Many children in the younger classes retain a new idea in school only in so far as it is presented to them in a context which engages their affectivity, whether it be funny, comic, moving, troubling, or frightening' (Mialaret, G., 1966, p. 133). Scott, L.E. (1972) states that this is the view of experienced competent teachers: 'Their view is that children learn best that which is concrete rather than abstract. Furthermore they believe that later ability to manage increasing abstraction is a function of the early base of concrete experiences' (p. 27). Insight reasoning experiments, where experimenters test understanding of logic statements, e.g. Goodwin, R.Q. and Wason, P.C. (1972); Johnson-Laird, P.N. and Wason, P.C. (1970a), give better results with concrete presentation as is shown by a logic task reported by Goodwin and Wason (1972, p. 206). They report that Wason and Shapiro (1971) used coloured cards and symbols which enabled the subjects to reason correctly. I believe this is possibly because the cards and symbols have more associated feelings which the subjects could use to aid their thinking.

Gilhooly, K.J. and Falconer, K.J. (1974) investigated the effect of all four combinations of abstract (*a*) or concrete (*c*), tasks (*t*) or relations (*r*), namely *at + ar, at + cr, ct + ar,* and *ct + cr*. The experimenters ran fifty subjects on each of the following conditions.

(1) 'Every time I go to Manchester I travel by car', representing concrete term and concrete relation: *ct + cr*;
(2) 'Every card which has Manchester on one side has car on the other side', representing concrete term and abstract relation: *ct + ar*
(3) 'Every time I go to *D*, I travel by 3', representing abstract term and concrete relation: *at + cr*
(4) 'Every card which has *D* on one side has 3 on the other', representing abstract term and abstract relation; *at + ar*.

Subjects in each condition were presented with four cards with appropriate symbols on each side and asked 'which of the four cards would you have to turn over to decide whether the following statement is true or false...? (p. 357). Then followed the statement for their particular condition. Using the correct number of answers (*p* and not *q*) the groups were ordered from the most correct as follows: both concrete, concrete terms, concrete relations, and then both abstract. This result supported earlier findings and the authors concluded: 'The results indicated that concreteness of the terms is the main factor leading to improved performance with "thematic" as against abstract material in the rule-testing task' (p. 355). Van Duyne, P.C. (1976) reviewing this, comments '. . .experiments have shown convincingly that the difficulties in reasoning correctly are overcome easily when the test sentence expresses a concrete relation which could occur in daily life. . . whereas sentences expressing an arbitrary relation between abstract symbols present almost insurmountable difficulties' (p. 86, four references given). Wason, P.C. (1966) also reports that information from positive instances can be assimilated and used more readily than information contained in negative instances.

Two more factors that make it easier for the subject to empathize with the problem were added in a similar experiment by Bracewell, R.J. and Hidi, S.E. (1974), namely 'natural' versus arbitrary order and temporal order. The authors cite previous studies which showed that thematic presentation of logical problems facilitated solution. They report the explanation as being that the themes acted by unifying the elements of the problem in different ways. In their experiment they used a $2 \times 2 \times 2$ design of natural versus arbitrary relationship, concrete versus abstract material, and order of presentation. This last treatment or order was new to this experiment, e.g. '1st order: every time I go to Ottawa I travel by car. 2nd order: I travel by car every time I go to Ottawa'. Ninety-six subjects were divided into eight groups. Significant results were for the two main factors, relationship and order, and the interaction factor of material by order. The authors part explained the results by noting that the natural rule 'seems distinctly odd' (p. 486) when in the second order and so inhibits S from making the error 'if p then q' implies 'if q then p'. The arbitrary relations did not show this effect. The Theory of Intuitive Thought shows this 'distinctly odd' feeling is available because of the ease with which the subject may empathize with the problem through this 'natural' presentation. Using presentations that do not carry such inherent information of non-reversability the authors found the relationship factor was not significant, i.e. 'every time I think of Ottawa, I remember car' (p. 486).

Clark, H.C. and Clark, E.V. (1968) have also found that a sentence which mentioned two sequential events in correct temporal order was recalled better than a sentence which mentioned the two events in reversed temporal order, which is consistent with the Theory of Intuitive Thought and pertinent to the discussion of anchor states in Section 3.2. Also in accordance with this interpretation Paivio, A. (1971) reports on the superiority of memory for concrete against abstract terms.

We utilize the intuitive process by empathizing with a situation to evoke feelings with which we may encode the situation and recall relevant information with concordant associated feelings. Metaphor, simile, analogy, and concrete situations help us to empathize. 'Poetry itself is so meaningful because it established relations between the abstract and the concrete. Poetry equates abstractions and ideals to simple acts and percepts. It requires the "almost seeing and feeling" of concrete things first' (Haefele, J.W., 1962, p. 56). Rothenberg, A. (1970) studying 'Inspiration, insight and the creative process in poetry' also says that we understand poetry through feeling and personal involvement. 'In other words the particular phrases, images, ideas or poetic metaphors which constitute inspirations and inceptions of poems are themselves metaphors for personal conflicts. The personal importance of these phrases etc., is *felt,* not conceived' (p. 176). The more modalities through which we may empathize, then the more physiological dimensions of feelings are available for intuitive recall. In mathematics we frequently make kinaesthetic representations to this end, e.g. 'a hole is to dig, a yard is to pace off, subtraction is to take away' (Bruner, J.S., 1962, p. 100). 'The concrete form is more quickly comprehended than the abstract form. A face is recognized before a geometrical figure, and both before numbers' (Haefele, J.W., 1962, p. 56).

The literature on creative mathematics is consistent with our interpretation that mathematics is created by the transformation of these 'feeling models', through the intuitive process of combining emotional sets, and then publicly transcribing: 'George Boole was showing the ability to model a subjective feeling about the sets of his experience' (Griffiths, H.B., 1972, p. 4; he gives other examples). Griffiths, H.B. and Howson, A.G. (1974) maintain that a common feature to all examples of insight is a familiar model '. . . a common feature is that "insight" into mathematical theory seems to be related to the realization that the theory has a model in physics, geometry, or some more familiar or accessible part of mathematics' (p. 215). They say: 'At all stages, one cannot make a good model of a situation without possessing a good intuitive experience of the situation' (p. 302). This view is also quoted by MacDonald, I. D. (1976) in his article on 'Insight and intuition in mathematics'. Section 2.2 on physiognomy shows how mathematical creativity uses the manipulation of these personal 'feeling models'. In seeking rigorous mathematical proofs Poincaré, H. (1969) used his intuitive knowledge of some concrete object: 'I seek to show that some property pertains to some object whose concept seems to me at first indefinable, because it is intuitive' (p. 208). He then abstracts from his intuition of the object a mathematical definition, a subset of the non-affective part of the intuition, to which the proof applies, i.e. some property of the object is used as an affective referent for the mathematical concept. 'At first I fail or must content myself with approximate proofs: finally I decide to give to my object a precise definition, and this enables me to establish this property in an irreproachable manner' (p. 208). Whether the final proof pertains to the original object or not depends upon the individual experience of the reader. 'Experience alone can teach us that some real and concrete object corresponds or does not correspond to some abstract definition. This second verify is not mathematically demonstrated, but neither can it be any more than can the empirical laws of the physical and natural sciences. It would be unreasonable to ask more' (p. 209). Although the subjective concrete affective referents are not published as part of the final abstract proof, these feelings are needed to give understanding and direction to the step-by-step analysis; a unity and understanding to the whole: '...and yet if the primitive image had totally disappeared from our recollection, how could we divine by what caprice all these inequalities were erected in this fashion one upon another?' (p. 210).

Symbolism, particularly in mathematics, is the bridge between people that allows us to communicate part of our 'feeling model' so that the other person in experiencing common associated feelings will share our understanding. Symbols that spark off many interrelated associations, that is evoke a high echelon emotional set, have much meaning. Whereas those symbols that evoke only limited associations have little meaning. We try to teach by conditioning symbols to feelings in common and associated with concrete situations, so that these symbols have a minimum consensus meaning defined by the shared feelings. Later personal transformation of these feelings during rehearsals allows 'abstract thought' and more understanding through the greater connectivity (redundancy) that the combination of emotional sets produces during the Intuitive Thought Process.

A 'good' symbol will easily evoke the feeling model by mapping, usually spatial features of the symbol on to features of the feeling model, thus easily recalling the represented concept e.g. $2^{\square}$ is a 'good' symbol for the volume of a cube of side two as the $\square$ maps on to, i.e. evokes, the volume of a cube in relation to its sides. Similarly IV is a 'good' symbol for four in that its spatial place system maps on to the relations between four one and five. However, as concepts grow, interpreted by the Theory of Intuitive Thought as increasing connectivity by combinations of emotional sets (Section 5.3), the feeling models are transformed accordingly. Thus the better a symbol is in recalling the lower concept, then the worse it is for recalling the extended concept because it powerfully evokes an inadequate feeling model restricting relevant thought.

> Perceiving, thinking, judging and related activities are profoundly affected by — perhaps even wholly dependent upon — a pre-established system or ordering or conceptual placement ...And yet this very dependence on a system of categories leads to a kind of conceptual closedness, reflected in a functional blindness to alternative evaluations that are not embodied in the conceptual framework employed at the moment. (Harvey, O.J. and Beverley, G.D., 1961, p. 125)

Hence 2^3, which commonly evokes the feeling of three twos separated by multiplication signs, is more appropriate to the extended concept of powers. Similarly the Hindu Arabic symbol 4 does not hamper thought by evoking probably the irrelevant feelings of the addition relations between 4, 1, and 5. As Haefele, J.W. (1962) says 'symbolization should be directed to move from the abstract towards a sense of experience, and to appeal to other senses than sight' (p. 56).

Sensitivity of Feeling Facilitates Intuition

As information for intuitive processing is coded by feelings, sensitivity to feelings will make this information more accessible. Burden, Virginia (1975) writing on 'The process of intuition' says: 'Intuition... is made available to man in a state of acute sensitivity' (p. 21). Bohart, A.C. (1972) hypothesizes that subjects 'open to their feeling life' were more likely to achieve insights (p. 435). Clark, F.V. (1973) says '...the subjective experience of receptivity is invariably associated with optimum intuitive functioning' (p. 160). Clark, J. (1973) says that when a subject '...utilizes intuition he is more receptive to experience' (p. 215). Developing sensitivity and self-awareness is used to encourage insight in 'project insight'. Besel, R.R. et al. (1970) report: 'One goal of project insight was to increase sensitivity and self-awareness' (p. 1).

Intuition may be facilitated by self-sensitivity developed using body movement exercises. These exercises are frequently accompanied by kinaesthetic imagery. Clark, F.V. (1973) says: 'Tuning in to bodily responses and kinaesthetic imagery in a given situation may give a subject information regarding unconscious reactions, which might otherwise be blocked from his awareness' (p. 161). This may explain insights facilitated by body movement exercises which are reported in the following paragraph.

Schofield, L.J. and Abbuhl, Stephanie, (1975) investigating 'The stimulation of insight and self-awareness through body movement exercise' have shown that body movement exercises enhance self-awareness and insight. They designed an experiment to test the hypothesis that self-awareness on a projective task is affective by related body movement exercises. Sixty-three female students were split into an experimental group and a control group. All were asked to name 'the animal you would most like to be'. The experimental group were given five minutes of modern dance exercises exploring emotion, texture, body awareness, and relaxing body movements. They then spent approximately five minutes acting out in movement the animal they had chosen. Both groups were asked to state why they had chosen their particular animal. These reasons were rated on six categories from (1) stereotyped descriptions to (6) considerable understanding of the animal and moderate connections with self (p. 746). A t-test was highly significant ($p < 0.001$) with the experimental group showing most 'awareness'. The authors say the reasons are unclear but suggest the following: 'It may be that the physical activity itself had the effect of lowering defenses and inhibitions for both experiencing and expressing thoughts and feelings. It also may be that general or rather specific body movements somehow directly stimulate cognitive functioning and thus permit greater insight and self-awareness' (p. 746). In the light of the Theory of Intuitive Thought a comment from Gellhorn, E. (1964) may be taken as support that the exercises make more feeling available for intuitive thought: 'The educational and therapeutic value of the control of the expressive movements, including that of the tone of the skeletal muscles, lies in the fact that they may be used to trigger or to inhibit the emotions by the employment of relatively simple physiological procedures' (p. 467). Samples, R. (1976)

predicts that to encourage intuition, future '...curriculum offerings will include the following... some students may use body movement as a medium to pursue concepts in physics' (p. 10).

It has been shown that relaxed atmospheres and permissive ego states facilitate intuitive thought, Section 2.3. This is partly because such internal and external environments help in a relaxed non-competitive atmosphere to encourage introspection of feelings. 'By maintaining an accepting, warm, and non judgmental attitude, the therapist develops feelings of trust, safety, and security in the patient. In this emotional climate, inhibitory to anxiety, the patient proceeds to talk about emotionally troublesome attitudes, feelings and experiences' (Brady, J.P., 1967, p. 307).

In a competitive atmosphere perceptual focusing occurs and subjects are less aware of both internal and external subliminal perceptions, Section 5.2.

Fox, Muriel (1960) showed that subjects who are subliminally sensitive 'are more guided by feelings'. While attending to external stimuli, internal stimuli reduce in amplitude (Lacey, J.I., 1967; Lacey, J.I. *et al.*, 1963), which reduces the threshold of feelings available for intuitive recall. Polanyi, M. (1966) realized that our attending to observable outcomes and reactions prevents us from being aware of and being able to identify the conditioning between our behaviour and our subliminal perceptions. For example when looking at a face by attending to the detailed characteristics we are not conscious of our awareness of its physiognomic features (p. 10).

Self-sensitivity is increased when we are in a relaxed state. Clark, F.V. (1973) in an excellent paper 'Exploring intuition' suggests: 'Participants should relax, free associate, and await spontaneous insight' (p. 168). He then recommends, in agreement with the above, that quiet attention to one's feelings in many modalities and across modalities will facilitate intuitive thought:

> ...take a few moments to focus on your own breathing and to clear or empty your mind. Having assumed a quiet receptive attitude... close your eyes and notice any other sense impressions which may be present. Since the dominance of visual impressions frequently blocks out other sense impressions, the temporary elimination of visual clues may activate more subtle perceptions. Optimum receptivity to kinaesthetic, auditory and visual imagery should be maintained in silence... the task should not be approached in a logical or intellectual manner. (pp. 167/168)

Intuition may be facilitated by increasing one's self-sensitivity using biofeedback and meditation. Relaxed states are characterized by wide frequencies of alpha rhythms down to the presence of theta rhythms. Although theta rhythms are initially too low for biofeedback, training in muscle relaxation will usually increase them so that the subject has something to work with (Green, E. *et al.*, 1970). Stoyva, J. (1973, p. 394) says that biofeedback muscle relaxation can produce alterations in quality of thinking, and distortions or changes of body image: vivid visual images are common, as are feelings of floating, turning, limb-moving, and disappearing.

Certain types of meditation have the same result as direct biofeedback training in promoting theta waves. Ornstein, R.E. (1972, p. 138) says that meditation, and deautomatization exercises intended to alter linear consciousness, can encourage the intuitive mode. A direct result showing that some meditation techniques induce the alpha and theta rhythms characteristic of the ego state facilitating intuition, has been found by Ghistra, D.N. *et al.* (1976), who write '...the alpha state has been noted to be associated with pleasant feeling, wellbeing, tranquility, relaxation, an abundance of alpha-wave activity is considered to represent a state of rest (not sleep), relaxation and relief from concentration' (p. 209). These authors monitored the physiological state of five subjects during a type of meditation called 'intuitional practice' where a subject concentrates on a selected part of his body and chants two-syllable words in time with his breathing. Results showed that frequency of brain waves during meditation as compared with that during concentration was different in that intuitional practice gave a wider band of frequency down to theta waves at 5·25 hz whereas frequency during concentration centred closely around the 10 hz range. It was found: 'During intuitional practice the percentage of waves in the alpha and theta bands increases: also the signal amplitude in this band increases markedly' (p. 209). Keefe, T. (1976) says '...that some varieties of meditation, especially those derived from Zen traditions, encourage behaviours that facilitate empathy'. They '...refine the worker's sensitivity to his own feeling responses to another person' (p. 13). It is proposed in this book that empathy is essential for intuition.

EEG alpha and theta measures, although indicative of states in which intuition occurs, are difficult to use for psychophysiological investigations of intuitions. This is because the large signal to noise ratio (Sternbach, R.A., 1960, 1966) necessitates repeated measures for statistically removing the noise. Repetition of the same intuition is not possible and to induce many different intuitions for this purpose may be considered to be impracticable.

An introspective description of feeling during a meditation state is given by Grim, P.F. (1975) in a paper on 'Relaxation, meditation, and insight'. His description shows some of the effects of sensitivity to feelings on cognition that have been discussed above. Grim describes how through a practice of 'autogenic training and progressive relaxation' (p. 125) he was able to cut out proprioceptive feedback while concentrating on a single image. He says it was evident that all words 'contained a fuzzy coating of emotional conditioning, not just four-letter words, but even definite articles like "the" ' (p. 128). It was this emotional content that caused his associations of thought: '...an image would no sooner be created than it would give way to a train of other images with apparently an associative relationship; or if not that, then it would shift to a series of related thoughts' (p. 128). When he was able to stop the bodily feelings that caused these associations, Grim describes: 'With all bodily reactions stopped at the moment of looking, images become neutral and language is reduced to a truly abstract symbol system. The connotative-denotative meaning of words and images split — only the denotative component remained' (p. 128). 'Proprioceptive sensations are not normally attended to unless unusual or painful' (p. 126).

I believe the sensitivity to feeling induced by some forms of religious meditation provides the link between western and eastern philosophical concepts of intuition, see Section 1.2 on studies involving religious views of intuition

Intuitive Understanding Using Feelings Evoked Through Empathy

The view is proposed here that intuitive information is accessed through appropriate feelings and these appropriate feelings are evoked mainly subconsciously through empathy with the concrete objects characterizing a situation. Dymond, Rosalind F. (1949) defines empathy as '...the imaginative transposing of oneself into the thinking, feeling and acting of another and so structuring the world as he does'. This use of empathy is extended to objects and in the following section discussed in more detail. This section serves to show that empathy evokes feelings used to give intuitive understanding.

Rust, R.M. (1948) quotes the artist Nicolaides' instructions to art students: 'To be able to see the gesture you must be able to feel it in your own body. If you do not respond in like manner to what the model is doing, you cannot understand what you see'. This is called the Empathy Theory of Movement, see Allport, G.W. (1937). Similar advice is given in Method Acting, e.g. to act the part of a rose one must feel as a rose feels.

In the synectic method of creative production Gordon, W.J.J. (1961) makes much use of empathy and intuition. However, he finds because of their abstract nature he must develop the products of intuition through introspection of the feelings evoked through empathy. 'Abstractions such as intuition and empathy are almost impossible to teach because of their lack of concreteness, i.e. they are non-operational. However, the mechanisms like personal analogy, fantasy analogy, are psychological tools which at the conscious level almost everybody has experienced to a lesser or greater degree' (p. 53). 'Considerable use is made of personification and anthropomorphization. How would I feel if I were it? As a further special case of feeling as an inanimate object would feel, we have experimented successfully with attempts to empathize, to feel, kinaesthetically, in interrelation of the muscles themselves the state of an inanimate object, a motion or a relationship' (pp. 30/31). From formal interviews many inventors agreed that they went through these psychological states. This was later found by Gordon to be universal (p. 19).

6.3   EMPATHY AND PROJECTION ESSENTIAL TO INTUITION

Empathy is the twelfth property of intuition with six references to it in Section 1.3.

Writers have described intuition in terms of empathic ability. Previous sections and chapters have established that information is encoded and retrieved through feeling cues. This section proposes that these feelings are evoked through empathy. To retrieve and process information appropriate to some situation the intuitive type empathizes with the elements of the situation to evoke appropriate feelings for retrieval and processing. He projects these feelings to the situation so he feels in fantasy as the elements feel in this situation. This is a temporary identification.

Through the transformation of his feelings, via the intuitive process of combining the emotional sets to which the feelings are conditioned, he feels the relations between the elements of the situation. As detailed in Section 5.4 the conscious realization in the terminating emotional set marks the conclusion of the intuitive process, feelings and associated cognitions are the intuition about the situation. This process of 'simultaneously' empathizing and projecting one's feelings in a temporary identification is fundamental to the intuitive process and is here called empathic projection.

Empathic projection may be thought of as the two-way channel of empathy and projection which allows the person to use his body as an intuitive processor. This is a necessary ability for intuition. The Selected Phrase Empathic Ability Key is a mental instrument designed to measure it and may be used to predict the intuitive type.

The literature describes intuition in terms of empathy and vice versa. Many writers define empathy in terms of intuition. Allport, G.W. (1960), commenting on Lipps' concept of empathy, says it consists of two aspects: intuition and inference. 'The intuition factor seems quite close to the Gestalt concept of direct perception. Inference begins to point to an associationist theory of understanding.' Both of these ideas are included in the Theory of Intuitive Thought. Conklin, K.R. (1970) equates empathy with intuition, '...empathy is the power of intuition when applied to give knowledge of someone's state of mind' (pp. 330/331). Fenichel, O. (1953) defines empathy as '...the intuitive grasp of the real psychic states of another person'. These last two definitions of empathy are in terms of intuition about people as in Szalita-Pemow A.B.'s, (1955) definition of the empathic process which he postulated as identical to the intuitive process: 'Whenever two people deal with each other, there is a tendency on the part of each to relate to the other on his own level ... Now this process is very similar, if not identical to the intuitive or creative process described above' (p. 13). However, one may also empathize with any object. The object is not required to be a person. Feelings evoked through empathy with the object are projected on to the object so the subject feels intuitively as the object does, '...empathy is the capacity of the subject instinctively and intuitively to feel as the object does' (Olden, Christine, 1953). Allport, G.W. (1929) includes empathy and sensation in his 'intuitive method' for the study of personality (pp. 26/27).

The association of intuition and empathy is emphasized by writers who consider them contiguously (e.g. Davitz, J.R., 1964, p. 2), as do Beres, D. and

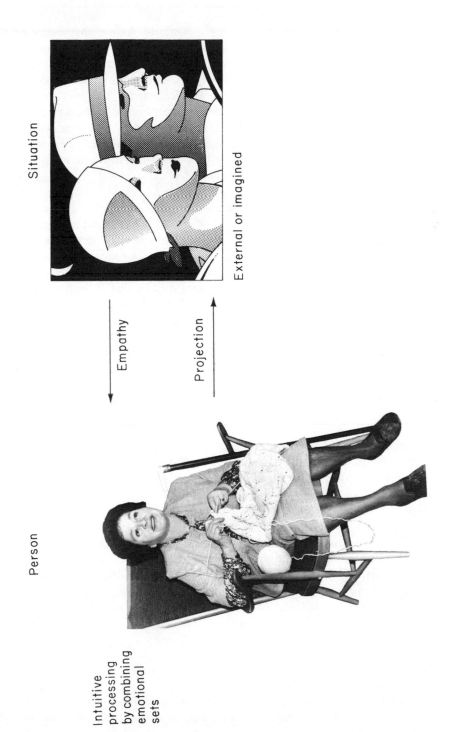

Situation

External or imagined

Empathy

Projection

Person

Intuitive
processing
by combining
emotional
sets

Fig. 6.3/1 Illustrating the role of empathic projection in the intuitive process

Arlow, J.A. (1974) when discussing the role of 'Fantasy and identification in empathy': 'The intuitive understanding of a therapist follows his empathic response ...the therapeutic situation requires that empathy and intuition go on to interpretation and insight... empathy and intuition play a basic role' (pp. 28, 46). They say empathy '...facilitates the emergence of intuition and leads by way of interpretation to insight' (p. 47). Rapaport, D. (1951) not only associates intuition and empathy, he admits our ignorance of these important processes: 'Though empathy and intuition certainly are the archetypes of our knowledge about our fellow human beings, their nature is still a closed book to us'. Clark, F.V. (1973) says intuition is reached 'through empathic identification with the totality...' (p. 166). This also refers to the global nature of intuition which we discussed in Section 5.5.

Stocks, J.L. (1939) describes intuition as used in mathematics in the same terms as those used to describe empathy. He also notes the feeling property of intuition (Section 6.2) and its global knowledge property of understanding 'wholeness' (Section 5.5). 'He feels it in himself; he understands his wholeness in and from his own being' (p. 12). Both Wild, K.W. (1938) and Guiora, A.Z. et al. (1965, p. 111) quote Bergson as defining intuition in the terms used to define empathy. 'By intuition is meant the kind of intellectual sympathy by which one places oneself within an object in order to coincide with what is unique in it and consequently inexpressible', and again 'by placing himself back within the object by a kind of sympathy, in breaking down, by an effort of intuition, the barrier that space puts between him and his model'. This is an example of what we are calling empathic projection.

Walkup, L.E. (1965) discusses examples of intuitive understanding through feelings evoked by empathy with objects.

> It is almost a feeling like the object being visualized. One can feel the pressure of contacting objects, or the erosion of material by friction, or the flow of heat from one point to another, or the swing of the oscillating electrical circuit, or the bending of light as it passes from one medium to another, or the appropriateness of a well-designed structure to hold a maximum load, with every part equally strained in the process, or the external bouncing about of the molecules of a gas or the almost physical transfer of energy from the gasoline, through the motor, transmission, and to the driving wheels of the automobile. It is as though one's own kinaesthetic sensing mechanisms were associated with the physical object and that he thus sensed directly what was going on in the external system. In highly-developed visualizers, this process probably is carried over for other than physical phenomena. (p. 39)

An example of this use of empathy as ascribed to intuition is given by Eyring, H. (1959) in a story of a man who by empathizing with a lost horse used the feelings generated to know where he would go if he were, in fantasy, the lost horse. He went there and found it. This story is recounted in Section

1.3 to illustrate that empathy is a property (property 12) of intuition. There are many similar examples of scientific intuition that the creators say from introspection were derived from empathy with the objects of their intuition, see Section 7.3.

Aldenbrand, Martha L. (1974) designed an experiment to investigate the relation between intuition, feeling and empathy. Unfortunately she used the Myers-Briggs scale to find the intuitive type and she used an accurate empathy method which produced the usual non-significant or paradoxical results of using, in this field, scales which are based on accuracy.

Empathic Projection

Empathy evokes subjectively appropriate feelings to be intuitively processed. The projection of these processed feelings on to the object with which the subject empathized, applies the intuition to the object. Because this is an ongoing process with the two processes concurrent and interacting, they merge to give what has been described as a temporary identification with the object. Cronbach, L.J. (1958) says empathy, like identification and projection, was regarded as an '...intuitive pervasive feeling state which preceded any cognition' (p. 376). In our present study we have termed the ability to evoke feelings empathically and project them on to the object of the empathy 'empathic projection'. This is similar to how Schachtel, E.G. (1950) describes perception of Rorschach M responses:

> In this process the psychomotor impulses are 'objectified', to a certain extent, and lead to the kinaesthetically enlivened percept in which the motor experience of the subject is projected onto the object seen ... He feels the movement or posture which to him seems to animate the ink blot. He experiences it as if he knew, not merely from outside but from inside how the human figure seen in the ink blot moves or holds its posture. It is as if he were, for a moment and to some extent, inside the figure seen. This is an experience similar to that which one has in the act of kinaesthetic empathy ... Thus, the perception of his own body in the kinaesthetic sensation is inextricably fused with the object perception ... by a feeling of inner evidence ... [giving] one's intuition... (pp. 70-72)

Empathy Used to Evoke Feelings Used in the Intuitive Process

Empathy is defined by Dymond, Rosalind F. (1949) as '...the imaginative transposing of oneself into the thinking, feeling and acting of another and so structuring the world as he does'. Spence, K. W. (1960) also considers empathy to mean that one experiences a situation from another person's point of view. But although the term is now commonly used as applicable to people, as in these two examples, it can be used to apply to how objects feel or how a person would feel in another situation. Later in this section we consider how the meaning of the term empathy has changed.

King, G.F. (1958) mentions many uses of the term empathy including that of Bochner and Halpern, who describe empathy in these egocentric terms, '...ability to put oneself in the place of another or to put oneself in different situations' (p. 2). Whereas Schafer, R. (1968) is one of the many writers who uses the term in its original meaning, the meaning in which it is used in this investigation, as applicable to objects '...the highest form of empathy ...the subject, so far as his own experience goes, feels that he is one with the object; he feels what the object feels' (p. 153). There is no consideration of accuracy here, for who can measure how an inanimate object might feel? There are only considerations of appropriateness which the logical verification of the intuition later establishes, see Section 8.1 on intuition need not be correct. It is the insistence that empathy can only be accurate that, in my view, is partially responsible for the previously poor results in experimentally establishing the dependence of intuition on empathy.

Feelings Projected to the Object of the Intuition

Schachtel, E.G. (1950) clearly associates: 'The capacity for empathic projection and for creative experience... [with] ...intuitive understanding' (pp. 96/97). This is particularly so in the parallel spatial-kinaesthetic modes which we have discussed as being common for intuitive thinking.

'Kinaesthetic thinking consists of having a mental "feeling" of the texture, contours, and consistency of the environment. It is as though the "mind's hands" feel the composition and the spatial relations among objects in the environment' (Bissell, Joan et al., 1971, p. 131). While the evoked feelings are transformed during the intuitive process, the transformed feelings are projected back to the original situation so that the subject is, in fantasy, feeling as the object in the situation is feeling. 'This direction of attribution — from self to another person — is projection, not empathy, as Chandler (1974) has noted' (Shantz, Carolyn Y., 1975, p. 19).

In this present investigation, projection is considered as defined by Bellak, L. (1944) as the ascribing of wishes, needs, thoughts, and sentiments which one has oneself, to subjects or objects of the external world without realizing that one does, and not necessarily as a defence mechanism as in Freud's work (p. 364). Schachtel, E.G. (1950) also infers that this process is preconscious (property 3).

In every act of kinaesthetic and other empathy there is an element of projection ...This, his personal kinesthetic or other feeling, aroused by what he sees, is projected onto the person or object seen and merges completely, without the subject's being aware of it, with the percept of the person or object empathically perceived ...The form of the object perceived stimulates kinesthetic sensations in the subject; these are then projected by the subject onto the object and seem to give life to it, to animate it, and to endow it with movement . . . in other words, while the content of the projection may or may not be conscious to the person as being part of himself, the process of projection usually takes place outside of awareness. (pp. 73/74)

The following relate empathy and projection with the intuitive process. Axelson, J.A. (1967) found from his investigations on a number of variables that: 'Self projection was most related to empathic perception'. Guiora, A.Z. et al. (1965) give a brief recapitulation of intuition as they found it was reflected in the literature, in which they emphasize '. . . the projective character of intuition', and that '. . . empathy is essential to it' (p. 118). And also Hathaway, S.R. (1955) comments: 'It is possible, however, that some features of all empathy, projection, and the like, would turn out to be intuitional if the pertinent data were available' (p. 224). In this book we have drawn attention to experimental procedures which interested readers may use to make such pertinent data available.

Temporary Identification During the Intuitive Process

Although it is recognized that empathy and projection are essential to the intuitive process, the literature does not differentiate their roles in the intuitive process as is done here in the Theory of Intuitive Thought; 'There is a thin line between projection, vicarious experience, empathy, and the ability to creatively solve human problems which escapes me' (Provus, M.M., 1966, p. 139). This involvement of empathy and projection in the intuitive process is a temporary identification with the objects to which the intuition is applied. This combination of empathy and projection as temporary identification in intuition is reported in the literature.

Burden, Virginia (1975) says: 'Intuition. . . is identification. . .' (p. 21). Sliker, Gretchen P. (1972) mentions 'an inside identification with the object' (p. 27) during the creative act. Suzuki, D.T. (1957) says '. . . the act of intuition is considered complete when a state of identification takes place between the object and the subject' (p. 89). Clark, F.V. (1973) says that '. . . intuitive insights result from identification. . . breaking down distinctions between subject and object' (p. 165). Gordon, W.J.J. (1961) reports that this temporary identification particularly involving kinaesthetic empathy is used during the intuitive phase of creativity:

. . . the chemist may personally identify with the molecules in action. Faraday 'looked . . . into the very heart of the electrolyte endeavoring to render the play of its atom visible to his mental eyes' (Tyndall, 1868, pp. 66/67). The creative technical person can think himself to be a dancing molecule, discarding the detachment of the expert and throwing himself into the activity of the elements involved. He becomes one of the molecules. He permits himself to be pushed and pulled by the molecular forces. He remains a human being but acts as though he were a molecule. For the moment the rigid formulae don't govern, and he feels what happens to a molecule. (p. 23)

He gives many examples from his own research of scientists identifying with objects in order to use their empathic feelings to aid invention. Gordon says

All the synectics groups (within as well as outside the parent group) had shown a recurrent tendency to identify as the altimeter inventor did when he asked himself: 'What would I feel like if I were a spring?' 'How would a spring feel if it were human?' We deliberately fed this tendency back into group sessions, and since its use led to successful solutions we concluded that this was one mechanism for initiating and sustaining inventive effort. This particular mechanism was injected by persuading participants to imagine how they would feel if they were the inanimate elements of the problem under consideration. For instance, in a session devoted to the invention of an unbreakable yet translucent plastic glass the group was encouraged to describe their subjective response at 'being' an actual piece of glass. How did they feel? Which way were they pulled? Did they want to stay close to their brother particles? (p. 28)

Suzuki, D.T. (1957) says that in Buddhist philosophy, during intuition: 'What is seen and the one who sees are identical' (p. 85).

In this present investigation, temporary identification is used in the same sense as the 'trial' or 'temporary identification' discussed by Fenichel, O. (1945) and what Schafer, R. (1959) calls identification in fantasy. This is not a permanent modification within the ego as is usually understood by identification but rather the person feels at one with the object or part of the object while maintaining his individuality. In Section 8.2 the ability to maintain one's individuality during empathic projection is considered as a learned development from egocentricity. Rogers, C.R. (1951) considers this 'empathic identification' as one of the three basic features of empathy. Stotland, E. and Dunn, R.E. (1963) similarly embody this idea of identification in their definition of empathy, '...the special case of identification in which the identifier acquires the model's level of anxiety (or any other emotion)' (p. 532).

Beres, D. and Arlow, J.A. (1974) recognize this ability in empathy to feel as the object and yet retain some separateness: 'There are two distinguishing features to empathy: one, it is a transient identification; second, the empathizer preserves his separateness from the object' (p. 33); '...the ego must stand aside in order to permit the experience' (Clark, F.V., 1973, p. 162). Clark uses the term 'empathic identification' (p. 166). It is this transient preconscious nature of the identification during empathy that distinguishes it from the traditional type of permanent identification. As Greenson, R.R. (1960) says, traditional identification '...is essentially an unconscious and permanent phenomenon, whereas empathy is preconscious and temporary' (p. 418); and the aim of empathy is 'to understand' but identification is to 'overcome anxiety, guilt or loss'. Kohut, H. (1959) describes empathy as 'vicarious introspection'.

An associated concept is 'sympathy' which writers seem to use to mean the helping component of empathy, '...arousing in one's self of the attitude of the individual whom one is assisting' (Mead, G.H., 1934, p. 366). Most studies of sympathy (e.g. Lenrow, P.B., 1965) deal with sympathy with people in various social conflicts using descriptive and ill-defined terms traditional to the psychoanalytic approach. I can find no studies of sympathy with inanimate objects. Buchheimer, A. (1963) defines sympathy as a parallel rather than shared feelings as in empathy. 'A sympathetic person feels along with another person but not necessarily into a person' (p. 63), and he criticizes many empathy studies using ratings in that: 'Most of these researches appear to be dealing with the phenomenon of sympathy rather than with that of empathy' (p. 65).

Imagined Extension of Body Boundary to Include the Object of Intuition

We may use empathic projection to give intuitive understanding by imagining our body boundary to be extended to include the object of the intuition. In this way we are in fantasy part of the object and the object is part of us. In particular as we share feelings the information from these feelings pertains to the object. This is the intuitive understanding of the object.

Polanyi, M. (1966) discusses how we may understand an object intuitively using empathy, we '...incorporate it in our body − or extend our body to include it − so that we come to dwell in it' (p. 16). He calls this 'indwelling', and writes '...that it is not by looking at things, but by dwelling in them that we understand their joint meaning' (p. 18). This 'breaking down' of the self/other awareness barriers is what we have referred to as temporary identification. A subject's defined body image is measured by his high barrier score. High barrier scores have already been associated with intuitive types (Roe, Anne, 1953; Holtzman, W.H. and Bitterman, M.E., 1956 and in Section 3.3).

Guiora, A. Z. (1965) defines empathy in terms of this temporary lack of definite body boundary used to give intuitive understanding. 'Empathy is a process of comprehending in which a temporary fusion of self-object boundaries, as in the earliest pattern of object relation, permits an immediate emotional apprehension of the affective experience of another, this sensing being used by the cognitive functions to gain understanding of the other.' It has been pointed out that this primary-process thinking is more likely to happen in relaxed ego-permissive states (Klein, G.S., 1970 and Section 8.2).

Kinaesthetic Empathy Gives Rise to Intuitive Understanding

Allport, G.W. (1960) explains that empathy works by judgments being made by the empathizer about the feeling state of the other person or object on the basis of associations the empathizer makes to various postural similarities. The original experience was initially imbued with specific kinaesthetic cues. When one physically puts oneself in the other's shoes by assuming the posture of the other, the kinaesthetic cues recur and reinstate the same original experience. Frijda, N.H. (1970) suggests that a person recognizes the meaning of expressive behaviour by representing the experience to themselves, making '...fractional empathic expressive movements himself'. These would be similar to the myographic responses accompanying imagery, see Section 3.1. Vernon, P.E. (1972) concurs with this view when he quotes Lipps, T. as saying: 'We empathize by copying the movements of others — e.g. straining upwards whilst watching a high jumper'. He uses this to explain the attribution of emotional qualities to objects. Vernon says '...we project the feelings on to the person rather than infer that the person feels the same as we do under similar circumstances' (pp. 48/49). Wolff, W. and Precker, J.A. (1951) define empathy in terms of identification through these movements. They define a principle of empathy '...according to which the expression of movements is an attempt at imitation and identification with the object to which the movement is related' (p. 490).

An interesting experiment was performed by Huntley, C.W. (1940) on the recognition of movement. His subjects were dressed in loose fitting concealing garments and filmed walking. A person rarely recognizes his own voice, hands, or mirrored handwriting. However, his subjects easily identified the movement of their own trunk and limbs, presumably using projective empathy. The perception of the total swing immediately arouses like muscular impulses which we promptly recognize as our own. Note the strange feeling when we copy another person's characteristic movements. However, Shapiro, T. (1974) points out that such empathy gives more than recognition. It allows understanding, '...empathy which Schafer, R. (1959) analogizes to a creative process ...permits comprehension of another's predicament rather than simple recognition' (p. 22).

Inanimate objects with which a person empathizes and then to which he projects his intuitively transformed feelings will have a physiognomic expression through this process. Arnheim, R. (1949) says Gestalt psychologists '...consider it indispensable to speak also of the expression conveyed by inanimate objects, such as mountains, clouds, sirens, machines' (p. 156). 'Instances of such direct expression are not limited to the appearance and behaviour of the subject's own body. They are also found in such "projective" material as the stirring red of a woman's favourite dress or the "emotional" character of the music she prefers. In addition, inanimate objects are said to convey direct expression' (p. 157), e.g. aggressive stroke of lightning, the soothing rhythm of rain etc. '...[T]he primary task, of the

Gestalt Theory of Expression, consists in making plausible the fact that the perception of shape, movement, etc., may convey to the observer the direct experience of an expression which is structurally similar to the organization of the observed stimulus pattern' (p. 162).

The Theory of Intuitive Thought does make this plausible: 'A weeping willow does not look sad because it looks like a sad person. It is more adequate to state that since the shape, direction and flexibility of willow branches convey the expression of passive hanging, a comparison with the structurally similar psychophysical pattern of sadness in humans may impose itself secondarily' (pp. 164/165).

Asch, S.E. (1946a) considers that environmental objects, e.g. sky, mountains, sea, possess expressive qualities by reason of the congruence of their structure with the structure of expressive movements occurring during periods of emotion. It is the co-ordination of the experience of the body with the structural qualities of the physical world that he believes also gives rise to the perception of expressive or physiognomic qualities of the environment. In Section 2.2 we have discussed how physiognomy of mathematical concepts leads to understanding and creative mathematics. Poincaré, H. (1969), talking of the great mathematician M. Hermite, recalls how he invested 'abstract' concepts with life: '...he never evoked a sensuous image, and yet you soon perceived that most abstract entities were for him like living beings' (p. 211).

It may be because the kinaesthetic and visual modalities are such common preference and ability modes that empathy is often considered in these terms. Although in this study experiments involving these modes are recommended for the investigation of intuition because they are of common occurrence, the theory allows for empathy in all modalities and across modalities. However, the kinaesthetic mode does seem to predominate in considerations of empathy. Hastorf, H.A. and Bender, I.E. (1952) conclude a series of studies on empathy with the summary that empathic ability '...seems to be a combination of sensory, imaginative, and intellectual processes. Imitative factors, particularly of a kinaesthetic nature, may well aid the process'. Meuller, W. and Abeles, N. (1964) have tried to correlate empathy with a number of kinaesthetic responses in the protocols of trainee psychotherapists.

Mialaret, G.'s (1966) description of how a spectator intuitively understands that which he sees acted, shows clearly the use of kinaesthetic empathy and projection for the intuitive process. He says empathy phenomena

> ...occur when a spectator of an action performed by another person 'lives' it himself to some extent and does not merely try to comprehend it in a purely intellectual way by classifying it into one conceptual category or another ...using incipient movements which are generalized and affect the whole of the motor apparatus. When that happens there is usually a real fusion between the visual data, movements of the actor, and the proprioceptive tactile-kinaesthetic data, movements of the

spectator, to the point where for the spectator there is only a single movement and things are happening in more or less the same way from his point of view as when he watches one of his own limbs moving ...this is ...emotional empathy to which are closely bound the empathy of feelings, of mental attitudes, of judgments, of thoughts. (pp. 126-128)

The developmental explanation of this process offered by Robinson, G. (1973) is consistent with the views presented in this chapter and conforms to the interpretation by the Theory of Intuitive Thought of evidence on the property 'understanding by feeling' cited in Section 6.2. Robinson defines projection and empathy as follows: 'Projection means that certain sensations, and perceptions, are referred to locations outside oneself' (p. 80). 'By empathy I mean the imaginal or mental projection of oneself into the elements of any object' (p. 77). On the extension of body boundaries he says that the notion of self and notself arises from experiences of differences and similarities of active and passive tactile kinaesthetic sensations. 'These sensation-patterns plus the difference between them, equal notself. This is unworded thinking, experienced in tactile kinaesthetic sensation-patterns' (p. 81). In empathy ideas of self and notself merge. 'This result follows because the proprioceptive sensations, existing wholly within the body of self, do not yield any distinction between active and passive, and therefore between self and notself and also because these sensations are the ones that give us knowledge or posture, the verb' (p. 81). He says the sensations of an enacted posture (imitation) are '...mediated by proprioceptive receptors' (p. 82), and cannot be distinguished from the imaged tactile kinaesthetic sensation patterns of self. 'The two are identical; the imagined posture of notself is the imagined posture of self... Self and outer object have seemed to become the outer object. What was once mysteriously both oneself and not oneself has seemed to project outwardly. This then is empathy; the imaged projection of oneself into an outer object' (p. 82). This, including other modalities, is the meaning of 'empathic projection' as used in this investigation.

Measuring Empathy

It is because empathy and projection are necessary to the intuitive process, that a measure of empathic projection would indicate a group of people which would include intuitive types. There are many extant measures of empathy which are based on various definitions of the term. 'Where definitions exist, they often vary from study to study, so that empathy is frequently discussed in terms of varying psychological processes' (Urist, J., 1976, p. 573). Harty, M.K. (1970) says the disagreement among psychoanalysts on the meaning of the term 'empathy' centres around the relationship of 'empathy' to identification. The original meaning of the term empathy was a temporary identification to understand an object, as used in this investigation, but it has now been developed, mainly by psychotherapists, to mean the ability to assess the opinions of another accurately. In the literature there is much criticism of this use of the term and the rating scale methods of assessing it.

The measures of empathy most suitable to use in investigations of intuition are the direct physiological measures and the projective psychological instruments like TAT, Rorschach, and Feffer's Role Taking Task, etc. However, an instrument designed to incorporate the relevant principles of these projective tests with measures of other necessary abilities described by the Theory of Intuitive Thought Processes is the Selected Phrase Empathic Ability Key (SPEAK) published by The Test Agency, Cournswood House, North Dean, High Wycombe, Bucks., England. SPEAK has been verified using physiological measures of empathy.

Changing Meanings of the Term 'Empathy'

Because measures of empathy depend upon the operational definition of the term 'empathy' the changing meaning of this term is now considered in relation to its use in this investigation.

The concept of Einfuhlung, meaning 'feeling together with' (Deutsch, Francine and Madle, R.A., 1975) was first introduced by Lipps, T. in 1900 (Allport, G.W., 1965) and used in this way by Lipps, T., 1909, Ribot, T., 1897, and Titchner, E.B., 1910. Titchner first translated the German word Einfuhlung to mean 'feeling oneself into' signified by 'empathy' in 1909 (Robinson, G., 1973, p. 77). It was used as a relationship between self and an object like an abstract picture.

Later Lipps (1926, 1935) extended the concept to person empathy where common feelings were created by inner cues evoked through slight imitations of expressions or postures. The feelings were derived mainly through motor mimicry; a kinaesthetic inference. Köhler, W. (1929, 1947) extended empathy to mean understanding another's emotion, but there was no self/other differentiation in his use of the term as it has now been developed, e.g. '. . . the worker must consciously separate feelings held by himself alone from those sensed and shared with the client' (Keefe, T. 1976, p. 12).

Mead, G.H. (1934) emphasized the cognitive as well as affective components of empathy. This is further accentuated in the role-play aspect of empathy. Role play was introduced and gave the term the meaning of imaginative transposing of oneself into the thinking and feeling of another. This now departs from the meaning of the term empathy as we use it in this investigation as the 'other' is a designated person and not an object. Empathy was at this point 'situational' rather than predictive in that the cognitive and affective empathy responses were to the situation. It now means accurate prediction of another's judgment of some situation or characteristic.

There are two approaches to measuring empathy with people. One is measures involving accurate assessment of situations from another's point of view, using role-taking. The other is the rating method where a subject's self-ratings of a characteristic are compared with a mean rating of that characteristic to give an accuracy score. Both of these accuracy measures have been severely criticized in the literature.

Measuring Person Empathy Using Role-taking

Bronfenbrenner, U. *et al.* (1958) say interpersonal judgments related to role-taking are intuitive. Role-taking is relevant to the encouragement of intuition in that its methods, atmosphere, etc., encourage intuitive thought. However, when used as a method of deriving accuracy measures of empathy it has given non-significant and contradictory results about the theory of empathy and its relation to intuition.

In spite of this shortcoming there are definitions of empathy in terms of the accuracy with which a subject puts himself into the situation of another, notably in the field of psychotherapy. Truax, C.B. and Carkhuff, R.R. (1967) narrowly define empathy in these accuracy terms but retain the 'sensitivity to feelings' characteristic of intuition in their definition of empathy as '...both the therapist's sensitivity to current feelings and his verbal facility to communicate this understanding in a language attuned to the client's current feelings' (p. 46). Jessor, R. and Richardson, S. (1968) define empathy in accuracy terms without even an affective component. 'First the individual must be able to take the role of another accurately; he must be able to correctly predict the impact the various lines of action will have on the other's definitions of the situation. This is what is meant by empathy if we strip the concept of its affective overtones' (p. 41). This is a far cry from how the term is used in our investigation. This last definition contradicts Johnson, Relda, J.'s (1971) definition which includes the affective component in accurate empathy: 'Empathy, delimited to the component of affective sensitivity, which is the ability to detect and describe the immediate affective state of another'. She used Campbell's Scale to measure 'affective sensitivity, empathy'. This is an accuracy measure.

The work of Heilman, K.A. (1972) is an abundant source of accurate prediction-type empathy measures. He considered theoretically predicted personality correlates, *viz.* cognitive complexity as a characteristic of good judges, i.e. the tendency to use many dimensions in perceiving and evaluating stimuli. This characteristic is also predicted by the Theory of Intuitive Thought, because intuitive individuals assess stimuli on a multitude of dimensions. Heilman, in common with many who have used accurate empathy measures, obtained disappointing results. Schultz, E.W. (1972) using Carkhuff scales for empathy and Bice, D.T. (1973) using the same scale, are other examples of experiments whose negative results are possibly due to the use of accurate empathy measures.

Other authors have severely criticized accurate empathy, for, as the Theory of Intuitive Thought shows, only the appropriateness rather than the accuracy of empathic feelings may be later determined by analysis, and it is possible to empathize inappropriately, see Section 8.1 which shows that intuition need not be correct. Empathy measures based on the accuracy of empathy, assume that no empathy has taken place unless it is accurate. However, 'People might be empathic without being able to predict and might be able to predict accurately without the process being an empathic one' (Cartwright, Rosalind F. née Dymond, 1961). Cooper, L. (1970) explains the poor results of many accurate empathy experiments by saying that they use measures that relate to different developmental levels of empathy (p. 173).

Measuring Person Empathy Using Rating Scales

Rating scales are used to measure empathic ability in many ways (see Marwell, G., 1964), e.g. comparing the correctness of prediction of others' assessment of oneself with one's own assessment, (Dymond, Rosalind F., 1949). For example, McClelland, W.A. (1951) asked subjects to rate six friends and these ratings were compared with the six self-ratings previously given on a cutdown version of the MMPI questionnaire. Epstein, S. and Smith, R. (1956) asked thirty-two subjects to *Q* sort thirty-two cards bearing their names, including their own name, according to how hostile they were. Authors measured insight by the difference in the subject's self-rating shown by the position he gave himself and the mean rating of him of the other subjects. This assumes I believe incorrectly, that subjects try to project their self-image accurately. In fact an experiment was performed by Feldman, M.J. and Bullock, D.H. (1955) that showed this assumption is true. They asked each of their subjects to rate herself twice: (1) 'as only they know themselves' and (2) 'as they thought other members of the class would rate them' (p. 145), i.e. (1) as I see myself and (2) as I think others see me. Results showed that self-image is not always projected. The two scales were not interchangeable.

Although Londgren, H.C. and Robinson, J. (1953) used measures of accuracy of character assessment by comparing similarity of self-assessment with that of group assessment, they admit that it is possible to empathize incorrectly: 'A check is made to see whether he has empathized correctly'. The insight score they obtain is a similar accuracy measure, i.e. comparison of self-ratings with how others rate oneself. 'The concept of insight employed by Dymond was Allport's criterion: the relation of what an individual thinks he has to what others think he has' (p. 172). This criterion is from Allport, G.W. (1937) used by Dymond, Rosalind F. (1950).

Assuming empathy by using the accuracy of ratings scales was one reason that I believe Aldenbrand, Martha L. (1974) was unable to confirm her theoretical association between intuition and empathy. She used predictive empathy defined as 'the ability to accurately predict the feelings, thoughts, and behaviours another person would ascribe to himself'. White, B.L. and Watts, Jean C. (1973, p. 42) had to drop an empathy measure from their experiment because it was unsatisfactory.

There is much criticism of the rating method of measuring accurate empathy. Chinsky, J.M. and Rappaport, J. (1970) severely criticized the meaning of 'accurate empathy' and the experimental rating procedure for assessing reliability: '...an even more fundamental question, "What is actually being rated in the Accurate Empathy judgment?" remains unanswered' (p. 381). Marwell, G. (1964) presents two 'literary' and operational definitions of empathy and identification, the latter in terms of 'rating scales'. His paper is a detailed criticism of the rating method of measuring empathy. 'Much has been said about the almost total inadequacy of the rating scale in eliciting interpretable responses for this type of research' (p. 89). Self-rating scales of empathy should not be used in investigations of intuition.

Measuring Empathy Using Projective and Fantasy Tests

Projective and fantasy tests can be used to measure empathy with objects. They have a strong psychoanalytical background. This is because 'serious attempts to conceptualize empathy in more than just the superficial descriptive way have generally only been made by theorists with a psychoanalytic orientation' (Harty, M.K., 1970, p. 6).

The Thematic Apperception Test (TAT) may be scored for empathy. Dymond (1948) used the standard instructions, as in the TAT manual with ten pictures shown on each of two weekly interviews. She found that TAT analysed in terms of interpersonal relationships gave a high validity. She gives a method of scoring TAT for empathy. She used twenty subjects which she split into high and low empathy groups and compared her results from interviews with the designated empathy group of the subject and found: 'These conditions suggest that empathy may be one of the underlying mechanisms on which insight is based'. Elms, A.C. (1966) also used TAT cards 7BM, 4, and 2 to measure empathy. Dymond (1949) scored fifty-three subjects on self-rating empathy on six items and compared the five highest and five lowest on their TAT protocols scored for empathy. Of the five low-rating scorers, four were also low on TAT and one high. She does not mention the other five subjects. The statistical analysis is just as poor in her 1948 paper.

Although the TAT pictures seem to structure a subject's response rather too much for the type of empathy applicable to intuitive thought, the theory on which they are based seems to indicate that they could be used in an investigation of intuition particularly cards 7BM, 2, and 4.

The Rorschach Ink Blot cards can also be used to measure empathy. 'The capacity for seeing human figures in the Rorschach blot materials is related to the capacity for good empathic relationships with other human beings' (Klopfer, B. et al., 1954, p. 264). Berry, Joyce H. (1970) wrote her PhD on 'The Rorschach Inkblot Test as an indication of empathy'. She says 'The Rorschach Inkblot Test has been assumed by its developer and by authorities in the use of the instrument as being capable of indicating empathy in an individual. The variables in the Rorschach that are assumed indicators of empathy are movement responses, form-colour responses and human content'. These are called M scores for human movement. Unfortunately in her own experiments she used an accurate empathy criterion scale which I believe was responsible for her poor results. She suggests that '...the lack of support for the hypotheses may be the lack of an adequate criterion to measure empathy. Construct validity has not been reported for the Accurate Empathy Scale, only face validity'.

King, G.F. (1958) reviews interpretations of *M,* mainly interpretations as empathy or insight, '*M* reflects the ability to empathize' (p. 3). He suggests the basic meaning of *M* as '*M* reflects the ability in fantasy to project the self into time and space in the interpersonal sphere' (p. 4). As this is how I have used empathy, but with objects, it indicates that *M* is a suitable measure of empathy in investigations of intuition. Roe, Anne (1951) found the number of *M* responses correlated significantly with the tendency for her subjects to complete their TAT stories by including a future.

Elms, A.C. (1966) used the five Rorschach cards, I, II, III, VII, and IX scored for *M* as he says these have been reported to be particularly relevant to empathic fantasy behaviour (p. 38). He also gives a method for scoring *M*. However Rust, R.M. (1948) reports that there is no standard method for scoring *M*. He says Rorschach intended to score *M* '...only when it was accompanied by actual empathy of the perceived movement or kinaesthesia' (p. 372).

Another point in favour of using *M* for scoring empathic projection is the experiments that show it has the same personality correlates as predicted for the intuitive type, e.g. preference for complexity in the Barron-Welsh Art Scale and field independence as measured in the embedded figures test (Bieri, J. *et al.,* 1958).

Feffer, M.H. (1959) and Feffer, M.H. and Gourevitch, Vivian (1960) developed a projective test based on MAPS material. Feffer called it a role-taking test (RTT). Subjects invent a story about people in a picture situation and then give each person's point of view of the story in a personal interview. The test gives two scores which go towards a measure of cognitive development and which agree with a measure of cognitive development developed from Rorschach protocols. The two scores are of actor description and perspective-taking. Actor description is a measure of the degrees of abstraction of definition of the characters scored on reported feelings. Perspective-taking is scored on the continuity of role-taking. Swinson, M. E. (1966) found a significant correlation between RTT and concrete operations with and without age and IQ partialled out; remember we discussed that intuition is facilitated by concrete examples in Section 6.2.

Actor-description scoring is similar to TAT scoring for empathy. Perspective-taking is a measure suitable for measuring the control of ego-state needed for successful applications of intuition to creativity. These theoretical considerations, taken with Weisskopf's E.A. (1950) proposed Transcendence Index measure of the TAT, *viz.* the mean number of comments per subject which go beyond pure description, have been used for the development of the Selected Phrase Empathic Ability Key (SPEAK).

Physiological Measures of Empathy

The feelings evoked by empathy are susceptible to physiological measurement, particularly if they are extreme. The following works illustrate successful physiological measures of empathy.

Lemineur, R. and Meurice, E. (1972) defined empathy in terms of similar physiological changes in the subject and the human object of the empathy. They operationally defined empathy as the occurrence of the same type of neurovegetative response in the observer and the subject observed while submitting to a painful stimulus which they called the sociometric state. Using nine subjects they measured empathy by GSR and found a significant correlation ($p < 0.05$) between the GSR-measured empathy and the sociometric states.

Kagan, J. and Phillips, W. (1964) used heart rate and respiration to measure 'identification'. Sixteen children (five- to eight-years-old) watched their same-sexed parent compete with a stranger. Subjects' heart rate and respiration was measured and they were watched by an observer. It was observed that subjects smiled more at their parents' successes and at the strangers' failures. Also their heart rate accelerated with examiner's praise of their parents' successes. They found heart rate for parents' success and strangers' failure was higher than vice versa. The results confirmed the hypothesis that if a child identifies with a model, the child should behave as if the events occurring to the model were occurring to him. 'The major purpose of this note is to communicate to others the feasibility of measuring affective involvement in a laboratory setting and to stimulate other investigators to develop measures of identification that rely on vicarious involvement with a model.' Lacey, J. I. *et al.* (1963), using taped drama, found that subjects anticipating a recording of angry exchanges between peers showed a correlation between palmar conductance and heart-rate response which was highly significant, compared with subjects anticipating angry exchanges between a son expressing anger to his mother which showed practically zero correlation.

Craig, K.D. and Wood, K. (1970) designed an experiment to compare GSR and heart rate of subjects with their hands in $-4°C$ brine solution and with subjects observing them whom they monitored simultaneously. Their results showed that the anticipatory power of the imagination produces a greater effect than the actual experience. They give four references to show: 'Studies of vicariously instigated conditioned emotional responses have implied that the pattern of arousal instigated vicariously is similar to the pattern elicited by direct contact with the noxious situation'. Bloemkolb, D. *et al.* (1971) showed the possibility that internal cognitive events can be used to induce or evoke emotional experience. Like Valins, S. (1966) Bloemkolb *et al.* showed slides to subjects but used unattractive slides, e.g. of wounded people, as well as attractive slides with which the subjects could empathize. Gellen, M.I. (1970), using finger blood volume, showed significantly more vascular constriction indicating physiological arousal in counsellors and counsellor trainees than with college science majors when both were given an empathy test with slides and dialogue: indicating that the counsellors were more empathic. Cohen, H.D. and Harvey, D. (1975) however, found no stress effect on the respiration rate of twenty-eight subjects when viewing stressful films. Barron, F. and Mordkoff, A. M. (1968) used a skin resistance measure simultaneously on pairs of identical twins in different rooms and looked for simultaneous responses to indicate empathy. A film and TAT cards were used as stimuli for one twin but no empathy responses were recorded in the other twin. A negative correlation between Rorschach *M* and Palmar Skin Potential fluctuations in response to completing emotionally involving sentences was found by Learmonth, G.J. *et al.* (1959).

These experiments point to the suitability of heart rate, finger blood volume, GSR and respiration as means of measuring empathy in psycho-physiological investigations of intuition. Deutsch, Francine and Madle, R.A. (1975) criticize the construct validity of all psychometric empathy tests on '...whether or not the test discriminates between groups of individuals who should, theoretically, possess different levels of empathy... The extent to which empathy measures actually assess empathy, as opposed to other constructs, is a question that remains unanswered' (pp. 274/275). SPEAK is a psychometric test of empathy that has been validated using physiological tests of empathy as outlined above.

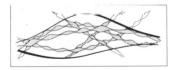

7

Creativity and Preverbal Immediacy of Intuition

7.1 INTUITION DESCRIBED AS A PREVERBAL CONCEPT

Preverbal concept is property 14, with five references to it in Section 1.3. This property of intuition arises mainly from 'guess the rule' insight experiments that use the sudden change to correct responses as an indication of insight. Experimenters find from interviews at this point that the subjects cannot verbalize the rule, hence the preverbal concept as a property of intuition. For example, Wason, P.C. (1966) reports that the ability to discriminate positive from negative instances frequently precedes the ability to formulate the concept in words.

This property of intuition is also supported by descriptions of intuition as non-verbal, which occur for two reasons. Firstly because intuitive perception and processing is speedy on many parallel modalities whereas the verbal mode is linear and slow in comparison. This 'speedy parallel' versus 'slow linear' comparison is also a reason behind the contrast of intuition with logic discussed in Section 2.1. Secondly and related to this, the amount and the sensory quality of the knowledge of which the subject becomes aware through the intuition precedes verbalization and makes its complete verbal communication impossible. It seems words only assist in the ongoing intuitive process by reason of their connotations and affective associations. They are however a means of communicating and verifying after the intuition in the later stages of the creative process.

It is because of the reasons outlined above that intuition is defined as a preverbal concept. Berne, E. (1949) considering 'The nature of intuition' believes that perception for intuition is preverbal body language communication. He considers intuitive knowledge to be based on previous experience of receiving 'latent' messages and it is acquired by means of 'pre-verbal unconscious or preconscoius functions' through sensory contact with the other person (communicant) and occurs without the intuiter (receiver)

298

being able to formulate exactly how he arrived at his judgment. Baldwin, A. (1966) on having considered 'The development of intuition' summarizes three aspects of intuition, one of which is 'unverbalizable beliefs and understanding' (p. 85). Hebb, D.O. (1946) says that intuitive judgments can remain 'unverbalized' (p. 89). Robinson, G. (1973) says that: 'It has been necessary to devise a concept to describe objects and postures insusceptible of verbalization' (p. 79). We propose here that this concept is intuitive understanding through empathy. De Groot, A.D. (1965, p. 147) says intuition cannot be verbalized. Bayles, E.E. (1952) writing on 'Development of insight' says that by insight: 'We refer to what lies back of any word statement; to that which one catches even before he has words to express it...' (p. 67).

Lorenz, K.Z. (1951) defines intuition as recognition of a category without a definition of the category, e.g. recognizing all types of dog without being 'able consciously to abstract the zoological diagnosis of *Canis familiaris Linnaeus'*. This is a common lay attribution to intuition and is explained as intuitive acceptance by the Theory of Intuitive Thought in Section 5.5. This criterion of being able to categorize before being able to verbalize the rules for categorization has been used to define insight operationally by Pickford, R. (1938), Snapper, A. (1956) and others, see Section 1.3.

Obviously one must know before one can verbalize this knowledge. However, after conversations with people who have verbal preference modes, it seems that for these people some knowledge is held in this mode and so such a statement would not be so obvious. I have found that such people tend to have a kinaesthetic non-spatial ability mode for intuitive thinking.

Some psychologists of my acquaintance who have pronounced verbal ability modes have arrogantly claimed that language is necessary for thought. Perhaps this is because the constant chatter in their minds or thinking restrictively about details can focus and associate analytic thought. Some are unaware of the spatial kinaesthetic aspects of arithmetic that we have discussed in Section 6.2, and expecting arithmetic to require a solely verbal ability are surprised to find activity in the left cerebral hemisphere corresponding to arithmetical activity. Because intuition is non-verbal it is feasible that the lack of prominence in the literature of this fundamental and important ability is partially due to the greater contribution to the literature made by the more articulate psychologists with high verbal ability and preference modes. This may be so particularly because psychologists' ideas of how people think and act at this integrated level have their roots in introspection.

Inadequacy of the Verbal Mode

Verbal Mode Inadequate for Intuitive Perception

Intuitive perception involves simultaneous perception through all modalities. Intuition is defined in the Oxford Dictionary as '...an immediate apprehension by sense'. Langer, Suzanne K (1969) says 'Locke meant by it [intuition] the kind of direct perception that may go through any available avenue of sense' (p. 325). Although hearing is one of these senses the complicated and mainly linear process of decoding sounds into meaningful words is not suitable for the speedy parallel intake of information during intuitive perception.

Baldwin, A. (1966) says, when discussing intuition, that '. . . all elements of imagery seem instantaneous whereas the verbal descriptions are sequential' (p. 90). Further Krebs, G.M. (1975) has shown that where there is a choice between verbal and non-verbal cues, the non-verbal cues are more influential than the verbal cues in evoking feelings (p. 44).

The unsuitability of the verbal mode for intuitive perception because of the non-linear parallel nature of such perception is further discussed in Section 5.3.

Verbal Mode Inadequate for Intuitive Processing

Intuitive processing manipulates feelings and only involves words through their connotative and affective associations. It is because of the multimodal parallel nature of this processing that the linear verbal mode is not only unsuitable but is consciously inhibiting. Kinaesthetic imagery is the most commonly reported modality of intuitive thought. 'Albert Einstein apparently believed that thought consisted entirely of dealing with mechanical images and not at all of words. The mathematician Jacques Hadamard reported that he thought exclusively in visual pictures' (Walkup, L.E., 1965, p. 39). These men had the '. . . ability to visualize in manipulative images' (p. 39). The unsuitability of the verbal mode for intuitive processing is discussed further in Section 5.3.

The 'tip-of-the-tongue phenomena' indicates that intuitive knowledge is not stored verbally. Here the words are stored by their associated feelings and we use our 'feeling of knowing' as retrieval cues for these words, see Section 3.2. Blake, M. (1973) ascribes to the 'feeling of knowing phenomenon', this important functional role of the attribute of the target memory (p. 318).

Verbal Mode Inadequate for Communicating Intuitions

Because the intuition is a sudden awareness of knowledge coded by feelings on a multitude of physiological dimensions, it is an understatement to say that the verbal mode is unsuitable for communicating such knowledge. 'The "intuitive process" depends on the rapidity of connections and availability of channels of communication,' (Szalita-Pemow, A.B., 1955, p. 17). Clinchy, Blythe (1975) says that intuition is 'wordless' (p. 48), and implies that intuitive understanding cannot be verbalized. 'Yet our inferences of a child's understanding, or lack of it, are derived from the child's verbal skill to communicate an answer hence we are not as teachers often aware of a child's intuitive understanding' (p. 49). Hebb, D.O. (1946) says of intuitive judgments that they especially 'cannot be put into words' (p. 89). Sliker, Gretchen P. (1972) mentions: 'Before words are associated with discovery the solution to the problem is felt in ways that involve motor responses as well as certain types of non-verbal thinking' (p. 27).

We cannot put our intuitive knowledge, coded by these feelings of which we are mostly not conscious, into words. This problem is discussed in Section 5.5. Polanyi, M. (1966) refers to it as: 'The fact that we can know more than we can tell' (p. 4). He gives examples of non-verbal methods by which we may attempt to communicate our intuitive knowledge, e.g. we may be able to recognize one face from a million but not know how. The police Identikit pictures have been developed to communicate this information (p. 5).

Watching the body language of a gesticulating person will indicate the kinaesthetic models with which he codes his ideas. Hammer, E.F. (1973), studying creativity, found 'Communication through sense images' to be a more basic and effective communication. In fact Haefele, J.W. (1962) links increased verbal thinking with a decrease in creativity (p. 56).

7.2   IMMEDIACY OF INTUITION

The quick, immediate and sudden appearance of intuition is the first property of intuition, with four references to it in Section 1.3. 'Insight is sudden: one moment you haven't a clue and the next moment all the pieces have fallen into place' (Beadle, M., 1971, p. 180). Lorenz, K.Z. (1951) says intuition happens 'suddenly . . . all at once [it] jumps out at him with the suddenness of a revelation'. Clark, F. V. (1973) also notes the suddenness of intuition whilst contrasting intuition with reasoning, property 4. 'On a mental level, intuition operates as an irrational factor in problem solving, as when the solution is reached suddenly by a leap of imagination, rather than as a result of deductive reasoning' (p. 161). Sliker, Gretchen P. (1972) refers to '. . . a flash of insight in which a solution is suddenly clear' (p. 27). Beveridge, W.I.B. (1950) defines intuition as: 'A clarifying idea that comes suddenly to mind'.

The speed of the intuitive process and the suddenness with which the intuition comes is a commonly noted property of intuition. Because there has been no satisfactory theory of intuitive thought to explain the relation of the intuition to previous experience and the environmental factors occasioning its appearance, it has seemed to appear unbidden and logically unrelated to the environment in which it appears. Such appearances have given intuition a mystical nature and have drawn attention to its suddenness.

There are four aspects of the suddenness of the intuition to which the literature refers. Firstly the immediate intuitive knowledge, understanding or judgments occurring simultaneously with the perception of the object of the intuition. Secondly the sudden appearance of the intuition spontaneously after an incubation period and apparently unconnected with the situation in which it occurs. Thirdly the Behaviourists' view of insight as a sudden increase in the number of correct responses during a learning task. Lastly the speed of the intuitive process makes it appear sudden in relation to the time that might be needed to reach the same result using, if possible, a step-by-step analysis.

Bahm, A.J. (1960) says: 'The fact that intuition is immediacy does not exclude the existence of mediating factors' (p. 1). The Theory of Intuitive Thought accounts simply for these four aspects of the suddenness of all intuitive products through the mediating factors of emotional sets.

Intuition Synchronous with Perception

It is frequently reported that an intuition is immediate with the perception of the object of the intuition. The Oxford Dictionary defines intuition as '. . . an immediate apprehension of an object by the mind without the intervention of any reasoning process'. Drever, J. (1974) similarly defines insight as 'direct apprehension' also Beres, D. and Arlow, J.A. (1974) define intuition as follows: '. . . the process of intuition, that is, of the immediate knowing or learning something without the conscious use of reasoning' (p. 28). Jung, C. G. (1926) defines intuition as '. . . intuition is an immediate awareness of relationships' (p. 381).

Such descriptions are of intuitive perception which, it has been shown in Section 5.2, acts on a wide field including subliminal perception simultaneously in all modalities, and so is a much faster method of receiving information than the traditional linear modes for reasoning: see Section 7.1 on non-verbal intuitive perception.

The Theory of Intuitive Thought shows that immediate intuitive products of acceptance, understanding, and judgments use such multimodal perception and result when the feelings evoked by these perceptions are concordant with the present emotional set; 'Section 5.5. The definition of intuition given by Guiora, A.Z. *et al.* (1965, pp. 118/119) and Guiora, A.Z. (1965) is fully in agreement with our explanation.

> Intuition is a mode of comprehending in which external cues normally inadequte for logical judgment and/or prediction give rise to apparently direct, immediate, and accurate judgment and/or prediction through the mediation of idiosyncratic associations and organized according to allological principles.

Although intuition appears instantaneously synchronous with the perception, it would obviously take some time for the subject to evoke through empathy the feelings appropriate to the object of the intuition. Dinero, T.E. (1970), considering the speed with which words evoke 'affective components contributing to the connotation of a term', says that the time span for the process $S \rightarrow r \rightarrow s \rightarrow R$ 'depends on the individual and is usually one to two seconds' (p. 260). Most everyday situations to which the observations of 'immediate' intuition refer involve more cues on more immediate modalities, prior to cross-modal transfer, than do 'words'. Also these everyday 'immediate' intuitions use instinctive responses (included in a to f of Fig. 5.3/2) which one might generally expect to be faster than learnt word associations; see also Section 8.3 on instinctive knowledge. 'One or two seconds' of primary-process thinking might be subjectively judged 'immediate'. Hence I would assume that in such situations Dinero's time of one to two seconds would be markedly reduced to subjective immediacy, which is consistent with the observations in the literature.

Intuitions that arise spontaneously with the initial perception of the object of the intuition are explained by the Theory of Intuitive Thought as produced by combining emotional sets by embedding. The other two methods of combining emotional sets (Section 5.4), explained the arrival of intuitions after continually working on a problem and the arrival of intuitions 'out of the blue' long after the problem has been consciously 'shelved'.

Spontaneous Intuition After an Incubation Period

The traditional scenario of *Eureka* experiences is of a scientist emotionally immersed in a problem, working through the early hours of the morning to no avail. He consciously shelves the problem and some time later, maybe years after, whilst engaged in an apparently completely unrelated, usually physical activity, the intuition suddenly comes, bringing the solution accompanied by great emotional satisfaction. This is explained by intuitions resulting from combining emotional sets by the recentring method. Rosenbloom, P.C. (1972) reports the sudden illumination of the Eureka experience. 'People remark on the suddenness, the "moment of illumination". After this moment of insight the world doesn't look the same. We may have seen something all our lives, but now, and forever after, we notice it' (p. 88).

Another scenario is when the inventor is working continually on the problem, sometimes for many hours, when suddenly it 'clicks' and he has the solution. This type of intuition is explained by combining emotional sets using the drifting method. The description of intuitive judgment by Clinchy, Blythe (1975) as sudden and disconnected follows this scenario: 'They [intuitive judgments] seem to occur suddenly, out of nowhere, rather than as the logical outcome of a step-by-step analytic procedure, although the sudden insight may follow upon long hours of seemingly fruitless pondering' (p. 48). Board, R. (1958) says that it is this sudden, spontaneous appearance without apparent effort: '. . . This relative isolation of intuitive insights [which] often lends them an uncanny, even mystical quality' (p. 234); see Section 1.1 on the mystique of intuition. Other writers also report this spontaneous occurrence of intuition. Weil, A. (1972) considers intuition as a 'transient spontaneous occurrence' (p. 150). Sinnott, E.W. (1959) calls it a 'flash' (p. 24), and Haefele, J.W. (1962) agrees: 'The breakthrough type of insight comes by sudden arrival' (p. 86).

Intuition Suddenly Erupts into Consciousness

Board, R. (1958), describing intuition and insight in his paper on 'Intuition', comments on '...their usually sudden appearance in consciousness' (p. 236).

The Theory of Intuitive Thought describes intuitions as the highly redundant responses conditioned to an emotional set, responses made conscious by an awareness of the feelings accompanying the increase in redundancy. The redundancy is increased by the combination of emotional sets to produce this terminating emotional set. This is discussed in more detail in Section 5.4 (see Fig. 5.4/7).

During the intuitive process one is mostly unaware of the transposition of feelings due to combining emotional sets to which they are conditioned. Polanyi, M. (1966) says these feelings are '. . . hardly noticeable in themselves previous to their transposition' (p. 14). The subject will be aware of only a large proportionate resolution of tension accompanying a correspondingly large increase in redundancy. When such a change is large enough, depending upon the self-sensitivity of the subject, the resultant emotional set will terminate the intuitive process because the subject, being consciously aware of his feelings, needs to attribute these to the cognitive components of his emotional set. So the intuition suddenly erupts into consciousness.

This view is consistent with the general view of intuition suddenly coming to mind illustrated by Szalita-Pemow, A.B. (1955) who quotes '. . . a very creative inventor' who described how intuitive thoughts came to him. Szalita-Pemow comments on this: 'Our modern explanation for this would be that the answer came to him from the unconscious, from the part of himself which he did not know. . . perhaps it would be more exact to say that it (intuitive knowledge) erupts into the conscious mind rather than enters it' (p. 9).

Intuitions 'Out of the Blue'

Intuitions seem to come 'out of the blue' when after a long incubation period of days or even years in which the problem has been mentally 'shelved', the intuition suddenly appears in an environment that seems to have no logical connection with the problem. However, there are affective similarities. The time taken to reach the terminal emotional set by combining emotional sets is the incubation time. The methods of combining emotional sets as detailed in Section 5.4 clearly show how incubation periods of different lengths arise. In particular all methods of combining emotional sets reorganize the responses whose conditioning to these emotional sets represents the individual's experience. In this respect the Theory of Intuitive Thought is consistent with descriptions of intuition as a reorganization of experience illustrated by the examples given below.

Section 4.1 detailed how combinations of emotional sets through the method of recentring, resulting in the Eureka experience, are instigated by responses in common between the original problem emotional set and the present solution emotional set which represents the intuition. These responses are in common not because of a logical connection between the problem and solution, but because of common feelings, i.e. responses from the two sets are coded similarly on the many common physiological dimensions. Hutchinson,

E.D. (1941) refers to '...the mood set up by the event or accident which originally occasioned insight' (p. 37). This explains why the environment in which the intuition appears does not have the logical relevance to the problem, as is commonly looked for and expected. The response instigating the recentring is commonly reported to be kinaesthetic, a particular movement that causes the recentring.

Recentring is sudden and the chain of emotional associations back to the time of the original problem is irrelevant as recentring directly links the two points of the chain rather than tracing it back. Further, the chain of emotional associations is irrelevant because in the time between the original problem and the solution any original responses would probably have been dropped, at least once, from the succession of emotional sets the person occupied. Tracing the chain of emotional associations is only relevant to original responses that are retained, or one would be led by continuous association from the original response through the subject's entire concept map.

The following descriptions of insight are consistent with our explanation of the changed experience, as a sudden reorganization of experience. Hutchinson, E.D. (1941) describes insights as follows:

> But suddenly, usually in a moment when the work has been temporarily abandoned, or when the attention is absorbed by irrelevant matters, comes an unpredicted insight into the solution, usually interpreted as a reorganization of the perceptual field, especially in regard to the relationship between means and end. As if 'inspired' 'given' ideas arise which constitute a real integration of previously accumulated experience — an answer, a brilliant hypothesis, a useful 'hunch', forming, it seems, a short-cut to artistic or scientific advance. (p. 31)

Similarly George, F.H. (1962) defines insight as '...the sudden adaptive reorganization of experience' (p. 36). Board, R. (1958) says: 'A new organization of the subject matter takes place' (p. 236).

Insight Defined as a Sudden Increase in Correct Responses on a Learning Task

This definition of insight as '...insight is inferred whenever an organism exhibits a dramatic upswing in his ability to solve a particular problem or class of problems' (Pollio, H.R., 1974, p. 134), is one legacy of the Gestalt versus Behaviourists Insight Controversy, discussed in Section 1.1. Similarly George, F.H. (1962) defines: 'Insight learning is the sudden production of a new adaptive response ...' (p. 36). Gestalt 'insight' meant how learning occurred. 'Gestalt Field psychologists' (GFP) definition of learning is the developing of new insights or the modifying of old ones' (Bigge, M.L. and Hunt, M.P., 1965, p. 296). The Behaviourists had great success in describing other psychological concepts in terms of quantitative behaviour but not this concept of insight.

The above definition illustrates a modern compromise in saying that by a behaviour change insight is inferred. In operational terms however, insight is merely the name given to the observation of a sudden increase in the number of correct responses on a learning task. For example: 'Insight was considered to be an apparently "sudden" learning of the relationships underlying the task. For this study insight was operationally defined as a rather consistent initial performance at chance level, followed by a rapid rise to a high level of performance' (Viesti, C.R. Jr., 1971, p. 181).

The above Behaviourist definition is inadequate as an operational definition of the compromise meaning given to insight, for the tasks have to be different but dependent upon one underlying relationship, and the degree to which each task is distinctly new yet related to this underlying relationship, is seldom, if ever, quantified, though it is necessary. 'Insight is used throughout this report to designate varieties of experience which in us are accompaniments of sudden, effective, individually wrought adaptations to more or less distinctly new and problematic situations' (Yerkes, R.M., 1927, p. 155).

Pechstein, L.A. and Brown, F.D. (1939) in an 'Experimental analysis of the alleged criteria of insight learning' investigated this behavioural definition of insight: 'Those describing learning in terms of insight contend that if there is evidence of mental activity preceding the overt adaptive act, that is indicative of insight' (p. 40), embodying the criterion: 'Sudden solution — rapid change in the learning curve,' and similar behaviourist criteria (p. 40). They conclude: 'The criteria of insight learning do not differentiate this as a mode of behaviour from trial-and-error. The term insight may be used only to describe the fact of learning, the end-product, and not as descriptive of the learning process, that is, how learning takes place' (p. 52).

Speed of the Intuitive Process

One of the 'critical factors' of intuition according to Kaplan, H.A. (1973) in his study of 'Intuitive problem solving' is its 'speed' (p. 4). Freund, C.J. (1976) says: 'Intuition is simply a case of the mind's performing rapidly below the level of consciousness,' (p. 419). The intuitive process is fast in comparison with the step-by-step logical analysis which leads to comparable conclusions. 'Intuition implies the act of grasping the meaning or significance or structure of a problem without explicit reliance upon the analytic apparatus of one's craft. It is the intuitive mode that yields hypotheses quickly' (Bruner, J.S., 1962, p. 102). Also '...intuition, the class of non-rigorous ways by which mathematicians speed towards solutions or cul-de-sacs' (p. 99).

The Theory of Intuitive Thought shows on several counts why the process of intuition is fast compared with logical analysis. We have shown the contrast between logical and intuitive thought in Section 2.1, where logical analysis is described as a linear step-by-step process whereas the intuitive process is shown as a parallel process advancing on many fronts through affective associations on a multitude of dimensions.

Szalita-Pemow, A.B. (1955) says of intuition: 'This is a short cut as compared with a person's ordinary thinking habits' (p. 9). Board, R. (1958) contrasts this with 'linear thought ...which might be called linear induction, which involves a methodical ordering of symbols and carefully noting empirical observations' (p. 236). He says: 'Often it is obvious that the hypotheses so advanced [by intuition] might never have been forthcoming through linear induction' (p. 236).

Further there is a subjective effect of time passing allowed by the step-by-step logical process which is diminished when this process is absent, making the intuitive process seem more rapid. Suzuki, D.T. (1957) says intuition is like a 'flash of lightning' (p. 87). Its quickness does not refer to the progress of time. He says it refers to the point that there is '...no intervening moment for reflection or analysis or interpretation' (p 86); '...it [intuition] means immediacy, absence of deliberation, no allowance for an intervening proposition, no passing from premises to conclusion' (p. 87).

Intuitive thought is also faster than detailed analysis because it involves probabilistic matching of hierarchical emotional sets by inclusion and accepting the match if details mismatched are not sufficiently discordant. Whereas analysis has to match precisely all details and check any mismatches before progressing, even though the mismatched details that slow down the process of analysis may from a later, even closer, scrutiny, be found to match.

Timing the Intuitive Process

The time for the intuitive process, from perception to final intuition, depends on many variables, some of which may be experimentally controlled and some of which are psychological characteristics of the intuiter. The speed of information intake has been controlled in many ways, see Section 5.1. The need to find a solution, i.e. the intrinsic motivation, can be partially controlled, by careful transference from rewards or threats. If the initial tension is relatively great then a partial solution will be subjectively accepted sooner to resolve this tension.

The recentring method of combining emotional sets to achieve an intuition is difficult to control as it depends a great deal on the experimental history of the subject, e.g. his idiosyncratic coding of experience. This was not controlled in the practical insight experiments cited in Section 1.3. For example, illustrating this Pechstein, L.A. and Brown, F.D. (1939), using a locked puzzle box in a test for insight, found a child easily opened it because, as the child unexpectedly said: 'This one is like the latch on our gate' (p. 51).

Experiment procedures giving hints and leaving practical apparatus 'around' are interpreted by the Theory of Intuitive Thought as guiding the drift of emotional sets by offering common associations. Maier, N.R.F. and Burke, R.J. (1967) used the hat rack problem to investigate the 'Influence of timing of hints on their effectiveness in problem solving'. They found the timing did not matter but the value of the hint depends on the incorrect activity it eliminated. This is explained in this present investigation as guiding the drift of combinations of emotional sets, not by leading it through allowing the hints to empathically evoke guiding associations, but by preventing detouring associations.

A similar experiment, also using the hat rack problem, was conducted by Dominowski, R.L. and Jenrick, Regina (1972) into the 'Effects of hints and interpolated activity on the solution of an insight problem'. Results again showed that the effect of the hints was not to put subjects on the right track but to stop them going on wrong leads. A Gestalt transformation test was used as a measure of insight problem-solving ability. The experimenters found some interaction between hints and interpolated activity only for high-ability subjects. Murray, G.H. and Denny, P.J. (1969) investigated this 'Interaction of ability level and interpolated activity in human problem solving'. These experimenters placed balls in a cylinder on a tray which had to be placed in another cylinder which was immovable. Both were out of reach. The tools for the insightful solution were string, a wire coat hanger and lots of newspaper. The interesting point is that the experimenters used the interpolated activity as an 'opportunity for incubation'. The interaction of the experimental materials with the subjects' experience was again not considered.

The speed of combination of emotional sets to give the terminating solution emotional set by drift, partially depends on how different the solution emotional set is from the problem emotional set. Collins, A.M. and Quillian, M.R. (1972a) found '. . . the closer two nodes are in the semantic network, the longer it takes to decide that they are not related in a particular manner'. Such a conclusion parallels the finding of Moyer, R.S. and Landauer, T.K. (1967) that 'the smaller the difference between two digits, the longer it takes to decide which is larger' (p. 125). There is also the intuitive ability of the subject to consider. In this type of experiment the experimenters do not usually consider the subject's intuitive ability, that is all the psychophysiological factors that cause the subject to redundantly code similar information to dissimilar emotional sets, although it is now apparent from our study of intuition that the subject's intuitive ability is the prominent effect in this type of experiment.

From common experience Cowen, E.L. (1952) found that 'insight problems' like water jar problems, joining dots, etc., take about two and a half minutes to solve, indicating the solution to this type of problem is found by combining emotional sets using the drifting method. The following experimenters also investigated the speed of the intuitive process. Jensen, K. (1960) considered 'Conditions influencing insight and problem solving behaviour'. He used block assembly problems and considered various peripheral cues as conditions. He found irrelevant cues inhibited problem-solving (a tautology) and that the subject's maturity relates to the speed of intuitive problem-solving. This result could be explained by Harlow H.F.'s (1949) classic experiment. Harlow worked with monkeys solving a protracted series of discrimination problems and came to the conclusion that they seemed to 'learn to learn'. He interpreted this following data: before the formation of a discrimination set, a single training trial produces negligible gain, after the formation of a discrimination learning set, a single training trial constitutes problem solution: as showing 'clearly' that animals can gradually learn insight. Or as Beadle, M. (1971) says: 'In other words, insight is not really a bolt from the blue; it simply reflects the learner's mastery of the principles that govern any systematic task. Insight is predictive' (pp. 183/184). It seems obvious that people acquire learning sets. For example a man who has learnt nine languages would probably have found some relevant general learning principles that make his acquisition of the tenth language easier than the acquisition of his first language.

Duncan, C.P. (1962) considered 'Probability versus latency of solution of an insight problem' where latency of solution is the incubation period, etc., which comprises the time defining the speed of the intuitive process. Using anagram solving and Maier's two-string pendulum problem, nine hundred and three subjects were plotted on their probability of obtaining a solution against log time of solution. Duncan found this gives almost straight lines with a higher probability for men than for women. He interprets this as showing that most of the insightful hypotheses come in a flood at the beginning then slow down considerably. This is consistent with an associative theory of thought such as our Theory of Intuitive Thought, as is shown by free word association experiments where the number and speed of word associations is similarly distributed and is inverse to the time between associated groups of free word associations.

7.3   INTUITION AND CREATIVITY

Intuition is associated with creativity. This is the seventh property of intuition with four references to it in Section 1.3.

Intuition is the first and a necessary stage of creativity. The intuition is followed, in scientific and mathematical creativity and also in creative problem-solving, by the logical verification of the intuition. The selection of analytic methods for verifying the intuition and the direction of their use is also guided by intuition. In creative art verification is often irrelevant, e.g. proof of logical consistency with an extant body of knowledge is not necessary as is the case in scientific creativity. The intuition and its attempted communication in the art form may completely comprise the artistic creative act. This communication, in art as in mathematics and science, assumes a knowledge of methods and materials for communicating and a technical proficiency in their use. It is because intuition is a necessary part of creativity that the properties, problems of definition and measurement, personality characteristics and correlates of intuition are also associated with creativity. Because of the lack of understanding of intuitive thought, most quantitative studies of creativity have avoided or ignored it and so I consider those studies to be incomplete.

It is hoped that the findings of this investigation, particularly applications of the Theory of Intuitive Thought, will contribute to the general advancement of creativity study, because intuitive thought is a necessary major constituent of all creativity.

Intuition is Essential to Creativity

Intuition and creativity have so many properties in common that Tauber, E.S. and Green, M.R. (1959) consider them to be essentially identical. Guiora, A.Z. *et al.* (1965) summarize Jung's position on intuition and they say he equates intuition with creativity, '...intuition seems to be a sort of teleological sense and also of power, that is to say creativity' (p. 113). Sinnott, E.W. (1959) says that the creative process may not exist without the initial spark of intuition '...without this flash the creative process might never have been able to get started' (p. 24). Baldwin, A. (1966) writing on 'The development of intuition' says that the intuitive processes are important for achieving understanding and creativity (p. 84).

Board, R. (1958) recognized that 'intuition and creative insight are similar' (p. 236), and concurs: 'Frequently, however, scientific advance is achieved by creative insight' (p. 236). Beveridge, W.I.B. (1950) also equates intuition with creativity. 'To speak more directly, and without metaphor, of the true relationship between intuition and intellect, intuition is the creative advance toward reality.' It is reported by Rossman, B.B. and Horn, J.J. (1972) that '...creative people are often said to be intuitive' (p. 280). Hutchinson, E.D. (1941) talking of '...the richness of emotions involved' says: 'It is in this phase of the intuitive experience that the identity of the creative aspects of science and art is to be discovered' (p. 38).

Intuition is recognized to be essential to creativity in specific fields, e.g. painting, literature, science, and mathematics. Poincaré, H. (1969) argues that '...intuition is in mathematics the most usual instrument of invention' (p. 212). Hill, J.C. (1976) quotes Sir Peter Medawar as saying: 'Intuition is the main-spring of all scientific action' (p. 46); and Hill concludes: 'For the writers I have quoted, intuition is part of the scientific method'. (p. 47). Rallo, J. (1974) discusses how artists may use '...the intuitive psychoanalytic perspective' to create their characters in literature or painting.

Intuition is the First Phase of Creativity

Four phases of the creative process are recognized in the literature: '...preparation, incubation, illumination and verification' (Clinchy, Blythe, 1975, p. 50). Hutchinson, E.D. (1941) expands on these four phases of the creative cycle under the following headings: 'A Period of Preparation Trial and Error Activity; A Period of Renunciation of the Problem during which effort is temporarily abandoned; A Period or Moment, of Insight: and A Period of Verification, Elaboration or Evaluation' (p. 32).

The first three stages of this creative cycle have been incorporated by the

Theory of Intuitive Thought into the one phase of 'intuition' so that the creative process may be thought of as just two stages, *viz.* intuition followed by verification. MacKinnon, D.W. (1962) writing on 'The nature and nurture of creative talent' also considers creativity in these two stages, creativity '...involves an elaboration of the initial novel insight so that it is adequately developed'. He gives this as a criterion of creativity. Zajonc, A.G. (1976) also considers that intuition followed by formal expression are the two stages of creativity, '...the intuition of the law which generally precedes its more formal expression...' (p. 332). Sliker, Gretchen P. (1972) mentions '...the felt thought of discovery followed by a logical thinking of verification' (p. 27). Simonton, D.K. (1975) conducted an experiment on the relation of 'intuition versus analysis' to 'creativity' in problem-solving. His results showed that high creatives improved in their ability to solve problems under the instruction to intuit and low creatives improved their problem-solving ability under the instruction to analyse: '...the results do tend to support the conclusions that (a) intuition and analysis may indeed be distinctive modes of thought and (b) the relative effectiveness of each may depend on both the nature of a problem and the cognitive style of the individual' (p. 353). The relevance of an individual's cognitive style to his intuitive ability has been discussed in Section 5.2, also intuitive and analytic thought as separate modes are discussed in Section 2.1. Although creativity may be considered in two phases, *viz.* intuition verified by analysis, it is shown below that intuition also guides the analysis stage.

Meaning of the Term 'Creativity' in Relation to the Literature on Intuition

The creativity literature is very large and contains varying definitions of creativity. It is not appropriate to consider these definitions in detail in this investigation except to say that because intuition is poorly understood in the literature, the definitions of creativity concerned with the psychology of the process reflect this insubstantiality. 'Establishing such an association [between intuition and creativity] is complicated by fact that "creativity" is a term as slippery as "intuition" ' (Frick, R.C., 1970, p. 10). Operational definitions of creativity are often not relevant to intuition.

Another problem of definition concerns 'originality'. Some definitions require that creativity be '...unique and singular originality' (Ausubel, D. P., 1968, p. 552). However, many definitions require only that creativity should be original to the person. So for example in teaching by the 'creative method' the students learn by 'recreating' (Peters, W. H., 1975). In this present investigation the term is used in this sense, to include subjective originality so that even if the subject has at some previous time expressed a specific creation and then, perhaps through lack of rehearsal or lesion the experience has been lost or forgotten, it is possible to again relive that specific creativity. This happens under the rare conditions in which an intuition may be repeated as if for the first time.

Apart from the originality there is a problem of 'purpose'. Most complex random states are original by virtue of the large possible number of combinations of their constituents. Even the order of stones thrown on the ground may be considered original and hence creative where originality is the only criterion of creativity. In this study creativity is considered as subjectively original and the originality being a product of intuition thus satisfying the tension evoked by some preconditions to the process. This precondition is incorporated in Provus M.M.'s (1966) definition of creativity as '...a human activity which produces a self-generated solution to a new and pressing problem, e.g. a fantastic scribble of coloured lines is creative only when it satisfies pre-existent conditions' (p. 128). Selections of preorganized material, patterning, assembly or even logical analysis are transformations that may lead to creativity, as does the internal combination of emotional sets, providing the results of these external transformations cause the personal combinations of emotional sets resulting in the personal intuition. It is not possible to tell from the final transformed 'problem set' or solution whether the solution was reached by personal intuition, and therefore it is no guide to whether creativity has occurred in the sense used in this investigation. On these considerations of subjective originality, purpose and personal insight, an end-result which indicates creativity for one subject in no way guarantees creativity has occurred for another subject. Yet many definitions of creativity use the result, rather than the method, as a criterion.

The following definition of creativity by Mednick, S.A. (1962) is clearly consistent with the previously discussed structure of emotional sets and their combinations that result in intuition. Particularly, Mednick's expressed view endorses the facilitating of intuition through similar responses conditioned to dissimilar emotional sets which encourages their combination. Mednick gives a definition of creativity in terms of

> serendipity, similarity and mediation — forming of associate elements into new combinations which either meet specified requirements or are in some way useful ...any ability or tendency which serves to bring otherwise mutually remote ideas into contiguity will facilitate a creative solution; any ability or tendency which serves to keep remote ideas from contiguous evocation will inhibit the creative solution. (pp. 221/222)

'...to perform creatively. This is, he [the subject] is asked to form associate elements into new combinations by providing mediating connective links' (p. 226). Pollio, H.R. (1974, p. 134) reports on Gordon W.J.J.'s (1961) synectics theory which Pollio says means the fitting together of diverse elements which, according to Gordon, is the heart of the creative act.

'Creativity' Considered as Intuition Verified by Intuitively Guided Analysis

In creativity the function of the initial intuition is to discover, to generate hypotheses (Bruner, J., 1962, p. 102), whereas the function of logical thought and analysis is to verify this intuition. Arnheim, R. (1970) quotes Henri Poincaré as saying 'it is by logic that we prove. It is by intuition that we discover' (p. 274). In agreement Bruner (1962) says of intuition: 'It produces interesting combinations of ideas before their worth is known. It precedes proof; indeed it is what the techniques of analysis and proof are designed to test and check' (p. 102). In the field of teaching and learning mathematics he says analysis is used for 'the translation of intuitive ideas into mathematics' (p. 99).

Analysis is a step-by-step process which needs direction, just as a man looking only at his feet can walk step by step but needs direction. Intuition gives that direction through its property of global knowledge. It sees the end from afar and also the approximate route (see Section 5.1). Intuition is also needed to select, untried, one method of analysis from the many available; to select with sufficient confidence for one to invest in the effort of logical verification. In respect of choice and guidance, intuition is the foundation of analysis. Accordingly. Baldwin, A. (1966) intimates about the intuitive processes 'that they may be the foundation upon which rests the process of analysis and formal explanation' (p. 84). Suzuki, D.T. (1957) says reason must have intuition behind it and cannot work without it (p. 85) and Bunge, M. (1962) agrees '...it [intuition] helps us in conceiving the rigorous demonstration' (p. 110). Hadamard, J. (1945) says: 'That an affective element is an essential part in every discovery or invention is only too evident, and has been insisted upon by several thinkers' (p. 31). He considers the rules which guide invention, particularly mathematical invention: 'The rules which must guide it are extremely fine and delicate. It is almost impossible to state them precisely; they are felt rather than formulated' (pp. 30/31). The Theory of Intuitive Thought attempts to state these rules precisely.

Beveridge, W.I.B. (1950) attributes to the intellect the technically proficient function of communicating the intuition as well as verifying it. However, we have seen that such technical proficiency also has an intuitive as well as an intellectual element. 'Intellect needs first to perform the valuable and necessary function of interpreting, i.e. of translating, verbalizing in acceptable mental terms, the results of intuition; second to check its validity; and third, to co-ordinate and to include it into the body of already accepted knowledge.' Bunge, M. (1962) in his book *Intuition and Science* confirms that intuition guides analysis during verification. 'Intuition serves as a guide in demonstrations, pointing to the way we must follow in order to attain perfect rigor' (p. 110).

Throughout the verification we use the analysis to transform information against the constant check of our intuition. Our intuition might allow us a slight digression, felt as an increase in discordance, an increasing anxiety, on the promise of an imminent reduction in tension or a great future resolution of anxiety. However, our intuition will not allow us to sustain such a detour without this promise. For example, in creative mathematics in proving an intuited conclusion, one's intuition would not sustain a path of increasing complexity unless it promised a sudden simplification. Similarly proofs which increase in complexity before simplification appear 'artificial', that is they do not reproduce in the reader the intuitive confidence of the gradual reduction in anxiety accompanying increasing simplification. Polanyi, M. (1966) argues that the solution of scientific problems rests on this ability to alternate between analytic and intuitive thinking. Beveridge, W.I.B. (1950) discusses how in the creative process both the intuition and the analytic modes of thought work together. An 'harmonious interplay between the two can work perfectly in a successive rhythm; intuitional insight, interpretation, further insight and its interpretation and so on'. Although Jung describes personality types as either mainly 'thinking' or 'intuitive' they can be mixed. (Dry, A.M., 1961). Such a controlled dual personality would be ideal for creativity.

Kurt Gödel's famous mathematical paper of 1931 implies that we may not rely on logical consistency as an infallible verification and so, as some philosophies have maintained, we must turn again to our intuition for the final acceptance of any analytic verification.

Correlates of Intuition and Creativity

Properties of intuition are also attributed to creativity. This further substantiates intuition as a major constituent of creativity. In particular correlates of intuition described and predicted by the Theory of Intuitive Thought are also attributed in the literature to creativity. This further endorses the Theory of Intuitive Thought as a description of intuition and its role in creativity. Some of the correlates of intuition and creativity themselves intercorrelate. The following characteristics of creativity, given by Sliker, Gretchen P. (1972) may also be considered characteristics of emotional sets as described in this study by the Theory of Intuitive Thought. 'There are four characteristics . . . which are pertinent to creativity theory. It has uninterrupted access to perceptual experience, it allows flow of imagery between conscious and unconscious; associated with it are patterns of ideomotor action in the form of motor adjustments, incipient movements, and anticipatory sets of attitudes; it facilitates organization of symbolic material' (p. 27).

Personality Correlates of Intuition and Creativity

There is a wide range of literature on the personality correlates of creativity, which reflects the need to identify creative types and the desirability of improving creativity by, wherever possible, educing its concomitant personality traits. Cattell, R.B. and Butcher, H.J. (1968) illustrate this need through their comment on the importance of creativity to the advancement of science and mathematics: '...it has been frequently pointed out that the individual, fertile originator remains the crucial factor in scientific progress: and this applies even more strongly in theoretical fields, perhaps especially in mathematics'. See also Tuska, C.D. (1957). Williams, F.E. (1966), recognizing this importance, calls for research into the 'personality of the creator' (p. 359).

The Theory of Intuitive Thought indicates the high-intuitive type as having similar responses conditioned to very dissimilar emotional sets. This structure will allow the same or a similar response to evoke these very different emotional sets along with their cognitive associations. This structure predicts the personality correlates of the intuitive type, e.g. the ability to recall many different associations from the same word because that word is associated with different words in the dissimilar emotional sets to which it is conditioned. This is Mednick's criterion for creativity and was found as a correlate of creativity in an experiment on 'An analysis of associative behaviour and creativity' by Riegel, K.F. *et al.* (1966) who had forty-eight subjects give word associations to stimulus words under certain restrictions, e.g. free associations, opposites, other words in the same group, etc. The subjects had previously been graded as high or low creatives on the Creative Personality Scale (p. 52). The results confirmed Mednick's hypotheses that creative subjects have a flatter probability distribution of choice of words and that non-creative subjects choose the same words more often. The experimenters suggest that creativity is shown in the high level of associating classes; classes which are represented by emotional sets in our proposed structure of cognitive/affective organization of the intuitive type.

This structure proposed by the Theory of Intuitive Thought shows that the ability to recall remote associates and divergent thinking are the same. Divergent thinking, e.g. thinking of uses for a brick, comprises a fluency (the number of responses considered statistically original) and flexibility (the number of categories used). Both fluency and flexibility are predicted from the structure used by the Theory of Intuitive Thought. Divergent thinking correlates with other creativity tests and is used to measure creativity, e.g. Guilford, J.P. (1956, 1959, 1967) and other more recent research.

The structure proposed by the theory, coding the same or a similar response to different emotional sets (categories), shows that flexibility in divergent thinking may be considered the same as preference for complexity and the cognitive style defined by preference for many categories of description. Many researchers have found that measures of creativity correlate with preference for complexity on the Barron-Welsh Art Scale (Barron, F., 1953). Cognitive styles indicative of the creative type, defined on the above multicategorization dimension and other dimensions, were discussed in relation to the intuitive type in Sections 5.2 and 5.3.

The ambiguity of categorization, natural to the intuitive type, is embodied in this structure of conditioning similar responses to dissimilar emotional sets. 'Tolerance of ambiguity' was found to be a correlate of intuition by Westcott,

M.R. and Ranzoni, J.H. (1963) and also found to be a correlate of creativity by many other researchers, e.g. Rossman, B.B. and Horn, J.J. (1972), Barron, F. (1963b). Provus, M.M. (1966) found problem-solvers were high in their ability to hold a variety of perspectives based on conflicting value assumptions.

This same ambivalent coding necessitates a delay in evaluating one's ideas while, according to the Theory of Intuitive Thought, the emotional sets combine to give the most probable acceptable coding for evaluation. Clinchy, Blythe (1975) is just one of many writers who have found that: 'Some evidence suggests that one characteristic of creative thinkers is the ability to delay evaluation of their own ideas' (p. 50). This same delay, while combining emotional sets, necessitates enduring the decreasing anxiety and discomfort, initially self-induced for resolving during the intuitive process. There is anecdotal literature suggesting that creative types are more prepared to suffer discomfort for the fruition of their ideas, e.g. the artists or inventors who choose to buy paint, tools, and materials rather than spend their meagre incomes on creature comforts or even on necessary food.

Amorphous categorization of responses conditioned to dissimilar emotional sets by personal experience is the opposite of dogmatism, conservatism, and authoritarianism scales, e.g. Barron, F. (1963a), Yamomoto, K.A. (1964), and also Drevdahl, J.E. (1956) found high creatives were significantly different from low creatives on Cattell's 16PF scale $Q1+$, i.e. not 'conservative, respecting established ideas, tolerant of traditional difficulties'. Cattell, R.B. and Drevdahl, J.E. (1955) studied the 16PF questionnaire responses of forty-six research physicists, forty-six research biologists, and fifty-two researchers in psychology in order to discover how the personality profile of creative workers differed from that of the average man. They found five factors at $p < 0.01$, viz. $A-$, $B+$, $F-$, $I+$ and $Q1+$. They concluded, in agreement with our thesis, that: 'Researchers are also significantly more emotionally sensitive $(I+)$, more radical $(Q1+)$, and somewhat more given to controlling their behaviour by an exacting self-concept'.

Westcott, M.R. (1964) found intuitive types were conservative (p. 43). Rossman, B.B. and Horn, J.J. (1972) found that the Rokeach Dogmatism scale loaded negatively on their creativity factor (p. 280). Our proposed structure associates the above personality correlates of creativity and explains Gerber's L.A. (1972) findings, using TAT empathy score, that preference for complexity correlates with field independence and negatively with dogmatism. The intuitive type is dependent upon his own experience to give him the subjective categories that he uses for evaluation. He needs to depend less than the non-intuitive type upon others' judgments and rules. Having his own system of evaluation 'independent' of authority and dogmatism makes the intuitive type more self-sufficient and willing than the non-intuitive type to take a risk with ideas. Rossman, B.B. and Horn, J.J. (1972) identified two factors of creativity, one of which was 'self-sufficient — calculated — risk taking' (p. 265). Hammer, E.F. (1973) also found a 'prerequisite' for creativity 'includes the "moral courage" to take a risk and explore ordinarily tabooed or forbidden areas'. Westcott, M.R. (1961, 1964, 1966, 1968), defines his intuitive type as one prepared to take the risk of making a guess at an answer when given little information and getting the answer right. So risk-taking is another correlate of intuition and creativity that is predicted by the Theory of Intuitive Thought. Risk-taking is encouraged by non-censuring atmospheres (Kogan, N. and Wallach, M., 1964) just as intuition and creativity are facilitated in these permissive environments.

The Theory of Intuitive Thought describes how the intuiter evokes through empathy feelings enabling him to become emotionally involved with the object of his intuition, and describes then how he depends upon his sensitivity to these feelings in order to reorganize them through the combination of emotional sets. This description is further supported by the following. Rosett, H.L. et al. (1968) found in a pilot test on mathematicians and chemists using the physiognomic cue test that: 'Subjects designated as more creative were more physiognomic' (p. 708). This agrees with the common use of physiognomic perception in the intuitive process discussed in Section 2.2. Rossman, B.B. and Horn, J.J. (1972) found that 16PF I (sensitivity) was indicative of creative types. Westcott, M.R. (1964) showed that intuitive types tended to be tensely involved in what they were doing and more sensitive to awareness of 'inner states' (p. 43). Torrance, E.P. (1973) also found creative types became emotionally involved.

From a self-concept study where the intuitive and the non-intuitive thinkers tick self-descriptions from an adjective check list, Westcott, M.R. (1964) gives lists of the words checked by both intuitive and non-intuitive categories. These self-descriptions correspond with the descriptions of personality correlates of creativity found by many other researchers and predicted by the Theory of Intuitive Thought.

The global knowledge property of intuition shows that intuitive types tend not to be concerned with details. Yamomoto, K.A. (1964) in agreement with this noted one of the traits of the creative personality was that creative types were 'unenthusiastic about details'. Thinking by analogy, which Ribot, T. (1906) says is essential and fundamental to the creative imagination, we consider to be a part of the intuitive process where the analogies are defined by common feelings (Section 6.2) rather than by 'logical parallels that exist between descriptive systems' (Griesinger, D.W., 1974, p. 50). The creative act of choosing appropriate 'logical parallels' rests on the similarity of feelings associated with the logical parallels. It has been shown that Rorschach M and TAT assess empathy and projection, which are essential to intuition, and therefore may be used to indicate the intuitive type (Section 6.3). These tests associate intuition and creativity through the work of King, G.F. (1958) who quotes Vernier and Kendig as finding a high relationship between M and TAT rated for creativity (p. 4).

Personality Differences Between Creative Scientists and Artists

The reluctance of the intuitive type to be 'rule-bound' is explained by the structure of amorphous emotional categorization. This trait is seen, through our proposed structure of cognitive/affective organization for intuitive thought, to be the same as anti-dogmatic, anti-authoritarianism, and anti-conservative traits. This 'unwilling to accept things on mere say-so' was found in the 'Nature of the creative person' by Guilford, J.P., (1966).

Barron, F. (1963b) reports that the creative are often said to be intuitive and not rule-bound. The second stage of creativity, the verification stage, is one thing that distinguishes scientific creativity from artistic creativity. In scientific creativity this verification requires intuition to guide analysis and to relate the intuitive insight to the extant body of knowledge which is not necessarily the case in artistic creativity. The extant body of knowledge is consistent because of rules of interrelation. The intuitive choice of methods of analysis needs an intuitive judgment that the analysis is suitable because its rules are analogous to the structure to be analysed, e.g. the use of right-hand axes from electromagnet theory is suggested by kinaesthetic analogy for the analysis of knotting and linking numbers in topology. This intuitive feeling for rules distinguishes artistic creativity from scientific creativity, and to a lesser extent distinguishes it from pure mathematical creativity which need not be restricted by rules of nature. Rossman, B.B. and Horn, J.J. (1972) found in their study of creative engineering and art students that the 'rule-orientated versus intuitive factor' distinguished between the art and engineering subjects (p. 265).

Cattell, R.B. and Butcher, H.J. (1968) found some differences between creative scientists and artists by using the 16PF scale. The authors discuss the personality of creative scientists considered from their biographies. e.g. scientists like Cavendish and Dalton as $A-$, $H+$, $F-$. They suggest that the second-order (stratum) factor 'introversion' has a structure in which traits are positively correlated for the general population but negatively correlated for creative scientists. This, the authors say, is the most marked difference between creative scientists and artists, applying least to composers and most to painters who were generally high on $E+$ and $L+$, i.e. socially uncongenial, undemocratic, and dominant. For an investigation into more specific types of creativity, for example into mathematical creativity which is similar to both artistic and scientific creativity, a second-order factor scale that distinguishes only scientific creativity is not a suitable indicator. For example Eysenck H.J.'s (1953) extroversion/neuroticism would be less suitable than a multi-first-order factor scale like Cattell's 16PF, although this particular scale is receiving much criticism. It has long been recognized that these creative scientists are high on $Q2+$, a high degree of intellectual self-sufficiency, departing freely from the usual judgments and accepting the freedom to be 'odd' which the average man does not. This $Q2+$ factor Cattell and Butcher say, usually connotes 'a rich supply of inner resources and interests', as is proposed for the intuitive type. To find any differences between innovators in art and science, the authors combined the results of previous researches in this field and contrasted with Drevdahl, J.E. and Cattell, R.B. (1958) who studied one hundred and fifty-three writers of imaginative literature. The results showed that profiles of creative workers are similar. Artists were more bohemian, $M+$, emotional sensitive, $I+$, and at a high ergic tension, $Q4+$. Any emotional instability or immaturity is due to high $I+$ rather than ego weakness, $C-$. This could be an effect of youth as it is found decreasingly in older engineers.

Physiological Concomitants of Intuition and Creativity

It has been shown in Section 5.2 that intuitive thought is associated with the right hemisphere of the brain. It has also been shown in Section 6.2 that alpha and theta waves are prominent during the intuitive mode of thought. Theta rhythms denote a regressed state of primary thinking which facilitates intuition and the intuitive stages of creativity. These ideas, taken with a hypothesis from the work of Miller, W.C. (1976), associate these physiological concomitants of intuition with creativity. His hypothesis is '. . .that during creative work, there would be a greater incidence of alpha and theta waves'. He used thirteen artists and one scientist and studied their brain waves from the right parietal and temporal lobes. His hypothesis was not confirmed. 'Instead, it was found that four subjects (three of whom were professional writers) were producing virtually 100 per cent beta waves when they seemed most involved in their work.' This could be due to the writers using the non-intuitive verbal mode, see Section 7.1 on intuition considered as a preverbal concept.

Properties of Intuition as Correlates of Creativity

It has been shown that empathy and emotional involvement are properties of intuition, Sections 6.3 and 3.1. This subsection further endorses intuition as a part of creativity by showing that empathy and emotional involvement are also correlates of creativity.

Gordon, W.J.J. (1961) says: 'Psychological states such as empathy are, as we have seen, basic to the creative process' (p. 33). He 'considers that the mediating process behind creativity is involved in nine phases. One of the most important is personal analogy, in which the inventor tries to become one of the objects looked at so that he can feel, think, and act as that object. This goes beyond mere role-playing, in that the inventor is encouraged to be an inanimate, as well as an animate, object or being' (Pollio, H.R., 1974, p. 134). Rogers, C.R. (1959) working 'Toward a theory of creativity' says that to encourage 'Understanding empathically . . .is a basic fostering of creativity' (p. 80). Schafer, R. (1959) considers associations of the empathizer as analogous to the inspirational phase of a creative process.

It has been shown that in the intuitive process empathy is used to evoke feelings, to get the intuiter emotionally involved so that he may use his sensitivity to his feelings during the intuitive process. Zajonc, A.G. (1976) agrees that such feelings are necessary during the first intuitive stage of creativity when he refers to '...the initial necessary element is the feeling of wonder without which the investigator can make little or no progress' (p. 332). Pine, F. and Holt, R.R. (1960) report: 'At the moment of creation, thinking is more fluid and ...less logical than usual; it is generally pervaded by intense emotionality — feelings of omnipotence, intense pleasure and/or pain' (p. 370).

Izard, C.E. and Tomkins, S.S. (1966) refer to emotion as 'affect' and say that positive affect provides the background motivation to creativity. May, R. (1959) writing on 'The nature of creativity' notes that self-awareness, another necessity of intuition discussed in Section 6.2, and emotional involvement are necessary to give insight during creativity. 'Hence the heightened awareness we are speaking of does not always mean increased self-consciousness. It is rather correlated more with abandon, absorption, and involves a heightening of awareness in the whole personality ...unconscious insights...come only in the areas to which the person is intensively committed in his conscious living' (p. 62). Sherman, V. (1977) suggests '...ego-involved self-experiences... personal meanings ...in sensory-laden forms' enable students to '...conceive of themselves as "creative". They learn to flow with natural, dynamic processes of their own mind/body systems' (p. 83).

Intuition and Creativity are Both Primary Processes

Intuition has been described in Sections 4.1 and 8.2 as primary-process thinking in regressed ego states. This present subsection further implicates intuition as the first stage of creativity by showing that the initial stage of creativity is considered in the literature as primary-process thinking in a regressed ego state. Further, the permissive relaxed environment that facilitates intuition also facilitates creativity.

Rothenberg, A. (1970) in a study of 'Inspiration, insight and the creative process' says that 'Ernest Kris applies his term "regression in the service of the ego" most particularly to inspiration' (p. 173). Pine, F. and Holt, R.R. (1960) use Kris's (1952) idea of 'regression in the service of the ego' as '...a momentary and at least partially controlled use of primitive, non-logical and drive-dominated modes of thinking in the early stages of the creative process' (p. 370), which agrees with what we have already seen in this section, namely that the early stages of the creative process are intuitive. Creativity being a primary process is supported by Hammer, E.F. (1973) who says that creatives have to be '...attuned to more primary thought processes while maintaining touch with reason and reality'. This also necessitates control of change and constancy of ego state. Hartmann, H. *et al.* (1947) consider primary-process thinking as regressive and productive modes of intuitive thinking which give rise to novel and creative ideas. One of the 'mechanisms' Freud described as characteristic of primary processes is: 'Condensation, which results in the fusion of two or more ideas or images' (Klein, G.S., 1970, p. 283), which is explained by the Theory of Intuitive Thought as a result of combining emotional sets.

Pollio, H.R. (1974) clearly implicates primary-process thinking with the production of insights in the early stages of creativity, and implicates secondary-process thinking with the verification of these insights. He implies insights are global, not detailed, reorganization. This global reorganization is described by the Theory of Intuitive Thought. He says intuitive thought is a

> ...primary process ideally suited to breaking down patterns of usual thought. If this is true, then an individual who can occasionally 'dip down' into such thinking, and not get lost in its labyrinth, is precisely that person who might be able to come up with a new insight, or a new work of art. ...In order to do this [make novel experiential associations] he 'regresses' to a time when all things are possible and none impossible, reverting back to secondary process only after new combinations have been established. Once such new combinations have been formed, secondary process thinking is required to fill in the details of this new recombination. (pp. 152/153)

This again needs ego control to change at will between secondary- and primary-process thinking. Non-judgmental, permissive atmospheres encourage creativity and intuition, and promote regression to primary-process thinking. Wallach, M.A. and Kogan, N. (1965) quote the conditions for creativity as 'relaxed and permissive to characterize the attitude deemed necessary for creative insights' (p. 19). Haefele, J.W. (1962) gives similar conditions for insight and for creativity. 'The breakthrough type of insight... is not susceptible to logical attack and can gain consideration only in a relaxed mental state or in disassociated thought' (p. 86). 'Environment for creativity — abeyance of judgment, relaxation of censorship, spirit of play' (p. 55).

We see from the foregoing that creativity starts with an intuition which is then verified by intuitively guided analysis and that, in the second verification stage of creativity, ego control is needed to change between primary and secondary thought in order to apply the intuitively guided analysis that brings the initial intuition to fruition as a creation.

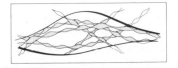

Intuitive Knowledge and its Correctness

8.1 INTUITION NEED NOT BE CORRECT

This is property 9, with four references supporting the correctness of intuition, and two references contradicting the correctness of intuition, in Section 1.3.

Intuition is defined by some writers as necessarily correct, whereas others disagree, saying that intuition like an educated guess is a useful guide often right but sometimes wrong. Intuition lost its place as a diviner of absolute truth as philosophic, scientific, and mathematical thought began to consider relative truth and subjective truth. In particular, mathematical ideas were rigorously substantiated that contradicted intuition, e.g. continuous lines without slopes, lines filling planes, etc. These failures of mathematical intuition seem to be related to a lack of relevant experience particularly of infinitesimals. When appropriate 'feeling model analogies' have been developed for the infinitesimals, however, intuition continues to be a correct guide.

In experimental situations, where the answers are known, it is clear whether or not a subject's intuitive answer is correct. It seems that all experiments evoking intuition by using a problem only accept that intuition has occurred if a correct or partially correct answer is given. Behaviourists, in particular, define insight as a dramatic increase in the number of correct solutions in such a learning experiment. However, the use of such 'accuracy criterion' experiments by researchers concerned with the theory of intuition, e.g. confirming personality traits of the intuitive type, all seem to give insignificant or paradoxical results; due, I believe, to using an accuracy criterion for intuition.

It is contended in this investigation that intuition is always considered to be subjectively correct but where there is an accepted answer for comparison, intuition may not always completely agree with this answer. This is true not only in intuitions giving scientific advance, where such a disagreement is the

322

most usual cause of the advance, but in everyday living experiences of intuition, and even in laboratory conditions for intuitive experiments. The Theory of Intuitive Thought clearly shows how intuitive perception, intuitive processing, and communicating the intuition are sources of error. Intuitive perception and the intuitive process, because of their descriptive idiosyncratic nature, can only be subjectively appropriate rather than correct. Even where noise-free information is available, its perception interacts with emotional sets to give a 'weighted' selection of the information. This weighted selected information is coded into feelings for intuitive processing. The accuracy and suitability of this coding depends upon the subject's self-sensitivity and his developed ability empathically to evoke appropriate feelings. Error first exists where this subjectively appropriate perception does not closely correspond to the available information.

The combination of emotional sets during the intuitive process further transforms this intuitive information according to its associations with the subject's past experience and present physiological state. This process may interact with the perception of the original information if the stimulus is still available, but otherwise this further transformation is independent of the original information and a second source for further error.

When the transformed information is harmonious with the person's other intuitive information, the intuitive process stops and the content of the emotional set, which is the intuition, usually has to be decoded and communicated. Precise decoding depends on correct and accurate introspection. The accuracy of introspection again depends on the subject's sensitivity. The correctness of introspection depends upon the subject's developed ability to attribute his feelings appropriately to the original information that evoked them, i.e. accurate decoding. For public verification the lack of technical proficiency in choosing 'symbols' commonly evoking his present feelings and associated cognitions is a source of error in communicating.

It is intended that, as detailing the intuitive process in other chapters indicates how intuitive ability may be improved, so in this section detailing these sources of errors to the correctness of intuition will indicate how accuracy of intuition may be improved.

Controversy on the Correctness of Intuition

Table 1.3/2 shows that four references attributed correctness to intuition, mostly from 'definitions' of intuition in psychological use, but that a further two references from insight in psychological use show that intuition need not be correct. In respect of this property, insight in psychological use is most different from insight in operational use where it is defined by an increase in the number of correct responses. Some theorists consider intuition must be correct, though most say it is only a useful guide that may rarely mislead. In contrast other investigators contend that no faith may be placed in intuition as it is often wrong. The cases cited by investigators who maintain that intuition is often wrong are usually technical, concerning infinity and limits, of which the intuiter had either inappropriate or no feeling model analogies.

Some writers consider that intuition is necessarily correct. Burden, Virginia (1975) writing on 'The process of intuition — a psychology of creativity' is one of many writers who consider: 'Intuition is always and invariably right...' (p. 31). Clark, F.V. (1973) says '...intuition may be true by definition...' (p. 160). Pechstein, L.A. and Brown, F.D. (1939) give the following criteria for insight: 'Immediate solution — a correct solution to a novel situation without trial' (p. 40).

Kaplan, H.A. (1973) says 'investigators have focused on four critical factors for analysis of intuition', one of which is 'accuracy' (p. 4). Examples are the use of rating scales where insight is defined as accuracy of self-rating, examples are given by Allport, G.W. (1937), or accuracy according to some criteria known to the experimenter but not to the subject as in Behaviourists' insight experiments. Sometimes this accuracy criterion is coupled to another property, e.g. low information demand (Westcott, M.R.) or preconscious process (Bouthilet, Lorraine, 1948).

Bouthilet experiments with 'The measurement of intuitive thinking' and operationally defines intuition as more than chance correctness based on 'guesses' or 'hunch-like' emergence of the recognition of classificationary schemes and relationships (p. 49); '...the capacity to make correct guesses without knowing why' (p. 57). Using ten male and ten female subjects her procedure was to use forty pairs of words serially presented for two seconds each. Subjects were instructed to learn the pairs. A subject had to find the matching word from five other words presented in a list. The unknown rule was that the matching word was made from some of the letters in the word from the matched pair. Subjects were asked to guess if they were not sure. The results were the usual insight curves.

Westcott has been most influential in the field of intuition. His lack of consideration for the theory and many properties of intuition are criticized elsewhere in this book. His procedure in measuring intuition is to give subjects clues, e.g. successive terms of a series. The subject has to guess a logically predicted result, e.g. the sixth or seventh terms of the series. Westcott measures intuition by the number of successful answers (S) divided by the number of clues required (I). He operationally defines intuition as the number S/I. This measure gave a retest reliability $p < 0.01$ over three years with ninety-five female students (Westcott, M.R., 1966, p. 194). I feel his influence on the study of intuition with a measure so unrelated to the nature of intuition lies in the recognized need for a quantitative measure in a field so obviously lacking in quantitative instruments and even a consensus definition of intuition.

Unfortunately many researchers have followed Westcott's lead. One such worker is Frick, R.C. (1970) who, proposing 'A study of intuition as inference', defines intuition as follows: 'Propensity for intuitive thinking as measured by accuracy of inference from little information' (p. 4). He used one

CLUES

1	2	3	4	5
over under	in out	short long	down up	black white
B C	C D	D E	E F	F G
DRAB BAR	LOT TO	TRAP PAR	TAPS SPA	TRAM MAR
Z	X	V	T	R
312-4	8-2	15-4	351-1	242-2
N	N E	E	S E	S
12321	23432	34543	45654	56765
carouse	arouse	rouse	ouse	use
ADZ	BOY	COX	DEW	ELV
326-1957	732-2619	573-2619	957-3261	195-7326
boat ship send	tar pitch toss	tavern bar rod	fee tip end	thin lean tilt
stripe 123456	strip 12345	trip 2345	pier 5463	pest 5612
DOC DUD	RID ROE	SEW SIX	COD CUE	TAM TEN
3692-4	216874-6	31-2	26915-5	9-1
KIT	KIVT	KVIIT	KXT	KXIIIT
9N	8E	6S	4F	7S
12	2	23	3	34
carts cart	holds hold	form for	howl how	bar ba
no tone	ma name	at star	10 fold	mi time

Fig. 8.1/1 Examples of Westcott's measures of intuitive thinking (based on Kaplan, H.A., 1973)

hundred and forty subjects from six schools who took an 'incomplete picture' test. The eight pictures in each sequence of the test become more complete and the subject must guess as soon as possible what the picture is. Twelve sequences were used. Results showed 'willingness to make inferences from little information was significantly greater among blacks than whites'. This was the only significant result. The two scores he used were the number of guesses and the number of the picture in the sequence of completion before the correct guess for that sequence. Frick quotes previous similar ineffectual research using accuracy measures and he recognizes the need for research into instruments more successful in identifying the intuitive thinker (p. 35). The Selected Phrase Empathic Ability Key has since been developed and this instrument successfully identifies intuitive thinkers.

The behaviourist definition of insight, as a dramatic increase in the number of correct responses up to 100 per cent correct, was used and found wanting in an experiment by Irwin, F.W. *et al.* (1934). The experimenters gave twelve subjects a series of words and asked for instant associations which they timed to one-fifteenth of a second. Subjects were paid according to their score which was inversely proportional to the total time and to the number of 'right' or 'wrong' responses as required, defined as being on one of two lists of ten words compiled by some criteria unknown to the subjects. Results were that even when subjects guessed or were taught the criteria they still did not get 100 per cent correct results. The authors say this contradicts the idea of Thorndike, E.L. and Rock, R.T. (1934) that knowledge of the criteria will soon lead to near perfection in responses. Further criticism of the use of accuracy measures leading at best to inconclusive results is given later in this section.

Other writers, concerned with the theory of intuition, have also contended that intuition must be correct. Szalita-Pemow, A. (1955) writing on 'The intuitive process' considers the 'inevitable accuracy of intuitive perceptions' (p. 9). Bunge, M. (1962) in his book *Intuition and Science* says insight is 'the sound judgment that usually comes from experience' (pp. 89/90). Guiora, A.Z. *et al.* (1965) in their paper 'Intuition: a preliminary statement' state their case as '...the writers feel that accuracy is an essential quality in intution' (p. 199).

Daniels, U.P. (1973) says: 'Definitions of intuition are numerous' (p. 2). Perhaps he means that descriptions of intuition are varied. He sees Westcott's ideas of intuition in the psychological definitions to which he refers including that 'the observation or conclusion arrived upon is accurate' (p. 2). He gives no evidence for this accuracy but says: 'Throughout these definitions it is usually assumed that the intuitive solution must be accurate' (p. 3).

Some writers consider intuition to be mostly correct. When an intuitive solution occurs it brings with it a subjective feeling of correctness, see Section 4.3 on confidence in intuitive products. However, if another solution later becomes available, through another means, the intuitions are occasionally reported to disagree. 'The brute power of logic is useless somehow, you get the clue and that's that. The moment it comes there is no question about the right solution. Occasionally you are wrong, but most of the time you are correct' (Garard, R.W., 1962, p. 118). Thus intuition is considered useful in generating hypotheses and guiding their verification, see Section 7.3 on 'creativity' considered as intuition verified by intuitively guided analysis, but sometimes it is reported to be misleading: 'Intuition is a useful guide but sometimes an unreliable one' (Adler, I., 1968, p. 80). Bigge, M.L. and Hunt, M.P. (1965) say of intuitive judgments, '...they are a worthwhile source of hypothesis. The mistake is to take them authoritatively' (p. 305).

It is because intuition is seen as occasionally misleading that Bahm, A.J. (1960) in his book *Types of Intuition* says we should not completely trust in it: '...we intuit error as well as truth ...Hence intuition, merely by itself, is not completely trustworthy' (p. 7). It is perhaps through this recognition that intuitions are occasionally wrong that Brunger, J.S. (1963) refers to the fruits of intuitive thinking as 'educated guesses': '...encouraging intuitive thinking in children, will bear later rewards in "educated guesses" in situations where an immediate right answer is lacking'. Often it seems that wrong intuitions are called 'bad guesses' and forgotten, whereas the accurate intuitions are selectively remembered, contributing to the supposition that intuitions are mostly correct.

There are some researchers who use the Behaviourists' criterion of correct answers to indicate insight but use it on a 'sliding scale' so that partially correct answers indicate a partial insight. This ignores the 'all or nothing' nature of insight. Van Duyne, P.C. (1976) used the term 'insight' to mean understanding of a logic sentence, inferred from the subject's score on a zero to four scale called the 'insight score'. Zero implies no insight, one to three 'partial insight' and four 'complete insight' (pp. 93/94). Subjects were asked to select and reject from the four truth values that would imply the truth of two conditoinal statements 'if a then b'. Namely, true antecedent, true consequent, false antecedent, and false consequent. Each correct decision contributed to the 'insight score', a maximum of four for each sentence. The subjects were asked to compose five 'necessary' and 'contingent' sentences from which E selected one of each for the experiment on each subject, e.g. necessary condition '1A. If it is a camera then it has a lens'. Contingency Condition '1B. If it is a tomato then it is red'. Results showed that overall performance in the contingency condition was better than that in the necessity condition, mainly E says because subjects seemed to want to find verifying conditions rather than falsifying conditions.

In a similar 'logic type' insight experiment Gilhooly, K.J. and Falconer, K.J. (1974) ordered subjects' responses by their degree of correctness which authors call 'partial insight'. Results again showed that accuracy favours concrete presentation which the authors found 'surprising' (p. 358) but which we would expect from our discussion in Section 6.2 on abstract thought as personalized feeling models of concrete analogies.

Some writers consider intuitions as mostly incorrect. These writers maintain that intuition can tell us nothing about the correctness of situations. For example Jones, E. (1953), quoting Freud on Goethe and Holmholtz, writes: 'It is once again an illusion to expect anything from intuition and introspection; they can give us nothing but particulars about our own mental life, which are hard to interpret' (p. 327). Other writers agree that these intuitions are mostly incorrect: 'An equally evident fact is that intuitive judgments are often wrong' (Hebb, D.O., 1946, p. 89); and also Clinchy, Blythe (1958) writing on the 'Role of intuition in learning' says '...intuitions are often wrong' (p. 36).

Claims of correctness of mathematical and scientific ideas have been made chronologically in three stages using (1) immediate usefulness, (2) intuitive appeals to experience and nature, and (3) consistency. In passing from stage (2) to stage (3) it was not only the mathematical and scientific ideas that were changed, e.g. Euclidean Parallel Axiom changed to give curved spaced geometries, but the appeal to intuition as verification was seen to be wrong and so intuition came to be associated with incorrect conceptualization. Criticisms against the use of intuition have, according to Ewing, A.C. (1941), been founded on the assumption that intuitions are necessarily correct. He says this position is no longer tenable: '...it seems to me that the advocate of intuition can only defend his position if he makes one concession. He must abandon the claim to certainty and infallibility which has been commonly advanced for intuition in the past' (p. 89).

Hahn, H. (1953) writing on 'The crisis in intuition' states that mathematics has forsaken intuitive results for formalization because results that were thought to have been intuitively obvious have since been formally disproved.

He gives several examples all of which are cases of limits, e.g. a plane defined by a series of points, a curve with a tangent at no point, a curve whose every point is a branch point, etc. Similarly Poincaré, H. (1969) writing on 'Intuition and logic in mathematics' notes the historic swing away from intuitive mathematics because: 'Intuition cannot give us rigor, nor even certainty' (p. 207). He cites several examples in mathematics where intuition fails us, e.g. continuous functions lacking derivatives and other examples.

The Theory of Intuitive Thought shows that intuition is inadequate in these situations because the experience of infinitesimals, which would perhaps have led to correct intuition, was not available to the intuitive process. Komar, A. (1962) describes what 'correctness' may be expected from a theory and decries the use of intuition that is not based on experience as erroneous. He says that one may only expect of the theory, in his example quantum theory, that its formalism and interpretation be precise so that predictions may be investigated. 'Anything more is a vacuous play upon words and an appeal to man's notoriously poor intuition into realms where one has no experience' (p. 369), see Section 2.4 on how intuition is influenced by experience. Clinchy, Blythe (1975) gives examples of children's intuitions that are wrong, e.g. that the force only emanates from a hand on the desk rather than the interaction between them. She says Bruner has suggested presenting 'counter-intuitive' facts or ideas to jolt them into a correct awareness (p. 49).

However, it is contended in this investigation that in the same way as a child's concept of 'force and equal and opposite reaction' changes by thinking intuitively in appropriate feeling model analogies, so mathematicians do think intuitively correctly about infinitesimals through similarly learnt idiosyncratic feeling model analogies — see Section 6.2 on abstract thought as intuitive processing of personalized feeling models of originally concrete analogies. Thus the Theory of Intuitive Thought shows that because concepts are represented by idiosyncratic feeling models, providing the intuiter has appropriate feeling models for his concepts, he can think intuitively and correctly about his concepts. No matter how abstract or generalized the concept, it always has, according to the Theory of Intuitive Thought, a concrete feeling model referent to make correct intuitive thought possible.

Tests on the Correctness of Intuition

Some experiments reported in the literature, that are concerned with intuition, use problems with known solutions and compare the subject's assumed intuitive solution against these criteria. Thus these experiments, unlike the accurate rating definition of intuition and the Behaviourist definition of insight as only correct solutions, admit to intuiting errors.

There are mainly two types of such experiments. One type uses known statistical parameters, e.g. means, correlations, etc., which the subject has to estimate or infer, and use in prediction. The characteristics of the original distributions are then used to account for the distribution of intuitive errors, usually by least squares regression.

The second type of experiment concerned with the correctness of intuition uses problems that may be solved both intuitively or analytically. The problems are presented in two or more ways, each intended in different degrees to evoke intuitive processing. The distribution of the errors under the types of presentation is compared and attributed to intuitive or analytic processes according to the presentation, usually spatial or linear (verbal) respectively. It is found that answers resulting from intuitive processes tend to be more or less correct with few exactly correct answers and few extremely erroneous answers, unlike answers from the analytic process that tend to be either exactly correct or greatly in error. Hence the pedagogic recommendation of using intuitive estimates first as a check on later analytic results.

The accuracy criterion for intuition is criticized in the same way as accuracy measures of empathy. For one may intuit incorrectly and be subjectively certain of the correctness at the time of the intuition. Shrauger, S. and Altrocchi, J. (1964) criticize accuracy measures and say that free description methods 'show promise' whereas research on accuracy and assumed similarity 'has primarily led to blind alleys' (p. 289). Hence in investigations of intuition free description methods are recommended. Two independent studies using accuracy measures of intuition found, against the general belief that women are more intuitive than men (Reid, L. A., 1976), that men were more intuitive (accurate) than women, viz. Valentine, C. (1929) and Levy, P.K. (1964, p. 54), who quotes similar findings from other researchers. Sex was recorded by Bastick, T. (1979) in an attempt to clarify whether men or women are more intuitive. He found that the constituent abilities necessary for intuition were sex-related.

Gitter, A.G. et al. (1971) used an accuracy measure. Like many others mentioned elsewhere their main results were insignificant. They did find, however, that accuracy improved with age, indicating that one's ability to evoke increasingly appropriate feelings improves with age. Age should therefore be considered as a variable to be recorded in investigations of intuition.

Correctness of Intuitive Estimates of Statistical Parameters

Wolfe, Mary L. (1975) asked thirty-three students to guess the means of lists of two-digit numbers. The twenty-seven lists varied in distribution, i.e. their length, standard deviation, and skewness. She entered these variables as predictors into a multiple regression against error in estimation as the criterion. She found that these variables accounted for nearly all the error (multiple $R = 0.87$). The standard deviation was by far the best predictor of error in intuitive judgment. Wolfe also reports that the subjects used the mid-range and corrected this for skewness. Our model of intuitive thought explains these results by the recency effect of series conditioning. An intuitive feeling for similarity or repeated difference may be derived from the concordance or repeated discordance associated with successively presented pairs of data. A feeling for a moving average will be built up so that earlier differences which would contribute to a measure of standard deviation, would not contribute so much to the latter feelings of difference, so the predicted effect would be to intuit a mean closer to the last moving average with the error mainly accounted for by the actual standard deviation, as Wolfe found. Our theory also predicts that the order of presentation will influence the correctness of intuition, e.g. a trend from small to large data should give a larger intuitive mean than the same data presented in a decreasing trend. This is an easily testable prediction.

The above explanation of intuitive feelings of similarity and difference between successive pairs, implies accuracy of intuitive estimation of correlation accompanying the presentation of pairs of numbers. The following two results support this implication. Gray C.W.'s (1968) subjects had to predict from seeing pairs of cards, a number on each, what number goes with a presented card. There was a correlation between the numbers, but as our Theory of Intuitive Thought predicts, matching rather than optimization was used for prediction. Birnbaum, M.H. (1976) experimented on 'Intuitive numerical prediction', using two successions of correlated pairs. He gave subjects x values and asked them to predict y values; x values were given in pairs where the first had a correlation of 0·447 with y and the second a correlation of 0·894 with y. E then fitted various equations to the subject's estimates (models) and found intuitive predictions are most consistent 'with the relative-weight averaging model in which regressed subjective values are averaged using weights that depend on their validities' (p. 428). The validities are measured by the correlations showing, as we would expect, that subjects could not get a fairly accurate feeling for two correlations simultaneously, which would have needed them to build two different emotional sets simultaneously, one for each correlation. There are other reports of intuitive inference against known statistical parameters. Johnson, E.M. (1974) using a set of data of known reliability, asked twenty-two subjects to state which of two hypotheses the presented data supported and to state their subjective odds on this support for data of varying reliability. Compared with a Bayesian model E found that subjects' intuitive results could be explained by incorporating the reliability as a multiplicative weighting factor which leads to increasing inaccuracy as the reliability decreases. Evans, J. St. B. and Dusoir, A. E. (1977) experimented to find the effects of sample size on 'intuitive statistical judgment'. They asked subjects to judge parent population asymmetry from pairs of binomial samples. Results showed only one-third considered the sample size but in a simpler presentation of the same problem one-half considered the sample size. This again shows the considerable effect of presentation on the encouragement of intuitive judgment. Bogartz, R.S. (1976) found intuitive analysis and prediction of statistical interactions were often wrong. Fischbein, E. *et al.* (1967, 1970) considered the intuitive judgment of the number of combinations of five objects, also the intuitive estimation of the probability of throwing a double with two dice. For similar experiments see Kahneman, D. and Tversky, A. (1973), Levin, I.P. (1975), Parducci, A. and Sandusky, A. (1965), and Peterson, C.R. and Beach, L.R. (1957).

Distribution of Intuitive Errors

Brunswik, E. (1956) proposed that intuitive and analytical processes be identifiable by their effects upon performance. In particular, results of intuitive thought processes are 'uncertainty geared' and characterized by a preponderance of approximately correct responses. In contrast analytic thinking, he says, involves measurement and calculation, is 'certainty geared' and is characterized by a preponderance of precisely correct responses with an occasional bizarre response. To illustrate the different effects, Brunswik compared performance in a size-consistency task with performance in an arithmetic task involving numerical equivalence of perceptual clues. Peters, Joan T. *et al.* (1974) tested this prediction of Brunswik's by asking subjects for the fourth vertex of a parallelogram given three vertices under two presentations, (a) three points on a grid, and (b) three pairs of co-ordinates. Method (a) was considered intuitive and method (b) was considered analytical. The spread of errors was found to be as predicted by Brunswik, *viz.* intuitive errors were approximately correct with few precisely correct or highly erroneous whereas analytical errors were either completely correct or very wrong with fewer approximately correct answers. The authors say that these results indicate that whether or not an intuitive or analytic mode is used depends not only on the individual but also on the task. This experiment again shows, as Earle, T.C. (1972) and others have shown, that the type of presentation of the problem affects the elicitation of the intuitive approach as some presentations allow subjects to empathize more appropriately by experimenters using a perceptual visual concrete presentation.

Newton, J.R. (1963) in 'An investigation of intuitive and analytical thinking' also used Brunswik's definition of intuitive thinking as 'uncertainty geared' whereas: 'The certainty geared process of analytical thinking, however, was considered to be based on a few cues, and to operate in a single track all or none fashion' (p. 1). Newton gave two problems and considered first the subject's use of cues and secondly the error distribution. He asked the subjects to guess student grades from information about the students. He found in agreement with Brunswik's prediction that analytic errors gave a leptokurtic distribution whereas intuitive errors gave a normal distribution.

Sources of Error in the Intuitive Process

Intuition is seen here as a natural function most suitable to the immediate needs of the individual. As it satisfies these immediate needs, the intuition may always be considered as correct in the immediate situation. However, by other later or external criteria the intuition may be considered inappropriate or wrong. Being geared to the immediate need introduces to the intuition errors of perception due to present availability of information and the present emotional state of the intuiter. Intuitive processing by combinations of emotional sets determined by past experience introduces allo-logical errors, again only detectable by external criteria. Pushing the feeling model analogies past the point where they are no longer appropriate makes the decoded intuition incorrect in terms of the objects originally evoking feelings for the intuition.

The intuition is subjectively correct at the moment, harmonizing the present available data. It is only in comparison to later or other external data that the inaccuracies of intuition are apparent. However, the subject may have conflicting intuitions in different situations because of compartmentalized knowledge.

Distortions During Intuitive Perception

Four sources of error during intuitive perception are the actual noise of the information available, see Section 8.3 on how incomplete knowledge contributes to 'incorrect' intuitions; the interaction of perception with the emotional set; empathically evoking inappropriate feelings; and an innate lack of sensitivity resulting in crude encoding. This is not seen here as a fault but as a natural adaptation of the subject suitable to his present situation. Empathic projection may not provide an accurate translation of reality, it merely provides a 'workable fit': 'the most accurate grasp of reality is not necessarily the most efficient one' (Gardner, R.W. *et al.*, 1959, p. 6). Only by later criteria may the perception be shown to be inadequate and not by the subject's present needs.

Clark, F.V. (1973) points out that '. . . intuition which is filtered through the senses, the emotions or the rational mind is more susceptible to distortion' (p. 160). The first source of error to intuition is in the perception of its information where this very perception transforms the information through interaction with the present emotional set; yet the intuiter 'believes his assumptions to be true' (Bigge, M. L. and Hunt, M. P., 1965, p. 305).

There are experiments where subjects' perceptual judgment has been shown to be influenced by changed emotional states. Callaway, E. and Thompson, S.V. (1953) asked subjects to stand with one foot in iced water and select a standard stimulus equal to a distant object. The results were that subjects overestimated the size of the stimuli compared with control conditions. Singer, J. L. (1952) found the comparative stimuli were overestimated by subjects when (1) they held meaningful rather than meaningless symbols; (2) when subjects were motivated by betting on the size; (3) when subjects had been frustrated by fifteen minutes of insoluble tasks with *E* feigning alarm and despondency at their performance prior to the experiment. In a review of the relevant literature, Jenkins, N. (1957) concludes that the size of valued objects is accentuated in perception. For example Dukes, W. and Bevan, W. (1952)

asked children to judge the weight of jars filled with sweets and jars containing sand and sawdust. The sweets were judged heavier and with less variability. We often see what we want to see or what we expect to see: '...our imagination is another and still more serious source of error; for if from the nature of the circumstances we expect to see any expression, we readily imagine its presence' (Darwin, C., 1872).

Stang, D.J. (1974) points out that intuitions are based on the perception of information in the same way as the results of other experiments: '...intuitions are reality based and data produced by intuitions would be no different than data directly produced by the (experimental) manipulation' (p. 652). However, his experiments also show that subjects perceive according to what they expect, even if what they expected was wrong. Benjafield, J. (1969) used the Sander parallelogram optical illusion, Fig. 5.1/1. He showed that '...the strong perceptual effects' make the subjects go wrong in their comparisons (p. 286).

Allo-logical Errors of the Intuitive Process

That intuitive associations are made on criteria of common feeling rather than logical similarity is a further source of error. The Theory of Intuitive Thought claims that during the combination of emotional sets, responses are associated because of their common feelings which have been conditioned to the emotional set through the subject's idiosyncratic experience. For example, a person may be unique in frequently associating Hawaii with salt because once unknown to him someone spilt salt over his pineapple and its unexpected taste conditioned this association. The idiosyncratic conditioning of experiences may have a cultural commonality, as implied by Osgood's Semantic Differential, which would be a source of varying accuracy of intuitive perception between cultures as well as between individuals: 'The degree of exactness of the intuition of space may be different in different individuals, perhaps even in different races...' (Klein, F., 1894, p. 46).

This description by the Theory of Intuitive Thought is in agreement with Arieti, S. (1955) who calls this association on idiosyncratic experience 'palaeologic' or 'allo-logic' association. Arieti finds the schizophrenic and the intuitive are similar in that both accept identity based on identical predicates whereas Aristotelian logic accepts identity only on the basis of identical subjects. The predicate selected is called the 'identifying link'. He says emotional factors and idiosyncratic association determine which of the many predicates will be chosen as an 'identifying link', e.g. dogs have hair and teeth, cats have hair and teeth, therefore dogs and cats are intuitively the same, as they have the same feelings associated with them. This violates the Aristotelian principle of identity, contradiction, and excluded middle.

Similarly Guiora, A.Z. et al. (1965) quote Bergson's writings as suggesting 'that intuition is something that lies outside the boundaries of Aristotelian logic' (p. 111). They also associate intuition with schizophrenia through this allo-logical or palaeological thought based on 'identifying links' determined by emotional factors and idiosyncratic association (p. 116). They imply the difference in the process common to intuitive and the schizophrenic is that intuition is more accurate because appropriate feelings are evoked through empathy whereas schizophrenia lacks this empathy. Also intuition they say is a more voluntary involvement: 'In the teaching of some of the philosophers the distinction would be in the presence (in intuition) or absence (in schizophrenia) of empathy' (p. 117). This is consistent with the dual role of intuition in temporarily identifying with the object of the intuition while maintaining the integrity of the ego, see Section 6.3 on empathic projection, temporary identification through empathy and projection which is essential to the intuitive process.

Because intuitive processing depends upon associations to the present emotional set it is possible that '...intuitions in different situations may be in conflict' (Bahm, A.J., 1960, p. 7). Such a possibility guarantees that one of the intuitions will be incorrect by external criteria. Such a state of having different conflicting understanding for different situations is referred to as 'compartmentalization'. The Theory of Intuitive Thought would interpret this as the subject's concept map being such that the conflicting knowledge will be represented by different emotional sets far from each other (near zero transition probability). It is only when the intuitive process causes the association of these sets, usually through recentring, that such compartmentalization is annulled and the conflicting understanding intuitively recognized.

Subjective Consistency Makes Intuition Seem Correct

The intuition is correct in that it harmonizes all the subjective information presently available. This is felt as a concordance of feelings associated with the information in the emotional set of the intuition. Clark, F. V. (1973) points out that intuitive perceptions 'are experienced as true in the same way that sensory data is experienced as true' (p. 159).

Bayles, E.E. (1950) gives two criteria for the correctness of a solution to a problem. His first criterion is satisfied by the above explanation of the intuitive process. 'A problem can be considered solved beyond reasonable doubt when and only when (1) one proposed solution presents a pattern which harmonises all the data which have been obtained, (2) there are no data which are incompatible with that proposal' (pp. 108/109). In respect of his second criterion, the intuition only satisfying present data may be considered incorrect where other contradictory data are found. As the amendment of our concepts with new data is a natural development, it may be more plausible to consider an intuition as appropriate to the present situation and approximate to the correct answer rather than as an incorrect intuition. Where an absolute truth is considered to exist, insight has been defined as an approximation to this truth, e.g. Woodworth, R.S. (1940) defines insight as: 'Some penetration into the true nature of things' (p. 299).

Some philosophers and theologians believe that not all knowledge, absolute or otherwise, can be represented by true propositions. Hence such intuitive knowledge cannot be logically deemed incorrect against such propositions.

> The Western world and its education have been dominated by a prejudice about the nature of knowledge so powerful that it is hard to know how to begin to question it with any effect. The prejudice is, briefly, that all that can genuinely and properly be called 'knowledge' can be adequately stated or expressed in true propositions for which sufficient reasons can be given. (Reid, L.A., 1976)

Gödel has proved that true statements can exist beyond the proof of an axiomatic system.

For moral, religious, some mathematical problems and more mundane problems where there is no certain solution or where the complexity of a logical solution is beyond us, we have again to rely on the correctness of our intuition that may not be disproved through logical consideration. 'Intuition does not ordinarily function well in helping us know scientific facts about the physical world, but intuition is absolutely essential for knowing moral truths, for knowing the intended meanings of someone's physical products, and for knowing someone's general personality or a particular state of mind' (Conklin, K.R., 1970, p. 330). Reid (1976) says moral problems are '...done within a context which requires a cognitively intuitive feeling for the whole situation' (p. 16).

As discussed in Section 4.2 on the satisfaction accompanying confidence, intuitive knowledge brings with it a feeling of certainty which guarantees its authenticity and its immediate subjective correctness, but not its validity against some external criteria. Reid says: 'The feeling for the situation as a whole may give rise to cognitive claims stated with strong belief or conviction. But this is of course no guarantee of validity or truth'. Conklin, also gives examples of how intuition may be used to test the validity of knowledge outside of one's analytic understanding, e.g. '...the problem the citizen has in politically evaluating the pronouncements of experts' (p. 311); or a teacher assessing a student's original work which goes beyond the teacher's knowledge: '...the teacher must always rely upon the power of his empathy or intuition to certify the validity of any evidence produced by a student... the grade must be determined by the teacher's intuitive insight into the student's intended meanings and frame of mind' (pp. 330, 332).

The errors of intuition are apparent only when the immediate self-consistently correct intuition is later compared with external criteria. Hebb, D.O. (1946) says of intuitive judgments that '...as long as they remain intuitive and unverbalized their flaws are not demonstrable' (p. 89). The intuitive process of itself makes no such public comparison. 'Intuitive structures are different from logical structures in that intuitive structures cannot be used to substantiate an argument' (Giordana, G., 1976, p. 6). It is recognized that '. . . intuition is less rigorous with respect to proof' (Bruner, J. and Clinchy, B., 1966, p. 71). This is because, as Bigge, M.L. and Hunt, M.P. (1965) describe: 'Intuitive thought does not make use of publicly verifiable data, runs no tests on its hypothesis, and totally ignores the fact that its assumptions may be false or debatable' (p. 305).

8.2   ASSOCIATIONS WITH EGOCENTRICITY AND HYPNOGOGIC REVERIE

Both egocentricity and hypnogogic reverie are two seemingly unrelated phenomena that have been associated with intuition. The Theory of Intuitive Thought incorporates both of these phenomena. Firstly we will consider egocentricity. This is the eighth property of intuition with three references to it in Section 1.3.

Egocentricity has been considered as an early stage of cognitive development in which the inability of a child to distinguish between his own point of view and that of others is deemed a 'poor' type of thought out of which the child develops.

It is noticed in this section that the characteristics of egocentric thought are also those of intuitive thought in the adult as well as in the child. Further, empathic projection, an essential ability for intuition and which also most closely describes the process of egocentric thinking, is explained through developmental models in the literature. This evidence, viewed in the light of the structure proposed by the Theory of Intuitive Thought, suggests that, far from being a childish mode of vestigian thought, egocentricity is increasingly developed, controlled, and projected; resulting in the appropriate empathic projection ability of the adult intuiter.

This suggestion is opposed to Piaget's scheme of increasingly abstract cognitive development away from egocentric thought. It is proposed here that egocentric thought is developed as a tool for abstract thinking in terms of concrete feeling model analogies discussed in Section 6.2. Changing modal preferences and increasing accuracy of cross-modal transposition during development reflects, it is considered here, a greater freedom for the use of this tool.

Concomitants of Egocentricity and Intuition

Descriptions of egocentric thought are also descriptions that apply to the intuitive process. Sliker, Gretchen P. (1972) gives seventeen criteria for egocentric thought adapted from works of Piaget and Flavell (pp. 127/129). Corresponding to each of these seventeen criteria for egocentricity, she gives characteristics of creativity and their references (pp. 44/45). It is apparent from previous sections of this present investigation that all the characteristics of creativity that she gives corresponding to the criteria of egocentricity are concomitants of the intuitive aspect of creativity and are not concerned with the analytic stage of creativity. Her PhD thesis could well be renamed from 'Creativity of adults in light of Piagetian theory' to 'Intuition in adults in the light of egocentricity'. As such it is the primary source for this section.

In illustration there follows a selection of some of the criteria for egocentricity and their associated creativity traits that have previously been mentioned in this book as concomitants of intuition. Criteria of egocentricity from Sliker are given with their correspondence in the Theory of Intuitive Thought inserted (in parentheses):

Pure egocentricity ...lack of differentiation of self from environment (temporary identification with the environment, Section 6.3). Ultimate criterion — pure assimilation. Thought polarized toward preoccupation with personal satisfaction. Is the response one that is enjoyed by the respondent? (This corresponds to directing intuitive thought by increasing personal satisfaction, Section 5.5.) Is there expenditure of affective energy, for example, is there personal involvement in the response? (emotional involvement, Section 3.1). Romance and invention on what is given in reality (fantasy, Section 5.4). Person judgments of value rather than collective judgments of value (reliance on one's own feelings, Section 7.3). Personal schemas of analogy — also memories of earlier reasoning which control present course of reasoning without openly manifesting their influence (preconscious process and influence of previous experience, Sections 4.1 and 2.4). Invocation of personalized images (the use of personal feeling model analogies in intuition, Section 6.2). Syncretism — multitude of diverse things grouped into global, all-encompassing schema (structure giving global knowledge, Chapter 5). Is there a causal relation suggested between elements which only occurred simultaneously (intuitive similarity of elements conditioned to the same emotional set, Section 5.5). Animism — physical objects and events are endowed with the attributes of life, consciousness, will, etc. (projection of one's own feelings into objects, Section 6.3). Preconcepts — concepts are action-ridden, imagistic (intuitive thinking in the common kinaesthetic and visual modalities, Sections 3.3 and 6.3), and concrete rather than schematic and abstract (concrete thought facilitates intuition, Section 6.2). Lack of stability of identity (changing body boundary particularly during temporary identification, Section 6.3). Mental experiment. Isomorphic replica of concrete actions and events (rehearsal through feeling model analogies of concrete experience, Section 6.2). Predominance in the response of representation of overt action (common kinaesthetic representation, Sections 2.1, 3.2, and 6.2). Not just the possibility of something happening. It is happening now. Present tense. (Projection of present feelings, Section 6.3.) Attention to single striking feature of object to neglect of others causing distortion (distortion in intuitive perception, Section 8.1).

The following are the corresponding traits of creativity given by Sliker (with references) and previously discussed in this present investigation as concomitants of intuition — creator as centre of own world: felt thought: incubation: off-conscious mind of relaxed concentration: flexibility: inside identification with object: idiosyncratic acts as aids to creation: lack of justification: self as source of values: patterns of ideomotor action: impelling reality of dream and daydream: Preference for complexity — asymmetry, etc.

Other writers have discussed intuition or defined insight in terms of these criteria of egocentricity, particularly the criteria that relate to empathy, see Section 6.3. Peters, R.S. (1970) defined insight as entry into one's own or another's emotions: '...imaginative type of entering into one's own and other peoples' more recondite emotions, for which we use the term "insight" ' (p. 198). Evered, R.D. (1977) found intuitives '...are internally rather than externally oriented ...are self-generative in terms of their identity'. Westcott, M.R. (1964) found that intuitive types — regardless of success — tend to be introspective (p. 43); a necessity of egocentricity and empathy.

Empathic Projection is Developed Egocentricity

In the literature egocentricity is discussed in the same terms as empathy and projection. It has been shown here that criteria for egocentricity are mostly descriptive of intuition in adults as well as in children. This evidence considered with developed models of empathy suggests that empathic projection is developed egocentricity, in contrast to Piaget's view that egocentricity is a passing stage in early cognitive development. The reverse will then also be true, that is egocentricity may be considered as uncontrolled empathy. The above criteria of egocentricity are most similar to descriptions of empathy, see Section 6.3. For example, empathy phenomena 'occur when a spectator of an action performed by another person "lives" it himself to some extent and does not merely try to comprehend it in a purely intellectual way by classifying it into one conceptual category or another' (Mialaret, G., 1966, pp. 126/127). Also: 'The word "empathy" ordinarily means "putting yourself in the other fellow's shoes" or "taking on the feeling of the other guy" ' (Conklin, K.R., 1970, p. 331).

Egocentric thought implies a lack of control in the feelings evoked and in their projection, so that the child assumes that other people and objects share his feelings. Drever, J. (1974) says '...the fact that an individual can interpret the thoughts and acts of another only through his own experience has been called the egocentric predicament' (p. 80).

Piaget actually implies that egocentric thought is poor thought (Flavell, J.H., 1968, p. 156, echoes the same theme) and that the child's goal is, and should be, to move toward functional equilibrium. It appears, however, that the only negative qualities of the egocentric thought pattern in the young child are his inability to control the assimilatory and accommodatory functions and the limitation in his intellectual range resultant from the lack of more advanced mental skills. (Slikcr, Gretchen P., 1972, p. 13)

Shantz, Carolyn Y. (1975) describes egocentricity using typical empathy descriptions and says that egocentrism is present in adults under a different name, implying that adult empathy is a similar process to the child-like egocentric thinking: '...self-judgments are essentially judgments of how one felt or how one would feel in a situation, assuming the other person would have the same feeling. The assumption of identity is often called "egocentrism" in young children and "assumed similarity" in adults' (p. 19). Baldwin, A. (1966) also associates the adult's intuition with child-like thought: 'While the adult's intuition retains some of its child-like character, it is not childish thinking' (p. 84).

Our interpretation of adult empathy is not as an evaluation of the feelings of another, but the controlled projection of an abstraction of one's feelings. This is supported by the work of Piaget, J. and Inhelder, B. (1956) who showed that '...it is easier to form an abstraction of one's own viewpoint,' (p. 235) and by Stotland, E. (1969) who showed that when observers become empathically aroused, it is by imagining how they themselves would feel in the same situation, i.e. through a displaced egocentricity equivalent to empathic projection.

Developmental Model of Egocentricity

We have just discussed egocentricity in terms of empathy. Now Borke, Helene (1972) points out that empathy is closely tied to cognitive development (p. 108). Beres, D. and Arlow, J.A. (1974) also link it to ego development, saying that empathic ability increases with age: 'Empathy consists of more than an immediate affective response; it requires considerable ego development. Accordingly, the capacity for empathy increases with age and experience' (p. 34). Mialaret, G. (1966) also says that empathy is related to age (p. 113).

We may infer from this information that egocentricity also develops with age. This inference is directly supported by the following three experiments, showing that judgments based on a 'displaced' (projected) egocentricity improve with age. Flavell, J.H. (1968) positioned a doll around models of mountains and asked different-aged subjects to identify which of several photographs represented the doll's view. His results were that at four- to six-years-old, subjects always produced their own viewpoint. From six- to seven-years-old the subject realizes the doll sees something different from his own view but the different view is chosen at random. Seven- to nine-year-old subjects give partially correct results usually in one dimension only. Subjects of nine- to ten-years-old give the correct viewpoint of the doll. Pufall, P. B. (1973) using a similar Piaget-type 'what does it look like from there' experiment (e.g. Piaget, J. and Inhelder, B., 1956) showed that: 'Self-reference, then rather than decreasing in its functional importance seems to be more encompassing' (p. 174). In an experiment on the 'Development of spatial egocentrism and conservation across the life span' Rubin, K.H. *et al.* (1973)

similarly used models to test subjects' ability to take the other's perspective and found an improved ability with age.

The views of Cooper, L. (1970) are in agreement with this developmental view of empathy, as used in the intuitive process, being a developed controlled egocentric thought process. He sees '. . . empathy as intricately related to other cognitive and affective functions evolved in the course of psychological development' (p. 169). He says that the major conceptions of empathy as seen by Gestaltists, social learning theorists and others, may be viewed as descriptions of the empathic process at different levels of psychological development (p. 169).

> The older child can be more discriminating and controlled, i.e. selectively responsive, about his effect and/or behaviours. While one form of the empathic response is observed in the infant's reaction (egocentricity), the acquisition of secondary process skills does not necessarily and should not normally mark the beginning of the end of the individual's capacity to respond empathically. . . . I am suggesting that with greater psychic development these modes of reacting become more prominent, they involve an integration of previous modes. The previous modes of experiencing never completely disappear, except perhaps under particular, neurotic, defensive operations, and it is through the conditions conducive to the processes involved in an adaptive regression that these prior modes of empathic experiencing become available to the individual along with a controlled reawakening of the prior effects and earlier ways of thinking. (p. 170)

Empathy may occur at any stage of cognitive development, and is recognized as egocentricity in its early uncontrolled stage. It then undergoes '. . . qualitative changes — reflecting — the new problems of inner organization and object relationships posed by each advance in development' (Schafer, R., 1959, p. 345). The developed control of egocentricity is lacking in the schizophrenic but is available to the adult.

> The fully matured and highly differentiated adult mind is capable, up to a certain extent, of voluntarily assuming different attitudes in his perception and experience of the environment. He can be at one moment the detached observer; the next moment he can open himself receptively to all the impressions from the environment and the feelings and pleasures aroused by them; and in the next he can project himself in empathic experience of some object of the environment. In looking at a tree, for example, he can in one moment be the detached botanist who observes, compares, classifies what he sees; in the next moment he may surrender to the color of the foliage and bark, the sound of leaves rustling in the breeze, their fresh scent after a shower of rain; and in the next moment he may try to feel, inside of himself, kinesthetically how

slight or solid the trunk stands and rises up, how calmly the branches spread, or how gracefully they move and yield to the wind. He can combine these different ways of experiencing the quality of the tree or he can separate them and concentrate on one or the other. This differentiation and specialization of attitudes and capacities in experience is a quite late development. The young child is neither capable of detached observation nor of voluntary maintenance of, and concentration on one or the other of the described attitudes. (Schachtel, E.G., 1950, pp. 97/98)

Clark, F.V. (1973) says that during intuition 'the ego must stand aside in order to permit the experience. Interpretation and evaluation must be temporarily suspended or held in abeyance . . .' (p. 162). I believe the creative adult learns to do this whereas the egocentric child has not got this control. Koffka, K. (1933) reports that to a child, stimuli are saturated with emotional and human attributes, e.g. a walking stick is proud, hard toffee is angry.

Sliker, Gretchen P. (1972) developed a Piagetian instrument to measure egocentricity in adults (p. 61). She found that explaining natural causes and telling stories were both unsuitable test formats as the results were unnatural and childish respectively. Her final choice was to ask adults for an explanation of common scientific phenomena for which there is an inadequate explanation at present. She had difficulty marking her test as the scoring categories she defined overlapped. However, the appendix to her test instructions encourages the relaxed enjoyable atmosphere necessary for intuition and for her test of adult egocentricity; and therefore its format is recommended for tests of intuition. Her format was: 'So remember just relax, enjoy yourself, and think about these activities in any way that pleases you. Just set out to amuse yourself and have a good time' (p. 124). These are similar to instructions for administrating the SPEAK test which measures empathic ability, empathic projection ability, and intuitive ability.

Hypnogogic Reverie

We now consider how and why hypnogogic reverie is associated with intuition. This is the seventeenth property of intuition, with three references to it in Section 1.3.

Hypnogogic reverie is the seemingly chaotic associations of images and ideas that occur during very relaxed, near sleep-like states. In the last section on allological errors of the intuitive process we reiterated our theory that during the combination of emotional sets responses are associated because of their common feelings which have been conditioned to the emotional sets through previous idiosyncratic experience. During sleep-like states without the self-induced anxiety that initiates the intuitive process, these combinations of emotional sets can result in hypnogogic reverie. It is possible that one purpose of sleep is to reduce ego control sufficiently to allow information to be transferred to long-term memory by interweaving the emotional contexts that hold this information into other high-redundant emotional sets. The minimum ego control afforded by sleep states would allow maximally redundant emotional sets to be combined. This would be accompanied by allo-logical associations as experienced in dreams and in hypnogogic reverie. Hypnogogic reverie has been associated with intuitive thought and been reported during the intuitive stage of creativity. There are anecdotes of intuitions arising from the associations of these images, e.g. the benzene ring from the image of a snake swallowing its tail. Cartwright, Mary L. (1955) reports that an insight on how to construct a seventeen-sided polygon came to Gauss while he was in bed (pp. 18/19).

Intuition and reverie are further associated by reported common concomitants. Reverie-like intuition is reported as primary-process thinking. The reverie states are characterized by theta rhythms and low-frequency alpha rhythms. So is intuition. The non-competitive relaxed atmosphere in which reverie occurs also facilitates intuitive thought.

The Theory of Intuitive Thought describes hypnogogic reverie simply as the drifting of emotional sets without the drive of the initially self-evoked anxiety that 'starts' the intuitive process. This 'free-wheeling' combines emotional sets in the usual fashion, through feeling responses in common between them. The drifting is accompanied by no significant anxiety reduction as no discordant elements, which are responsible for the initial anxiety and the direction of the intuitive process, are present. Consequently the only intuitions that may occur during hypnogogic reverie are through the recentring method of combining emotional sets which gives the Eureka experience (Section 3.2). This is consistent with the reported anecdotes of intuitions occurring in these reverie states which seem to be Eureka experiences only.

Hypnogogic Reverie Associated with the Intuitive Process

Intuition has been linked to the dream-like states of reverie and these states are reported in descriptions of the personality of intuitive thinkers. Messer, Eunice A. (1967) says that the '...intuitive person may be quite out of touch with reality, seeing visions or having revelations and dreams' (p. 40). Szalita-Pemow, A. (1955) considers that commerce with the unconscious and with what he calls dream-like awareness, is necessary for the demonstration of intuitive behaviour.

Those who deliberately employ intuition in their work can use this relaxed state to evoke imagery and give knowledge of their feelings through introspection. Rallo, J. (1974) says that an artist may use intuition through introspective use of dreams and disconnected series of images. Resisting this reverie state inhibits intuitive thinking. As Szalita-Pemow (1955) comments: 'The understandable resistance on the part of the therapist to enter the dream state of the patient inhibits the therapist's "intuitive thinking" '(p. 18).

Investigators have found the preference for these reverie states is prominent in the personalities of intuitive thinkers. Evered, R.D. (1977) found intuitives 'prefer intangible imagery to the tangible sensible world'. The findings of Rachelson, S.E. (1977) not only link intuition to these reverie states, but also link it with the previously mentioned properties of sudden appearance (Section 7.2), the use of the right cerebral hemisphere (Section 5.2), and with the intuitive generation of scientific hypotheses (Section 7.3). He associates timeless, metaphorical, guided imagery with intuitive thought, which is performed by the right cerebral hemisphere and he says generates hypotheses in scientific enquiry.

Intuition and Hypnogogic Reverie are Primary-Process Thinking

Intuition is further associated with hypnogogic reverie through both being described as primary-process thinking. The conditions that induce primary-process thinking also facilitate hypnogogic reverie and intuitive thought. The intervention of ego controls to allow secondary-process-thinking, inhibits both intuitive thought and hypnogogic reverie. During sleep ego control is most relaxed. In this state images are clearly chained by their associated feelings — as described by the Theory of Intuitive Thought. Kinaesthesis clearly has a pronounced influence, e.g. the joke of the man who dreamed he was eating a giant marshmallow and awoke to find he had half-eaten his pillow. Common experiences also support this description, feelings like dreaming of fighting to free your arm and awakening to find it trapped under your body, or dreaming a cat is clawing your body and awakening to find your own nail marks in that part of your body.

Intuition is considered as primary-process thinking. Guiora, A.Z. *et al.* (1965) put forward Berne's view of intuitive thinking as primary-process thinking which must necessarily be inhibited by controlled ego states. 'If, as Berne maintains, the intuitive process is a faculty of the archaic ego, child ego stage, then its function is repressed when the adult ego state prevails' (p. 115). Szalita-Pemow, A. (1955) also considers that many aspects of adult cognitive processes act so as to prevent regression; see also Section 5.4 on the global process of intuition being restricted by ego-threatening anxiety. Guilford, J.P. (1966) describes 'the intuitive thinker' as 'the person who regresses occasionally and is playful and childlike, the visionary individual' (p. 89). Hammer, E.F. (1973) gives the primary-process thinking conditions of '. . . the relaxation of rationality; and the willingness to reach down into the preconscious and maintain an attitude of unfocused concentration [as] . . . Another factor in the liberation of a greater creative responsiveness and active intuition'.

Reverie states are similarly considered as primary-process thinking. Klein G.S.'s (1970) description of primary-process thinking could well be a description of hypnogogic reverie or intuitive thinking. 'Primary-process thinking is unreflective and lacking temporal orderliness; contradictory ideas are tolerated side by side; ideas freely shift about, and reversals of figure and ground occur easily' (p. 282): for example, as with the alternating perceptions of the facing profiles/vase of Rubin's illusion. Klein says that the characteristics of primary-process thought are to be found in 'reverie' states (p. 283). Primary and secondary processes are traditionally associated with wish fulfilment of the early development of the child and with defensive reactions in the psychiatric patient (e.g. Freud, S., 1916). However, Pollio, H.R. (1974) considers primary-process thinking in the same fashion as it is considered in this present investigation, that is not as regression in the usual derogatory sense but as allowing intuitive thought in normal adults. 'There are, however, in adult life a number of significant functions still motorized by primary process, slips of the tongue, dreams' (p. 152). He has attributed to primary processes the '. . . seemingly chaotic topic jumping that is extremely important in analysing the stream of free association, as well as the content of dreams and slips of the tongue' (p. 151).

Associations of Hypnogogic Reverie with Other Properties of Intuition

The existence of 'child-like' thinking of regressed ego stages in which adult intuition and reverie occur, supports the interpretation of the adult ability of empathic projection, essential to intuition, as developed, controlled egocentricity (Section 8.2). Beres, D. and Arlow, J.A. (1974) describe this experience: 'As self and object are one in their fantasy' (p. 35). Imagery, particularly kinaesthetic imagery as occurs in reverie, is a prominent modality for intuitive thought, see Section 3.1. The Theory of Intuitive Thought explains that the image/ideas of reverie are associated by their common feelings, which give them meaning. This idea is supported by Bower, G.H. (1972) in his model of 'Mental imagery and associative learning' in which he likewise considers the meaning of imagery as the mediator in mental associations. He also points out that concrete nouns produce the most vivid imagery as would be expected from the discussion in Section 6.2 which shows intuition is facilitated by concrete exemplars.

The Theory of Intuitive Thought proposes that anxiety is initially self-evoked and its gradual reduction is used by the intuiter to guide his intuitive process, Section 4.2. In this present subsection and elsewhere, intuition has been presented as primary-process thinking, e.g. see Section 7.3 on intuition and creativity as primary-process thinking. Independent support linking these two aspects of the Theory of Intuitive Thought comes from Zac, J. (1974). He considered Piagetian and general psychoanalytic primary-process thinking to outline the development of thought. He bases the origin of thought in the capacity to tolerate anxiety caused by the delay of action. As the Theory of Intuitive Thought proposes that intuitive processes do this, they may be considered as primary processes defined independently of the fact that they also fit the category of ego-regressed processes. 'Moreover, it is this capacity to bear frustration caused by delay that gives origin to thought' (p. 58). See

Section 7.3 which discusses how intuitive types are more willing to suffer discomfort during the delay in producing the fruits of their creativity.

At this stage of having considered seventeen properties of intuition, each described independently by the Theory of Intuitive Thought, it gives some confidence in the theory when so much independent evidence is increasingly interrelated by such a simple structure.

8.3   INTUITION CONSIDERED AS INSTINCTIVE OR AS INCOMPLETE KNOWLEDGE DEPENDENT ON THE ENVIRONMENT

Intuitive knowledge is sometimes considered to be innate or instinctive. We also sometimes use our intuition to arrive at judgments or courses of action although our knowledge seems too incomplete to justify such judgments or actions. 'Woman's intuition' appears to be of this kind. In this section we discuss firstly how the structure of emotional sets allows for a description of intuition as 'instinctive knowledge'. Then we will consider how too little or too much information can result in us having incomplete knowledge which we complement with what knowledge we do have, thus enabling us to use our intuitive process.

Why Intuition is Considered to be Instinctive

The consideration of intuition as instinctive knowledge is the thirteenth property of intuition with two references to it in Section 1.3.

Some writers consider intuition as an innate, instinctive knowledge or ability. Bouthilet, Lorraine (1948) in her PhD thesis on 'The measurement of intuitive thinking' found the word 'instinct' was frequently associated with intuition in the literature. Bergson, H. (1944) for example, says that intuition is a restricted type of insight which is related to other characteristics of intuition noted in this investigation. 'By intuition' Bergson says, 'I mean instinct that has become disinterested, self-conscious, capable of reflecting upon its object and of enlarging it indefinitely.'

Writers probably consider intuition as instinctive because:

(a) the immediate intuitive action seems involuntary as instinctive actions are;
(b) the dependence of intuition on the previous experience and learning has not been elucidated and is generally not recognized;
(c) intuition is a mode of thought that, in contrast to reasoning, is particularly noticeable in the young, who are more guided by instincts;
(d) the word instinctive is used in the lay sense to mean a natural preconscious unexplained process, which also describes intuition;
(e) Intuition it seems is common in varying degrees to all people in the same way as instincts.

Instinctive and Learned Intuitive Responses

The Theory of Intuitive Thought has described the intuitive process in terms of a structure of responses conditioned to emotional sets. However, many of these responses, associated with the physiological states instrumental in deciding emotional sets, are instinctive, see Section 3.2 on instinctive responses in emotional sets.

Peters, R.S. (1970) says that these instinctive responses can result from immediate intuitive appraisal. 'There is, too, the intermediary class of some reactions, which is typical of an unco-ordinated, protopathic type, that springs from an intuitive, sometimes subliminal type of appraisal of a situation' (p. 91). He gives an example of such an instinctive response resulting from an immediate intuitive appraisal. 'If we jump when we see a face at the window, our appraisal is immediate and intuitive, and our jump has an involuntary, protopathic character — quite unlike that of the high jumper' (p. 194). Intuitive actions based on instinctive responses to emotional sets are also discussed in Section 3.2, which shows how intuitive decision and action is derived from instinctive responses to evoked emotional sets. Clark, F.V. (1973) also notes how these instinctive 'approach-avoidance responses' may be used as the basis of intuitive evaluation.

> Sensations of constriction, tension, tingling, lightness, heaviness, trembling, and so forth, may give an early indication of personal response to another person or a situation which has not yet developed sufficiently for any rational evaluation to make sense. Likewise, intuitive awareness on a feeling level frequently performs an evaluative function in terms of approach-avoidance responses, or like and dislike responses, with no apparent justification. (p. 161).

The individual's experience gradually conditions other concordant responses to the same emotional sets that include these instinctive responses. So as he develops he may use his instinctive responses and learned responses to guide his intuitive thinking more appropriately to increasingly subtle variations in his environment, from the mainly instinctive intuitive response of the child to the more differentiated intuitive behaviour of the adult. However, Guiora, A. Z. *et al.* (1965) report that Bergson only attributes these instinctive, rather than learned, responses to intuition: 'True intuition differs from the capacity resulting from learning, experiencing and routine ...understanding' (p. 111). Our proposed structure of emotional sets incorporates instinctive stimuli/responses, learned stimuli/responses and non-discordant contiguous stimuli/responses. This allows us to infer that a baby's intuition is composed predominantly of instinctive stimuli/responses and that we include more learned stimuli-responses in our intuition as we develop.

Hence, through experience a person's behaviour, which is initially instinctive, becomes more differentiated and appropriate to differing situations: from a pure instinctive response to an immediate emotional stimulus developed to the stage of including an instinctive response with learned responses subjectively appropriate to the feeling evoked through empathic projection, appropriate even to imagined situations. For example, the instinctive drive to escape from a threatening closed space might later provide feeling model analogies in a variety of 'pressure' situations. Examples are highly idiosyncratic and therefore may not be appreciated by the reader, who probably is not in the regressive mood necessary to evoke the appropriate meaningful feelings. Feelings, for instance, evoked through a temporary identification with a liquid under an increasing pressure in a closed container. So he may intuitively feel how the liquid will try to escape, searching the inner surfaces of the container for any crack or weakness more frantically as the pressure increases until forcing a fissure gives the sudden relief of freedom and an associated drop in pressure. Examples abound in the lay literature and the literature on scientific creativity (Section 6.3) of such personification of natural events which may be appreciated through a temporary identification engaging the reader's instinctive as well as learnt responses. Piaget's consideration of intuitive thinking as concurrent with his concrete operational stage of development may be interpreted as the external stimuli representing the concrete object being necessary to engage the intuitive responses in the young, whereas at a later stage the same instinctive feelings may be evoked through their inextricable association with the memory of the stimuli.

The body feedback processes on which intuition and retaining homeostasis depend, is also an instinctive ability. Although this interpretation is consistent with intuition as instinctive it is also consistent with a developmental (egocentricity to adult empathic projection) and controlled sensitivity (biofeedback), view of intuition that indicates intuitive ability may be pedagogically improved.

Incomplete Knowledge

Incomplete knowledge is the sixteenth property of intuition with two references to it in Section 1.3.

Writers have commented that we use intuition in situations where we have incompleete knowledge. Our knowledge may be incomplete because the information is too sparse to allow an analytic solution or because the information is so complex that we are unable to comprehend it all. In both cases we resort to the intuitive mode of thought. 'Faced with a problem where the data are too sparse or too complex to suggest a clear route to solution, one chooses, intuitively, a path that seems possible or probable' (Clinchy, Blythe, 1975, p. 50). In Section 5.1 it is pointed out that under such circumstances, where the information is either insufficient or too complex for the analytic process, the intuitive mode of thought is the default mode. Bruner, J.S. (1963) also pointed out how intuition is most effective in a complex situation which highlights our incomplete knowledge. 'At the risk of redundancy, the point is repeated that a teacher has few knowns in a classroom; within this complex situation, the more willing and effective intuitional behaviour is more likely to lead to whatever learning goals are specified.'

Incomplete knowledge characterizes 'uncertainty' situations suitable for intuitive thought. Brunswik, E. (1956) considers intuition as an 'uncertainty geared process' (Section 8.1) and Baldwin, A. (1966) analyses this as an aspect of intuition from his considerations of its general usage, *viz.* '...formation of hunches in uncertain situations' (p. 85).

Incomplete Knowledge Incorporated with Internal Information for Intuitive Processing

It was discussed in Section 5.1 how by deliberately giving incomplete information experimenters have tried to encourage subjects' use of the intuitive mode. In particular evidence was cited to support the proposition that inadequate external information is supplemented by the subject's own redundancy-rich internal information, incorporating it into his global knowledge for intuitive processing. Allport, G.W. (1929) defines intuition as '...grasping events as fraught with meaning in relation to a totality' (p. 14), i.e. it is part of the intuitive process to attribute meaning to the incomplete knowledge in order to incorporate it into the intuiter's total global knowledge.

By incorporating the incomplete knowledge into his redundancy-rich internal information the subject has the potential ability to process it intuitively, giving, for instance, the confidence of intuitive judgments which seems objectively unjustified by the externally available evidence. De Groot, A.D. (1965) gives an example of this working in chess, where the player naturally recognizes his incomplete knowledge in the light of many variables including the vast number of complex combinations of moves and their outcomes. Yet De Groot recognizes that the player uses his intuition to give him the confidence to make a move in the face of such objectively inadequate knowledge. 'In chess nearly every argumentation is incomplete and decisions are based on necessarily incomplete evidence. There is a strong need for "intuitive completion" to enable the subject to build up the subjective certainty he requires for actual decisions' (p. 150), see Section 4.2 on the subjective certainty that intuitions are correct. Naturally, the more sparse the immediate knowledge then the greater is the likelihood that it is incorporated with inappropriate internal knowledge, increasing the probability of objectively incorrect intuitions discussed in Section 8.1 where we considered that intuition need not be correct.

Incomplete Knowledge Contributing to 'Incorrect' Intuitions

Bigge, M.L. and Hunt, M.P. (1965) point out that '...one's direction or purposeful activity in his life space is dependent upon its cognitive structure. A completely new situation would be cognitively unstructured and a person would have no knowledge of what would lead or point to what. Thus at that moment his behaviour would be completely random' (p. 357). Such a situation illustrates 'no knowledge' rather than 'incomplete knowledge'. However, no situation is ever 'completely new' and the subject is always able to use what is not new in the situation to evoke the subjectively appropriate emotional set in which to incorporate the incomplete knowledge available from the situation, i.e. to 'see it' or understand it in his own way. As he then acts according to his total internal information his behaviour is never random, i.e. without purpose, even in such a fairly new situation. It may be that the vacillating behaviour observed in new situations or in frustration is an attempt to enhance physiological variability to increase the probability of evoking an emotional set with more appropriate responses, i.e. more easily associated knowledge with which to incorporate the incomplete knowledge of the new situations and the probable cause of frustration.

Dependence on Environment

This is the nineteenth property of intuition with one reference to it in Section 1.3. 'Degrees of intuitive awareness may be affected by such factors as time, place, mood, attitude, state of consciousness, and innumerable idiosyncratic variables' (Clark, F.V., 1973, p. 166).

The environment is particularly important to the intuitive process in three ways.

(1) The cultural and specific situations in which the subject develops contribute to fashioning the personality characteristics that promote intuitive thinking and contribute to the specific experiences that condition his responses to particular emotional sets.
(2) The immediate environment for intuition should be relaxed, familiar, and free from stress.
(3) During periods of relaxed disassociated thought a particular experience from the immediate environment, usually associated with non-vigorous familiar movement, can 'spark' the recentring type of insight resulting in the Eureka experience.

We will now consider each of these effects of the environment on intuition.

Cultural Influences on the Intuitive Type

Comella, T. (1971) says '...environment can be demonstrated to have influences upon creative development' (p. 177). Although there are immediate environments that facilitate intuition and creativity (see below), Comella points out that cultural environments can inhibit the '...psychological qualities which creative personalities display' (p. 177). He gives the following five cultural environmental influences that inhibit creativity:

(1) Desire to be accepted by others works toward the elimination of individualistic traits, promoting conformity.
(2) Progressive encounter with civil laws and social rules prompts most people to adopt prescribed patterns of thought, as well as behaviour.
(3) Systematic methodology of educational systems inadvertently stifles curiosity and restricts intellectual activity to conventional techniques. Our institutes of learning are oriented more toward teaching what to think rather than how to think.
(4) The learned axiom 'the majority rules' is equated with 'the majority is right' in the minds of many people. This error further restricts the thinking process. Majority opinions and approaches are heavily relied upon.
(5) People develop habits of thought which are as resistant to change as behavioural habits. Newton's first law of motion — describing how an object's momentum resists changes in speed and direction unless acted upon by an external force — is equally descriptive of the mental ruts people dig for themselves. (p. 177)

In agreement with (3) above cultural influences that have inhibited and are inhibiting intuitive thought in education, particularly in mathematical education, are further discussed in Chapter 9 of Bastick, T. (1979).

How the environment in which a person develops gives him the experiences conditioning particular responses to various emotional sets for later intuitive processing is discussed in Section 2.4, which is concerned with the influence of experience, property 5.

Non-repressive Environments Facilitate Intuitive Thought

Writers have commented on the need for a non-repressive environment during the intuitive stage of creative thought. Yanoff, J.M. (1972) points out that an environment that eliminates repression will encourage intuitive thinking. In repressive environments subjects' failures are punished by an attack on their egos. An example is personal criticism in the presence of peers. While the subject is not free to risk failure he will tend to use the analytic mode which enables him to justify his results. 'A social climate is essential which will balance stress and reward in such a way that the student will feel free to risk failure and loss of self-esteem in an attempt to cope with a problem which is meaningful to the group with whom he has identified' (Provus, M.M., 1966, p. 133). Similarly Bruner, J.S. (1962) says of intuition: 'It is founded on a kind of combinatiorial playfulness that is only possible when the consequences of error are not overpowering or sinful' (p. 102).

Writers have said that creative people know the rules and when to break them. In repressive environmnts this necessitates taking the risk of public censure. Risk-taking has already been discussed as a correlate of intuitive thinking in Section 7.3. Many of the practical insight experiments are seen to imply taboos, e.g. experiments requiring the breaking of beads in order to rearrange them (Bulbrook, Mary, E., 1932). The inhibiting factor in such cases seems to be an acceptance of these inferred restrictions and the 'trick' is to ignore the restrictions. I believe that ignoring them is influenced by the 'risk' implied in the degree of repression of the immediate environment. To facilitate creative thought experimenters have given 'warm encouragement' to their subjects (e.g. Jensen, K. 1960, p. 27). Thus a permissive environment should be used during testing and experiments concerned with intuition.

The inhibiting effect of stress on the subject's ability to build and use the structure proposed by the Theory of Intuitive Thought has been discussed in Sections 2.3 and 3.1. Cowen's view that the subject's ability 'to form broad comprehensive cognitive maps' in a stress-free environment supports the use of the proposed structure in the facilitory rather than inhibitory direction (Cowen, E.L., 1952). In particular, in a stress-free environment a subject is more able to form the emotional sets and their linkings which are the base of concept formation and intuitive thought. In Cowen's experiments on problem-solving he found in such a stress-free environment 'he [the subject] is able to form broad comprehensive maps which later allow him to shift readily to a more parsimonious problem-solving behaviour when the external situation makes such a path to the goal available' (p. 517).

The contrast between intuitive and analytic thought (Section 2.1) is reflected in the contrast between the environments facilitating each of these modes of thought. 'Highly restricted learning situations seem to produce Skinner-type results. Considerable amount of freedom during the learning situation, favours insightful learning' (Bigge, M.L. and Hunt, M.P., 1965, p. 297). Castadena, A. et al. (1956) similarly found that an environment with a lack of anxiety is a requirement for creativity. Anxiety, e.g. competition, encourages rote learning but hinders creativity and complex learning tasks, especially in new situations. Other experimental studies have reached the same conclusion, e.g. Taylor, J.A. and Spence, K.W. (1952) agree that a low-anxiety environment encourages creativity and the opposite is true for rote learning.

The need for a non-repressive environment, in which the intuiter is free to take risks without having to defend his ego, relates to the previously discussed view of intuition as a primary rather than secondary process in Sections 4.1, 7.3, and 8.2. For as Klein, G.S. (1970) points out: 'A great loss of ego autonomy from drives is reflected in primary-process dominated thought; on the other hand, rigidly emphasized secondary-process thinking exemplified either an undue fealty of the ego to environmental fact or to be constantly geared for defense' (p. 283). Non-repressive, relaxed, non-threatening environments that encourage both intuitive thought and reverie (Section 4.1) have also been found to encourage subliminal perception which has been shown to be part of intuitive perception (Section 5.2). Eagle, M. (1962) reports some conclusions concerning these same conditions under which a subliminal effect is most likely to be facilitated. Namely (1) a state of dispersed attention or relaxation; (2) a suspension of reality testing; (3) provision of a task which allows response on the basis of guesses, intuitions, vague cues, memory impressions, subjective evaluation; and (4) stimuli which are unstructured and unclear. Comella, T. (1971) similarly says: 'It [insight] usually comes when the conscious mind is passive' (p. 175).

Environments Sparking Eureka Experiences

When the environment is such that the above conditions for intuitive thinking are satisfied, it may offer a particular experience, usually an often repeated familiar kinaesthetic experience, that triggers the recentring type of insight resulting in the Eureka experience. For example, Newton observing the falling apple, Archimedes taking a bath, James Watt watching the kettle boil, Poincaré's Fuchsian functions that occurred to him whilst getting on a bus (Comella, T., 1971, p. 176; Cartwright, Mary L., 1955, p. 19). Section 4.1 shows that the Theory of Intuitive Thought explains this by the feelings aroused through such activity being in common with those of the 'problem' emotional set which allows recentring. The subject is particularly sensitive to such feelings during regressed ego states. Hutchinson, E.D. (1941) describes these same conditions as those in which the recentring type of insight, as appears after an incubation period, is reported to occur:

> Insights, aside from those which appear while one is deliberately engaged upon the problem come most frequently, I believe, under three preferred conditions: during or just after periods of rest and relaxation; in periods characterized by a slight degree of mental dissociation; during periods of light physical activity, usually of a more or less repetitive and automatic character. (p. 33)

It is clear from the examples he gives that such insight is occasioned by emotional and kinaesthetic stimuli often during 'mental disassociation' or 'reverie' states (pp. 34/35).

Comella, T. (1971) gives an explanation that also shows that the environment in which reverie may occur can trigger an insight that links the present experience to the emotional sets to which the problem was associated, which supports the interpretation of the evidence by the proposed structure of the Theory of Intuitive Thought. 'Insight is triggered by a specific experience, whether that experience is in the form of an actual event, a dream, or a vision ...Elements in the triggering experience are transposed into the framework of the problem providing what seems to be the last crucial link in the emerging concept' (p. 175).

Environments Created by Eccentrics

The social and personal eccentricities of creative workers are well documented. For example Haefele, J.W. (1962) reports that Carlyle tried to build a soundproof room; Emerson left his family and rented a hotel room; Freud chain-smoked; Kipling could not write creatively with a lead pencil (p. 90). These are seen, in the light of the Theory of Intuitive Thought, as an effort to induce the body state necessary for intuitive thought by deliberately duplicating selected environmental stimuli which were present in previous non-repressive environments in which intuitions were experienced. Cartwright, Mary L. (1955) quotes Professor J. E. Littlewood as stating in agreement with this: 'the truth [is] that for serious work one does best with a background of familiar routine' (p. 14).

During an effort of creative thought in such a personally familiar environment, some creative people are observed to have nervous or anxious mannerisms and to take the most eccentric stances to go through unusual limb movements. The paradoxical nervous or anxious mannerisms in such non-stressful familiar environments are seen here as behavioural responses associated with the self-induced internal environment of anxiety necessary for the guidance of the intuitive process explained in Section 4.2. The eccentric posturings are interpreted as a means of encouraging drift to more appropriate emotional sets through common kinaesthetic responses. These occur at points in the intuitive process when the gradual release of the initial tension is temporarily halted and felt as a momentary frustration.

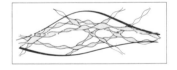

Organization for Describing Thought and Behaviour

Our theory is simply that we emotionally encode information. Our thoughts and behaviours are the decoded versions of this information which, associated by their contiguous common feelings, tend to be recalled when we re-experience these emotions. Often, similar information is associated with different emotions. Our thoughts and behaviours tend to increase this, assuring content duplication.

The theory is presented in this chapter as an organization for describing thought and behaviour. This organization synthesizes the ideas and research findings discussed in Chapters 1 to 8. It shows that intuition is a fundamental process of thought and behaviour that results from this organization.

9.1   THEORETICAL BACKGROUND

The organization is a consideration of thought/behaviour resulting from processing information coded by 'feelings' and organized by being associated as response tendencies to overlapping emotional sets. The content of thought is then the cognitive components of the responses realized when a subject is in a particular emotional set.

Thought and behaviour change as the subject drifts from one emotional set to the next. The next emotional set occupied by the subject will tend to be the one which most overlaps the present emotional set. During the change, the duplicated response tendencies will be reinforced, making the path of drift more probable in future. The overlapping duplication of response tendencies between emotional sets is here termed 'redundancy'.

Before describing the organization and how we use it we will clarify how we are using the term 'redundancy'. During the early 1980s the word redundancy gained the bad connotations of unemployment. If a machine duplicated your job then you were made redundant. So redundancy, which means duplication, became associated with unemployment. In this book the word redundancy does not refer to losing your job but has the same meaning as it does in information theory. It means duplicated or common information. Duplication gives us alternative ways of doing things, which is useful because it allows us to have several options open. Duplication of information allows us to check consistency to reduce errors, which is also useful. The concept of redundancy as used in this book refers to something useful that we wish to increase, namely duplicated information. If someone has two things to tell you, and they are completely independent, he has one Binary digIT's worth of information. This is abbreviated as one BIT of information. But if the two things are not independent, that is one thing partially duplicates the other so that knowing one you will know part of the other, then he has less than one bit of information. If they duplicate say a quarter of their information then there is a quarter of a bit redundancy and only three-quarters of a bit information. The twenty-six letters of the alphabet illustrate how we all intuitively use redundancy. If we see the letters one at a time and have no idea what letter is coming next, then each letter holds $\log_2 26 = 4 \cdot 2$ bits of information. But when used for spelling words, the letters are not uniformly random. For example in 'queen', 'quiet', 'quarry', and 'quantity' a 'u' follows 'q'. When we see a 'q' we expect a 'u' next so 'q' and 'qu' are redundant: the 'qu' is merely duplicating the 'q'. Redundancy in spelling cuts the information in each letter to about $1 \cdot 4$ bits. We use the $4 \cdot 2 - 1 \cdot 4 = 2 \cdot 8$ bits of redundancy to know intuitively when a word in English is misspelt, even if we have never seen the word before. Words like 'qhom', 'xcft' and 'zcmx' intuitively just do not look right. Thought and behaviour, particularly intuitive thought and behaviour, use redundant information which is encoded by the stimuli and responses that make up our feelings and is duplicated by our senses. For example, when what we see does duplicate what we hear, then we are more likely to accept it intuitively, but a baby that talks with a man's voice, a bee that 'chugs' instead of 'buzzes', a strawberry-flavoured egg, etc., would not be intuitively acceptable. Information duplicated by different senses allows cross-modal transfer and transposition.

A tendency to increase redundancy – a natural parsimony – is postulated as a basic organizing principle of thought and behaviour.

This organization describes and relates many thought and behaviour processes.

Primary-process thinking may be described as a result of combining highly redundant emotional sets whereas secondary thinking may be described as a result of combining 'smaller' less redundant emotional sets. Intuitive thought is directed primary-process thinking. It is directed by the need to resolve an initiating non-ego-threatening anxiety due to a problem situation tending to evoke different emotional sets in the intuiter which have conflicting response tendencies, giving cognitive dissonance. The resolution of this initiating anxiety is concomitant with increasing redundancy. The resolution of anxiety is the cue by which the subject is aware that he is on the right track, without knowing the goal, and by which he identifies the final intuition. The last large proportional decrease in this anxiety, to an acceptable level, causes the subject to notice the change to the emotional set terminating the intuitive process and consciously to label its responses as the intuition. The theory points to a fundamental difference between people. The essential difference between the intuitive type and the non-intuitive type is the highly redundant structure of the emotional sets available to the high-intuitive type but not to the low-intuitive type. Further, to use this structure the intuitive type needs to be emotionally self-sensitive and able to evoke the initiating anxiety. The initiating self-evoked anxiety is identified with 'curiosity'. Its resolution through the intuitive process reinforces the future choice of this mode of thought.

The theory predicts that individuals will exhibit certain abilities. The organization of information by emotional sets requires the use of empathy to evoke feelings subjectively appropriate to the information, often initially emotionally neutral information from the environment. Attributing the processed information to the appropriate situation, requires projection of these feelings to the objects associated through empathy with the feelings. Hence, empathic projection is a necessary ability of the intuitive type. From the intuitive type's ease of emotional drift and combination of emotional sets it follows that the intuitive type is more emotionally variable than the non-intuitive type.

Control of ego state allows an individual to control and change the level of redundancy at which he processes his organization. This control distinguishes the intuitive type from the creative type. The creative type has a control over his ego state that enables him both to keep constant and to shift more easily between directed primary thought (intuitive processing) and secondary thinking (for analytic processing). In this way, the intuitive process is used to furnish the original idiosyncratic inspiration and to guide the analytic verification in creativity.

> The manner in which the mathematician works his way towards discovery, by shifting his confidence from intuition to computation and back again from computation to intuition, while never releasing his hold on either of the two, represents in miniature the whole range of operations by which articulation disciplines and expands the reasoning powers of man. (Polanyi, M., 1966, p. 131)

One example of the use of this proposed organization which has traditionally given some difficulties is to identify differences between types of creativity. To identify for example the different aptitudes contributing to scientific, artistic, or mathematical creativity. The basic difference in types of creative ability is not in the content-specific technical ability but is determined by combinations of the degree of ego control of the creator and the redundancy of his emotional sets. The degree of redundancy which decides his level of intuitive ability, matches the freedom in accepting the initial problem constraints. The control of constancy of ego state matches the required continued intuitive or analytic thought, and control of frequent switching of ego state matches the choice and guidance of analytic verification. The controlled change from secondary to primary thinking allows a tolerance of incompleteness not acceptable in secondary thought.

The theory's description of the processes evolved in creativity may be summarized as follows:

(1) secondary-process thinking results from the combination of sparsely redundant emotional sets;
(2) primary-process thinking requires the combination of highly redundant emotional sets;
(3) intuitive types utilize this redundant structure by evoking an initial anxiety in a low level of redundancy that they resolve by combining emotional sets at a higher level of redundancy to give the intuition, which is the response tendencies of the terminating emotional set;
(4) creative types are intuitive types with control of constancy and change of ego state determining their level of redundancy.

Other phenomena of thought and behaviour, rather than intuitive thought in particular, occur if the initiating non-ego-threatening anxiety is not available in a relaxed ego state, allowing the combination of emotional sets at a high level of redundancy.

We may illustrate the organization by a hierarchical network of emotional sets as illustrated in Fig. 9.1/1. Phenomena such as personality type, cognitive style and creative, intuitive, and empathic ability, may be described more precisely in terms of this structure and in terms of how we process this structure by our progress through it.

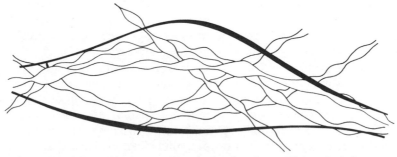

Fig. 9.1/1 Hierarchical network of emotional sets illustrating the organization

358

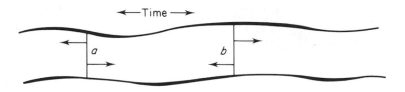

Fig. 9.2/1   Band of continually changing emotional states

9.2   STRUCTURE OF THE ORGANIZATION

The following diagrams and explanations build stage by stage to illustrate this hierarchical network of emotional sets. In Fig. 9.2/1 the wavy band represents all the detectable stimuli amplitudes and stimuli changes in the subject. These include all the slightest skeletal hormonal, visceral, muscular, etc., etc., stimuli to which the body is self-sensitive. The width of the band represents the range of these stimuli. The vertical line *a* represents the emotional state of the subject at an instant in time. The emotional state is the totality of all these stimuli at a particular instant. This emotional state is continually changing in time as the myriad stimuli change. This change is represented by the horizontal arrows. Similarly line *b* represents the emotional state of the subject at some other instant in time when there is a different totality of stimuli within the body giving this different emotional state. However, because of the integrating regulatory feedback systems of the body the myriad detectable stimuli do not change independently but at some times conglomerations of stimuli act in accord. This, for example, helps to retain homeostatis, co-ordinate stimuli to precipitate integrated responses, etc., etc. Groups of stimuli precipitate responses which act as further stimuli. Because internal stimuli and responses may both act as stimuli we shall make no distinction between them and will refer to them as internal stimuli/responses. These common characteristics of the emotional states are preserved over time.

These more lasting characteristics of the transient emotional states we refer to as a physiological set. The undulations in the band of emotional states in Fig. 9.2/2 which illustrate the changing range of stimuli/responses as they reinforce or cancel each other, represent the building and decay of the common characteristics of these emotional states over time.

Combinations of these conglomerations of stimuli acting in accord define more and less integrated response tendencies. A particular response tendency may be realized as a response if more of the stimuli/responses that comprise the emotional state are constituents of that particular response tendency rather than some other competing response tendency. These response tendencies, which include cognitive response tendencies, are associated with the physiological set. Extreme physiological sets like hunger or fear get their names from their response tendencies. Here we are also considering much less

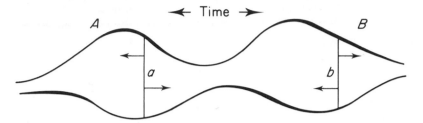

← Time →

Key A and B are physiological sets
         a and b are changing instantaneous emotional states

Fig. 9.2/2 Physiological set as a succession of emotional states in which
stimuli act in accord

extreme and more subtle physiological sets in which a person may be found at
any time.

The response tendencies may be instinctive or conditioned. There will also
be contiguous stimuli/responses which, if conditioned, will become future
response tendencies. Together with the physiological set these response
tendencies comprise the emotional set. All of our response tendencies
represent our total knowledge. The more we have the more we know.

Fig. 9.2/3 illustrates two similar emotional sets with some response
tendencies in common, i.e. some redundancy. The arrows denote that being in
an emotional set gives the possibility of a particular response. Also the
occurrence of a particular response/stimulus gives the possibility of evoking

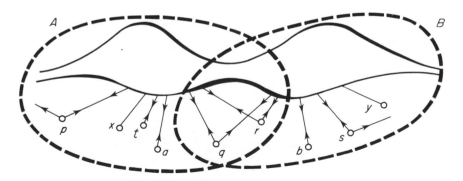

Key A and B are emotional sets
         a and b represent instinctive responses
         p, q, r, s and t represent conditioned stimuli/responses
         x and y represent contiguous stimuli/responses

Fig. 9.2/3 Two emotional sets with some redundancy

the emotional set to which it is conditioned. For example, when we are in a sexy mood or emotional set, we tend to have sexual thoughts and behaviour. Or if we experience a sexual stimulus or sexual behaviour, this tends to evoke a sexy mood. Similarly, for much less physiologically extreme emotional sets as when a particular noise 'puts us in mind of' a situation in which we usually expect to hear that noise.

It will be noticed that the redundant responses, q and r, contribute to the drift between emotional sets; for being in emotional set A one will tend to realize responses q and r which, acting as stimuli, will tend to evoke emotional set B. The probability of going from emotional set A to emotional set B is termed the transition probability T_{AB}. This transition probability results from the natural directional change of physiological sets p_{AB} and the contribution of the redundant (shared) response tendencies.

The transition probabilities between emotional sets define chains of probable associations. These chains can be linked by highly redundant emotional sets, i.e. emotional sets with many response tendencies in common with more than two other emotional sets. This is illustrated in Fig. 9.2/4 where while occupying emotional set Q, it is highly likely, because of the shared response tendencies, to drift to any of the emotional sets R, S, T, or U.

For example, if Q is an emotional set categorizing emotional contexts to do with cars, then it is possible to go from this emotional set to R, S, T, or U where each of these emotional sets, although different from all the others, shares response tendencies with Q concerning cars. Emotional set R may categorize emotional contexts of driving, perhaps a driving holiday. Emotional set S may categorize the emotional contexts of car parts, perhaps their safety or maintenance. Emotional set T may categorize the emotional contexts of the costs associated with running the car, perhaps tax, insurance,

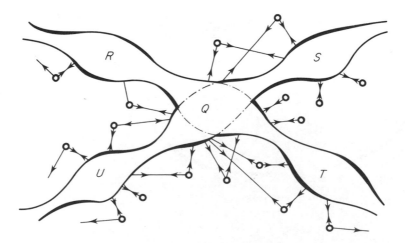

Fig. 9.2/4 Highly redundant emotional sets linking chains of probable associations

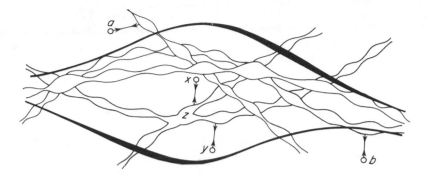

Fig. 9.2/5 Highly redundant nodes in the network of emotional sets of high transition probability

fuel, whereas emotional set U may categorize the emotional context of ownership concerned with perhaps a macho image if one owns a sports car. Any one of $R, S, T,$ or U will lead on to other emotional sets with common associations which have probably less in common with Q. Or one may return again from any of $R, S, T,$ or U back to Q.

The transition probabilities between emotional sets define a network of such linking emotional sets which are the most probable paths of associations. Part of this network is illustrated by Fig. 9.2/5. As an aid to visualization it is what you might see if you 'stood back' so to speak from the part of the network shown in Fig. 9.2/4 and could see the wider field of view shown in Fig. 9.2/5. The parsimony of using different combinations of similar concordant stimuli to constitute physiological sets, and the responses in common between emotional sets, ensures the redundancy of this network. This redundancy is illustrated in Fig. 9.2/5 by the links between the emotional sets. Emotional sets which form nodes of the network are highly redundant because they have many response tendencies in common with the many adjacent emotional sets of high transition probability, rather than only having responses in common with two emotional sets, namely one on either side as in a linear chain. In Fig. 9.2/5 many emotional sets are shown unconnected because their transition probabilities are low; that is it is unlikely that the subject will occupy two such emotional sets consecutively. The nodes or junctions of the network that allow us different ways to associate our knowledge, represent our understanding. This defines understanding as ways of associating knowledge. The more nodes, or highly redundant emotional sets, we have in our network then the more understanding we have. In general the more redundancy then the more understanding we have. If similar knowledge is conditioned to two emotional sets with low transition probability, say in the unlinked chains at a and b of Fig. 9.2/5, then this knowledge is compartmentalized. That is, it is not associated or understood. Although we know a and b we do not understand their similarity because we cannot associate them. For example, a child may know $2 \times 4 = 8$ and may know $4 \times 2 = 8$ but treat these as two unrelated number facts. But if the similar knowledge is conditioned to two emotional sets with high transition probability, say in the linked chains at x and y of Fig. 9.2/5 then the link Z gives a means of associating this similar knowledge; a means for better understanding their similarity. In the above example Z might be explicit understanding of multiplicative commutality or understanding through frequently discovering that 'multiplication is the same the other way around'. Then Z is the understanding that $4 \times 2 = 8$ is the same as $2 \times 4 = 8$ and the child may associate $4 \times 2 = 8$ with $2 \times 4 = 8$ through the understanding of commutivity or the understanding that 'multiplication is the same the other way around'.

A neighbourhood of linked emotional sets represents a concept. A core concept is shown in our example illustrating how the emotional set Q in Fig. 9.2/4, categorizing emotional contexts to do with cars, allows drift to R, S, T, or U which each categorize different emotional contexts associated with cars. This part of the network Q, R, S, T, and U will hold the core concept of cars. This concept becomes more diffuse as we include more of the network of emotional sets with lower transition probabilities from Q. These emotional sets which are peripheral to the concept of cars will probably be part of some other concept. The whole network may therefore be considered as consisting of overlapping concepts, that is redundant concepts. Everything we feel about cars gives us an overall attitude to them which is our emotional set categorizing our concept of cars. As each concept has its own emotional set, the model is hierarchical. Fig. 9.2/5 illustrates how a neighbourhood of linked emotional sets may be considered as one concept defined by its own emotional set.

We can only have an overall attitude about cars say, in a relaxed state when we do not have to consider more detailed aspects of cars. When we look in detail at such an overall attitude we find it is ambivalent because such an overall attitude consists of so many highly redundant emotional sets which overall contain dissimilar response tendencies. The complete network of emotional sets may be considered at this higher level to be associated concepts each defined by an extremely redundant emotional set whose large integrated response tendencies are the smaller emotional sets comprising the concept. The response tendencies to our overall attitude to cars will be the emotional contexts like Q on a lower level of redundancy. The model is hierarchical so we can continue down to greater detail at lower levels of redundancy. For example, we may consider some aspect of driving cars, represented by a response tendency conditioned to emotional set R. We may move between a great many very low-level redundant emotional sets which corresponds to the possibility of consecutively considering a great many details which, being details, are composed of less information and so will have less in common with each other. We need to concentrate on the details at hand for this more analytic work and not let our minds wander at higher levels of redundancy as we could in more relaxed states. Or we may relax and go higher and higher in redundancy levels and include our attitude to cars within a very general attitude, that is within our emotional set of our way of life. And so we may move between fewer extremely redundant emotional sets at this very high level of redundancy which represents concepts of concepts.

Primary-process thinking combines the emotional sets high in the hierarchy while secondary-process thinking combines emotional sets low in the hierarchy. We reiterate that knowledge may be described by the quantity of response tendencies whereas understanding is reflected by the amount of redundancy, the links and nodes of the network. This hierarchical network of emotional sets that we have just derived is the structure whose dynamics describes how we think and act. We will consider the dynamics of the structure in Section 9.4 but many phenomena of thought and behaviour are described merely by various aspects of this simple structure. We will now look at some of these. In doing so I expect you will also see how this structure can describe other phenomena in which you may have a particular knowledge or interest.

9.3   PHENOMENA DESCRIBED BY THE STRUCTURE

We shall now see how just one aspect of the structure, namely the high versus low redundancy levels, describes primary and secondary thought, emotional variability, functional fixation, frustration, behaviour, multicategorization and tolerance of ambiguity as well as dogmatic and authoritarian personality traits. We now consider the high versus low levels of redundancy or shared responses that are available to us as we progress through our network of emotional sets.

For comparison Figs. 9.3/1 and 9.3/2 show two chains of emotional sets of high and low redundancy respectively. For simplicity the probable links with other emotional sets because of their high redundancy are not shown in Fig. 9.3/1. The only difference between the two chains is that the highly redundant emotional sets in Fig. 9.3/1 have many responses in common between different emotional sets. If these cross-over lines representing the redundancy were removed, the two figures would be identical. There are two reasons why such a difference may exist. Firstly they could represent similar hierarchical levels in two different individuals; one of whom through hereditary or enriched experience has been blessed with high redundancy whilst the other person has not. Or these structures could represent two different levels of redundancy in the hierarchy of the same person who has a highly redundant network, as shown in Fig. 9.3/1, but under certain conditions this is temporarily degraded to the low redundancy of Fig. 9.3/2. The level of redundancy available to anyone may be temporarily degraded by internal ego control as when we deliberately concentrate on details; or temporarily degraded by external ego threat, when accentuated attention to the external environment gives less emotional sensitivity to the stimulus response information peripheral to his emotional set. Redundancy may be degraded by ego threat accentuating attention to the external environment at the expense of sensitivity to emotionally coded peripheral information. You will notice from

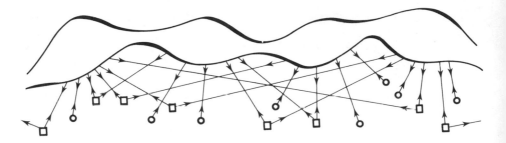

Fig. 9.3/1 Highly redundant structure

Fig. 9.3/1 that the redundant stimuli/responses tend to be on the periphery rather than near the centre of the emotional sets. Hence when these peripheral stimuli/responses are unavailable, the redundancy is lost. Without the availability of these redundant responses the person's generalized behavioural state disassociates into less redundant emotional sets at a lower level in his hierarchy with their more predictable and specialized responses.

An inherent lack of emotional sensitivity to these peripheral cues may prevent a person utilizing his experience to build a highly redundant structure. Conversely and with pedagogic implications, possibly training in emotional sensitivity to an enriched environment may encourage the development of such a highly redundant network. Occupying successive emotional sets at high or low levels of redundancy exhibits the characteristics of primary and secondary thought. The characteristics of primary thought result from occupying a succession of highly redundant emotional sets as along the chain illustrated in Fig. 9.3/1. This stream of consciousness, comprised of the succession of highly redundant cognitive responses from the chain of emotional sets, will be accompanied by their concordant affective responses giving characteristics such as idiosyncratic multimodal associations rich in connotation and inconsistency typical of primary thought. Whereas the characteristics of secondary thought result from occupying a succession of low redundant emotional sets as along the chain illustrated in Fig. 9.3/2. This stream of consciousness comprised of sparsely redundant cognitive responses with very few affective or other associations will have characteristics such as predictable associations, step-by-step analytic deduction devoid of feeling and connotation typical of secondary thought. At a low level in the hierarchy emotional sets, as illustrated in Fig. 9.3/2, have few specific response tendencies and so have little in common with other emotional sets, i.e. redundancy is low so the probability density of transition probabilities has a small variance, from which it follows that the emotional sets will be associated with greater predictability which is consistent with the predictability of responses in secondary thought compared with the variability of responses in primary thought. Essentially secondary/primary thought is a continuum through the hierarchical levels of redundancy but for clarity only high and low

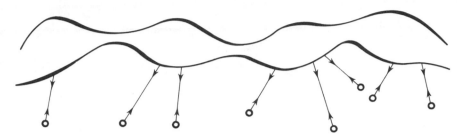

Fig. 9.3/2 Sparsely redundant structure

redundancy levels are contrasted here. It takes some effort to retain either the extremely low redundancy level of concentrated restricted response or the extremely high Nirvana-type level of redundancy.

Intuitive thought is described later as primary thought, highly redundant thought directed to resolve an initial cognitive dissonance. Intuitive individuals, needing to be capable of primary thought, have a redundant structure as illustrated in Fig. 9.3/1 whereas lack of redundancy inhibits intuitive thought. The redundant structure of the intuitive type predicts that he will be more emotionally variable, or moody, than the non-intuitive person. This is because the redundant responses greatly encourage the change of emotional sets. Whereas in the low-redundant chain of Fig. 9.3/2 only the natural physiological change contributes to the change of emotional sets. This critical prediction, that the intuitive type is necessarily more emotionally variable than the non-intuitive type, has been used successfully to test the veracity of the theory by physiologically monitoring and comparing the emotional variability of high- and low-intuitive types (Bastick, T., 1979).

These levels of redundancy also describe functional fixation. It sometimes happens that one response becomes heavily conditioned to its emotional set, as when we are very familiar with the standard solution to a problem. We find it difficult to think of any other solution but the familiar one. The heavy conditioning tends to restrict our responses to this most probable response. For being in the emotional set of a familiar problem we tend to give the familiar response, which in turn tends to evoke the same emotional set, keeping us in this emotional set so that we continue to give the familiar response.

Fig. 9.3/3 and 9.3/4 illustrate functional fixation in a non-intuitive type and in an intuitive type respectively. The intuitive type, being more emotionally variable, has more chance of escaping from this functional fixation by drifting to another emotional set to which other responses are likely. Without this redundancy, the non-intuitive type has less chance of escaping from this functional fixation. He only has the natural change in physiological set to help him escape. In the absence of high redundancy, this change in psychological set can be encouraged by vacillating vigorous physical and mental activity

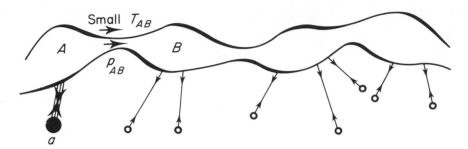

Fig. 9.3/3 Functional fixedness in non-intuitive thought

which is observed in such situations as frustration behaviour. A prediction from this organization is that as ego threat reduces redundancy, we would expect more functional fixations and frustration behaviour under ego threat, and that intuitive types would have a preference for permissive non-ego-threatening environments in which their highly redundant structures may operate.

Emotionally coding information implies that we categorize contexts by emotional sets of various complexity. Redundancy allows the same stimuli to be associated with different emotional sets. Fig. 9.3/4 illustrates how stimulus *a* may be categorized both by emotional set *A* in one context and by emotional set *B* in another context. This may happen because stimulus *a* continues while the subject changes from emotional set *A* to emotional set *B,* or because stimulus *a* occurred whilst the subject was in emotional set *A* and then occurred again whilst the subject was in emotional set *B,* or because stimulus *a* is a common constituent of two different responses, one conditioned to emotional set *A* and the other conditioned to emotional set *B*. This multicategorization is a parameter of enriched environments often overshadowed by emphasis on multiplicity of stimuli. The intuitive person has a greater ability to multicategorize objects, represented by stimuli/responses like *a,* than has the non-intuitive person. The redundant response tendencies of Fig. 9.3/1 are variously multicategorized. The intuitive type has a correspondingly greater tolerance of apparent ambiguity of multicategorizing

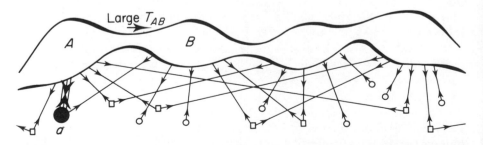

Fig. 9.3/4 Redundant structure for intuitive thought overcomes functional fixedness

than has the non-intuitive person, whose single method of categorizing, illustrated in Fig. 9.3/2 is exhibited as dogmatic, authoritarian personality traits. The intuitive type's ability to multicategorize stimuli allows him to handle more easily a multiplicity of differing stimuli that would perhaps evoke cognitive dissonance in a non-intuitive type, e.g. intuitive types can handle global instruction procedures better than non-intuitive types. Cognitive dissonance is discussed later.

9.4   PROCESSING OUR NETWORK OF EMOTIONAL SETS

We process our network by our progress through it. We have previously presented a simplified view of a network of emotional sets through which we may drift, leaving unaltered the emotional sets through which we pass. However, our progress through our network does alter it leaving each emotional set changèd. As we change from one emotional set to another 'refreshing' some responses, the relative conditioning of the response tendencies within the emotional set changes, so that the new emotional set entered is not identical to the next chosen extant emotional set in the network. It is rather a combination of this next extant emotional set with the present emotional set. The present emotional set is combined with the next to form a new emotional set. So as we drift through the network of emotional sets, combining the present with the next, these refreshed emotional sets of the network are left changed. We learn by this revision and rehearsal as well as by direct conditioning The transition probabilities between emotional sets on the chosen path are increased by this rehearsal; thus tending to make a similar future 'train of thought, feeling and behaviour' habitual, more likely to be chosen. It is dominant responses that tend to be reinforced particularly under drive conditions thus increasing this conservation.

Reducing Dissonance

Dissonance occurs when we try to give conflicting responses simultaneously. We may be in a situation which requires our usual consistent response and then notice something unusual about the situation that makes a conflicting response seem more appropriate. The tendency to give the usual response and the conflicting response causes dissonance. It is felt as an anxiety, the tension of a frustrated drive to give a response, but which one?

An example of dissonance is when we are on a slimming diet and have the response not to eat chocolate. But presenting us with chocolate makes us want to eat it. We want to eat it and not eat it at the same time. This is dissonance. Our Theory that stimuli evoke emotional sets which in turn precipitate responses describes the phenomena of dissonance and shows that combining emotional sets may reduce dissonance.

We perceive our internal and external environment at any instant through the concurrent stimuli/responses we can detect at that instant. We can only be

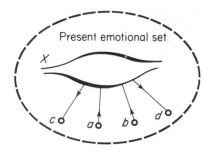

Fig. 9.4/1 Concordance

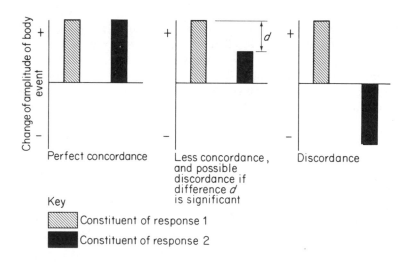

Fig. 9.4/2 Similarity or dissimilarity of response constituents giving concordant or discordant responses

in one emotional set at a time, in X say in Fig. 9.4/1. If two concurrent stimuli/responses a and b both tend to evoke this one emotional set with its response tendencies c and d then a, b, c, and d are concordant stimuli/responses, being from the same physiological set. Response tendencies from the same physiological set are concordant because the differences in amplitudes and changes of the multitude of minute self-detectable stimuli and responses or body events, whose combinations comprise these responses, little no effect. That is they are concordant because their constituents are similar.

This is illustrated in Fig. 9.4/2 which diagrammatically shows the amplitudes and changes of some particular body event that is a constituent of two different response tendencies. If the difference d between them has no effect then the response tendencies are concordant and can co-exist within one physiological set. For example if one response tendency is precipitated by a combination of body events which include an adrenalin constituent then a concordant response tendency will not be precipitated by a combination of body events which include a noradrenalin constituent. The responses will be more concordant if the levels of the adrenalin constituents are similar, given all else is the same. If two concurrent stimuli/responses *a* and *b* tend to evoke two different emotional sets Y and Z say, as in Fig. 9.4/3 with their conflicting response tendencies *c* and *d,* from two different physiological sets, then *a* and *b* are discordant. Their concurrence is marked by an anxiety due to the tendency to give dissonant responses *c* and *d*. This discordance can be resolved if the two emotional sets Y and Z could be combined to give one emotional set like the emotional set X in Fig. 9.4/1. This will have concordant response tendencies.

In our diet example where the dissonance is wanting to eat the chocolate and not wanting to eat it at the same time, the emotional set Y in Fig. 9.4/3 would represent the emotional set of the diet. Response *c* would be not wanting to eat chocolate. Stimuli *a* and *b* would be the chocolate. Stimulus *a* is concordant with emotional set A in that it is recognized that it is chocolate evoking response *c* that it must not be eaten. However, stimulus *b* is the delicious smell of the chocolate that is simultaneously tending to evoke the non-diet emotional set Z with its 'eat me'· response *d*. The dissonance can be resolved if we could eat the chocolate and still be on a slimming diet.

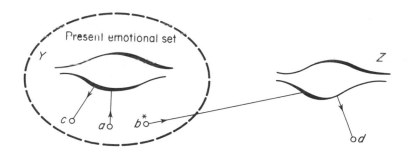

Fig. 9.4/3 Discordance

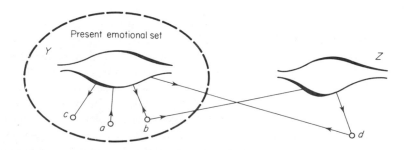

Fig. 9.4/4 Redundancy resolving discordance

These different emotional sets may be combined by combining the present emotional set Y with a succession of only slightly different emotional sets to give a new present emotional set that is increasingly similar to Z, so that it can eventually be combined with Z. Methods of combining emotional sets are described later. The direction of combining emotional sets is decided by the natural physiological change and the redundant responses they have in common which together define the transition probability. We may increase this transition probability, which will give more guidance to the direction of combination, making it more likely to combine emotional sets Y and Z, by redundantly also associating b with emotional set Y and redundantly also associating d with emotional set Y as in Fig. 9.4/4. Now taking Y as our present emotional set and Z as a next emotional set, this increased redundancy increases the probability that we will combine with increasingly different emotional sets in the direction of Z until our present conglomerate emotional set is sufficiently similar to Z for us to combine them to give a new emotional set which, like X in Fig. 9.4/1 at the high level of redundancy, has a, b, c, and d concordantly associated with it.

The redundant associations of b and d with emotional set Y may be made available in two ways. We could change to a higher level of redundancy where these peripheral responses may then become available, or we may try to associate b and d with emotional set Y at the lower level of redundancy. In the example of dissonance caused by wanting to eat chocolate when on a slimming diet, resolution of this dissonance by changing to a higher level of redundancy would correspond to taking a wider view, e.g. in the grand scheme of things one bar of chocolate is not going to make a significant difference to how fat we are, or we will exercise it off, or we will eat less tomorrow. So we resolve the dissonance and eat the chocolate even though we are on a diet. The second method of helping to resolve the dissonance by associating the chocolate b and eating d with the emotional set of the diet A would correspond to being told that the chocolate contained a special chemical that by breaking down fatty tissue helped slimming. Now eating the chocolate is more compatible (concordant) with slimming. The associations help us to resolve the dissonance and eat the chocolate while remaining on a slimming diet.

To summarize, combining emotional sets can resolve discordance, reducing its anxiety by releasing the tension through the realization of concordant responses associated with the conglomerate emotional set. Also redundancy helps to direct the combinations of emotional sets.

Combinations of emotional sets without the resolution of dissonance result in general thought and behaviour. However, combinations of emotional sets that resolve a dissonance result in intuitive thought. If the dissonance is associated with a problem then the accompanying anxiety and its resolution by combining emotional sets results in intuitive problem-solving. A problem may be defined as a situation which contains discordant stimuli tending to give conflicting responses as illustrated in Fig. 9.4/3. These discordant stimuli are some of the elements that form the problem. For example 'how do you get a quart into a pint pot?'. The first part of this problem namely 'how do you get a quart into a...' evokes an emotional set whose affective and cognitive response tendencies are our knowledge of putting quarts into things. Response tendencies commonly conditioned to this emotional set that are likely to be realized are thoughts and feelings of pouring two pints of liquid completely into ... as yet an unspecified container. The second part of the problem, namely '...a pint pot', evokes an emotional set that specifies the container. The response tendencies representing the pint pot are discordant with the response tendencies of our present emotional set evoked by the first part of the problem. This discordance makes the situation into a problem. If for some reason there was no discordance, for example, if we thought the quart and the pint were the same volume, the liquid would compress on pouring, the pint would stretch on receiving the liquid, half of the liquid would disappear when being poured, putting sawdust in the pint pot would absorb half the liquid, etc., etc., then there would be no discordance and no problem. Otherwise we need to combine emotional sets which would allow these responses to be concordant with our present emotional set. The other responses of this emotional set that allow the resolution of this original dissonance will represent the solution of the problem. The problem is considered solved when the problem elements are categorized in one context with its emotional set having concordant consistent responses as in Fig. 9.4/1. The solution responses to the combined sets resolve the anxiety evoked by the problem.

In the illustrative example of the quart into a pint pot we are consciously aware of our involvement with this problem. However, in the majority of our day-to-day intuitive thoughts we are not really consciously aware that we are dealing with problems, e.g. in a room we may replace an object that has been moved from its usual setting or we may pick up a dropped pencil, do the washing up because we want clean dishes, turn the page of a book because we cannot read the other side unless we do, etc., etc. We do these things intuitively. Their difference from our great intuitions is only one of degree with a correspondingly smaller reduction in anxiety, depending on how much these things irk us in the first place.

Combining Emotional Sets

The likelihood of combining two particular emotional sets depends on their transition probability, but any two emotional sets may be combined whether they have a high, medium, or low transition probability providing they are similar. It may take one or many combinations to bring them together and these combinations can only occur if the emotional sets are sufficiently similar to allow any slight discordance to be accommodated in opposite peripheries of the emotional sets. For example, going back to Fig. 9.2/3, the more peripheral response tendencies p and r in emotional set A can have less in common than the more central similar response tendencies a and t, while still being included in emotional set A. And if these two emotional sets A and B were combined into a 'larger' more redundant emotional set it would follow that the more dissimilar response tendencies p and s, would be included. Their slight discordance would be 'diluted' so to speak, because their tendency to be realized as responses has been reduced relative to the increased number of responses available and relative to the increased probability of giving more similar and combined responses.

This organization predetermines three methods of combining emotional sets corresponding to a high, medium, or low transition probability, each resulting in increasing redundancy. The increased redundancy results from the combination concordantly associating response tendencies into one emotional set that had not previously been associated. That is, the responses have been slightly changed by the combination so that they now have a larger proportion of constituent body events in common, the same combinations of minute body events are duplicated constituents in those responses thus giving increased redundancy. These three methods of combining emotional sets are, in order of increasing resulting redundancy: embedding, drifting, and recentring. This processing will be discussed in the context of intuitive problem-solving so that the reader may see how the processing easily describes thoughts and behaviours commonly associated with intuitive problem-solving while clarifying and unifying some fundamental phenomena of intuitive thought that have been inadequately conceptualized by traditional theory.

The three methods of combining emotional sets describe intuitive problem-solving over three types of incubation period. Embedding describes intuitions that are synchronous with the perception of the problem. An extension of embedding to higher redundancy levels, namely hierarchical embedding, describes the least satisfying type of intuition which involves relaxing the problem constraints by generalization. Combining by drifting describes intuitive solutions that come after a continuous period of working on a problem. Recentring describes intuitions that come 'out of the blue' days or months after one has consciously stopped working on the problem. Although we consider these three methods separately, all three could contribute to a particular intuition. If the resolution of discordance is omitted from our discussion, then the processing will describe non-intuitive thought and behaviour.

Combining by Hierarchical Embedding

This method of combining emotional sets describes intuitions that are synchronous with the perception of the problem and describes problems intuitively solved by generalization. Combining by embedding is most likely to occur when two emotional sets A and B are very similar and their transition probability is very high. This is illustrated by the adjacent emotional sets A and B in Fig. 9.4/5. Because the transition probability T_{AB} is very high, emotional set A has many of the problem elements p conditioned to it and some of the solution elements s. Similarly, emotional set B has many of the

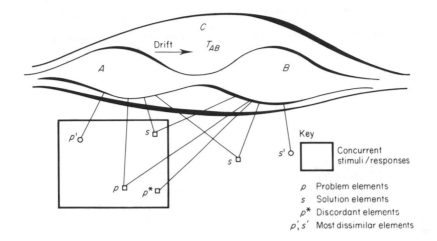

Fig. 9.4/5 Increased redundancy by hierarchical embedding of similar
emotional sets with a high transition probability

solution elements conditioned to it and some of the problem elements. In addition, some of the problem elements are composed of slightly discordant stimuli/responses which are concurrent with the stimuli/responses of emotional set A but are conditioned to the slightly different emotional set B. Both emotional sets have many problem and solution elements in common. This similarity, reinforced by the drift in physiological set, prevents the problem-solver from being able to differentiate between them. A and B are embedded in one emotional set C. The few elements that were not in common between A and B, namely p^*, p' and s' are now both associated with C, producing a small increase in redundancy and a decrease in the slight anxiety attributed to the initial slight discordance. A simple example of combining by embedding would be a child's problem of not being able to add 3 apples and 2 pears because the units are different. However, the emotional set categorizing apples and the emotional set categorizing pears both have in common associated response tendencies representing fruit, which enables the emotional sets to be combined by embedding in the one emotional set categorizing fruit, allowing the response of 3 apples + 2 pears = 5 fruits. Psychologically the effect of combining by embedding is to generalize, therefore sufficient discordance is 'diluted' in the generalization to allow its acceptance.

Hierarchical embedding is combining emotional sets by embedding them into one larger emotional set. This is the least satisfying method of achieving an intuitive solution because the release of tension is similarly 'diluted' by the increased number of possible responses rather than being achieved quickly through a few decisive responses. Further, if the embedding stops after having combined two very similar emotional sets this indicates that there was very little initial anxiety, whose resolution could give this satisfaction. This process

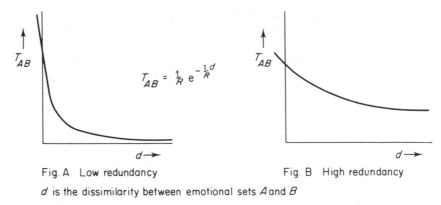

$$T_{AB} = \frac{1}{R} e^{-\frac{1}{R}d}$$

Fig. A Low redundancy   Fig. B High redundancy

d is the dissimilarity between emotional sets A and B

Fig. 9.4/6 Distribution of transition probabilities T_{AB} at different redundancy levels R

of hierarchical embedding is reversible so that under ego threat or ego control a focusing occurs, making available only part of the larger emotional set. Many response tendencies that were held in common, are then no longer held in common, so that the redundancy level is degraded. In our fruit example above, we may focus on the apples say, concerning ourselves only with how any apple is similar to any other apple. By ego control or under ego threat related to apples we are able to blot out the peripheral information that apples are also fruit; that is we blot out the duplicated information defining fruit which is in common with other emotional sets.

When just two similar emotional sets are embedded this is equivalent to combining by drifting to the next most similar emotional set, which is the method of combination resulting in least increase in redundancy and the method most probable in low levels of redundancy where combinations result in secondary thinking. In a low level of redundancy the natural change in physiological set contributes predominantly to the transition probabilities, making the combination with a very similar emotional set even more probable. This gives the characteristics of predictability, affect-free, step-by-step thought typical of secondary thought. But when the redundancy level is high then the natural physiological change contributes less to the transition probability. This increases the possibility of more dissimilar emotional sets being brought into combination. Fig. 9.4/6 suggests how transition probability may be distributed at different redundancy levels. When redundancy is small the probability rapidly drops off making the combination of similar emotional sets giving similar responses more probable as in Fig. 9.4/6A. As redundancy increases we get a more uniform distribution as illustrated in Fig. 9.4/6B, giving a greater probability of combining with a more dissimilar emotional set resulting in less predictable responses. This distribution of transition probabilities fits the results of dissimilar associations given by subjects in primary thought when redundancy is high as opposed to similar associations given in secondary thought when redundancy is low.

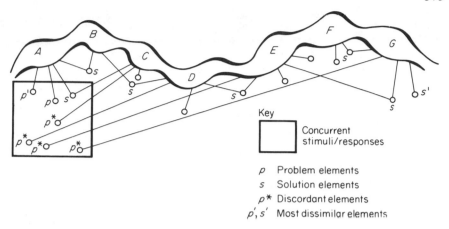

Fig. 9.4/7 Drifting through a chain of emotional sets with high transition probabilities

Combining by Continued Drifting

This method of combining emotional sets describes intuitions that arise at the end of a continuous period of working on a problem. Combining by continued drifting through a succession of increasingly different emotional sets makes it more probable that response tendencies conditioned to the original emotional set may be associated with increasingly different emotional sets, particularly if the initial response tendencies have some components in common with successive extant emotional sets. If initial response tendencies have few components in common with successive emotional sets, then these response tendencies will tend to be dropped from the train of present emotional sets. The composition of response tendencies with more components in common with successive emotional sets will be slightly changed as these common (redundant) components are reinforced by refreshing (re-experiencing) during the combination. Response tendencies will be dropped during drifting if the emotional sets are of low redundancy or if the response tendencies are not particularly physiologically enduring, unlike the anxiety responses initiating the intuitive process. Fig. 9.4/7 illustrates a distribution of problem and solution responses along a chain of increasingly different emotional sets which leads to intuitive problem-solving by drifting, without changing the hierarchical level of redundancy. The process starts with emotional set *A* as the present emotional set which is sustained by some of the problem elements while other problem elements are comprised of concurrent discordant stimuli tending to evoke other emotional sets of increasing dissimilarity, e.g. emotional sets *C, D, E,* and *G* in Fig. 9.4/7.

We then drift through this chain successively combining adjacent emotional sets by selectively embedding their concordant problem and solution responses. The shared (redundant) response tendencies encourage this combining and continued drift. Hence this process is more likely to occur in higher redundancy levels where each of the emotional sets illustrated in Fig. 9.4/7 would represent part of the network at a lower level of redundancy, as illustrated in Fig. 9.2/5. Successive combinations at this higher level cause rearrangements of the nodes at the lower levels which are the response tendencies for the higher level. The reinforced components of response tendencies at the higher level are new and coalesced nodes at the lower level. You will remember that nodes, or in particular redundancy, represent our understanding, hence this increased redundancy represents increased understanding, particularly at a lower level. For instance, when we realize that two things are similar then the many details about them also fit into place. Therefore combining just two things at the higher level gives many detailed associations at a lower level. By drifting through emotional sets of increasing dissimilarity from the one initially evoked by the problem elements, retaining the problem stimuli, collecting solution responses and dropping irrelevant responses on the way, we gradually build an emotional set quite different from the one initially evoked. Combining by drifting, gathering up duplicated response tendencies, increases redundancy more than combining by embedding. It takes some time to drift to a solution, some time to change through increasingly different emotional sets. And it takes some ego control to stay constantly at this one hierarchical level of redundancy without relaxing more to a higher level or hampering the drift by concentrating on details at a lower level of redundancy. But this is usually done during one continuous period of problem-solving. We tackle a problem and work our way towards a solution. The initiating discordance is gradually resolved as we drift along the chain combining our gradually changing emotional set with the emotional sets which the original discordant elements were tending to evoke. The concordant responses of the present conglomerate emotional set are solution responses. The solution responses collected during the drift are accompanied by a continual decrease in the initial anxiety evoked by the problem. This is how the problem-solver intuitively feels he is progressing towards a solution, even though he does not know what that solution is.

If the drift is not accompanied by this gradual resolution of the initiating dissonance then the intuiter feels he is 'getting nowhere'. If he drifts so as to combine emotional sets that increase the dissonance he feels 'he is going in the wrong direction'. He might accept short-term increases in anxiety, which corresponds to detours in the direction of the mind, providing that the increase in anxiety is less than the resolution of anxiety anticipated by the solution. As this temporary increase in anxiety builds, the intuiter increasingly feels he is 'going down a blind alley' which further reduces his tendency to drift in that direction. Without the anticipated resolution of anxiety created by the original discordance, such short-term increases in anxiety would be resisted as is the case for many 'second-hand' explanations, like some mathematical proofs that seem to get more complicated before simplifying. They do not feel satisfying and we feel the proof or explanation is using a 'trick'.

Combining by Drastic Recentring

This method of combining emotional sets describes intuitions that arise 'out of the blue' some time after the problem has been mentally shelved and when the intuiter is doing something which is seemingly unrelated to the original problem. Recentring can occur at a high level of redundancy when the initiating response tendencies have been dropped from the present emotional set. An incubation period is necessary to allow time for the original response tendencies to be dropped from the train of present emotional sets. To precipitate recentring there then occurs an emotional set so similar to the original emotional set that was left in the network with its unresolved response tendencies, that some mild, usually kinaesthetic, stimulus causes the present emotional set to be combined with the original emotional set. The two emotional sets previously had near-zero transition probability being distinct local centres of the network, but now are 'recentred', i.e. combined. This drastically restructures transition probabilities in the immediate neighbourhood of the network by creating new links, new understanding.

Combining by recentring quickly produces the most redundancy. Recentring describes the Eureka experience. When an obstinate problem has been mentally shelved, then later, as with Archimedes in his bath or Newton under his apple tree, the intuitive solution seems to come out of the blue! We can use Fig. 9.4/8 followed by Fig. 9.4/9 to illustrate recentring. We refer to Fig. 9.4/8 first. As with the other methods of combining, the problem initially evokes an emotional set P, but working on the problem, represented by drifting to Q, does not resolve the anxiety with a satisfying answer. This particularly happens when the discordant problem elements fall into two or more categories where each of these categories is associated with some emotional sets of high transition probability in different chains. Working on the problem, partially solving it by making just one of the categories concordant, is felt as a satisfying further clarification of the problem. We get the feeling that we are so near the solution but just cannot make that final connection. In which ever direction we continue to work on the problem, represented in our model by combining emotional sets of high transition probability, it brings us no closer to the solution than this. Although we are tantilizingly near the solution, we have no option but mentally to shelve the problem.

The emotional set Q of the unresolved problem is left in the network. Some time later, whilst drifting through a different chain of emotional sets we occupy an emotional set O, very similar in physiological set to the emotional set Q of the shelved problem. Although Q and O have responses in common, being in different chains their transition probability is practically zero. Whilst in O a chance stimulus/response occurs that had previously been associated with Q, usually a body movement. Without the peripheral distractions originally associated with the emotional set Q of the shelved problem that might have been instrumental in initially clarifying or partially solving the problem and then had tended to misdirect our drift to P or R, this increased

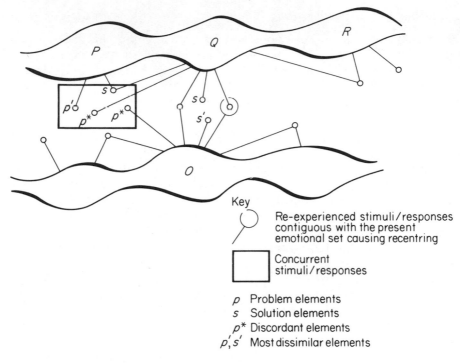

Key

○ Re-experienced stimuli/responses contiguous with the present emotional set causing recentring

▢ Concurrent stimuli/responses

p Problem elements
s Solution elements
p* Discordant elements
p', s' Most dissimilar elements

Fig. 9.4/8 Highly redundant chains of emotional sets before recentring

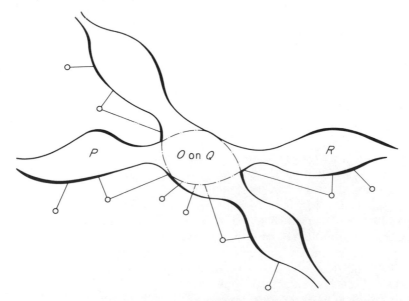

Fig. 9.4/9 Highly redundant chains of emotional sets after recentring

redundancy, their new common links, causes the two emotional sets to be combined by recentring on one another as illustrated in Fig. 9.4/9. The concordance of stimuli/responses not previously associated provides new insights. The linking of the two chains provides new paths of association, and drastically restructures the network at the lower redundancy levels, coalescing and creating many new nodes. The large sudden increase in redundancy, shared stimuli/responses, accompanying this drastic restructuring of the network is felt as the euphoric release of tension traditionally associated with great intuitions occurring after long incubation periods. These intuitions appear to 'come out of the blue' because one cannot seem to find a similarity between the conscious cognitive components of the originally unresolved problem and the conscious cognitive components of the situation in which the intuition appeared. However, the similarity is at the preconscious level between the myriad of affective stimuli/responses encoding the emotional context of the unresolved problem and also encoding much of the emotional context in which the intuition appears. The re-experiencing of more of these stimuli/responses is sufficient to cause the recentring. The anecdotal literature reports that these re-experienced stimuli responses are commonly spatial and kinaesthetic. This is consistent with spatial kinaesthesis being a common and most suitable ability mode for intuitive thought. The link between the apparently unrelated problem and the situation in which the intuition appears is that many of the physiological stimuli/responses of the present emotional set also encode the emotional context of the problem.

Intuitive thought is initiated by some concurrent stimuli/responses discordantly tending to evoke different emotional sets with their simultaneous discordant response tendencies. By combining redundant emotional sets which successively reduce the anxiety accompanying these conflicting response tendencies, a concordant emotional set is reached. The sudden proportionate decrease in anxiety effected by the concordant responses of this emotional set becomes noticeable, causing the intuiter to label his present responses as the intuition. Section 5.5 shows how this organization accounts for different intuitive products, *viz.* immediate and delayed intuitive recognition, intuitive judgment of the similarity of recognized and novel stimuli, intuitive acceptance and intuitive judgment of suitabiity.

During problem-solving one or all of these methods of combination may occur as the problem-solver changes the hierarchical levels of redundancy in which he works. However, at low levels of redundancy in which secondary thinking occurs the method of combining tends to be by successively embedding only two most similar emotional sets at a time. The redundancy directing this combination and the resolution of the initiating anxiety reinforces the direction. Other thought and behaviour rather than intuitive thought and behaviour would result in the absence of the initiating driving anxiety. The response tendencies of any emotional set are less likely to be preserved through successive combinations when they are not linked to this continuing anxiety. And so non-intuitive thought and behaviour proceed by combining successively different emotional sets without necessarily preserving the original response tendencies, that is a step-by-step process in which each step is not necessarily dependent on the initial emotional set as in, for example, hypnogogic reverie at a high level of redundancy or in analytic thought at a low level of redundancy.

Mild recentring, without the accompanying eurphoric release of the tension that initiates the intuitive process, gives rise to *déjà vu* experiences. This again happens when usually in a relaxed state of high redundancy a kinaesthetic spatial stimulus/response gives us the feeling that we have previously done what we are doing at that moment. That is, our present emotional set is so similar to a previous emotional set in another chain that re-experiencing some common stimuli/responses causes a mild recentring so that we then suddenly have available other conditioned affective and cognitive response tendencies whose concordant associations with our present cognitive responses are experienced as a familiarity and as different cognitive associations.

The greatest relaxation of ego control, and the corresponding highest redundancy level, is during sleep. During sleep, combining highly redundant emotional sets regardless of inconsistency results in allo-logical surrealist dream sequences associated by feelings, and the intuitive solutions of problems during sleep. Skilfully composed music, story and joke-telling use our culturally conditioned response tendencies to evoke in us emotional sets and mild dissonance and lead us to combine emotional sets, giving us the pleasant reductions in anxiety accompanying these choreographed combinations terminating in the associated satisfaction of a resolved chord, or the tying up of loose ends of a story, or the punch line of a joke, or of a sense of beauty. Beauty is minimum stimuli/responses which give maximum redundancy. Four examples are: 'To see a World in a Grain of Sand,/ And a Heaven in a Wild Flower,/ Hold Infinity in the palm of your hand,/ and Eternity in an hour.' (Blake: *Auguries of Innocence*). Thus artists play on our feelings using stimuli to evoke emotional sets and dissonance. They use our expected responses, give and use other stimuli leading us to evoke and combine our emotional sets, helping us to reduce the dissonance they have created. Our choreographed feelings and the resolution of dissonance are our experience and enjoyment of their art. Some disconcerting art deliberately creates only dissonance and does not lead us to resolve it. Such work feels similar to an unresolved problem.

Thought and Behaviour Tend to Increase Redundancy

We have seen that our progress through our network of emotional sets, and the responses we give, are not chaotic but are probabilistic. We progress through our network by successively combining emotional sets in a direction of high redundancy because the duplicated response tendencies contribute to the transition probabilities and thus guide our progress. We have also considered how our progress through our network increases redundancy by increasing the conditioning of the common response tendencies during the combinations. When the combinations result in realizing concordant responses that resolve the discordant stimuli initiating intuitive thought, satisfaction accompanying this resolution reinforces the redundancy responsible for the combinations.

This conditioning increases their tendencies to be realized as a response, making them more central to the conglomerate emotional set. Thus through refreshing we tend to embed emotional sets, allowing us to use the same responses redundantly for more situations. For example, without considering new aspects of two situations, dwelling on their similarities gives their similarity a priority that enables us to treat both situations subjectively as the same. We tend to use the same responses for both situations, continuously mulling over things without new stimuli; we tend to develop generalized attitudes with less specific responses. With age we lose the impetuosity of youth. With contemplation we lose the impulsiveness of the moment: 'And thus the native hue of resolution/ Is sicklied o'er with the pale cast of thought,/ And enterprises of great pith and moment/ With this regard their currents turn awry,/ And lose the name of action' (*Hamlet, III,* i, 56).

Similarly, we will sometimes tend to use the response tendencies of our present emotional set rather than change to an emotional set whose different response tendencies would be more appropriate to our environment. That is we tend to generalize the use of responses from our present emotional set rather than make an effort to create new ones. Change to a new emotional set, with perhaps more appropriate responses might sometimes be inhibited by a subjectively disabilitating dissonance. This is because responses that are necessary and available in our present emotional set, may not be so immediately available in the new emotional set where the different, more appropriate, responses might be available. Staying in the present emotional set with its few necessary responses and many non-suitable responses is preferable to changing to a new emotional set which would entail losing the present availability of the necessary responses in order to perhaps make available the different, more appropriate responses, of the new emotional set. Generalizing a present certainty to deal inadequately with a pressing situation produces less anxiety than discarding the present certainty on just a chance of then precisely dealing with the situation: a case of 'the devil you know being better than the devil you do not know'. Examples that are a result of this, at a low level of redundancy, include misperception and selective perception as when we make unwarranted preconscious assumptions in order to get on more efficiently with what we are doing. We may misread a word, make Gestalt completions, e.g.

see ◯ as ◯ , make a Freudian slip and generally perceive what we expect to be there. Examples at a high level of redundancy include rationalization, as when we restructure whole situations to fit our attitudes, amply illustrated by Jonathan Swift's phrase 'there's none so blind as those who won't see'.

In the next section we will discuss how dissonance may be resolved by changing to a higher redundancy level. Less specific response tendencies are available at a higher redundancy level. Not having relevant specific response tendencies available is potentially disabilitating in an ego-threatening situation. Hence it is a testable prediction from this theory that more misperceptions and preconscious assumptions like those noted above will occur in non-permissive ego-threatening environments, as when assumed taboos and restrictions prevent solution of practical insight problems under test stress conditions (Section 1.3). In a similar fashion it is sometimes considered disabilitating to change from a high redundancy level to a low redundancy level. For example when working with general principles, overall aims and goals, we often deliberately ignore possibly conflicting details whose consideration at a lower level of redundancy would hinder our progress.

From our considerations, it seems that the cognitive and behavioural response tendencies we realize have the effect of increasing the redundancy of our network of emotional sets.

Unified theory — redundancy principle

This tendency of our thoughts and actions to increase redundancy is proposed as a fundamental principle of thought and behaviour.

Creativity and Resolving Cognitive Dissonance

Combining emotional sets at a high level of redundancy can resolve cognitive dissonance evoked at a low level of redundancy which initiates intuitive problem-solving. As illustrated in Fig. 9.4/3, in a low level of redundancy two stimuli *a* and *b*, present together, are discordant because they tend to evoke different emotinal sets *Y* and *Z* which have conflicting response tendencies *c* and *d*. We cannot be in two different emotional sets at one time. But in a high level of redundancy the intuitive person is able to combine *Y* and *Z* into one emotional set as illustrated in Fig. 9.4/1 and so resolve the dissonance. Because ego threat reduces the level of redundancy, this predicts that cognitive dissonance is more likely to be unresolved under ego threat. The ego control necessary to change hierarchical levels of redundancy is a necessary ability for creativity, considered as an intuition verified by analysis. The dissonance of the problem arises in a low level of redundancy. By changing to a high level of redundancy the creative person may use his intuitive process to resolve this dissonance. Then changing to a low level of redundancy, the intuition may be verified using step-by-step analytical secondary thought. The choice of analytic techniques if often intuitively guided, so a frequent change in redundancy level may be required during this last verification stage of bringing the creation to fruition. Thus a creative person is an intuitive person who has ego control of both the change and constancy of his redundancy level. This predicts that non-intuitive and uncreative people are less likely to resolve cognitive dissonance. We have defined creativity as intuition plus analytic verification and defined a creative person as being an intuitive person who has ego control.

Perhaps at this point we should pause for a moment, for we have discussed many varied phenomena that are not usually associated by traditional theories. This may give the reader the feeling that we are merely proliferating *ad hoc* assumptions, which would weaken the synthesis offered by the theory. However, these phenomena follow from the simple organization we have described without any added assumptions. Their variety, which may at first give this false impression, is intended to illustrate the range of synthesis achieved by this simple organization.

For example, the theory shows that because people encode information using personal feeling models and evoke these feelings to recall the information, we may use body language as a guide to whether a person is recalling memories or inventing lies. For when recalling information coded by feelings a person will move and gesture more, as kinaesthetic responses associated with the cognitive memory are also recalled and used to help evoke the chain of emotional sets whose conditioned cognitive responses are the remembered verbalized information. A person who is inventing such information has less need for the movement and gesticulation used in recall. Hence, contrary to popular belief, when a person is fidgeting and gesticulating he is more probably telling the truth.

In contrast to this description, in illustration of the theory's range of synthesis, the satisfaction accompanying the resolution of dissonance explains how this reward reinforces the choice of the intuitive mode for problem-solving. That this reward may be sought by deliberately creating non-disabilitating dissonance would predict that we learn to be curious and learn to need the stimulation of variety.

Meditation, bio-feedback training, and sensitivity training can help us to control the change and constancy of our redundancy levels. We also inadvertently learn to create environments which aid our ego control of change and constancy of redundancy level. Perhaps you will recognize some of the following procedures you might have used to help you work. The anecdotal introspective literature on creative thinking is replete with descriptions of such techniques used by creative workers; techniques which make sense in terms of our proposed structure of emotional sets.

Extraneous stimuli can act to change the redundancy level and thus interfere with the present type of thought. At a low level of redundancy we may wish to restrict ourselves to one response like the short-term memory of a telephone number, or restrict ourselves to very similar responses as when thinking of synonyms for the same word. In these examples we need to be in a low redundancy level which we may achieve by affecting a mood of self-anger to the point of annoyance and frustration with ourselves. Once at this low level of redundancy we need to stay in one sparsely redundant emotional set in order to realize its most probable central response tendency, the one on which we are concentrating. We may do this in two ways. We try to retain the emotional set by repeating the central stimulus/response. In the examples above, we may continually repeat the telephone number or the word. In addition we add multimodal reinforcements such as associating repetition with rhythm or some such accompanying movement. Secondly, we may reduce the peripheral stimuli that would tend to distract us. For example, if someone were to talk to us we would irritatedly tell them not to interrupt while we continue to repeat the problem over and over, trying to retain its precise feeling and encouraging functional fixation with the required response as illustrated in Fig. 9.3/4. At a slightly higher level of redundancy we sometimes need to do continuous repetitive work like housework or copy-typing. Some people find it easier to retain this level of redundancy (prolong the required level of arousal) with a continuous background noise, for example traffic noise, the noise of factory machines or background music. This engages most of the affective responses and leaves the cognitive responses free for the repetitive work. One effect is to stop drifting at a higher redundancy level, e.g. day-dreaming. However, if the background noise becomes cognitively demanding then it competes with the cognitive requirements of the task.

At this level of redundancy if a background noise is not available one can use the constant chatter in one's head to help retain this level. Your thoughts are a silent continuous conversation inside your head, retaining the associative links at this level of redundancy.

We use a higher level of redundancy when our work needs inspiration, for example ideas for a book or for a painting, or ideas to solve some problem intuitively. To encourage such intuitive ideas to come, creative people try to recreate environments in which they have previously experienced such intuitions. This may involve props to act as stimuli, for example, a man may prefer to work with a particular pen or on a special type of paper, or in a particular room or chair. Sometimes 'getting into the creative mood' involves an idiosyncratic ritual, for example, the preliminary walk in the garden, cigarette, cup of coffee, eccentric posturing, etc. Sometimes the rituals chosen happen unfortunately to be restrictive, as if one could only work creatively in the early hours of the morning or after a heavy meal. The environments for creativity must have no ego-threatening anxiety and therefore familiar surroundings are used.

At an even higher level of redundancy the insights are not so tied to a particular problem. These are general insights, for example insights into the nature of one's existence. To attain this high level of redundancy one must reduce the power of internal and external stimuli to evoke emotional sets at a lower level of redundancy. The techniques of meditation are useful here, to think of nothing in particular but be aware of everything. When the chatter in your head is stopped your mind grabs for details to hold on to, a sound, a sensation or some visual detail. As these details are rejected the mind diffuses away from the restrictions of associated thought to a general awareness of sensation.

As well as controlling the constancy of the redundancy level, the creative person has to control the change in redundancy level, so that the initial insight occurring at a high level may be analytically worked on at a low level. The redundancy level during this later stage of bringing the intuition to creative fruition is frequently changed because the analytic techniques are intuitively chosen and other problems arise that are set as subgoals to be intuitively solved and themselves analytically verified. Creative people manipulate their environment to aid their ego control to change redundancy levels. The most common example is perhaps to change chains of emotional sets by stopping work and doing something completely different as a break before returning to the task, hopeful of new associations, of new ideas and with refreshed strength to retain the required redundancy level (level of arousal). To change from a high level to a lower level in order to concentrate on some detail, one may self-induce a mood of annoyance with the detail to be considered. This focuses attention on the detail and allows one to work at the lower level. Taking up a restrained physical position and excluding distracting stimuli also helps, for example sitting on a hard stool at a desk to work in a quiet room. This helps to reduce the range of affective stimuli responses that define the higher level of redundancy. To return again to a higher level in order to continue more intuitive work, one only has to relax physically and use the thoughts and feelings associated with the problem at the higher level to maintain the relevant emotional sets. It helps to identify temporarily with the elements of the problem and be sensitive to one's empathic thoughts and feelings.

Intuition and Types of Creativity

One difference between creative ability in art and creative ability in science is that, although both fields require technical expertise to communicate the original intuition, in scientific creativity the intuition must be verified by being consistent with present knowledge whereas this restriction does not necessarily apply to artistic creativity. The technical expertise for communicating the intuition in both fields requires an intuitive understanding of the analytic techniques available so that the choice of technique and guidance in its use may be intuitively directed.

Scientific creativity has a futher restriction in that it must describe nature. Pure mathematical creativity as opposed to applied mathematics, although similar to scientific creativity in requiring consistency, is, however, like artistic creativity in being free from the restriction of being isomorphic to nature. Considering these freedoms and restrictions in terms of intuitive and secondary thought respectively enables our theory to describe the inherent structural differences between intuition, in artistic, scientific, and mathematical creative ability.

To summarize, the process of intuition and creativity may be described by the theory as follows. In primary thought, the intuiter allows environmental stimuli to evoke conflicting response tendencies through *empathy*. He resolves the dissonance of these conflicting responses by combining redundant emotional sets. He gives as the intuitive response a response conditioned to the terminating emotional set. Note that empathy is essential to the process. Given the technical prowess to communicate the intuition, this description satisfies general artistic creativity. However, some artists self-impose consistency restrictions similar to scientific and mathematical creativity. This requires a subsequent disassociation of the terminating highly redundant emotional set to give secondary thinking by combining sparsely redundant emotional sets, resulting in analytic associations. The ability to control the change of ego state between primary and secondary thinking, distinguishes the intuitive from the creative type. The creative type is an intuitive type with this ego-state control. Without this control the intuitive type would continue to produce only highly idiosyncratically associated primary thought responses. With this control he is able to produce very similar responses associated with a restricted (sparsely redundant) emotional set of his intuitive response.

Scientific creativity places restraint on the range of different emotional sets that may be combined during the intuitive process. This is because such emotional sets that are allowed to come into combination must have a restricted range of response tendencies corresponding to the restriction of nature under which the scientist must work, i.e. be highly analogous. Hence in terms of the range of different emotional sets brought into combination, the creative scientist will be less intuitive than the creative artist, i.e. he will have response tendencies in common between more similar emotional sets than the creative artist. However, the creative scientist's need for controlled change between primary and secondary thought will be greater than that required by the creative artist, who is not so restricted by the requirements of consistency.

The creative mathematician, in common with the artist, is unrestricted by the need to combine more similar emotional sets describing nature. Hence the creative mathematician is as intuitive as the creative artist. However, the creative mathematician, in common with the creative scientist, is restricted by the need for validation in the form of consistency. So after the creative mathematician has given his unrestricted intuitive response he must switch to secondary thinking to produce less idiosyncratic responses for analytic verification of his intuitive response. Although both the creative scientist and creative mathematician subsequently frequently change modes of thought in guiding and using the techniques of verification, the initial change from primary to secondary thinking is generally greater for the creative mathematician. From this we can predict that one would find a greater range of control of ego states in mathematicians than in scientists, who have more ego-state control than artists; with artists and mathematicians being more intuitive than scientists. The creative mathematician's greater control of ego states may extend to controlled interchange of dual personalities; expansive, diffused, permissive, interchanged with the discreet, precisely detailed, authoritative.

To increase the likelihood of objectively original and true verifiable intuitions, the creative person needs a global knowledge of his field of study. You will remember how we defined knowledge as all the stimuli/responses conditioned to emotional sets. In other words, the originally creative person must have an extensive feeling for his field of work. The redundancy will furnish him with intuition and the extent of his consistent global knowledge increases the likelihood that his intuition will be objectively consistent and hence not untrue. The public 'truth' of a creative work is whether its content is chosen and arranged so as to evoke in the public the dissonance of the problem and choreograph their feelings to resolve this dissonance. This is true for artistic, scientific, mathematical, or other creativity. Subjective creativity, as opposed to public creativity, does this only within the creator rather than consistently within the public.

Surveying the literature on comparative personality traits of artists, scientists, and mathematicians for verification or refutation, one unfortunately finds a lack of rigorous differentiation between the creative and the merely technically competent.

Cognitive Styles

We have seen how the organization can be used to describe phenomena in terms of the levels of redundancy and control of change and constancy of these levels. Other writers define cognitive styles in terms of these phenomena and so this organization simplifies and relates these proliferating definitions of cognitive style.

Thought and Behavioural Phenomena

Low redundancy	High redundancy	Ego control
High cognitive dissonance	Low cognitive dissonance	Resolution of cognitive dissonance
Authoritarian, dogmatic	Multicategorizing	Creative
Frustration behaviour	Tolerance of ambiguity	
Functional fixation	Emotional sensitivity	
Secondary thought	Primary thought	Primary and secondary thought
Stable mood	Emotional variability	
Cue focusing	Multimodal and subliminal sensitivity	

Cognitive Styles

Focusing	Levelling	Controlled change between levelling and focusing as convenient
Local thinking	Global thinking	
Serialistic	Holistic	
Vertical thinking	Lateral thinking	
Convergent thinking	Divergent thinking	
High barrier	Low barrier	Changing body image
Yielding	Independent	Flexible

388

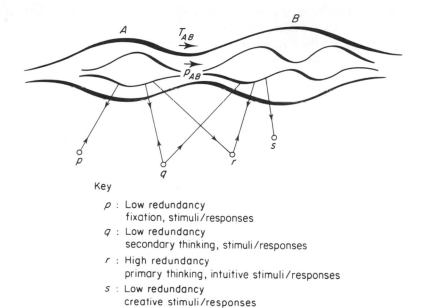

Key

p : Low redundancy
    fixation, stimuli/responses
q : Low redundancy
    secondary thinking, stimuli/responses
r : High redundancy
    primary thinking, intuitive stimuli/responses
s : Low redundancy
    creative stimuli/responses

Fig. 9.5/1 Summary diagram illustrating the probability of experiencing
the processes involved in creativity

9.5   FORMAL SUMMARY

Using Fig. 9.5/1 we may now summarize how the organization formally describes the processes involved in creativity. Given stimulus p the responses characteristic of these processes may be described by combinations of paths through the structure illustrated in Fig. 9.5/1. The tendency to give different responses may be described by the probability of following these paths. For convenience of illustration these probabilities are assumed to be independent so that the probabilities of following successive paths may be multiplied, and assumed to be mutually exclusive, so that the probabilities of alternative paths may be summed. For simplicity the most direct paths are considered: p and q are stimuli/responses concurrent with emotional set A. Initially a stimulus/response, represented by p evokes an associated emotional set A. In secondary thought, a very similar stimulus/response q may be given, or even the same stimulus response p may be given. The arrowed path from p to A represents the probability that p will evoke A. This is denoted P_{pA}. The arrowed path from A back to p represents the probability of being in A and giving the stimulus/response of p. This is denoted by P_{Ap}. The path pA followed by path Ap represents stimulus/response p resulting in stimulus/response p, that is functional fixation. Whereas the path from p to A and then from A to the very similar stimulus/response q describes secondary thinking. In reality, there are many stimulus/responses like p present, that evoke this emotional set, and there are many stimuli/responses like q that go to make up an integrated response. The sum of all possible paths between stimuli/responses like p and q via A will more accurately describe secondary thinking, i.e.

$$\sum_{p,q,} P_{qA} \cdot P_{Ap} \qquad\qquad \sum_{p} P_{pA} \cdot P_{Ap}$$

secondary thinking   *functional fixation*

This includes $p = q$ for functional fixation which is an extreme form of secondary thought. This expression is symmetrical in p and q. That is if p and q are interchanged the expression still denotes secondary thinking. This conforms to the preference for symmetry in uncreative people. In a more relaxed ego state p or q may evoke an emotional set of high redundancy, or a creative person may change to a higher level of redundancy. Now in primary thought, helped by the redundancy of stimuli/responses q and r, he may drift to emotional set B, making more probable the primary response r. The probability of giving the primary response r is described by the following paths: by going from p or q to A and then from A to r, or from q to B and then from B to r. For the many stimuli/responses like p, q, and r the sum of all these paths leads to the primary response. The change in emotional set is also helped by the natural change in physiological set P_{AB}. The paths to a primary response r are:

$$\sum_{p,\,q,\,r} [(P_{pA} + P_{qA}) \cdot P_{Ar} + P_{qB} P_{Br}] + P_{AB}$$

$\longleftarrow$ primary response r $\longrightarrow$

Dissonance is described if the concurrent stimulus/response q tends to evoke a different emotional set B more than it tends to evoke the present emotional set A. That is:

$$\sum_{q} P_{qA} \; < \; < \sum_{q} P_{aB}$$

$\longleftarrow$ dissonance $\longrightarrow$

Such dissonance may be resolved in intuitive thinking by combining emotional sets A and B by drifting from A to B (embedding). We see in the expression for primary thinking above that if the P_{qA} term is so small that it can be neglected we get the following expression for an intuitive response r which will be concordant with the other stimuli/responses in the conglomerate emotional set:

$$\sum_{q,r} (P_{qA} \cdot P_{Ar} + P_{qB} \cdot P_{Br}) + P_{AB} \qquad\qquad q \neq r$$

$\longleftarrow$ intuitive response r $\longrightarrow$

The highly redundant emotional sets available to the intuitive type allow him to drift easily between emotional sets. The sparsely redundant emotional sets available to the non-intuitive type do not allow such emotional variability. The intuitive person may continue in primary thought to other redundant emotional sets, giving increasingly idiosyncratic scatterbrained responses.

Creatives are intuitive types who can control this emotional drift. Through control of ego state they may change from the combination of highly redundant emotional sets to combining sparsely redundant emotional sets which gives the objectively closer associated responses characteristic of secondary (analytical) thought rather than giving continued primary responses which would appear 'scatterbrained'. The creative person can focus his attention after giving this intuitive stimulus response r, reducing his level of redundancy, and in secondary thought he is able to give similar stimulus response s representing creativity. Having given an intuitive response r, this may be followed with the creative response s by returning from r to the degraded emotional set B and then from B to s for all the different stimulus responses like r and s. That is a creative response s results from the paths:

$$\left[\sum_{q,r} (P_{qA} \cdot P_{Ar} + P_{qB} \cdot P_{Br}) + P_{AB} \right] \cdot \sum_{r,s} P_{rB} \cdot P_{Bs} \qquad r \neq s$$

$\longleftarrow$ intuitive response r $\longrightarrow$
$\longleftarrow$ creative response s $\longrightarrow$

The terms P_{qA} and P_{qB} contributing to the intuitive response above represent an empathic ability to allow the stimulus q to evoke emotionals sets A and B. The terms P_{Ar} and P_{Br} also contributing to the intuitive response above represent a projection.

Thus, excluding the contribution of the naturally changing physiological set P_{AB}, empathic projection, represented by the terms $P_{qA} \cdot P_{Ar} + P_{qB} \cdot P_{Br}$, is **essential** for an intuitive response or for a creative response.

Empathic projection involves personal involvement, through empathy with otherwise non-emotionally involving elements in the environment. The intuiter allows any such neutral object of his perception, not necessarily animate but inanimate or even abstract, to evoke through empathy subjectively appropriate feelings which are the information for his intuitive process. In empathic projection the feelings evoked through empathy are directed by projection to the object evoking these feelings, and so the feelings are temporarily shared with the object. This is a major construct, for the theory may be proved false if intuitive types cannot allow this empathic projection with neutral objects, as represented formally by

$$\sum_{q,r} (P_{qA} \cdot P_{Ar} + P_{qB} \cdot P_{Br})$$

in the probability description of intuition and creativity.

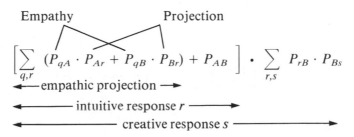

SPEAK (Bastick, T., 1981), is a general mental instrument that assesses the propensity of these structures in an individual's organization and therefore may be used to assess subjects in relation to any of the many phenomena of thought and behaviour described by these structures.

Apart from being used for qualitative clinical diagnosis and as a tool for understanding personality, SPEAK is designed to measure quantitatively a subject's preference for secondary or primary thought, for intuitive thought, control of change in modes of thought and the necessary ability for intuitive and creative thought of empathic projection. One of the ways in which the theory has been tested is by psychophysiological experiments with subjects whose performance on an intuitive problem-solving task, an empathy task, and an empathic projection task agrees with their SPEAK assessment on these abilities. The validity of the organization is supported through these and other experimental results reported in Bastick T. (1979).

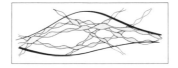

Bibliography

Abel, I.M., 1930. Attitudes and galvanic reflex, *Journal of Experimental Psychology,* no. 13, 47–60.

Adamson, R.E., 1952. Functional fixedness as related to problem solving: A repetition of three experiments, *Journal of Experimental Psychology, no. 44, 288*–291.

Adamson, R.E. and Taylor, D.W., 1954. Functional fixedness as related to elapsed time and to set, *Journal of Experimental Psychology,* no. 47, 122–126.

Adler, I., 1968. *Mathematics and Mental Growth,* Dennis Dobson, London.

Aldenbrand, Martha L., 1974. The Effects of Intuition, Feeling and Similarity on Predictive Empathy, PhD thesis, Michigan State University.

Allport, F.H., 1955. *Theories of Perception and the Concept of Structure,* John Wiley, New York.

Allport, G.W., 1929. A study of personality by the intuitive method, *Journal of Abnormal and Social Psychology,* no. 24, 14–27.

Allport, G.W., 1937. *Personality, A Psychological Interpretation,* Henry Holt, New York.

Allport, G.W., 1960. *Personality, A Psychological Interpretation,* Henry Holt, New York.

Allport, G.W., 1965. *Pattern and Growth in Personality.* Holt, Rinehart & Winston, New York.

Allport, G.W., and Odbert, H.S., 1936. Trait names: a psycholexical study, Psychological Monographs: General and Applied. no. 47 (whole no. 211).

Anderson, H.A., 1959. Creativity in perspective, in Anderson, H.A. (ed), *Creativity and its Cultivation — Collection of Papers,* Harper & Row, New York, Chapter 15, p. 237.

Anderson, J.R., 1972. Fran: a simulation model of free recall, *The Psychology of Learning and Motivation. Advances in Research and Theory,* **5,** Academic Press, London, pp. 315ff.

Anderson, J.R., and Bower, G.H., 1973. *Human Associative Memory,* V.H. Winson & Sons, Washington.

Andreassi, J.L., 1966. Some psychological correlates of verbal learning task difficulty, *Psychonomic Science,* **6** (2), 69–70.

Andreassi, J.L., and Whalen, Patricia M., 1967. Some Psychological correlates of learning and overlearning, *Psychophysiology,* **3,** no. 4, 406–413.

Arieti, S., 1955. *Interpretation of Schizophrenia,* Brunner, New York.

Arieti, S., 1970. Cognition and feeling, in Arnold, M.B. (ed), *Feelings and Emotions —
The Loyola Symposium,* Academic Press, London, New York, Chapter 9.

Armstrong, H., 1964. The Relationship Between A Dimension of Body Image and Two
Dimensions of Conditioning, unpublished doctoral dissertation, Syracuse
University.

Arnheim, R., 1949. The Gestalt theory of expression, *Psychological Review,* no. 56,
156–171.

Arnheim, R., 1970. *Visual Thinking,* Faber and Faber, London.

Arnold, Magda B., 1961. *Emotion and personality, Neurological and Physiological
Aspects.* Cassell, London.

Arnold, Magda B., 1970. Perennial problems in the field of emotion, in Arnold, M.B.
(ed), *Feelings and Emotions — The Loyola Symposium,* Academic Press, New
York, London, Chapter 12, pp. 169ff.

Asch, S.E., 1964a. Forming impressions of personality, *Journal of Abnormal and
Social Psychology.* **41,** 258–290.

Asch, S.E., 1946b. Max Wertheimer's contribution to modern psychology, *Social
Research,* no. 13, 81–102.

Assagioli, R., 1965. *Psychosynthesis,* Hobbs Dorman, New York.

Assagioli, R., 1971. *Psychosynthesis,* Viking Press, New York, 217–224.

Atkinson, J.W., 1951. Recall of Successes and Failures Related to Difference in
Achievement, paper delivered at the APA Meeting.

Atkinson, R.C., and Shiffrin, R.M., 1968. Human memory: a proposed system and its
control processes, in Spence, K.W., and Spence, J.T. (eds), *The Psychology of
Learning and Motivation,* **2,** Academic Press, London.

Ausubel, D.P., 1968. *Educational Psychology (A Cognitive View),* Holt, Rinehart &
Winston, New York.

Ax, A.F., 1953. The physiological differentiation between fear and anger in humans,
Psychosomatic Medicine, **15,** 433–442.

Axelson, J.A. 1967. The relationship of counselor candidates' empathic perception and
rapport in small group interaction, *Counselor Education and Supervision,* no. 6(4),
287–292.

Baccelli, G., Guazzi, M., Libretti, A., and Zanchetti, A., 1965. Pressoceptive and
chemoceptive aortic reflexes in decorticate and decerebrate cats, *American Journal
of Physiology,* no. 208, 708–714.

Baer, R.A. Jr., 1976. A seminar on ecology and play: new directions in environmental
education, *Journal of College Science Teaching,* **6,** Part 1, 27–29.

Bahm, A.J. 1960. *Types of Intuition,* University of New Mexico Publications in Social
Sciences and Philosophy, no. 3, University of New Mexico Press.

Bahrick, H.P., Fotts, P.M., and Rankin, R.E., 1952. Effect of incentives upon reactions to peripheral stimuli, *Journal of Experimental Psychol.,* no. 44, 400–406.

Baldwin, A., 1966. The development of intuition, in Bruner, J. (ed), *Learning About
Learning,* no. 15, Bureau of Research (Co-Operation Research Monograph), USA
Printing Office, Washington DC.

Bandura, A., 1969. *Principles of Behaviour Modification,* Holt, Rinehart & Winston,
New York.

Barber, T.X., and Hahn, K.W. Jr., 1962. Physiological and subjective responses to
pain producing stimulation under hypnotically-suggested and waking-imagined
'analgesia', *J. Abnormal and Social Psychol.,* **65,** 411–418.

Barron, F., 1953. Complexity — simplicity as a personality dimension, *Journal of
Abnormal and Social Psychology,* **48,** no. 2.

Barron, F., 1963a. *Creativity and Psychological Health.* Van Nostrand, Princeton, NJ.

Barron, F., 1963b. The disposition toward originality, in Taylor, C.W., and Barron, F.
(eds), *Scientific Creativity: Its Recognition and Development.* John Wiley, New York.

Barron, F., and Mordkoff, A.M., 1968. An attempt to relate creativity to possible extrasensory empathy as measured by physiological arousal in identical twins, *Journal of the American Society for Psychical Research,* **62,** no. 1, 73–79.

Bartlett, E.S., 1971. A Dimensional and Typological Investigation of the Subjective Experience of Emotion, PhD thesis, Vanderbilt University.

Bartlett, F.C., 1932. *Remembering: A Study in Experimental and Social Psychology,* The University Press, Cambridge.

Bartlett, F.C., 1958. *Thinking,* George Allen & Unwin, London.

Bartlett, F.C., 1968. Adventurous thinking, in Wason, P.C., and Johnson-Laird, P.N. (eds), *Thinking and Reasoning,* Penguin Books, Harmondsworth, Chapter 11, 133–144.

Bassin, F.V., and Bein, E.S., 1961. Application of electromyography to the study of speech, in O'Connor, N. (ed), *Recent Soviet Psychology,* Liveright, New York.

Bastick, T., 1979. Psychophysiological Investigation of Intuitive Thought Processes and Creative Mathematical Problem-solving, PhD thesis (Education), Brunel University, Uxbridge, England.

Baumgardner, S.R., 1973. The impact of college experiences in conventional logic, *Journal of Counselling Psychology,* **23,** part 1, Jan, 40–45.

Bayles, E.E., 1950. *Theory and Practice of Teaching,* Hamish Hamilton, London.

Bayles, E.E., 1952. The idea of learning as development of insight, *Educational Theory,* **2,** no. 2, April, 65–71.

Beadle, M., 1971. *A Child's Mind,* Anchor Press, New York.

Beck, S.J., 1967. Emotional experience as a necessary constituent in knowing, in Reymert, M.L. (ed), *Feelings and Emotions – The Mooseheart Symposium,* Hafner, New York.

Becker, J.D., 1970. An Information-processing Model of Intermediate Cognition, Standford Artificial Intelligence Project, Memo A1-119.

Bellak, L., 1944. The concept of projection – an experimental investigation and study of the concept, *Psychiatry – Journal for the Study of Interpersonal Processes,* **7,** 353–370.

Benjafield, J., 1969. Logical and empirical thinking in a problem-solving task, *Psychonomic Science,* **14,** 285–286.

Bereiter, C., and Hidi, Suzanne, 1977. Biconditional Versus Factual Reasoning in Children, paper presented at the Biennial Meeting of the Society for Research in Child Development, New Orleans, Louisiana.

Beres, D., and Arlow, J.A., 1974. Fantasy and identification in empathy, *Psychoanalytic Quarterly,* **43**(1), 26–50.

Bergson, H., 1944, *Creative Evolution,* Modern Library, New York.

Berne, E., 1949. The nature of intuition, *Psychiatric Quarterly,* no. 23, 203–226.

Berne, E., 1955. Intuition IV. Primal images and printed judgment, *Psychiatric Quarterly,* no. 29, 634–658.

Berne, E., 1957. Intuition V. The ego image, *Psychiatric Quarterly,* no. 31, 611–627.

Berry, Joyce H., 1970. The Rorschach Inkblot Test as an Indication of Empathy, PhD thesis, University of Kentucky.

Bertelson, P., and Tisseyre, F., 1966. Choice reaction time as a function of stimulus versus response relative frequency of occurrence, *Nature,* no. 212, 1069–1070.

Besel, R.R., Kappenberger, R., Lees, Ruth, Sheehan, J.T., and Wesman, M., 1970. Evaluation Report: Project Insight 1969–1970, Department of Health, Education and Welfare, US Office of Education.

Beveridge, W.I.B., 1950. *The Art of Scientific Investigation,* Random House, New York.

Bice, D.T., 1973. Relationship Between Introversion – Extroversion and Learning Empathic Understanding, PhD thesis, University of Missouri, Columbia.

Bieri, J., Bradburn, W., and Gelinsky, M.D., 1958. Six differences in perceptual behaviour, *Journal Personality,* no. 26, 1–12.

Bigge, M.L., 1968. *Learning Theories for Teachers,* Harper & Row & John Weatherhill, New York.

Bigge, M.L., and Hunt, M.P., 1965. *Psychological Foundations of Education,* Harper & Row, New York.

Birch, H.G., 1945. The relation of previous experience to insightful problem-solving, *Journal of Comparative Psychology,* **38**, 367–383.

Birnbaum, M.H., 1976. Intuitive numerical prediction, *American Journal of Psychology,* **89**, no. 3, 417–429.

Birren, ,J.E., 1952. A factorial analysis of the Wechisier–Bellevue scale given to an elderly population, *Journal of Consulting Psychology,* no. 16, 399–405.

Bishop, A.J., 1973. Use of structural apparatus and spatial ability: a possible relationship, *Research in Education,* **9**, 43–49.

Bissell, Joan, White, Sheldon, and Zivin, Gail, 1971. Sensory modalities in children's learning, in Lesser, G.S. (ed), *Psychology and Educational Practice,* Scott, Foresman, London, Chapter 6.

Blake, M., 1973. Prediction of recognition when recall fails: exploring the feeling-of-knowing phenomenon, *Journal of Verbal Learning and Verbal Behaviour,* no. 12, 311–319.

Blake, R.W., 1976. Composing for the Left Hand: Writing Activities for the Intermediate Grades, Report, State University College at Brockport.

Blakeshlee, T.R., 1980. *The Right Brain,* Macmillan, Great Britain, London and Basingstoke.

Blatt, S., 1960. Experimental Evidence of Preconscious Functioning in Efficient Problem-solving, paper Read at EPA Meeting, New York.

Blatt, S., 1961. Patterns of cardiac arousal during complex mental activity, *Journal of Abnormal and Social Psycholoty,* no. 63, 272–282.

Bledsoe, J.L., 1976. Why, when, and how to use each of your four communicating styles, *Training,* **13**, Part 3, 18–21.

Block, J., and Petersen, P., 1955. Some personality correlates of confidence, caution, and speed in a decision situation, *Journal of Abnormal Social Psychology,* **51**, 34–41.

Bloemkolb, D., Defares, P., Van Enckevert, G., and Van Gelderen, M., 1971. Cognitive processing of information on varied physiological arousal, *European Journal of Social Psychology,* no. 1–1, 31–46.

Bloom, B.S., 1956. Report on Creativity Research at the University of Chicago, First University of Utah Research Conference on the Identification of Creative Scientific Talent, University of Utah Press, Salt Lake City.

Blumenthal, M., 1959. Lingual Myographic Responses During Directed Thinking, an abstract of a Dissertation presented to the Faculty of Graduate College, University of Denver.

Board, R., 1958. Intuition in the methodology of psychoanalysis, *Psychiatry,* **21**, 233–239.

Bodnar, W.A., 1975. The Relationship of Cognitive Controls to Psychological Types and Functions and Anxiety Level, PhD thesis, Boston University Graduate School.

Bogartz, R.S., 1976. On the meaning of statistical interactions, *Journal of Experimental Child Psychology,* **22**(1), 178–183.

Bohart, A.C., 1972. Roleplaying and the reduction of interpersonal conflict, *Dissertation Abstracts International,* **33**(1-B), July, 435–436. (University of California, Los Angeles, PhD thesis)

Bonvallet, M., and Allen, M.B., 1963. Prolonged spontaneous and evoked reticular activation following discrete bulbar lesions, *Electroenceph. Clin. Neurophysiol,* no. 15, 969–988.

Borke, Helene, 1972. Chandler and Greenspan's 'Ersatz Egocentricism', a rejoinder, *Developmental Psychology,* **7**, no. 2, 107–109.

Bousfield, W.A., Steward, Judith R., and Cowan, T.M., 1964. The use of free association norms for the prediction of clustering, *The Journal of General Psychology,* no. 70, 205–214.

Bouthilet, Lorraine, 1948. The Measurement of Intuitive Thinking, PhD thesis, Department of Psychology, University of Chicago.

Bower, G.H., 1967. A multicomponent theory of the memory trace, in Spence, K.W., and Spence, J.T. (eds), *Advances in the Psychology of Learning and Motivation Research and Theory,* vol. 1, Academic Press, New York.

Bower, G.H., 1972. Mental imagery and associative learning, in Gregg, L.W. (ed), *Cognition in Learning and Memory,* John Wiley, London, Chapter 3.

Bracewell, R.J., and Hidi, S.E., 1974. The solution of an inferential problem as a function of stimulus materials, *Quarterly Journal of Experimental Psychology,* no. 26, 480–488.

Brady, J.P., 1967. Psychotherapy learning theory and insight, *Archives of General Psychiatry,* **16**(3), 304–311.

Brady, J.V., 1970a. Emotion: some conceptual problems and psychophysiological experiments, in Arnold, M.B. (ed), *Feelings and Emotions — The Loyola Symposium,* Academic Press, New York, London.

Brady, J.V., 1970b. Endocrine and automatic correlates of emotional behaviour, in Black, P. (ed), *Physiological Correlates of Emotion,* Academic Press, New York, London.

Bridger, W.H., and Mandel, I.J.A., 1964. Comparison of GSR fear responses produced by threat and electric shock, *Journal of Psychiatric Research,* no. 2, 31–40.

Brindley, G.S., and Merton, P.A., 1960. The absence of position sense in the human eyes, in Bender, M.B. (ed), *The Oculomotor System,* Harper & Row, New York, 314–320.

Broadbent, D.E., 1958. *Perception and Communication,* Pergamon Press, London.

Bronfenbrenner, U., Harding, J., and Gallwey, M., 1958. The measurement of skill in social perception, in McClelland, D.C., Bronfenbrenner, U., Baldwin, A.L., and Stordtbeck, F.L.F. (eds), *Talent and Society,* Van Nostrand, Princeton.

Brosgole, L., and Neylon, Ann, 1973. Kinetic Visual imagery, *Perceptual and motor skills,* no. 37, 423–425.

Brown, C.H., 1937. The relation of magnitude of galvanic skin response and resistance levels to the rate of learning, *Journal of Experimental Psychology,* **20**, 262–278.

Brown, J.J., and Farber, I.E., 1951. Emotions conceptualized as intervening variables — with suggestions toward a theory of frustration, *Psychological Bulletin,* no. 48, 465–495.

Brown, R., 1975. The gut impact of the visual media, *Media and Methods,* **11**, part 9, 28–29.

Brown, R., and McNeill, D., 1966. The 'tip-of-the-tongue' phenomenon, *Journal of Verbal Learning and Verbal Behaviour,* no. 5, 325–337.

Brown, T., 1860. *Lectures on the Philosophy of the Human Mind,* 20th Edn, William Tegg, London.

Bruner, J.S., 1960. *The Process of Education,* Harvard University Press.

Bruner, J.S., 1962. *On Knowing — Essays for the Left Hand,* Belknap Press of Harvard University.

Bruner, J.S., 1963. *The Process of Education,* Vintage Books, Random House, New York.

Bruner, J.S., 1964. The act of discovery in Ripple, R.E. (ed), *Readings in Learning and Human Abilities,* Harper & Row, New York, Chapter 19, p. 242.

Bruner, J.S., and Clinchy, B., 1966. Towards a disciplined intuition, in Bruner, J. (ed),

Learning About Learning, no. 15, Bureau of Research (Co-Operative Research Monograph).

Bruner, J.S., and Kenney, H.J., 1965. Representation and mathematics learning, in Wason, P.C., and Johnson Laird, P.N. (eds), *Monograph of the Society for Research in Child Development,* **30,** Serial no. 99, 50–59.

Bruner, J.S., and Tagiuri, R., 1954. The perception of people, in Lindzey, G. (ed), *Handbook of Social Psychology,* vol. 2, Addison Wesley, Cambridge, Mass., Chapter 17.

Brunswik, E., 1956. *Perception and the Representative Design of Experiments,* University of California Press, Berkeley.

Brunswik, E., 1966. Reasoning as a universal behaviour model and a functional differentiation between 'perception' and 'thinking', in Hammond, K.R. (ed), *The Psychology of Egon Brunswik,* Holt, Rinehart & Winston, New York.

Buchheimer, A., 1963. The development of ideas about empathy, *Journal of Counselling Psychology,* **10,** part 1, 61–70.

Buckminster Fuller, R., 1972. *Intuition,* Doubleday, Garden City, New York.

Bugelski, B., 1956. *Psychology of Learning,* Holt, Rinehart & Winston, New York.

Bulbrook, Mary E., 1932. An experimental inquiry into the existence and nature of 'insight', *The American Journal of Psychology,* **XLIV,** no. 3, July, 409–453.

Bunge, M., 1962. *Intuition and Science,* Prentice-Hall, Englewood Cliffs, NJ.

Burden, Virginia, 1975. *The Process of Intuition — A Psychology of Creativity,* The Theosophical Publishing House, London.

Burke, R.J., and Maier, N.R.F., 1965. Attempts to predict success on an insight problem, *Psychological Reports,* no. 17, 303–310.

Byrne, D., 1966. *An Introduction to Personality — A Research Approach,* Prentice-Hall, Englewood Cliffs, NJ.

Callaway, E., and Thompson, S.V., 1953. Sympathetic activity and perception, *Psychosom. Med.,* no. 15, 443–455.

Camp, Bonnie W., and Zimet, Sara G., 1973. Recall of aggressive words by kindergarten children, *Psychological Reports,* **33,** no. 2, 575–578.

Campbell, H.J., and Eayrs, J.T., 1965. Influence of hormones on the central nervous system, *British Medical Bulletin,* no. 21, 81–86.

Cannon, W.B., 1932. *The Wisdom of the Body,* Norton, New York, 38.

Cantril, H., and Hunt, W.A., 1932. Emotional effects produced by the injection of adrenalin, *American Journal of Psychology,* no. 44, 300–307.

Cartwright, Mary L., 1955. The mathematical mind, James Boyce Memorial Lecture, Oxford University Press.

Cartwright, Rosalind, née Dymond, 1961. Comments on Presentation: Empathy in Counselling, American Personnel & Guidance Association, Denver, Colorado.

Castadena, A., Palermo, D.S., and McCandless, B.R., 1956. Complex learning and performance as a function of anxiety in children and task difficulty, *Child Development,* **27,** 327–332.

Cattell, R.B., 1946. Description and measurement of personality, World Book Co., Yonkers, New York.

Cattell, R.B., and Butcher, H.J., 1968. The prediction of achievement and creativity, Bobbs-Merrill, New York, 276–278, 289–96.

Cattell, R.B., and Drevdahl, J.E., 1955. A comparison of the personality profile (16PF) of eminent researchers with that of eminent teachers and administrators and of the general population, *British Journal of Psychology,* **46,** 248–261.

Chappell, Marcia H., 1976. The place of reference service in Ranganathan's theory of librarianship, *Library Quarterly,* **46,** no. 4, 378–396.

Chase, W.G., 1973. Visual Information Processing, Proceedings of the 8th Annual Carnegie Symposium on Cognition held at the Carnegie-Melton University, Pittsburgh, Pennsylvania, Academic Press, New York.

398

Chesterton, G.K., 1950. The Wrong Shape, *The Father Brown Stories,* Cassell, London.

Child, D., and Smithers, A., 1971. Some cognitive and affective factors in subject choice, *Research in Education,* no. 5, 1–9.

Chinsky, J.M., and Rappaport, J., 1970. Brief critique of the meaning and reliability of 'accurate empathy' ratings, *Psychological Bulletin,* **73,** no. 5, 379–382.

Christie, L.S., and Luce, R.D., 1956. Decision structure and time relations in simple choice behaviour, *Bull. Maths. Biophys.,* no. 18, 89–111.

Clark, F.V., 1973. Exploring intuition: prospects and possibilities, *Journal of Transpersonal Psychology,* **3,** 156–169.

Clark, H.C., and Clark, E.V., 1968. Semantic distinctions and memory for complex sentences, *Quarterly Journal of Experimental Psychology,* no. 20, 129–138.

Clark, J., 1973. Observation as moderator of reason and intuition in clinical training, *Psychology in the Schools,* **10,** no. 2, 214–221.

Clinchy, B., 1958. The role of intuition in learning, *National Education Association Journal,* **LVII,** Feb., 33–37.

Clinchy, B., 1975. The role of intuition in learning, *Today's Education,* **64**(2), April, 48–51.

Cobb, S., 1952. *Foundations of Neuropsychiatry,* 5th edn., Williams & Wilkins, Baltimore.

Cohen, D., 1978. Psychologists on psychology, *Journal of National Association of Teachers in Further and Higher Education,* no. 2, 18 (Routledge & Kegan Paul).

Cohen, H.D., and Harvey, D., 1975. The effects of stress on components of the respiration cycle, *Psychophysiology,* **12,** no. 4, 377–388.

Cohen, M.J., 1962. The peripheral organization of sensory systems, Chapter 13 in Reizz, R.F. (ed) (1964), *Neutral Theory and Modelling — Proceedings of the 1962 Ojai Symposium,* Stanford University Press.

Colgan, D.M., 1970. Effects of instructions on the skin resistance response, *Journal of Experimental Psychology,* **86,** no. 1, 108–112.

Collins, A.M., and Quillian, M.R., 1972a. Experiments on semantic memory and language comprehension, in Gregg, L.W. (ed), *Cognition in Learning and Memory,* John Wiley, New York, Chapter 5.

Collins, A.M., and Quillian, M.R., 1972b. How to make a language user, in Tulving, E., (ed), *Organization of Memory,* Academic Press, London, Chapter 8.

Combs, A.W., and Taylor, C., 1952. The effect of the perception of mild degrees of threat on performance, *Journal of Abnormal and Social Psychology,* no. 47, 420–424.

Comella, T., 1971. Understanding creativity for use in managerial planning, in Davis, G.A., and Scott, J.A. (eds), *Training Creative Thinking,* Holt, Rinehart & Winston, New York, Chapter 13.

Conklin, K.R., 1970. Educational evaluation and intuition, *Educational Forum,* **34,** part 3, 323–332.

Conrad, R., 1964. Accoustic confusions in immediate memory, *British Journal of Psychology,* no. 55, 75–84.

Cooper, L., 1970. Empathy: a developmental model, *Journal of Nervous and Mental Disease,* **151**(3), 169–178.

Costello, C.G., 1961. Constant errors in the measurement of kinaesthetic figural aftereffects, *American Journal of Psychology,* no. 74, 473–474.

Courtney, R., 1968. *Play, Drama and Thought,* Cassell, London.

Cowen, E.L., 1952. The influence of varying degrees of psychological stress on problem-solving rigidity, *Journal of Abnormal and Social Psychology,* **47,** 512–519.

Craig, K.D., and Wood, K., 1970. Physiological differentiation of direct and vicarious affective arousal, *Canadian Journal of Behavioural Science,* **1,** no. 2, 98–105.

Cronbach, L.J., 1958. Proposals leading to analytic treatment of social perception scores, in Tagiuri, R., and Petrullo, L. (eds), *Person Perception and Interpersonal Behaviour,* Stanford University Press, Stanford.

Cronbach, L.J., and Meehl, P.E., 1955. Construct validity in psychological tests, *Psychological Bulletin,* **52,** 281–302.

Crutchfield, R.S., 1960. Male superiority in 'intuitive' problem-solving, *American Psychologist,* **15,** 429.

Daniels, U.P., 1973. The Effect of Perceived Locus of Control and Psychological Stress on Intuitive Problem Solving, PhD thesis, York University, Toronto, Ontario.

Darwin, C., 1872. *The Expression of the Emotions in Man and Animals,* Murray, London.

Davis, G.A., and Scott, J.A., 1971. *Training Creative Thinking,* Holt, Rinehart & Winston, New York.

Davitz, J.R., 1964. Personality, perceptual and cognitive correlates of emotional sensitivity, in Davitz, J.R. (ed), *The Communication of Emotional Meaning,* McGraw-Hill, New York, Chapter 5, 57–68.

Davitz, J.R., and Ball, S., 1970. *Psychology of the Educational Process,* McGraw-Hill, New York, 169–170.

Deese, J., 1959. Influence on inter-item associative strength upon immediate free recall, *Psychological Reports,* **5,** 305–312.

De Groot, A.D., 1965. *Thought and Choice in Chess,* Sections 58 and 62, Mouton, NV.

De Soto, C., London, M., and Handel, S., 1965. Social reasoning and spatial paralogic, *Journal Pers. Soc. Psychology,* no. 2, 513–521.

Delgado, J.M.R., 1970. Modulation of emotions by cerebral radio stimulation, in Black, P. (ed), *Physiological Correlates of Emotion,* Academic Press, London, Chapter 9.

Deutsch, Francine, and Madle, R.A., 1975. Empathy: historic and current conceptualizations, measurement and a cognitive theoretical perspective, *Human Development,* **18,** no. 4, 267–287.

Dinero, T.E., 1970. The Prediction of Semantic Differential Responses Using Denotative Referents: Validation of a Mathematical Model for the Generation of Affect to Words in Isolation, PhD thesis (Education, Psychology), May, State University of New York at Buffalo.

Dittmann, A.T., 1972. *Interpersonal Messages of Emotion,* Springer, New York.

Doktor, R., and Bloom, D.M., 1977. Selective lateralization of cognitive style related to occupation as determined by EEG alpha asymmetry, *Psychophysiology,* **14**(4), 385–387.

Dominowski, R.L., and Jenrick, Regina, 1972. Effects of hints and interpolated activity on solution of an insight problem, *Psychon. Science,* **26,** no. 6, 335–337.

Drevdahl, J.E., 1956. Factors of importance to creativity, *Journal of Clinical Psychology,* **2,** 21–26.

Drevdahl, J.E., and Cattell, R.B., 1958. Personality and creativity in artists and writers, *Journal of Clinical Psychology,* **14,** 107–111.

Drever, J., 1934. The pre-insight period in learning, *British Journal of Psychology,* **25,** 197–203.

Drever, J., 1974. *A Dictionary of Psychology,* Penguin Books, Harmondsworth.

Dry, Avis M., 1961. *The Psychology of Jung,* John Wiley, New York.

Dukes, W., and Bevan, W., 1952. Accentuation and response variability in the perception of personally relevant objects, *Journal Person,* no. 20, 457–467.

Duncan, C.P., 1962. Probability vrs. latency of solution of an insight problem, *Psychological Reports,* no. 20, 119–121.

Duncker, K., 1945. On problem solving, *Psychological Monographs: General and Applied,* Greenwood Press, Westport, Connecticut.

Dunlap, K., 1932. Are emotions teleological constructs? *American Journal of Psychology,* no. 44, 572–576.

Duval, S., and Wickland, R.A., 1972. *A Theory of Objective Self-Awareness,* Academic Press, London.

Dwyer, J.H., III, 1975. Contextual Inferences and the Right Cerebral Hemisphere: Listening with the Left Ear. PhD thesis, Psychology Social, University of California, Santa Cruz.

Dymond, Rosalind F., 1948. A preliminary investigation of the relation of insight and empathy, *Journal of Consulting Psychology,* no. 12, 228–233.

Dymond, Rosalind F., 1949. A scale for the measurement of empathic ability, *Journal of Consulting Psychology,* no. 13, 127–133.

Dymond, Rosalind F., 1950. Personality and empathy, *Journal of Consulting Psychology,* no. 14, 343–350.

Eagle, M., 1962. Personality correlates of sensitivity to sublimal stimulation, *Journal of Nervous and Mental Diseases,* no. 134, 1–17.

Earle, T.C., 1972. Intuitive and Analytical Thinking in Consistent and Inconsistent Multiple-Cue Learning Tasks, PhD thesis, University of Oregon.

Easterbrook, J.A., 1959. The effect of emotion on cue utilization and the organization of behaviour, *Psychological Review,* **66,** no. 3, 183–201.

Elder, Connie Z., 1973. Miniature sand environments: a new way to see and feel and explain from young children, **28**(5), 283–286.

Elms, A.C., 1966. Influence on fantasy ability on attitude change through role playing, *Journal of Personality and Social Psychology,* **4,** no. 1, 36–43.

English, H.B., and English, Ava C., 1958. *A Comprehensive Dictionary of Psychological and Psychoanalytical Terms,* Longmans, Green, New York.

Epstein, S., and Smith, R., 1956. Repressions and insight as related to reaction to cartoons, *Journal of Consulting Psychology,* **20,** no. 5, 391–395.

Eriksen, G.W., and Kuethe, J.L., 1956. Avoidance conditioning of verbal behaviour without awareness: a paradigm of repression, *Journal of Abnormal and Social Psychology,* **53,** 203–209.

Eutsch, M.D., 1954. Field theory in social psychology, in Gardner Lindzer (ed), *Handbook of Social Psychology,* Addison-Wesley, New York, 191.

Evans, J. St. B., and Dusoir, A.E., 1977. Proportionality and sample size as factors in intuitive statistical judgment, *Acta Psychologica,* **41**(2-3), 129–237.

Evered, R.D., 1977. Organizational activism and its relation to 'reality' and mental imagery, *Human Relations,* **30**(4), 311–334.

Everitt, B., 1978. *Graphical Techniques for Multivariate Date,* Heinemann Educational Books, London.

Ewing, A.C., 1941. Reason and intuition, *Proceedings of the British Academy,* **55,** 67–107.

Eyring, H., 1959. Scientific creativity, in Anderson, H.H. (ed) *Creativity and Its Cultivation,* Harper & Row, New York, Chapter 1, 6.

Eysenck, H.J., 1953. *The Structure of Human Personality,* John Wiley, New York.

Farmer, C., 1961. An Experimental Approach to the Measurement of Intuition, unpublished manuscript, Teachers' College, Columbia University.

Feffer, M.H., 1959. The cognitive implications of role-taking behaviour, *Journal of Personality,* **27,** 152–168.

Feffer, M.H., and Gourevitch, V., 1960. Cognitive aspects of role-taking in children, *Journal of Personality.* part 28, 383–396.

Fehr, F.S., and Stern, J.A., 1970. Peripheral physiological variables and emotion: the James Lange theory revisited, *Psychological Bulletin,* no. 74, 411–424.

Feilberg, L., 1949. On offensive physiognomy, in *Saulede Skrifter* (Collected Papers), 3rd Edn., vol. 2, Copenhagen, p. 284ff.

Feldman, M.J., and Bullock, D.H., 1955. Some factors related to insight, *Psychological Reports,* no. 1, 143–152.

Fenichel, O., 1945. *Psychoanalytic Theory of the Neuroses,* Norton, New York.

Fenichel, O., 1953. Identification, in *Collected Papers,* First Series, Norton, New York, 97–112.

Fernald, Grace M., 1943. *Remedial Techniques in Basic School Subjects,* McGraw-Hill, New York.

Festinger, L., and Kirkpatrick, C.L., 1965. Information about spatial location based on knowledge about efference, *Psychological Review,* **72,** no. 5, 373–384.

Finesmith, S., 1959. Systematic Changes in GSR Activity as a Physiological Correlate of Paired-associates Learning. Paper presented at the Meeting of the Third Conference on Learning, Remembering, and Forgetting, Western Psychological Association, May, Chicago.

Fischbein, E., 1972. Notes on Intuition and Comprehension in Mathematical Education, paper given at Second International Congress on Mathematical Education, Exeter University, England.

Fischbein, E., Pampu, I., and Minzat, J., 1967. Intuition probabiliste chez l'enfant, *Enfance,* no. 2, 193–208.

Fischbein, E., Pampu, I., and Minzat, J., 1970. Comparison of ratios and the chance concept in children, *Child Development,* **41,** no. 2, 377–389.

Fisher, S.A., 1958. *A Body Image and Personality,* Van Nostrand, Princeton, NJ.

Fisher, S.A., 1959. Prediction of body exterior vrs. body interior reactivity from a body image scheme, *Journal of Personality,* no. 27, 56–62.

Fisher, S.A., 1963. A further appraisal of the body boundary concept, *Journal of Consulting Psychology,* no. 27, 62–74.

Fisher, S.A., 1964. Sex differences in body perception, *Psychological Monographs: General and Applied,* **78,** no. 14 (Whole no. 591).

Fisher, S.A., 1968. *Body Image and Personality,* 2nd rev. edn, Dover, New York.

Fisher, S.A., and Cleveland, S.E., 1968 *Body Image and Personality,* Dover, New York.

Flavell, J.H., 1968. *The Development of Role-taking and Communication Skills in Children,* John Wiley, London.

Folkins, C.H., 1970. Temporal factors and the cognitive mediators of stress reaction, *Journal of Person. Soc. Psychol.,* no. 14, 172–183.

Foulkes, D., 1966. *The Psychology of Sleep,* Scribner, New York.

Fox, H.M., Murawski, J., Bartholamay, A.F., and Gifford, S., 1961. Adrenal steroid excretion patterns in 18 healthy subjects, *Psychosomatic Medicine,* no. 23, 33–40.

Fox, Muriel, 1960. Regression as an aid to subliminal sensitivity, *American Psychologist,* **15,** 429.

Franco, Laura, and Sperry, R.W., 1977. Hemisphere lateralization for cognitive processing of geometry, *Neuropsychologia,* **15,** 107–114.

Frankle, A.H., 1953. Rorschach Human Movement and Human Content Responses as Indices of the Adequacy of Interpersonal Relationships of Social Work Students, doctoral dissertation, University of Chicago.

Frederick, W.C., 1967. Information processing and concept learning at Grades Six, Eight and Ten as a function of cognitive styles, *Dissertation Abstracts International,* no. 28, 4478–A.

French, Elizabeth, 1958. Development of a measure of complex motivation, in Atkinson, J.W. (ed), *Motives in Fantasy, Action and Society,* Van Nostrand, Princeton.

Freud, S., 1916. Metapsychological supplement to the theory of dreams, *Collected Papers 4,* Hogarth Press, London, 1948, 137–151.

Freund, C.J., 1976. Training for technological toss-ups, *Engineering Education,* **66,** part 5, 418–422.

Frick, R.C., 1970. A Study of Intuition and Inference, Atlanta University, School of Education, Georgia.

Frijda, N.H., 1970. Emotion and recognition of emotion, in Arnold, M.L. (ed), *Feelings and Emotions — The Loyola Symposium*, Academic Press, New York, London, 241–250.

Fromm-Reichmann, F., 1955. Clinical significance of intuitive process of the psychoanalyst, *Journal of the American Psychoanalysis Association*, no. 3, 82–88.

Fuhrer, M.J., and Baer, P.E., 1965. Differential classical conditioning: verbalization of stimulus contingencies, *Science*, no. 150, 1479–1481.

Furth, H.G., and Terry, R.A., 1961. Autonomic responses and serial learning, *Journal of Comparative and Physiological Psychology*, **54**, no. 2, 139–142.

Gagne, R.M., 1965. *Conditions of Learning*. Hold, New York.

Garard, R.W., 1962. How the brain creates ideas, in Parnes, S.J., and Harding, H.F. (eds), *A Source Book for Creative Thinking*, Selection 11, Scribner, New York.

Gardner, R.W., Holzman, P.S., Klein, G.S., Linton, J.R., and Spence, D.P., 1959. Cognitive control — a study of individual consistencies in cognitive behaviour, *Psychological Issues*, **1**, no. 4, monograph 4.

Garvill, J., and Milander, B., 1968. Asymmetric effects in cross-modal transfer, *UMEA Psychological Reports*, no. 3.

Gaughran, E., 1963. Physiognomic Perception: A Study of a Cognitive Style in Relation to Qualities of Body Experience, PhD thesis (Psychology, clinical), New York University.

Gellen, M.I., 1970. Finger blood volume response of counselors, counselor trainees, and non-counselors to stimuli from an empathy test, *Counselor-Education and Supervision*, **10**, no. 1, 64–74.

Gellhorn, E., 1957. *Autonomic Imbalance and the Hypothalamus, Implications for Physiology, Medicine, Psychology and Neuropsychiatry*, University of Minnesota Press.

Gellhorn, E., 1964. Motion and emotion: The role of proprioception in the physiology and pathology of the emotions, *Psychological Review*, **71**, no. 6, 457–472.

Gellhorn, E., and Loufbourrow, G.N., 1963. *Emotions and Emotional Disorders*, Hoeber, New York.

George, F.H., 1962. *Cognition*. Methuen, London.

Gerard, R.W., 1966. How the brain creates ideas, in Taylor, C.W., and Williams, F.E. (eds), *Instructional Media and Creativity*, Utah Creativity 6th Research Conference 1964, John Wiley, New York.

Gerber, L.A., 1972. Measurement of statements made about emotion: an investigation of the affect-cognition scale, *Psychological Reports*, no. 30, 231–235.

Germana, J., 1964. Autonomic Correlates of Acquisition and Extinction, unpublished Master's thesis, Rutgers — The State University.

Germana, J., 1966. Activational Peaking: The Role of General Activation in the Elaboration of Conditioned Responses, doctorial thesis, Rutgers — The State University.

Germana, J.J., 1968. Psychophysiological correlates of conditioned response formation, *Psychological Bulletin*, **70**, no. 2, 105–114.

Germana, J.J., and Pavlik, W.B., 1964. Autonomic correlates of acquisition and extinction, *Psychonomic Science*, no. 1, 109–110.

Ghistra, D., Nandagopal, D., Ramamurthi, B., Das, A., Mukherji, A., and Sprinivasan, T.M., 1976. Physiological characterisation of the 'meditative state' during intuitional practice (The Ananda Marga System of Meditation) and its therapeutic value, *Medical and Biological Engineering*, **14**, part 2, 209–214.

Gibson, J.J., 1962. Observations on active-touch, *Psychological Review*, **69**, no. 6, 477–491.

Gilbert, G.S., and Rappaport, L., 1975. Categories of thought and variations in meaning: a demonstration experiment, *Journal of Phenomenological Psychology,* **5**(2), 419–424.

Gilhooly, K.J., and Falconer, K.J., 1974. Concrete and abstract terms and relations in testing a rule, *Quarterly Journal of Experimental Psychology,* no. 26, 355–359.

Giordana, G., 1976. Disciplinary organization in critical reading, *Reading World,* **16**(1), 5–8.

Gitter, A.G., Mostofsky, D.I., and Quincy, A.J., 1971. Race and sex differences in the child's perception of emotion, *Child Development,* no. 42, 2071–2075.

Goodwin, R.Q., and Wason, P.C., 1972. Degrees of insight, *British Journal of Psychology,* no. 63(2), 205–212.

Gopal Rao, G.S., Penfold, D.M., and Penford, A.P., 1970. Modern and traditional mathematics teaching, *Educational Research,* no. 13, 61–65.

Gordon, F.R., and Flavell, J.H., 1977. The development of intuitions about cognitive cueing, *Child Development,* no. 48, 1027–1033.

Gordon, W.J.J., 1961. *Synectics, The Development of Creative Capacity,* Harper & Row, New York.

Govinda, L.A., 1974. *Foundations of Tibetan Mysticism,* Samuel Weiser, New York.

Gray, C.W., 1968. Predicting with intuitive correlations, *Psychon. Science,* **11**(2), 41–42.

Green, E., Green, A., and Walters, D., 1970. Voluntary control of internal states: psychological and physiological, *Journal of Transpersonal Psychology,* no. 1, 1–26.

Greeno, J.G., 1972. On the acquisition of a simple cognitive structure, in Tulving, E. (ed), *Organization of Memory,* Academic Press, London, Chapter 9.

Greenson, R.R., 1960. Empathy and its vicissitudes, *International Journal of Psycho-analysis,* **41**, 418–434.

Griesinger, D.W., 1974. The physics of behavioural systems, *Behavioural Science,* **19**, part 1, 35–51.

Griew, S., 1958. Age changes and information loss in performance on a pursuit-tracking task involving interrupted preview, *Journal of Experimental Psychology,* no. 55, 486–489.

Griffiths, H.B., 1972. Mathematical insight and mathematical curricula, *Mathematics in School,* **1**, part 3, 3–7.

Griffiths, H.B., and Howson, A.G, 1974. *Mathematics Society and Curricula,* Cambridge University Press.

Grim, P.F., 1975. Relaxation, meditation and insight, *Psychologia,* no. 18, 125–333.

Grings, W.W., 1973. The role of consciousness and cognition in autonomic behaviour change, in McGuigan, F.H., and Schoonover, R.A. (eds), *The Psychophysiology of Thinking,* Academic Press, London, Chapter 7.

Grossman, D., 1951. The construction and validation of two insight inventories, *Journal of Consulting Psychology,* no. 15, 109–114.

Guilford, J.P., 1950. Creativity: Its Measurement and Development, Presidential Address of the American Psychological Association at Pennsylvania State College.

Guilford, J.P., 1956. The structure of intellect, *Psychological Bulletin,* no. 53, 267–293.

Guilford, J.P., 1959. Traits of creativity, in Anderson, H.H. (ed), *Creativity and its Cultivation,* Harper & Row, New York, Chapter 10.

Guilford, J.P., 1966. Basic problems in teaching for creativity, in Taylor, C.W., and Williams, F.E. (eds), *Instructional Media and Creativity.* John Wiley, London, Chapter 3.

Guilford, J.P., 1967. *The Nature of Human Intelligence,* McGraw-Hill, New York.

Guilford, J.P., and Fruchter, B., 1973. *Fundamental Statistics in Psychology and Education,* McGraw-Hill, New York.

Guiora, A.Z., 1965. On clinical diagnosis and prediction, *Psychological reports,* no. 17, 779–784.

Guiora, A.Z., Bolin, R.K., Dutton, C.E., and Meer, B., 1965. Intuition: a preliminary statement, *Psychiatric Quarterly,* **39,** part 1, 110–122.

Gupta, G.C., 1973. Effect on lateral body tilts and visual frames on perception of the apparent vertical, *Journal of Experimental Psychology,* **100,** no. 1, 162–167.

Haber, W.B., 1956. Observations on phantom limb phenomena, *American Medical Association: Archives of Neurology and Psychiatry,* no. 75, 624–636.

Hadamard, J., 1945. *The Psychology of Invention in the Mathematical Field,* Princeton University Press.

Haddon, F.A., and Lytton, H., 1968. Teaching approach and the development of divergent thinking abilities in primary schools, *The British Journal of Educational Psychology,* no. 38, 171–180.

Haefele, J.W., 1962. *Creativity and Innovation,* Reinhold Publishing Corporation, New York.

Hahn, H., 1953. The crisis in intuition, in J.R. Newman (ed), *The World of Mathematics,* **3,** George Allen & Unwin, London, 1956–1976.

Hamlyn, D.W., 1961. Sensation and perception: a history of the philosophy of perception, in Ayer, A.J. (ed), Routledge & Kegan Paul, London.

Hammer, E.F., 1973. Creativity in the therapy situation, *Art Psychotherapy,* **1**(1), 1–6.

Hammond, L.J., 1970. Conditioned emotional states, in Black, P. (ed), *Physiological Correlates of Emotion,* Academic Press, New York, London, 245–259.

Hanfmann, E., 1941. A study of personal patterns in an intellectual performance, *Character and Personality,* no. 9, 315–325.

Harlow, H.F., 1949. The formation of learning sets, *Psychological Review,* no. 56, 51–65.

Hartmann, G.W., 1931. The concept and criteria of insight, *Psychological Review,* **38,** 243–253.

Hartmann, G.W., 1933. Insight vrs. trial and error in the solution of problems, *American Journal of Psychology,* **XLV,** 663–677.

Hartmann, H., 1939. *Ego Psychology and the Problem of Adaptations,* International Universities Press, New York (Pub. 1958).

Hartmann, H., Kris, E., and Lowenstein, R.M., 1947. Comments on the formation of psychic structure, in Freud, A. (ed), *The Psychoanalytic Study of the Child,* Volume 11. International Universities Press, New York, 11–38.

Harty, M.K., 1970. The Capacity for Adaptive Regression as a Component of Empathic Ability, PhD thesis (psychology clinical), The University of Michigan.

Harvey, O.J., 1965. Cognitive Aspects of Affective Arousal in Tomkins, S.S., and Izard, C.E. (eds), *Affect, Cognition and Personality,* Springer Pub., New York.

Harvey, O.J., and Beverley, G.D., 1961. Some personality correlates of concept change through role playing, *J. Abnormal Social Psychology,* **63,** 125–130.

Hastorf, A.H., and Bender, I.E., 1952. A caution respecting the measurement of empathic ability, *Journal of Abnormal and Social Psychology,* no. 47, 574–576.

Hathaway, S.R., 1955. Clinical intuition and inferential accuracy, *Journal of Personality,* no. 24, 223–250.

Hayward, A.L., and Sparkes, J.J., 1970. *English Dictionary,* Cassell, London.

Hebb, D.O., 1946. Emotion in Man and Animals: An Analysis of the Intuitive Processes of Recognition, *Yerkes Laboratories of Primate Biology Psychological Review,* **53,** 88–106.

Hebb, D.O., 1949. *Organization of Behaviour,* John Wiley, New York.

Hebb, D.O., 1968. Concerning imagery, *Psychological Review,* **75**(6), 466–477.

Hefferline, R.F., Keenan, B., and Hartford, R.A., 1959. Escape and avoidance conditioning in human subjects without their observation of the response, *Science,* **130,** November, 1338–1339.

Hefferline, R.F., and Perera, T.B., 1963. Proprioceptive discrimination of a covert operant without its observation by the subject, *Science,* **139**, March, 834–835.

Heilman, K.A., 1972. Empathy, The Construct and its Measurement, PhD thesis, Purdue University, University Microfilms 72-30904.

Helson, H., 1927. 'Insight' in the white rat, *Journal of Experimental Psychology,* no. 10, 378–396.

Henderson, A., 1946. Science and art: an approach to a new synthesis, *American Scientist,* no. 34, 453–463.

Herring, F.H., 1956. Response during anaesthesia and surgery, *Psychosom. Med.,* no. 18, 234–251.

Hilgard, E.R., 1959. Creativity and problem-solving, in Anderson, H.H. (ed), *Creativity and its Cultivation,* Harper & Row, New York, Chapter 11, pp. 164ff.

Hill, J.C., 1976. The unconscious and the scientific method, *Reiss Davis Clinical Bulletin,* **13**(1), 45–48.

Hoff, Phyllis A., 1971. Scales of selected aspects of kinaesthesis, *Perception and Psychophysics,* **9**(1B).

Hohle, R.H., 1965. Inferred components of reaction times as functions of fore-period duration, *Journal of Experimental Psycholoyg,* **69**, 382–386.

Hohmann, G.W., 1962. The Effect of Dysfunctions of the Autonomic Nervous System on the Experienced Feelings and Emotions, paper presented at the Conference on Emotions and Feelings at the New School for Social Research, October, New York.

Hohmann, G.W., 1966. Some effects of spinal cord lesions on experienced emotional feelings, *Psychophys.,* no. 3, 143–156.

Holst, E. Von., 1954, Relations between the central nervous system and peripheral organs, *British Journal of Animal Behaviour,* **3**, 89–94.

Holtzmann, W.H., and Bitterman, M.E., 1956. A factorial study of adjustment to stress, *Journal of Abnormal and Social Psychology,* no. 52, 179–185.

Honkavaara, S., 1961. The psychology of expressions, *British Journal of Psychology: Monogram Supplement,* no. 32.

Hudson, L., 1968. *Frames of Mind,* Methuen, London.

Hull, C.L., 1943. *Principles of Behaviour,* Appleton-Century-Crofts, New York.

Huntley, C.W., 1940. Judgments of self based upon records of expressive behaviour, *Journal of Abnormal and Social Psychology,* no. 35, 398–427.

Hutchinson, E.D., 1941. The nature of insight, *Psychiatry — Journal for the Study of Interpersonal Processes.* **4**, 31–43.

Irwin, F.W., Kauffman, K., Prior, G., and Weaver, H.B., 1934. On learning without awareness of what is being learned, *Journal of Exp. Psychology,* no. 17, 823–827.

Israel, N.R., 1969. Levelling-sharpening and anticipatory cardiac resonse, *Psychosomatic Medicine,* no. 31, 499–509.

Izard, C.E., and Tomkins, S.S., 1966. Affect and behaviour: anxiety as negative affect, in Spielberger, G.D. (ed), *Anxiety and Behaviour,* Academic Press, New York, London.

Jackson, P.W., 1971. The way teachers think, in Lesser, G.S. (ed), *Psychology and Educational Practice,* Scott, Foresman, Glenview, Illinois. p. 10.

Jacobson, E., 1932. Electrophysiology of mental activities, *American Journal of Psychology,* **44**, 677–694.

Jacbson, E., 1967. *Biology of Emotions,* Charles C. Thomas, Springfield, Ill. 91–120.

Jacobson, E., and Kraft, F.L., 1942. Contraction potentials (right *quadricepts femoris*) in man during reading, *American Journal of Psychology,* **137**, 1–5.

Jacobson, R.W., 1944. A method of psychobiologic evaluation, *Amer. Journal Psychiat.,* **101**, 343–348.

Jaensčh, E.R., 1930. *Eidetic Imagery,* Kegan Paul, London.

James, W., 1950. *Principles of Psychology,* Holt, New York.

Jenkins, J.M., and Russell, W.A., 1952. Associative clustering during recall, *Journal of Abnormal and Social Psychology,* no. 47, 818–821.

Jenkins, N., 1957. Affective processes in perception, *Psychological Bulletin,* no. 54, 100–127.

Jensen, K., 1960. Conditions Influencing Insight and Problem-solving Behaviour in the Mentally Retarded, Report No. CRP-150, Wisconsin University, Madison, School of Education.

Jessor, R., and Richardson, S., 1968. Psychological deprivation and personality development, *Perspectives on Human Deprivation,* Washington DC, Dept. of Health, Education and Welfare.

John, E.R., 1957. Contributions to the study of the problem-solving process, *Psychological Monographs: General and Applied,* **71,** no. 18 (Whole no. 447).

Johnson, D.M., 1972. *Systematic Introduction to the Psychology of Thinking,* Harper & Row, New York.

Johnson, E.M., 1974. The Effect of Data Source Reliability on Intuitive Inference, Army Research Institute for the Behavioural and Social Sciences — Technical Paper, no. 251.

Johnson, Relda J., 1971. An Exploration of Relationships Between and Among Empathy, Trust and Ego Stage Development in the Adult Learner, PhD thesis, Michigan State University.

Johnson-Laird, P.N., and Wason, P.C., 1970a. Insight into a logical relation, *Q.J. Exp. Psycol.,* **22,** 49–61.

Johnson-Laird, P.N., and Wason, P.C., 1970b. A theoretical analysis of insight into a reasoning task, *Cognitive Psychology,* no. 1, 134–148.

Jones, B., 1972. Outflow and inflow in movement duplication, *Perception and Psychophysics,* **12**(1B).

Jones, B., 1973. When are vision and kinaesthesis comparable? *British Journal of Psychology,* **64,** no. 4, 587–591.

Jones, E., 1953. *Sigmund Freud: Life and Works,* vol. 1, Hogarth Press, London.

Jung, C.G., 1926. *Psychological Types,* translated by Byrnes, H.G., Harcourt, Brace, New York.

Jung, C.G., 1969. Psychological types, in De Laszco (ed), *The Basic Writings of C.G. Jung.* Random House, New York.

Kagan, J., Moss, H.A., and Sigel, I.E., 1963. Psychological significance of styles of conceptualization, *Monographs of the Society for Research in Child Development,* no. 28, 73–112.

Kagan, J., and Phillips, W., 1964. Measurement of identification, *Journal of Abnormal and Social Psychology,* **69,** no. 4, 442–444.

Kagan, J., Rosman, B.L., Day, D., Albert, J., and Phillips, W., 1964. Information processing in the child: significance of analytic and reflective attitudes, *Psychological Monograms,* no. 78 (Whole no. 578).

Kahneman, D., Tursky, B., Shapiro, D., and Crider, A., 1969. Pupillary, heart rate and skin resistance changes during a mental task, *Journal of Expt. Psychology,* **79,** no. 1, 164–167.

Kahneman, D., and Tversky, A., 1973. On the psychology of prediction, *Psychological Review,* **80,** no. 4, 237–251.

Kantor, J.R., 1966. Feelings and emotions as scientific events, *The Psychological Record,* no. 16, 377–404.

Kaplan, H.A., 1973. Intuitive Preference, Conditions of Arousal and their Effects On Intuitive Problem-Solving, University of Kansas, PhD thesis, (Psychology, clinical).

Katkin, E.S., and Murray, E.N., 1968. Instrumental conditioning of autonomically mediated behaviour, *Psychological Bulletin,* no. 70, 52–68.

Kaufman, M.L., 1972. Transfer of laboratory experience to day-to-day use, *Training and Development Journal,* **26,** no. 2, 41–42.

Keefe, T., 1976. Empathy: the critical skill, *Social Work,* **21,** part 1, June, 10–14.

Kelly, G.A., 1955. *The Psychology of Personal Constructs,* vol. 1, Norton, New York.

Kilpatrick, D.G., 1972. Differential responsiveness of two electrodermal indices to psychological stress and performance of a complex cognitive task, *Psychophysiology,* **9,** no. 2, 218–226.

King, G.F., 1958. A theoretical and experimental consideration of the Rorschach human movement response, *Psychological Monographs: General and Applied,* **72,** no. 5 (Whole no. 458).

Kintsch, W., 1965. Habituation of the GSR component of the orienting reflex during paired associate learning before and after learning has taken place, *Journal of Mathematical Psychology,* no. 2, 330–340.

Kirchmer, W.K., 1958. Age differences in short-term retention of rapidly changing information, *Journal Experimental Psychol.,* no. 55, 352–358.

Klein, F., 1894, *The Evanston Colloquium Lectures on Mathematics,* Macmillan, New York, 46.

Klein, G.S, 1970. *Perception, Motives and Personality,* Alfred A. Knopf, New York.

Kline, M., 1970. Logic versus pedagogy, *The American Mathematical Monthly,* **77,** no. 3, 264–282.

Kline, M., 1976. NACOME: implications for curriculum design, *Mathematics Teacher,* **69,** part 6, 449–454.

Klopfer, B., & Ainsworth, Mary D., Klopfer, W.G., and Holt, R.R., 1954. *Development in the Rorschach Technique, Technique and Theory,* vol. 1, World Book Co., New York.

Knight, J., 1950. *Story of my Psychoanalysis,* McGraw-Hill, New York.

Koestler, A., 1959. *The Sleepwalkers,* Macmillan, New York.

Koffka, K., 1933. *Principles of Gestalt Psychology,* Harcourt, Brace, New York, 655–661.

Kogan, N, and Wallach, M., 1964. *Risk Taking,* Holt, Rinehart & Winston, New York.

Köhler, W., 1925. *The Mentality of Apes,* Harcourt, Brace, New York.

Köhler, W., 1929. *Gestalt Psychology,* Liveright, New York.

Kohler, W., 1947. *Gestalt Psychology,* The New American Library, New York and Toronto; The New English Library, London.

Kohut, H., 1959. Introspection, empathy and psychoanalysis. An examination of the relationship between mode of observation and theory, *Journal of the American Psychoanalysis Association,* **VII,** 459–483.

Komar, A., 1962. Indeterminate character of the wave packet in quantum theory, *Psychological Review,* no. 126, 365–369.

Krauss, R., 1930. Uber graphischen ausdruck, *Zschr. Angew Psychol,* 48.

Krebs, G.M., 1975. Utilization of Incongruent Communication, PhD thesis, University of Missouri, Columbia.

Kris, E., 1950. On preconscious mental processes, *Psychoan. Quart.,* **19,** 542–552.

Kris, E., 1952. *Psychoanalytic Explorations in Art,* International Universities Press, New York.

Kubie, L.S., 1958. *Neurotic Distortion of the Creative Process,* University of Kansas Press.

Kumberger, Dorothy, and Kardash, Kay, 1948. An Experiment Exemplifying 'Learning' as Induction and 'Insight' as Deduction, paper presented at a meeting in Philadelphia of the Eastern Psychological Association.

Kvascev and Popov, 1972. Imaginative approach to solutions of problem situations, *Psiholoske Razprave: IV Kongkes Pshihologove Serj,* V Ljublj Ank Press, Ljubljana, Yugoslavia, p. 502.

Laabs, C.J., 1971. Cue Effect in Motor Short-term Memory, unpublished doctoral dissertation, University of Oregon.

Lacey, J.I., 1967. Somatic response patterning and stress: some revisions of activation theory, in Appleby, M.A., and Trumbull, R. (eds), *Psychological Stress: Issues in Research,* Appleton-Century-Crofts, New York, 14–39.

Lacey, J.I., Kagan, J., Lacey, B.C., and Moss, H.A., 1963. The visceral level: situational determinants and behavioural correlates of autonomic response patterns, in Knapp, P.H. (ed), *Expression of the Emotions in Man,* International Universities Press, New York, 161–96.

Lacey, J.I., and Lacey, B.C., 1970. Some automatic-central nervous system interrelationships, in Black, P. (ed), *Physiological Correlates of Emotion,* Academic Press, New York, London.

Lacey, J.I., and Smith, R.L., 1954. Conditioning and generalization of unconscious anxiety, *Science,* no. 120, 1–8.

Laming, D.R.J., 1968. *Information Theory of Choice-reaction Times.* Academic Press, London and New York.

Landis, C., 1924. Studies of emotional reactions: II. General behaviour and facial expression, *Journal of Comparative Psychology,* no. 4, 447–501.

Langer, Suzanne K., 1969. The great shift: instinct to intuition, in Eisenberg, J.F., and Dillon, W.S. (eds), *Comparative Social Behaviour,* Smithsonian Institution Press, Washington, Chapter 10.

Lanzetta, J.T., and Kleck, R.E., 1970. Encoding and decoding of nonverbal affect in humans, *Journal of Personality and Social Psychology,* no. 16, 12–19.

Lazarus, R.S., Averill, J.R., and Option, E.M. Jr., 1970. Towards a cognitive theory of emotion, in Arnold, Magda (ed), *The Loyola Symposium — Feelings and Emotions,* Academic Press, London, New York, Chapter 14, 207–232.

Lazarus, R.S., and McCleary, R.A., 1949. Autonomic discrimination without awareness: an interim report, *Journal of Personality,* **18,** 171–179.

Learmonth, G.J., Ackerly, W., and Kaplan, M, 1959. Relationships between palmar skin potential during stress and personality variables, *Psychosomatic Medicine,* **21,** no. 2, 150–157.

Lee, W., 1971. *Decision Theory and Human Behaviour,* John Wiley, New York.

Lehmann, A., 1913. Om stemninger i naturen (On moods in nature), *Oversigt — Kongeltige D Anske Videnskabernes Selskabs Forhandlinger,* no. 5, 382.

Lemineur, R., and Meurice, E., 1972. Relations between empathy and sociometric status, *Journal of Psychologie Normale et Pathologique,* no. 3, 327–332.

Lenrow, P.B., 1965. Studies of sympathy, in Tomkins, S.S., and Izard, C.E. (eds), *Affect, Cognition, and Personality,* Springer Publishing, New York, Chapter 9, pp. 264ff.

Levin, I.P., 1975. Information integration in numerical judgments and decision processes, *Journal of Experimental Psychology: General,* **104,** no. 1, 39–53.

Levy, P.K., 1964. The ability to express and perceive vocal communications of feeling, in Davitz, J.R. (ed), *The Communication of Emotional Meaning,* McGraw-Hill, New York, Chapter 4, 43–55.

Lewis, Ann T.C., 1976. The Relation Between Intuition and Affective Sensitivity, PhD thesis, University of Notre Dame.

Lipps, T., 1926. *Psychological Studies.* Williams & Wilkins, Baltimore.

Lipps, J., 1935. Empathy, inner imitation of sense feelings, in Ruder, M., *A Modern Book of Esthetics,* Holt, New York.

Locke, J., 1690. *An Essay Concerning Human Understanding.* London.

Lollo, V.Di, and Cassedy, J.H., 1965. Graded contrast effects in the judgment of lifted weights, *Journal of Experimental Psychology,* no. 70, 234–235.

Londgren, H.C., and Robinson, J., 1953. An evaluation of Dymond's test of insight and empathy, *Journal of Consulting Psychology,* **17,** no. 3, 172–176.

Lorenz, K.Z., 1951. The role of Gestalt perception in animal and human behaviour, in White, L.L. (ed), *Symposium on Aspects of Form,* Lund Humphries, London.

Lykken, D.T., and Venables, P.H., 1971. Direct measurement of skin conductance: a proposal for standardization, *Psychophysiology,* **8,** no. 5, 656–672.

409

MacDonald, I.D., 1976. Insight and Intuition in Mathematics, private communication (personal), University of Stirling.

MacFarlane Smith, I., 1964. *Spatial Ability — Its Educational and Social Significance.* University of London Press.

MacKinnon, D.W., 1962. The nature and nurture of creative talent, *American Psychologist,* **17**, 484–495.

Mackworth, N.H., 1950. *Researches in the Measurement of Human Performance,* Medical Research Council Special Report, Series No. 268, HMSO, London.

Maier, N.R.F., 1931. Reasoning in humans II. The solution of a problem and its appearance in consciousness, *Journal of Comparative Psychology,* **12**, 181–194.

Maier, N.R.F., 1956. Frustration theory: restatement and extension, *Psychological Review,* **63**, no. 6, 370–388.

Maier, N.R.F., and Burke, R.J., 1967. Influence of timing of hints on their effectiveness in problem-solving, *Psychological Reports,* **20**, 3–8.

Maier, N.R.F., and Casselman, G.G., 1970. Locating the difficulty in insight problems: individual sex differences, *Psychological Reports,* no. 26, 103–117.

Malone, T.W., 1975. System simulation — computer simulation of two-person interactions, *Behavioural Science,* **20**, part 4, 260–267.

Mandler, G., 1967. Organization and memory, in Spence, K.W., and Spence, J.T. (eds), *The Psychology of Learning and Motivation,* Vol. 1, Academic Press, London.

Mandler, G., 1972. Organization and recognition, in Tulving, E. (ed), *Organization of Memory,* Academic Press, London, Chapter 4.

Mandler, G., and Pearlstone, Z., 1966. Free and constrained concept learning and subsequent recall, *Journal of Verbal Learning and Verbal Behaviour,* **5**, 126–131.

Manso, A.V., Grey, L., and Haggard, Martha, 1977. Psychological approaches for the reading specialist: a reclamation project, *Reading World,* **16**(3), 188–195.

Martin, B., 1961. The assessment of anxiety by physiological behavioural measures, *Psychological Bulletin,* **58**, no. 3, 234–255.

Marwell, G., 1964. Problems of operational definitions of 'empathy', 'identification', and related concepts, *The Journal of Social Psychology,* no. 63, 87–102.

May, R., 1959. The nature of creativity, in H.H. Anderson (ed), *Creativity and its Cultivation,* Harper, New York, 56–68.

McClelland, D.C., and Liberman, A.M., 1949. The effect of need for achievement on recognition of need related words, *Journal Pers.,* **18**, 236–251.

McClelland, D.C., Atkinson, J.W., Clark, R.A., and Lovell, E.L., 1953. *The Achievement Motive,* Appleton-Century-Croft, New York.

McClelland, W.A., 1951. A preliminary test of role-playing ability, *Journal of Consulting Psychology,* no. 15, 102–108.

McFarland, J.H., 1962. Visual and proprioceptive changes during visual exposure to a tilted line, *Perceptual and Motor Skills,* no. 15, 322.

McGill, W.J., 1963. Stochastic latency mechanisms, in Luce, R.D., Bush, R.R., and Galanter, E. (eds), *Handbook of Mathematical Psychology,* vol. 1, John Wiley, New York.

McGuigan, F.J., 1973. Muscular-neural encoding process, in McGuigan, F.H., and Schoonover, R.A. (eds), *The Psychophysiology of Thinking,* Academic Press, London, Chapter 7.

Mead, G.H., 1934. *Mind, Self and Society.* University of Chicago Press, Chicago.

Mednick, S.A., 1962. The associative basis of the creative process, *Psychological Review,* **69**, no. 3, 220–232.

Mehrabian, A., and Ferris, S.R., 1967. Inference of attitudes from nonverbal communication in two channels, *Journal of Consulting Psychology,* no. 31, 248–252.

Melzack, R., and Casey, K.L., 1970. The affective dimension of pain, in Arnold, M.B. (ed), *Feelings and Emotions — The Loyola Symposium,* Academic Press, London, New York, Chapter 4, pp. 55ff.

410

Merton, P.A., 1964. Absence of conscious position sense in the human eyes, in Bender, M.B. (ed), *The Oculomotor System,* Harper & Row, New York, 314–320.

Messer, Eunice A., 1967. *Children, Psychology, and the Teacher,* McGraw-Hill, New York.

Meuller, W., and Abeles, N., 1964. The components of empathy and their relationship to the projection of human movement responses, *Journal of Projective Techniques,* no. 28, 322–330.

Meyer, D.E., 1970. On the representation and retrieval of stored semantic information, *Cognitive Psychology,* no. 1, 242–299.

Mialaret, G., 1966. *The Psychology of the Use of Audio-Visual Aids in Primary Education,* Harrap, London.

Miller, G.A., 1956. The magical number seven, plus or minus two: some limits on our capacity to process information, *Psychological Review,* no. 63, 81–97.

Miller, G.A., 1964. What is information measurement? in Miller, G.A. (ed), *Mathematics and Psychology,* John Wiley, London, pp. 171ff.

Miller, G.A., 1967. Psycholinguistic approaches to the study of communication, in Arm, D.L. (ed), *Journeys in Science: Small steps — Great Strides,* University of New Mexico Press, Albuquerque.

Miller, N.E., 1951. Learning drives and rewards, in Stevens, S.S. (ed), *Handbook of Experimental Psychology,* Wiley, New York.

Miller, N.E., and Dollard, J., 1941. *Social Learning & Imitation,* Yale University Press, New Haven, Conn.

Miller, R., 1973. The use of concrete and abstract concepts by children and adults, *Cognition,* **2**, no. 1, 49–58.

Miller, W.C., 1976. Brainwaves and the creative state, *Behavioural Engineering,* **3**(3), 73–75.

Mira, E., 1940. Myokenitic psychodiagnosis, *Proceedings of the Royal Society of Medicine,* **33**, 173–194.

Montessori, Maria, 1965a. *Dr. Montessori's Own Handbook,* Schocken Books, New York.

Montessori, Maria, 1965b. *The Montessori Method,* Robert Bentley, Cambridge, Mass.

Montessori, Maria, 1969. *The Absorbent Mind,* Dell Publishing, New York.

Mowrer, H.O., 1946. The law of effect and ego psychology, *Psychol. Rev.,* **53**, 321–334.

Mowrer, H.O., 1950. *Learning Theory and Personality Dynamics,* The Ronald Press, New York.

Mowrer, H.O., 1960a. *Learning Theory and Behaviour,* John Wiley, New York.

Mowrer, H.O., 1960b. *Learning Theory and the Symbolic Process,* John Wiley, New York.

Moyer, R.S., and Landauer, T.K., 1967. Time required for judgments of numerical inequality, *Nature,* **125**, 1519–1520.

Murphy, G., 1965. Discussion, in Tomkins, S.S., and Izard, C.E. (eds), *Affect, Cognition, and Personality.* Springer Pub., New York, Chapter 15, pp. 4444ff.

Murray, G.H., and Denny, P.J., 1969. Interaction of ability level and interpolated activity (opportunity for incubation) in human problem-solving, *Psychological Reports,* no. 24, 271–276.

Myers, I.B., 1958. Some Findings with Regard to Type and Manual for Myers-Briggs Type Indicator, Form E, Swarthmore: privately printed.

Myers, I.B., 1962. *The Myers–Briggs Type Indicator,* Educational Testing Service, Princeton, NJ.

Neisser, U., 1963a. The imitation of man by machine, *Science,* no. 139, 193–197.

Neisser, U., 1963b. The multiplicity of thought, *British Journal of Psychology,* **54**, 1–14.

Newell, A., and Simon, H.A., 1972. *Human Problem-Solving,* Prentice-Hall, Englewood Cliffs, NJ.

Newton, J.R., 1963. An Investigation of Intuitive and Analytical Thinking, PhD thesis, (psychology, general), University of Colorado.

Nicholls, J.G., 1972. Some effects of testing procedure on divergent thinking, *Child Development,* no. 42, 1647–1651.

Norman, D.A., 1970. *Models of Human Memory.* Academic Press, London.

Norman, D.A., and Rumelhart, D.E., 1970. A system for perception and memory, in Norman, D.A. (ed), *Models of Human Memory,* Academic Press, London, Chapter 2.

Nuttall, D.L., 1971. Modes of Thinking and Their Measurement, PhD thesis, University of Cambridge.

Nuttall, D.L., 1973. Convergent and divergent thinking, in Butcher, H.J., and Pont, H.B. (eds), *Educational Research in Britain 3,* University of London Press, 112–129.

Olden, Christine, 1953. On adult empathy with children, *Psychoanalytic Study of the Child,* no. 8, 111–126.

Ornstein, R.E., 1972. *The Psychology of Consciousness,* Viking Press, New York.

Osgood, C.E., 1952a. Studies on the generality of affective meaning systems, *American Psychologist,* no. 17, 10–28.

Osgood, G.E., 1952b. The nature and measurement of meaning, *Psychol. Bull.,* **49,** 197–237.

Paivio, A., 1971. *Imagery and Verbal Process,* Holt, Rinehart & Winston, New York.

Parducci, A., and Sandusky, A., 1965. Distribution and sequence effects in judgement, *Journal of Exp. Psychol.,* no. 69, 450–459.

Parkinson, A.M., 1970. The lateralization of emotional tone, *Speech Synthesis and Perception: Progress Reports,* no. 3, 27–38.

Pechstein, L.A., and Brown, F.D., 1939. An experimental analysis of the alleged criteria of insight learning, *Journal of Educational Psychology,* **30,** 38–52.

Peters, G.A., and Merrifield, P.R., 1958. Graphic representation of emotional feelings, *Clinical Psychology,* **14,** 375–378.

Peters, Joan T., Hammond, K.R., and Summers, D.A., 1974. A note on intuitive vs. analytic thinking, *Organizational Behaviour and Human Performance,* no. 12, 125–131.

Peters, R.S., 1970. The education of the emotions, in Arnold, M.B. (ed), *Feelings and Emotions — The Loyola Symposium,* Academic Press, London, New York, Chapter 13, pp. 187ff.

Peters, W.H., 1975. The open classroom and creative teaching, *High School Journal,* **59**(3), 112–121.

Peterson, C.R., and Beach, L.R., 1957. Man as an intuitive statistician, *Psychological Bulletin,* no. 68, 29–46.

Pettigrew, T.F., 1958. The measurement and correlates of category width as a cognitive variable, *Journal of Personality,* **26,** 532–544.

Piaget, J., and Inhelder, B., 1956. *The Child's Conception of Space,* Routledge & Kegan Paul, London.

Pickford, R., 1938. An experiment on insight, *British Journal of Psychology,* no. 28, 412–423.

Pine, F., and Holt, R.R., 1960. Creativity and primary process: a study of adaptive regression, *Journal of Abnormal and Social Psychology,* **61,** no. 3, 370–379.

Piotrowski, Z.A., 1971. System of all sciences, in Vetter, H.J., and Smith, B.D. (eds), *Personality Theory: A Source Book,* Meredith Corporation, New York.

Pishkin, V., and Shurley, J.T., 1968. Electrodermal and electromyographic parameters in concept identification, *Psychophysiology,* no. 5, 112–118.

Poincaré, H., 1969. Intuition and logic in mathematics, *Mathematics Teacher,* **62,** part 3, 205–212. (Reprinted from the *Foundations of Science: Science and Education 1.* The Science Press, New York and Lancaster, 1929.)

Polanyi, M., 1966. *The Tacit Dimension,* Routledge & Kegan Paul, London.

Pollio, H.R., 1974. *The Psychology of Symbolic Activity,* Addison-Wesley, New York.

Posner, M.I., 1967. Characteristics of visual and kinaesthetic memory codes, *Journal of Exp. Psychology,* **75,** no. 1, 103–107.

Prentice, W.C.H., 1949. Continuity in human learning, *Journal of Experimental Psychology,* no. 39, 187–194.

Pribram, K.H., 1970. Feelings as monitors, in Arnold, M.B. (ed), *Feelings and Emotions — The Loyola Symposium,* Academic Press, London, New York.

Provus, M.M., 1966. Some personal observations on creativity, in Taylor, C.W., and Williams, F.E. (eds), *Instructional Media and Creativity,* John Wiley, London, Chapter 5.

Pufall, P.B., 1973. Analysis of the development of children's spatial reference system, *Cognitive Psychology,* **5,** 151–175.

Rachelson, S.E., 1977. An Identification of the Characteristics of Hypothesis Generation in Scientific Inquiry with Applications to Guided Imagery and to the Science Curriculum Improvement Study and Essence Curricula, PhD dissertation, Georgia State University.

Rallo, J., 1974. A discussion of the paper by G.H. Allinson and J.C. Ullman on 'The intuitive psychoanalytic perspective of galdos in fortunata and jacinta', *International Journal of Psychoanalysis,* no. 55, 345–347.

Rapaport, D., 1950. *Diagnostic Psychological Testing,* vol. 1, Year Book Publishers, Chicago.

Rapaport, D., 1951. *Organization and Pathology of Thought,* Columbia University Press, New York.

Rashbass, C., 1961. The relationship between saccadic and smooth tracking eye movements, *Journal of Physiology,* **159,** 326–338.

Reese, H.W., 1968. *The Perception of Stimulus Relations, Discrimination Learning and Transposition,* Academic Press, London.

Reid, L.A., 1976. Feeling and aesthetic knowing, *Journal of Aesthetic Education,* **10**(3/4), 11–27.

Restle, F., 1961. *The Psychology of Judgment and Choice,* John Wiley, New York.

Ribot, T., 1897. *The Psychology of the Emotions,* Scott, London.

Ribot, T., 1906. *Essay on the Creative Imagination,* Open Court, Chicago.

Richards, P.N., and Bolton, N., 1971. Type of mathematics teaching, mathematical ability and divergent thinking in junior school children, *British Journal of Educational Psychology,* no. 41, 32–37.

Riegel, K.F., Riegel, Ruth M., and Levine, R.S., 1966. An analysis of associative behaviour and creativity, *Journal of Personality and Social Psychology,* **4,** no. 1, 50–56.

Ripple, R., 1964. *Readings in Learning and Human Abilities,* Harper & Row, New York.

Roback, H.B., 1974. Insight: a bridging of the theoretical and research literatures, *The Canadian Psychologist,* **15,** no. 1, Jan., 61–88.

Robinson, G., 1973. Empathy and identification on the first developmental level, *The Journal of Asthma Research,* **11,** no. 2, Dec., 77–92.

Roe, Anne, 1951. Psychological tests of research scientists, *Journal of Consulting Psychology,* no. 15, 492–495.

Roe, Anne, 1952. *The Making of a Scientist,* Dodd, Mead, New York.

Roe, Anne, 1953. A psychological study of eminent psychologists and anthropologists and a comparison with biological and physical scientists, *Psychological Monograms,* **67,** no. 2, (Whole no. 352).

Rogers, C.R., 1951. Client-centred therapy: its current practice, implications and theory, Houghton-Mifflin, New York.

Rogers, C.R., 1959. Toward a theory of creativity, in Anderson, H.H. (ed), *Creativity and its Cultivation,* Harper & Row, New York, Chapter 6, 80.

Rollo, May, 1959. The nature of creativity, in Anderson, H.H. (ed), *Creativity and its Cultivation,* Harper & Row, New York, Chapter 5, pp. 62ff.

Rommetveit, R., 1968. *Words, Meanings and Messages,* Academic Press, New York.

Rose, J., and Mountcastle, Y.B., 1959. Touch and kinaesthesis, *Handbook of Physiology. Section 1. Neurophysiology,* vol. 1, American Physiological Society, Washington, 387–429.

Rose, R.G., 1975. Introspective evaluations of bilingual memory processes, *Journal of General Psychology,* no. 93, 149–150.

Rosenbloom, P.C., 1972. Some aspects of learning and teaching modern mathematics, in Lamon, W.E. (ed), *Learning and the Nature of Mathematics,* Science Research Associates, Chicago, Chapter 7.

Rosenzweig, M.R., 1957. *Année Psychologique,* no. 57, 23–532.

Rosenzweig, M.R., 1961. *American Journal of Psychology,* no. 74, 347–360.

Rosett, H.L., Robbins, H., and Watson, W.S., 1968. Physiognomic perception as a cognitive control principle, *Perceptual and Motor Skills,* no. 26, 707–719.

Rossman, B.B., 1970. Cognitive, Motivational and Temperamental Indicants of Creativity, unpublished doctoral dissertation, University of Denver.

Rossman, B.B., and Horn, J.J., 1972. Cognitive, motivational and temperamental indicants of creativity and intelligence, *Journal of Educational Measurement,* **9,** no. 4, 265–286.

Rothenberg, A., 1970. Inspiration, insight and the creative process in poetry, *College English,* **32**(2), 172–176, 181–183.

Rubin, K.H., Attwell, P.W., and Teirney, M.C., 1973. Development of spatial egocentrism and conservation across the life span, *Developmental Psychology,* **9,** no. 3, 432.

Rust, R.M., 1948. Some correlates of the movement response, *Journal of Personality,* **16,** 369 401.

Ryan, T.J., and Watson, P., 1968. Frustrative non reward theory applied to children's behaviour, *Psychological Bulletin,* **69,** 111–125.

Samples, R., 1976. Neurophysiology and a new look at curriculum, *Thrust for Education Leadership,* **5**(3), 8–10.

Sanford, R.N., Adkins, M.M., Muller, R.B., and Cobb, E., 1943. Physique, personality and scholarship, *Monographs of the Society for Research in Child Development,* no. 7, Serial no. 34.

Sanford, N., Webster, H., and Freedman, M., 1957. Impulse expression as a variable of personality, *Psychological Monographs,* **71,** no. 11 (Whole of No. 440).

Sarbin, T.R., Taft, R., and Bailey, D.E., 1960. *Clinical Inference and Cognitive Theory,* Holt, Rinehart & Winston, New York.

Schachtel, E.G., 1950. Projection and its relation to character attitudes and creativity in the kinaesthetic responses, *Psychiatry — Journal for the Study of Interpersonal Processes,* **13,** 69–100.

Schachtel, E.G., 1959. *Metamorphosis,* Basic Books, New York.

Schachter, J., 1957. Pain, fear and anger in hypertensives and normotensives, *Psychosom. Med.,* no. 19, 17–29.

Schachter, S., 1964. The interaction of cognitive and physiological determinants of emotional state, in Berkowitz, L. (ed), *Advances in Experimental Social Psychology,* **1,** 49–79.

Schachter, S., 1971. Emotion, obesity and crime, Academic Press, New York and London.

Schachter, S., and Singer, J.E., 1962. Cognitive, social and physiological determinants of emotional state, *Psychological Review,* **69,** no. 5, 379–389.

Schafer, R., 1959. Generative empathy in the treatment situation, *Psychoanalytic Quarterly,* no. 28, 342–373.

Schafer, R., 1968. *Aspects of Internalization,* International Universities Press, New York.

Scheerer, M., and Lyons, J., 1957. Line drawing and matching responses to words, *Journal of Personality,* **25,** 251–273.

Schneider, J.B., 1971. Solving urban location problems: human intuition versus the computer, *Journal American Institute of Planners, Research Report,* **37,** part 2, 95–99.

Schofield, L.J. Jr., and Abbuhl, Stephanie, 1975. The stimulation of insight and self-awareness through body movement exercise, *Journal of Clinical Psychology,* **31,** part 4, 745–746.

Schultz, E.W., 1972. The influence of teacher behaviour and dyad compatibility on clinical gains in arithmetic tutoring, *Journal for Research in Mathematics Education,* **3**(1), Jan., 33–41.

Schwartz, G.E., Davidson, R.J., and Maer, F., 1975. Right hemisphere lateralization for emotion in the human brain: interactions with cognition, *Science,* **190,** Oct., 286–288.

Scott, L.F., 1972. Increasing mathematics learning through improved instructional organization, in Lamon, W.E. (ed), *Learning and the Nature of Mathematics.* Science Research Associates, New York, Chapter 3.

Seymour, R.B., 1950. Personality Correlates of Electrodermal Resistance to Response, PhD dissertation, University of California.

Shantz, Carolyn Y., 1975. Empathy in relation to social cognitive development, *Counselling Psychologist,* **5,** no. 2, 18–21.

Shapiro, T., 1974. The development and distortions of empathy, *Psychoanalytic Quarterly,* **43**(1), 4–25.

Shepard, R., and Metzler, Jacqueline, 1971. Mental rotation of three-dimensional objects, *Science,* **171,** 701–703.

Shepard, R.N., and Chipman, Susan, 1970. Second-order isomorphism of internal representations: shapes of states, *Cognitive Psychology,* no. 1, 1–17.

Shepard, R.N., and Feng, Christine, 1972. A chronometric study of mental paper folding, *Cognitive Psychology,* no. 3, 228–243.

Sherman, V., 1977. An interplay approach to system modification, *Viewpoints,* **53,** part 3, 81–90.

Shrauger, S., and Altrocchi, J., 1964. The personality of the perceiver as a factor in person perception. *Psychological Bulletin,* **62,** no. 5, Nov.

Shiffrin, R.M., 1970. Memory search. in Norman, D.A. (ed), *Models of Human Memory,* Academic Press, London, Chapter 12.

Simon, H.A., 1967. Motivational and emotional controls of cognition, *Psychological Review,* **74,** no. 1, 29-39.

Simon, H.A., 1972. What is visual imagery? An Information Processing Interpretation, in Gregg, L.W. (ed), *Cognition in Learning and Memory,* John Wiley, London, Chapter 7.

Simon, H.A., and Barenfield, M., 1969. Information processing analysis of perceptual processes in problem-solving, *Psychological Review,* **76,** no. 5, 473–483.

Simonton, D.K., 1975. Creativity, task complexity, and intuition vrs. analytical problem-solving, *Psychological Reports,* no. 37, 351–354.

Singer, J.L., 1952. Personal and environmental determinants of perception in a size constancy experiment, *Journal of Experimental Psychol.,* no. 43, 420–427.

Sinnott, E.W., 1959. The creativeness of life, in Anderson, H.H. (ed), *Creativity and its Cultivation,* Harper & Row, New York, Chapter 2, 24–25.

Skemp, R.R., 1971. *The Psychology of Learning Mathematics,* Penguin Books, Harmondsworth.

Skinner, B.F., 1969. *Contingencies of Reinforcement.* Appleton-Century-Crofts, New York.

Sliker, Gretchen Paula, 1972. Creativity of Adults in Light of Piagetian Theory, PhD thesis, Case Western Reserve University.

Smith, E.E., Shoben, E.J., and Rips, L.T., 1974. Structure and process in semantic memory. A featural model of semantic decisions, *Psychological Review,* **81**, part 3, 214–241.

Snapper, A., 1956. Mediating Verbal Responses in Transfer of Training, unpublished AB Honours thesis, Harvard University.

Sokolov, E.N., 1960. Neuronal models and the orienting reflex, in Brazier, M.A.B. (ed), *The Central Nervous System and Behaviour* (3rd Conference), Josia Macy, Nr. Foundation, New York.

Solley, C.M., and Messick, S.J., 1957. Probability learning, the statistical structure of concepts, and the measurement of meaning, *American Journal of Psychology,* no. 70, 163–173.

Solley, C.M., and Murphy, G., 1960. *Development of the Perceptual World,* Basic Books, New York.

Solley, C.M., and Snyder, F.W., 1958. Information processing and problem-solving, *Journal of Experimental Psychology,* **55**, no. 4, 384–388.

Solomon, R.L., and Wynne, L.C., 1950. Avoidance conditioning in normal dogs and in dogs deprived of normal autonomic functioning, *American Psychologist,* No. 5, 264.

Solomon, R.L., and Wynne, L.C., 1954. Traumatic avoidance learning: the principles of anxiety conservation and partial irreversibility, *Psychological Review,* no. 61, 353–385.

SPEAK, Selected Phrase Empathic Ability Key, 1981. The Test Agency, Cournswood House, North Dean, High Wycombe, Bucks.

Spence, K.W., 1960. *Behaviour Theory and Learning,* Prentice-Hall, Englewood Cliffs, NJ.

Spencer, B., 1972. An Investigation of the Relationship Between Three Measures of GSR and Activational Peaking in Two Concept Identification Tasks, doctoral dissertation, Baylor University, Waco, Texas.

Spencer, W.B., and Olmedo, E.L., 1969. Activational Peaking and Concept Identification, unpublished research paper, Baylor University, Waco, Texas.

Springbett, B., 1957. An approach to the measurement of creative thinking, *Canadian Journal of Psychology,* **11**, 9–20.

Stang, D.J., 1974. Intuition as artifact in mere exposure studies, *Journal of Personality and Social Psychology,* **30**, no. 5, 647–653.

Stern, R.M., 1973. Voluntary control of GSRS and reports of sweating, *Perceptual and Motor Skills,* no. 36, 1342.

Sternbach, R.A., 1960. Some relationships among various 'dimensions' of autonomic activity, *Psychosom. Med.,* no. 22, 430–434.

Sternbach, R.A., 1962. Assessing differential autonomic patterns in emotions, *Journal of Psychosomatic Research,* no. 6, 87–91.

Sternbach, R.A., 1966. *Principles of Psychophysiology,* Academic Press, London.

Stocks, J.L., 1939. *Reason and Intuition,* Oxford University Press.

Stotland, E., 1969. Exploratory investigations of empathy, in Berkowitz, L. (ed), *Advances in Experimental Social Psychology,* vol. 4, Academic Press, New York.

Stotland, E., and Dunn, R.E., 1963. Empathy, self-esteem and birth order, *Journal of Abnormal and Social Psychology,* no. 66, 532–540.

Stoyva, J., 1973. Biofeedback techniques and the conditions for hallucinatory activity, in McGuigan, F.H., and Schoonover, R.A. (eds), *The Psychophysiology of Thinking,* Academic Press, London, Chapter 11.

Strongman, K.T., 1973. *The Psychology of Emotion,* John Wiley, London.

Sudjanen, W.W., 1976. Creativity, management and the minds of man, *Human Resource Management,* **15**, part 1, 19–27.

Summers, Roni, 1976. A Phenomenological Approach to the Intuitive Experience, PhD thesis (psychology, clinical), California School of Professional Psychology.

Suzuki, D.T., 1957. Reason and intuition in Buddhist philosophy, in Humphreys, C. (ed), *Studies in Zen — The Complete Works of Suzuki,* Rider, Chapter IV, 85–128.

Swinson, M.E., 1966. The development of cognitive skills and role taking, *Dissert. Abstract,* **26**(7), 4082.

Szalita-Pemow, A.B., 1955. The 'intuitive process' and its relation to work with schizophrenics, *Journal of the American Psychoanalytic Association,* **3**, 7–18.

Taft, R., 1955. The ability to judge people, *Psychological Bulletin,* no. 52, 1–23.

Taft, R., 1960. Judgement and judging in person cognition, in David, H., and Brengelmann, J.C. (eds), *Perspectives in Personality Research,* Crosby Lockwood, London, 196–209.

Taft, R., 1969. Peak experiences and ego-permissiveness: an exploratory factor study of their dimensions in normal persons, *Acta Psychol.,* no. 29, 35–54.

Tauber, E.S., and Green, M.R., 1959. Prelogical experience, basic machine, *Sci. Amer.,* **203**, 60–68.

Taylor, Janet, 1953. A personality scale of manifest anxiety, *Journal of Abnormal and Social Psychology,* **48**, 285–290.

Taylor, J.A., and Spence, K.W., 1952. Anxiety level and serial learning, *Journal of Experimental Psychology,* **44**, 61–64.

Teghtsoonian, Martha, and Teghtsoonian, R., 1965. Seen and felt length, *Psychon. Sci.,* **3**, 465–466.

Thorndike, E.L., and Rock, R.T. Jr., 1934. Learning without awareness of what is being learned or intent to learn it, *Journal of Exp. Psychology,* **17**, 1–19.

Thorsland, M.N., 1971. Formative Evaluation in An Audio-tutorial Physics Course with Emphasis on Intuitive and Analytic Problem-solving Approaches, PhD thesis (education), Cornell University.

Thorsland, M.N., and Novak, J.D., 1972. The Identification and Significance of Intuitive and Analytic Problem-solving Approaches Among College Physics Students, paper delivered at the National Association for Research in Science Teaching Annual Meeting, Chicago, Ill., 4 April.

Thurstone, L.L., 1962. The scientific study of inventive talent, in Parnes, S.J., and Harding, H.F. (eds), *A Source Book for Creative Thinking,* Scribner, New York.

Titchener, E.B., 1900. *An Outline of Psychology,* Macmillan, New York.

Titchener, E.B., 1910. *Textbook of Pscyhology,* Macmillan, New York.

Tomkins, S.S., 1965. Affect and the psychology of knowledge, in Tomkins, S.S., and Izard, C.E. (eds), *Affect, Cognition and Personality.* Springer, New York, pp. 72ff.

Torrance, E.P., 1973. Dyadic Interaction in Creative Thinking and Problem-solving, paper prepared for Annual Meeting of the American Education Research Associations, 25 February to 1 March.

Trabasso, T., and Bower, G.H., 1964. Memory in concept identification, *Psychonomic Science,* **1**, 133–134.

Triandis, H.C., 1964. Cultural influences upon cognitive processes, in Berkowitz, L. (ed), *Advances in Experimental Social Psychology,* **7**, Academic Press, London, 2–4.

Truax, C.B., and Carkhuff, R.R., 1967. *Toward Effective Counselling and Psychotherapy: Training and Practice,* Aldine, Chicago.

Tuska, C.D., 1957. *Inventors and Inventions,* McGraw-Hill, New York.

Underwood, B.J., 1964. The representativeness of rote learning, in Melton, A.W. (ed), *Categories of Human Learning,* Academic Press, New York, 47–78.

Underwood, B.J., 1969. Attributes of memory, *Psychological Review,* no. 76, 559–573.

Urist, J., 1976. Some structural considerations in the relationship between M and empathy, *Journal of Personality Assessment,* **40**, no. 6, 573–578.

Valentine, C., 1929. The relative reliability of men and women in intuitive judgments of character, *British Journal of Psychology,* no. **XIX**, part 3, 213–238.

Valins, S., 1966. Cognitive effects of false heart-rate feedback, *Journal Person. Soc. Psychol.,* no. 4, 400–408.

Van Duyne, P.C., 1976. Necessity and contingency in reasoning, *Acta Psychologica,* no. 40, 85–101.

Vernon, Lee, 1912. *Beauty and Ugliness and Other Studies in Psychological Aesthetics,* J. Lane, London.

Vernon, P.E., 1971. Effects of administration and scoring on divergent thinking tests, *British Journal of Educational Psychology,* no. 41, 245–257.

Vernon, P.E., 1972. *Personality Assessment, a Critical Survey,* Methuen, London.

Viesti, C.R. Jr., 1971. Effect of monetary rewards on an insight learning task, Psychonomic Science, **23**, no. 2, 181–183.

Voss, J.F., 1972. On the relationship of associative and organizational processes, in Tulving, E. (ed), *Organization of Memory,* Academic Press, London, Chapter 5.

Vygotsky, L.S., 1962. *Thought and Language,* MIT Press, Cambridge, Mass.

Wagenaar, W.A., and Sabato, S.D., 1975. Misperception of exponential growth, *Perception and Psychophysics,* **18**(6), 416–422.

Walkup, L.E., 1965. Creativity in science through visualisation, *Perceptual and Motor Skills,* no. 21, 35–41.

Wallach, M.A., and Kogan, N., 1965. *Modes of Thinking in Young Children: A Study of the Creativity — Intelligence Distinction,* Holt, Reinhart & Winston, New York.

Waller, A.D., 1919. Concerning emotive phenomena II. Periodic variations of conductance of the palm of the human hand, *Proceedings of the Royal Society,* no. 91, 17–32.

Watson, G., 1964. What psychology can we trust? in R.E. Ripple (ed), *Readings in Learning and Human Abilities,* Harper & Row, New York.

Watson, J.B., 1930. *Behaviourism,* Norton, New York.

Watson, L., 1974. *Supernature,* Coronet Books, Hodder Paperbacks, London, 276–279.

Wason, P.C., 1966. Reasoning, in Foss, B.M. (ed), *New Horizons in Psychology,* Penguin, Harmondsworth.

Wason, P.C., and Shapiro, D., 1971. Natural and contrived experience in a reasoning problem, *Quarterly Journal of Experimental Psychology,* **23**, no. 1, 63–71.

Weil, A., 1972. *The Natural Mind,* Houghton Miffin, New York.

Weingartner, H., 1963. The free recall of sets of associatively related words, *Journal of Verbal Learning and Verbal Behaviour,* no. 3, 6–10.

Weiskrantz, L., 1968. Emotion, in Weiskrantz, L. (ed), *Analysis of Behaviour Change,* Harper & Row, New York, London.

Weisskopf, E.A., 1950. A transcendence index as a proposed measure of the TAT, *Journal of Psychology,* no. 29, 379–390.

Welford, A.T., 1951. *Skill and Age: An Experimental Approach,* Oxford University Press, London.

Wenger, M.A., 1941. The measurement of individual differences in autonomic balance, *Psychosom. Med.,* no. 3, 427–434.

Wenger, M.A., 1947. Preliminary study of the significance of measure of autonomic balance, *Psychosom. Med.,* no. 9, 301–309.

Wenger, M.A., and Cullen, T.D., 1958. ANS response patterns to fourteen stimuli, *American Psychologist,* no. 13, 423.

Werner, H., 1948. *Comparative Psychology of Mental Development,* International Universities Press, New York.

Werner, H., 1940. Perception of spatial relationships in mentally deficient children, *Journal Genetic Psychology,* **57**, 93–100.

Werner, H., 1954. *On Expressive Language,* Clarke University Press, Worcester, Mass.

Werner, H., and Kaplan, B., 1967. *Symbol Formation. An Organismic-development Approach to Language and the Expression of Thought,* John Wiley, London.

Werner, H., and Wapner, S., 1949. Sensory-tonic field theory of perception, *Journal Personality,* no. 18, 88–107.

Wertheimer, M., 1959. *Productive Thinking,* Harper & Row, New York.

Westcott, M.R., 1961. On the measurement of intuitive leaps, *Psychological Reports,* no. 9, 267–274.

Westcott, M.R., 1964. Empirical studies of intuition, in Taylor, C.W. (ed), *Widening Horizons,* John Wiley, New York, Chapter 4.

Westcott, M.R., 1966. A note on the stability of intuitive thinking, *Psychological Reports,* no. 19, 194.

Westcott, M.R., 1968. *Toward A Contemporary Psychology of Intuition,* Holt, Rinehart & Winston, New York.

Westcott, M.R., and Ranzoni, Jane H., 1963. Correlates of intuitive thinking. *Psychological Reports,* no. 12, 595–613.

Wheeler, R.H., 1931. *The Science of Psychology: An Introductory Study,* Jarrolds, London.

White, B.L., and Carew Watts, Jean, 1973. *Experience and Environment — Major Influences on the Development of the Young Child,* Prentice-Hall, Englewood Cliffs, NJ.

White, S.H., and Plum, G., 1964. Eye movement photography during children's discrimination learning, *Journal of Experimental Child Psychology,* no. 1, 327–338.

Whitfield, J.W., 1951. An experiment in problem-solving, *Quarterly Journal Experimental Psychology,* **3,** 184–197.

Wilcoxon, H.C., 1952. 'Abnormal fixation' and learning, *Journal Experimental Psychology,* no. 44, 324–333.

Wild, K.W., 1938. *Intuition,* Cambridge University Press, London.

Wilkins III, W.W., 1970. Cognitive and Physiological Determinants of Emotion, PhD thesis (psychology, clinical), University of Washington.

Williams, F.E., 1966. Conference overview with models and summary lists of tenable ideas and research areas, in Taylor, C.W., and Williams, F.E. (cd), *Instructional Media and Creativity,* John Wiley, London, Chapter 13.

Wishner, J., 1953. Neurosis and tension: an exploratory study of the relationship of physiological and Rorschach measures, *Journal of Abnormal and Social Psychology,* no. 48, 253–260.

Wishner, J., 1955. The concept of efficiency in psychological health and in psychopathology, *Psychological Review,* no. 62, 69–80.

Witkin, H.A., Kyk, R.B., Faterson, H.F., Goodenough, D.R., and Karp, S.A., 1962. *Psychological Differentiation. Studies of Development,* John Wiley, New York.

Witkin, H.A., Lewis, H.B., Hertzman, M., Machover, K., Meissner, P.B., and Wapner, S., 1954. *Personality Through Perception,* Harper & Row, New York.

Wolfe, Mary L., 1975. Distribution characteristics as predictors of error in intuitive estimation of means, *Psychological Reports,* no. 36, 367–370.

Wolff, W., and Precker, J.A., 1951. Expressive movement and the methods of experimental depth psychology, in Anderson, H.H., and Anderson, G.L. (eds), *Introduction to Projective Techniques,* Prentice-Hall, Englewood Cliffs, NJ., Chapter 16, 490.

Woodworth, R.S., 1940. *Psychology,* Holt, New York, 299–300.

Woodworth, R.S., 1947. Reinforcement of perception, *American Journal of Psychology,* **60'** 119–124.

Yamamoto, K., 1972. *The Child and His Image,* Houghton Mifflin, New York.

Yamomoto, K., 1964. A further analysis of the role of creative thinking in high school achievement, *Journal of Psychology,* **58,** 277–283.

Yanoff, J.M., 1972. The function of the mind in the learning process, in Silberman (ed), *The Psychology of Open Teaching and Learning: An Inquiry Approach*. Little, Brown, Boston.

Yavuz, H.S., and Bousfield, W̄.A., 1959. Recall of connotative meaning, *Psychological Reports*, no. 5, 319–320.

Yerkes, R.M., 1927. The mind of a gorilla, *Genetic Psychology Monographs*, **11**, Jan., March, 1–193.

Younie, W.J., 1967. *Instructional Approaches to Slow Learning*, Teachers College, New York, 28.

Zac, J., 1974. Thinking as the goal of intraphysic adequacy, *Contemporary Psychoanalysis*, **1**, no. 1, 57–69.

Zajonc, A.G., 1976. Goethe's theory of colour and scientific intuition, *American Journal of Physics*, **44**, no. 4, April, 327–333.

Zavalishina, D.N., 1973. Two functions of visualization while problem-solving, *Voprosy Psikhologii*, **19**, no. 4, 17–27.

Zimmerman, W.S., 1954. The influence of item complexity upon the factor composition of a spatial visualization test, *Educational Psychology Measurement*, no. 14, 106–19.

Zimring, F., Nauman, C., and Blacombe, J., 1970. Listening with the second ear: selective attention and emotion, *Proceedings of the American Psychological Association*, no. 5, 471–472.

Name Index

424

426

Subject Index

B

C

438

—————————— **D** ——————————

———————— E ————————

———————— **F** ————————

G

H

462

L

M

──────────── **N** ────────────

O

P

488

T

U

V

W

Y